ISBN: 9781290835633

Published by:
HardPress Publishing
8345 NW 66TH ST #2561
MIAMI FL 33166-2626

Email: info@hardpress.net
Web: http://www.hardpress.net

THE OUTLINE OF HISTORY

NEANDERTHAL MANKIND
(*Homo Neanderthalensis*)
By Sir H. H. Johnston

"Half ape, half monkey, it ran upon its hind legs; it had clever hands. . . It was our ancestor."

The Outline of History

Being a Plain History of Life and Mankind

By

H. G. Wells

Written with the Advice and Editorial Help of
Mr. Ernest Barker, Sir H. H. Johnston, Sir E. Ray Lankester *and* Professor Gilbert Murray
And Illustrated by J. F. Horrabin

Revised and Corrected Edition
(With Several New Maps and Diagrams)

VOLUME I

The Waverley Book Company, Limited
96 Farringdon Street, London, E.C.4
1920

INTRODUCTION

"*A philosophy of the history of the human race, worthy of its name, must begin with the heavens and descend to the earth, must be charged with the conviction that all existence is one—a single conception sustained from beginning to end upon one identical law.*"—FRIEDRICH RATZEL.

THIS *Outline of History* is an attempt to tell, truly and clearly, in one continuous narrative, the whole story of life and mankind so far as it is known today. It is written plainly for the general reader, but its aim goes beyond its use as merely interesting reading matter. There is a feeling abroad that the teaching of history considered as a part of general education is in an unsatisfactory condition, and particularly that the ordinary treatment of this "subject" by the class and teacher and examiner is too partial and narrow. But the desire to extend the general range of historical ideas is confronted by the argument that the available time for instruction is already consumed by that partial and narrow treatment, and that therefore, however desirable this extension of range may be, it is in practice impossible. If an Englishman, for example, has found the history of England quite enough for his powers of assimilation, then it seems hopeless to expect his sons and daughters to master universal history, if that is to consist of the history of England, plus the history of France, plus the history of Germany, plus the history of Russia, and so on. To which the only possible answer is that universal history is at once something more and something less than the aggregate of the national histories to which we are accustomed, that it must be approached in a different spirit and dealt with in a different manner. This book seeks to justify that answer. It has been written primarily to show that *history as one whole* is amenable to a more broad and comprehensive handling than is the history of special nations and periods, a broader handling that will bring it within the normal limitations of time and energy set to the reading and education of an ordinary citizen. This outline deals with ages and races and nations, where the ordinary history deals with reigns and pedigrees and campaigns; but it will not be found to be more crowded with names and dates, nor more difficult to follow and understand. History is no exception amongst the sciences; as the gaps fill in, the outline simplifies; as the outlook broadens, the clustering multitude of details dissolves into general laws. And many topics of quite primary interest to mankind, the first appearance and the growth of scientific knowledge for example, and its effects upon human life, the elaboration of the ideas of money and credit, or the story of the origins and spread and influence of Christianity, which must be treated fragmentarily or by elaborate digressions in any partial history, arise and flow completely and naturally in one general record of the world in which we live.

The need for a common knowledge of the general facts of human history throughout the world has become very evident during the tragic happenings of the last few years. Swifter means of communication have brought all men closer to one another for good or for evil. War becomes a universal disaster, blind and monstrously destructive; it bombs the baby in its cradle and sinks the food-ships that cater for the non-combatant and the neutral. There can be no peace now, we realize, but a common peace in all the world; no prosperity but a general prosperity. But *there can be no common peace and prosperity without common historical ideas.* Without such ideas to hold them together in harmonious co-operation, with nothing but narrow, selfish, and conflicting nationalist traditions, races and peoples are bound to drift towards conflict and destruction. This truth, which was apparent to that great philosopher Kant a century or more ago—it is the gist of his tract upon universal peace—is now plain to the man in the street. Our internal policies and our economic and social ideas are profoundly vitiated at present by wrong and fantastic ideas of the origin and historical relationship of social classes. A sense of history as the common adventure of all mankind is as necessary for peace within as it is for peace between the nations.

Such are the views of history that this *Outline* seeks to realize. It is an attempt to tell how our present state of affairs, this distressed and multifarious human life about us, arose in the course of vast ages and out of the inanimate clash of matter, and to estimate the quality and amount and range of the hopes with which it now faces its destiny. It is one experimental contribution to a great and urgently necessary educational reformation, which must ultimately restore universal history, revised, corrected, and brought up to date, to its proper place and use as the backbone of a general education. We say "restore," because all the great cultures of the world hitherto, Judaism and Christianity in the Bible, Islam in the Koran, have used some sort of cosmogony and world history as a basis. It may indeed be argued that without such a basis any really binding culture of men is inconceivable. Without it we are a chaos.[1]

Remarkably few sketches of universal history by one single author have been written. One book that has influenced the writer very strongly is Winwood Reade's *Martyrdom of Man*. This *dates*, as people say, nowadays, and it has a fine gloom of its own, but it is still an extraordinarily inspiring presentation of human history as one consistent process. Mr. F. S. Marvin's *Living Past* is also an admirable summary of human progress. There is a good *General History of the World* in one volume by Mr. Oscar Browning. America has recently produced two well-illustrated and up-to-date class books, Breasted's *Ancient Times* and Robinson's *Medieval and Modern Times*, which together give a very good idea of the story of mankind since the beginning of human societies. There are, moreover, quite a number of nominally Universal Histories in existence, but they are really not histories at all, they are encyclopædias of history; they lack the unity of presentation attainable only when the whole subject has been passed through one single mind. These universal histories are compilations, assemblies of separate national or regional histories by different hands, the parts being necessarily unequal in merit and authority and disproportionate one to another. Several such universal histories in thirty or forty volumes or so, adorned with allegorical title pages and illustrated by folding maps and plans of Noah's Ark, Solomon's Temple, and the Tower of Babel, were produced for the libraries of gentlemen in the eighteenth century. Helmolt's *World History*, in eight massive volumes, is a modern compilation of the same sort, very useful for reference and richly illustrated, but far better in its parts than as a whole. Another such collection is the *Historians' History of the World* in 25 volumes. *The Encyclopædia Britannica* contains, of course, a complete encyclopædia of history within itself, and is the most modern of all such collections. F. Ratzel's *History of Mankind*, in spite of the promise of its title, is mainly a natural history of man, though it is rich with suggestions upon the nature and development of civilization. That publication and Miss Ellen Churchill Semple's *Influence of Geographical Environment*, based on Ratzel's work, are quoted in this *Outline*, and have had considerable influence upon its plan. F. Ratzel would indeed have been the ideal author for such a book as our present one. Unfortunately neither he nor any other ideal author was available.[2]

The writer will offer no apology for making this experiment. His disqualifications are manifest. But such work needs to be done by as many people as possible, he was free to make his contribution, and he was greatly attracted by the task. He has read sedulously and made the utmost use of all the help he could obtain. There is not a chapter that has not been examined by some more competent person than himself and very carefully revised. He has particularly to thank his friends Sir E. Ray Lankester, Sir H. H. Johnston, Professor Gilbert Murray, and Mr. Ernest Barker for much counsel and direction and editorial help. Mr. Philip Guedalla has toiled most efficiently and kindly through all the proofs. Mr. A. Allison, Professor T. W. Arnold, Mr. Arnold Bennett, the Rev. A. H. Trevor Benson, Mr. Aodh de Blacam, Mr. Laurence Binyon, the Rev. G. W. Broomfield, Sir William Bull, Mr. L. Cranmer Byng, Mr. A. J. D. Campbell, Mr. A. Y. Campbell, Mr. L. Y. Chen, Mr. A. R. Cowan, Mr. O. G. S. Crawford, Dr. W. S. Culbertson, Mr. R. Langton Cole, Mr. B. G. Collins, Mr. J. J. L. Duyven-

[1] See upon this an excellent pamphlet by F. J. Gould, *History, the Supreme Subject in the Instruction of the Young* (Watts & Co.).

[2] A compact and inspiring book to be noted here is Fairgrieve's *Geography and World Power*. Another very suggestive book is Andrew Reid Cowan's *Master Clues in World History*.

dak, Mr. O. W. Ellis, Mr. G. S. Ferrier, Mr. David Freeman, Mr. S. N. Fu, Mr. G. B. Gloyne, Sir Richard Gregory, Mr. F. H. Hayward, Mr. Sydney Herbert, Dr. Fr. Krupicka, Mr. H. Lang Jones, Mr. C. H. B. Laughton, Mr. B. I. Macalpin, Mr. G. H. Mair, Mr. F. S. Marvin, Mr. J. S. Mayhew, Mr. B. Stafford Morse, Professor J. L. Myres, the Hon. W. Ormsby-Gore, Sir Sydney Olivier, Mr. R. I. Pocock, Mr. J. Pringle, Mr. W. H. R. Rivers, Sir Denison Ross, Dr. E. J. Russell, Dr. Charles Singer, Mr. A. St. George Sanford, Dr. C. O. Stallybrass, Mr. G. H. Walsh, Mr. G. P. Wells, Miss Rebecca West, and Mr. George Whale have all to be thanked for help, either by reading parts of the MS. or by pointing out errors in the published parts, making suggestions, answering questions or giving advice. The amount of friendly and sympathetic assistance the writer has received, often from very busy people, has been a quite extraordinary experience. He has met with scarcely a single instance of irritation or impatience on the part of specialists whose domains he has invaded and traversed in what must have seemed to many of them an exasperatingly impudent and superficial way. Numerous other helpful correspondents have pointed out printer's errors and minor slips in the serial publication which preceded this book edition, and they have added many useful items of information, and to those writers also the warmest thanks are due. But of course none of these generous helpers are to be held responsible for the judgments, tone, arrangement or writing of this *Outline*. In the relative importance of the parts, in the moral and political implications of the story, the final decision has necessarily fallen to the writer. The problem of illustrations was a very difficult one for him, for he had had no previous experience in the production of an illustrated book. In Mr. J. F. Horrabin he has had the good fortune to find not only an illustrator but a collaborator. Mr. Horrabin has spared no pains to make this work informative and exact. His maps and drawings are a part of the text, the most vital and decorative part. Some of them, the hypothetical maps, for example, of the western world at the end of the last glacial age, during the "pluvial age" and 12,000 years ago, and the migration map of the Barbarian invaders of the Roman Empire, represent the reading and inquiry of many laborious days.

The index to this edition is the work of Mr. Strickland Gibson of Oxford. Several correspondents have asked for a pronouncing index and accordingly this has been provided.

The writer owes a word of thanks to that living index of printed books, Mr. J. F. Cox of the London Library. He would also like to acknowledge here the help he has received from Mrs. Wells. Without her labour in typing and re-typing the drafts of the various chapters as they have been revised and amended, in checking references, finding suitable quotations, hunting up illustrations, and keeping in order the whole mass of material for this history, and without her constant help and watchful criticism, its completion would have been impossible.

THE OUTLINE OF HISTORY

CONTENTS OF VOLUME I

BOOK I

THE MAKING OF OUR WORLD

BOOK II

THE MAKING OF MAN

BOOK III

THE DAWN OF HISTORY

CHAPTER XIX. GODS AND STARS, PRIESTS AND KINGS

CHAPTER XX. SERFS, SLAVES, SOCIAL CLASSES, AND FREE INDIVIDUALS

BOOK IV

JUDEA, GREECE, AND INDIA

CHAPTER XXI. THE HEBREW SCRIPTURES AND THE PROPHETS

CHAPTER XXII. THE GREEKS AND THE PERSIANS

CHAPTER XXIII. GREEK THOUGHT AND LITERATURE

CHAPTER XXIV. THE CAREER OF ALEXANDER THE GREAT

CHAPTER XXV. SCIENCE AND RELIGION AT ALEXANDRIA

CHAPTER XXVI. THE RISE AND SPREAD OF BUDDHISM

BOOK V

THE RISE AND COLLAPSE OF THE ROMAN EMPIRE

CHAPTER XXVII. THE TWO WESTERN REPUBLICS

CHAPTER XXVIII. FROM TIBERIUS GRACCHUS TO THE GOD-EMPEROR IN ROME

CHAPTER XXIX. THE CÆSARS BETWEEN THE SEA AND THE GREAT PLAINS OF THE OLD WORLD

LIST OF MAPS AND ILLUSTRATIONS

COLOUR PLATES

PHOTOGRAVURES

MAPS AND CHARTS

TEXT ILLUSTRATIONS

BOOK I

THE MAKING OF OUR WORLD

THE OUTLINE OF HISTORY

I

THE EARTH IN SPACE AND TIME

THE earth on which we live is a spinning globe. Vast though it seems to us, it is a mere speck of matter in the greater vastness of space.

Space is, for the most part, emptiness. At great intervals there are in this emptiness flaring centres of heat and light, the "fixed stars." They are all moving about in space, notwithstanding that they are called fixed stars, but for a long time men did not realize their motion. They are so vast and at such tremendous distances that their motion is not perceived. Only in the course of many thousands of years is it appreciable. These fixed stars are so far off that, for all their immensity, they seem to be, even when we look at them through the most powerful telescopes, mere points of light, brighter or less bright. A few, however, when we turn a telescope upon them, are seen to be whirls and clouds of shining vapour which we call nebulæ. They are so far off that a movement of millions of miles would be imperceptible.

One star, however, is so near to us that it is like a great ball of flame. This one is the sun. The sun is itself in its nature like a fixed star, but it differs from the other fixed stars in appearance because it is beyond comparison nearer than they are; and because it is nearer men have been able to learn something of its nature. Its mean distance from the earth is ninety-three million miles. It is a mass of flaming matter, having a diameter of 866,000 miles. Its bulk is a million and a quarter times the bulk of our earth.

These are difficult figures for the imagination. If a bullet fired from a Maxim gun at the sun kept its muzzle velocity unimpaired, it would take seven years to reach the sun. And yet we say the sun is near, measured by the scale of the stars. If the earth were a small ball, one inch in diameter, the sun would be a globe of nine feet diameter; it would fill a small bedroom. It is spinning round on its axis, but since it is an incandescent fluid, its polar regions do not travel with the same velocity as its equator, the surface of which rotates in about twenty-five days. The surface visible to us consists of clouds of incandescent metallic vapour. At what lies below we can only guess. So hot is the sun's atmosphere that iron, nickel, copper, and tin are present in it in a gaseous state. About it at great distances circle not only our earth, but certain kindred bodies called the planets. These shine in the sky because they reflect the light of the sun; they are near enough for us to note their movements quite easily. Night by night their positions change with regard to the fixed stars.

It is well to understand how empty is space. If, as we have said, the sun were a ball nine feet across, our earth would, in proportion, be the size of a one-inch ball, and at a distance of 323 yards from the sun. The moon would be a speck the size of a small pea, thirty inches from the earth. Nearer to the sun than the earth would be two other very similar specks, the planets Mercury and Venus, at a distance of a hundred and twenty-five and two hundred and fifty yards respectively. Beyond the earth would come the planets Mars, Jupiter, Saturn, Uranus, and Neptune, at distances of 500, 1,680, 3,000, 6,000, and 9,500 yards respectively. There would also be a certain number of very much smaller specks, flying about amongst these planets, more particularly a number called the asteroids circling between Mars and Jupiter, and occasionally a little puff of more or less luminous vapour and dust would drift into the system from the almost limitless emptiness beyond. Such a puff is what we call a comet. *All the rest of the space about us and around us and for unfathomable distances beyond is cold, lifeless, and void.* The nearest fixed star to us, *on this minute scale*, be it remembered—the earth as a one-inch ball, and the moon a little pea—would be over 40,000 miles away.

The science that tells of these things and how men have come to know about them is Astronomy, and to books of astronomy the reader must go to learn more about the sun and stars. The science and description of the world on which we live are called respectively Geology and Geography.

The diameter of our world is a little under 8,000 miles. Its surface is rough, the more projecting parts of the roughness are mountains, and in the hollows of its surface there is a film of water, the oceans and seas. This film of water is about five miles thick at its deepest part—that is to say, the deepest oceans have a depth of five miles. This is very little in comparison with the bulk of the world.

About this sphere is a thin covering of air, the atmosphere. As we ascend in a balloon or go up a mountain from the level of the sea-shore the air is continually less dense, until at last it becomes so thin that it cannot support life. At a height of twenty miles there is scarcely any air at all—not one hundredth part of the density of air at the surface of the sea. The highest point to which a bird can fly is about four miles up—the condor, it is said, can struggle up to that; but most small birds and insects which are carried up by aeroplanes or balloons drop off insensible at a much lower level, and the greatest height to which any mountaineer has ever climbed is under five miles. Men have flown in aeroplanes to a height of over four miles, and balloons with men in them have reached very nearly seven miles, but at the cost of considerable physical suffering. Small experimental balloons, containing not men, but recording instruments, have gone as high as twenty-two miles.

It is in the upper few hundred feet of the crust of the earth, in the sea, and in the lower levels of the air below four miles that life is found. We do not know of any life at all except in these films of air and water upon our planet. So far as we know, all the rest of space is as yet without life. Scientific men have discussed the possibility of life, or of some process of a similar kind, occurring upon such kindred bodies as the planets Venus and Mars. But they point merely to questionable possibilities.

Astronomers and geologists and those who study physics have been able to tell us something of the origin and history of the earth. They consider that, vast ages ago, the sun was a spinning, flaring mass of matter, not yet concentrated into a compact centre of heat and light, considerably larger than it is now, and spinning very much faster, and that as it whirled, a series of fragments detached themselves from it, which became the planets. Our earth is one of these planets. The flaring mass that was the material of the earth broke into two masses as it spun; a larger, the earth itself, and a smaller, which is now the dead, still moon. Astronomers give us convincing reasons for supposing that sun and earth and moon and all that system were then whirling about at a speed much greater than the speed at which they are moving to-day, and that at first our earth was a flaming thing upon which no life could live. The way in which they have reached these conclusions is by a very beautiful and interesting series of observations and reasoning, too long and elaborate for us to deal with here. But they oblige us to believe that the sun, incandescent though it is, is now much cooler than it was, and that it spins more slowly now than it did, and that it continues to cool and slow down. And they also show that the rate at which the earth spins is diminishing and continues to diminish—that is to say, that our day is growing longer and longer, and that the heat at the centre of the earth wastes slowly. There was a time when the day was not a half and not a third of what it is to-day; when a blazing hot sun, much greater than it is now, must have moved visibly—had there been an eye to mark it—from its rise to its setting across the skies. There will be a time when the day will be as long as a year is now, and the cooling sun, shorn of its beams, will hang motionless in the heavens.

It must have been in days of a much hotter sun, a far swifter day and night, high tides, great heat, tremendous storms and earthquakes, that life, of which we are a part, began upon the world. The moon also was nearer and brighter in those days and had a changing face.[1]

[1] For a convenient recent discussion of the origin of the earth and its early history before the seas were precipitated and sedimentation began, the student should consult Professor Burrell's contribution to the Yale lectures, *The Evolution of the Earth and its Inhabitants* (1918), edited by President Lull.

II

THE RECORD OF THE ROCKS

§ 1. *The First living Things.* § 2. *How Old is the World?*

§ 1

WE do not know how life began upon the earth.[1]

Biologists, that is to say, students of life, have made guesses about these beginnings, but we will not discuss them here. Let us only note that they all agree that life began where the tides of those swift days spread and receded over the steaming beaches of mud and sand.

The atmosphere was much denser then, usually great cloud masses obscured the sun, frequent storms darkened the heavens. The land of those days, upheaved by violent volcanic forces, was a barren land, without vegetation, without soil. The almost incessant rain-storms swept down upon it, and rivers and torrents carried great loads of sediment out to sea, to become muds that hardened later into slates and shales, and sands that became sandstones. The geologists have studied the whole accumulation of these sediments as it remains to-day, from those of the earliest ages to the most recent. Of course the oldest deposits are the most distorted and changed and worn, and in them there is now no certain trace to be found of life at all. Probably the earliest forms of life were small and soft, leaving no evidence of their existence behind them. It was only when some of these living things developed skeletons and shells of lime and such-like hard material that they left fossil vestiges after they died, and so put themselves on record for examination.

The literature of geology is very largely an account of the fossils that are found in the rocks, and of the order in which layers after layers of rocks lie one on another. The very oldest rocks must have been formed before there was any sea at all, when the earth was too hot for a sea to exist, and when the water that is now sea was an atmosphere of steam mixed with the air. Its higher levels were dense with clouds, from which a hot rain fell towards the rocks below, to be converted again into steam long before it reached their incandescence. Below this steam atmosphere the molten world-stuff solidified as the first rocks. These first rocks must have solidified as a cake over glowing liquid material beneath, much as cooling lava does. They must have appeared first as crusts and clinkers. They must have been constantly remelted and recrystallized before any thickness of them became permanently solid. The name of Fundamental Gneiss is given to a great underlying system of crystalline rocks which probably formed age by age as this hot youth of the world drew to its close. The scenery of the world in the days when the Fundamental Gneiss was formed must have been more like the interior of a furnace than anything else to be found upon earth at the present time.

After long ages the steam in the atmosphere began also to condense and fall right down to earth, pouring at last over these warm primordial rocks in rivulets of hot water and gathering in depressions as pools and lakes and the first seas. Into those seas the streams that poured over the rocks brought with them dust and particles to form a sediment, and this sediment accumulated in layers, or as geologists call them, *strata*, and formed the first Sedimentary Rocks. Those earliest sedimentary rocks sank into depressions and were covered by others; they were bent, tilted up, and torn by great volcanic disturbances and by tidal strains that swept through the rocky crust of the earth. We find these first sedimentary rocks still coming to the surface of the land here and there, either not covered by later strata or exposed after vast ages of concealment by the wearing off of the rock that covered them later—there are great surfaces of them in Canada especially; they are cleft and bent, partially remelted, recrystallized, hardened and compressed, but recognizable

[1] Here in this history of life we are doing our best to give only known and established facts in the broadest way, and to reduce to a minimum the speculative element that must necessarily enter into our account. The reader who is curious upon this question of life's beginning will find a very good summary of current suggestions done by Professor L. L. Woodruff in President Lull's excellent compilation *The Evolution of the Earth* (Yale University Press). Professor H. F. Osborn's *Origin and Evolution of Life* is also a very vigorous and suggestive book upon this subject, but it demands a fair knowledge of physics and chemistry. Two very stimulating essays *for the student* are A. H. Church's *Botanical Memoirs* Nos. 1 and 3 (Ox. Univ. Press).

for what they are. And they contain no single certain trace of life at all. They are frequently called *Azoic* (lifeless) Rocks. But since in some of these earliest sedimentary rocks a substance called graphite (black lead) occurs, and also red and black oxide of iron, and since it is asserted that these substances need the activity of living things for their production, which may or may not be the case, some geologists prefer to call these earliest sedimentary rocks *Archæozoic* (primordial life). They suppose that the first life was soft living matter that had no shells or skeletons or any such structure that could remain as a recognizable fossil after its death, and that its chemical influence caused the deposition of graphite and iron oxide. This is pure guessing, of course, and there is at least an equal probability that in the time of formation of the Azoic Rocks, life had not yet begun.

Long ago there were found in certain of these ancient first-formed rocks in Canada, curious striped masses, and thin layers of white and green mineral substance which Sir William Dawson considered were fossil vestiges, the walls or coverings of some very simple sort of living thing which has now vanished from the earth. He called these markings *Eozoon Canadense* (the Canadian dawn-animal). There has been much discussion and controversy over this Eozoon, but to-day it is agreed that Eozoon is nothing more than a crystalline marking. Mixed minerals will often intercrystallize in blobs or branching shapes that are very suggestive of simple plant or animal forms. Anyone who has made a lead tree in his schooldays, or lit those queer indoor fireworks known as serpents' eggs, which unfold like a long snake, or who has seen the curious markings often found in quartz crystals, or noted the tree-like pattern on old stone-ware beer mugs, will realize how closely non-living matter can sometimes mock the shapes of living things.

Overlying or overlapping these Azoic or Archæozoic rocks come others, manifestly also very ancient and worn, which do contain traces of life. These first remains are of the simplest description; they are the vestiges of simple plants called algæ, or marks like the tracks made by worms in the sea mud. There are also the skeletons of the microscopic creatures called Radiolaria. This second series of rocks is called the Proterozoic (beginning of life) series, and marks a long age in the world's history. Lying over and above the Proterozoic rocks is a third series, which is found to contain a considerable number and variety of traces of living things. First comes the evidence of a diversity of shell-fish, crabs, and such-like crawling things, worms, seaweeds, and the like; then of a multitude of fishes and of the beginnings of land plants and land creatures. These rocks are called the Palæozoic (ancient life) rocks. They mark a vast era, during which life was slowly spreading, increasing, and developing in the seas of our world. Through long ages, through the earliest Palæozoic time, it was no more than a proliferation of such swimming and creeping things in the water. There were creatures called trilobites; they were crawling things like big sea woodlice that were probably related to the American king-crab of to-day. There were also sea-scorpions, the prefects of that early world. The individuals of certain species of these were nine feet long. These were the very highest sorts of life. There were abundant different sorts of an order of shellfish called brachiopods. There were plant animals, rooted and joined together like plants, and loose weeds that waved in the waters.

It was not a display of life to excite our imaginations. There was nothing that ran or flew or even swam swiftly or skilfully. Except for the size of some of the creatures, it was not very different from, and rather less various than, the kind of life a student would gather from any summer-time ditch nowadays for microscopic examination. Such was the life of the shallow seas through a hundred million years or more in the early Palæozoic period. The land during that time was apparently absolutely barren. We find no trace nor hint of land life. Everything that lived in those days lived under water for most or all of its life.

Between the formation of these Lower Palæozoic rocks in which the sea scorpion and trilobite ruled, and our own time, there have intervened almost immeasurable ages represented by layers and masses of sedimentary rocks. There are first the Upper Palæozoic Rocks, and above these the geologists distinguish two great divisions. Next above the Palæozoic come the Mesozoic (middle life) rocks, a second vast system of fossil-bearing rocks, representing perhaps a hundred millions of swift years, and containing a wonderful array of fossil remains, bones of giant reptiles and the like, which we will presently describe; and above these again are the Cainozoic (recent life) rocks, a third great volume in the history of life, an unfinished volume of which the sand and mud that was carried out to sea yesterday by the rivers of the world, to bury the bones and scales and bodies and tracks that will become at last fossils of the things of to-day, constitute the last written leaf.

(It is, we may note, the practice of many geologists to make a break between the rest of the Cainozoic system of rocks and those which contain traces of humanity, which latter are cut off as a separate system under the name of Quaternary. But that, as we shall see, is rather like taking the last page of a book, which is really the conclusion of the last chapter, and making a separate chapter of it and calling it the last chapter.)

These markings and fossils in the rocks and the rocks themselves are our first historical documents. The history of life that men have puzzled out and are still puzzling out from them is called the Record of the Rocks. By studying this record men are slowly piecing together a story of life's beginnings, and of the beginnings of our kind, of which our ancestors a century or so ago had no suspicion. But when we call these rocks and the fossils a record and a history, it must not be supposed that there is any sign of an orderly keeping of a record. It is merely that whatever happens leaves some trace, if only we are intelligent enough to detect the meaning of that trace. Nor are the rocks of the world in orderly layers one above the other, convenient for men to read. They are not like the books and pages of a library. They are torn, disrupted, interrupted, flung about, defaced, like a carelessly arranged office after it has experienced in succession a bombardment, a hostile military occupation, looting, an earthquake, riots, and a fire. And so it is that for countless generations this Record of the Rocks lay unsuspected beneath the feet of men. Fossils were known to the Ionian Greeks in the sixth century B.C.,[1] they were discussed at Alexandria by Eratosthenes and others in the third century B.C., a discussion which is summarised in Strabo's *Geography* (? 20–10 B.C.). They were known to the Latin poet Ovid, but he did not understand their nature. He thought they were the first rude efforts of creative power. They were noted by Arabic writers in the tenth century. Leonardo da Vinci, who lived so recently as the opening of the

Note its general resemblance, except for size, to the microscopic summer ditchwater life of to-day.

[1] Theophrastus, quoting Xenophanes.

sixteenth century (1452—1519), was one of the first Europeans to grasp the real significance of fossils,[1] and it has been only within the last century and a half that man has begun the serious and sustained deciphering of these long-neglected early pages of his world's history.

§ 2.

Speculations about geological time vary enormously.[2] Estimates of the age of the oldest rocks by geologists and astronomers starting from different standpoints have varied between 1,600,000,000, and 25,000,000. The lowest estimate was made by Lord Kelvin in 1867. Professor Huxley guessed at 400,000,000 years. There is a summary of views and the grounds upon which the estimates have been made in Osborn's *Origin and Evolution of Life;* he inclines to the moderate total of 100,000,000. It must be clearly understood by the reader how sketchy and provisional all these time estimates are. They rest nearly always upon theoretical assumptions of the slenderest kind. That the period of time has been vast, that it is to be counted by scores and possibly by hundreds of millions of years, is the utmost that can be said with certainty in the matter. It is quite open to the reader to divide every number in the appended time diagram by ten or multiply it by two; no one can gainsay him. Of the relative amount of time as between one age and another we have, however, stronger evidence; if the reader cuts down the 800,000,000 we have given here to 400,000,000, then he must reduce the 40,000,000 of the Cainozoic to 20,000,000.

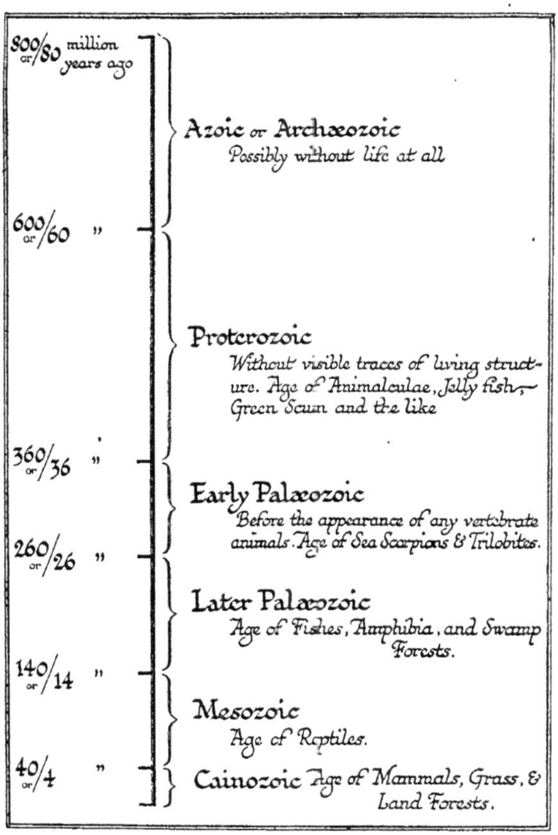

And be it noted that whatever the total sum may be, most geologists are in agreement that *half or more than half of the whole of geological time had passed before life had developed to the Later Palæozoic level.* The reader reading quickly through these opening chapters may be apt to think of them as a mere swift prelude of preparation to the apparently much longer history that follows, but in reality that subsequent history is longer only because it is more detailed and more interesting to us. It looms larger in perspective. For ages that stagger the imagination this earth spun hot and lifeless, and again for ages of equal vastness it held no life above the level of the animalculæ in a drop of ditch-water.

Not only is Space from the point of view of life and humanity empty, but Time is empty also. Life is like a little glow, scarcely kindled yet, in these void immensities.

[1] There is a discussion of fossils in the Holkham Hall Leonardo MS.

[2] An admirable recent book, short and written in a style intelligible to the general reader, is Arthur Holmes, *The Age of the Earth.* He gives a good summary of this most interesting discussion, and sustains the maximum estimate of 1,600 million years.

A MESOZOIC SCENE
SHOWING DEINOTHERIA

Drawing by Alice B. Woodward

"The Mesozoic reptiles attained enormous proportions." Here, two Ceratosauriens are hunting. One has bowled over a Stegosaurus (so as to get at the soft part of him and avoid the armour), the other has sighted a herd of Cetiosauriens and is in full cry. The latter are making for the water.

III

NATURAL SELECTION AND THE CHANGES OF SPECIES

NOW here it will be well to put plainly certain general facts about this new thing, *life*, that was creeping in the shallow waters and intertidal muds of the early Palæozoic period, and which is perhaps confined to our planet alone in all the immensity of space.

Life differs from all things whatever that are without life in certain general aspects. There are the most wonderful differences among living things to-day, but all living things past and present agree in possessing *a certain power of growth*, all living things *take nourishment*, all living things *move about* as they feed and grow, though the movement may be no more than the spread of roots through the soil, or of branches in the air. Moreover, living things reproduce ; they give rise to other living things, either by growing and then dividing or by means of seeds or spores or eggs or other ways of producing young. *Reproduction* is a characteristic of life.

No living thing goes on living for ever. There seems to be *a limit of growth* for every kind of living thing. Among very small and simple living things, such as that microscopic blob of living matter the *Amœba*, an individual may grow and then divide completely into two new individuals, which again may divide in their turn. Many other microscopic creatures live actively for a time, grow, and then become quiet and inactive, enclose themselves in an outer covering and break up wholly into a number of still smaller things, spores, which are released and scattered and again grow into the likeness of their parent. Among more complex creatures the reproduction is not usually such simple division, though division does occur even in the case of many creatures big enough to be visible to the unassisted eye. But the rule with almost all larger beings is that the individual grows up to a certain limit of size. Then, before it becomes unwieldy, its growth declines and stops. As it reaches its full size it *matures*, it begins to produce young, which are either born alive or hatched from eggs. But all of its body does not produce young. Only a special part does that. After the individual has lived and produced offspring for some time, it ages and dies. It does so by a sort of necessity. There is a practical limit to its life as well as to its growth. These things are as true of plants as they are of animals. And they are not true of things that do not live. Non-living things, such as crystals, grow, but they have no set limits of growth or size, they *do not move of their own accord* and there is *no stir within them*. Crystals once formed may last unchanged for millions of years. There is *no reproduction* for any non-living thing.

This growth and dying and reproduction of living things leads to some very wonderful consequences. The young which a living thing produces are either directly, or after some intermediate stages and changes (such as the changes of a caterpillar and butterfly), like the parent living thing. But they are never exactly like it or like each other. There is always a slight difference, which we speak of as *individuality*. A thousand butterflies this year may produce two or three thousand next year ; these latter will look to us almost exactly like their predecessors, but each one will have just that slight difference. It is hard for us to see individuality in butterflies because we do not observe them very closely, but it is easy for us to see it in men. All the men and women in the world now are descended from the men and women of A.D. 1800, but not one of us now is exactly the same as one of that vanished generation. And what is true of men and butterflies is true of every sort of living thing, of plants as of animals. Every species changes all its individualities in each generation. That is as true of all the minute creatures that swarmed and reproduced and died in the Archæozoic and Proterozoic seas, as it is of men to-day.

Every species of living things is continually dying and being born again, as a multitude of fresh individuals.

Consider, then, what must happen to a new-born generation of living things of any species. Some of the individuals will be stronger or sturdier or better suited to succeed in life in some way than the rest, many individuals will be weaker or less suited. In particular single cases any sort of luck or accident may occur, but *on the whole* the better equipped individuals will live and grow up and reproduce themselves and the weaker will *as a rule* go under. The latter will be less able to get food, to fight their enemies and pull through. So that in each generation there is as it were a picking over of a species, a picking out of most of the weak or unsuitable and a preference for the strong and suitable. This process is called *Natural Selection* or the *Survival of the Fittest.*[1]

old sort of individual that used to prosper and dominate will fail and die out and the new sort of individual will become the rule, —until the general character of the species changes.

Suppose, for example, there is some little furry whitey-brown animal living in a bitterly cold land which is usually under snow. Such individuals as have the thickest, whitest fur will be least hurt by the cold, less seen by their enemies, and less conspicuous as they seek their prey. The fur of this species will thicken and its whiteness increase with every generation, until there is no advantage in carrying any more fur.

DIAGRAM OF LIFE IN THE LATER PALÆOZOIC AGE.

Life is creeping out of the water. An insect, like a dragon-fly, is shown. There were amphibia like gigantic newts and salamanders, and even primitive reptiles in these swamps.

It follows, therefore, from the fact that living things grow and breed and die, that every species, so long as the conditions under which it lives remain the same, becomes more and more perfectly fitted to those conditions in every generation.

But now suppose those conditions change, then the sort of individual that used to succeed may now fail to succeed and a sort of individual that could not get on at all under the old conditions may now find its opportunity. These species will change, therefore, generation by generation; the

[1] It might be called with more exactness the *Survival of the Fitter.*

Imagine now a change of climate that brings warmth into the land, sweeps away the snows, makes white creatures glaringly visible during the greater part of the year and thick fur an encumbrance. Then every individual with a touch of brown in its colouring and a thinner fur will find itself at an advantage, and very white and heavy fur will be a handicap. There will be a weeding out of the white in favour of the brown in each generation. If this change of climate come about too quickly, it may of course exterminate the species altogether; but if it come about gradually, the species, although it may have a hard time, may yet be able to change itself and adapt itself generation by generation. This change and adaptation is called the *Modification of Species.*

Perhaps this change of climate does not occur all over the lands inhabited by the species; maybe it occurs only on one side of some great arm of the sea or some great mountain range or such-like divide, and not on the other. A warm ocean current like the Gulf Stream may be deflected, and flow so as to warm one side of the barrier, leaving the other still cold. Then on the cold side this species will still be going on to its utmost possible furriness and whiteness and on the other side it will be modifying towards brownness and a thinner coat. At the same time there will probably be other changes going on; a difference in the paws perhaps, because one half of the species will be frequently scratching through snow for its food, while the other will be scampering over brown earth. Probably also the difference of climate will mean differences in the sort of food available, and that may produce differences in the teeth and the digestive organs. And there may be changes in the sweat and oil glands of the skin due to the changes in the fur, and these will affect the excretory organs and all the internal chemistry of the body. And so through all the structure of the creature. A time will come when the two separated varieties of this formerly single species will become so unlike each other as to be recognizably different species. Such a splitting up of a species in the course of generations into two or more species is called the *Differentiation of Species.*

And it should be clear to the reader that given these elemental facts of life, given growth and death and reproduction with individual variation in a world that changes, life *must* change in this way, modification and differentiation *must* occur, old species *must* disappear, and new ones appear. We have chosen for our instance here a familiar sort of animal, but what is true of furry beasts in snow and ice is true of all life, and equally true of the soft jellies and simple beginnings that flowed and crawled for hundreds of millions of years between the tidal levels and in the shallow, warm waters of the Proterozoic seas.

The early life of the early world, when the blazing sun rose and set in only a quarter of the time it now takes, when the warm seas poured in great tides over the sandy and muddy shores of the rocky lands and the air was full of clouds and steam, must have been modified and varied and species must have developed at a great pace. Life was probably as swift and short as the days and years; the generations, which natural selection picked over, followed one another in rapid succession.

Natural selection is a slower process with man than with any other creature. It takes twenty years or more before an ordinary human being in western Europe grows up and reproduces. In the case of most animals the new generation is on trial in a year or less. With such simple and lowly beings, however, as first appeared in the primordial seas, growth and reproduction was probably a matter of a few brief hours or even of a few brief minutes. Modification and differentiation of species must accordingly have been extremely rapid, and life had already developed a great variety of widely contrasted forms before it began to leave traces in the rocks. The Record of the Rocks does not begin, therefore, with any group of closely related forms from which all subsequent and existing creatures are descended. It begins in the midst of the game, with nearly every main division of the animal kingdom already represented.[1] Plants are already plants, and animals animals. The curtain rises on a drama in the sea that has already begun, and has been going on for some time. The brachiopods are discovered already in their shells, accepting and consuming much the same sort of food that oysters and mussels do now; the great water scorpions crawl among the seaweeds, the trilobites roll up into balls and unroll and scuttle away. In that ancient mud and among those early weeds there was probably as rich and abundant and active a life of infusoria and the like as one finds in a drop of ditch-water to-day. In the ocean waters too, down to the utmost downward limit to which light could filter, then as now, there was an abundance of minute and translucent, and in many cases phosphorescent, beings.

But though the ocean and intertidal waters already swarmed with life, the land above the high-tide line was still, so far as we can guess, a stony wilderness without a trace of life.

[1] See Evans, The Sudden Appearance of the Cambrian Fauna (*Proc. of XIe Congress Geolog. Inst.*, 1910) for a discussion of this.

IV

THE INVASION OF THE DRY LAND BY LIFE

§ 1. *Life and Water.* § 2. *The Earliest Animals.*

§ 1

WHEREVER the shore line ran there was life, and that life went on in and by and with water as its home, its medium, and its fundamental necessity.

The first jelly-like beginnings of life must have perished whenever they got out of the water, as jelly-fish dry up and perish on our beaches to-day. Drying up was the fatal thing for life in those days, against which at first it had no protection. But in a world of rain-pools and shallow seas and tides, any variation that enabled a living thing to hold out and keep its moisture during hours of low tide or drought met with every encouragement in the circumstances of the time. There must have been a constant risk of stranding. And, on the other hand, life had to keep rather near the shore and beaches in the shallows because it had need of air (dissolved of course in the water) and light.

No creature can breathe, no creature can digest its food, without water. We talk of breathing air, but what all living things really do is to breathe oxygen dissolved in water. The air we ourselves breathe must first be dissolved in the moisture in our lungs; and all our food must be liquefied before it can be assimilated. Water-living creatures which are always under water, wave their freely exposed gills by which they breathe in that water, and extract the air dissolved in it. But a creature that is to be exposed for any time out of the water, must have its body and its breathing apparatus protected from drying up. Before the seaweeds could creep up out of the Early Palæozoic seas into the intertidal line of the beach, they had to develop a tougher outer skin to hold their moisture. Before the ancestor of the sea scorpion could survive being left by the tide it had to develop its casing and armour. The trilobites probably developed their tough covering and rolled up into balls, far less as a protection against each other and any other enemies they may have possessed, than as a precaution against drying. And when presently, as we ascend the Palæozoic rocks, the fish appear, first of all the back-boned or vertebrated animals, it is evident that a number of them are already adapted by the protection of their gills with gill covers and by a sort of primitive lung swimming-bladder, to face the same risk of temporary stranding.

Now the weeds and plants that were adapting themselves to intertidal conditions were also bringing themselves into a region of brighter light, and light is very necessary and precious to all plants. Any development of structure that would stiffen them and hold them up to the light, so that instead of crumpling and flopping when the waters receded, they would stand up outspread, was a great advantage. And so we find them developing fibre and support, and the beginning of *woody fibre* in them. The early plants reproduced by soft spores, or half-animal "gametes," that were released in water, were distributed by water and could only germinate under water. The early plants were tied, and most lowly plants to-day are tied, by the conditions of their life cycle, to water. But here again there was a great advantage to be got by the development of some protection of the spores from drought that would enable reproduction to occur without submergence. So soon as a species could do that, it could live and reproduce and spread above the high-water mark, bathed in light and out of reach of the beating and distress of the waves. The main classificatory divisions of the larger plants mark stages in the release of plant life from the necessity of submergence by the development of woody support and of a method of reproduction that is more and more defiant of drying up. The lower plants are still the prisoner attendants of water. The lower mosses must live in damp, and even the development of the spore of the ferns demands at certain stages extreme wetness. The highest plants have carried freedom from water so far that they can live and reproduce if only there is some moisture in the soil below them. They have solved their problem of living out of water altogether.

The essentials of that problem were worked out through the vast æons of the Proterozoic Age and the early Palæozoic Age by nature's method of experiment and trial. Then slowly, but in great abundance,

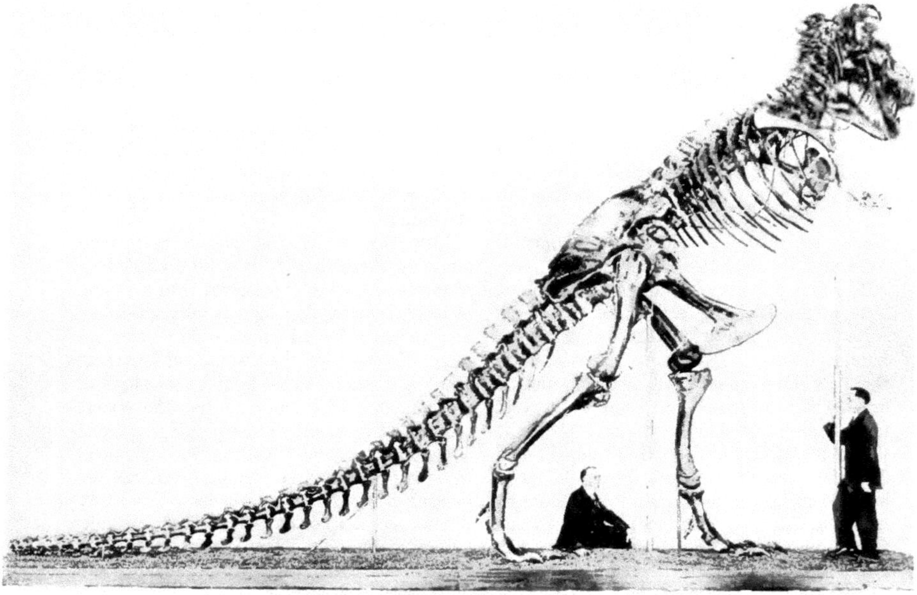

SKELETON OF THE TYRANNOSAURUS

In the American Museum of Natural History, New York

It stood eighteen feet hign and was the fighting animal of his age.

THE TYRANNOSAURUS REX AT HOME

"The last word in frightfulness among living things . . . forty feet from snout to tail, with muscles of a quite miraculous quality."

a variety of new plants began to swarm away from the sea and over the lower lands, still keeping to swamp and lagoon and water-course as they spread.

§ 2

And after the plants came the animal life.

There is no sort of land animal in the world, as there is no sort of land plant, whose structure is not primarily that of a water-inhabiting being which has been adapted through the modification and differentiation of species to life out of the water. This adaptation is attained in various ways. In the case of the land scorpion the gill-plates of the primitive sea scorpion are sunken into the body so as to make the lung-books secure from rapid evaporation. The gills of crustaceans, such as the crabs which run about in the air, are protected by the gill-cover extensions of the back shell or carapace. The ancestors of the insects developed a system of air pouches and air tubes, the tracheal tubes, which carry the air all over the body before it is dissolved. In the case of the vertebrated land animals, the gills of the ancestral fish were first supplemented and then replaced by a bag-like growth from the throat, the primitive lung swimming-bladder. To this day there survive certain mudfish which enable us to understand very clearly the method by which the vertebrated land animals worked their way out of the water. These creatures (*e.g.* the African lung fish) are found in tropical regions in which there is a rainy full season and a dry season, during which the rivers become mere ditches of baked mud. During the rainy season these fish swim about and breathe by gills like any other fish. As the waters of the river evaporate, these fish bury themselves in the mud, their gills go out of action, and the creature keeps itself alive until the waters return by swallowing air, which passes into its swimming-bladder. The Australian lung fish, when it is caught by the drying up of the river in stagnant pools, and the water has become deaerated and foul, rises to the surface and gulps air. A newt in a pond does exactly the same thing. These creatures still remain at the transition stage, the stage at which the ancestors of the higher vertebrated animals were released from their restriction to an under-water life.

The amphibia (frogs, newts, tritons, etc.) still show in their life history all the stages in the process of this liberation. They are still dependent on water for their reproduction; their eggs must be laid in sunlit water, and there they must develop. The young tadpole has branching external gills that wave in the water; then a gill cover grows back over them and forms a gill chamber. Then, as the creature's legs appear and its tail is absorbed, it begins to use its lungs, and its gills dwindle and vanish. The adult frog can live all the rest of its days in the air, but it can be drowned if it is kept steadfastly below water. When we come to the reptile, however, we find an egg which is protected from evaporation by a tough egg case, and this egg produces young which breathe by lungs from the very moment of hatching. The reptile is on all fours with the seeding plant in its freedom from the necessity to pass any stage of its life cycle in water.

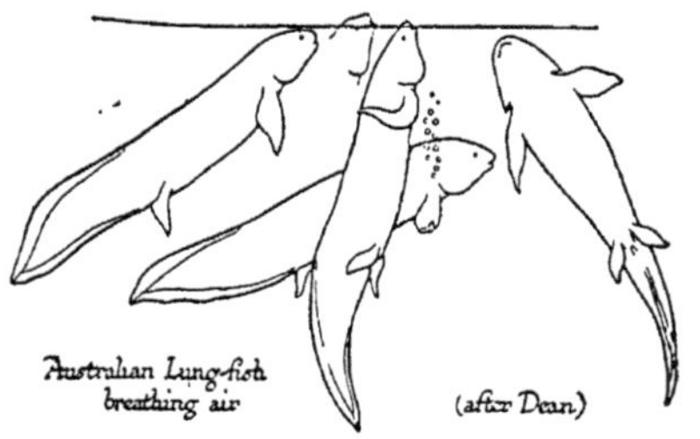

The later Palæozoic Rocks of the northern hemisphere give us the materials for a series of pictures of this slow spreading of life over the land. Geographically, all round the northern half of the world it was an age of lagoons and shallow seas very favourable to this invasion. The new plants, now that they had acquired the power to live this new aerial life, developed with an extraordinary richness and variety.

There were as yet no true flowering plants,[1] no grasses nor trees that shed their leaves in winter[2]; the first "flora" consisted of great tree ferns, gigantic equisetums, cycad ferns, and kindred vegetation. Many of these plants took the form of huge-stemmed trees, of which great multitudes of trunks survive fossilized to this day. Some of these trees were over a hundred feet high, of orders and classes now vanished from the world. They stood with their stems in the water, in which no doubt there was a thick tangle of soft mosses and green slime and fungoid growths that left few plain vestiges behind them. The abundant remains of these first swamp forests constitute the main coal measures of the world to-day.

Amidst this luxuriant primitive vegetation

[1] Phanerogams. [2] Deciduous trees.

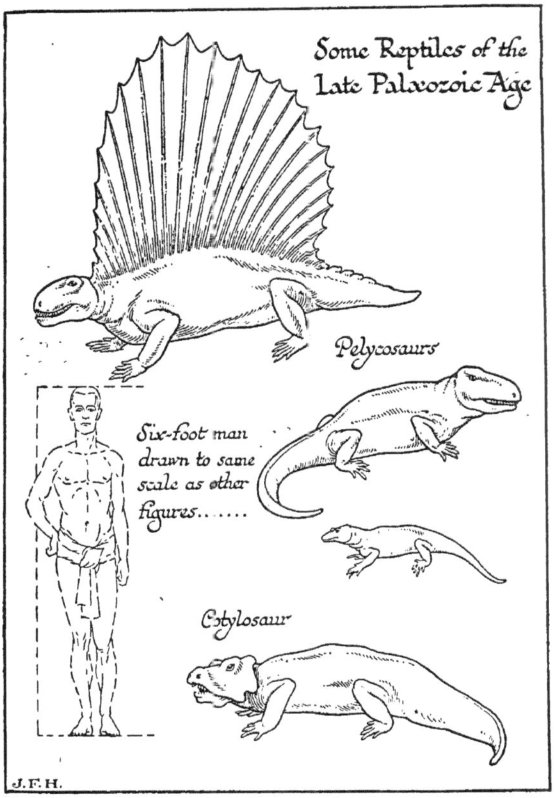

crawled and glided and flew the first insects. They were rigid-winged, four-winged creatures, often very big, some of them having wings measuring a foot in length. There were numerous dragon flies—one found in the Belgian coal-measures had a wing span of twenty-nine inches! There were also a great variety of flying cockroaches. Scorpions abounded, and a number of early spiders, which, however, had no spinnerets for web making.[1] Land snails appeared. So too did the first-known step of our own ancestry upon land, the amphibia. As we ascend the higher levels of the Later Palæozoic record, we find the process of air adaptation has gone as far as the appearance of true reptiles amidst the abundant and various amphibia.

The land life of the Upper Palæozoic Age was the life of a green swamp forest without flowers or birds or the noises of modern insects. There were no big land beasts at all; wallowing amphibia and primitive reptiles were the very highest creatures that life had so far produced. Whatever land lay away from the water or high above the water was still altogether barren and lifeless. But steadfastly, generation by generation, life was creeping away from the shallow sea-water of its beginning.

V

CHANGES IN THE WORLD'S CLIMATE

§ 1. *Why Life must Change Continually.*
§ 2. *The Sun a Steadfast Star.*
§ 3. *Changes from Within the Earth.*
§ 4. *Life may control Change.*

§ 1

THE Record of the Rocks is like a great book that has been carelessly misused. All its pages are torn, worn and defaced, and many are altogether missing. The outline of the story that we sketch here has been pieced together slowly and painfully in an investigation that is still incomplete and still in progress. The Carboniferous Rocks, the "coal-measures," give us a vision of the first great expansion of life over the wet lowlands. Then come the torn

[1] This, says Mr. R. I. Pocock, has to be qualified. There were Carboniferous spiders with spinnerets, though they may have used the silk only for egg cases. And he thinks that the Carboniferous myriapods point to *ground* beneath the trees.

pages known as the Permian Rocks (which count as the last of the Palæozoic), that preserve very little for us of the land vestiges of their age. Only after a long interval of time does the history spread out generously again.

It must be borne in mind that great changes of climate have always been in progress, that have sometimes stimulated and sometimes checked life. Every species of living thing is always adapting itself more and more closely to its conditions. And conditions are always changing. There is no finality in adaptation. There is a continuing urgency towards fresh change.

About these changes of climate some explanations are necessary here. They are not regular changes; they are slow fluctuations between heat and cold. The reader must not think that because the sun and earth were once incandescent, the climatic history of the world is a simple story of cooling down. The centre of the earth is certainly very hot to this day, but we feel nothing of that internal heat at the surface; the internal heat, except for volcanoes and hot springs, has not been perceptible at the surface since first the rocks grew solid. Even in the Azoic or Archæozoic Age there are traces in ice-worn rocks and the like of periods of intense cold. Such cold waves have always been going on everywhere, alternately with warmer conditions. And there have been periods of great wetness and periods of great dryness throughout the earth.

A complete account of the causes of these great climatic fluctuations has still to be worked out, but we may perhaps point out some of the chief of them.[1] Prominent among them is the fact that the earth does not spin in a perfect circle round the sun. Its path or orbit is like a hoop that is distorted; it is, roughly speaking, elliptical (ovo-elliptical), and the sun is nearer to one end of the ellipse than the other. It is at a point which is a focus of the ellipse. And the shape of this orbit never remains the same. It is slowly distorted by the attractions of the other planets, for ages it may be nearly circular, for ages it is more or less elliptical. As the ellipse becomes most nearly circular, then the focus becomes most nearly the centre. When the orbit becomes most elliptical, then the position of the sun becomes most remote from the middle or, to use the astronomer's phrase most eccentric. When the orbit is most nearly circular, then it must be manifest that all the year round the earth must be getting much the same amount of heat from the sun; when the orbit is most distorted, then there will be a season in each year when the earth is nearest the sun (this phrase is called *Perihelion*) and getting a great deal of heat comparatively, and a season when it will be at its farthest from the sun (*Aphelion*) and getting very little warmth. A planet at *aphelion* is travelling its slowest, and its fastest at *perihelion*; so that the hot part of its year will last for a much less time than the cold part of its year. (Sir Robert Ball calculated that the greatest difference possible between the seasons was thirty-three days.) During ages when the orbit is most nearly circular there will therefore be least extremes of climate, and when the orbit is at its greatest eccentricity, there will be an age of cold with great extremes of seasonal temperature. These *changes in the orbit of the earth* are due to the varying pull of all the planets, and Sir Robert Ball declared himself unable to calculate any regular cycle of orbital change, but Professor G. H. Darwin maintained that it is possible to make out a kind of cycle between greatest and least eccentricity of about 200,000 years.

But this change in the shape of the orbit is only one cause of the change of the world's climate. There are many others that have to be considered with it. As most people know, the change in the seasons is due to the fact that the equator of the earth is inclined at an angle to the plane of its orbit. If the earth stood up straight in its orbit, so that its equator was in the plane of its orbit, there would be no change in the seasons at all. The sun would always be overhead at the equator, and the day and night would each be exactly twelve hours long throughout the year everywhere. It is this inclination which causes the difference in the seasons and the unequal length of the day in summer and winter. There is, according to Laplace, a possible variation of nearly three degrees (from 22° 6′ to 24° 50′) in this inclination of the equator to the orbit, and when this is at a maximum, the difference between summer and winter is at its greatest. Great importance has been attached to this variation in the inclination of the equator to the orbit by Dr. Croll in his book *Climate and Time*. At present the angle is 23° 27′. Manifestly when the angle is at its least, the world's

[1] See Sir R. Ball's *Causes of the Great Ice Age*, and Dr. Croll's *Climate and Time*. These are sound books to read still, but the reader will find many of their conclusions modified in Wright's *The Quaternary Ice Age*, which is a quarter of a century more recent.

climate, other things being equal, will be most equable.

And as a third important factor there is what is called the *precession of the equinoxes.* This is a slow wabble of the pole of the spinning earth that takes 25,000 odd years. Any one who watches a spinning top as it "sleeps," will see its axis making a slow circular movement, exactly after the fashion of this circling movement of the earth's axis. The north pole, therefore, does not always point to the same north point among the stars; its pointing traces out a circle in the heavens every 25,000 years.

Now, there will be times when the earth is at its extreme of aphelion or of perihelion, when one hemisphere will be most turned to the sun in its midsummer position and the other most turned away at its midwinter position. And as the precession of the equinoxes goes on, a time will come when the summer-winter position will come not at aphelion and perihelion, but at the half-way points between them. When the summer of one hemisphere happens at perihelion and the winter at aphelion, it will be clear that the summer of the other hemisphere will happen at aphelion and its winter at perihelion. One hemisphere will have a short hot summer and a very cold winter, and the other a long cold summer and a briefer warmish winter. But when the summer-winter positions come at the half-way point of the orbit, and it is the spring of one hemisphere and the autumn of the other that is at aphelion or perihelion, there will not be the same wide difference between the climate of the two hemispheres.

Here are three wavering systems of change all going on independently of each other; the precession of the equinoxes, the change in the obliquity of the equator to the orbit, and the changes in the eccentricity of the orbit. Each system tends by itself to produce periods of equability and periods of greater climatic contrast. And all these systems of change interplay with each other. When it happens that at the same time the orbit is most nearly circular, the equator is at its least inclination from the plane of the earth's orbit, and the spring and autumn are at perihelion and aphelion, then all these causes will be conspiring to make climate warm and uniform; there will be least difference of summer and winter. When, on the other hand, the orbit is in its most eccentric stage of deformation, when also the equator is most tilted up and when

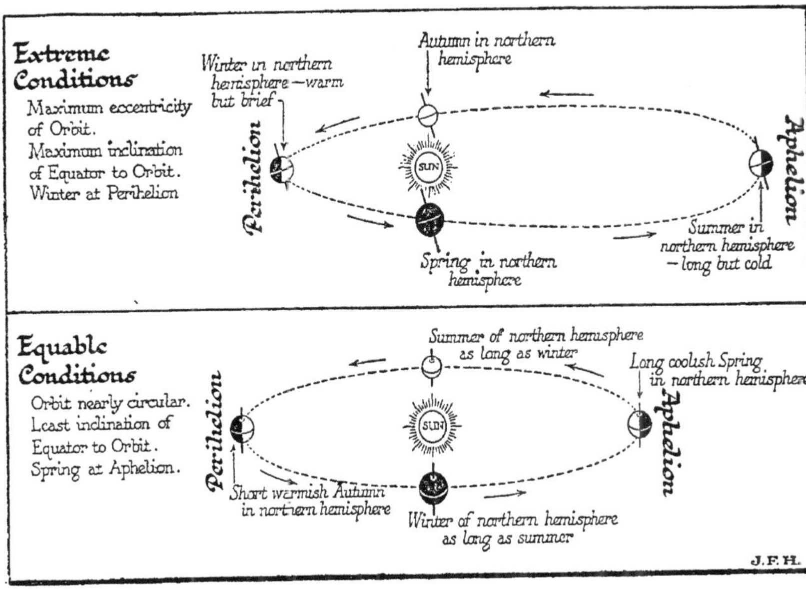

DIAGRAM TO ILLUSTRATE ONE SET OF CAUSES, THE ASTRONOMICAL VARIATIONS, WHICH MAKE THE CLIMATE OF THE WORLD CHANGE SLOWLY BUT CONTINUOUSLY.

It does not change in regular periods. It fluctuates through vast ages. As the world's climate changes, life must change too or perish.

VEGETATION IN THE CARBONIFEROUS AGE

By W. E. Robinson

The Sigillaria (plural, Sigillariæ,) or Club Mosses (2) were branchless and reached 100 ft. in height, while the Lepidodendrons (5) were branched and were 14 ft. higher. The Cordaites or Cycaid Conifers (6) grew on high ground, averaged 90 ft. in height, and were the only then existing species bearing flowers. The Giant Horsetails or Calamites (8) grew to 60 ft., and everywhere was an abundance (7 centre) of ferns. All these formed the coal measures, and their roots are in the underlying clay beds. In the Carboniferous Age were myriads of winged insects (1), dragon flies (3) with bodies 18 in. long, and small amphibians, Keraterpeton (4), were frequent.

further the summer and winter are at aphelion and perihelion, then climates will be at their extremest and winter at its bitterest. There will be great accumulations of ice and snow in winter; the heat of the brief hot summer will be partly reflected back into space by the white snow, and it will be unequal to the task of melting all the winter's ice before the earth spins away once more towards its chilly aphelion. The earth will accumulate cold so long as this conspiracy of extreme conditions continues.

So our earth's climate changes and wavers perpetually as these three systems of influence come together with a common tendency towards warmth or severity, or as they contradict and cancel each other.

We can trace in the Record of the Rocks an irregular series of changes due to the interplay of these influences; there have been great ages when the separate rhythms of these three systems kept them out of agreement and the atmosphere was temperate, ages of world-wide warmth, and other ages when they seemed to concentrate bitterly to their utmost extremity, to freeze out and inflict the utmost stresses and hardship upon life.

And in accordance we find from the record in the rocks that there have been long periods of expansion and multiplication when life flowed and abounded and varied, and harsh ages when there was a great weeding out and disappearance of species, genera, and classes, and the learning of stern lessons by all that survived. Such a propitious conjunction it must have been that gave the age of luxuriant low-grade growth of the coal measures; such an adverse series of circumstances that chilled the closing æons of the Palæozoic time.

It is probable that the warm spells have been long relatively to the cold ages. Our world to-day seems to be emerging with fluctuations from a prolonged phase of adversity and extreme conditions. Half a million years ahead it may be a winterless world with trees and vegetation even in the polar circles. At present we have no certainty in such a forecast, but later on, as knowledge increases, it may be possible to reckon with more precision, so that our race will make its plans thousands of years ahead to meet the coming changes.

§ 2

Another entirely different cause of changes in the general climate of the earth may be due to variations in the heat of the sun. We do not yet understand what causes the heat of the sun or what sustains that undying fire. It is possible that in the past there have been periods of greater and lesser intensity. About that we know nothing; human experience has been too short; and so far we have been able to find no evidence on this matter in the geological record. On the whole, scientific men are inclined to believe that the sun has blazed with a general steadfastness throughout geological time. It may have been cooling slowly, but, speaking upon the scale of things astronomical, it has certainly not cooled very much.

§ 3

A third great group of causes influencing climate are to be found in the forces within the world itself. Throughout the long history of the earth there has been a continuous wearing down of the hills and mountains by frost and rain and a carrying out of their material to become sedimentary rocks under the seas. There has been a continuous process of wearing down the land and filling up the seas, by which the seas, as they became shallower, must have spread more and more over the land. The reverse process, a process of crumpling and upheaval, has also been in progress, but less regularly. The forces of upheaval have been spasmodic; the forces of wearing down continuous. For long ages there has been comparatively little volcanic upheaval, and then have come periods in which vast mountain chains have been thrust up and the whole outline of land and sea changed. Such a time was the opening stage of the Cainozoic period, in which the Alps, the Himalayas, and the Andes were all thrust up from the sea-level to far beyond their present elevations, and the main outlines of the existing geography of the world were drawn.

Now, a time of high mountains and deep seas would mean a larger dry land surface for the world, and a more restricted sea surface, and a time of low lands would mean a time of wider and shallower seas. High mountains precipitate moisture from the atmosphere and hold it out of circulation as snow and glaciers, while smaller oceans mean a lesser area for surface evaporation. Other things being equal, lowland stages of the world's history would be ages of more general atmospheric moisture than periods of relatively greater height of the mountains and greater depth of the seas. But even small increases in the amount of moisture in the air have a powerful influence upon the transmission of radiant heat through that air. The sun's heat will pass much more freely through dry air than through moist air, and so a greater amount of heat would reach the land surfaces of the globe under the conditions of extremes of elevation and depth, than during the periods of relative lowness and shallowness. Dry phases in the history of the earth mean, therefore, hot days. But they also mean cold nights, because for the same reason that the heat comes abundantly to the earth, it will be abundantly radiated away. Moist phases mean, on the other hand, cooler days and warmer nights. The same principle applies to the seasons, and so a phase of great elevations and depressions of the surface would also be another contributory factor on the side of extreme climatic conditions.

And a stage of greater elevation and depression would intensify its extreme conditions by the gradual accumulation of ice caps upon the polar regions and upon the more elevated mountain masses. This accumulation would be at the expense of the sea, whose surface would thus be further shrunken in comparison with the land.

Here then is another set of varying influences that will play in with and help or check the influence of the astronomical variations stated in § 1 and § 2. There are other more localized forces at work into which we cannot go in any detail here, but which will be familiar to the student of the elements of physical geography; the influence of great ocean currents in carrying warmth from equatorial to more temperate latitudes; the interference of mountain chains with the moisture borne by prevalent winds and the like. As in the slow processes of nature these currents are deflected or the mountain chains worn down or displaced by fresh upheavals, the climate over great areas will be changed and all the conditions of life changed with it. Under the incessant slow variations of these astronomical, telluric, and geographical influences life has no rest. As its conditions change it must change or perish.

§ 4

And while we are enumerating the forces that change climate and the conditions of terrestrial life, we may perhaps look ahead a little and add a fourth set of influences, at first unimportant in the history of the world so far as the land surface is concerned, but becoming more important after the age of Reptiles, to which we shall proceed in our next chapter. These are the effects produced upon climate by life itself. Particularly great is the influence of vegetation, and especially that of forests. Every tree is continually transpiring water vapour into the air; the amount of water evaporated in summer by a lake surface is far less than the amount evaporated by the same area of beech forest. As in the later Mesozoic and the Cainozoic Age, great forests spread over the world, their action in keeping the air moist and mitigating and stabilizing climate by keeping the summer cool and the winter mild must have become more and more important. Moreover, forests accumulate and protect soil and so prepare the possibility of agricultural life.

Water-weeds again may accumulate to choke and deflect rivers, flood and convert great areas into marshes, and so lead to the destruction of forests or the replacement of grass-lands by boggy wildernesses.

Finally, with the appearance of human communities, came what is perhaps the most powerful of all living influences upon climate. By fire and plough and axe man alters his world. By destroying forests and by irrigation man has already affected the climate of great regions of the world's surface. The destruction of forests makes the seasons more extreme; this has happened, for instance, in the north-eastern states of the United States of America. Moreover, the soil is no longer protected from the scour of rain, and is washed away, leaving only barren rock beneath. This has happened in Spain and Dalmatia and, some thousands of years earlier, in South Arabia. By irrigation, on the other hand, man restores the desert to life and mitigates climate. This process is going on in North-west India and Australia. In the future, by making such operations world-wide and systematic, man may be able to control climate to an extent at which as yet we can only guess.

VI

THE AGE OF REPTILES

§ 1

WE know that for hundreds of thousands of years the wetness and warmth, the shallow lagoon conditions that made possible the vast accumulations of vegetable matter which, compressed and mummified,[1] are now coal, prevailed over most of the world. There were some cold intervals, it is true; but they did not last long enough to destroy the growths. Then that long age of luxuriant low-grade vegetation drew to its end, and for a time life on the earth seems to have undergone a period of world-wide bleakness.

When the story resumes again, we find life entering upon a fresh phase of richness and expansion. Vegetation has made great advances in the art of living out of water. While the Palæozoic plants of the coal measures probably grew with swamp water flowing over their roots, the Mesozoic flora from its very outset included palm-like cycads and low-ground conifers that were distinctly land plants growing on soil above the water level. The lower levels of the Mesozoic land were no doubt covered by great fern brakes and shrubby bush and a kind of jungle growth of trees. But there existed as yet no grass, no small flowering plants, no turf nor greensward. Probably the Mesozoic was not an age of very brightly coloured vegetation. It must have had a flora green in the wet season and brown and purple in the dry. There were no gay flowers, no bright autumn tints before the fall of the leaf, because there was as yet no fall of the leaf. And beyond the lower levels the world was still barren, still unclothed, still exposed without any mitigation to the wear and tear of the wind and rain.

When one speaks of conifers in the Mesozoic the reader must not think of the pines and firs that clothe the high mountain slopes of our time. He must think of low-growing evergreens. The mountains were still as bare and lifeless as ever. The only colour effects among the mountains were the colour effects of naked rock, such colours as make the landscape of Colorado so marvellous to-day.

Amidst this spreading vegetation of the lower plains the reptiles were increasing mightily in multitude and variety. They were now in many cases absolutely land animals. There are numerous anatomical points of distinction between a reptile and an amphibian; they held good between such reptiles and amphibians as prevailed in the carboniferous time of the Upper Palæozoic; but the fundamental difference between reptiles and amphibia which matters in this history is that the amphibian must go back to the water to lay its eggs, and that in the early stages of its life it must live in and under water. The reptile, on the other hand, has cut out all the tadpole stages from its life cycle, or, to be more exact, its tadpole stages are got through before the young leave the egg case. The reptile has come out of the water altogether. Some had gone back to it again, just as the hippopotamus and the otter among mammals have gone back, but that is a further extension of the story to which we cannot give much attention in this *Outline*.

In the Palæozoic period, as we have said, life had not spread beyond the swampy river valleys and the borders of sea lagoons and the like; but in the Mesozoic, life was growing ever more accustomed to the thinner medium of the air, was sweeping boldly up over the plains and towards the hill-sides. It is well for the student of human history and the human future to note that. If a disembodied intelligence with no knowledge of the future had come to earth and studied life during the early Palæozoic age, he might very reasonably have concluded that life was absolutely confined to the water, and that it could never spread over the land. It found a way. In the Later Palæozoic Period that visitant might have been equally sure that life could not go beyond the edge of a swamp. The Mesozoic Period would still have found him setting bounds to life far more limited than the bounds that are set to-day. And so to-day, though we mark how life and man are

[1] Dr. Marie Stopes, *Monograph on the Constitution of Coal.*

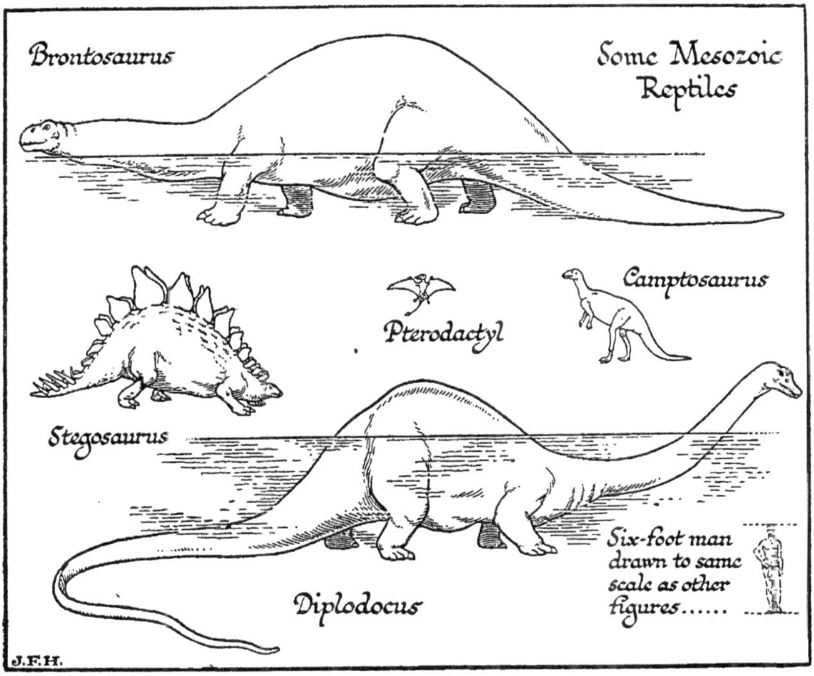

still limited to five miles of air and a depth of perhaps a mile or so of sea, we must not conclude from that present limitation that life, through man, may not presently spread out and up and down to a range of living as yet inconceivable.

The earliest known reptiles were beasts with great bellies and not very powerful legs, very like their kindred amphibia, wallowing as the crocodile wallows to this day; but in the Mesozoic they soon began to stand up and go stoutly on all fours, and several great sections of them began to balance themselves on tail and hind-legs, rather as the kangaroos do now, in order to release the fore limbs for grasping food The bones of one notable division of reptiles which retained a quadrupedal habit, a division of which many remains have been found in South African and Russian Early Mesozoic deposits, display a number of characters which approach those of the mammalian skeleton, and because of this resemblance to the mammals (beasts) this division is called the *Theriomorpha* (beastlike). Another division was the crocodile branch, and another developed towards the tortoises and turtles. The *Plesiosaurs* and *Ichthyosaurs* were two groups which have left no living representatives; they were huge reptiles returning to a whale-like life in the sea. *Pliosaurus*, one of the largest plesiosaurs, measured thirty feet from snout to tail tip—of which half was neck. The *Mosasaurs* were a third group of great porpoise-like marine lizards. But the largest and most diversified group of these Mesozoic reptiles was the group we have spoken of as kangaroo-like, the *Dinosaurs*, many of which attained enormous proportions. In bigness these greater *Dinosaurs* have never been exceeded, although the sea can still show in the whales creatures as great. Some of these, and the largest among them, were herbivorous animals; they browsed on the rushy vegetation and among the ferns and bushes, or they stood up and grasped trees with their fore-legs while they devoured the foliage. Among the browsers, for example, were the *Diplodocus carnegii*, which measured eighty-four feet in length, and the *Atlantosaurus*. The *Gigantosaurus*, disinterred by a German expedition in 1912 from rocks in East Africa, was still more colossal. It measured well over a hundred feet! These greater monsters had legs, and they are usually figured as standing up on them; but it is very doubtful if they could have supported their weight in this way, out of water. Buoyed up by water or mud they may have got along. Another noteworthy

THE GIGANTOSAURUS

Prehistoric aquatic reptile, disinterred from rocks, 1912

From a reconstruction drawing by A. Forestier

"It measured well over a hundred feet, is usually figured as standing up, but it is doubtful if it could support its own weight out of water or mud." Note crocodile for comparative size.

type we have figured is the *Triceratops.* There were also a number of great flesh-eaters who preyed upon these herbivores. Of these, *Tyrannosaurus* seems almost the last word in "frightfulness" among living things. Some species of this genus measured forty feet from snout to tail. Apparently it carried this vast body kangaroo fashion on its tail and hind-legs. Probably it reared itself up. Some authorities even suppose that it leapt through the air. If so, it possessed muscles of a quite miraculous quality. A leaping elephant would be a far less astounding idea. Much more probably it waded half submerged in pursuit of the herbivorous river saurians.

§ 2

One special development of the dinosaurian type of reptile was a light, hopping, climbing group of creatures which developed a bat-like web between the fifth finger and the side of the body, which was used in gliding from tree to tree after the fashion of the flying squirrels. These bat-lizards were the *Pterodactyls.* They are often described as *flying* reptiles, and pictures are drawn of Mesozoic scenery in which they are seen soaring and swooping about. But their breastbone has no keel such as the breastbone of a bird has for the attachment of muscles strong enough for long sustained flying. They must have flitted about like bats. They must have had a grotesque resemblance to heraldic dragons, and they played the part of bat-like birds in the Mesozoic jungles. But bird-like though they were, they were not birds nor the ancestors of birds. The structure of their wings was altogether different from that of birds. The structure of their wings was that of a hand with one long finger and a web; the wing of a bird is like an arm with feathers projecting from its hind edge. And these Pterodactyls had no feathers.

§ 3

Far less prevalent at this time were certain other truly bird-like creatures, of which the earlier sorts also hopped and clambered and the later sorts skimmed and flew. These were at first—by all the standards of classification—Reptiles. They developed into true birds as they developed wings and as their reptilian scales became long and complicated, fronds rather than scales, and so at last, by much spreading and splitting, feathers. Feathers are the distinctive covering of birds, and they give a power of resisting heat and cold far greater than that of any other integumentary covering except perhaps the thickest fur. At a very early stage this novel covering of feathers, this new heat-proof contrivance that life had chanced upon,

enabled many species of birds to invade a province for which the pterodactyl was ill equipped. They took to sea fishing—if indeed they did not begin with it—and spread to the north and south polewards beyond the temperature limits set to the true reptiles. The earliest birds seem to have been carnivorous divers and water birds. To this day some of the most primitive bird forms are found among the sea birds of the Arctic and Antarctic seas, and it is among these sea birds that zoologists still find lingering traces of teeth, which have otherwise vanished completely from the beak of the bird.

The earliest known bird (the *Archæopteryx*) had no beak; it had a row of teeth in a jaw like a reptile's. It had three claws at the forward corner of its wing. Its tail too was peculiar. All modern birds have their tail feathers set in a short compact bony rump; the *Archæopteryx* had a long bony tail with a row of feathers along each side.

§ 4

This great period of Mesozoic life, this second volume of the book of life, is indeed an amazing story of reptilian life proliferating and developing. But the most striking thing of all the story remains to be told. Right up to the latest Mesozoic Rocks we find all these reptilian orders we have enumerated still flourishing unchallenged. There is no hint of an enemy or competitor to them in the relics we find of their world. Then the record is broken. We do not know how long a time the break represents; many pages may be missing here, pages that may represent some great cataclysmal climatic change. When next we find abundant traces of the land plants and the land animals of the earth, this great multitude of reptile species had gone. For the most part they have left no descendants. They have been "wiped out." The pterodactyls have gone absolutely, of the plesiosaurs and ichthyosaurs none is alive; the mosasaurs have gone; of the lizards a few remain, the monitors of the Dutch East Indies are the largest; all the multitude and diversity of the dinosaurs have vanished. Only the crocodiles and the turtles and tortoises carry on in any quantity into Cainozoic times. The place of all these types in the picture that the Cainozoic fossils presently unfold to us is taken by other animals not closely related to the Mesozoic reptiles and certainly not descended from any of their ruling types. A new kind of life is in possession of the world.

This apparently abrupt ending up of the reptiles is, beyond all question, the most striking revolution in the whole history of the earth before the coming of mankind. It is probably connected with the close of a vast period of equable warm conditions and the onset of a new austerer age, in which the winters were bitterer and the summers brief but hot. The Mesozoic life, animal and vegetable alike, was adapted to warm conditions and capable of little resistance to cold. The new life, on the other hand, was before all things capable of resisting great changes of temperature.

Whatever it was that led to the extinction of the Mesozoic reptiles, it was probably some very far-reaching change indeed, for the life of the seas did at the same time undergo a similar catastrophic alteration. The crescendo and ending of the Reptiles on land was paralleled by the crescendo and ending of the Ammonites, a division of creatures like squids with coiled shells which swarmed in those ancient seas. All through the rocky record of this Mesozoic period there is a vast multitude and variety of these coiled shells; there are hundreds of species, and towards the end of the Mesozoic period they increased in diversity and produced exaggerated types. When the record resumes these too have gone. So far as the reptiles are concerned, people may perhaps be inclined to argue that they were exterminated because the Mammals that replaced them, competed with them, and were more fitted to survive; but nothing of the sort can be true of the Ammonites, because to this day their place has not been taken. Simply they are gone. Unknown conditions made it possible for them to live in the Mesozoic seas, and then some unknown change made life impossible for them. No genus of Ammonite survives to-day of all that vast variety, but there still exists one isolated genus very closely related to the Ammonites, the Pearly Nautilus. It is found, it is to be noted, in the warm waters of the Indian and Pacific Oceans.[1]

And as for the Mammals competing with and ousting the less fit reptiles, a struggle of which people talk at times, there is not a scrap of evidence of any such direct competition. To judge by the Record of the Rocks as we know it to-day, there is much more reason for believing that first the reptiles in some inexplicable way perished, and then that later on, after a very hard time for all life upon the earth, the mammals, as conditions became more genial again, developed and spread to fill the vacant world.

Hesperornis
(Reptilian wingless water-bird)

[1] See article "Cephalopoda" in the *Encyclopædia Britannica* for its anatomy.

§ 5

Were there mammals in the Mesozoic period?

This is a question not yet to be answered precisely. Patiently and steadily the geologists gather fresh evidence and reason out completer conclusions. At any time some new deposit may reveal fossils that will illuminate this question. Certainly either mammals, or the ancestors of the mammals, must have lived throughout the Mesozoic period. In the very opening chapter of the Mesozoic volume of the Record there were those Theriomorphous Reptiles to which we have already alluded, and in the later Mesozoic a number of small jaw-bones are found, entirely mammalian in character. But there is not a scrap, not a bone, to suggest that there lived any Mesozoic Mammal which could look a dinosaur in the face. The Mesozoic mammals or mammal-like reptiles—for we do not know clearly which they were—seem to have been all obscure little beasts of the size of mice and rats, more like a down-trodden order of reptiles than a distinct class; probably they still laid eggs and were developing only slowly their distinctive covering of hair. They lived away from big waters, and perhaps in the desolate uplands, as marmots do now; probably they lived there beyond the pursuit of the carnivorous dinosaurs. Some perhaps went on all fours, some chiefly went on their hind-legs and clambered with their fore limbs. They became fossils only so occasionally that chance has not yet revealed a single complete skeleton in the whole vast record of the Mesozoic rocks by which to check these guesses.

These little Theriomorphs, these ancestral mammals, developed hair. Hairs, like feathers, are long and elaborately specialized scales. Hair is perhaps the clue to the salvation of the early mammals. Leading lives upon the margin of existence, away from the marshes and the warmth, they developed an outer covering only second in its warmth-holding (or heat-resisting) powers to the down and feathers of the Arctic sea-birds. And so they held out through the age of hardship between the Mesozoic and Cainozoic ages, to which most of the true reptiles succumbed.

All the main characteristics of this flora and sea and land fauna that came to an end with the end of the Mesozoic age were such as were adapted to an equable climate and to shallow and swampy regions. But in the case of their Cainozoic successors, both hair and feathers gave *a power of resistance to variable temperatures* such as no reptile possessed, and with it they gave a range far greater than any animal had hitherto attained.

The range of life of the Lower Palæozoic Period was confined to warm water.

The range of life of the Upper Palæozoic Period was confined to warm water or to warm swamps and wet ground.

The range of life of the Mesozoic Period as we know it was confined to water and fairly low-lying valley regions under equable conditions.

Meanwhile in each of these periods there were types involuntarily extending the range of life beyond the limits prevailing in that period; and when ages of extreme conditions prevailed, it was these marginal types which survived to inherit the depopulated world.

That perhaps is the most general statement we can make about the story of the geological record; it is a story of widening range. Classes, genera, and species of animals appear and disappear, but the range widens. It widens always. Life has never had so great a range as it has to-day. Life to-day, in the form of man, goes higher in the air than it has ever done before; man's geographical range is from pole to pole, he goes under the water in submarines, he sounds the cold, lifeless darkness of the deepest seas, he burrows into virgin levels of the rocks, and in thought and knowledge he pierces to the centre of the earth and reaches out to the uttermost star. Yet in all the relics of the Mesozoic time we find no certain memorials of his ancestry. His ancestors, like the ancestors of all the kindred mammals, must have been creatures so rare, so obscure, and so remote that they have left scarcely a trace amidst the abundant vestiges of the monsters that wallowed rejoicing in the steamy air and lush vegetation of the Mesozoic lagoons, or crawled or hopped or fluttered over the great river plains of that time.[1]

[1] And here the genius of a great humorous artist E. T. Reed) obliges us to add a footnote to clear (away a common misconception. He was the creator of a series of fantastic pictures, *Prehistoric Peeps*, which have had a deserved and immense vogue, and it was his whim to represent primitive men as engaged in an unending wild struggle with great Plesiosaurs and the like. His fantasy has become a common belief. As we shall see, millions of years elapsed between the vanishing of the last great Mesozoic reptile and the first appearance of man upon this earth. Early man had as contemporaries some monstrous animals, as we shall note, but not these extreme monsters.

In these opening six chapters we have been much indebted, in addition to the books already named in the text or in footnotes, to Ray Lankester's *Extinct Animals*, Osborn's *Age of Mammals*, Jukes Browne's, Lyell's and Pirsson and Schuchert's text-books of geology, and the collections and catalogues of the Natural History Museum at South Kensington. H. R. Knipe's *From Nebula to Man* and his *Evolution in the Past* have also been very useful and suggestive. These two books are full of admirable illustrations of extinct monsters by Miss G. M. Woodward and Mr. Bucknall. There are good figures also in *Extinct Monsters* and *Creatures of Other Days* by H. N. Hutchinson.

VII

THE AGE OF MAMMALS

§ 1

THE third great division of the geological record, the Cainozoic, opens with a world already physically very like the world we live in to-day. Probably the day was at first still perceptibly shorter, but the scenery had become very modern in its character. Climate was, of course, undergoing, age by age, its incessant and irregular variations; lands that are temperate to-day have passed, since the Cainozoic age began, through phases of great warmth, intense cold, and extreme dryness; but the landscape, if it altered, altered to nothing that cannot still be paralleled to-day in some part of the world or other. In the place of the cycads, sequoias, and strange conifers of the Mesozoic, the plant names that now appear in the lists of fossils include birch, beech, holly, tulip trees, ivy, sweet gum, bread-fruit trees. Flowers had developed concurrently with bees and butterflies. Palms were now very important. Such plants had already been in evidence in the later levels of the (American Cretaceous) Mesozoic, but now they dominated the scene altogether. Grass was becoming a great fact in the world. Certain grasses too had appeared in the later Mesozoic, but only with the Cainozoic period came grass plains and turf spreading wide over a world that was once barren stone.

The period opened with a long phase of considerable warmth; then the world cooled. And in the opening of this third part of the record, this Cainozoic period, a gigantic crumpling of the earth's crust and an upheaval of mountain ranges was in progress. The Alps, the Andes, the Himalayas, are all Cainozoic mountain ranges; the background of an early Cainozoic scene to be typical should display an active volcano or so. It must have been an age of great earthquakes.

Geologists make certain main divisions of the Cainozoic period, and it will be convenient to name them here and to indicate their climate. First comes the *Eocene* (dawn of recent life), an age of exceptional warmth in the world's history, subdivided into an older and newer Eocene; then the *Oligocene* (but little of recent life), in which the climate was still equable. The *Miocene* (with living species still in a minority) was the great age of mountain building, and the general temperature was falling. In the *Pliocene* (more living than extinct species), climate was very much at its present phase; but with the *Pleistocene* (a great majority of living species) there set in a long period of extreme conditions—it was the Great Ice Age. Glaciers spread from the poles towards the equator, until England to the Thames was covered in ice. Thereafter to our own time came a period of partial recovery.

§ 2

In the forests and following the grass over the Eocene plains there appeared for the first time a variety and abundance of mammals. Before we proceed to any description of these mammals, it may be well to note in general terms what a mammal is.

From the appearance of the vertebrated animals in the Lower Palæozoic Age, when the fish first swarmed out into the sea, there has been a steady progressive development of vertebrated creatures. A fish is a vertebrated animal that breathes by gills and can live only in water. An amphibian may be described as a fish that has added to its gill-breathing the power of breathing air with its swimming bladder in adult life, and that has also developed limbs with five toes to them in place of the fins of a fish. A tadpole is for a time a fish, it becomes a land creature as it develops. A reptile is a further stage in this detachment from water; it is an amphibian that is no longer amphibious; it passes through its tadpole stage—its fish stage that is—in an egg. From the beginning it must breathe in air; it can never breathe under water as a tadpole can do. Now a modern mammal is really a sort of reptile that has developed a peculiarly effective protective covering, hair; and that also retains its eggs in the body until they hatch so that it brings forth living young (viviparous), and even after birth it cares for them and feeds them by its mammæ for a longer or shorter period. Some reptiles, some vipers for example, are viviparous, but none stand by their young as the real mammals do. Both the birds and the mammals, which escaped whatever destructive forces made an end to the Mesozoic reptiles, and which survived to dominate the Cainozoic world, have these two things in common; first, a far more effective protection against changes of temperature than any other variation of the reptile type ever produced, and, secondly, a peculiar care for their eggs, the bird by incubation and the mammal by retention, and a disposition to look after the young for a certain period after hatching or birth. There is by comparison the greatest carelessness about offspring in the reptile.

Hair was evidently the earliest distinction of the mammals from the rest of the reptiles. It is doubtful if the particular Theriodont reptiles who were developing hair in the early Mesozoic were viviparous. Two mammals survive to this day which not only do not suckle their young,[1] but which lay eggs, the *Ornithorhynchus* and the *Echidna*, and in the Eocene there were a number of allied forms. They are the survivors of what was probably a much larger number and variety of small egg-laying hairy creatures, hairy reptiles, hoppers, climbers, and runners, which included the Mesozoic ancestors of all existing mammals up to and including man.

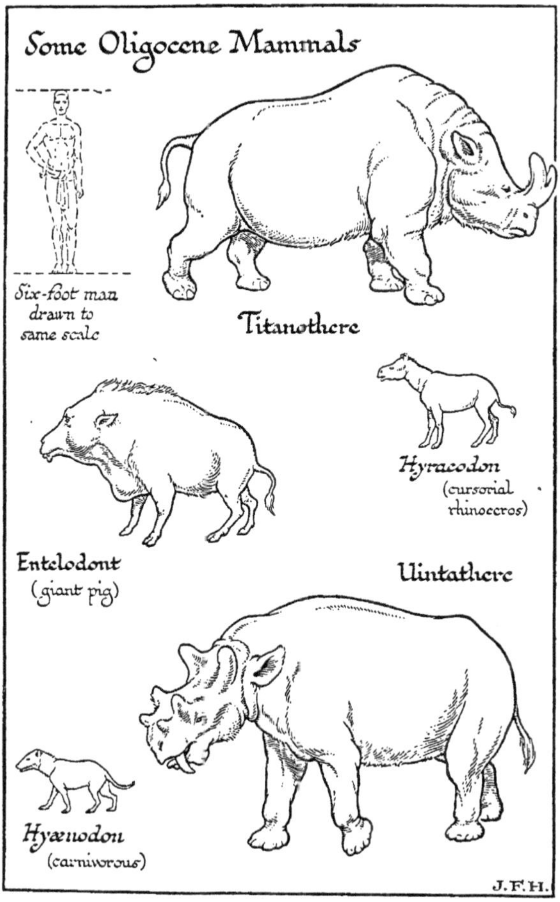

Now we may put the essential facts about mammalian reproduction in another way. *The mammal is a family animal.* And the family habit involved the possibility of a new sort of continuity of experience in the world. Compare the completely closed-in life of an individual lizard with the life of even a quite lowly mammal of almost any kind. The former has no mental continuity with anything beyond itself; it is a little self-contained globe of experience that serves its purpose and ends; but the latter "picks up" from its mother, and "hands on" to its offspring. All the mammals, except for the two genera we have named, had already before the lower Eocene age arrived at this stage of pre-adult dependence and imitation. They were all more or less imitative in youth and capable of a certain modicum of education; they all, as a part of their development, received a certain amount of care and example and even direction from their mother. This is as true of the hyæna and rhinoceros as it is of the dog or man; the difference of educability is enormous, but the

[1] They secrete a nutritive fluid on which the young feeds from glands scattered over the skin. But the glands are not gathered together into mammæ with nipples for suckling. The stuff oozes out, the mother lies on her back, and the young browse upon her moist skin.

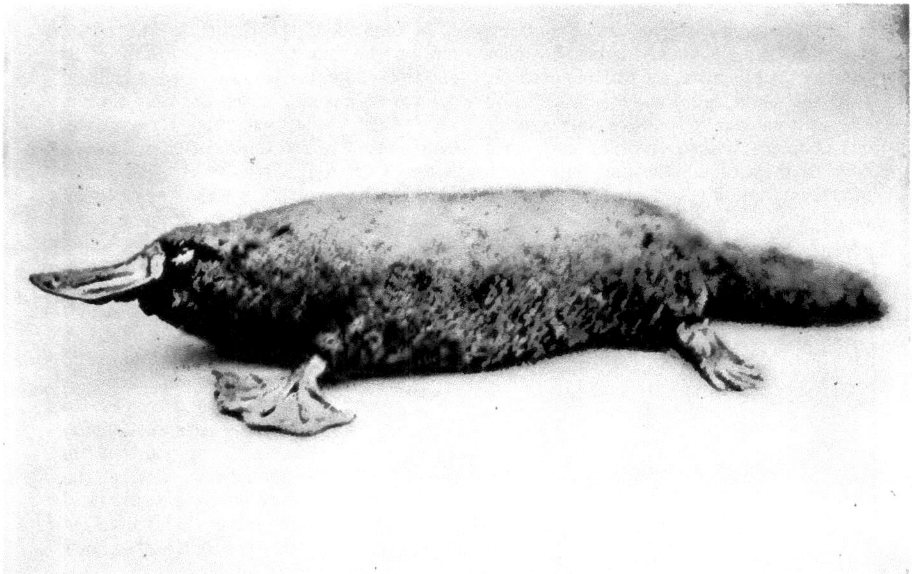

PLATYPUS, OR DUCKBILL

Photo: W. S. Berridge, F.Z.S.

"The *Ornithorhynchus* [Platypus] survive to this day."

ECHIDNA OR SPINY ANT-EATER

Supplied by Sir H. H. Johnston

"An egg-laying mammal—with the Platypus, the Mesozoic ancestors of all existing mammals, up to and including man."

fact of protection and educability in the young stage is undeniable. So far as the vertebrated animals go, these new mammals, with their viviparous, young-protecting disposition, and these new birds, with their incubating, young-protecting disposition, introduce at the opening of the Cainozoic period a fresh thing into the expanding story of life, namely, social association, the addition to hard and inflexible instinct of *tradition*, and the nervous organisation necessary to receive tradition.

All the innovations that come into the history of life begin very humbly. The supply of blood-vessels in the swimming bladder of the mudfish in the lower Palæozoic torrent-river, that enabled it to pull through a season of drought, would have seemed at that time to that bodiless visitant to our planet we have already imagined, a very unimportant side fact in that ancient world of great sharks and plated fishes, sea-scorpions, and coral reefs and seaweed; but it opened the narrow way by which the land vertebrates arose to predominance. The mudfish would have seemed then a poor refugee from the too crowded and aggressive life of the sea. But once lungs were launched into the world, every line of descent that had lungs went on improving them. So too in the upper Palæozoic, the fact that some of the Amphibia were losing their "amphibiousness" by a retardation of hatching of their eggs, would have appeared a mere response to the distressful dangers that threatened the young tadpole. Yet that prepared the conquest of the dry land for the triumphant multitude of the Mesozoic reptiles. It opened a new direction towards a free and vigorous land-life along which all the reptilian animals moved. And this viviparous, young-tending training that the ancestral mammalia underwent during that age of inferiority and hardship for them, set going in the world a new continuity of perception, of which even man to-day only begins to appreciate the significance.

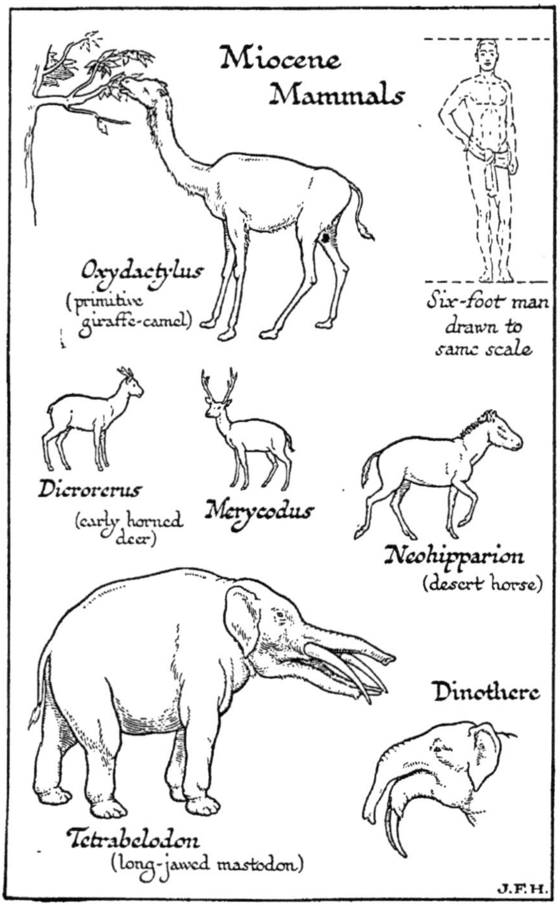

§ 3

A number of types of mammal already appear in the Eocene. Some are differentiating in one direction, and some in another, some are perfecting themselves as herbivorous quadrupeds, some leap and climb among the trees, some turn back to the water to swim, but all types are unconsciously exploiting and developing the brain which is the instrument of this new power of acquisition and educability. In the Eocene rocks are found small early predecessors of the horse (Eohippus), tiny camels, pigs, early tapirs, early hedgehogs, monkeys and lemurs, opossums and carnivores. Now, all these were more or less ancestral to living forms, and all have brains relatively much smaller than their living representatives. There is, for instance, an early rhinoceros, *Titanotherium*, with a brain not one tenth the size of that of the existing rhinoceros. The latter is by no means a perfect type of the attentive and submissive student, but even so it is ten times more observant and teachable than its predecessor. This sort of thing is true of all primitive dogs, some as big as bears, and the first cats, one in particular (*Smilodon*), a small fierce-looking creature with big knife-like canines, the first sabre-toothed tiger, which was to develop into greater things. American deposits in the Miocene display a great variety of camels, giraffe camels with long necks, gazelle camels, llamas, and true camels. North America, throughout most of the Cainozoic period, appears to have been in open and easy continuation with Asia, and

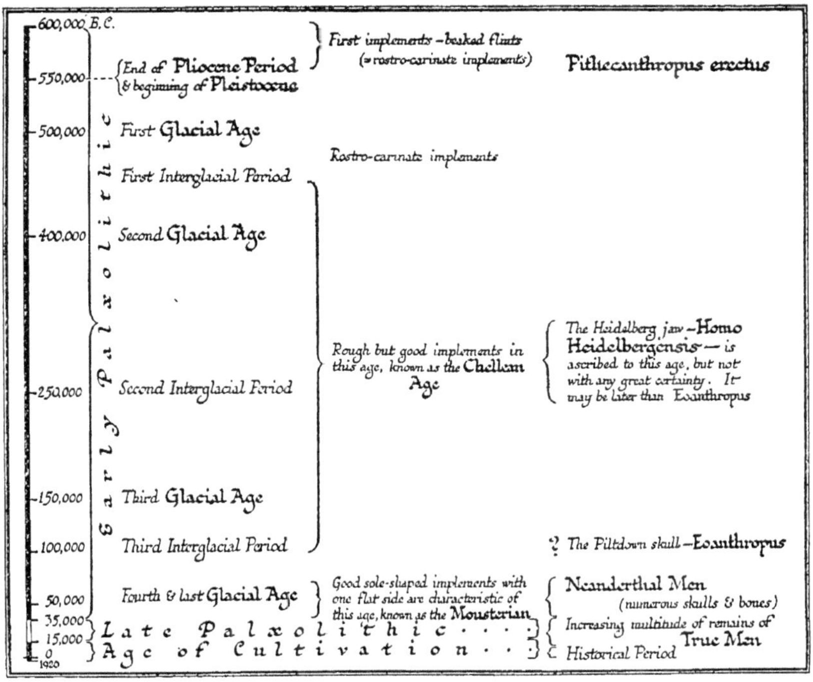

TIME DIAGRAM OF THE GLACIAL AGES.

The reader should compare this diagram carefully with our first time diagram, Chapter II, § 2, p. 8. That diagram, if it were on the same scale as this one, would be between 41 and 410 feet long. The position of the Eoanthropus is very uncertain; it may be as early as the Pliocene.

the orders and families that survive until to-day. All the Cainozoic mammals were doing this one thing in common under the urgency of a common necessity; they were all growing brain. It was a parallel advance. In the same order or family to-day, the brain is usually from six to ten times what it was in the Eocene ancestor.

Grass was now spreading over the world, and with this extension arose some huge graminivorous brutes of which no representative survives to-day. Such were the Uintatheres and the Titanotheres. And in pursuit of such beasts came great swarms of when at last the glaciers of the Great Ice Age, and then the Bering Strait, came to separate the two great continental regions, the last camels were left in the old world and the llamas in the new.

In the Eocene the first ancestors of the elephants appear in northern Africa as snouted creatures; the elephant's trunk dawned on the world in the Miocene.

One group of creatures is of peculiar interest in a history that is mainly to be the story of mankind. We find fossils in the Eocene of monkeys and lemurs, but of one particular creature we have as yet not a.

IN THE PLEISTOCENE AGE—

1. Summer : The mastodon, ancient ox, and horse
2. Autumn : Moose, and a tapir-like animal
3. Winter's verge: Migration of the mammoth ; herd of elk at left

"An Arctic fauna ushers in the Pleistocene. Over Europe for thousands of years the ice advanced. The age of mammals culminated in ice and hardship and man."

single bone. It was half ape, half monkey; it clambered about the trees and ran, and probably ran well, on its hind-legs upon the ground. It was small-brained by cur present standards, but it had clever hands with which it handled fruits and beat nuts upon the rocks and perhaps caught up sticks and stones to smite its fellows. It was our ancestor.

§ 4

Through millions of simian generations the spinning world circled about the sun; slowly its orbit, which may have been nearly circular during the equable days of the early Eocene, was drawn by the attraction of the circling outer planets into a more elliptical form. Its axis of rotation, which had always heeled over to the plane of its orbit, as the mast of a yacht under sail heels over to the level of the water, heeled over by imperceptible degrees a little more and a little more. And each year its summer point shifted a little further from perihelion round its path. These were small changes to happen to a one-inch ball, circling at a distance of 330 yards from a flaming sun nine feet across, in the course of a few million years. They were changes an immortal astronomer in Neptune, watching the earth from age to age, would have found almost imperceptible. But from the point of view of the surviving mammalian life of the Miocene, they mattered profoundly. Age by age the winters grew on the whole colder and harder and a few hours longer relatively to the summers in a thousand years; age by age the summers grew briefer. On an average the winter snow lay a little later in the spring in each century, and the glaciers in the northern mountains gained an inch this year, receded half an inch next, came on again a few inches. . . .

The Record of the Rocks tells of the increasing chill. The Pliocene was a temperate time, and many of the warmth-loving plants and animals had gone. Then, rather less deliberately, some feet or some inches every year, the ice came on.

An arctic fauna, musk ox, woolly mammoth, woolly rhinoceros, lemming, ushers in the Pleistocene. Over North America, and Europe and Asia alike, the ice advanced. For thousands of years it advanced, and then for thousands of years it receded, to advance again. Europe down to the Baltic shores, Britain down to the Thames, North America down to New England, and more centrally as far south as Ohio, lay for ages under the glaciers. Enormous volumes of water were withdrawn from the ocean and locked up in those stupendous ice caps so as to cause a world-wide change in the relative levels of land and sea. Vast areas were exposed that are now again sea bottom.

The world to-day is still coming slowly out of the last of four great waves of cold. It is not growing warmer steadily. There have been fluctuations. Remains of bog oaks, for example, which grew two or three thousand years ago, are found in Scotland at latitudes in which not even a stunted oak will grow at the present time. And it is amidst this crescendo and diminuendo of frost and snow that we first recognize forms that are like the forms of men. The Age of Mammals culminated in ice and hardship and man.

§ 5

Guesses about the duration of the great age of cold are still vague, but in the Time diagram on page 28 we follow H. F. Osborn in accepting as our guides the estimates of Albrecht Penck[1] and C. A. Reeds.[2]

[1] *Die Alpen in Eiszeitalters*, vol. iii.

[2] "Graphic Projection of the Pleistocene," "Climatic Oscillations," in *Bulletin of Geological Soc. Am.*, vol. xxvi.

BOOK II

THE MAKING OF MAN

VIII

THE ANCESTRY OF MAN[1]

§ 1. *Man descended from a walking Ape.* § 2. *First Traces of Man-like Creatures.* § 3. *The Heidelberg Sub-man.* § 4. *The Piltdown Sub-man.* § 5. *The Riddle of the Piltdown Remains.*

§ 1

THE origin of man is still very obscure. It is commonly asserted that he is "descended" from some man-like ape such as the chimpanzee, the orang-utang, or the gorilla, but that of course is as reasonable as saying that I am "descended" from some Hottentot or Esquimaux as young or younger than myself. Others, alive to this objection, say that man is descended from the common ancestor of the chimpanzee, the orang-utang, and the gorilla. Some "anthropologists" have even indulged in a speculation whether mankind may not have a double or treble origin; the negro being descended from a gorilla-like ancestor, the Chinese from a chimpanzee-like ancestor, and so on. These are very fanciful ideas, to be mentioned only to be dismissed. It was formerly assumed that the human ancestor was "probably arboreal," but the current idea among those who are qualified to form an opinion seems to be that he was a "ground ape," and that the existing apes have developed in the arboreal direction.

Of course if one puts the skeleton of a man and the skeleton of a gorilla side by sida, their general resemblance is so great that it

[1] In this and the next chapters the writer has used Osborn's *Men of the Stone Age*, Sollas' *Ancient Hunters*. Dr. Keith's *Antiquity of Man*, W. B. Wright's *The Quaternary Ice Age*, Worthington Smith's *Man, the Primeval Savage*, F. Wood Jones' *Arboreal Man*, H. G. F. Spurrell's *Modern Man and his Forerunners*, O. T. Mason's *Origins of Invention*, Parkyn s *History of Prehistoric Art* Salomon Reinach's *Répertoire de l'Art Quaternaire*, and various of the papers in Ray Lankester's *Science from an Easy Chair*.

is easy to jump to the conclusion that the former is derived from such a type as the latter by a process of brain growth and general refinement. But if one examines closely into one or two differences, the gap widens. Particular stress has recently been laid upon the tread of the foot. Man walks on his toe and his heel; his great toe is his chief lever in walking, as the reader may see for himself if he examines his own footprints on the bathroom floor and notes where the pressure falls as the footprints become fainter. His great toe is the king of his toes.

Among all the apes and monkeys, the only group that have their great toes developed on anything like the same fashion as man are some of the lemurs. The baboon walks on a flat foot and all his toes, using his middle toe as his chief throw off, much as the bear does. And the three great apes all walk on the outer side of the foot in a very different manner from the walking of man.

POSSIBLE APPEARANCE OF THE SUB-MAN *PITHECANTHROPUS.*

The face, jaws, and teeth are mere guess-work (*see* text). The creature may have been much less human-looking than this.

The great apes are forest dwellers; their walking even now is incidental; they are at their happiest among trees. They have very distinctive methods of climbing; they swing by the arms much more than the monkeys do and do not, like the latter, take off with a spring from the feet. They have a specially developed climbing style of their own. But man walks so well and runs so swiftly as to suggest a very long ancestry upon the ground. Also, he does not climb well now; he climbs with caution and hesitation. His ancestors may have been running creatures for long ages. Moreover, it is to be noted that he does not swim naturally; he has to learn to swim, and that seems to point to a long-standing separation from rivers and lakes and the sea. Almost certainly that ancestor was a smaller and slighter creature than its human descendants. Conceivably the human ancestor at the opening of the Cainozoic period was a running ape living chiefly on the ground, hiding among rocks rather than trees. It could still climb trees well and hold things between its great toe and its second toe (as the Japanese can to this day), but it was already coming down to the ground again from a still remoter, a Mesozoic arboreal ancestry. It is quite understandable that such a creature would very rarely die in water in such circumstances as to leave bones to become fossilized.

It must always be borne in mind that among its many other imperfections the Geological Record necessarily contains abundant traces only of water or marsh creatures or of creatures easily and frequently drowned. The same reasons that make any traces of the ancestors of the mammals rare and relatively unprocurable in the Mesozoic rocks, probably make the traces of possible human ancestors rare and relatively unprocurable in the Cainozoic rocks. Such knowledge as we have of the earliest men, for example, is almost entirely got from a few caves, into which they went and in which they left their traces. Until the hard Pleistocene times they lived and died in the open, and their bodies were consumed or decayed altogether.

But it is well to bear in mind also that the record of the rocks has still to be thoroughly examined. It has been studied only for a few generations, and by only a few men in each generation. Most men have been too busy making war, making profits out of their neighbours, toiling at work that machinery could do for them in a tenth of the time, or simply playing about, to give any attention to these more interesting things. There may be, there probably are, thousands of deposits still untouched containing countless fragments and vestiges of man and his progenitors. In Asia particularly, in India or the East Indies, there may be hidden the most illuminating clues. What we know to-day of early men is the merest scrap of what will presently be known.

The apes and monkeys already appear to have been differentiated at the beginning of the Cainozoic Age, and there are a number of Oligocene and Miocene apes whose relations to one another and to the human line have still to be made out. Among these we

THE CHATHAM ELEPHANT

From fossil remains 400,000 years old discovered in 1913 near Chatham

From a reconstruction drawing by A. Forestier

"In the Eocene the first ancestors of the elephants appear . . . the elephant's trunk dawned on the world in the Miocene."

may mention *Dryopithecus* of the Miocene Age, with a very human-looking jaw. In the Siwalik Hills of northern India remains of some very interesting apes have been found, of which *Sivapithecus* and *Palæopithecus* were possibly related closely to the human ancestor. Possibly these animals already used implements. Charles Darwin represents baboons as opening nuts by breaking them with stones, using stakes to prise up rocks in the hunt for insects, and striking blows with sticks and stones.[1] The chimpanzee makes itself a sort of tree hut by intertwining branches. Stones apparently chipped for use have been found in strata of Oligocene Age at Boncelles in Belgium. Possibly the implement-using disposition was already present in the Mesozoic ancestry from which we are descended.[2]

[1] Darwin's *Descent of Man.*

[2] In *Conquest* for February, 1920, Mr. R. I. Pocock published a very useful criticism of this section as it stood in the first version of the *Outline.* It has been carefully modified in accordance with his views. In addition, we take the liberty of quoting the following:

"It was formerly held, I believe, that, so far as habits are concerned, the transitional steps in man's descent were to be traced from an active arboreal monkey to the equally active arboreal gibbon, and thence to the less active, but still mainly arboreal, orang-utang; from the latter to the half arboreal, half terrestrial chimpanzee, thence, through the mainly terrestrial gorilla, to wholly terrestrial man. In other words, the stages of man's evolution were a series of structural modifications resulting from the gradual dropping of the ancestral habit of living in trees in favour of life on the ground. But such a conception leaves unexplained the great differences between monkeys and gibbons in arboreal and terrestrial activity. Were it correct, we should expect the gibbons to show a transition between monkeys and other apes in their method of moving through trees and on the ground. They show no such transition. It is necessary, therefore, to formulate another theory.

"Since all the active climbing monkeys have well-developed tails, and since the tail tends to shorten or disappear in species of less active habits which live, like the monkey of Gibraltar, on rocky hillsides, the absence of the tail in apes suggests very forcibly that their ancestor had to a great extent given up living in trees. Moreover, the short broad foot of the apes, their ability to stand and walk erect, their peculiar way of climbing, all point to the conclusion that they are descended, not from a truly arboreal ape, but from an ape which had already taken to terrestrial life, with partly bipedal, partly quadrupedal progression; an ape which, while still retaining the power to ascend trees for purposes of feeding and escaping from carnivorous foes, was, at best, probably a slow, inactive climber, certainly not an arboreal leaper like a monkey. A large ape of that mode of life, with hands and feet not very different from those of a chimpanzee or gorilla, but with stronger legs and shorter arms, is my conception of the ancestor of existing apes and of man. And the progenitor of that hypothetical ancestor was probably a big ground monkey."

§ 2

Among the earliest evidences of some creature, either human or at least more man-like than any living ape upon earth, are a number of flints and stones very roughly chipped and shaped so as to be held in the hand. These were probably used as hand-axes. These early implements ("Eoliths") are often so crude and simple that there was for a long time a controversy whether they were to be regarded as natural or artificial productions.[3] The date of the earliest of them is put by geologists as Pliocene—that is to say, *before the First Glacial Age.* They occur also throughout the First Interglacial period. We know of no bones or other remains in Europe or America of the quasi-human beings of half a million years ago, who made and used these implements. They used them to hammer with, perhaps they used them to fight with, and perhaps they used bits of wood for similar purposes.[4]

But at Trinil, in Java, in strata which are said to correspond either to the later Pliocene or to the American and European First Ice Age, there have been found some scattered bones of a creature, such as the makers of these early implements may have been. The top of a skull, some teeth, and a thigh-bone have been found. The skull shows a brain-case about half-way in size between that of the chimpanzee and man, but the thigh-bone is that of a creature as well adapted to standing and running as a man, and as free, therefore, to use its hands. The creature was not a man, nor was it an arboreal ape like the chimpanzee. It was a walking ape. It has been named by naturalists *Pithecanthropus erectus* (the walking ape-man). We cannot say that it is a direct human ancestor, but we may guess that the creatures who scattered these first stone tools over the world must have been closely similar and kindred, and that our ancestor was a

[3] Among the earlier pioneers of the latter view was Mr. Harrison, a grocer of Ightham in Kent, one of those modest and devoted observers to whom British geology owes so much. At first his "Eoliths" were flouted and derided by archæologists, but to-day he has the scientific world with him in the recognition of the quasi-human origin of many of his specimens. With him we must honour Mr. W. J. Lewis Abbott, a jeweller of St. Leonards, whose intimate knowledge of stone structure has been of the utmost value in these discussions. See "Occ. Papers." No. 4, of the Royal Anthropl. Inst., for a description by Sir E. R. Lankester of one of the better formed of these early implements.

[4] Some writers suppose that a Wood and Shell age preceded the earliest Stone Age. South Sea Islanders, Negroes, and Bushmen still make use of wood and the sharp-edged shells of land and water molluscs as implements.

beast of like kind. This little trayful of bony fragments from Trinil is, at present, apart from stone implements, the oldest relic of early humanity, or of the close blood relations of early humanity, that is known.

While these early men or "sub-men" were running about Europe four or five hundred thousand years ago, there were mammoths, rhinoceroses, a huge hippopotamus, a giant beaver, and a bison and wild cattle in their world. There were also wild horses, and the sabre-toothed tiger still abounded. There are no traces of lions or true tigers at that time in Europe, but there were bears, otters, wolves, and a wild boar. It may be that the early sub-man sometimes played jackal to the sabre-toothed tiger, and finished up the bodies on which the latter had gorged itself.[1]

§ 3

After this first glimpse of something at least sub-human in the record of geology, there is not another fragment of human or man-like bone yet known from that record for an interval of hundreds of thousands of years. It is not until we reach deposits which are stated to be of the Second Interglacial period, 200,000 years later, 200,000 or 250,000 years ago, that another little scrap of bone comes to hand. Then we find a jaw-bone.

This jaw-bone was found in a sandpit near Heidelberg, at a depth of eighty feet from the surface,[2] and it is not the jaw-bone of a man as we understand man, but it is man-like in every respect, except that it has absolutely no trace of a chin; it is more massive than a man's, and its narrowness behind could not, it is thought, have given the tongue sufficient play for articulate speech. It is not an ape's jaw-bone; the teeth are human. The owner of this jaw-bone has been variously named *Homo Heidelbergensis* and *Palæoanthropus Heidelbergensis*, according to the estimate formed of his humanity or sub-humanity by various authorities. He lived in a world not remotely unlike the world of the still earlier sub-man of the first implements; the deposits in which it is found show that there were elephants, horses, rhinoceroses, bison, a moose, and so forth with it in the world, but the sabre-toothed tiger was declining and the lion was spreading over Europe. The implements of this period (known as the Chellean period) are a very considerable advance upon those of the Pliocene Age. They are well made but *very much bigger* than any truly human implements. The Heidelberg man may have had a very big body and large forelimbs. He may have been a woolly strange looking creature.

[1] For some interesting suggestions on the origin of flint implements see Elliot Smith's presidential address to the Anthropl. Sect. of the Brit. Assn., 1912.

[2] Sollas' *Ancient Hunters*, p. 40.

§ 4

We must turn over the Record for, it may be, another 100,000 years for the next remains of anything human or sub-human. Then in a deposit ascribed to the Third Interglacial period, which may have begun 100,000 years ago and lasted 50,000 years,[3] the smashed pieces of a whole skull turn up. The deposit is a gravel which may have been derived from the washing out of still earlier gravel strata, and this skull fragment may be in reality as old as the First Glacial Period. The bony remains discovered at Piltdown in Sussex display a creature still ascending only very gradually from the subhuman.

The first scraps of this skull were found in an excavation for road gravel in Sussex. Bit by bit other fragments of this skull were hunted out from the quarry heaps until most of it could be pieced together. It is a thick skull, thicker than that of any living race of men, and it has a brain capacity intermediate between that of Pithecanthropus and man. This creature has been named *Eoanthropus*, the dawn man. In the same gravel-pits were found teeth of rhinoceros, hippopotamus, and the leg-bone of a deer with marks upon it that may be cuts. A curious bat-shaped instrument of elephant bone has also been found.[4]

There was moreover a jaw-bone among these scattered remains, which was at first assumed naturally enough to belong to *Eoanthropus*, but which it was afterwards suggested was probably that of a chimpanzee. It is extraordinarily like that of a chimpanzee, but Dr. Keith, one of the greatest authorities in these questions, assigns it, after an exhaustive analysis in his *Antiquity of Man* (1915), to the skull with which it is found. It is, as a jaw-bone, far less human in character than the jaw of the much more ancient *Homo Heidelbergensis*, but the teeth are in some respects more like those of living men.

[3] We follow Penck.

[4] For sixpence and postage the reader can get from the British Museum, South Kensington, a very fully illustrated pamphlet *A Guide to the Fossil Remains of Man* showing the Piltdown material in great detail.

Dr. Keith, swayed by the jaw-bone, does not think that *Eoanthropus*, in spite of its name, is a creature in the direct ancestry of man. Much less is it an intermediate form between the Heidelberg man and the Neanderthal man we shall presently describe. It was only related to the true ancestor of man as the orang is related to the chimpanzee. It was one of a number of sub-human running apes of more than ape-like intelligence, and if it was not on the line royal, it was at any rate a very close collateral.

After this glimpse of a skull, the Record for very many centuries gives nothing but flint implements, which improve steadily in quality. A very characteristic form is shaped like a sole, with one flat side stricken off at one blow and the other side worked. The archæologists, as the Record continues, are presently able to distinguish scrapers, borers, knives, darts, throwing stones, and the like. Progress is now more rapid; in a few centuries the shape of the hand-axe shows distinct and recognizable improvements. And then comes quite a number of remains. The Fourth Glacial Age is rising towards its maximum. Man is taking to caves and leaving vestiges there; at Krapina in Croatia, at Neanderthal near Düsseldorf, at Spy, human remains have been found, skulls and bones of a creature that is certainly a man. Somewhen about 50,000 years ago, if not earlier, appeared *Homo Neanderthalensis* (also called *Homo antiquus* and *Homo primigenius*), a quite passable human being. His thumb was not quite equal in flexibility and usefulness to a human thumb, he stooped forward and could not hold his head erect, as all living men do, he was chinless and perhaps incapable of speech, there were curious differences about the enamel and the roots of his teeth from those of all living men, he was very thick-set, he was, indeed, not quite of the human species; but there is no dispute about his attribution to the genus *Homo*. He was certainly not descended from Eoanthropus, but his jawbone is so like the Heidelberg jaw-bone, as to make it possible that the clumsier and heavier *Homo Heidelbergensis*, a thousand centuries before him, was of his blood and race.

§ 5

Upon this question of the Piltdown jawbone, it may be of interest to quote here a letter to the writer from Sir Ray Lankester, discussing the question in a familiar and luminous manner. It will enable the reader to gauge the extent and quality of the evidence that we possess at present upon the nature of these early human and sub-human animals. Upon these fragile Piltdown fragments alone more than a hundred books, pamphlets, and papers have been written. These scraps of bone are guarded more carefully from theft and wilful damage than the most precious jewels, and in the museum cases one sees only carefully executed *facsimiles*.

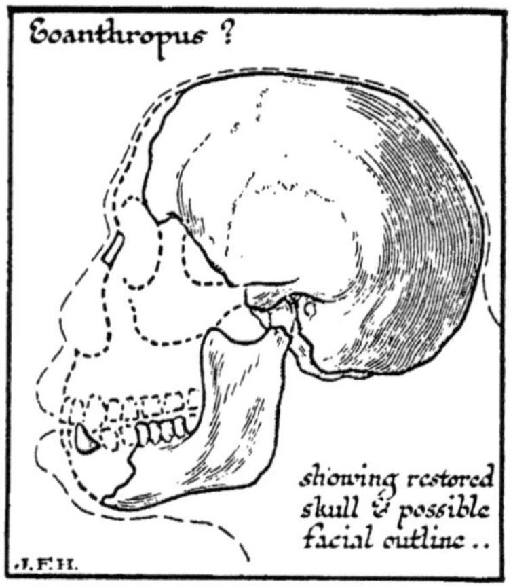

DIAGRAM TO ILLUSTRATE THE RIDDLE OF THE PILTDOWN SUB-MAN.

"As to the Piltdown jaw-bone, the best study of it is that by Smith Woodward, who first described it and the canine found later. The jaw is imperfect in front, but has the broad, flat symphysis of the Apes. G. S. Miller, an American anthropologist, has made a very good comparison of it with a chimpanzee's jaw, and concludes that it is a chimpanzee's. (His monograph is in the *Am. Jour. of Phys. Anthrop.* Vol. I., no. 1.) The one point in the Piltdown jaw itself against chimpanzee identification is the smooth, flat, worn surface of the molars. This is a *human* character, and is due to lateral movement of the jaw, and hence rubbing down of the tubercles of the molars. This is not worth much. But the serious question is, are we to associate this jaw with the cranium found close by it? If so, it is certainly not chimpanzee nor close to the Apes, but decidedly hominid. Two other small fragments of crania and a few more teeth have been found in the gravel two miles from Piltdown, which agree with the Piltdown cranium in having superciliary ridges fairly strong for a human skull, but not anything like the great superciliary ridges of Apes. The fact one has to face is this; here you have an imperfect cranium, very thick-walled and of small cubical contents (1,100 or so), but much larger in that respect than any ape's. A few yards distant from it in the same layer of gravel is found a jaw-bone having rather large pointed canines, a flat, broad symphysis, and other points about the inner face of the ramus and ridges which resemble those of the chimpanzee. Which is the more likely: (*a*) that these two novel fragments tending apewards from man were parts of the same individual; or (*b*), that the sweeping of the Wealden valley has brought there together a half-jaw and a broken cranium *both* more ape-like in character than any known human corresponding bits, and yet derived from two separate anthropoid beasts, one (the jaw) more simian, and the other (the cranium) much less so? As to the probabilities, we must remember that this patch of gravel at Piltdown, clearly and definitely, is a wash-up of remains of various later tertiary and post-tertiary deposits. It contains fragments of Miocene mastodon and rhinoceros teeth. These latter differ entirely in mineral character from the Eoanthropus jaw and the cranium. But (and this needs re-examination and *chemical* analysis) the Piltdown jaw and the Piltdown cranium do not seem to me to be quite alike in their mineral condition. The jaw is more deeply iron-stained, and, I should say (but not confidently), harder than the cranium. Now, it is easy to attribute too much importance to that difference, since in a patch of iron-stained gravel, such as that at Piltdown, the soaking of water and iron salts into bones embedded may be much greater in one spot than in another only a yard off, or a few inches deeper!

"So I think we are stumped and baffled! The most prudent way is to keep the jaw and the cranium apart in all argument about them. On the other hand, on the principle that hypotheses are not to be multiplied beyond necessity, there is a case for regarding the two—jaw and cranium—as having been parts of one beast—or man."

To which Sir H. H. Johnston adds: "Against the chimpanzee hypothesis it must be borne in mind that so far no living chimpanzee or fossil chimpanzee-like remains have been found nearer England than north equatorial Africa or North-west India, and no remains of great apes at all nearer than Southern France and the upper Rhine—and those widely different from the *Eoanthropus* jaw."

IX

THE NEANDERTHAL MEN, AN EXTINCT RACE

(The Early Palæolithic Age[1])

§ 1. *The World 50,000 Years Ago.* § 2. *The Daily Life of the First Men.* § 3. *The last Palæolithic Men.*

§ 1

IN the time of the Third Interglacial period the outline of Europe and western Asia was very different from what it is to-day. Vast areas to the west and north-west which are now under the Atlantic waters were then dry land; the Irish Sea and the North Sea were river valleys. Over these northern areas there spread and receded and spread again a great ice cap such as covers central Greenland to-day (see Map on p. 39). This vast ice cap, which covered both polar regions of the earth, withdrew huge masses of water from the ocean, and the sea-level consequently fell, exposing great areas of land that are now submerged again. The Mediterranean area was probably a great valley below the general sea-level, containing two inland seas cut off from the general ocean. The climate of this Mediterranean basin was perhaps cold temperate, and the region of the Sahara to the south was not then a desert of baked rock and blown sand, but a well-watered and fertile country. Between the ice sheets to the north and the Alps and Mediterranean valley to the south stretched a bleak wilder-

[1] Three phases of human history before the knowledge and use of metals are often distinguished. First there is the so-called Eolithic Age (dawn of stone implements), then the Palæolithic Age (old stone implements), and finally an age in which the implements are skilfully made and frequently well finished and polished (Neolithic Age). The Palæolithic Period is further divided into an earlier (sub-human) and a later (fully human) period. We shall comment on these divisions later.

ness whose climate changed from harshness to a mild kindliness and then hardened again for the Fourth Glacial Age.

Across this wilderness, which is now the great plain of Europe, wandered a various fauna. At first there were hippopotami, rhinoceroses, mammoths, and elephants. The sabre-toothed tiger was diminishing towards extinction. Then, as the air chilled, the hippopotamus, and then other warmth-loving creatures, ceased to come so far north, and the sabre-toothed tiger disappeared altogether. The woolly mammoth, the woolly rhinoceros, the musk ox, the bison, the aurochs, and the reindeer became prevalent, and the temperate vegetation gave place to plants of a more arctic type. The glaciers spread southward to the maximum of the Fourth Glacial Age (about 50,000 years ago), and then receded again. In the earlier phase, the Third Interglacial period, a certain number of small family groups of men (*Homo Neanderthalensis*) and probably of sub-men (*Eoanthropus*) wandered over the land, leaving nothing but their flint implements to witness to their presence. They probably used a multitude and variety of wooden implements also; they had probably learnt much about the shapes of objects and the use of different shapes from wood, knowledge which they afterwards applied to stone; but none of this wooden material has survived; we can only speculate about its forms and uses. As the weather hardened to its maximum of severity, the Neanderthal men, already it would seem acquainted with the use of fire, began to seek shelter under rock ledges and in caves—and so leave remains behind them. Hitherto they had been accustomed to squat in the open about the fire, and near their water supply. But they were sufficiently intelligent to adapt themselves to the new and harder conditions. (As for the sub-men, they seem to have succumbed to the stresses of this Fourth Glacial Age altogether. At any rate, the rudest type of Palæolithic implements presently disappears.)

Not merely man was taking to the caves. This period also had a cave lion, a cave bear, and a cave hyæna. These creatures had to be driven out of the caves and kept out of the

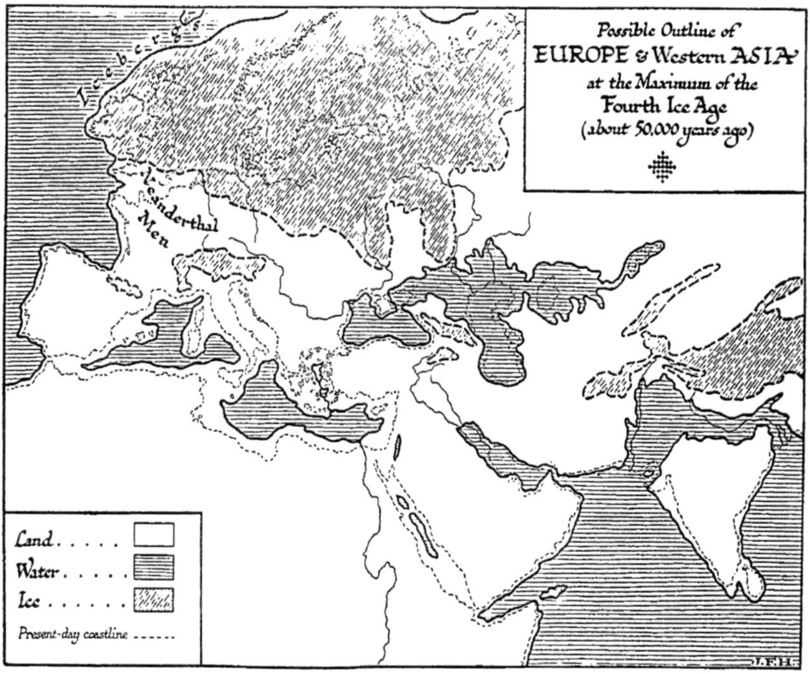

THIS MAP REPRESENTS THE PRESENT STATE OF OUR KNOWLEDGE OF THE GEOGRAPHY OF EUROPE AND WESTERN ASIA AT A PERIOD WHICH WE GUESS TO BE ABOUT 50,000 YEARS AGO, THE NEANDERTHALER AGE.

Much of this map is of course speculative, but its broad outlines must be fairly like those of the world in which meu first became men.

caves in which these early men wanted to squat and hide; and no doubt fire was an effective method of eviction and protection. Probably early men did not go deeply into the caves, because they had no means of lighting their recesses. They got in far enough to be out of the weather, and stored wood and food in odd corners. Perhaps they barricaded the cave mouths. Their only available light for going deeply into the caverns would be torches.

What did these Neanderthal men hunt? Their only possible weapons for killing such giant creatures as the mammoth or the cave bear, or even the reindeer, were spears of wood, wooden clubs, and those big pieces of flint they left behind them, the "Chellean" and "Mousterian" implements;[1] and probably their usual quarry was smaller game.

Neanderthal Man

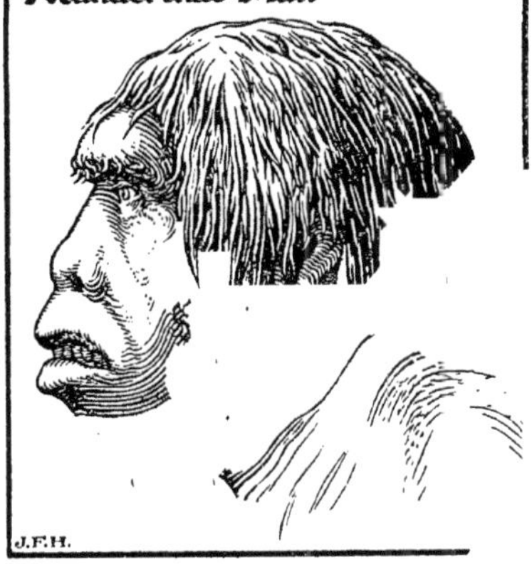

But they did certainly eat the flesh of the big beasts when they had a chance, and perhaps they followed them when sick or when wounded by combats, or took advantage of them when they were bogged or in trouble with ice or water. (The Labrador Indians still kill the caribou with spears at awkward river crossings.) At Dewlish, in Dorset, an artificial trench has been found which is supposed to have been a Palæolithic trap for elephants.[2] We know that the Neanderthalers partly ate their kill where it fell; but they brought back the big marrow bones to the cave to crack and eat at leisure, because few ribs and vertebræ are found in the caves, but great quantities of cracked and split long bones. They used skins to wrap about them, and the women probably dressed the skins.

[1] From Chelles and Le Moustier in France.

[2] Osmond Fisher, quoted in Wright's *Quaternary Ice Age.*

We know also that they were right-handed like modern men, because the left side of the brain (which serves the right side of the body) is bigger than the right. But while the back parts of the brain which deal with sight and touch and the energy of the body are well developed, the front parts, which are connected with thought and speech, are comparatively small. It was as big a brain as ours, but different. This species of *Homo* had certainly a very different mentality from ours; its individuals were not merely simpler and lower than we are, they were on another line. It may be they did not speak at all, or very sparingly. They had nothing that we should call a language.

§ 2

In Worthington Smith's *Man the Primeval Savage* there is a very vividly written description of early Palæolithic life, from which much of the following account is borrowed. In the original, Mr. Worthington Smith assumes a more extensive social life, a larger community, and a more definite division of labour among its members than is altogether justifiable in the face of such subsequent writings as J. J. Atkinson's memorable essay on Primal Law.[3] For the little tribe Mr. Worthington Smith described, there has been substituted, therefore, a family group under the leadership of one Old Man, and the suggestions of Mr. Atkinson as to the behaviour of the Old Man have been worked into the sketch.

Mr. Worthington Smith describes a squatting-place near a stream, because primitive man, having no pots or other vessels, must needs have kept close to a water supply, and with some chalk cliffs adjacent from which flints could be got to work. The air was bleak, and the fire was of great importance, because fires once out were not easily relit in those days. When not required to blaze it was probably banked down with ashes. The most probable way in which fires were started was by hacking a bit of iron pyrites with a flint amidst dry dead leaves; concretions of iron pyrites and flints are found together in England where the gault and chalk approach each other.[4] The little group of people would be squatting about amidst a litter of fern, moss, and such-like

[3] *Social Origins*, by Andrew Lang, and *Primal Law*, by J. J. Atkinson. (Longmans, 1903.)

[4] This first origin of fire was suggested by Sir John Lubbock (*Prehistoric Times*), and Ludwig Hopf, in *The Human Species*, says that "Flints and pieces of pyrites are found in close proximity in palæolithic settlements near the remains of mammoths."

dry material. Some of the women and children would need to be continually gathering fuel to keep up the fires. It would be a tradition that had grown up. The young would imitate their elders in this task. Perhaps there would be rude wind shelters of boughs on one side of the encampment.

The Old Man, the father and master of the group, would perhaps be engaged in hammering flints beside the fire. The children would imitate him and learn to use the sharpened fragments. Probably some of the women would hunt good flints; they would fish them out of the chalk with sticks and bring them to the squatting-place.

There would be skins about. It seems probable that at a very early time primitive men took to using skins. Probably they were wrapped about the children, and used to lie upon when the ground was damp and cold. A woman would perhaps be preparing a skin. The inside of the skin would be well scraped free of superfluous flesh with trimmed flints, and then strained and pulled and pegged out flat on the grass, and dried in the rays of the sun.

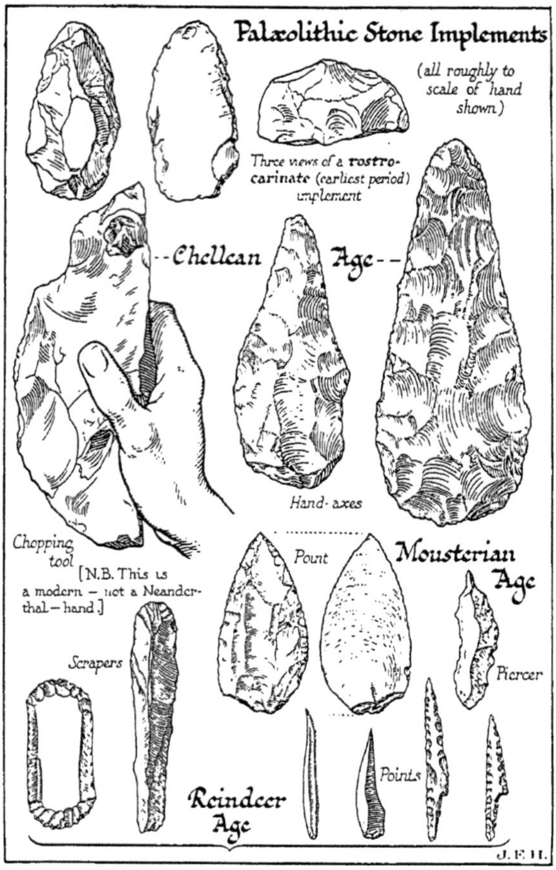

EARLY STONE IMPLEMENTS.

The Mousterian Age implements, and all above it, are those of Neanderthal men or, possibly in the case of the rostro-carinates, of sub-men. The lower row (Reindeer Age) are the work of true men. The student should compare this diagram with the time diagram attached to Chapter VII, § 6, and he should note the relatively *large size* of the pre-human implements.

Away from the fire other members of the family group prowl in search of food, but at night they all gather closely round the fire and build it up, for it is their protection against the wandering bear and such-like beasts of prey. The Old Man is the only fully adult male in the little group. There are women, boys and girls, but so soon as the boys are big enough to rouse the Old Man's jealousy, he will fall foul of them and either drive them off or kill them. Some girls may perhaps go off with these exiles, or two or three of these youths may keep together for a time, wandering until they come upon some other group, from which they may try to steal a mate. Then they would probably fall out among themselves. Some day, when he is forty years old perhaps or even older, and his teeth are worn down and his energy abating, some younger male will stand up to the old man and kill him and reign in his stead. There is probably short shrift for the old at the squatting-place. So soon as they grow weak and bad-tempered, trouble and death come upon them.

What did they eat at the squatting-place?

"Primeval man is commonly described as a hunter of the great hairy mammoth, of the bear, and the lion, but it is in the highest degree improbable that the human savage ever hunted animals much larger than the hare, the rabbit, and the rat. Man was probably the hunted rather than the hunter.

"The primeval savage was both herbivorous and carnivorous. He had for food hazel-nuts, beech-nuts, sweet chestnuts, earth-nuts, and acorns. He had crab-apples, wild pears, wild cherries, wild gooseberries, bullaces, sorbs, sloes, blackberries, yewberries, hips and haws, watercress, fungi, the larger and softer leaf-buds, Nostoc (the vegetable substance called 'fallen stars' by countryfolk), the fleshy, juicy, asparagus-like rhizomes or subterranean stems of the *Labiatæ* and like plants, as well as other delicacies of the vegetable kingdom. He

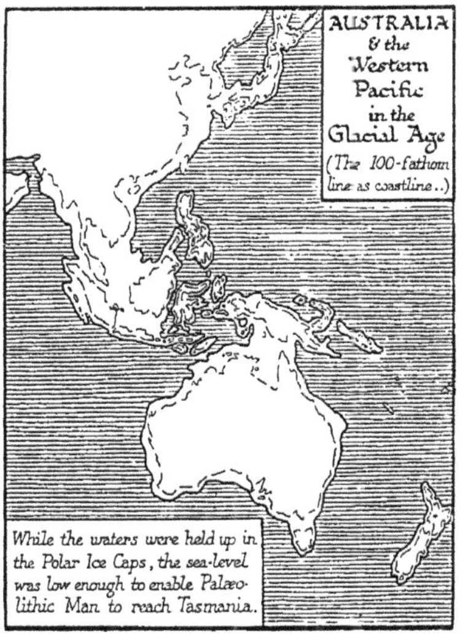

AUSTRALIA & the Western Pacific in the Glacial Age (The 100-fathom line as coastline..)

While the waters were held up in the Polar Ice Caps, the sea-level was low enough to enable Palæolithic Man to reach Tasmania.

had birds' eggs, young birds, and the honey and honeycomb of wild bees. He had newts, snails, and frogs—the two latter delicacies are still highly esteemed in Normandy and Brittany. He had fish, dead and alive, and fresh-water mussels; he could easily catch fish with his hands and paddle and dive for and trap them. By the seaside he would have fish, mollusca, and seaweed. He would have many of the larger birds and smaller mammals, which he could easily secure by throwing stones and sticks, or by setting simple snares. He would have the snake, the slow-worm, and the crayfish. He would have various grubs and insects, the large larvæ of beetles and various caterpillars. The taste for caterpillars still survives in China, where they are sold in dried bundles in the markets. A chief and highly nourishing object of food would doubtlessly be bones smashed up into a stiff and gritty paste.

"A fact of great importance is this—primeval man would not be particular about having his flesh food over-fresh. He would constantly find it in a dead state, and, if semi-putrid, he would relish it none the less—the taste for high or half-putrid game still survives. If driven by hunger and hard pressed, he would perhaps sometimes eat his weaker companions or unhealthy children who happened to be feeble or unsightly or burthensome. The larger animals in a weak and dying state would no doubt be much sought for; when these were not forthcoming, dead and half-rotten examples would be made to suffice. An unpleasant odour would not be objected to; it is not objected to now in many continental hotels.

"The savages sat huddled close together round their fire, with fruits, bones, and half-putrid flesh. We can imagine the old man and his women twitching the skin of their shoulders, brows, and muzzles as they were annoyed or bitten by flies or other insects. We can imagine the large human nostrils, indicative of keen scent, giving rapidly repeated sniffs at the foul meat before it was consumed; the bad odour of the meat, and the various other disgusting odours belonging to a haunt of savages, being not in the least disapproved.

"Man at that time was not a *degraded* animal, for he had never been higher; he was therefore an exalted animal, and, low as we esteem him now, he yet represented the highest stage of development of the animal kingdom of his time."

That is at least an acceptable sketch of a Neanderthal squatting-place. But before extinction overtook them, even the Neanderthalers learnt much and went far.

Whatever the older Palæolithic men did with their dead, there is reason to suppose that the later *Homo Neanderthalensis* buried some individuals at least with respect and ceremony. One of the best-known Neanderthal skeletons is that of a youth who apparently had been deliberately interred. He had been placed in a sleeping posture, head on the right fore-arm. The head lay on a number of flint fragments carefully piled together "pillow fashion." A big hand-axe lay near his head, and around him were numerous charred and split ox bones, as though there had been a feast or an offering.

To this appearance of burial during the later Neanderthal age we shall return when we are considering the ideas that were inside the heads of primitive men.

This sort of men may have wandered, squatted about their fires, and died in Europe for a period extending over 100,000 years, if we assume, that is, that the Heidelberg jaw-bone belongs to a member of the species, a period so vast that all the subsequent history of our race becomes a thing of yesterday. Along its own line this species of men was accumulating a dim tradition, and working out its limited possibilities. Its thick skull imprisoned its brain, and to the end it was low-browed and brutish.

§ 3

When the Dutch discovered Tasmania, they found a detached human race not very greatly advanced beyond this Lower Palæolithic stage. But over most of the world the Lower Palæolithic culture had developed into a more complicated and higher life twenty or thirty thousand years ago. The Tasmanians were not racially Neanderthalers;[1] their brain-cases, their neck-bones, their jaws and teeth, show that; they had no Neanderthal affinities; they were of the same species as ourselves. There can be little doubt that throughout the hundreds of centuries during which the scattered little groups of Neanderthal men were all that represented men in Europe, real men, of our own species, in some other part of the world, were working their way along parallel lines from much the same stage as the Neanderthalers ended at, and which the Tasmanians preserved, to a higher level of power and achievement. The Tasmanians, living under unstimulating conditions, remote from any other human competition or example, lagged behind the rest of the human brotherhood.[2]

About 200 centuries ago or earlier, real men of our own species, if not of our own race, came drifting into the European area.

X

THE LATER POSTGLACIAL PALÆOLITHIC MEN, THE FIRST TRUE MEN

(Later Palæolithic Age)

§ 1. *The Coming of men like ourselves.*
§ 2. *Subdivision of the later Palæolithic.*
§ 3 *The Earliest True Men were splendid Savages.*
§ 4. *Hunters give Place to Herdsmen.*
§ 5. *No Sub-men in America.*

§ 1

THE Neanderthal type of man prevailed in Europe at least for tens of thousands of years. For ages that make all history seem a thing of yesterday, these nearly human creatures prevailed. If the Heidelberg jaw was that of a Neanderthaler, and if there is no error in the estimate of the age of that jaw, then the Neanderthal Race lasted out for more than 200,000 years! Finally, between 40,000 and 25,000 years ago, as the Fourth Glacial Age softened towards more temperate conditions (see Map on p. 45), a different human type came upon the scene, and, it would seem, exterminated *Homo Neanderthalensis.*[3] This new type was probably developed in South Asia or North Africa, or in lands now submerged in the Mediterranean basin, and, as more

[1] But compare Sollas' *Ancient Hunters.* Elliot Smith (*Primitive Man.* Proceedings Brit. Acad., Vol. VII) says they approach the Neanderthal type.

[2] What is known of the Tasmanian Old Stone men is to be found in Roth and Butler's *Aborigines of Tasmania.* See also footnote on the Tasmanian language to Chapter XIII.

[3] The opinion that the Neanderthal race (*Homo Neanderthalensis*) is an extinct species which did not interbreed with the true men (*Homo sapiens*) is held by Professor Osborn, and it is the view to which the writer inclines and to which he has pointed in the treatment of this section; but it is only fair to the reader to note that many writers do not share this view. They write and speak of living "Neanderthalers" in contemporary populations. One observer has written in the past of such types in the west of Ireland; another has observed them in Greece. These so-called "living Neanderthalers" have neither the peculiarities of neck, thumb, nor teeth that distinguish the Neanderthal race of pre-men. The cheek teeth of true men, for instance, have what we call fangs, long fangs; the Neanderthaler's cheek tooth is a *more complicated and specialized* cheek tooth, a long tooth with short fangs, and his canine teeth were *less* marked, *less* like dog-teeth, than ours. Nothing

remains are collected and evidence accumulates, men will learn more of their early stages. At present we can only guess where and how, through the slow ages, parallel with the Neanderthal cousin, these first *true men* arose out of some more ape-like progenitor. For hundreds of centuries they were acquiring skill of hand and limb, and power and bulk of brain, in that still unknown environment. They were already far above the Neanderthal level of achievement and intelligence, when

first they come into our ken, and they had already split into two or more very distinctive races.

These newcomers did not migrate into Europe in the strict sense of the word, but rather, as century by century the climate ameliorated, they followed the food and plants to which they were accustomed, as those spread into the new realms that opened to them. The ice was receding, vegetation was increasing, big game of all sorts was becoming more abundant. Steppe-like conditions, conditions of pasture and shrub, were bringing with them vast herds of wild horse. Ethnologists (students of race) class these new human races in one same species as ourselves, and with all human races subsequent to them, under one common specific name of *Homo sapiens*. They had quite human brain-cases and hands. Their teeth and their necks were anatomically as ours are.

Now here again, with every desire to be plain and explicit with the reader, we have still to trouble him with qualified statements and notes of interrogation. There is now an enormous literature about these earliest true men, the men of the Later Palæolithic Age, and it is still for the general reader a very confusing literature indeed. It is confusing because it is still confused at the source. We know of two distinct sorts of skeletal remains in this period, the first of these known as the Cro-Magnon race, and the second the Grimaldi race; but the great bulk of the human traces and appliances we find are either without human bones or with insufficient bones for us to define their associated physical type. There may have been many more distinct races than these two. There may have been intermediate types. In the grotto of Cro-Magnon it was that complete skeletons of one main type of these Newer Palæolithic men, these true men, were first found, and so it is that they are spoken of as Cro-Magnards.

These Cro-Magnards were a tall people with very broad faces, prominent noses, and, all things considered, astonishingly big brains. The brain capacity of the woman in the Cro-Magnon cave exceeded that of the average male to-day. Her head had been smashed by a heavy blow. There were also in the same cave with her the complete skeleton of an older man, nearly six feet high, the fragments of a child's skeleton, and the skeletons of two young men. There were also flint implements and perforated sea-shells, used no doubt as ornaments. Such is one sample of the earliest true men. But at the Grimaldi cave, near Mentone, were discovered two skeletons also of the later Palæolithic Period, but of a widely contrasted type, with negroid characteristics that point rather to the negroid type. There can be no doubt that we have to deal in this period with at least two, and probably more, highly divergent races of true men. They may have overlapped in time, or Cro-Magnards may have followed the Grimaldi race, and either or both may have been contemporary with the late Neanderthal men. Various authorities have very strong opinions upon these points, but they are, at most,

could show more clearly that he was on a different line of development. We must remember that so far only western Europe has been properly explored for Palæolithic remains, and that practically all we know of the Neanderthal species comes from that area (see Map, p. 39). No doubt the ancestor of *Homo sapiens* (which species includes the Tasmanians) was a very similar and parallel creature to *Homo neanderthalensis*. And we are not so far from that ancestor as to have eliminated not indeed "Neanderthal," but "Neanderthaloid" types. The existence of such types no more proves that the Neanderthal species, the makers of the Chellean and Mousterian implements, interbred with *Homo sapiens* in the European area than do monkey-faced people testify to an interbreeding with monkeys; or people with faces like horses, that there is an equine strain in our population.

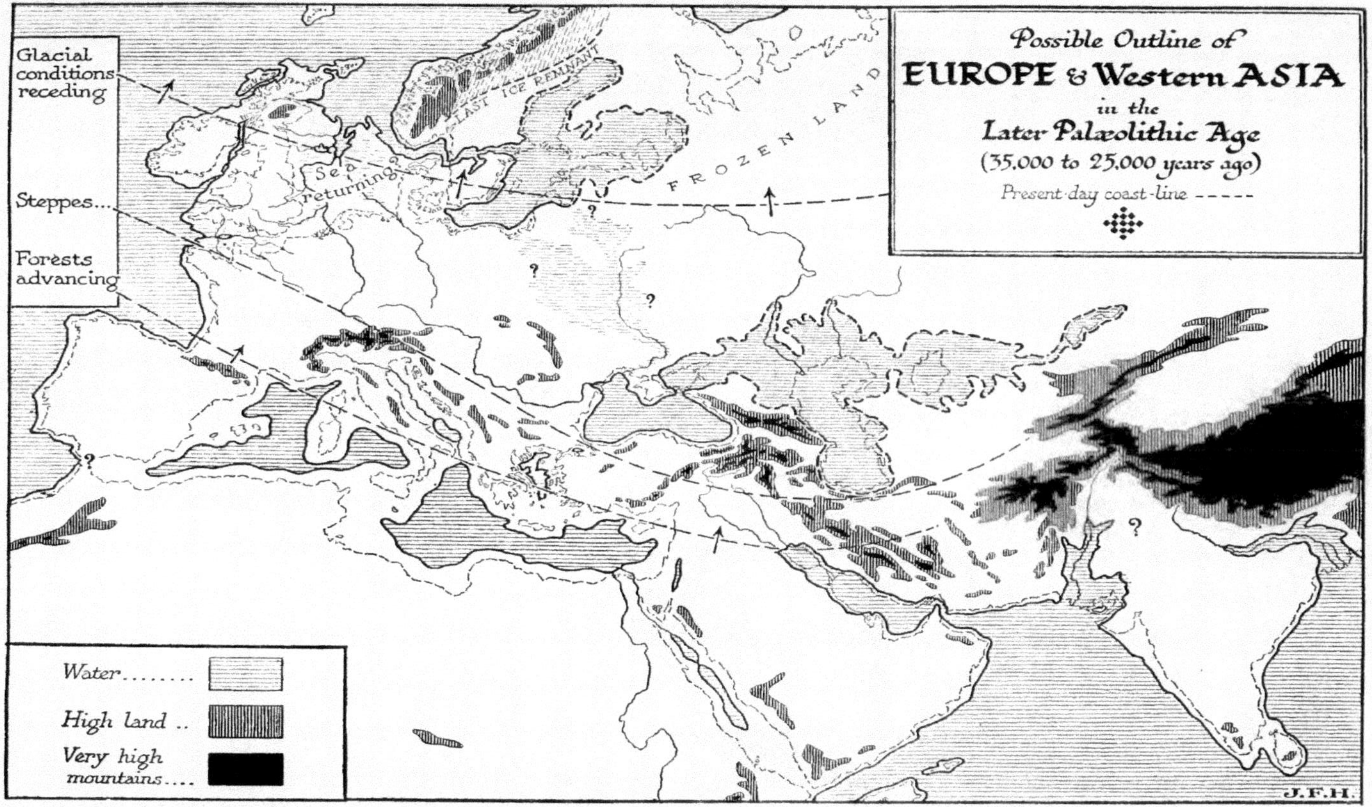

MAP SHOWING EUROPE AND WESTERN ASIA ABOUT THE TIME THE TRUE MEN WERE REPLACING THE NEANDERTHALERS IN WESTERN EUROPE.

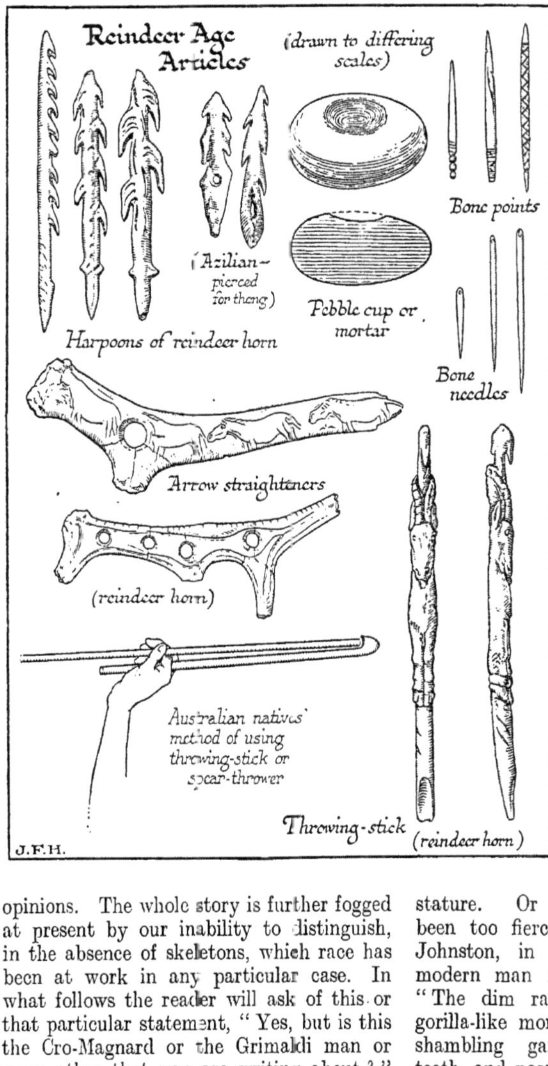

fore-brain, a human hand, an intelligence very like our own. They dispossessed *Homo Neanderthalensis* from his caverns and his stone quarries. And they agreed with modern ethnologists, it would seem, in regarding him as a different species. Unlike most savage conquerors, who take the women of the defeated side for their own and interbreed with them, it would seem that the true men would have nothing to do with the Neanderthal race, women or men. There is no trace of any intermixture between the races, in spite of the fact that the newcomers, being also flint users, were establishing themselves in the very same spots that their predecessors had occupied. We know nothing of the appearance of the Neanderthal man, but this absence of intermixture seems to suggest an extreme hairiness, an ugliness, or a repulsive strangeness in his appearance over and above his low forehead, his beetle brows, his ape neck, and his inferior stature. Or he—and she—may have been too fierce to tame. Says Sir Harry Johnston, in a survey of the rise of modern man in his *Views and Reviews:* "The dim racial remembrance of such gorilla-like monsters, with cunning brains, shambling gait, hairy bodies, strong teeth, and possibly cannibalistic tendencies, may be the germ of the ogre in folklore. . . ."

These true men of the Palæolithic Age, who replaced the Neanderthalers, were coming into a milder climate, and although they used the caves and shelters of their predecessors, they lived largely in the open. They were hunting peoples, and some or all of them appear to have hunted the mammoth and the wild horse as well as the reindeer, bison, and aurochs. They ate much horse. At a great open-air camp at Solutré, where they seem to have had annual gatherings for many centuries, it is estimated that there

opinions. The whole story is further fogged at present by our inability to distinguish, in the absence of skeletons, which race has been at work in any particular case. In what follows the reader will ask of this or that particular statement, "Yes, but is this the Cro-Magnard or the Grimaldi man or some other that you are writing about?" To which in most cases the honest answer is, "As yet we do not know." Confessedly our account of the newer Palæolithic is a jumbled account. There are probably two or three concurrent and only roughly similar histories of these newer Palæolithic men as yet, inextricably mixed up together. Some authorities appear to favour the Cro-Magnards unduly and to dismiss the Grimaldi people with as little as possible of the record.

The appearance of these truly human post glacial Palæolithic peoples was certainly an enormous leap forward in the history of mankind. Both of these main races had a human

are the bones of 100,000 horses, besides reindeer, mammoth, and bison bones. They probably followed herds of horses, the little bearded ponies of that age, as these moved after pasture. They hung about on the flanks of the herd, and became very wise about its habits and dispositions. A large part of these men's lives must have been spent in watching animals.

Whether they tamed and domesticated the horse is still an open question. Perhaps they learnt to do so by degrees as the centuries passed. At any rate, we find late Palæolithic drawings of horses with marks about the heads that are strongly suggestive of bridles, and there exists a carving of a horse's head showing what is perhaps a rope of twisted skin or tendon. But even if they tamed the horse, it is still more doubtful whether they rode it or had much use for it when it was tamed. The horse they knew was a wild pony with a beard under its chin, not up to carrying a man for any distance. It is improbable that these men had yet learnt the rather unnatural use of animal's milk as food. If they tamed the horse at last, it was the only animal they seem to have tamed. They had no dogs, and they had little to do with any sort of domesticated sheep or cattle.

It greatly aids us to realize their common humanity that these earliest true men could draw. Both races, it would seem, drew astonishingly well. They were by all standards savages, but they were artistic savages. They drew better than any of their successors down to the beginnings of history. They drew and painted on the cliffs and cave walls that they had wrested from the Neanderthal men. And the surviving drawings come to the ethnologist, puzzling over bones and scraps, with the effect of a plain message shining through guesswork and darkness. They drew on bones and antlers; they carved little figures.

These later Palæolithic people not only drew remarkably well for our information, and with an increasing skill as the centuries passed, but they have also left us other information about their lives in their graves. They buried. They buried their dead, often with ornaments, weapons, and food; they used a lot of colour in the burial, and evidently painted the body. From that one may infer that they painted their bodies during life. Paint was a big fact in their lives. They were inveterate painters; they used black, brown, red, yellow, and white pigments, and the pigments they used endure to this day in the caves of France and Spain. Of all modern races, none have shown so pictorial a disposition; the nearest approach to it has been among the American Indians.

These drawings and paintings of the later Palæolithic people went on through a long period of time, and present wide fluctuations in artistic merit. We give here some early sketches, from which we learn of the interest taken by these early men in the bison, horse, ibex, cave bear, and reindeer. In its early stages the drawing is often primitive like the drawing of clever children; quadrupeds are usually drawn with one hindleg and one foreleg, as children draw them to this day. The legs on the other side were too much for the artist's technique. Possibly the first drawings began as children's drawings begin, out of idle scratchings. The savage scratched with a flint on a smooth rock surface, and was reminded of some line or gesture. But their solid carvings are at least as old as their first pictures. The earlier drawings betray a complete incapacity to group animals. As the centuries progressed, more skilful

A Reindeer Age Masterpiece

Painting in four colours (Cave of Altamira, Spain)

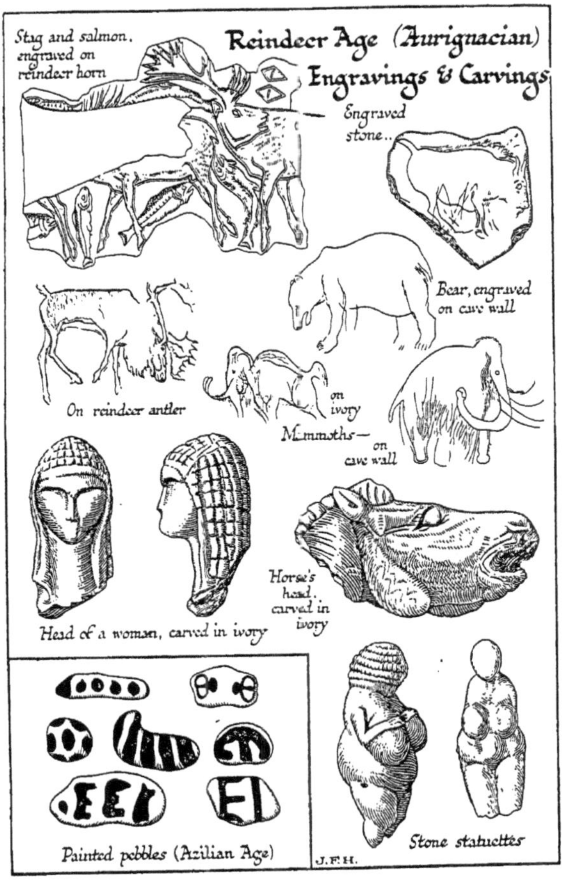

artists appeared. The representation of beasts became at last astonishingly vivid and like. But even at the crest of their artistic time they still drew in profile as children do; perspective and the foreshortening needed for back and front views were too much for them.[1] They rarely drew themselves. The vast majority of their drawings represent animals. The mammoth and the horse are among the commonest themes. Some of the people, whether Grimaldi people or Cro-Magnon people, also made little ivory and soapstone statuettes, and among these are some very fat female figures. These latter suggest the physique of Grimaldi rather than of Cro-Magnon artists. They are like Bushmen women. The human sculpture of the earlier times inclined to caricature, and generally such human figures as they represent are far below the animal studies in vigour and veracity.

Later on there was more grace and less coarseness in the human representations. One little ivory head discovered is that of a girl with an elaborate coiffure. These people at a later stage also scratched and engraved designs on ivory and bone. Some of the most interesting groups of figures are carved very curiously round bone, and especially round rods of deer bone, so that it is impossible to see the entire design altogether. Figures have also been found modelled in clay, although no Palæolithic people made any use of pottery.

Many of the paintings are found in the depths of unlit caves. They are often difficult of access. The artists must have employed lamps to do their work, and shallow soapstone lamps in which fat could have been burnt have been found. Whether the seeing of these cavern paintings was in some way ceremonial or under what circumstances they were seen, we are now altogether at a loss to imagine.

§ 2

Archæologists distinguish at present three chief stages in the history of these newer Palæolithic men in Europe, and we must name these stages here. But it may be as well to note at the same time that it is a matter of the utmost difficulty to distinguish which of two deposits in different places is the older or newer. We may very well be dealing with the work of more or less contemporary and different races when we think we are dealing with successive ones. We are dealing, the reader must bear in mind, with little disconnected patches of material, a few score altogether. The earliest stage usually distinguished by the experts is the *Aurignacian* (from the grotto of Aurignac); it is characterized by very

[1] R. I. Pocock.

well-made flint implements, and by a rapid development of art and more particularly of statuettes and wall paintings. The most esteemed of the painted caves is ascribed to the latter part of this the first of the three subdivisions of the newer Palæolithic. The second subdivision of this period is called the *Solutrian* (from Solutré), and is distinguished particularly by the quality and beauty of its stone implements; some of its razor-like blades are only equalled and not surpassed by the very best of the Neolithic work. They are of course unpolished, but the best specimens are as thin as steel blades and almost as sharp. Finally, it would seem came the *Magdalenian* (from La Madeleine) stage, in which the horse and reindeer were dwindling in numbers and the red deer coming into Europe.[1] The stone implements are smaller, and there is a great quantity of bone harpoons, spearheads, needles, and the like. The hunters of the third and last stage of the later Palæolithic Age appear to have supplemented a diminishing food supply by fishing. The characteristic art of the period consists of deep reliefs done upon bone and line engraving upon bone. It is to this period that the designs drawn round bones belong, and it has been suggested that these designs upon round bones were used to print coloured designs upon leather. Some of the workmanship on bone was extraordinarily fine. Parkyn quotes from de Mortillet, about the Reindeer Age (Magdalenian) bone needles, that they "are much superior to those of later, even historical, times, down to the Renaissance. The Romans, for example, never had needles comparable to those of the Magdalenian epoch."

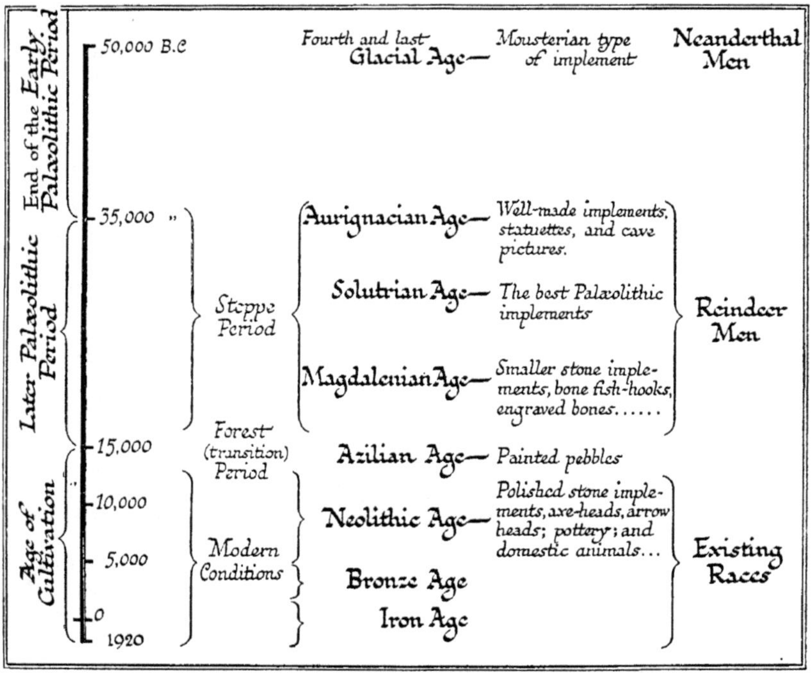

TIME DIAGRAM SHOWING THE ESTIMATED DURATION OF THE TRUE HUMAN PERIODS.

This time diagram again is on a larger scale than its predecessors. The time diagram on page 28, if it were on this scale, would be nearly 4 feet long, and the diagram of the whole of geological time (page 8), between 500 and 5,000 feet long. (Or perhaps even as much as 10,000 feet.)

It is quite impossible at present to guess at the relative lengths of these ages. We are not even positive about their relative relationship. Each lasted perhaps for four or five or more thousand years, more than double the time from the Christian Era to our own day.

At last it would seem that circumstances began to turn altogether against these hunting Newer Palæolithic people who had

[1] So Osborn in his *Men of the Old Stone Age*. But see Wright's *Quaternary Ice Age* for a different view of the Magdalenian Age.

flourished for so long in Europe. They disappeared. New kinds of men appeared in Europe, replacing them. These latter seem to have brought in bow and arrows; they had domesticated animals and cultivated the soil. A new way of living, the Neolithic way of living, spread over the European area; and the life of the Reindeer Age and of the races of Reindeer men, the Later Palæolithic men, after a reign vastly greater than the time between ourselves and the very earliest beginnings of recorded history, passed off the European stage.

§ 3

There is a disposition on the part of many writers to exaggerate the intellectual and physical qualities of these later Palæolithic men and make a wonder of them.[1] Collectively considered, these people had remarkable gifts, but a little reflection will show they had almost as remarkable deficiencies. The tremendous advance they display upon their Neanderthalian predecessors and their special artistic gift must not blind us to their very obvious limitations. For all the quantity of their brains, the quality was narrow and special. They had vivid perceptions, an acute sense of animal form, they had the real artist's impulse to render; so far they were fully grown human beings. But that disposition to paint and draw is shown to-day by the Bushmen, by Californian Indians, and by Australian black fellows; it is not a mark of all-round high intellectual quality. The cumulative effect of their drawings and paintings is very great, but we must not make the mistake of crowding all these achievements together in our minds as though they had suddenly flashed out upon the world in a brief interval of time, or as though they were all the achievements of one people. These races of Reindeer men were in undisturbed possession of Western Europe for a period at least ten times as long as the interval between ourselves and the beginning of the Christian Era, and through all that immense time they were free to develop and vary their life to its utmost possibilities. Their art constitutes their one claim to be accounted more than common savages.

They were in close contact with animals, but they never seemed to have got to terms with any animal unless it was the horse. They had no dogs. They had no properly domesticated animals at all. They watched and drew and killed and ate. They do not seem to have cooked their food. Perhaps they scorched and grilled it, but they could not have done much more, because they had no cooking implements. Although they had clay available, and although there are several Palæolithic clay figures on record, they had *no pottery*. Although they had a great variety of flint and bone implements, they never rose to the possibilities of using timber for permanent shelters or such-like structures. They never made hafted axes or the like that would enable them to deal with timber. There is a suggestion in some of the drawings of a fence of stakes in which a mammoth seems to be entangled. But here we may be dealing with superimposed scratchings. They had *no buildings*. It is not even certain that they had tents or huts. They may have had simple skin tents. Some of the drawings seem to suggest as much. It is doubtful if they knew of the bow. They left no good arrowheads behind them. Certain of their implements are said to be "arrow-straighteners" by distinguished authorities, but that is about as much evidence as we have of arrows. They may have used sharpened sticks as arrows. They had *no cultivation* of grain or vegetables of any sort. Their women were probably squaws, smaller than the men; the earlier statuettes represent them as grossly fat, almost as the Bushmen women are often fat to-day. (But this may not be true of the Cro-Magnards.)

They clothed themselves, it would seem, in skins, if they clothed themselves at all. These skins they prepared with skill and elaboration, and towards the end of the age they used bone needles, no doubt to sew these pelts. One may guess pretty safely that they painted these skins, and it has even been supposed, printed off designs upon them from bone cylinders. But their garments were mere wraps; there are no clasps or catches to be found. They do not seem to have used grass or such-like fibre for textiles. Their statuettes are naked. They were, in fact, except for a fur wrap in cold weather, naked painted savages.

These hunters lived on open steppes for two hundred centuries or so, ten times the length of the Christian era. They were, perhaps, overtaken by the growth of the European forests, as the climate became milder and damper. When the wild horse and the reindeer diminished in Europe, and a newer type of human culture, with a greater power over food supply, a greater tenacity of settlement, and probably a larger social organization, arose, the Reindeer men had to learn fresh ways of living or disappear.

[1] See, for example, H. G. F. Spurrell, *Modern Man and His Forerunners*, end of Chapter III.

How far they learnt and mingled their strain with the new European populations, and how far they went under we cannot yet guess. Opinions differ widely. Wright lays much stress on the "great hiatus" between the Palæolithic and Neolithic remains, while Osborn traces the likeness of the former in several living populations. In the region of the Doubs and of the Dordogne in France, many individuals are to be met with to this day with skulls of the "Cro-Magnon" type. Apparently the Grimaldi type of men has disappeared altogether from Europe. Whether the Cro-Magnon type of men mingled completely with the Neolithic peoples, or whether they remained distinct and held their own in favourable localities to the north and west, following the reindeer over Siberia and towards America, which at that time was continuous with Siberia, or whether they disappeared altogether from the world, is a matter that can be only speculated about at present. There is not enough evidence for a judgment. Possibly they mingled to a certain extent. There is little to prevent our believing that they survived without much intermixture for a long time in north Asia, that "pockets" of them remained here and there in Europe, that there is a streak of their blood in most European peoples to-day, and that there is a much stronger streak, if not a predominant strain, in the Mongolian and American races.[1]

§ 4

It was about 12,000 or fewer years ago that, with the spread of forests and a great change of the fauna, the long prevalence of the hunting life in Europe drew to its end. Reindeer vanished. Changing conditions frequently bring with them new diseases. There may have been prehistoric pestilences. For many centuries there may have been no men in Britain or Central Europe (Wright). For a time there were in Southern Europe drifting communities of some little known people who are called the Azilians.[2] They may have been transition generations; they may have been a different race. We do not know. Some authorities incline to the view that the Azilians were the first wave of a race which, as we shall see later, has played a great part in populating Europe, the dark-white or Mediterranean or Iberian race. These Azilian people have left behind them a multitude of pebbles, roughly daubed with markings of an unknown purport (see illus. p. 48). The use or significance of these Azilian pebbles is still a profound mystery. Was this some sort of token writing? Were they counters in some game? Did the Azilians play with these pebbles or tell a story with them, as imaginative children will do with bits of wood and stone nowadays? At present we are unable to cope with any of these questions.

We will not deal here with the other various peoples who left their scanty traces in the world during the close of the New Palæolithic period, the spread of the forests where formerly there had been steppes, and the wane of the hunters, some 10,000 or 12,000 years ago. We will go on to describe the new sort of human community that was now spreading over the northern hemisphere, whose appearance marks what is called the *Neolithic Age*. The map of the world was assuming something like its present outlines, the landscape and the flora and fauna were taking on their existing characteristics. The prevailing animals in the spreading woods of Europe were the royal stag, the great ox, and the bison; the mammoth and the musk ox had gone. The great ox, or aurochs, is now extinct, but it survived in the German forests up to the time of the Roman Empire. It was never domesticated.[3] It stood eleven feet high at the shoulder, as high as an elephant. There were still lions in the Balkan peninsula, and they remained there until about 1,000 or 1,200 B.C. The lions of Würtemberg and South Germany in those days were twice the size of the modern lion. South Russia and Central Asia were thickly wooded then, and there were elephants in Mesopotamia and Syria, and a fauna in Algeria that was tropical African in character.

Hitherto men in Europe had never gone farther north than the Baltic Sea or the English midlands, but now Ireland, the Scandinavian peninsula, and perhaps Great Russia were becoming possible regions for human occupation. There are no Palæolithic remains in Sweden or Norway, nor in Ireland or Scotland. Man, when he entered these countries, was apparently already at the Neolithic stage of social development.

§ 5

Nor is there any convincing evidence of man in America before the end of the

[1] Upon this question W. J. Sollas' *Ancient Hunters* is very full and suggestive.

[2] From the cave of Mas d'Azil.

[3] But our domestic cattle are derived from some form of aurochs—probably from some lesser Central Asiatic variety.—H. H. J.

Pleistocene.[1] The same relaxation of the climate that permitted the retreat of the reindeer hunters into Russia and Siberia, as the Neolithic tribes advanced, may have allowed them to wander across the land that is now cut by Bering Strait, and so reach the American continent. They spread thence southward, age by age. When they reached South America, they found the giant sloth (the *Megatherium*), the glyptodon, and many other extinct creatures, still flourishing. The glyptodon was a monstrous South American armadillo, and a human skeleton has been found by Roth buried beneath its huge tortoise-like shell.[2]

All the human remains in America, even the earliest, it is to be noted, are of an Amer-Indian character. In America there does not seem to have been any preceding races of sub-men. Man was fully man when he entered America. The old world was the nursery of the sub-races of mankind.

XI

NEOLITHIC MAN IN EUROPE[3]

§ 1. *The Age of Cultivation Begins.*
§ 2. *Where did the Neolithic Culture Arise?*
§ 3. *Everyday Neolithic Life.*
§ 4. *How did Sowing Begin.*
§ 5. *Primitive Trade.*
§ 6. *The Flooding of the Mediterranean Valley.*

§ 1

THE Neolithic phase of human affairs began in Europe about 10,000 or 12,000 years ago. But probably men had reached the Neolithic stage elsewhere some thousands of years earlier.[4] Neolithic men came slowly into Europe from the south or south-east as the reindeer and the open steppes gave way to forest and modern European conditions.

The Neolithic stage in culture is characterized by: (1) the presence of polished stone implements, and in particular the stone *axe*, which was perforated so as to be the more effectually fastened to a wooden handle, and which was probably used rather for working wood than in conflict. There are also abundant arrow heads. The fact that some implements are polished does not preclude the presence of great quantities of implements of unpolished stone. But there are differences in the make between even the unpolished tools of the Neolithic and of the Palæolithic Period. (2) The beginning of a sort of agriculture, and the use of plants and seeds. But at first there are abundant evidences that hunting was still of great importance in the Neolithic Age. Neolithic man did not at first sit down to his agriculture. He took snatch crops. He settled later. (3) Pottery and proper cooking. The horse is no longer eaten. (4) Domesticated animals. The dog appears very early. The Neolithic man had domesticated cattle, sheep, goats, and pigs. He was a huntsman turned herdsman of the herds he once hunted.[5] (5) Plaiting and weaving.

These Neolithic people probably "migrated" into Europe, in the same way that the Reindeer Men had migrated before them; that is to say, generation by generation and century by century, as the climate changed, they spread after their accustomed food.

[1] "The various finds of human remains in North America for which the geological antiquity has been claimed have been thus briefly passed under review. In every instance where enough of the bones is preserved for comparison, the evidence bears witness against the geological antiquity of the remains and for their close affinity to or identity with the modern Indian." (Smithsonian Institute, Bureau of American Ethnology, Bulletin 33. Dr. Hrdlicka.)

But J. Deniker quotes evidence to show that eoliths and early palæoliths have been found in America. See his compact but full summary of the evidence and views for and against in his *Races of Man*, pp. 510, 511.

[2] "Questioned by some authorities," says J. Deniker in *The Races of Man*.

[3] A good account of Palæolithic and Neolithic man is to be found in Rice Holmes' *Ancient Britain*, 1907. Otis T. Mason's *Origins of Invention* also illuminates this period.

[4] The deposits at Susa show Neolithic remains perhaps more than 20,000 years old. See Monteliu's *Congrès Internat. d'Anthrop. Prehist.*, 1906, p. 32. Sir Arthur Evans says the Neolithic age began in Crete more than 14,000 years ago.—G. Wh.

[5] See Peisker, *Cambridge Medieval History*. Vol. 1, or some interesting views upon domestication.—E. B.

SWISS LAKE DWELLINGS, IN THE NEOLITHIC AGE

By Alice B. Woodward

"The Swiss pile-dwellers seem to have lived in practically self-contained villages."

They were not "nomads." Nomadism, like civilization, had still to be developed. At present we are quite unable to estimate how far the Neolithic peoples were new-comers and how far their arts were developed or acquired by the descendants of some of the hunters and fishers of the Later Palæolithic Age.

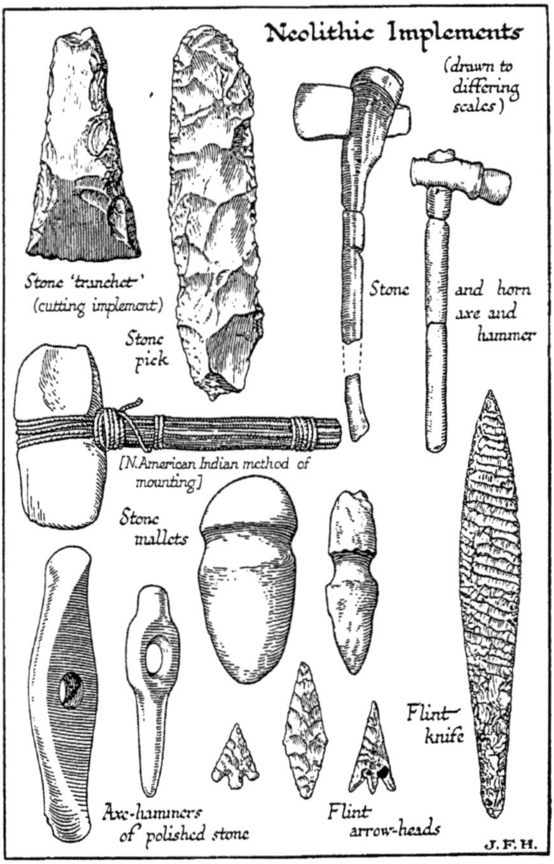

Whatever our conclusions in that matter, this much we may say with certainty; there is no great break, no further sweeping away of one kind of man and replacement by another kind between the appearance of the Neolithic way of living and our own time. There are invasions, conquests, extensive emigrations and intermixtures, but the races as a whole carry on and continue to adapt themselves to the areas into which they began to settle in the opening of the Neolithic Age. The Neolithic men of Europe were white men ancestral to the modern Europeans. They may have been of a darker complexion than many of their descendants; of that we cannot speak with certainty. But there is no real break in culture from their time onward until we reach the age of coal, steam, and power-driven machinery that began in the eighteenth century.

After a long time gold, the first known of the metals, appears among the bone ornaments with jet and amber. Irish Neolithic remains are particularly rich in gold. Then, perhaps 6,000 or 7,000 years ago in Europe, Neolithic people began to use copper in certain centres, making out of it implements of much the same pattern as their stone ones. They cast the copper in moulds made to the shape of the stone implements. Possibly they first found native copper and hammered it into shape.[1] Later—we will not venture upon figures—men had found out how to get copper from its ore. Perhaps, as Lord Avebury suggested, they discovered the secret of smelting by the chance putting of lumps of copper ore among the ordinary stones with which they built the fire pits they used for cooking. In China, Hungary, Cornwall, and elsewhere copper ore and tinstone occur in the same veins; it is a very common association, and so, rather through dirtiness than skill, the ancient smelters, it may be, hit upon the harder and better bronze, which is an alloy of copper and tin.[2] Bronze is not only harder than copper, but the mixture of tin and copper is more fusible and easier to reduce. The so-called "pure-copper" implements usually contain a small proportion of tin, and there are no tin implements known, nor very much evidence to show that early men knew of tin as a separate

[1] Native copper is still found to-day in Italy, Hungary, Cornwall, and many other places.

[2] This view of the origin of bronze is that of Dr. Gowland, *The Metals in Antiquity* (Huxley Lecture, 1912). But Lord Avebury quotes the verbal opinion of the late Lord Swansea against this view, and sets it aside without further argument.

metal.[1] [2] The plant of a prehistoric copper smelter has been found in Spain, and the material of bronze foundries in various localities. The method of smelting revealed by these finds carries out Lord Avebury's suggestion. In India, where zinc and copper ore occur together, brass (which is an alloy of the two metals) was similarly hit upon.

So slight was the change in fashions and methods produced by the appearance of bronze, that for a long time such bronze axes and so forth as were made were cast in moulds to the shape of the stone implements they were superseding.

Finally, perhaps as early as 3,000 years ago in Europe, and even earlier in Asia Minor, men began to smelt iron. Once smelting was known to men, there is no great marvel in the finding of iron. They smelted iron by blowing up a charcoal fire, and wrought it by heating and hammering. They produced it at first in comparatively small pieces [3]; its appearance worked a gradual revolution in weapons and implements; but it did not suffice to change the general character of men's surroundings. Much the same daily life that was being led by the more settled Neolithic men 10,000 years ago, was being led by peasants in out-of-the-way places all over Europe at the beginning of the eighteenth century.[4]

People talk of the Stone Age, the Bronze Age, and the Iron Age in Europe, but it is misleading to put these ages as if they were of equal importance in history. Much truer is it to say that there was:

(1) An *Early Palæolithic Age*, of vast duration; (2) a *Later Palæolithic Age*, that lasted not a tithe of the time; and (3) the *Age of Cultivation*, the age of the white men in Europe, which began 10,000 or at most 12,000 years ago, of which the Neolithic Period was the beginning, and which is still going on.

§ 2

We do not know yet the region in which the ancestors of the white and whitish Neolithic peoples worked their way up from the Palæolithic stage of human development. Probably it was somewhere about south western Asia, or in some region now submerged beneath the Mediterranean Sea or the Indian Ocean, that, while the Neanderthal men still lived their hard lives in the bleak climate of a glaciated Europe, the ancestors of the white men developed the rude arts of *their* Later Palæolithic period. But they do not seem to have developed the artistic skill of their more northerly kindred, the European Later Palæolithic races. And through the hundred centuries or so while Reindeer men were living under comparatively unprogressive conditions upon the steppes of France, Germany, and Spain, these more-favoured and progressive people to the south were mastering agriculture, learning to develop their appliances, taming the dog, domesticating cattle, and, as the climate to the north mitigated and the equatorial climate grew more tropical, spreading northward. All these early chapters of our story have yet to be disinterred. They will probably be found in Asia Minor, Persia, Arabia, India, or north Africa, or they lie beneath the Mediterranean waters. Twelve thousand years ago, or thereabouts—we are still too early for anything but the roughest chronology—Neolithic peoples were scattered all over Europe, north Africa, and Asia. They were peoples at about the level of many of the Polynesian islanders of the last century, and they were the most advanced peoples in the world.

§ 3

It will be of interest here to give a brief account of the life of the European Neolithic people before the appearance of metals. We get our light upon that life from various sources. They scattered their refuse about, and in some places (*e.g.* on the Danish coast) it accumulated in great heaps, known as the kitchen-middens. They buried some of their people, but not the common herd, with great care and distinction, and made huge heaps of earth over their sepulchres; these heaps are the barrows or dolmens which contribute a feature to the European, Indian, and American scenery in many districts to this day. In connection with these mounds, or

[1] Ridgeway (*Early Age of Greece*) says a lump of tin has been found in the Swiss pile-dwelling deposits.

[2] Tin was known as a foreign import in Egypt under the XVIIIth Dynasty; there is (rare) Mycenæan tin, and there are (probably later, but not clearly dated) tin objects in the Caucasus. But it is very difficult to distinguish tin from antimony. There is a good deal of Cyprus bronze which contains antimony; a good deal which seems to be tin is antimony—the ancients trying to get tin, but actually getting antimony and thinking it was tin.—J. L. M.

[3] In connection with iron, note the distinction of ornamental and useful iron. Ornamental iron, a rarity, perhaps meteoric, as jewellery or magical stuff, occurs in east Europe sporadically in the time of the XVIIIth Dynasty. This must be distinguished from the copious useful iron which appears in Greece much later from the North.—J. L. M.

[4] People were probably healthier and longer lived in the Bronze than in the Neolithic age. The disparity of stature between male and female was much less.—G. Wh.

IN ENGLAND 2,000 YEARS AGO

The landing stage of prehistoric lake village near Glastonbury

From a reconstruction drawing by A. Forestier

"Lake dwellings existed in England and Ireland from the Neolithic Age up to the days when O'Neil of Tyrone was fighting against the English."

Restoration of a Lake Dwelling

(after a drawing in Déchelette's "Manuel d'Archéologie")

independently of them, they set up great stones (megaliths), either singly or in groups, of which Stonehenge in Wiltshire and Carnac in Brittany are among the best-known examples. In various places their villages are still traceable.

One fruitful source of knowledge about Neolithic life comes from Switzerland, and was first revealed by the very dry winter of 1854, when the water level of one of the lakes, sinking to an unheard-of lowness, revealed the foundations of prehistoric pile dwellings of the Neolithic and early Bronze Ages, built out over the water after the fashion of similar homes that exist to-day in Celebes and elsewhere. Not only were the timbers of those ancient platforms preserved, but a great multitude of wooden, bone, stone, and earthenware utensils and ornaments, remains of food and the like, were found in the peaty accumulations below them. Even pieces of net and garments have been recovered. Similar lake dwellings existed in Scotland, Ireland, and elsewhere—there are well-known remains at Glastonbury in Somersetshire; in Ireland lake dwellings were inhabited from prehistoric times up to the days when O'Neil of Tyrone was fighting against the English before the plantation of Scotch colonists to replace the Irish in Ulster in the reign of James I of England. These lake villages had considerable defensive value, and there was a sanitary advantage in living over flowing water.

Probably these Neolithic Swiss pile dwellings did not shelter the largest communities that existed in those days. They were the homes of small patriarchal groups. Else-

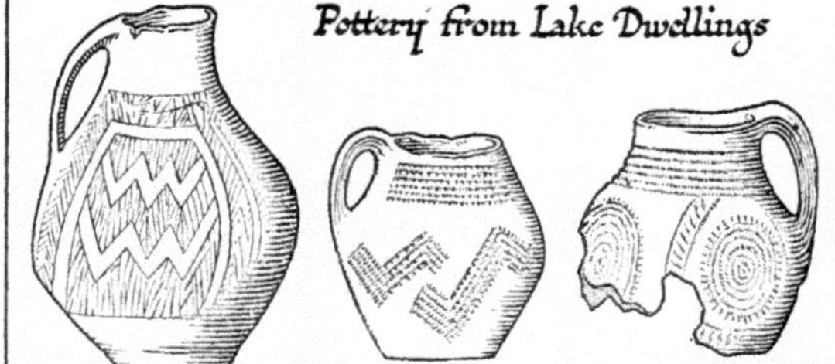

Pottery from Lake Dwellings

where upon fertile plains and in more open country there were probably already much larger assemblies of homes than in those mountain valleys. There are traces of such a large community of families in Wiltshire in England, for example; the remains of the stone circle of Avebury near Silbury mound were once the "finest megalithic ruin in Europe."[1] It consisted of two circles of stones surrounded by a larger circle and a ditch, and covering altogether twenty-eight and a half acres. From it two avenues of stones, each a mile and a half long, ran west and south on either side of Silbury Hill. Silbury Hill is the largest prehistoric artificial mound in England. The dimensions of this centre of a faith and a social life now forgotten altogether by men indicate the concerted efforts and interests of a very large number of people, widely scattered though they may have been over the west and south and centre of England. Possibly they assembled at some particular season of the year in a primitive sort of fair. The whole community "lent a hand" in building the mounds and hauling the stones. The Swiss pile-dwellers, on the contrary, seem to have lived in practically self-contained villages.

These lake-village people were considerably more advanced in methods and knowledge, and probably much later in time than the early Neolithic people who accumulated the shell mounds, known as kitchen middens, on the Danish and Scotch coasts. These kitchen midden folk may have been as early as 10,000 B.C. or earlier; the lake dwellings were probably occupied continuously from 5,000 or 4,000 B.C. down almost to historic times. Those early kitchen-midden people were among the most barbaric of Neolithic peoples, their stone axes were rough, and they had no domesticated animal except the dog. The lake-dwellers, on the other hand, had, in addition to the dog, which was of a medium-sized breed, oxen, goats, and sheep. Later on, as they were approaching the Bronze Age, they got swine. The remains of cattle and goats prevail in their débris, and, having regard to the climate and country about them, it seems probable that these beasts were sheltered in the buildings upon the piles in winter, and that fodder was stored for them. Probably the beasts lived in the same houses with the people, as the men and beasts do now in Swiss chalets. The people in the houses possibly milked the cows and goats, and milk perhaps played as important a part in their economy as it does in that of the mountain Swiss of to-day. But of that we are not sure at present. Milk is not a natural food for adults; it must have seemed queer stuff to take at first; and it may have been only after much breeding that a continuous supply of milk was secured from cows and goats. Some people think that the use of milk, cheese, butter, and other milk products came later into human life when men became nomadic. The writer is, however, disposed to give the Neolithic men credit for having discovered milking. The milk, if they did use it (and, no doubt, in that case sour curdled milk also, but not well-made cheese and butter), they must have kept in earthenware pots, for they had pottery, though it was roughly hand-made pottery and not the shapely product of the potter's wheel. They eked out this food supply by hunting. They killed and ate red deer and roe deer, bison and wild boar. And they ate the fox, a rather high-flavoured meat, and not what any one would eat in a world of plenty. Oddly enough, they do not seem to have eaten the hare, although it was available as food. They are supposed to have avoided eating it, as some savages are said to avoid eating it to this day, because they feared that the flesh of so timid a creature might make them, by a sort of infection, cowardly.[2]

Of their agricultural methods we know very little. No ploughs and no hoes have been found. They were of wood and have perished. Neolithic men cultivated and ate wheat, barley, and millet, but they knew nothing of oats or rye. Their grain they roasted, ground between stones and stored in pots, to be eaten when needed. And they made exceedingly solid and heavy bread, because round flat slabs of it have been got out of these deposits. Apparently they had no yeast. If they had no yeast, then they had no fermented drink. One sort of barley that they had is the sort that was cultivated by the ancient Greeks, Romans, and Egyptians, and they also had an Egyptian variety of wheat, showing that their ancestors had brought or derived this cultivation from the south-east. The centre of diffusion of wheat was somewhere in the eastern Mediterranean region. A wild form is still found in the neighbourhood of Mt. Hermon (see Footnote to Chap. XVI, § 1). When the lake dwellers

[1] Lord Avebury. For a good account of Avebury, Stonehenge, and the traces of a well-developed social system in England before the coming of the Keltic peoples, see Hippisley Cox, *The Green Roads of England.*

[2] Caesar *de Bello Gallico* says the Britons tabooed hare, fowl and goose.—G. Wh.

THE KITCHEN MIDDENERS AT HOME

By W. Paget

"The kitchen midden folk, maybe as early as 10000 B.C. or earlier, were amongst the most barbaric of the Neolithic peoples."

sowed their little patches of wheat in Switzerland, they were already following the immemorial practice of mankind. The seed must have been brought age by age from that distant centre of diffusion. In the ancestral lands of the south-east men had already been sowing wheat perhaps for thousands of years.[1] Those lake dwellers also ate peas, and crab-apples—the only apples that then existed in the world. Cultivation and selection had not yet produced the apple of to-day.

They dressed chiefly in skins, but they also made a rough cloth of flax. Fragments of that flaxen cloth have been discovered. Their nets were made of flax; they had as yet no knowledge of hemp and hempen rope. With the coming of bronze, their pins and ornaments increased in number. There is reason to believe they set great store upon their hair, wearing it in large shocks with pins of bone and afterwards of metal. To judge from the absence of realistic carvings or engravings or paintings, they either did not decorate their garments or decorated them with plaids, spots, interlacing designs, or similar conventional ornament. Before the coming of bronze there is no evidence of stools or tables; the Neolithic people probably squatted on their clay floors. There were no cats in these lake dwellings; no mice or rats had yet adapted themselves to human dwellings; the cluck of the hen was not as yet added to the sounds of human life, nor the domestic egg to its diet.[2]

The chief tool and weapon of Neolithic man was his axe; his next the bow and arrow. His arrow heads were of flint, beautifully made, and he lashed them tightly to their shafts. Probably he prepared the ground for his sowing with a pole, or a pole upon which he had stuck a stag's horn. Fish he hooked or harpooned. These implements no doubt stood about in the interior of the house, from the walls of which hung his fowling-nets. On the floor, which was of clay or trodden cow-dung (after the fashion of hut floors in India to-day), stood pots and jars and woven baskets containing grain, milk, and such-like food. Some of the pots and pans hung by rope loops to the walls. At one end of the room, and helping to keep it warm in winter by their animal heat, stabled the beasts. The children took the cows and goats out to graze, and brought them in at night before the wolves and bears came prowling.

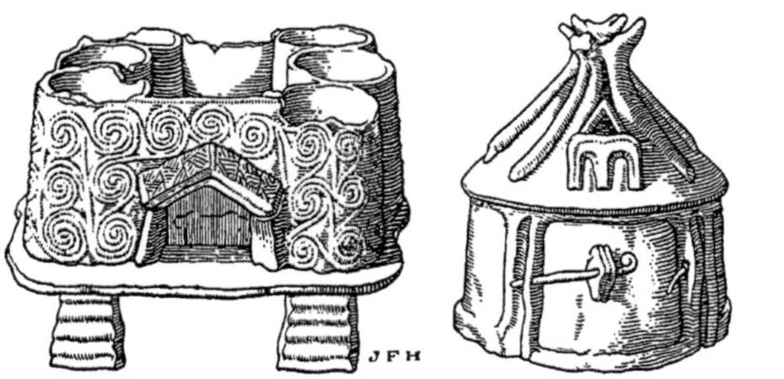

Hut urns, the first probably representing a lake-dwelling ... After Lubbock.

Since Neolithic man had the bow, he probably also had stringed instruments, for the rhythmic twanging of a bow-string seems almost inevitably to lead to that. He also had earthenware drums across which skins were stretched; perhaps also he made drums by stretching skins over hollow tree stems.[3] We do not know when man began to sing, but evidently he was making music, and since he had words, songs were no doubt

[1] All Old World peoples who had entered upon the Neolithic stage grew and ate wheat, but the American Indians must have developed agriculture independently in America after their separation from the Old World populations. They never had wheat. Their cultivation was maize, Indian corn, a new-world grain.

[2] Poultry and hens' eggs were late additions to the human cuisine, in spite of the large part they now play in our dietary. The hen is not mentioned in the Old Testament (but note the allusion to an egg, Job vi, 6) nor by Homer. Up to about 1,500 B.C. the only fowls in the world were jungle denizens in India and Burmah. The crowing of jungle cocks is noted by Glasfurd in his admirable accounts of tiger shooting as the invariable preliminary of dawn in the Indian jungle. Probably poultry were first domesticated in Burmah. They got to China, according to the records, only about 1,100 B.C. They reached Greece via Persia before the time of Socrates. In the New Testament the crowing of the cock reproaches Peter for his desertion of the Master.

[3] Later Palæolithic bone whistles are known. One may guess that reed pipes were an early invention.

being made. To begin with, perhaps, he just let his voice loose as one may hear Italian peasants now behind their ploughs singing songs without words. After dark in the winter he sat in his house and talked and sang and made implements by touch rather than sight. His lighting must have been poor, and chiefly firelight, but there was probably always some fire in the village, summer or winter. Fire was too troublesome to make for men to be willing to let it out readily. Sometimes a great disaster happened to those pile villages, the fire got free, and they were burnt out. The Swiss deposits contain clear evidence of such catastrophes.

All this we gather from the remains of the Swiss pile dwellings, and such was the character of the human life that spread over Europe, coming from the south and from the east with the forests as, 10,000 or 12,000 years ago, the reindeer and the Reindeer men passed away. It is evident that we have here a way of life already separated by a great gap of thousands of years of invention from its original Palæolithic stage. The steps by which it rose from that condition we can only guess at. From being a hunter hovering upon the outskirts of flocks and herds of wild cattle and sheep, and from being a co-hunter with the dog, man by insensible degrees may have developed a sense of proprietorship in the beasts and struck up a friendship with his canine competitor. He learnt to turn the cattle when they wandered too far; he brought his better brain to bear to guide them to fresh pasture. He hemmed the beasts into valleys and enclosures where he could be sure to find them again. He fed them when they starved, and so slowly he tamed them. Perhaps his agriculture began with the storage of fodder. He reaped, no doubt, before he sowed. The Palæolithic ancestor away in that unknown land of origin to the south-east first supplemented the precarious meat supply of the hunter by eating roots and fruits and wild grains. Man storing graminiferous grasses for his cattle might easily come to beat out the grain for himself.

§ 4

How did man learn to sow in order that he might reap?

We may hesitate here to guess at the answer to that question. But a very great deal has been made of the fact that wherever sowing occurs among primitive people in any part of the world, it is accompanied by a human sacrifice or by some ceremony which may be interpreted as the mitigation and vestige of an ancient sacrificial custom. This is the theme of Sir J. G. Frazer's *Golden Bough*. From this it has been supposed that the first sowings were in connection with the burial of a human being, either through wild grain being put with the dead body as food or through the scattering of grain over the body. It may be argued that there is only one reason why man should have disturbed the surface of the earth before he took to agriculture, and that was to bury his dead; and in order to bury a dead body and make a mound over it, it was probably necessary for him to disturb the surface over a considerable area. Neolithic man's chief apparatus for mound-making consisted of picks of deer's horn and shovels of their shoulder-blades, and with this he would have found great difficulty in making a deep excavation. Nor do we find such excavations beside the barrows. Instead of going down into tough sub-soil, the mound-makers probably scraped up some of the surface soil and carried it to the mound. All this seems probable, and it gives just that wide area of bared and turned-over earth upon which an eared grass, such as barley, millet, or primitive wheat, might have seeded and grown. Moreover, the mound-makers, being busy with the mound, would not have time to hunt meat, and if they were accustomed to store and eat wild grain, they would be likely to scatter grain, and the grain would be blown by the wind out of their rude vessels over the area they were disturbing. And if they were bringing up seed in any quantity in baskets and pots to bury with the corpse, some of it might easily blow and be scattered over the fresh earth. Returning later to the region of the mound, they would discover an exceptionally vigorous growth of food grain, and it would be a natural thing to associate it with the buried person, and regard it as a consequence of his death and burial. He had given them back the grain they gave him increased a hundredfold.

At any rate, there is apparently all over the world a traceable association in ancient ceremonial and in the minds of barbaric people between the death and burial of a person and the ploughing and sowing of grain. From this it is assumed that there was once a world-wide persuasion that it was necessary that some one should be buried before a crop could be sown, and that out of this persuasion arose a practice and tradition of human sacrifice at seedtime, which has produced profound effects in the religious development of the race. There may have been some idea of refreshing the earth by a blood draught or revivifying it with the life of the sacrificed person. We state these considerations here merely as suggestions that have been made of the way in which the association of seedtime and sacrifice arose. They are, at the best, speculations; they have a considerable vogue at the present time, and we have to note them, but we have neither the space nor the time here to examine them at length. The valuable accumulation of suggestions due to the industry and ingenuity of Sir J. G. Frazer still await a thorough critical examination, and to his works the reader must go for the indefatigable expansion of this idea.

§ 5

All these early beginnings must have taken place far back in time, and in regions of the world that have still to be effectively explored by the archæologists. They were probably going on in Asia or Africa, in what is now the bed of the Mediterranean, or in the region of the Indian Ocean, while the Reindeer man was developing his art in Europe. The Neolithic men who drifted over Europe and Western Asia 12,000 or 10,000 years ago were long past these beginnings; they were already close, a few thousand years, to the dawn of written tradition and the remembered history of mankind. Without any very great shock or break, bronze came at last into human life, giving a great advantage in warfare to those tribes who first obtained it. Written history had already begun before weapons of iron came into Europe to supersede bronze.

Already in those days a sort of primitive trade had sprung up. Bronze and bronze weapons, and such rare and hard stones as jade, gold because of its plastic and ornamental possibilities, and skins and flax-net and cloth, were being swapped and stolen and passed from hand to hand over great stretches of country. Salt also was probably being traded. On a meat dietary men can live without salt, but grain-consuming people need it just as herbivorous animals need it. Hopf says that bitter tribal wars have been carried on by the desert tribes of the Soudan in recent years for the possession of the salt deposits between Fezzan and Murzuk. To begin with, barter, blackmail, tribute, and robbery by violence passed into each other by insensible degrees. Men got what they wanted by such means as they could.[1]

§ 6

So far we have been telling of a history without events, a history of ages and periods and stages in development. But before we conclude this portion of the human story, we must record what was probably an event of primary importance and at first perhaps of tragic importance to developing mankind, and that was the breaking in of the Atlantic waters to the great Mediterranean valley.

The reader must keep in mind that we are endeavouring to give him plain statements that he can take hold of comfortably. But both in the matter of our time charts and the three maps we have given of prehistoric geography there is necessarily much speculative matter. We have dated the last Glacial Age and the appearance of the true men as about 40,000 or 35,000 years ago. Please bear that "about" in mind. The truth may be 60,000 or 20,000. But it is no good saying "a very long time" or "ages" ago, because then the reader will not know whether we mean centuries or millions of years. And similarly in these maps we give, they represent not the truth, but something like the truth. The outline of the land was "some such outline." There were such seas and such land masses. But both Mr. Horrabin, who has drawn these maps, and I, who have incited him to do so, have preferred to err on the timid side.[2] We are not geologists enough to launch out into original research in these matters, and so we have stuck to the 40-fathom line and the recent deposits as our guides for our post-glacial map and for the map of 12,000 to 10,000 B.C. But in one matter we have gone beyond these guides. It is practically certain that at the end of the last Glacial Age the Mediterranean was a couple of land-locked sea basins, not connected—or only connected by a torrential overflow river. The eastern basin was the fresher; it was fed by the Nile, the "Adriatic" river, the "Red-Sea" river, and perhaps by a river that poured down amidst the mountains that are now the Greek Archipelago from the very much bigger Sea of Central Asia that then existed. Almost certainly human beings, and possibly even Neolithic

[1] In addition to authorities already cited, we have used for this and the following chapters Lord Avebury's *Prehistoric Times*, Schrader and Jevons' *Prehistoric Antiquities of the Aryan Peoples*, and A. H. Keane's *Man Past and Present*.

[2] Among other books we have used Jukes Browne's *Building of the British Isles*.

men, wandered over that now lost Mediterranean valley.

The reasons for believing this are very good and plain. To this day the Mediterranean is a sea of evaporation. The rivers that flow into it do not make up for the evaporation from its surface. There is a constant current of water pouring into the Mediterranean from the Atlantic, and another current streaming in from the Bosphorus and Black Sea. For the Black Sea gets more water than it needs from the big rivers that flow into it; it is an overflowing sea, while the Mediterranean is a thirsty sea. From which it must be plain that when the Mediterranean was cut off both from the Atlantic Ocean and the Black Sea it must have been a shrinking sea with its waters sinking to a much lower level than those of the ocean outside. This is the case of the Caspian Sea to-day. Still more so is it the case with the Dead Sea

But if this reasoning is sound, then where to-day roll the blue waters of the Mediterranean there must once have been great areas of land, and land with a very agreeable climate. This was probably the case during the last Glacial Age, and we do not know how near it was to our time when the change occurred that brought back the ocean waters into the Mediterranean basin. Certainly there must have been Grimaldi people, and perhaps even Azilian and Neolithic people going about in the valleys and forests of these regions that are now submerged. The Neolithic Dark Whites, the people of the Mediterranean race, may have gone far towards the beginnings of settlement and civilization in that great lost Mediterranean Valley.

Mr. W. B. Wright [1] gives us some very stimulating suggestions here. He suggests that in the Mediterranean basin there were two lakes, "one a fresh-water lake, in the eastern depression, which drained into the other in the western depression. It is interesting to think what must have happened when the ocean level rose once more as a result of the dissipation of the ice-sheets, and its waters began to pour over into the Mediterranean area. The inflow, small at first, must have ultimately increased to enormous dimensions, as the channel was slowly lowered by erosion and the ocean level slowly rose. If there were any unconsolidated materials on the sill of the Strait, the result must have been a genuine debacle, and if we consider the length of time which even an enormous torrent would take to fill such a basin as that of the Mediterranean, we must conclude that this result was likely to have been attained in any case. Now, this may seem all the wildest speculation, but it is not entirely so, for if we examine a submarine contour map of the Straits of Gibraltar, we find there is an enormous valley running up from the Mediterranean deep, right through the Straits, and trenching some distance out on to the Atlantic shelf. This valley or gorge is probably the work of the inflowing waters of the ocean at the termination of the period of interior drainage."

[1] *The Quaternary Ice Age.*

This refilling of the Mediterranean, which by the rough chronology we are employing in this book may have happened somewhen between 30,000 and 10,000 B.C., must have been one of the greatest single events in the pre-history of our race. If the later date is the truer, then, as the reader will see plainly enough after reading the next two chapters, the crude beginnings of civilization, the first lake dwellings and the first cultivation, were probably round that eastern Levantine Lake into which there flowed not only the Nile, but the two great rivers that are now the Adriatic and the Red Sea. Suddenly the ocean waters began to break through over the westward hills and to pour in upon these primitive peoples—the lake that had been their home and friend, became their enemy; its waters rose and never abated; their settlements were submerged; the waters pursued them in their flight. Day by day and year by year the waters spread up the valleys and drove mankind before them. Many must have been surrounded and caught by the continually rising salt flood. It knew no check; it came faster and faster; it rose over the tree-tops, over the hills, until it had filled the whole basin of the present Mediterranean and until it lapped the mountain cliffs of Arabia and Africa. Far away, long before the dawn of history, this catastrophe occurred.

XII

EARLY THOUGHT[1]

§ 1

BEFORE we go on to tell how 6,000 or 7,000 years ago men began to gather into the first towns and to develop something more than the loose-knit tribes that had hitherto been their highest political association, something must be said about the things that were going on inside these brains of which we have traced the growth and development through a period of 500,000 years from the Pithecanthropus stage.

What was man thinking about himself and about the world in those remote days?

At first he thought very little about anything but immediate things. At first he was busy thinking such things as: "Here is a bear; what shall I do?" Or "There is a squirrel; how can I get it?" Until language had developed to some extent there could have been little thinking beyond the range of actual experience, for language is the instrument of thought as book-keeping is the instrument of business. It records and fixes and enables thought to get on to more and more complex ideas. It is the hand of the mind to hold and keep. Primordial man, before he could talk, probably saw very vividly, mimicked very cleverly, gestured, laughed, danced, and lived, without much speculation about whence he came or why he lived. He feared the dark, no doubt, and thunderstorms and big animals and queer things and whatever he dreamt about, and no doubt he did things to propitiate what he feared or to change his luck and please the imaginary powers in rock and beast and river. He made no clear distinction between animate and inanimate things; if a stick hurt him, he kicked it; if the river foamed and flooded, he thought it was hostile. His thought was probably very much at the level of a bright little contemporary boy of four or five. He had the same subtle unreasonableness of transition and the same limitations. But since he had little or no speech he would do little to pass on the fancies that came to him, and develop any tradition or concerted acts about them.

The drawings even of Late Palæolithic man do not suggest that he paid any attention to sun or moon or stars or trees. He was preoccupied only with animals and men. Probably he took day and night, sun and stars, trees and mountains, as being in the nature of things—as a child takes its meal times and its nursery staircase for granted. So far as we can judge, he drew no fantasies, no ghosts or anything of that sort. The Reindeer Men's drawings are fearless familiar things, with no hint about them of any religious or occult feelings. There is scarcely anything that we can suppose to be a religious or mystical symbol at all in his productions. No doubt he had a certain amount of what is called *fetishism* in his life; he did things we should now think unreasonable to produce desired ends, for that is all fetishism amounts to; it is only incorrect science based on guess-work or false analogy, and entirely different in its nature from religion. No doubt he was excited by his dreams, and his dreams mixed up at times in his mind with his waking impressions and puzzled him. Since he buried his dead, and since even the later Neanderthal men seem to have buried their dead, and apparently with food and weapons, it has been argued that he had a belief in a future life. But it is just as reasonable to suppose that early men buried their dead with food and weapons because

[1] Our treatment of this chapter is written for the general reader and is broad and general. But the student who wishes to go more thoroughly into the development of the civilized mentality out of the elements of the primitive human mind should read and study very carefully that very illuminating book, Jung's *Psychology of the Unconscious* (English translation by Beatrice M. Hinkle), and especially the opening two chapters. That book is a most important contribution to the mental history of mankind.

they doubted if they were dead, which is not the same thing as believing them to have immortal spirits, and that their belief in their continuing vitality was reinforced by dreams of the departed. They may have ascribed a sort of were-wolf existence to the dead, and wished to propitiate them.

The Reindeer man, we feel, was too intelligent and too like ourselves not to have had some speech, but quite probably it was not very serviceable for anything beyond direct statement or matter of fact narrative. He lived in a larger community than the Neanderthaler, but how large we do not know. Except when game is swarming, hunting communities must not keep together in large bodies or they will starve. The Indians who depend upon the caribou in Labrador must be living under circumstances rather like those of the Reindeer men. They scatter in small family groups, as the caribou scatter in search of food; but when the deer collect for the seasonal migration, the Indians also collect. That is the time for trade and feasts and marriages. The simplest American Indian is 10,000 years more sophisticated than the Reindeer man, but probably that sort of gathering and dispersal was also the way of Reindeer men. At Solutré in France there are traces of a great camping and feasting place. There was no doubt an exchange of news there, but one may doubt if there was anything like an exchange of ideas. One sees no scope in such a life for theology or philosophy or superstition or speculation. Fears, yes; but unsystematic fears; fancies and freaks of the imagination, but personal and transitory freaks and fancies.

Perhaps there was a certain power of suggestion in these encounters. A fear really felt needs few words for its transmission; a value set upon something may be very simply conveyed.

In these questions of primitive thought and religion, we must remember that the lowly and savage peoples of to-day probably throw very little light on the mental state of men before the days of fully developed language. Primordial man could have had little or no tradition before the development of speech. All savage and primitive peoples of to-day, on the contrary, are soaked in tradition—the tradition of thousands of generations. They may have weapons like their remote ancestors and methods like them, but what were slight and shallow impressions on the minds of their predecessors are now deep and intricate grooves worn throughout the intervening centuries generation by generation.

§ 2

Certain very fundamental things there may have been in men's minds long before the coming of speech. Chief among these must have been fear of the Old Man of the tribe. The young of the primitive squatting-place grew up under that fear. Objects associated with him were probably forbidden. Every one was forbidden to touch his spear or to sit in his place, just as to-day little boys must not touch father's pipe or sit in his chair. He was probably the master of all the women. The youths of the little community had to remember that. The idea of *something forbidden*, the idea of things being, as it is called, *tabu*, not to be touched, not to be looked at, may thus have got well into the human mind at a very early stage indeed. J. J. Atkinson, in an ingenious analysis of these primitive tabus which are found among savage peoples all over the world, the tabus that separate brother and sister, the tabus that make a man run and hide from his step-mother, traces them to such a fundamental cause as this.[1] Only by respecting this primal law could the young male hope to escape the Old Man's wrath. And the Old Man must have been an actor in many a primordial nightmare. A disposition to propitiate him even after he was dead is quite understandable. One was not sure that he *was* dead. He might only be asleep or shamming. Long after an Old Man was dead, when there was nothing to represent him but a mound and a megalith, the women would convey to their children how awful and wonderful he was. And being still a terror to his own little tribe, it was easy to go on to hoping that he would be a terror to other and hostile people. In his life he had fought for his tribe, even if he had bullied it. Why not when he was dead? One sees that the Old Man idea was an idea very natural to the primitive mind and capable of great development.[2]

§ 3

Another idea probably arose early out of the mysterious visitation of infectious diseases, and that was the idea of uncleanness and of being accurst. From that, too, there may have come an idea of avoiding particular places and persons, and persons in particular phases of health. Here was the root of another set of tabus. Then man, from the very dawn of his mental life, may have had a feeling of the sinister about places and things.

[1] J. J. Atkinson's *Primal Law*.

[2] See Frazer, *Belief in Immortality*.

Animals, who dread traps, have that feeling. A tiger will abandon its usual jungle route at the sight of a few threads of cotton.[1] Like most young animals, young human beings are easily made fearful of this or that by their nurses and seniors. Here is another set of ideas, ideas of repulsion and avoidance, that sprang up almost inevitably in men.

As soon as speech began to develop, it must have got to work upon such fundamental feelings and begun to systematize them, and keep them in mind. By talking together men would reinforce each other's fears, and establish a common tradition of tabus of things forbidden and of things unclean. With the idea of uncleanness would come ideas of cleansing and of removing a curse. The cleansing would be conducted through the advice and with the aid of wise old men or wise old women, and in such cleansing would lie the germ of the earliest priestcraft and witchcraft.

Speech from the first would be a powerful supplement to the merely imitative education and to the education of cuffs and blows conducted by a speechless parent. Mothers would tell their young and scold their young. As speech developed, men would find they had experiences and persuasions that gave them or seemed to give them power. They would make secrets of these things. There is a double streak in the human mind, a streak of cunning secretiveness and a streak perhaps of later origin that makes us all anxious to tell and astonish and impress each other. Many people make secrets in order to have secrets to tell. These secrets of early men they would convey to younger, more impressionable people, more or less honestly and impressively in some process of initiation. Moreover, the pedagogic spirit overflows in the human mind; most people like "telling other people not to." Extensive arbitrary prohibitions for the boys, for the girls, for the women, also probably came very early into human history.

Then the idea of the sinister has for its correlative the idea of the propitious, and from that to the idea of making things propitious by ceremonies is an easy step.[2]

§ 4

Out of such ideas and a jumble of kindred ones grew the first quasi-religious elements in human life. With every development of speech it became possible to intensify and develop the tradition of tabus and restraints and ceremonies. There is not a savage or barbaric race to-day that is not held in a net of such tradition. And with the coming of the primitive herdsman there would be a considerable broadening out of all this sort of practice. Things hitherto unheeded would be found of importance in human affairs. Neolithic man was nomadic in a different spirit from the mere daylight drift after food of the primordial hunter. He was a herdsman, upon whose mind a sense of direction and the lie of the land had been forced. He watched his flock by night as well as by day. The sun by day and presently the stars by night helped to guide his migrations; he began to find after many ages that the stars are steadier guides than the sun. He would begin to note particular stars and star groups, and to distinguish any individual thing was, for primitive man, to believe it individualized and personal. He would begin to think of the chief stars as persons, very shining and dignified and trustworthy persons looking at him like bright eyes in the night. His primitive tillage strengthened his sense of the seasons. Particular stars ruled his heavens when seedtime was due. The beginnings of agriculture were in the sub-tropical zone, or even nearer the equator, where stars of the first magnitude shine with a splendour unknown in more temperate latitudes.

And Neolithic man was counting, and falling under the spell of numbers. There are savage languages that have no word for any number above five. Some peoples cannot go above two. But Neolithic man in the lands of his origin in Asia and Africa even more than in Europe was already counting his accumulating possessions. He was beginning to use tallies, and wondering at the triangularity of three and the squareness of four, and why some quantities like twelve were easy to divide in all sorts of ways, and others, like thirteen, impossible. Twelve became a noble, generous, and familiar number to him, and thirteen rather an outcast and disreputable one.

Probably man began reckoning time by the clock of the full and new moons. Moonlight is an important thing to herdsmen who no longer merely hunt their herds, but watch and guard them. Moonlight too, was, perhaps, his time for love-making, as indeed it may have been for primordial man and the ground ape ancestor before him. But from the phases of the moon, as his tillage increased, man's attitude would go on to the greater

[1] Glasfurd's *Rifle and Romance in the Indian Jungle*, 1915.

[2] For some interesting suggestions here, see Sigismund Freud, *Totem and Taboo, Resemblances between the Psychic Life of Savages and Neurotics.*

cycle of the seasons. Primordial man probably only drifted before the winter as the days grew cold. Neolithic man knew surely that the winter would come, and stored his fodder and presently his grain. He had to fix a seedtime, a propitious seedtime, or his sowing was a failure. The earliest recorded reckoning is by moons and by generations of men. The former seems to be the case in the Book of Genesis, where, if one reads the great ages of the patriarchs who lived before the flood as lunar months instead of

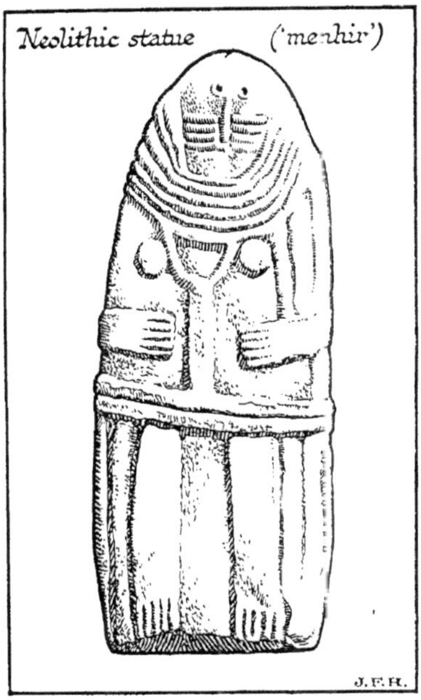

A CARVED STATUE ("MENHIR") OF THE NEOLITHIC PERIOD—A CONTRAST TO THE FREEDOM AND VIGOUR OF PALÆOLITHIC ART.

years, Methusaleh and the others are reduced to a credible length of life. But with agriculture began the difficult task of squaring the lunar month with the solar year; a task which has left its scars on our calendar to-day. Easter shifts uneasily from year to year, to the great discomfort of holiday-makers; it is now inconveniently early and now late in the season because of this ancient reference of time to the moon.

And when men began to move with set intention from place to place with their animal and other possessions, then they would begin to develop the idea of other places in which they were not, and to think of what might be in those other places. And in any valley where they lingered for a time, they would, remembering how they got there, ask, "How did this or that other thing get here?" They would begin to wonder what was beyond the mountains, and where the sun went when it set, and what was above the clouds.

§ 5

The capacity for telling things increased with their vocabulary. The simple individual fancies, the unsystematic fetish tricks and fundamental tabus of Palæolithic man began to be handed on and made into a more consistent system. Men began to tell stories about themselves, about the tribe, about its tabus and why they had to be, about the world and the why for the world. A tribal mind came into existence, a tradition. Palæolithic man was certainly more of a free individualist, more of an artist, as well as more of a savage, than Neolithic man. Neolithic man was coming under prescription; he could be trained from his youth and told to do things and not to do things; he was not so free to form independent ideas of his own about things. He had thoughts given to him; he was under a new power of suggestion. And to have more words and to attend more to words is not simply to increase mental power; words themselves are powerful things and dangerous things. Palæolithic man's words, perhaps, were chiefly just names. He used them for what they were. But Neolithic man was thinking about these words, he was thinking about a number of things with a great deal of verbal confusion, and getting to some odd conclusions. In speech he had woven a net to bind his race together, but also it was a net about his feet. Man was binding himself into new and larger and more efficient combinations indeed, but at a price. One of the most notable things about the Neolithic Age is the total absence of that free direct artistic impulse which was the supreme quality of later Palæolithic man. We find much industry, much skill, polished implements, pottery with conventional designs, co-operation upon all sorts of things, but no evidence of personal creativeness.[1] Self-suppression is beginning for men. Man has entered upon

[1] Ludwig Hopf, in *The Human Species*, calls the later Palæolithic art "masculine" and the Neolithic "feminine." The pottery was made by women, he says, and that accounts for it. But the arrowheads were made by men, and there was nothing to prevent Neolithic men from taking scraps of bone or slabs of rock and carving them—had they dared. We suggest they did not dare to do so.

the long and tortuous and difficult path towards a life for the common good, with all its sacrifice of personal impulse, which he is still treading to-day.

Certain things appear in the mythology of mankind again and again. Neolithic man was enormously impressed by serpents—and he no longer took the sun for granted. Nearly everywhere that Neolithic culture went, there went a disposition to associate the sun and the serpent in decoration and worship. This primitive serpent worship spread ultimately far beyond the regions where the snake is of serious practical importance in human life.

§ 6

With the beginnings of agriculture a fresh set of ideas arose in men's minds. We have already indicated how easily and naturally men may have come to associate the idea of sowing with a burial. Sir J. G. Frazer has pursued the development of this association in the human mind, linking up with it the conception of special sacrificial persons who are killed at seedtime, the conception of a specially purified class of people to kill these sacrifices, the first priests, and the conception of a *sacrament*, a ceremonial feast in which the tribe eats portions of the body of the victim in order to share in the sacrificial benefits.

Out of all these factors, out of the Old Man tradition, out of the desire to escape infection and uncleanness, out of the desire for power and success through magic, out of the sacrificial tradition of seedtime, and out of a number of like beliefs and mental experiments and misconceptions, a complex something was growing up in the lives of men which was beginning to bind them together mentally and emotionally in a common life and action. This something we may call *religion* (Lat. *religare*, to bind [1]). It was not a simple or logical something, it was a tangle of ideas about commanding beings and spirits, about gods, about all sorts of "musts" and "must-nots." Like all other human matters, religion has grown. It must be clear from what has gone before that primitive man—much less his ancestral

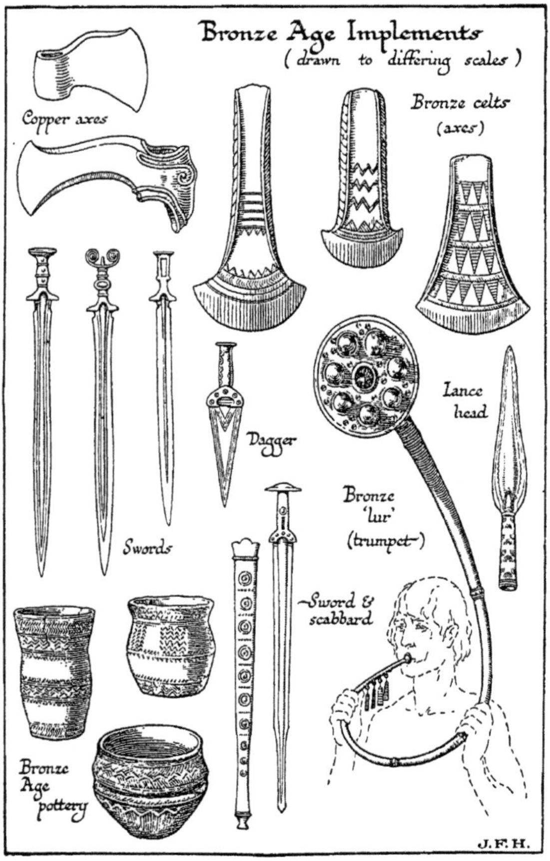

apes and his ancestral Mesozoic mammals—could have had no idea of God or Religion; only very slowly did his brain and his powers of comprehension become capable of such general conceptions. Religion is something that has grown up with and through human association, and God has been and is still being discovered by man.

This book is not a theological book, and it is not for us to embark upon theological

[1] But Cicero says relegere, "*to read over*," and the "binding" by those who accept *religare* is often written of as being merely the binding of a vow.

discussion; but it is a part, a necessary and central part, of the history of man to describe the dawn and development of his religious ideas and their influence upon his activities. All these factors we have noted must have contributed to this development, and various writers have laid most stress upon one or other of them. Sir J. G. Frazer we have already noted as the leading student of the deriva-

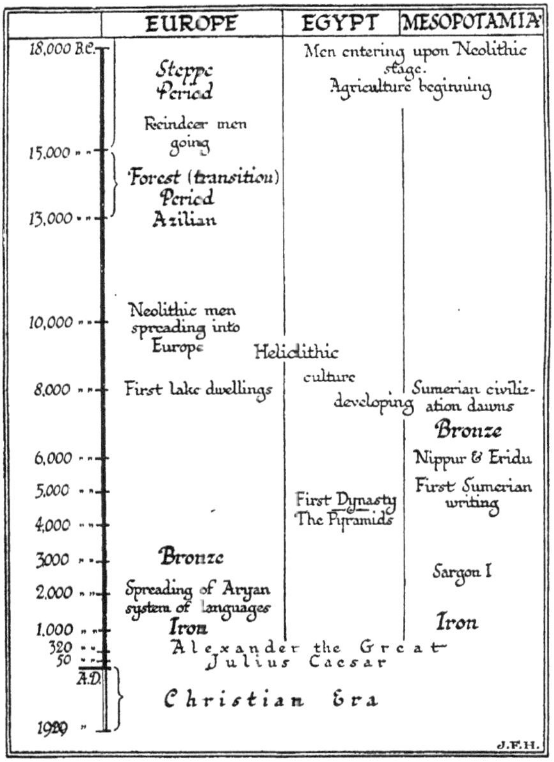

TIME DIAGRAM SHOWING THE GENERAL DURATION OF THE NEOLITHIC PERIOD IN WHICH EARLY THOUGHT DEVELOPED.

By this scale, three times of that on p. 49, the diagram on p. 28 of the period since the earliest subhuman traces would be 12 feet long, and the diagram of geological time (ch. ii, § 2) somewhere between 1,500 feet and three miles.

tion of sacraments from magic sacrifices. Grant Allen, in his *Evolution of the Idea of God*, laid stress chiefly on the posthumous worship of the "Old Man." Sir E. B. Tylor (*Primitive Culture*) gave his attention mainly to the disposition of primitive man to ascribe a soul to every object animate and inanimate. Mr. A. E. Crawley, in *The Tree of Life*, has called attention to other centres of impulse and emotion, and particularly to sex as a source of deep excitement. The thing we have to bear in mind is that Neolithic man was still mentally undeveloped, he could be confused and illogical to a degree quite impossible to an educated modern person. Conflicting and contradictory ideas could lie in his mind without challenging one another; now one thing ruled his thoughts intensely and vividly and now another; his fears, his acts, were still disconnected as children's are.

Confusedly under the stimulus of the need and possibility of co-operation and a combined life, Neolithic mankind was feeling out for guidance and knowledge. Men were becoming aware that personally they needed protection and direction, cleansing from impurity, power beyond their own strength. Confusedly in response to that demand, bold men, wise men, shrewd and cunning men were arising to become magicians, priests, chiefs, and kings. They are not to be thought of as cheats or usurpers of power, nor the rest of mankind as their dupes. All men are mixed in their motives; a hundred things move men to seek ascendancy over other men, but not all such motives are base or bad. The magicians usually believed more or less in their own magic, the priests in their ceremonies, the chiefs in their right. The history of mankind henceforth is a history of more or less blind endeavours to conceive a common purpose in relation to which all men may live happily, and to create and develop a common consciousness and a common stock of knowledge which may serve and illuminate that purpose. In a vast variety of forms this appearance of kings and priests and magic men was happening all over the world under Neolithic conditions. Everywhere mankind was seeking where knowledge and mastery and magic power might reside; everywhere individual men were willing, honestly or dishonestly, to rule, to direct, or to be the magic beings who would reconcile the confusions of the community.

In many ways the simplicity, directness, and detachment of a later Palæolithic rock-painter appeal more to modern sympathies than does the state of mind of these Neolithic men, full of the fear of some ancient Old Man who had developed into a tribal God, obsessed by ideas of sacrificial propitiation and magic murder. No doubt the reindeer hunter was a ruthless hunter and a combative and passionate creature, but he killed for reasons we can still understand; Neolithic man, under the sway of talk and a confused thought process, killed on theory, he killed for monstrous and now incredible ideas, he killed those he loved through fear and under direction. Those Neolithic men not only made human sacrifices at seedtime; there is every reason to suppose they sacrificed wives and slaves at the burial of their chieftains; they killed men, women, and children whenever they were under adversity and thought the gods were athirst. They practised infanticide.[1] All these things passed on into the Bronze Age.

Hitherto a social consciousness had been asleep and not even dreaming in human history. Before it awakened it produced nightmares.

Away beyond the dawn of history, 3,000 or 4,000 years ago, one thinks of the Wiltshire uplands in the twilight of a midsummer day's morning. The torches pale in the growing light. One has a dim apprehension of a procession through the avenue of stone, of priests, perhaps fantastically dressed with skins and horns and horrible painted masks—not the robed and bearded dignitaries our artists represent the Druids to have been—of chiefs in skins adorned with necklaces of teeth and bearing spears and axes, their great heads of hair held up with pins of bone, of women in skins or flaxen robes, of a great peering crowd of shock-headed men and naked children. They have assembled from many distant places; the ground between the avenues and Silbury Hill is dotted with their encampments. A certain festive cheerfulness prevails. And amidst the throng march the appointed human victims, submissive, helpless, staring towards the distant smoking altar at which they are to die—that the harvests may be good and the tribe increase. . . . To that had life progressed 3,000 or 4,000 years ago from its starting-place in the slime of the tidal beaches.

XIII
THE RACES OF MANKIND

§ 1. *Is Mankind Still Differentiating?* § 2. *The Main Races of Mankind.* § 3. *Was there an Alpine Race?* § 4. *The Brunet Peoples.* § 5. *How existing Races may be related to each other.*

§ 1

IT is necessary now to discuss plainly what is meant by a phrase, used often very carelessly, "The Races of Mankind."

It must be evident from what has already been explained in Chapter III that man, so widely spread and subjected therefore to great differences of climate, consuming very different food in different regions, attacked by different enemies, must always have been undergoing considerable local modification and differentiation. Man, like every other species of living thing, has constantly been tending to differentiate into several species; wherever a body of men has been cut off, in islands or oceans or by deserts or mountains, from the rest of humanity, it must have begun very soon to develop special characteristics, specially adapted to the local conditions. But, on the other hand, man is usually a wandering and enterprising animal, for whom there exist few insurmountable barriers. Men imitate men, fight and conquer them, interbreed, one people with another. Concurrently for thousands of years there have been two sets of forces at work, one tending to separate men into a multitude of local varieties, and another to remix and blend these varieties together before a separate species has been established.

These two sets of forces may have fluctuated in this relative effect in the past. Palæolithic man, for instance, may have been more of a wanderer, he may have drifted about over a much greater area,

[1] Bateman, *Ten Years' Digging in Celtic and Saxon Gravehills*, quoted by Lord Avebury in *Prehistoric Times*, p. 176.

than later Neolithic man; he was less fixed to any sort of home or lair, he was tied by fewer possessions. Being a hunter, he was obliged to follow the migrations of his ordinary quarry. A few bad seasons may have shifted him hundreds of miles. He may therefore have mixed very widely and developed few varieties over the greater part of the world.

The appearance of agriculture tended to tie those communities of mankind that took it up to the region in which it was most conveniently carried on, and so to favour differentiation. Mixing or differentiation is not dependent upon a higher or lower stage of civilization; many savage tribes wander now for hundreds of miles; many English villagers in the eighteenth century, on the other hand, had never been more than eight or ten miles from their villages, neither they nor their fathers nor grandfathers before them. Hunting peoples often have enormous range. The Labrador country, for instance, is inhabited by a few thousand Indians,[1] who follow the one great herd of caribou as it wanders yearly north and then south again in pursuit of food. This mere handful of people covers a territory as large as France. Nomad peoples also range very widely. Some Kalmuck tribes are said to travel nearly a thousand miles between summer and winter pasture.

It carries out this suggestion, that Palæolithic man ranged widely and was distributed, thinly indeed but uniformly, throughout the world, that the Palæolithic remains we find are everywhere astonishingly uniform. To quote Sir John Evans,[2] "The implements in distant lands are so identical in form and character with the British specimens that they might have been manufactured by the same hands. . . . On the banks of the Nile, many hundreds of feet above its present level, implements of the European types have been discovered; while in Somaliland, in an ancient river-valley at a great elevation above the sea, Sir H. W. Seton-Karr has collected a large number of implements formed of flint and quartzite, which, judging from their form and character, might have been dug out of the drift-deposits of the Somme and the Seine, the Thames or the ancient Solent."

Phases of spreading and intermixture have probably alternated with phases of settlement and specialization in the history of mankind. But up to a few hundred years ago it is probable that since the days of the Palæolithic Age at least mankind has on the whole been differentiating. The species has differentiated in that period into a very great number of varieties, many of which have reblended with others, which have spread and undergone further differentiation or become extinct. Wherever there has been a strongly marked local difference of conditions and a check upon intermixture, there one is almost obliged to assume a variety of mankind must have appeared. Of such local varieties there must have been a great multitude.

In one remote corner of the world, Tasmania, a little cut-off population of people remained in the early Palæolithic stage until the discovery of that island by the Dutch in 1642. They are now, unhappily, extinct. The last Tasmanian died in 1877. They may have been cut off from the rest of mankind for 15,000 or 20,000 or 25,000 years.

But among the numerous obstacles and interruptions to intermixture there have been certain main barriers, such as the Atlantic Ocean, the highlands, once higher, and the now vanished seas of Central Asia and the like, which have cut off great groups of varieties from other great groups of varieties over long periods of time. These separated groups of varieties developed very early certain broad resemblances and differences. Most of the varieties of men in eastern Asia and America, but not all, have now this in common, that they have yellowish buff skins, straight black hair, and often high cheek-bones. Most of the native peoples of Africa south of the Sahara, but not all, have black or blackish skins, flat noses, thick lips, and frizzy hair. In north and western Europe a great number of peoples have fair hair, blue eyes, and ruddy complexions; and about the Mediterranean there is a prevalence of white-skinned peoples with dark eyes and black hair. The black hair of many of these dark whites is straight, but never so strong and waveless as the hair of the yellow peoples. It is straighter in the east than in the west. In southern India we find brownish and darker peoples with straight black hair, and these as we pass eastward give place to more distinctly yellow peoples. In scattered islands and in Papua and New Guinea we find another series of black and brownish peoples of a more lowly type with frizzy hair.

But it must be borne in mind that these are very loose-fitting generalizations. Some of the areas and isolated pockets of mankind in the Asiatic area may have been under

[1] Cabot in *Labrador*, by Grenfell and others. Macmillan, New York.

[2] Quoted in *Ency. Brit.*, vol. ix, p. 850.

conditions more like those in the European area; some of the African areas are of a more Asiatic and less distinctively African type. We find a wavy-haired, fairish, hairy-skinned race, the Ainu, in Japan. They are more like the Europeans in their facial type than the surrounding yellow Japanese. They may be a drifted patch of the whites or they may be a quite distinct people. We find primitive black people in the Andaman Islands far away from Australia and far away from Africa. There is a streak of very negroid blood traceable in south Persia and some parts of India. These are the "Asiatic" negroids. There is little or no proof that all black people, the Australians, the Asiatic negroids and the negroes, derive from one origin, but only that they have lived for vast periods under similar conditions. We must not assume that human beings in the eastern Asiatic area were all differentiating in one direction and all the human beings in Africa in another. There were great currents of tendency, it is true, but there were also backwaters, eddies, admixtures, readmixtures, and leakages from one main area to the other. A coloured map of the world to show the races would not present just four great areas of colour; it would have to be dabbed over with a multitude of tints and intermediate shades, simple here, mixed and overlapping there.

In the early Neolithic Period in Europe—it may be 10,000 or 12,000 years ago or so—man was differentiating all over the world, and he had already differentiated into a number of varieties, but he has never differentiated into different *species*. A "species," we must remember, in biological language is distinguished from a "variety" by the fact that varieties can interbreed, while species either do not do so or produce offspring which, like mules, are sterile. All mankind can interbreed freely, can learn to understand the same speech, can adapt itself to co-operation. And in the present age, man is probably no longer undergoing differentiation at all. Readmixture is now a far stronger force than differentiation. Men mingle more and more. Mankind from the view of a biologist is an animal species in a state of arrested differentiation and possible re-admixture.

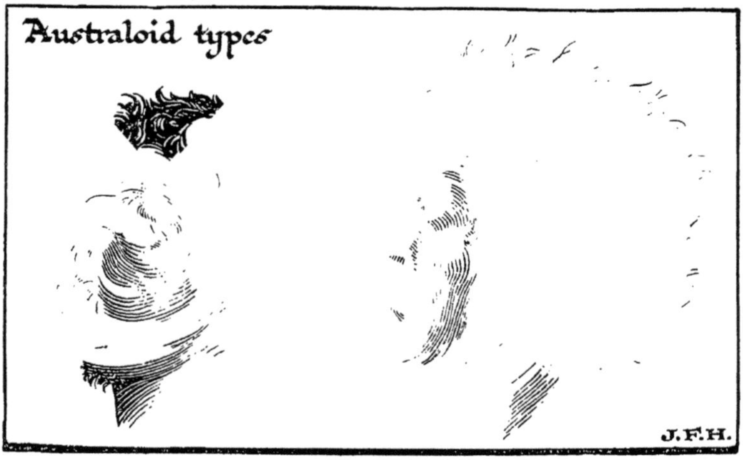

§ 2

It is only in the last fifty or sixty years that the varieties of men came to be regarded in this light, as a tangle of differentiations recently arrested or still in progress. Before that time students of mankind, influenced, consciously or unconsciously, by the story of Noah and the Ark and his three sons, Shem, Ham, and Japhet, were inclined to classify men into three or four great races, and they were disposed to regard these races as having always been separate things, descended from originally separate ancestors. They ignored the great possibilities of blended races and of special local isolations and variations. The classification has varied considerably, but there has been rather too much readiness to assume that mankind *must* be completely divisible into three or four main groups. Ethnologists (students of race) have fallen into grievous disputes about a multitude of minor peoples, as to whether they were of this or that primary race or "mixed," or strayed early forms, or what not. But all races are more or less mixed. There are, no doubt, four main groups, but each is a miscellany, and there are little groups that will not go into any of the four main divisions.

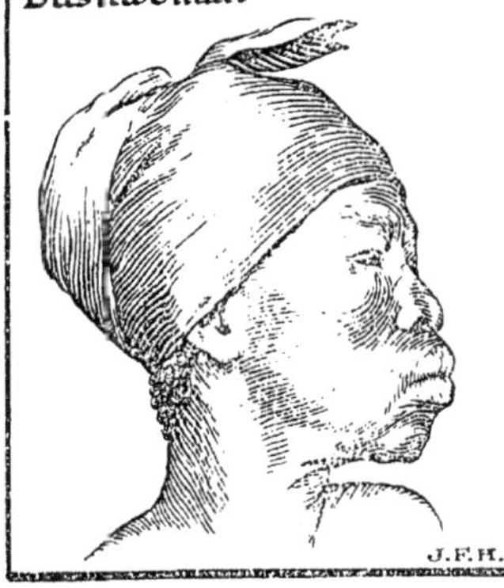

Bushwoman

Subject to these reservations, when it is clearly understood that when we speak of these main divisions we mean not simple and pure races, but groups of races, then they have a certain convenience in discussion. Over the European and Mediterranean area and western Asia there are, and have been for many thousand years, white peoples, usually called the CAUCASIANS,[1] subdivided into two or three subdivisions, the northern blonds, an alleged intermediate race about which many authorities are doubtful, and the southern dark whites; over eastern Asia and America a second group of races prevails, the MONGOLIANS, generally with yellow skins, straight black hair, and sturdy bodies; over Africa the NEGROES, and in the region of Australia and New Guinea the black, primitive AUSTRALOIDS. These are convenient terms, provided the student bears in mind that they are not exactly defined terms. They represent only the common characteristics of certain main groups of races; they leave out a number of little peoples who belong properly to none of these divisions, and they disregard the perpetual mixing where the main groups overlap.

[1] This is not a good name, and may perhaps drop out of use later. Blumenbach chose a particular skull as the "type" of this race and it happened to be a skull from the Caucasus.—G. S.

§ 3

Whether the "Caucasian" race is to be divided into two or three main subdivisions depends upon the classificatory value to be attached to certain differences in the skeleton and particularly to the shape of the skull. The student in his further reading will meet with constant references to round-skulled (Brachycephalic) and long-skulled (Dolichocephalic) peoples. No skull looked at from above is completely round, but some skulls (the dolichocephalic) are much more oblong than others; when the width of a skull is four-fifths or more of its length from back to front, that skull is called brachycephalic; when the width is less than four-fifths of the length, the skull is dolichocephalic. While some ethnologists regard the difference between brachycephaly and dolichocephaly as a difference of quite primary importance, another school—which the writer must confess has entirely captured his convictions—dismisses this as a mere secondary distinction. It seems probable that the skull shapes of a people may under special circumstances vary in comparatively few generations.[1] We do not know what influences alter the shape of the skull, just as we do not know why people of British descent in the Darling region of Australia ("Cornstalks") grow exceptionally tall, or why in New England their jawbones seem to become slighter and their teeth in consequence

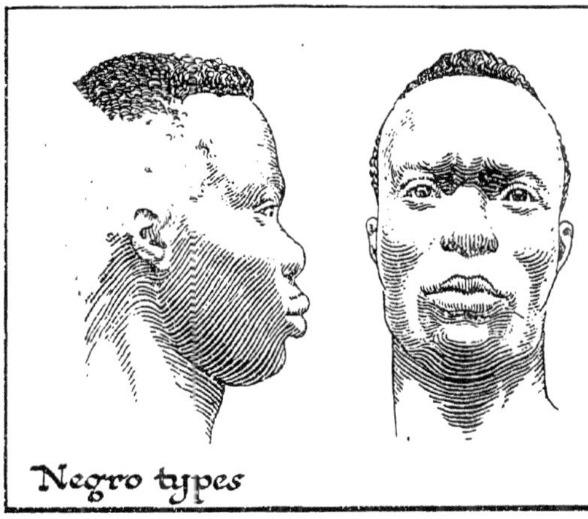

Negro types

[1] The skull shape of the Lombards, says Flinders Petrie, changed from dolichocephalic to brachycephalic in a few hundred years. See his Huxley Lecture for 1906, *Migrations*, published by the *Anthropological Institute*. Ripley is the great authority on the other side.

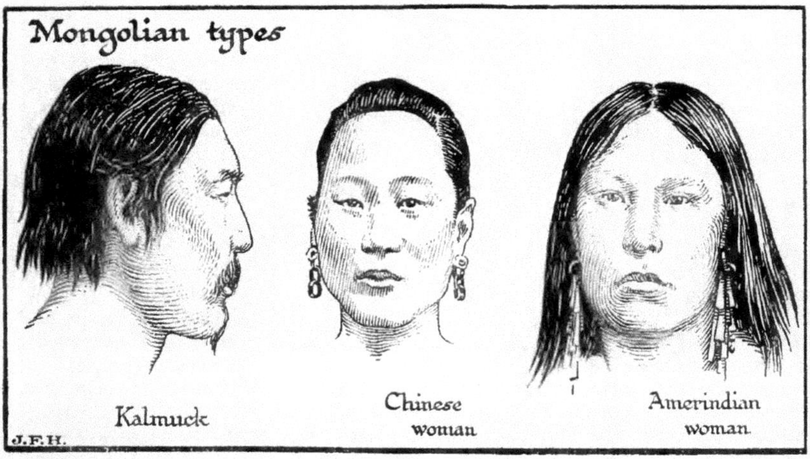

rather crowded. Even in Neolithic times dolichocephalic and brachycephalic skulls are found in the same group of remains and often buried together, and that is true of most peoples to-day. Some peoples, such as the mountain people of Central Europe, have more brachycephalic individuals per cent. than others; some, as the Scandinavians, are more prevalently dolichocephalic. In Neolithic Britain and in Scandinavia the earliest barrows (= tomb mounds) are long grave-shaped barrows and the late ones round, and the skulls found in the former are usually dolichocephalic and in the latter most frequently brachycephalic. This points perhaps to a succession of races in western Europe in the Neolithic Period (see Chapter XLV), but it may also point to changes of diet, habit, or climate.

But it is this study of skull shapes which has led many ethnologists to divide the Caucasian race not, as it was divided by Huxley, into two, the northern *blonds* and the Mediterranean and North African *dark whites* or brunets, but into three. They split his blonds into two classes. They distinguish a northern European type, blond and dolichocephalic, the Nordic; a Mediterranean or Iberian race, Huxley's dark whites, which is dark-haired and dolichocephalic, and between these two they descry this third race, their brachycephalic race, the Alpine race. The opposite school would treat the alleged Alpine race simply as a number of local brachycephalic varieties of Nordic or Iberian peoples. The Iberian peoples were the Neolithic people of the long barrows, and seem at first to have

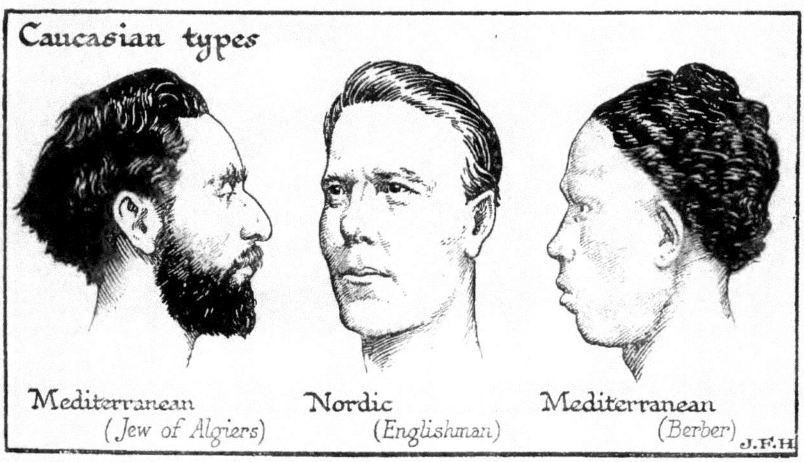

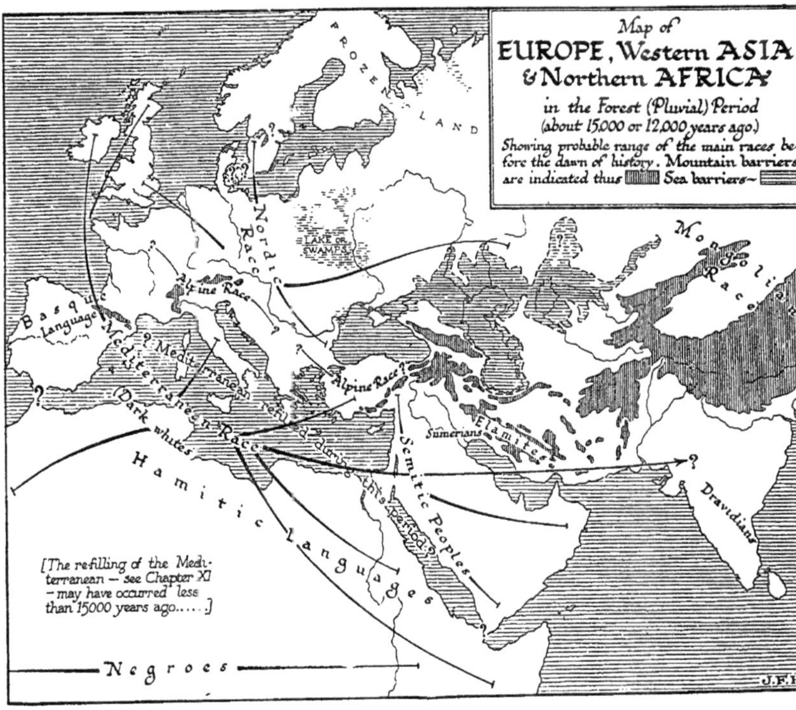

pervaded most of Europe and Western Asia.

§ 4

This Mediterranean or Iberian race certainly had a wider range in early times, and was a less specialized and distinctive race than the Nordic. It is very hard to define its southward boundaries from the Negro, or to mark off its early traces in Central Asia from those of early Dravidians or Mongolians. Wilfred Scawen Blunt[1] says that Huxley "had long suspected a common origin of the Egyptians and the Dravidians of India, perhaps a long belt of brown-skinned men from India to Spain in very early days." Across France and Great Britain these dark-white Iberian or Mediterranean people were ousted by a round-barrow-making "Alpine" or Alpine-Nordic race, and the dawn of history in Europe sees them being pressed westward and southward everywhere by the expansion of the fairer northern peoples.

It is possible that this "belt" of Huxley's of dark-white and brown-skinned men, this race of brunet-brown folk, ultimately spread even farther than India; that they reached to the shores of the Pacific, and that they were everywhere the original possessors of the Neolithic culture and the beginners of what we call civilization. The Nordic and the Mongolian peoples may have been but north-western and north-eastern branches from this more fundamental stem. Or the Nordic race may have been a branch, while the Mongolian, like the Negro, may have been another equal and distinct stem with which the brunet-browns met and mingled in South China. Or the Nordic peoples also may have developed separately from a palæolithic stage.

At some period in human history (see Elliot Smith's *Migrations of Early Culture*) there seems to have been a special type of Neolithic culture widely distributed in the world which had a group of features so curious and so unlikely to have been independently developed in different regions of the earth, as to compel us to believe that it was in effect one culture. It reached through all the regions inhabited by the brunet Mediterranean race, and beyond through India, Further India, up the Pacific coast of China, and it spread at last across the Pacific and to Mexico and Peru. It was a coastal culture not reaching deeply inland. (Here again we cover the ground of Huxley's

[1] *My Diaries*, under date of July 25, 1894.

ANCIENT PERUVIAN POTTERY

American Museum of Natural History

Evidences that "Huxley's 'race of brunet peoples'—everywhere the original possessors of the Neolithic Culture and the beginners of what we call civilization—were very widely distributed in the world."

"belt of brown-skinned men," and extend it far to the east across the stepping-stones of Polynesia. There are, we may note, some very striking resemblances between early Japanese pottery and so forth and similar Peruvian productions.) This peculiar development of the Neolithic culture, which Elliot Smith called the *heliolithic* [1] culture, included many or all of the following odd practices: (1) circumcision, (2) the very queer custom of sending the *father* to bed when a child is born, known as the *couvade*, (3) the practice of massage, (4) the making of mummies, (5) megalithic monuments [2] (*e.g.* Stonehenge), (6) artificial deformation of the heads of the young by bandages, (7) tattooing, (8) religious association of the sun and the serpent, and (9) the use of the symbol known as the swastika (see figure) for good luck. This odd little symbol spins gaily round the world; it seems incredible that

The Swastika

men would have invented and made a pet of it twice over. Elliot Smith traces these practices in a sort of constellation all over this great Mediterranean-India Ocean-Pacific area. Where one occurs, most of the others occur. They link Brittany with Borneo and Peru. But this constellation of practices does not crop up in the primitive homes of Nordic or Mongolian peoples, nor does it extend southward much beyond equatorial Africa. For thousands of years, from 15,000 to 1,000 B.C., such a heliolithic Neolithic culture and its brownish possessors may have been oozing round the world through the warmer regions of the world, drifting by canoes often across wide stretches of sea. And its region of origin may have been, as Elliot Smith suggests, the Mediterranean and North-African region. It must have been spreading up the Pacific Coast and across the island stepping-stones to America, long after it had passed on into other developments in its areas of origin. Many of the peoples of the East Indies, Melanesia and Polynesia were still in this heliolithic stage of development when they were discovered by European navigators in the eighteenth century. The

[1] "Sunstone" culture became of the sun worship and the megaliths. This is not a very happily chosen term. It suggests a division equivalent to palæolithic (old stone) and neolithic (new stone), whereas it is a sub-division of the neolithic culture.

[2] Megalithic monuments have been made quite recently by primitive Indian peoples.

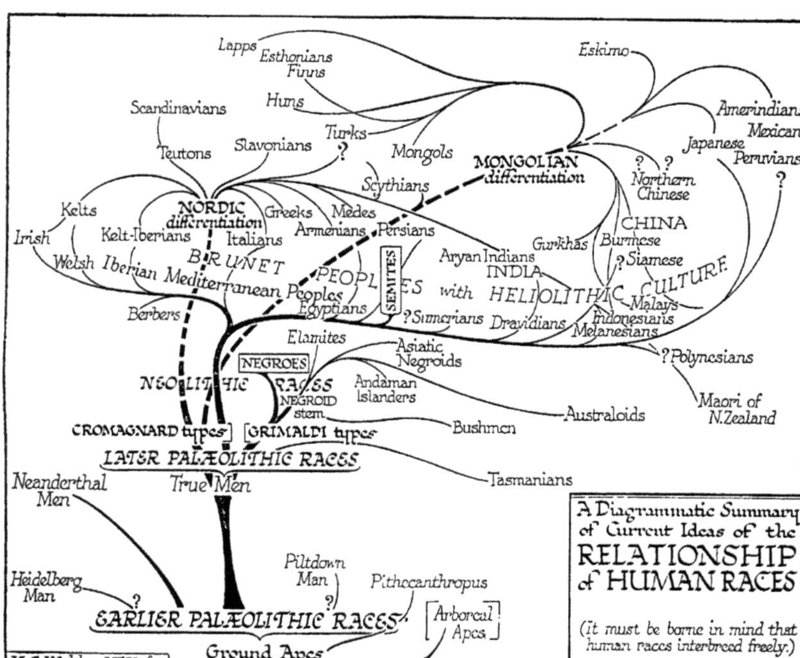

A Diagrammatic Summary of Current Ideas of the RELATIONSHIP of HUMAN RACES

(It must be borne in mind that human races interbreed freely.)

first civilizations in Egypt and the Euphrates-Tigris valley probably developed directly out of this widespread culture.[1] We will discuss later whether the Chinese civilization had a different origin. The Semitic nomads of the Arabian desert seem also to have had a heliolithic stage.

§ 5

It may clear up the necessarily rather confused discussion of this chapter to give a summary of the views expressed here in a diagram. This, on page 73, should be compared later with the language diagram on page 76.

We have put the Australoids as a Negroid branch, but many authorities would set back the Australoid stem closer to the Tasmanian, and there may even be sound reasons for transferring both Australoids and Tasmanians as separate branches to the left of the "Later Palæolithic Races." To avoid crowding we have omitted the Hairy Ainu. They may be the last vestiges of an ancient primitive Pre-Nordic Pre-Mongolian strain from which the Nordic races are descended.

XIV

THE LANGUAGES OF MANKIND

§ 1

IT is improbable that there was ever such a thing as a common human language. We know nothing of the language of Palæolithic man; we do not even know whether Palæolithic man talked freely.

We know that Palæolithic man had a keen sense of form and attitude, because of his drawings; and it has been suggested that he communicated his ideas very largely by gesture. Probably such words as the earlier men used were mainly cries of alarm or passion or names for concrete things, and in many cases they were probably imitative sounds made by or associated with the things named.[2]

The first languages were probably small collections of such words; they consisted of interjections and nouns. Probably the nouns were said in different intonations to convey different meanings. If Palæolithic man had a word for "horse" or "bear," he probably showed by tone or gesture whether he meant "bear is coming," "bear is going," "bear is to be hunted," "dead bear," "bear has been here," "bear did this," and so on. Only very slowly did the human mind develop methods of indicating action and relationship in a formal manner. Modern languages contain many thousands of words, but the earlier languages could have consisted only of a few hundred. It is said that even modern European peasants can get along with something less than a thousand words, and it is quite conceivable that so late as the Early Neolithic Period that was the limit of the available vocabulary. Probably men did not indulge in those days in conversation or description. For narrative purposes they danced and acted rather than told. They had no method of counting beyond a method of indicating two by a dual number, and some way of expressing many. The growth of speech was at first a very slow process indeed, and grammatical forms and the expression of abstract ideas may have come very late in human history, perhaps only 400 or 500 generations ago.

[1] For some interesting suggestions in this matter, see W. H. R. Rivers, "*Sun Cult and Megaliths in Oceana*" (*American Anthropologist* (N.S.), vol. xvii). Hose and MacDougall, *The Pagan Tribes of Borneo* contains some very interesting parallelisms between the culture of modern Borneo and the prehistoric culture of southern Europe. See also Dr. W. Warde Fowler's "Ancient Italy and Modern Borneo" in the *Journal of Roman Studies* (1916).

[2] Sir Arthur Evans suggests that in America sign-language arose before speech, because the sign-language is common to all Indians in North America, whereas the languages are different. See his *Anthropology and the Classics*.—G. M.

Samuel Butler (*Note Books*) suggests that language was "originally confined to a few scholars."—G. Wh.

§ 2

The students of languages (philologists) tell us that they are unable to trace with certainty any common features in all the languages of mankind. They cannot even find any elements common to all the Caucasian languages. They find over great areas groups of languages which have similar root words and similar ways of expressing the same idea, but then they find in other areas languages which appear to be dissimilar down to their fundamental structure, which express action and relation by entirely dissimilar devices, and have an altogether different grammatical scheme.[1] One great group of languages, for example, now covers nearly all Europe and stretches out to India; it includes English, French, German, Spanish, Italian, Greek, Russian, Armenian, Persian, and various Indian tongues. It is called the Indo-European or ARYAN family. The same fundamental roots, the same grammatical ideas, are traceable through all this family. Compare, for example, English *father*, *mother*, Gothic *fadar*, *moutar*, German *vater*, *mutter*, Latin *pater*, *mater*, Greek *pater*, *meter*, French *père*, *mère*, Armenian *hair*, *mair*, Sanscrit *pitar*, *matar*, etc., etc. In a similar manner the Aryan languages ring the changes on a great number of fundamental words, *f* in the Germanic languages becoming *p* in Latin, and so on. They follow a law of variation called Grimm's Law. These languages are not different things, they are variations of one thing. The people who use these languages think in the same way.

At one time in the remote past, in the Neolithic Age, that is to say 6,000[2] years or more ago, there may have been one simple original speech from which all these Aryan languages have differentiated. Somewhere between Central Europe and Western Asia there must have wandered a number of tribes sufficiently intermingled to develop and use one tongue. It is convenient here to call them the Aryan peoples. Sir H. H. Johnston has called them "Aryan Russians." They belonged mostly to the Caucasian group of races and to the blond and northern subdivision of the group, to the Nordic race that is.

Here one must sound a note of warning. There was a time when the philologists were disposed to confuse languages and races, and to suppose that people who once all spoke the same tongue must be all of the same blood. That, however, is not the case, as the reader will understand if he will think of the negroes of the United States who now all speak English, or of the Irish, who—except for purposes of political demonstration—no longer speak the old Erse language but English, or of the Cornish people, who have lost their ancient Keltic speech. But what a common language does do, is to show that a common intercourse has existed, and the possibility of intermixture; and if it does not point to a common origin, it points at least to a common future.

But even this original Aryan language, which was a spoken speech perhaps 4,000 or 3,000 B.C., was by no means a *primordial* language or the language of a savage race. Its speakers were in or past the Neolithic stage of civilization. It had grammatical forms and verbal devices of some complexity. The vanished methods of expression of the later Palæolithic peoples, of the Azilians, or of the early Neolithic kitchen-midden people for instance, were probably much cruder than the most elementary form of Aryan.

Probably the Aryan group of languages became distinct in a wide region of which the Danube, Dnieper, Don, and Volga were the main rivers, a region that extended eastward beyond the Ural mountains north of the Caspian Sea. The area over which the Aryan speakers roamed probably did not for a long time reach to the Atlantic or to the south of the Black Sea beyond Asia Minor. There was no effectual separation of Europe from Asia then at the Bosphorus.[3] The Danube flowed eastward to a great sea that extended across the Volga region of south-eastern Russia right into Turkestan, and included the Black, Caspian, and Aral Seas of to-day. Perhaps it sent out arms to the Arctic Ocean. It must have been a pretty effective barrier between the Aryan speakers and the people in north-eastern Asia. South of this sea stretched a continuous shore from the Balkans to Afghanistan.[4] North-west of it a region of swamps and lagoons reached to the Baltic.

§ 3

Next to Aryan, philologists distinguish another group of languages which seem to have been made quite separately from the Aryan languages, the Semitic. Hebrew and

[1] See article "Grammar" in the *Encyclopædia Britannica*.

[2] Sir H. H. Johnston gives this estimate in his *Comparative Study of the Bantu and Semi-Bantu Languages*.

[3] Greek—ox-ford.

[4] Ratzel (quoted in the *Ency. Brit.*, art. "Caspian").

Arabic are kindred, but they seem to have even a different set of root words from the Aryan tongues; they express their ideas of relationship in a different way; the fundamental ideas of their grammars are generally different. They were in all probability made by human communities quite out of touch with the Aryans, separately and independently. Hebrew, Arabic, Abyssinian, ancient Assyrian, ancient Phœnician, and a number of associated tongues are put together, therefore, as being derived from a second primary language, which is called the SEMITIC. In the very beginnings of recorded history we find Aryan-speaking peoples and Semitic-speaking peoples carrying on the liveliest intercourse of war and trade round and about the eastern end of the Mediterranean, but the fundamental differences of the primary Aryan and primary Semitic languages oblige us to believe that in early Neolithic times, before the historical period, there must for thousands of years have been an almost complete separation of the Aryan-speaking and the Semitic-speaking peoples. The latter seem to have lived either in south Arabia or in north-east Africa. In the opening centuries of the Neolithic Age the original Aryan speakers and the original Semitic speakers were probably living, so to speak, in different worlds with a minimum of intercourse. Racially, it would seem, they had a remote common origin; both Aryan speakers and Semites are classed as Caucasians; but while the original Aryan speakers seem to have been of Nordic race, the original Semites were rather of the Mediterranean type.

§ 4

Philologists speak with less unanimity of a third group of languages, the HAMITIC, which some declare to be distinct from, and others allied to, the Semitic. The weight of opinion inclines now towards the idea of some primordial connection of these two groups. The Hamitic group is certainly a much wider and more various language group than the Semitic or the Aryan, and the Semitic tongues are more of a family, have more of a common likeness, than the Aryan. The Semitic languages may have arisen as some specialized proto-Hamitic group, just as the birds arose from a special group of reptiles (Chap. IV). It is a tempting speculation, but one for which there is really no basis of justifying fact, to suppose that the rude primordial ancestor group of the Aryan tongues branched off from the proto-Hamitic speech forms at some still earlier

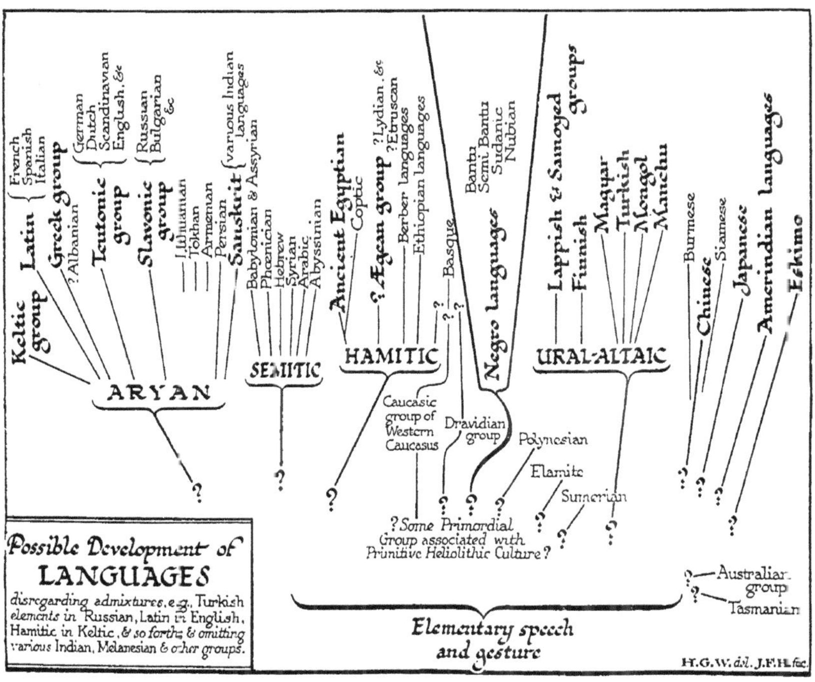

Possible Development of LANGUAGES disregarding admixtures, e.g., Turkish elements in Russian, Latin in English, Hamitic in Keltic, & so forth; & omitting various Indian, Melanesian & other groups.

date than the separation and specialization of Semitic. The Hamitic speakers to-day, like the Semitic speakers, are mainly of the Mediterranean Caucasian race. Among the Hamitic languages are the ancient Egyptian and Coptic, the Berber languages (of the mountain people of North Africa, the Masked Tuaregs, and other such peoples), and what are called the Ethiopic group of African languages in eastern Africa, including the speech of the Gallas and the Somalis. The general grouping of these various tongues suggests that they originated over some great area to the west, as the primitive Semitic may have arisen to the east, of the Red Sea divide. That divide was probably much more effective in Pleistocene times; the sea extended across to the west of the Isthmus of Suez, and a great part of lower Egypt was under water. Long before the dawn of history, however, Asia and Africa had joined at Suez, and these two language systems were in contact in that region. And if Asia and Africa were separated then at Suez, they may, on the other hand, have been joined by way of Arabia and Abyssinia.

These Hamitic languages may have radiated from a centre on the African coast of the Mediterranean, and they may have extended over the then existing land connections very widely into western Europe.

All these three great groups of languages, it may be noted, the Aryan, Semitic, and Hamitic, have one feature in common which they do not share with any other language, and that is grammatical gender; but whether that has much weight as evidence of a remote common origin of Aryan, Semitic, and Hamitic, is a question for the philologist rather than for the general student. It does not affect the clear evidence of a very long and very ancient prehistoric separation of the speakers of these three diverse groups of tongues.

The bulk of the Semitic and Hamitic-speaking peoples are put by ethnologists with the Aryans among the Caucasian group of races. They are "white." The Semitic and Nordic "races" have a much more distinctive physiognomy; they seem, like their characteristic languages, to be more marked and specialized than the Hamitic-speaking peoples.

§ 5

Across to the north-east of the Aryan and Semitic areas there must once have spread a further distinct language system which is now represented by a group of languages known as the TURANIAN, or URAL-ALTAIC group. This includes the Lappish of Lapland and the Samoyed speech of Siberia, the Finnish language, Magyar, Turkish or Tartar, Manchu and Mongol; it has not as a group been so exhaustively studied by European philologists, and there is insufficient evidence yet whether it does or does not include the Korean and Japanese languages. (A Japanese writer, Mr. K. Hirai, has attempted to show that Japanese and Aryan may have had a common parent tongue.[1])

§ 6

A fifth region of language formation was south-eastern Asia, where there still prevails a group of languages consisting of monosyllables without any inflections, in which the tone used in uttering a word determines its meaning. This may be called the Chinese or MONOSYLLABIC group, and it includes Chinese, Burmese, Siamese, and Tibetan. The difference between any of these Chinese tongues and the more western languages is profound. In the Pekinese form of Chinese there are only about 420 primary monosyllables, and consequently each of these has to do duty for a great number of things, and the different meanings are indicated either by the context or by saying the word in a distinctive tone. The relations of these words to each other are expressed by quite different methods from the Aryan methods; Chinese grammar is a thing different in nature from English grammar; it is a separate and different invention. Many writers declare there is no Chinese grammar at all, and that is true if we mean by grammar anything in the European sense of inflections and concords. Consequently any such thing as a literal translation from Chinese into English is an impossibility. The very method of the thought is different.[2] Their philosophy remains still largely a sealed book to the European on this account and vice versa, because of the different nature of the expressions.

[1] *Encyclopædia Britannica*, article "Japan."

[2] The four characters indicating "Affairs, query, imperative, old," placed in that order, for example, represent "Why walk in the ancient ways?" The Chinaman gives the bare cores of his meaning; the Englishman gets to it by a bold metaphor. He may be talking of conservatism in cooking or in bookbinding, but he will say: "Why walk in the ancient ways?" Mr. Arthur Waley, in the interesting essay on Chinese thought and poetry which precedes his book, *170 Chinese Poems* (Constable, 1918), makes it clear how in these fields Chinese thought is kept practical and restricted by the limitations upon metaphor the contracted structure of Chinese imposes. See also Hirst, *Ancient History of China*, ch. vii.

§ 7

In addition, the following other great language families are distinguished by the philologist. All the American-Indian languages, which vary widely among themselves, are separable from any Old World group. Here we may lump them together not so much as a family as a miscellany.[1] There is one great group of languages in Africa, from a little way north of the equator to its southern extremity, the BANTU, and in addition a complex of other languages across the centre of the continent about which we will not trouble here.[2] There are also two probably separate groups, the DRAVIDIAN in South India, and the MALAY-POLYNESIAN stretched over Polynesia, and also now including Indian tongues.

Now it seems reasonable to conclude from these fundamental differences that about the time when men were passing from the Palæolithic to Neolithic conditions, and beginning to form rather larger communities than the family herd, when they were beginning to tell each other long stories and argue and exchange ideas, human beings were distributed about the world in a number of areas which communicated very little with each other. They were separated by oceans, seas, thick forests, deserts or mountains from one another. There may have been in that remote time, it may be 10,000 years ago or more, Aryan, Semitic, Hamitic, Turanian, American, and Chinese-speaking tribes and families, wandering over their several areas of hunting and pasture, all at very much the same stage of culture, and each developing its linguistic instrument in its own way. Probably each of these original tribes was not more numerous altogether than the Indians in Hudson Bay Territory to-day. Agriculture was barely beginning, and until agriculture made a denser population possible men may have been almost as rare as the great apes have always been.

In addition to these early Neolithic tribes, there must have been various varieties of still more primitive forest folk in Africa and in India. Central Africa, from the Upper Nile, was then a vast forest, impenetrable to ordinary human life, a forest of which the Congo forests of to-day are the last shrunken remains.

Possibly the spread of men of a race higher than primitive Australoids into the East Indies,[3] and the development of the languages of the Malay-Polynesian type came later in time than the origination of these other language groups.

The language divisions of the philologist do tally, it is manifest, in a broad sort of way with the main race classes of the ethnologist, and they carry out the same idea of age-long separations between great divisions of mankind. In the Glacial Age, ice, or at least a climate too severe for the free spreading of peoples, extended from the north pole into Central Europe and across Russia and Siberia to the great tablelands of Central Asia. After the last Glacial Age, this cold north mitigated its severities very slowly, and was for long without any other population than the wandering hunters who spread eastward and across Bering Strait. North and Central Europe and Asia did not become sufficiently temperate for agriculture until quite recent times, times that is within the limit of 12,000 or possibly even 10,000 years, and a dense forest period intervened between the age of the hunter and the agricultural clearings.

This forest period was also a very wet period. It has been called the Pluvial or Lacustrine Age, the rain or pond period. It has to be remembered that the outlines of the land of the world have changed greatly even in the last hundred centuries. Across European Russia, from the Baltic to the Caspian Sea, as the ice receded there certainly spread much water and many impassable swamps; the Caspian Sea and the Sea of Aral and parts of the Desert of Turkestan, are the vestiges of a great extent of sea that reached far up to the Volga valley and sent an arm westward to join the Black Sea. Mountain barriers much higher than they are now, and the arm of the sea that is now the region of the Indus, completed the separation of the early Caucasian races from the Mongolians and the Dravidians, and made the broad racial differentiation of those groups possible.

Again the blown-sand Desert of Sahara—it is not a dried-up sea, but a wind desert, and was once fertile and rich in life—becoming more and more dry and sandy, cut the Caucasians off from the sparse primitive

[1] See Farrand *The American Nation* and E. S. Payne *History of the New World called America*, and note footnote to § 1 of this chapter.

[2] These are discussed compactly, but with very special knowledge, by Sir Harry Johnston in his little book on *The Opening up of Africa*, in the Home University Library. The student who finds this subject of philological history interesting, should read the introduction to the same writer's *Comparative Study of the Bantu and Semi-Bantu Languages*.

[3] The Polynesians appear to be a later eastward extension of the dark whites or brown peoples. See again § 4 of chap. xiii.

Negro population in the central forest region of Africa.

The Persian Gulf extended very far to the north of its present head, and combined with the Syrian desert to cut off the Semitic peoples from the eastern areas, while on the other hand the south of Arabia, much more fertile than it is to-day, may have reached across what is now the Gulf of Aden towards Abyssinia and Somaliland. The Mediterranean and Red Sea were probably still joined at Suez. The Himalayas and the higher and vaster massif of Central Asia and the northward extension of the Bay of Bengal up to the present Ganges valley divided off the Dravidians from the Mongolians, the canoe was the chief link between Dravidian and Southern Mongol, and the Gobi system of seas and lakes which presently became the Gobi desert, and the great system of mountain chains which follow one another across Asia from the centre to the north-east, split the Mongolian races into the Chinese and the Ural-Altaic language groups.

Bering Strait, when this came into existence, before or after the Pluvial Period, isolated the Amer-Indians.

These ancient separations must have remained effectual well into Neolithic times. The barriers between Africa, Asia, and Europe were lowered or bridged by that time, but mixing had not gone far. The practical separation of the west from Dravidian India and China continued indeed down almost into historical times; but the Semite, the Hamite, and the Aryan were already in close contact and vigorous reaction again in the very dawn of history.

We are not suggesting here, be it noted, that these ancient separations were absolute separations, but that they were effectual enough at least to prevent any great intermixture of blood or any great intermixture of speech in those days of man's social beginnings. There was, nevertheless, some amount of meeting and exchange even then, some drift of knowledge that spread the crude patterns and use of various implements, and the seeds of a primitive agriculture about the world.

§ 8

The fundamental tongues of these nine main language groups we have noted were not by any means all the human speech beginnings of the Neolithic Age. There may have been other, and possibly many other, ineffective centres of speech which were afterwards overrun by the speakers of still surviving tongues, and of elementary languages which faded out. We find strange little patches of speech still in the world which do not seem to be connected with any other language about them. Sometimes, however, an exhaustive inquiry seems to affiliate these disconnected patches, seems to open out to us tantalizing glimpses of some simpler, wider, and more fundamental and universal form of human speech. One language group that has been keenly discussed is the Basque group of dialects. The Basques live now on the north and south slopes of the Pyrenees; they number perhaps 600,000 altogether in Europe, and to this day they are a very sturdy and independent-spirited people. Their language, as it exists to-day, is a fully developed one. But it is developed upon lines absolutely different from those of the Aryan languages about it. Basque newspapers have been published in the Argentine and in the United States to supply groups of prosperous emigrants. The earliest "French" settlers in Canada were Basque, and Basque names are frequent among the French Canadians to this day. Ancient remains point to a much wider distribution of the Basque speech and people over Spain. For a long time this Basque language was a profound perplexity to scholars, and its structural character led to the suggestion that it might be related to some Amer-Indian tongue. A. H. Keane, in *Man, Past and Present*, assembles reasons for linking it—though remotely—with the Berber language of North Africa, and through the Berber with the general body of Hamitic languages, but this relationship is questioned by other philologists. They find Basque more akin to certain similarly stranded vestiges of speech found in the Caucasian Mountains, and they are disposed to regard it as a last surviving member, much changed and specialized, of a once very widely extended group of pre-Hamitic languages, otherwise extinct, spoken chiefly by peoples of that brunet Mediterranean race (round-barrow men) which once occupied most of western and southern Europe and western Asia, and which may have been very closely related to the Dravidians of India and the peoples with a heliolithic culture who spread eastward thence through the East Indies to Polynesia and beyond.

It is quite possible that over western and southern Europe language groups extended 10,000 years ago that have completely vanished before Aryan tongues. Later on we shall note, in passing, the possibility of three lost language groups represented by (1) Ancient Cretan, Lydian, and the like (though these may have belonged, says Sir H. H. Johnston, to the "Basque—Caucasian—Dravidian [!] group"), (2) Sumerian, and (3) Elamite. The suggestion has been made—it is a mere guess—that ancient Sumerian may have been a linking language between the early Basque-Caucasian and early Mongolian groups. If this is true, then we have in this "Basque-Caucasian-Dravidian-Sumerian-proto-Mongolian" group a still more ancient and more ancestral system of speech than the fundamental Hamitic.

The Hottentot language is said to have affinities with the Hamitic tongues, from which it is separated by the whole breadth of Bantu-speaking Central Africa. A Hottentot-like language with Bushman affinities is still spoken in equatorial East Africa, and this strengthens the idea that the whole of East Africa was once Hamitic-speaking. The Bantu languages and peoples spread, in comparatively recent times, from some centre of origin in West Central Africa and cut off the Hottentots from the other Hamitic peoples. But it is at least equally probable that the Hottentot is a separate language group.

Among other remote and isolated little patches of language are the Papuan speech of New Guinea and the native Australian. The now extinct Tasmanian language is but little known. What we do know of it is in support of what we have guessed about the comparative speechlessness of Palæolithic man.

We may quote a passage from Hutchinson's *Living Races of Mankind* upon this matter:—

"The language of the natives is irretrievably lost, only imperfect indications of its structure and a small proportion of its words having been preserved. In the absence of sibilants and some other features, their dialects resembled the Australian, but were of ruder, of less developed structure, and so imperfect that, according to Joseph Milligan, our best authority on the subject, they observed no settled order or arrangement of words in the construction of their sentences, but conveyed in a supplementary fashion by tone, manner, and gesture those modifications of meaning which we express by mood, tense, number, etc. Abstract terms were rare; for every variety of gum-tree or wattle-tree there was a name, but no word for 'tree' in general, nor for qualities such as hard, soft, warm, cold, long, short, round, etc. Anything hard was 'like a stone,' anything round 'like the moon,' and so on, usually suiting the action to the word and confirming by some sign the meaning to be understood."

§ 9

In reading this chapter it is well to remember how laborious and difficult are the tasks of comparative philology, and how necessary it is to understand the qualifications and limitations that are to be put upon its conclusions. The Aryan group of languages is much better understood than any other, for the simple reason that it has been more familiar and accessible to European science. The other groups have been less thoroughly investigated, because so far they have not been studied exhaustively by men accustomed to use them, and whose minds are set in the key of their structure. Even the Semitic languages have been approached at a disadvantage because few Jews think in Hebrew. But a time is fast approaching when Japanese, Chinese, Arabic, and Indian philologists will come to the rescue in these matters, and good reason may be found for revising much that has been said above about the native American, Ural-Altaic, primitive Chinese, and Polynesian groups of tongues.

Racial types......... From Egyptian tomb-paintings. (After Champollion.)

BOOK III

THE DAWN OF HISTORY

XV

THE ARYAN-SPEAKING PEOPLES IN PREHISTORIC TIMES

§ 1. *The Spreading of the Aryan-Speakers.* § 2. *Primitive Aryan Life.* § 3. *Early Aryan Daily Life.*

§ 1

WE have spoken of the Aryan language as probably arising in the region of the Danube and South Russia and spreading from that region of origin. We say "probably," because it is by no means certainly proved that that was the centre; there have been vast discussions upon this point and wide divergences of opinion. We give the prevalent view. As it spread widely, Aryan began to differentiate into a number of subordinate languages. To the west and south it encountered the Basque language, which was then widely spread in Spain, and also possibly various Hamitic Mediterranean languages.

The Neolithic Mediterranean race, the Iberian race, was distributed over Great Britain, Ireland, France, Spain, north Africa, south Italy, and, in a more civilized state, Greece and Asia Minor. It was probably closely related to the Egyptian. To judge by its European vestiges it was a rather small human type, generally with an oval face and a long head. It buried its chiefs and important people in megalithic chambers—*i.e.* made of big stones—covered over by great mounds of earth; and these mounds of earth, being much longer than they are broad, are spoken of as the long barrows. These people sheltered at times in caves, and also buried some of their dead therein; and from the traces of charred, broken, and cut human bones, including the bones of children, it is inferred that they were cannibals. These short dark Iberian tribes (and the Basques also if they were a different race) were thrust back westward, and conquered and enslaved by slowly advancing waves of a taller and fairer Aryan-speaking people, coming southward and westward through Central Europe, who are spoken of as the Kelts. Only the Basque resisted the conquering Aryan speech. Gradually these Keltic-speakers made their way to the Atlantic, and all that now remains of the Iberians is mixed into the Keltic population. How far the Keltic invasion affected the Irish population is a matter of debate at the present time; the Kelts may have been a mere caste of conquerors who imposed their language on a larger subject population. It is even doubtful if the north of England is more Aryan than pre-Keltic in blood. There is a sort of short dark Welshman, and certain types of Irishmen, who are Iberians by race. The modern Portuguese are also largely of Iberian blood.

The Kelts spoke a language, Keltic,[1] which was also in its turn to differentiate into the language of Gaul, Welsh, Breton, Scotch and Irish Gaelic, and other tongues. They buried the ashes of their chiefs and important people in round barrows. While these Nordic Kelts were spreading westward, other Nordic Aryan peoples were pressing down upon the dark white Mediterranean race in the Italian and Greek peninsulas, and developing the Latin and Greek groups of tongues. Certain other Aryan tribes were drifting towards the Baltic and across into Scandinavia, speaking varieties of the Aryan which became ancient Norse—the parent of Swedish, Danish, Norwegian, and Icelandic—Gothic, and Low and High German.

While the primitive Aryan speech was thus spreading and breaking up into daughter languages to the west, it was also spreading and breaking up to the east. North of the Carpathians and the Black Sea, Aryan-speaking tribes were increasing and spreading and using a distinctive dialect called Slavonian, from which came Russian, Serbian, Polish, Bulgarian, and other tongues; other

[1] "The Keltic group of languages, of which it has been said that they combined an Aryan vocabulary with a Berber (or Iberian) grammar." Sir Harry Johnston. See also Sir John Rhys, *The Welsh People*, Mac Neilh's *Phases in Irish History*, and various articles by Prof. Stewart Macalister in the *Irish Monthly* (1917–1919).

variations of Aryan distributed over Asia Minor and Persia were also being individualized as Armenian and Indo-Iranian, the parent of Sanscrit and Persian. In this book we have used the word Aryan for all this family of languages, but the term Indo-European is sometimes used for the entire family, and "Aryan" itself restricted in a narrower sense to the Indo-Iranian speech.[1] This Indo-Iranian speech was destined to split later into a number of languages, including Persian and Sanscrit, the latter being the language of certain tribes of fair-complexioned Aryan speakers who pushed eastward into India somewhen between 3,000 and 1,000 B.C. and conquered dark Dravidian peoples who were then in possession of that land.

§ 2

What sort of life did these prehistoric Aryans lead, these Nordic Aryans who were the chief ancestors of most Europeans and most white Americans and European colonists of to-day, as well as of the Armenians,[2] Persians, and high-caste Hindus?

In answering that question we are able to resort to a new source of knowledge in addition to the dug-up remains and vestiges upon which we have had to rely in the case of Palæolithic man. We have language. By careful study of the Aryan languages it has been found possible to deduce a number of conclusions about the life of these Aryan peoples 5,000 or 4,000 years ago. All these languages have a common resemblance, as each, as we have already explained, rings the changes upon a number of common roots. When we find the same root word running through all or most of these tongues, it seems reasonable to conclude that the thing that root word signifies must have been known to the common ancestors. Of course, if they have *exactly the same word* in their languages, this may not be the case; it may be the new name of a new thing or of a new idea that has spread over the world quite recently. "Gas," for instance, is a word that was made by Van Helmont, a Dutch chemist, about 1625, and has spread into most civilized tongues, and "tobacco" again is an American-Indian word which followed the introduction of smoking almost everywhere. But if the same word turns up in a number of languages, and *if it follows the characteristic modifications of each language*, we may feel sure that it has been in that language, and a part of that language, since the beginning, suffering the same changes with the rest of it. We know, for example, that the words for waggon and wheel run in this fashion through the Aryan tongues, and so we are able to conclude that the primitive Aryans, the more purely Nordic Aryans, had waggons, though it would seem from the absence of any common roots for spokes, rim, or axle that their wheels were not wheelwright's wheels with spokes, but made of the trunks of trees shaped out with an axe between the ends.

These primitive waggons were drawn by oxen. The early Aryans did not ride or drive horses; they had very little to do with horses. The Reindeer men were a horse-people, but the Neolithic Aryans were a cow-people. They ate beef, not horse; and after many ages they began this use of draught cattle. They reckoned wealth by cows. They wandered, following pasture, and "trekking" their goods, as the South African Boers do, in ox-waggons, though of course their waggons were much clumsier than any to be found in the world to-day. They probably ranged over very wide areas. They were migratory, but not in the strict sense of the word "nomadic"; they moved in a slower, clumsier fashion than did the later, more specialized nomadic peoples. They were forest and parkland people without horses. They were developing a migratory life out of the more settled "forest clearing" life of the earlier Neolithic period. Changes of climate which were replacing forest by pasture, and the accidental burning of forests by fire may have assisted this development.

When these early "Aryans" came to big rivers or open water, they built boats, at first hollow tree trunks and then skin-covered frameworks of lighter wood. Before history began there was already some Aryan canoe-traffic across the English Channel and in the Baltic, and also among the Greek islands. But the Aryans, as we shall see later, were probably not the first peoples to take to the sea.

We have already described the sort of home the primitive Aryan occupied and his household life, so far as the remains of the Swiss pile-dwellings enable us to describe

[1] See Schrader (translated by Jevons), *Prehistoric Antiquities of the Aryan Peoples*, p. 404. But though the word Aryan was undoubtedly in its original application the name only of the Indo-Iranian people, it has been used in modern discussion for more than half a century in the wider sense. A word was badly wanted for that purpose, and "Aryan" was taken; failing "Aryan" we should be obliged to fall back on "Indo-Germanic" or "Indo-European," terms equally open to objection and ugly and clumsy to employ.

[2] But these may have been an originally Semitic people who learnt an Aryan speech.

these things. Mostly his houses were of too flimsy a sort, probably of wattle and mud, to have survived, and possibly he left them and trekked on for very slight reasons. The Aryan peoples burnt their dead, a custom they still preserve in India, but their predecessors, the long-barrow people, the Iberians, buried their dead in a sitting position. In some ancient Aryan burial mounds (round barrows) the urns containing the ashes of the departed are shaped like houses, and these represent rounded huts with thatched roofs. (*See* Fig. page 57).

The grazing of the primitive Aryan was far more important to him than his agriculture. At first he cultivated with a rough wooden hoe; then, after he had found out the use of cattle for draught purposes, he began real ploughing with oxen, using at first a suitably bent tree bough as his plough. His first cultivation before that came about must have been rather in the form of garden patches near the house buildings than of fields. Most of the land his tribe occupied was common land on which the cattle grazed together.

He never used stone for building house walls until upon the very verge of history. He used stone for hearths (e.g. at Glastonbury), and sometimes stone sub-structures. He did, however, make a sort of stone house in the centre of the great mounds in which he buried his illustrious dead. He may have learnt this custom from his Iberian neighbours and predecessors. It was these dark whites of the heliolithic culture, and not the primitive Aryans, who were responsible for such primitive temples as Stonehenge or Carnac in Brittany.

His social life was growing. Man was ow living in clans and tribal communities. These clans and communities clashed; they took each other's grazing land, they sought to rob each other; there began a new thing in human life, *war*. For war is not a primeval thing; it has not been in this world for more than 20,000 years. To this day very primitive peoples, such as the Australian blackfellows, do not understand war. The Palæolithic Age was an age of fights and murder, no doubt, but not of the organized collective fighting of numbers of men.[1] But now men could talk together and group themselves under leaders, and they found a need of centres where they could come together with their cattle in time of raids and danger. They began to make camps with walls of earth and palisades, many of which are still to be traced in the history-worn contours of the European scenery. The leaders under whom men fought in war were often the same men as the sacrificial purifiers who were their early priests.

The knowledge of bronze spread late in Europe. Neolithic man had been making his slow advances age by age for 7,000 or 8,000 years before the metals came. By that time his social life had developed so that there were men of various occupations and men and women of different ranks in the community. There were men who worked wood and leather, potters and carvers. The women span and wove and embroidered. There were chiefs and families that were distinguished as leaderly and noble; and man varied the monotony of his herding and wandering, he consecrated undertakings and celebrated triumphs, held funeral assemblies, and distinguished the traditional seasons of the year, by *feasts*. His meats we have already glanced at; but somewhen between 10,000 B.C. and the broadening separation of the Aryan peoples towards 2,000 or 1,000 B.C., mankind discovered fermentation, and began to brew intoxicating drinks. He made these of honey, of barley, and, as the Aryan tribes spread southward, of the grape. And he got merry and drunken. Whether he first used yeast to make his bread light or to ferment his drink we do not know.

At his feasts there were individuals with a gift for "playing the fool," who did so no doubt to win the laughter of their friends,[2] but there was also another sort of men, of great importance in their time, and still more important to the historian, certain singers of songs and stories, the bards or rhapsodists. These *bards* existed among all the Aryan-speaking peoples; they were a consequence of and a further factor in that development of spoken language which was the chief of all the human advances made in Neolithic times. They chanted or recited stories of the past, or stories of the living chief and his people; they told other stories that they invented; they memorized jokes and catches.

[1] On this point see Perry. *An Ethnological Study of Warfare*, vol. lxi. Mem. Manchester Lit. and Phil. Soc., and also published separately 1917.—G. Wh.

[2] Fools, I think, were not wits, but deformed idiots, whom the company teased and laughed at. Certainly so in Roman and mediæval times. They do not occur in the Hellenic Age, except at courts in Asia Minor; but they must have been present in pre-Hellenic kingdoms; cf. end of *Iliad I*, where the gods laugh consumedly not at Hephaestus' wit, but at his lameness. The idealized Fool of Shakespeare is, like the idealized Hermit of the romances, the invention of later days.—G. M.

They found and seized upon and improved the rhythms, rhymes, alliterations, and such-like possibilities latent in language; they probably did much to elaborate and fix grammatical forms. They were the first great artists of the ear, as the later Aurignacian rock painters were the first great artists of the eye and hand. No doubt they used much gesture; probably they learnt appropriate gestures when they learnt their songs; but the order and sweetness and power of language was their primary concern.

And they mark a new step forward in the power and range of the human mind. They sustained and developed in men's minds a sense of a greater something than themselves, the tribe, and of a life that extended back into the past. They not only recalled old hatreds and battles, they recalled old alliances and a common inheritance. The feats of dead heroes lived again. A new thought came into men's minds, the desire to be remembered. Men began to live in thought before they were born and after they were dead.

Like most human things, this bardic tradition grew first slowly and then more rapidly. By the time bronze was coming into Europe there was not an Aryan people that had not a profession and training of bards. In their hands language became as beautiful as it is ever likely to be. These bards were living books, man-histories, guardians and makers of a new and more powerful tradition in human life. Every Aryan people had its long poetical records thus handed down, its sagas (Teutonic), its epics (Greek), its vedas (Old Sanscrit). The earliest Aryan people were essentially a people of the voice. The recitation seems to have predominated even in those ceremonial and dramatic dances and that "dressing-up" which among most human races have also served for the transmission of tradition.[1]

At that time there was no writing, and when first the art of writing crept into Europe, as we shall tell later, it must have seemed far too slow, clumsy, and lifeless a method of record for men to trouble very much about writing down these glowing and beautiful treasures of the memory. Writing was at first kept for accounts and matters of fact. The bards and rhapsodists flourished for long after the introduction of writing. They survived, indeed, in Europe as the minstrels into the Middle Ages.

Unhappily their tradition had not the fixity of a written record. They amended and reconstructed, they had their fashions and their phases of negligence. Accordingly we have now only the very much altered and revised vestiges of that spoken literature of prehistoric times. One of the most interesting and informing of these prehistoric compositions of the Aryans survives in the Greek *Iliad*. An early form of *Iliad* was probably recited by 1,000 B.C., but it was not written down until perhaps 700 or 600 B.C. Many men must have had to do with it as authors and improvers, but later Greek tradition attributed it to a blind bard named Homer, to whom also is ascribed the *Odyssey*, a composition of a very different spirit and outlook. To be a bard was naturally a blind man's occupation.[2] The Slavs called all bards *sliepac*, which was also their word for a blind man. The original recited version of the *Iliad* was older than that of the *Odyssey*. "The *Iliad* as a complete poem is older than the *Odyssey*, though the material of the *Odyssey*, being largely undatable folk-lore, is older than any of the historical material in the *Iliad*."[3] Both epics were probably written over and rewritten by some poet of a later date, in much the same manner that Lord Tennyson, the poet laureate of Queen Victoria, in his *Idylls of the King*, wrote over the *Morte d'Arthur* (which was itself a writing over by Sir Thomas Malory, *circ.* 1450, of pre-existing legends), making the speeches and sentiments and the characters more in accordance with those of his own time. But the events of the *Iliad* and the *Odyssey*, the way of living they describe, the spirit of the acts recorded, belong to the closing centuries of the prehistoric age. These sagas, epics, and vedas do supply, in addition

[1] The Aryans developed their languages and their ballads and epics between 10,000 B.C. and the historical period. Very much later in time, probably within the last 3,000 years, the nomadic Mongolian peoples of Asia began to develop their Ural-Altaic speech, under similar conditions, by similar poetic uses. Later we shall note the presence of bards at the court of Attila the Hun.

[2] It is suggested in the text that blind men became bards: Myres says that bards were (artificially) blinded to stop them from going elsewhere—the tribe wanted to keep them. The poetic touch is that "the Muses" blind the poet. Not a bit of it. (Homer, being a blind bard, describes things by sound—the twanging arrow, the far-thundering sea, the noise of the chariot going through the gate. He is audile, not visual.)—E. B.

But in this matter note the adjectives in the passage quoted here from the *Iliad;* they are all visual.—G. H. M.

Mr. L. Lloyd, of the experimental station at Cheshunt, tells me he has seen in Rhodesia the musician and singer of a troupe of native dancers who had been blinded by his chief to prevent him leaving the village.—H. G. W.

[3] G. M.

HOMER

By Harry Bates
By permission of Frederick Hollyer

"The *Iliad* and the *Odyssey* are both attributed to the blind bard Homer . . . They belong to the closing centuries of the prehistoric age."

to archæology and philology, a third source of information about those vanished times.

Here, for example, is the concluding passage of the *Iliad*, describing very exactly the making of a prehistoric barrow. (We have taken here Chapman's rhymed translation, correcting certain words with the help of the prose version of Lang, Leaf, and Myers.)

> " . . . Thus oxen, mules, in waggons straight they put,
> Went forth, and an unmeasur'd pile of sylvan matter cut;
> Nine days employ'd in carriage, but when the tenth morn shin'd
> On wretched mortals, then they brought the bravest of his kind
> Forth to be burned. Troy swam in tears. Upon the pile's most height
> They laid the body, and gave fire. All day it burn'd, all night.
> But when th' elev'nth morn let on earth her rosy fingers shine,
> The people flock'd about the pile, and first with gleaming wine
> Quench'd all the flames. His brothers then, and friends, the snowy bones
> Gather'd into an urn of gold, still pouring out their moans.
> Then wrapt they in soft purple veils the rich urn, digg'd a pit,
> Grav'd it, built up the grave with stones, and quickly piled on it
> A barrow. . . .
> . . . The barrow heap'd once, all the town
> In Jove-nurs'd Priam's Court partook a sumptuous fun'ral feast,
> And so horse-taming Hector's rites gave up his soul to rest."

There remains also an old English saga, *Beowulf*, made long before the English had crossed from Germany into England, which winds up with a similar burial. The preparation of a pyre is first described. It is hung round with shields and coats of mail. The body is brought and the pyre fired, and then for ten days the warriors built a mighty mound to be seen afar by the traveller on sea or land. *Beowulf*, which is at least a thousand years later than the *Iliad*, is also interesting because one of the main adventures in it is the looting of the treasures of a barrow already ancient in those days.

§ 3

The Greek epics reveal the early Greeks with no knowledge of iron, without writing, and before any Greek-founded cities existed in the land into which they had evidently come quite recently as conquerors. They were spreading southward from the Aryan region of origin. They seem to have been a fair people, newcomers in Greece, newcomers to a land that had been held hitherto by a darker people, people who are now supposed to have belonged to a dark white "aboriginal" race, a "Mediterranean" people allied to those Iberians whom the Kelts pressed westward, and to the Hamitic white people of North Africa.

Let us, at the risk of a slight repetition, be perfectly clear upon one point. The *Iliad* does not give us the primitive neolithic life of that Aryan region of origin; it gives us that life already well on the move towards a new state of affairs. The primitive neolithic way of living, with its tame and domesticated animals, its pottery and cooking, and its

Combat between Menelaus & Hector (in the Iliad)

From a platter ascribed to the end of the seventh century in the British Museum. This is probably the earliest known vase bearing a Greek inscription. Greek writing was just beginning. Note the Swastika.

patches of rude cultivation, we have sketched in Chapter XI. We have already discussed in § 4 of Chapter XIII the probability of a widespread *heliolithic* culture, a sort of sub-civilization, very like the Polynesian and Indonesian life of a hundred years ago, an elaboration of the earlier Neolithic stage. Between 15,000 and 6,000 B.C. the neolithic way of living had spread with the forests and abundant vegetation of the Pluvial Period, over the greater part of the old world, from the Niger to the Hwang-ho and from Ireland to the south of India. Now, as the climate of great portions of the earth was swinging towards drier and more open conditions again, the primitive neolithic life was developing along two divergent directions. One was leading to a more wandering life, towards at last a constantly migratory life between summer and winter pasture, which is called NOMADISM; the other, in certain sunlit river valleys, was towards a water-treasuring life of irrigation, in which men gathered into the first towns and made the first CIVILIZATION. The nature and development of civilization we shall consider more fully in the next chapter, but here we have to note that the Greeks, as the *Iliad* presents them, are neither simple neolithic nomads, innocent of civilization, nor are they civilized men. They are primitive nomads in an excited state, because they have just come upon civilization, and regard it as an opportunity for war and loot.[1] So far they are exceptional and not representative. But our interest in them in this chapter is not in their distinctively Greek and predatory aspect, but in what they reveal of the ordinary northward life from which they are coming.

These early Greeks of the *Iliad* are sturdy fighters, but without discipline—their battles

Horses & chariots—
(from an archaic Greek vase)

are a confusion of single combats. They have horses, but no cavalry; they use the horse, which is a comparatively recent addition to Aryan resources, to drag a rude fighting chariot into battle. The horse is still novel enough to be something of a terror in itself. For ordinary draught purposes, as in the quotation from the *Iliad* we have just made, oxen were employed.

The only priests of these Aryans are the keepers of shrines and sacred places. There are chiefs, who are heads of families and who also perform sacrifices, but there does not seem to be much mystery or sacramental feeling in their religion. When the Greeks go to war, these heads and elders meet in council and appoint a king, whose powers are very loosely defined. There are no laws, but only customs; and no exact standards of conduct.

The social life of the early Greeks centred about the households of these leading men. There were no doubt huts for herds and the like, and outlying farm buildings; but the hall of the chief was a comprehensive centre, to which everyone went to feast, to hear the bards, to take part in games and exercises. The primitive craftsmen were gathered there. About it were cowsheds and stabling and such-like offices. Unimportant people slept about anywhere as retainers did in the mediæval castles and as people still do in Indian households. Except for quite personal possessions, there was still an air of patriarchal communism about the tribe. The tribe, or the chief as the head of the tribe, owned the grazing lands; forest and rivers were the wild.

The Aryan civilization seems, and indeed all early communities seem, to have been without the little separate households that make up the mass of the population in western Europe or America to-day. The tribe was a big family; the nation a group of tribal families; a household often contained hundreds of people. Human society began, just as herds and droves begin among animals, by the family delaying its breaking up. Nowadays the lions in East Africa are apparently becoming social animals in this way, by the young keeping with the mother after they are fully grown, and hunting in a group. Hitherto the lion has been much more of a solitary beast. If men and women do not cling to their families nowadays as much as they did, it is because the state and the community supply now safety and help and facilities that were once only possible in the family group.

In the Hindu community of to-day these great households of the earlier stages of human society are still to be found. Mr. Bhupendranath Basu has recently described a typical Hindu household.[2] It is an Aryan household refined and made gentle by thousands of years of civilization, but its social structure is the same as that of the households of which the Aryan epics tell.

"The joint family system," he said, "has descended to us from time immemorial, the Aryan patriarchal system of old still holding sway in India. The structure, though ancient, remains full of life. The joint family is a co-operative corporation, in

[1] The *Iliad* describes what Chadwick calls a Heroic Age: i.e. a time when the barbarians or nomads are breaking up an old civilization. Men are led by chiefs, who live by plunder and conquest and make themselves kingdoms. The tribe is broken up; instead comes the comitatus of casual men who attach themselves to a particular chief, as Phœnix or Patroclus to Achilles. Religion is broken up, being by origin local. Hence there is almost no religion in the *Iliad* or the *Nibelungenlied*. Almost no magic. No family life. Tremendous booty, and *la carrière ouverte aux talents* with a vengeance.—G. M.

[2] *Some Aspects of Hindu Life in India.* Paper read to the Royal Society of Arts, Nov. 28, 1918.

which men and women have a well-defined place. At the head of the corporation is the senior member of the family, generally the eldest male member, but in his absence the senior female member often assumes control." (Cp. Penelope in the *Odyssey*.)

"All able-bodied members must contribute their labour and earnings, whether of personal skill or agriculture and trade, to the common stock; weaker members, widows, orphans, and destitute relations, all must be maintained and supported; sons, nephews, brothers, cousins, all must be treated equally, for any undue preference is apt to break up the family. We have no word for cousins—they are either brothers or sisters, and we do not know what are cousins two degrees removed. The children of a first cousin are your nephews and nieces, just the same as the children of your brothers and sisters. A man can no more marry a cousin, however removed, than he can marry his own sister, except in certain parts of Madras, where a man may marry his maternal uncle's daughter. The family affections, the family ties, are always very strong, and therefore the maintenance of an equal standard among so many members is not so difficult as it may appear at first sight. Moreover, life is very simple. Until recently shoes were not in general use at home, but sandals without any leather fastenings. I have known of a well-to-do middle-class family of several brothers and cousins who had two or three pairs of leather shoes between them, these shoes being only used when they had occasion to go out, and the same practice is still followed in the case of the more expensive garments, like shawls, which last for generations, and with their age are treated with loving care, as having been used by ancestors of revered memory.

"The joint family remains together sometimes for several generations, until it becomes too unwieldy, when it breaks up into smaller families, and you thus see whole villages peopled by members of the same clan. I have said that the family is a co-operative society, and it may be likened to a small state, and is kept in its place by strong discipline based on love and obedience. You see nearly every day the younger members coming to the head of the family and taking the dust of his feet as a token of benediction; whenever they go on an enterprise, they take his leave and carry his blessing. . . . There are many bonds which bind the family together—the bonds of sympathy, of common pleasures, of common sorrows; when a death occurs, all the members go into mourning; when there is a birth or a wedding, the whole family rejoices. Then above all is the family deity, some image of Vishnu, the preserver; his place is in a separate room, generally known as the room of God, or in well-to-do families in a temple attached to the house, where the family performs its daily worship. There is a sense of personal attachment between this image of the deity and the family, for the image generally comes down from past generations, often miraculously acquired by a pious ancestor at some remote time. . . . With the household gods is intimately associated the family priest. . . . The Hindu priest is a part of the family life of his flock, between whom and himself the tie has existed for many generations. The priest is not generally a man of much learning; he knows, however, the traditions of his faith. . . . He is not a very heavy burden, for he is satisfied with little—a few handfuls of rice, a few home-grown bananas or vegetables, a little unrefined sugar made in the village, and sometimes a few pieces of copper are all that is needed. . . . A picture of our family life would be incomplete without the household servants. A female servant is known as the 'jhi,' or daughter, in Bengal—she is like the daughter of the house; she calls the master and the mistress father and mother, and the young men and women of the family brothers and sisters. She participates in the life of the family; she goes to the holy places along with her mistress, for she could not go alone, and generally she spends her life with the family of her adoption; her children are looked after by the family. The treatment of men servants is very similar. These servants, men and women, are generally people of the humbler castes, but a sense of personal attachment grows up between them and the members of the family, and as they get on in years they are affectionately called by the younger members elder brothers, uncles, aunts, etc. . . . In a well-to-do house there is always a resident teacher, who instructs the children of the family as well as other boys of the village; there is no expensive school building, but room is found in some veranda or shed in the courtyard for the children and their teacher, and into this school low-caste boys are freely admitted. These indigenous schools were not of a very high order, but they supplied an agency of instruction for the masses which was probably not available in many other countries. . . .

"With Hindu life is bound up its traditional duty of hospitality. It is the duty of a householder to offer a meal to any stranger who may come before midday and ask for one; the mistress of the house does not sit down to her meal until every member is fed, and, as sometimes her food is all that is left, she does not take her meal until well after midday lest a hungry stranger should come and claim one." . . .

We have been tempted to quote Mr. Basu at some length, because here we do get to something like a living understanding of the type of household which has prevailed in human communities since Neolithic days, which still prevails to-day in India, China, and the Far East, but which in the west is rapidly giving ground before a state and municipal organization of education and a large-scale industrialism within which an amount of individual detachment and freedom is possible, such as these great households never knew. . . .

But let us return now to the history preserved for us in the Aryan epics.

The Sanscrit epics tell a very similar story to that underlying the *Iliad*, the story of a fair, beef-eating people—only later did they become vegetarians—coming down from Persia into the plain of North India and conquering their way slowly towards the Indus. From the Indus they spread over India, but as they spread they acquired much from the dark Dravidians they conquered, and they seem to have lost their bardic tradition. The vedas, says Mr. Basu, were transmitted chiefly in the households by the women. . . .

The oral literature of the Keltic peoples who pressed westward has not been preserved so completely as that of the Greeks or Indians; it was written down many centuries later, and so, like the barbaric, primitive English *Beowulf*, has lost any clear evidence of a period of migration into the lands of an antecedent people. If the pre-Aryans figure in it at all, it is as the fairy folk of the Irish stories. Ireland, most cut off of all the Keltic-speaking communities, retained to the latest date its primitive life; and the *Táin*, the Irish *Iliad*, describes a cattle-keeping life in which war chariots are still used, and war dogs also, and the heads of the slain are carried off slung round the horses' necks. The *Táin* is the story of a cattle raid. Here too the same social order appears as in the *Iliad*; the chiefs sit and feast in great halls, they build halls for themselves, there is singing and story-telling by the bards, and drinking and intoxication.[1] Priests are not very much in evidence, but there is a sort of medicine man who deals in spells and prophecy.

XVI

THE FIRST CIVILIZATIONS

§ 1

WHEN the Aryan way of speech and life was beginning to spread to the east and west of the region in which it began, and breaking up as it spread into a number of languages and nations, considerable communities of much more civilized men were already in existence in Egypt and in Mesopotamia, and probably also in China and in (still purely Dravidian) India. Our story has overshot itself in its account of the Aryans and of their slow progress from early Neolithic conditions to the heroic barbarism of the Bronze Age. We must now go back. Such a pre-Keltic gathering as we sketched at Avebury would have happened about 2,000 B.C., and the building of the barrow for Hector as the *Iliad* describes it, 1,300 B.C. or even later. It is perhaps natural for a European writer writing primarily for English-reading students to overrun his subject in this way. No great harm is done if the student does clearly grasp that there has been an overlap.

[1] No Greek heroes, in Homer or the heroic tradition, ever get drunk. In the comic tradition they do, and of course centaurs and barbarians do.—G. M.

Here then we take up the main thread of human history again. We must hark back to 6,000 B.C. or even earlier. But although we shall go back so far, the people we shall describe are people already in some respects beyond the Neolithic Aryans of three thousand years later, more particularly in their social organization and their material welfare. While excavations of the American expedition [1] at Nippur have unearthed evidence of a city community existing there at least as early as 5,000 B.C., and probably as early as 6,000 B.C., an earlier date than anything we know of in Egypt. De Candolle asserts that it is only in the Euphrates-Tigris district that wheat has ever been found growing wild.[2] It may be that from Mesopotamia as a

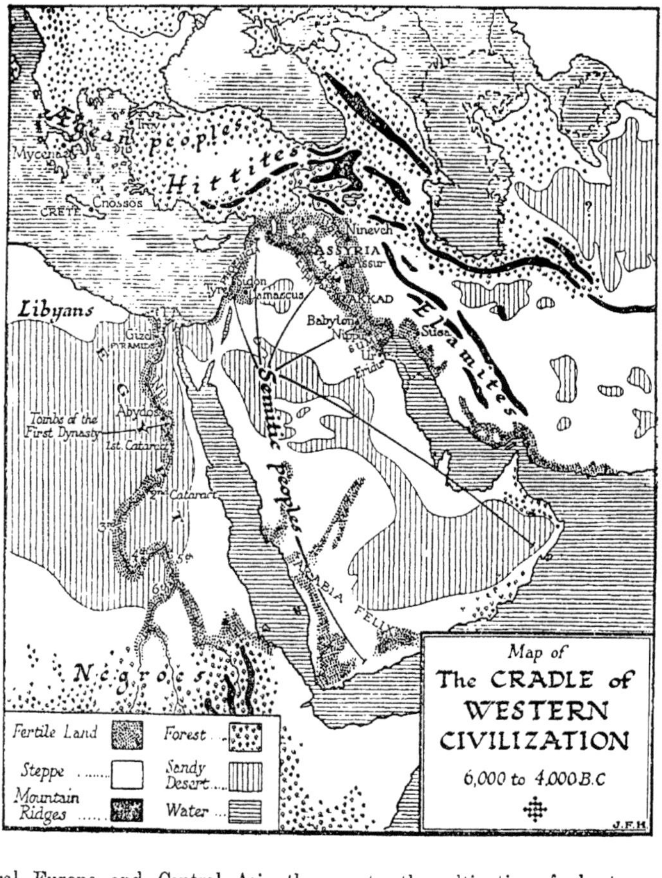

in Central Europe and Central Asia the primitive Neolithic way of life was becoming more migratory and developing into nomadism, in the great river valleys it is becoming more settled and localized. It is still doubtful whether we are to consider Mesopotamia or Egypt the earlier scene of the two parallel beginnings of settled communities living in towns. By 4,000 B.C., in both these regions of the earth, such communities existed, and had been going on for a very considerable time. The centre the cultivation of wheat spread over the entire eastern hemisphere. Or it may be that wheat grew wild in some regions now submerged. There may have been a

[1] Babylonian expedition of the University of Pennsylvania.

[2] H. R. Hall, *Ancient History of the Near East*, says it has been found in Palestine.—S. H.

The late Mr. Aaron Aaronson found a real wild wheat upon the slopes of Mt. Hermon. See Bulletin 274, Plant Indus. Bureau, U.S. Dept. of Agriculture; and Stapf in Suppt. to the ***Jour. of the Board of Agri., Lond.***, vol xvii, No. 3.—E. J. R.

wild wheat region in what is now the sea bottom of the eastern Mediterranean. But cultivation is not civilization; the growing of wheat had spread from the Atlantic to the Pacific with the distribution of the Neolithic culture by perhaps 10,000 or 9,000 B.C., before the beginnings of civilization. Civilization is something more than the occasional seasonal growing of wheat. It is the settlement of men upon an area continuously cultivated and possessed, who live in buildings continuously inhabited with a common rule and a common city or citadel. For a long time civilization may quite possibly have developed in Mesopotamia without any relations with the parallel beginnings in Egypt. The two settlements may have been quite independent, arising separately out of the widely diffused Heliolithic Neolithic culture. Or they may have had a common origin in the region of the Mediterranean, the Red Sea, and southern Arabia.

The first condition necessary to a real settling down of Neolithic men, as distinguished from a mere temporary settlement among abundant food, was of course a trustworthy all-the-year-round supply of water, fodder for the animals, food for themselves, and building material for their homes. There had to be everything they could need at any season, and no want that would tempt them to wander further. This was a possible state of affairs, no doubt, in many European and Asiatic valleys; and in many such valleys, as in the case of the Swiss lake-dwellings, men settled from a very early date indeed; but nowhere, of any countries now known to us, were these favourable conditions found upon such a scale, and nowhere did they hold good so surely year in and year out as in Egypt and in the country between the upper waters of the Euphrates and Tigris and the Persian Gulf.[1] Here was a constant water supply under enduring sunlight; trustworthy harvests year by year; in Mesopotamia wheat yielded, says Herodotus, two hundredfold to the sower; Pliny says that it was cut twice and afterwards yielded good fodder for sheep; there were abundant palms and many sorts of fruits; and as for building material, in Egypt there was clay and easily worked stone, and in Mesopotamia a clay that becomes a brick in the sunshine. In such countries men would cease to wander and settle down almost unawares; they would multiply and discover themselves numerous and by their numbers safe from any casual assailant. They multiplied, producing a denser human population than the earth had ever known before; their houses became more substantial, wild beasts were exterminated over great areas, the security of life increased so that ordinary men went about in the towns and fields without encumbering themselves with weapons, and among themselves, at least, they became peaceful peoples. Men took root as man had never taken root before.

But in the less fertile and more seasonal lands outside these favoured areas, there developed on the other hand a thinner, more active population of peoples, the primitive nomadic peoples. In contrast with the settled folk, the agriculturists, these nomads lived freely and dangerously. They were in comparison lean and hungry men. Their herding was still blended with hunting; they fought constantly for their pastures against hostile families. The discoveries in the elaboration of implements and the use of metals made by the settled peoples spread to them and improved their weapons. They followed the settled folk from Neolithic phase to Bronze phase. It is possible that in the case of iron, the first users were nomadic. They became more warlike with better arms, and more capable of rapid movements with the improvement of their transport. One must not think of a nomadic stage as a predecessor of a settled stage in human affairs. To begin with, man was a slow drifter, following food. Then one sort of men began to settle down, and another sort became more distinctly nomadic. The settled sort began to rely more and more upon grain for food; the nomad began to make a greater use of milk for food. He bred his cows for milk. The two ways of life specialized in opposite directions. It was inevitable that nomad folk and the settled folk should clash, that the nomads should seem hard barbarians to the settled peoples, and the settled peoples soft and effeminate and very good plunder to the nomad peoples. Along the fringes of the developing civilizations there must have been a constant raiding and bickering between hardy nomad tribes and mountain tribes and the more numerous and less warlike peoples in the towns and villages.

[1] We shall use "Mesopotamia" here loosely for the Euphrates-Tigris country generally. Strictly, of course, as its name indicates, Mesopotamia (mid-rivers) means only the country *between* those two great rivers. That country in the fork was probably very marshy and unhealthy in early times (Sayce), until it was drained by man, and the early cities grew up west of the Euphrates and east of the Tigris. Probably these rivers then flowed separately into the Persian Gulf

For the most part this was a mere raiding of the borders. The settled folk had the weight of numbers on their side; the herdsmen might raid and loot, but they could not stay. That sort of mutual friction might go on for many generations. But ever and again we find some leader or some tribe amidst the disorder of free and independent nomads, powerful enough to force a sort of unity upon its kindred tribes, and then woe betide the nearest civilization. Down pour the united nomads on the unwarlike, unarmed plains, and there ensues a war of conquest. Instead of carrying off the booty, the conquerors settle down on the conquered land, which becomes all booty for them; the villagers and townsmen are reduced to servitude and tribute-paying, they become hewers of wood and drawers of water, and the leaders of the nomads become kings and princes, masters and aristocrats. They too settle down, they learn many of the arts and refinements of the conquered, they cease to be lean and hungry, but for many generations they retain traces of their old nomadic habits, they hunt and indulge in open-air sports, they drive and race chariots, they regard work, especially agricultural work, as the lot of an inferior race and class.

This in a thousand variations has been one of the main stories in history for the last seventy centuries or more. In the first history that we can clearly decipher we find already in all the civilized regions a distinction between a non-working ruler class and the working mass of the population. And we find too that after some generations, the aristocrat, having settled down, begins to respect the arts and refinements and law-abidingness of settlement, and to lose something of his original hardihood. He intermarries, he patches up a sort of toleration between conqueror and conquered; he exchanges religious ideas and learns the lessons upon which soil and climate insist. He becomes a part of the civilization he has captured. And as he does so, events gather towards a fresh invasion by the free adventurers of the outer world.[1]

§ 2A

This alternation of settlement, conquest, refinement, fresh conquest, refinement, is particularly to be noted in the region of the Euphrates and Tigris, which lay open in every direction to great areas which are not arid enough to be complete deserts, but which were not fertile enough to support civilized populations. Perhaps the earliest people to form real cities in this part of the world, or indeed in any part of the world, were a people of mysterious origin called the Sumerians. They were neither Semites nor Aryans, and whence they came we do not know. Whether they were dark whites of Iberian or Dravidian affinities is less certainly to be denied.[2] They used a kind of

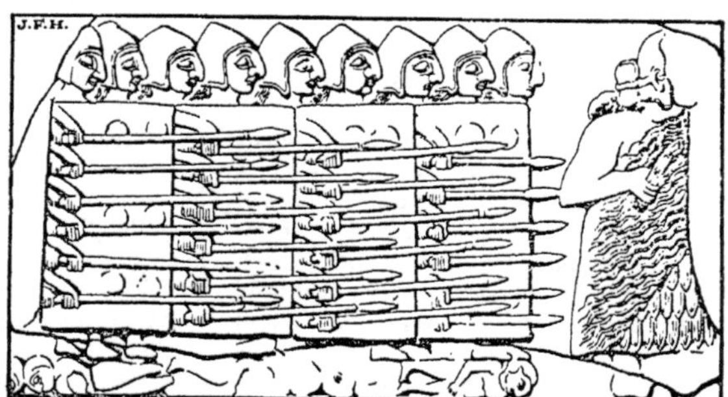

A very early Sumerian stone carving showing Sumerian warriors in phalanx

[1] My friend, Colonel Lawrence, tells me that the movement among the Arabs is somewhat as follows: (1) the sessile village cultivators are pushed out by over-population into the desert—very reluctantly; (2) they wander in the desert for a thousand years or so—as a stick pushed into the water gets carried about for a long way; (3) they are pushed again out of the desert, back again into sessile life, by starvation—very reluctantly (they have learned to love the desert); and when they come back into sessile life they are on the other side—i.e. having started in west Arabia, they land in Mesopotamia. Thus they wander a thousand years or so, and end up thousands of miles from where they started.—E. B.

[2] Sir H. H. Johnston is inclined to believe that a common late Neolithic and early bronze culture spread widely in this primitive world. He links the Dravidian languages of India—some of which group are to be found in Beluchistan and the eastern fringe of Persia—with certain languages in the Caucasian Mountains, and these again with Basque. He would bring the Sumerians, the early Cretans, and the early peoples of Asia Minor into this early "brown" or dark white culture before the Aryans, Semites, or Hamites developed their language cultures and thrust across this band of primordial civilization. He connects these "class and prefix" languages with the creation of the African Bantu, but that is a speculation beyond the scope of this present work. A series of articles on this subject by the Rev. W. Crabtree will be found in the *Journal of the African Society*. The connection of Sumerian and Bantu was first suggested by Sir Richard Burton in 1885. These views are in complete accordance with Elliot Smith's suggestion of a widespread heliolithic culture already dealt with in chap. xiii, § 4, page 72.

writing which they scratched upon clay, and their language has been deciphered.[1] It was a language more like the unclassified Caucasic language groups than any others that now exist. These languages may be connected with Basque, and may represent what was once a widespread group extending from Spain and western Europe to eastern India, and reaching southwards to Central Africa. These people shaved their heads and wore simple tunic-like garments of wool. They settled first on the lower courses of the great river and not very far from the Persian Gulf, which in those days ran up for a hundred and thirty miles [2] and more beyond its present head. They fertilized their fields by letting water run through irrigation trenches, and they gradually became very skilful hydraulic engineers; they had cattle, asses, sheep, and goats, but no horses; their collections of mud huts grew into towns, and their religion raised up tower-like temple buildings.

Clay, dried in the sun, was a very great fact in the lives of these people. This lower country of the Euphrates-Tigris valleys had little or no stone. They built of brick, they made pottery and earthenware images, and they drew and presently wrote upon thin tile-like cakes of clay. They do not seem to have had paper or to have used parchment. Their books and memoranda, even their letters, were potsherds.

At Nippur they built a great tower of brick to their chief god, El-lil (Enlil), the memory of which is supposed to be preserved in the story of the Tower of Babel. They seem to have been divided up into city states, which warred among themselves and maintained for many centuries their military capacity. Their soldiers carried long spears and shields, and fought in close formation. Sumerians conquered Sumerians. Sumeria remained unconquered by any stranger race for a very long period of time indeed. They developed their civilization, their writing, and their shipping, through a period that may be twice as long as the whole period from the Christian era to the present time.

The first of all known empires was that founded by the high priest of the god of the Sumerian city of Erech. It reached, says an inscription at Nippur, from the Lower (Persian Gulf) to the Upper (Mediterranean or Red ?) Sea. Among the mud heaps of the Euphrates-Tigris valley the record of that vast period of history, that first half of the Age of Cultivation, is buried. There flourished the first temples and the first priest-rulers that we know of among mankind.

§ 2B

Upon the western edge of this country appeared nomadic tribes of Semitic-speaking peoples who traded, raided, and fought with the Sumerians for many generations. Then arose at last a great leader among these Semites, Sargon (2,750 B.C.),[3] who united them, and not only conquered the Sumerians, but extended his rule from beyond the Persian Gulf on the east to the Mediterranean on the west. His own people were called the Akkadians and his empire is called the Sumerian Akkadian empire. It endured for over two hundred years.

But though the Semites conquered and gave a king to the Sumerian cities, it was the Sumerian civilization which prevailed over the simpler Semitic culture. The new-comers learnt the Sumerian writing (the "cuneiform" writing) and the Sumerian language; they set up no Semitic writing of their own. The Sumerian language became for these barbarians the language of knowledge and power, as Latin was the language of knowledge and power among the barbaric peoples of the middle ages in Europe. This Sumerian learning had a very great vitality. It was destined to survive through a long series of conquests and changes that now began in the valley of the two rivers.

§ 2C

As the people of the Sumerian Akkadian empire lost their political and military vigour, fresh inundations of a warlike people began from the east, the Elamites,[4] while from the west came the Semitic Amorites, pinching the Sumerian Akkadian empire between

[1] Excavations conducted at Eridu by Capt. R. Campbell Thompson during the recent war have revealed an early Neolithic agricultural stage, before the invention of writing or the use of bronze, beneath the earliest Sumerian foundations. The crops were cut by sickles of earthenware. Capt. Thompson thinks that these pre-Sumerian people were not of Sumerian race, but proto-Elamites. Entirely similar Neolithic remains have been found at Susa, once the chief city of Elam.

[2] Sayce, in *Babylonian and Assyrian Life*, estimates that in 6,500 B.C. Eridu was on the seacoast.

[3] Authorities vary upon this date. Some put back Sargon I to 3,750 B.C. This latter was his traditional date based on Babylonian records.

[4] Of unknown language and race, "neither Sumerians nor Semites," says Sayce. Their central city was Susa. Their archæology is still largely an unworked mine. They are believed by some, says Sir H. H. Johnston, to have been negroid in type. There is a strong negroid strain in the modern people of Elam.

NIMROD. A MIGHTY HUNTER

From the painting by Briton [illegible] R.A.

By permission of the [illegible]

"The Assyrians became mighty raiders . . . adopting the horse and war chariot . . . and conquered Babylon."

them. The Amorites settled in what was at first a small up-river town, named Babylon; and after a hundred years of warfare became masters of all Mesopotamia under a great king, Hammurabi (2,100 B.C.), who founded the first Babylonian empire.

Again came peace and security and a decline in aggressive prowess, and in another hundred years fresh nomads from the east were invading Babylonia, bringing with them the horse and the war chariot, and setting up their own king in Babylon. . . .

§ 2D

Higher up the Tigris, above the clay lands and with easy supplies of workable stone, a Semitic people, the Assyrians, while the Sumerians were still unconquered by the Semites, were settling about a number of cities of which Assur and Nineveh were the chief. Their peculiar physiognomy, the long nose and thick lips, was very like that of the commoner type of Polish Jew to-day. They wore great beards and ringletted long hair, tall caps and long robes. They were constantly engaged in mutual raiding with the Hittites to the west; they were conquered by Sargon I and became free again; a certain Tushratta, King of Mitanni, to the north-west, captured and held their capital, Nineveh, for a time; they intrigued with Egypt against Babylon and were in the pay of Egypt; they developed the military art to a very high pitch, and became mighty raiders and exacters of tribute; and at last, adopting the horse and the war chariot, they settled accounts for a time with the Hittites, and then, under Tiglath Pileser I, conquered Babylon for themselves (about 1,100 B.C.[1]). But their hold on the lower, older, and more civilized land was not secure, and Nineveh, the stone city, as distinguished from Babylon the brick city, remained their capital. For many centuries power swayed between Nineveh and Babylon, and sometimes it was an Assyrian and sometimes a Babylonian who claimed to be "king of the world."

For four centuries Assyria was restrained from expansion towards Egypt by a fresh northward thrust and settlement of another group of Semitic peoples, the Arameans, whose chief city was Damascus, and whose descendants are the Syrians of to-day. (There is, we may note, no connection whatever between the words Assyrian and Syrian. It is an accidental similarity.) Across these Syrians the Assyrian kings fought for power and expansion south-westward. In 745 B.C. arose another Tiglath Pileser, Tiglath Pileser III, the Tiglath Pileser of the Bible.[2] He not only directed the transfer of the Israelites to Media (the "Lost Ten Tribes" whose ultimate fate has exercised so many curious minds), but he conquered and ruled Babylon, so founding what historians know as the New Assyrian Empire. His son, Shalmaneser IV,[3] died during the siege of Samaria, and was succeeded by a usurper, who, no doubt to flatter Babylonian susceptibilities, took the ancient Akkadian Sumerian name of Sargon, Sargon II. He seems to have armed the Assyrian forces for the first time with iron weapons. It was probably Sargon II who actually carried out the deportation of the Ten Tribes.

Such shiftings about of population became a very distinctive part of the political methods of the Assyrian new empire. Whole nations who were difficult to control in their native country would be shifted *en masse* to unaccustomed regions and amidst strange neighbours, where their only hope of survival would lie in obedience to the supreme power.

Assyrian warrior
(Bas-relief from the palace of Sargon II

Sargon's son, Sennacherib, led the Assyrian hosts to the borders of Egypt. There Sennacherib's army was smitten by a pestilence, a

[1] For most of these dates here Winckler in *Helmolt's World History* has been followed.

[2] II. Kings xv. 29, and xvi. 7 *et seq.*

[3] II. Kings xvii. 3.

disaster described in the nineteenth chapter of the Second Book of Kings.

"And it came to pass that night, that the angel of the Lord went out, and smote in the camp of the Assyrians an hundred fourscore and five thousand: and when they arose early in the morning, behold, they were all dead corpses. So Sennacherib king of Assyria departed, and went and returned, and dwelt at Nineveh." [1]

Sennacherib's grandson, Assurbanipal (called by the Greeks Sardanapalus), did succeed in conquering and for a time holding lower Egypt.

§ 2E

The Assyrian empire lasted only a hundred and fifty years after Sargon II. Fresh nomadic Semites coming from the south-east, the Chaldeans, assisted by two Aryan peoples from the north, the Medes and Persians, combined against it, and took Nineveh in 606 B.C.

The Chaldean Empire, with its capital at Babylon (Second Babylonian Empire), lasted under Nebuchadnezzar the Great (Nebuchadnezzar II) and his successors until 539 B.C., when it collapsed before the attack of Cyrus, the founder of the Persian power. . . .

So the story goes on. In 330 B.C., as we shall tell later in some detail, a Greek conqueror, Alexander the Great, is looking on the murdered body of the last of the Persian rulers.

The story of the Tigris and Euphrates civilizations, of which we have given as yet only the bare outline, is a story of conquest following after conquest, and each conquest replaces old rulers and ruling classes by new; races like the Sumerian and the Elamite are swallowed up, their languages vanish, they interbreed and are lost, the Assyrian melts away into Chaldean and Syrian, the Hittites become Aryanized and lose distinction, the Semites who swallowed up the Sumerians give place to Aryan rulers, Medes and Persians appear in the place of the Elamites, the Aryan Persian language dominates the empire until the Aryan Greek ousts it from official life. Meanwhile the plough does its work year by year, the harvests are gathered, the builders build as they are told, the tradesmen work and acquire fresh devices; the knowledge of writing spreads, novel things, the horse and wheeled vehicles and iron, are introduced and become part of the permanent inheritance of mankind; the volume of trade upon sea and desert increases, men's ideas widen, and knowledge grows. There are set-backs, massacres, pestilence; but the story is, on the whole, one of enlargement. For four thousand years this new thing, civilization, which had set its root into the soil of the two rivers, grew as a tree grows; now losing a limb, now stripped by a storm, but always growing and resuming its growth. After four thousand years the warriors and conquerors were still going to and fro over this growing thing they did not understand, but men had now (330 B.C.) got iron, horses, writing and computation, money, a greater variety of foods and textiles, a wider knowledge of their world.

The time that elapsed between the empire of Sargon I and the conquest of Babylon by Alexander the Great was as long, be it noted, at the least estimate, as the time from Alexander the Great to the present day. And before the time of Sargon, men had been settled in the Sumerian land, living in towns, worshipping in temples, following an orderly Neolithic agricultural life in an organized community for at least as long again. "Eridu, Lagash, Ur, Uruk, Larsa, have already an immemorial past when first they appear in history." [2]

One of the most difficult things for both the writer and student of history is to sustain the sense of these time-intervals and prevent these ages becoming shortened by perspective in his imagination. Half the duration of human civilization and the keys to all its chief institutions are to be found *before* Sargon I. Moreover, the reader cannot too often compare the scale of the dates in these latter fuller pages of man's history with the succession of countless generations to which the time diagrams given on pages, 8, 28 and 49 bear witness.

§ 3

The story of the Nile valley from the dawn of its traceable history until the time of Alexander the Great is not very dissimilar from that of Babylonia; but while Babylonia lay open on every side to invasion, Egypt was protected by desert to the west and by desert and sea to the east, while to the south she had only negro peoples. Consequently her history is less broken by the invasions of strange races than is the history of Assyria and Babylon, and until towards the eighth century B.C., when she fell under an Ethiopian

[1] To be murdered by his sons.

[2] Winckler (Craig), *History of Babylonia and Assyria*.

ASSURBANIPAL ON HORSEBACK SPEARING LION

British Museum

"Sennacherib's grandson, Assurbanipal (the Assyrian King), is a particularly interesting figure."

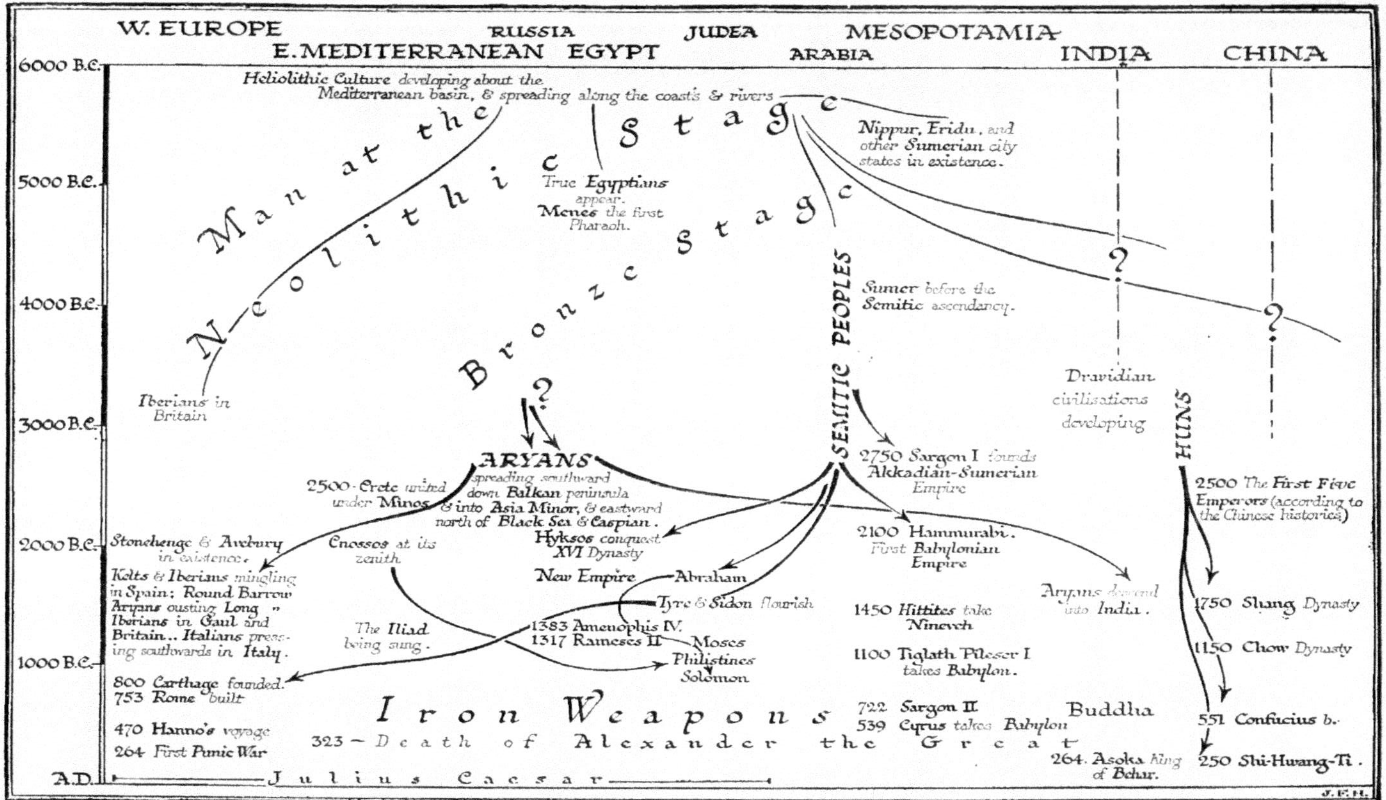
W. EUROPE
E. MEDITERRANEAN
RUSSIA
EGYPT
JUDEA
ARABIA
MESOPOTAMIA
INDIA
CHINA
6000 B.C.
5000 B.C.
4000 B.C.
3000 B.C.
2000 B.C.
1000 B.C.
A.D.
Heliolithic Culture developing about the Mediterranean basin, & spreading along the coasts & rivers
Man at the Neolithic Stage
Bronze Stage
Iron Weapons
True Egyptians appear.
Menes the first Pharaoh.
Nippur, Eridu, and other Sumerian city states in existence.
Sumer before the Semitic ascendancy.
SEMITIC PEOPLES
Dravidian civilisations developing
HUNS
Iberians in Britain
ARYANS spreading southward down Balkan peninsula & into Asia Minor, & eastward north of Black Sea & Caspian.
2500 - Crete united under Minos
2750 Sargon I founds Akkadian-Sumerian Empire
2500 The First Five Emperors (according to the Chinese historians)
Stonehenge & Avebury in existence.
Cnossos at its zenith
Hyksos conquest XVI Dynasty
2100 Hammurabi. First Babylonian Empire
New Empire
Abraham
Kelts & Iberians mingling in Spain; Round Barrow Aryans ousting Long " Iberians in Gaul and Britain.. Italians pressing southwards in Italy.
Tyre & Sidon flourish
1450 Hittites take Nineveh
Aryans descend into India.
1750 Shang Dynasty
The Iliad being sung.
1383 Amenophis IV.
1317 Rameses II
Moses
Philistines
Solomon
1100 Tiglath Pileser I takes Babylon.
1150 Chow Dynasty
800 Carthage founded.
753 Rome built
722 Sargon II
539 Cyrus takes Babylon
Buddha
551 Confucius b.
470 Hanno's voyage
264 First Punic War
323 – Death of Alexander the Great
264. Asoka King of Behar.
250 Shi-Hwang-Ti.
Julius Caesar
J. F. H.

H

dynasty, whenever a conqueror did come into her story, he came in from Asia by way of the Isthmus of Suez.

The Stone Age remains in Egypt are of very uncertain date; there are Palæolithic and then Neolithic remains. It is not certain whether the Neolithic pastoral people who left those remains were the direct ancestors of the later Egyptians. In many respects they differed entirely from their successors. They buried their dead, but before they buried them they cut up the bodies and apparently ate portions of the flesh. They seem to have done this out of a feeling of reverence for the departed; the dead were "eaten with honour" according to the phrase of Mr. Flinders Petrie. It may have been that the survivors hoped to retain thereby some vestige of the strength and virtue that had died. Traces of similar savage customs have been found in the long barrows that were scattered over western Europe before the spreading of the Aryan peoples, and they

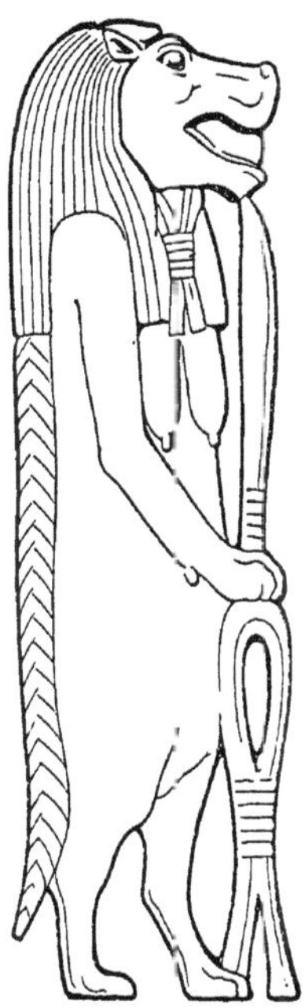

Early figure of the Egyptian hippopotamus goddess

have pervaded negro Africa, where they are only dying out at the present time.

About 5,000 B.C., or earlier, the traces of these primitive peoples cease, and the true Egyptians appear on the scene. The former people were hut builders and at a comparatively low stage of Neolithic culture, the latter were already a civilized Neolithic people; they used brick and wood buildings instead of their predecessors' hovels, and they were working stone. Very soon they passed into the Bronze Age. They possessed a system of picture writing almost as developed as the contemporary writing of the Sumerians, but quite different in character. Possibly there was an irruption from southern Arabia by way of Aden, of a fresh people, who came into upper Egypt and descended slowly towards the delta of the Nile. Dr. Wallis Budge writes of them as "conquerors from the East." But their gods and their ways, like their picture writing, were very different indeed from the Sumerian. One of the earliest known figures of a deity is that of a hippopotamus goddess, and so very distinctively African.[1]

The clay of the Nile is not so fine and plastic as the Sumerian clay, and the Egyptians made no use of it for writing. But they early resorted to strips of the papyrus reed fastened together, from whose name comes our word "paper."

The broad outline of the history of Egypt is simpler than the history of Mesopotamia. It has long been the custom to divide the rulers of Egypt into a succession of Dynasties, and in speaking of the periods of Egyptian history it is usual to speak of the first, fourth, fourteenth, and so on, Dynasty. The Egyptians were ultimately conquered by the Persians after their establishment in Babylon, and when finally Egypt fell to Alexander the Great in 332 B.C., it was Dynasty XXXI that came to an end. In that long history of over 4,000 years, a much longer period than that between the career of Alexander the Great and the present day, certain broad phases of development may be noted here. There was a phase known as the "old kingdom," which culminated in the IVth Dynasty; this

[1] "The original home or centre of development of this 'Dynastic' Egyptian type seems to have been in Southern or South-western Arabia. This region of South-western and Southern Arabia, ten to fifteen thousand years ago, was probably an even better favoured province than it is at the present day, when it still bears the Roman designation of Arabia Felix—so much of the rest of this gaunt, lava-covered, sand-strewn peninsula being decidedly 'infelix.' It has high mountains—a certain degree of rainfall on them, and was anciently clothed in rich forests before the camels, goats, and sheep of Neolithic and Bronze Age man nibbled away much of this verdure. Above all there grew trees oozing with delicious-scented resins or gums. These, when civilization dawned on the world, became very precious and an offering of sweet savour to the civilized man's gods, because so grateful to his own nostrils"—*Africa*, by Sir H. H. Johnston.

ISRAEL IN EGYPT

From the painting by Sir Edward J. Poynter, P.R.A.
By permission of J. C. Hawkshaw, Esq.

"The XIXth Dynasty included Rameses II, a great builder of temples, who reigned 77 years . . . the Pharaoh of Moses."

Dynasty marks a period of wealth and splendour, and its monarchs were obsessed by such a passion for making monuments for themselves as no men have ever before or since had a chance to display and gratify. It was Cheops [1] and Chephren and Mycerinus of this IVth Dynasty who raised the vast piles of the great and the second and the third pyramids at Gizeh. These unmeaning[2] sepulchral piles, of an almost incredible vastness,[3] erected in an age when engineering science had scarcely begun, exhausted the resources of Egypt through three long reigns, and left her wasted as if by a war.

The story of Egypt from the IVth to the XVth Dynasty is a story of conflicts between alternative capitals and competing religions, of separations into several kingdoms and reunions. It is, so to speak, an internal history. Here we can name only one of that long series of Pharaohs, Pepi II, who reigned ninety years, the longest reign in history, and left a great abundance of inscriptions and buildings. At last there happened to Egypt what happened so frequently to the civilizations of Mesopotamia. Egypt was conquered by nomadic Semites, who founded a "shepherd" dynasty, the Hyksos (XVIth), which was finally expelled by native Egyptians. This invasion probably happened while that first Babylonian Empire which Hammurabi founded was flourishing, but the exact correspondences of dates between early Egypt and Babylonia are still very doubtful. Only after a long period of servitude did a popular uprising expel these foreigners again.

After the war of liberation (*circa* 1,600 B.C.) there followed a period of great prosperity in Egypt, *the New Empire*. Egypt became a great and united military state, and pushed her expeditions at last as far as the Euphrates, and so the age-long struggle between the Egyptian and Babylonian-Assyrian power began.

For a time Egypt was the ascendant power. Thothmes III [4] and his son Amenophis III (XVIIIth Dynasty) ruled from Ethiopia to the Euphrates in the fifteenth century B.C. For various reasons these names stand out with unusual distinctness in the Egyptian record. They were great builders, and left many monuments and inscriptions. Amenophis III founded Luxor, and added greatly to Karnak. At Tel-el-Amarna a mass of letters has been found, the royal correspondence with Babylonian and Hittite and other monarchs, including that Tushratta who took Nineveh, throwing a flood of light upon the political and social affairs of this particular age. Of Amenophis IV we shall have more to tell later, but of one, the most extraordinary and able of Egyptian monarchs, Queen Hatasu, the aunt and stepmother of Thotmes III, we have no space to tell. She is represented upon her monuments in masculine garb, and with a long beard as a symbol of wisdom.

Thereafter there was a brief Syrian conquest of Egypt, a series of changing dynasties, among which we may note the XIXth, which included Rameses II, a great builder of temples, who reigned seventy-seven years (about 1,317 to 1,250 B.C.), and who is supposed by some to have been the Pharaoh of Moses, and the XXIInd, which included Shishak, who plundered Solomon's temple (*circa* 930 B.C.). An Ethiopian conqueror from the Upper Nile founded the XXVth Dynasty, a foreign dynasty, which went down (670 B.C.) before the new Assyrian Empire created by Tiglath Pileser III, Sargon II, and Sennacherib, of which we have already made mention.

The days of any Egyptian predominance over foreign nations were drawing to an end. For a time under Psammetichus I of the XXVIth Dynasty (664–610 B.C.) native rule was restored, and Necho II recovered for a time the old Egyptian possessions in Syria up to the Euphrates while the Medes and Chaldeans were attacking Nineveh. From those gains Necho II was routed out again after the fall of Nineveh and the Assyrians by Nebuchadnezzar II, the great Chaldean king, the Nebuchadnezzar of the Bible. The

[1] 3,733 B.C., Wallis Budge.

[2] But compare the citation of *Beowulf* in Chap. xv, § 2.—R. L. C.

[3] The great pyramid is 450 feet high and its side 700 feet long. It is calculated (says Wallis Budge) to weigh 4,883,000 tons. All this stone was lugged into place chiefly by human muscle.

[4] There are variants to these names, and to most Egyptian names, for few self-respecting Egyptologists will tolerate the spelling of their colleagues. One may find, for instance, Thethmosis, Thoutmosis, Tahutmes, Thutmose, or Tethmosis; Amunothph, Amenhotep or Amenothes. A pleasing variation is to break up the name, as, for instance, Amen Hetep. This particular little constellation of variants is given here not only because it is amusing, but because it is desirable that the reader should know such variations exist. For most names the rule of this book has been to follow whatever usage has established itself in English literature, regardless of the possible contemporary pronunciation. Amenophis, for example, has been so written in English books for two centuries. It came into the language by indirect routes, but it is now as fairly established as is Damascus as the English name of a Syrian town. Nevertheless, there are limits to this classicism. The writer, after some vacillation, has abandoned Oliver Goldsmith and Dr. Johnson in the case of "Peisistratus" and "Keltic," which were formerly spelt "Pisistratus" and "Celtic."

Jews, who had been the allies of Necho II, were taken into captivity by Nebuchadnezzar to Babylon.

When, in the sixth century B.C., Chaldea fell to the Persians, Egypt followed suit, a rebellion later made Egypt independent once more for sixty years, and in 332 B.C. she welcomed Alexander the Great as her conqueror, to be ruled thereafter by foreigners, first by Greeks, then by Romans, then in succession by Arabs, Turks, and British, until the present day.

Such briefly is the history of Egypt from its beginnings; a history first of isolation and then of increasing entanglement with the affairs of other nations, as increasing facilities of communication drew the peoples of the world into closer and closer interaction.

§ 4

The history we need to tell here of India is simpler even than this brief record of Egypt. Somewhere about the time of Hammurabi or later, a branch of the Aryan-speaking people who then occupied North Persia and Afghanistan, pushed down the north-west passes into India. They conquered their way until they prevailed over all the darker populations of North India, and spread their rule or influence over the whole peninsula. They never achieved any unity in India; their history is a history of warring kings and republics. The Persian empire, in the days of its expansion after the capture of Babylon, pushed its boundaries beyond the Indus, and later Alexander the Great marched as far as the border of the desert that separates the Punjab from the Ganges valley. But with this bare statement we will for a time leave the history of India.

§ 5

Meanwhile, as this triple system of White Man civilization developed in India and in the lands about the meeting-places of Asia, Africa, and Europe, another and quite distinct civilization was developing and spreading out from the then fertile but now dry and desolate valley of the Tarim and from the slopes of the Kuen-lun mountains in two directions down the course of the Hwang-ho, and into the valley of the Yang-tse-kiang. We know practically nothing as yet of the archæology of China, we do not know anything of the Stone Age in that part of the world, and at present our ideas of this early civilization are derived from the still very imperfectly explored Chinese literature. It has evidently been from the first and throughout a Mongolian civilization. Until after the time of Alexander the Great there are few traces of any Aryan or Semitic, much less of Hamitic influence. All such influences were still in another world, separated by mountains, deserts, and wild nomadic tribes until that time. The Chinese seem to have made their civilization spontaneously and unassisted. Some recent writers suppose indeed a connection with ancient Sumeria. Of course both China and Sumeria arose on the basis of the almost world-wide early Neolithic culture, but the Tarim valley and the lower Euphrates are separated by such vast obstacles of mountain and desert as to forbid the idea of any migration or interchange of peoples who had once settled down.

But though the civilization of China is wholly Mongolian (as we have defined Mongolian), it does not follow that the northern roots are the only ones from which it grew. If it grew first in the Tarim valley, then unlike all other civilizations (including the Mexican and Peruvian) it did not grow out of the heliolithic culture. We Europeans know very little as yet of the ethnology and pre-history of southern China. There the Chinese mingle with such kindred peoples as the Siamese and Burmese, and seem to bridge over towards the darker Dravidian peoples and towards the Malays. It is quite clear from the Chinese records that there were southern as well as northern beginnings of a civilization, and that the Chinese civilization that comes into history 2,000 years B.C. is the result of a long process of conflicts, minglings and interchanges between a southern and a northern culture of which the southern may have been the earlier. The southern Chinese perhaps played the rôle towards the northern Chinese that the Hamites or Sumerians played to the Aryan and Semitic peoples in the west, or that the settled Dravidians played towards the Aryans in India. They may have been the first agriculturalists and the first temple builders. But so little is known as yet of this attractive chapter in pre-history, that we cannot dwell upon it further here.

The chief foreigners mentioned in the early annals of China were a Ural-Altaic people on the north-east frontier, the Huns, against whom certain of the earlier emperors made war.

Chinese history is still very little known to European students, and our accounts of

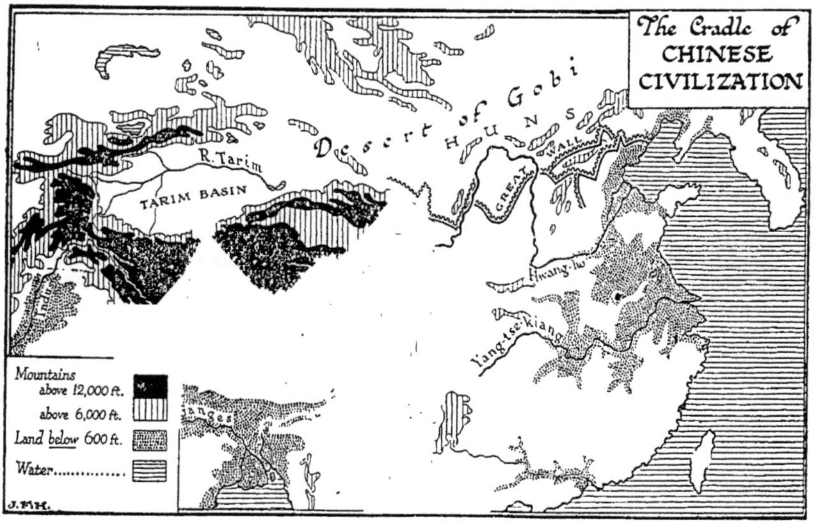

the early records are particularly unsatisfactory. About 2,700 to 2,400 B.C. reigned five emperors, who seem to have been almost incredibly exemplary beings.

There follows upon these first five emperors a series of dynasties, of which the accounts become more and more exact and convincing as they become more recent. China has to tell a long history of border warfare and of graver struggles between the settled and nomad peoples. To begin with, China, like Sumer and like Egypt, was a land of city states. The government was at first a government of numerous kings; they became loosely feudal under an emperor, as the Egyptians did; and then later, as with the Egyptians, came a centralizing empire. Shang (1,750 to 1,125 B.C.) and Chow (1,125 to 250 B.C.) are named as being the two great dynasties of the feudal period. Bronze vessels of these earlier dynasties, beautiful, splendid, and with a distinctive style of their own, still exist, and there can be no doubt of the existence of a high state of culture even before the days of Shang.

It is perhaps a sense of symmetry that made the later historians of Egypt and China talk of the earlier phases of their national history as being under dynasties comparable to the dynasties of the later empires, and of such early "Emperors" as Menes (in Egypt) or the First Five Emperors (in China). The early dynasties exercised far less centralized powers than the later ones. Such unity as China possessed under the Shang Dynasty was a religious rather than an effective political union. The "Son of Heaven" offered sacrifices for all the Chinese. There was a common script, a common civilization, and a common enemy in the Huns of the north-western borders.

The last of the Shang Dynasty was a cruel and foolish monarch who burnt himself alive (1,125 B.C.) in his palace after a decisive defeat by Wu Wang, the founder of the Chow Dynasty. Wu Wang seems to have been helped by allies from among the south-western tribes as well as by a popular revolt.

For a time China remained loosely united under the Chow emperors, as loosely united as was Christendom under the popes in the Middle Ages; the Chow emperors had become the traditional high priests of the land in the place of the Shang Dynasty and claimed a sort of overlordship in Chinese affairs, but gradually the loose ties of usage and sentiment that held the empire together lost their hold upon men's minds. Hunnish peoples to the north and west took on the Chinese civilization without acquiring a sense of its unity. Feudal princes began to regard themselves as independent. Mr. Liang-Chi-Chao,[1] one of the Chinese representatives at the Paris Conference of 1919, states that between the eighth and fourth centuries B.C. "there were in the Hwang-ho and Yang-tse valleys no less than five or six thousand small states with about

[1] *China and the League of Nations*, a pamphlet by Mr. Liang-Chi-Chao. (*Pekin Leader* Office.)

a dozen powerful states dominating over them." The land was subjected to perpetual warfare ("Age of Confusion"). In the sixth century B.C. the great powers in conflict were Ts'i and Ts'in, which were northern Hwang-ho states, and Ch'u, which was a vigorous, aggressive power in the Yang-tse valley. A confederation against Ch'u laid the foundation for a league that kept the peace for a hundred years; the league subdued and incorporated Ch'u and made a general treaty of disarmament. It became the foundation of a new pacific empire.

The knowledge of iron entered China at some unknown date, but iron weapons began to be commonly used only about 500 B.C., that is to say two or three hundred years or more after this had become customary in Assyria, Egypt, and Europe. Iron was probably introduced from the north into China by the Huns.

The last rulers of the Chow Dynasty were ousted by the kings of Ts'in, the latter seized upon the sacred sacrificial bronze tripods, and so were able to take over the imperial duty of offering sacrifices to Heaven. In this manner was the Ts'in dynasty established. It ruled with far more vigour and effect than any previous family. The reign of Shi-Hwang-ti (meaning "first universal emperor") of this dynasty is usually taken to mark the end of feudal and divided China. He seems to have played the unifying rôle in the east that Alexander the Great might have played in the west, but he lived longer, and the unity he made (or restored) was comparatively permanent, while the empire of Alexander the Great fell to pieces, as we shall tell, at his death. Shi-Hwang-ti, among other feats in the direction of common effort, organized the building of the Great Wall of China against the Huns. A civil war followed close upon his reign, and ended in the establishment of the Han Dynasty. Under this Han Dynasty the empire grew greatly beyond its original two river valleys, the Huns were effectively restrained, and the Chinese penetrated westward until they began to learn at last of civilized races and civilizations other than their own.

By 100 B.C. the Chinese had heard of India, their power had spread across Tibet and into Western Turkestan, and they were trading by camel caravans with Persia and the western world. So much for the present must suffice for our account of China. We shall return to the distinctive characters of its civilization later.

§ 6

And in these thousands of years during which man was making his way step by step from the barbarism of the heliolithic culture to civilization at these old-world centres, what was happening in the rest of the world? To the north of these centres, from the Rhine to the Pacific, the Nordic and Mongolian peoples, as we have told, were also learning the use of metals; but while the civilizations were settling down these men of the great plains were becoming migratory and developing from a slow wandering life towards a complete seasonal nomadism. To the south of the civilized zone, in central and southern Africa, the negro was making a slower progress, and that, it would seem, under the stimulus of invasion by whiter tribes from the Mediterranean regions, bringing with them in succession cultivation and the use of metals. These white men came to the black by two routes: across the Sahara to the west as Berbers and Tuaregs and the like, to mix with the negro and create such quasi-white races as the Fulas; and also by way of the Nile, where the Baganda (=Gandafolk) of Uganda, for example, may possibly be of remote white origin. The African forests were denser then, and spread eastward and northward from the Upper Nile.

The islands of the East Indies, three thousand years ago, were probably still only inhabited here and there by stranded patches of Palæolithic Australoids, who had wandered thither in those immemorial ages when there was a nearly complete land bridge by way of the East Indies to Australia. The islands of Oceania were uninhabited. The spreading of the heliolithic peoples by sea-going canoes into the islands of the Pacific came much later in the history of man, at earliest a thousand years B.C. Still later did they reach Madagascar. The beauty of New Zealand also was as yet wasted upon mankind; its highest living creatures were a great ostrich-like bird, the moa, now extinct, and the little kiwi which has feathers like coarse hair and the merest rudiment of wings.

In North America a group of Mongoloid tribes were now cut off altogether from the old world. They were spreading slowly southward, hunting the innumerable bison of the plains. They had still to learn for themselves the secrets of a separate agriculture based on maize, and in South America to tame the lama to their service, and so build up in Mexico and Peru two

GUFARS AT BAGDAD

Permission, Edmund Candler

"Basketwork caulked with bitumen. Such was Moses' 'ark of bulrushes.'"

DONEGAL NATIVES AND CORACLE

Photo: W. Lawrence, Dublin

"The first boats, early Neolithic, were hollowed trees, then hides expanded upon wickerwork, coracles. To this day coracles are used in Ireland."

civilizations roughly parallel in their nature to that of Sumer, but different in many respects, and later by six or seven thousand years. . . .

When men reached the southern extremity of America, the *Megatherium*, the giant sloth, and the *Glyptodon*, the giant armadillo, were still living. . . .

There is a considerable imaginative appeal in the obscure story of the early American civilizations. It was largely a separate development.[1] Somewhen at last the southward drift of the Amerindians must have met and mingled with the eastward, canoe-borne drift of the heliolithic culture. But it was the heliolithic culture still at a very lowly stage and probably before the use of metals. It has to be noted as evidence of this canoe-borne origin of American culture, that elephant-headed figures are found in Central American drawings. American metallurgy may have arisen independently of the old-world use of metal, or it may have been brought by these elephant carvers. These American peoples got to the use of bronze and copper, but not to the use of iron; they had gold and silver; and their stonework, their pottery, weaving, and dyeing were carried to a very high level. In all these things the American product resembles the old-world product *generally*, but always it has characteristics that are distinctive. The American civilizations had picture-writing of a primitive sort, but it never developed even to the pitch of the earliest Egyptian hieroglyphics. In Yucatan only was there a kind of script, the Maya writing, but it was used simply for keeping a calendar. In Peru the beginnings of writing were superseded by a curious and complicated method of keeping records by means of knots tied upon strings of various colours and shapes. It is said that even laws and orders could be conveyed by this code. These string bundles were called *quipus*, but though *quipus* are still to be found in collections, the art of reading them is altogether lost. The Chinese histories, Mr. L. Y. Chen informs us, state that a similar method of record by knots was used in China before the invention of writing there. The Peruvians also got to making maps and the use of counting-frames. "But with all this there was no means of handing on knowledge and experience from one generation to another, nor was anything done to fix and summarize these intellectual possessions, which are the basis of literature and science."[2]

When the Spaniards came to America, the Mexicans knew nothing of the Peruvians nor the Peruvians of the Mexicans. Intercourse there was none. Whatever links had ever existed were lost and forgotten. The Mexicans had never heard of the potato which was a principal article of Peruvian diet. In 5,000 B.C. the Sumerians and Egyptians probably knew as little of one another. America was 6,000 years behind the Old World.

XVII

SEA PEOPLES AND TRADING PEOPLES

§ 1. *The Earliest Ships and Sailors.*
§ 2. *The Ægean Cities before History.*
§ 3. *The First Voyages of Exploration.*
§ 4. *Early Traders.*
§ 5. *Early Travellers.*

§ 1

THE first boats were made very early indeed in the Neolithic stage of culture by riverside and lakeside peoples. They were no more than trees and floating wood, used to assist the imperfect natural swimming powers of men. Then came the hollowing out of the trees, and then, with the development of tools and a primitive carpentry, the building of boats. Men in Egypt and Mesopotamia also developed a primitive type of basketwork boat, caulked with bitumen. Such was the "ark of bulrushes" in which Moses was hidden by his mother. A kindred sort of vessel grew up by the use of skins and hides expanded upon a wicker framework. To this day cow-hide wicker boats (coracles)

[1] Here we touch on highly controversial matters. The reader interested in the question of the separate origin of the American civilization should consult *Nature*, Jan. 27, 1916, Spinden and Elliot Smith in discussion.

[2] F. Ratzel, *History of Mankind.*

are used upon the west coast of Ireland, where there is plenty of cattle and a poverty of big trees. They are also still used on the Euphrates, and on the Towy in South Wales. Inflated skins may have preceded the coracle, and are still used on the Euphrates and upper Ganges. In the valleys of the great rivers, boats must early have become an important means of communication; and it seems natural to suppose that it was from the mouths of the great rivers that man, already in a reasonably seaworthy vessel, first ventured out upon what must have seemed to him then the trackless and homeless sea.

No doubt he ventured at first as a fisherman, having learnt the elements of seacraft in creeks and lagoons. Men may have navigated boats upon the Levantine lake before the refilling of the Mediterranean by the Atlantic waters. The canoe was an integral part of the heliolithic culture, it drifted with that culture upon the warm waters of the earth from the Mediterranean to (at last) America. There were not only canoes, but Sumerian boats and ships upon the Euphrates and Tigris, when these rivers in 7,000 B.C. fell by separate mouths into the Persian Gulf. The Sumerian city of Eridu, which stood at the head of the Persian Gulf (from which it is now separated by a hundred and thirty miles of alluvium [1]), had ships upon the sea then. We also find evidence of a fully developed sea life six thousand years ago at the eastern end of the Mediterranean, and possibly at that time there were already canoes on the seas among the islands of the nearer East Indies. There are pre-dynastic Neolithic Egyptian representations of Nile ships of a fair size, capable of carrying elephants.[2]

Very soon the seafaring men must have realized the peculiar freedom and opportunities the ship gave them. They could get away to islands; no chief nor king could pursue a boat or ship with any certainty; every captain was a king. The seamen would find it easy to make nests upon islands and in strong positions on the mainland. There they could harbour, there they could carry on a certain agriculture and fishery; but their speciality and their main business was, of course, the expedition across the sea. That was not usually a trading expedition; it was much more frequently a piratical raid. From what we know of mankind, we are bound to conclude that the first sailors plundered when they could, and traded when they had to.

Because it developed in the comparatively warm and tranquil waters of the eastern Mediterranean, the Red Sea, the Persian Gulf, and the western horn of the Indian Ocean, the shipping of the ancient world retained throughout certain characteristics that make it differ very widely from the ocean-going sailing shipping, with its vast spread of canvas, of the last four hundred years. "The Mediterranean," says Mr. Torr,[3] "is a sea where a vessel with sails may lie becalmed for days together, while a vessel with oars would easily be traversing the smooth waters, with coasts and islands everywhere at hand to give her shelter in case of storm. In that sea, therefore, oars became the characteristic instruments of navigation, and the arrangement of oars the chief problem in shipbuilding. And so long as the Mediterranean nations dominated Western Europe, vessels of the southern type were built upon the northern coasts, though there generally was wind enough here for sails and too much wave for oars. . . . The art of rowing can first be discerned upon the Nile. Boats with oars are represented in the earliest pictorial monuments of Egypt, dating from about 2,500 B.C.; and although some crews are paddling with their faces towards the bow, others are rowing with their faces towards the stern. The paddling is certainly the older practice, for the hieroglyph *chen* depicts two arms grasping an oar in the attitude of paddling, and the

[1] Sayce.

[2] Mosso. *The Dawn of Mediterranean Civilization.* —R. L. C.

[3] Cecil Torr, *Ancient Ships.*

Boats on the Nile, about 2,500 B.C. [From Torr's "Ancient Ships."]

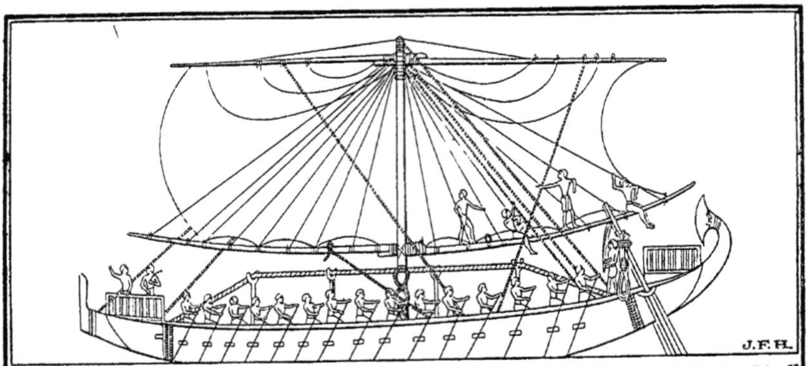

Egyptian ship on the Red Sea, about 1250 B.C. [From Torr's "Ancient Ships."]

Mr. Langton Cole calls attention to the rope *truss* in this illustration, stiffening the beam of the ship. No other such use of the truss is known until the days of modern engineering.

hieroglyphs were invented in the earliest ages. And that practice may really have ceased before 2,500 B.C., despite the testimony of monuments of that date; for in monuments dating from about 1,250 B.C., crews are represented unmistakably rowing with their faces towards the stern and yet grasping their oars in the attitude of paddling, so that even then Egyptian artists mechanically followed the turn of the hieroglyph to which their hands were accustomed. In these reliefs there are twenty rowers on the boats on the Nile, and thirty on the ships on the Red Sea; but in the earliest reliefs the number varies considerably, and seems dependent on the amount of space at the sculptor's disposal."

The Aryan peoples came late to the sea. The earliest ships on the sea were either Sumerian or Hamitic; the Semitic peoples followed close upon these pioneers. Along the eastern end of the Mediterranean, the Phœnicians, a Semitic people, set up a string of independent harbour towns of which Acre, Tyre, and Sidon were the chief; and later they pushed their voyages westward and founded Carthage and Utica in North Africa. Possibly Phœnician keels were already in the Mediterranean by 2,000 B.C. Both Tyre and Sidon were originally on islands, and so easily defensible against a land raid. But before we go on to the marine exploits of this great sea-going race, we must note a very remarkable and curious nest of early sea people whose remains have been discovered in Crete.[1]

[1] See Evans' *Prehistoric Tombs of Cnossos.*

§ 2

These early Cretans were of unknown race, but probably of a race akin to the Iberians of Spain and Western Europe and the dark whites of Asia Minor and North Africa, and their language is unknown. This race lived not only in Crete, but in Cyprus, Greece, Asia Minor, Sicily, and South Italy. It was a civilized people for long ages before the fair Aryan Greeks spread southward through Macedonia. At Cnossos, in Crete, there have been found the most astonishing ruins and remains, and Cnossos, therefore, is apt to overshadow the rest of these settlements in people's imaginations, but it is well to bear in mind that though Cnossos was no doubt a chief city of this Ægean civilization, these " Ægeans " had in the fullness of their time many cities and a wide range. Possibly, all that we know of them now are but the vestiges of a far more extensive heliolithic Neolithic civilization which is now submerged under the waters of the Mediterranean.

At Cnossos there are Neolithic remains as old or older than any of the pre-dynastic remains of Egypt. The Bronze Age began in Crete as soon as it did in Egypt, and there have been vases found by Flinders Petrie in Egypt and referred by him to the Ist Dynasty, which he declared to be importations from Crete. Stone vessels have been found in Crete of forms characteristic of the IVth (pyramid-building) Dynasty, and there can be no doubt that there was a vigorous trade between Crete and Egypt in the time of the XIIth Dynasty. This continued until about 1,000 B.C. It is clear that this island civilization arising upon the soil of Crete is at least as old as the Egyptian, and that it was already launched upon the sea as early as 4,000 B.C.

The great days of Crete were not so early as this. It was only about 2,500 B.C. that the island appears to have been unified under one ruler. Then began an age of peace and prosperity unexampled in the history of the ancient world. Secure from invasion, living in a delightful climate, trading with every civilized community in the world, the Cretans were free to develop all the arts and amenities of life. This Cnossos was not so much a town as the vast palace of the king and his people. It was not even fortified. The kings, it would seem, were called Minos always, as the kings of Egypt were all called Pharaoh; the king of Cnossos figures in the early legends of the Greeks as King Minos, who lived in the Labyrinth and kept there a horrible monster, half man, half bull, the Minotaur, to feed which he levied a tribute of youths and maidens from the Athenians. Those stories are a part of Greek literature, and have always been known, but it is only in the last few decades that the excavations at Cnossos have revealed how close these legends were to the reality. The Cretan labyrinth was a building as stately, complex, and luxurious as any in the ancient world. Among other details we find water-pipes, bathrooms, and the like conveniences, such as have hitherto been regarded as the latest refinements of modern life. The pottery, the textile manufactures, the sculpture and painting of these people, their gem and ivory work, their metal and inlaid work, is as admirable as any that mankind has produced. They were much given to festivals and shows, and, in particular, they were addicted to bull-fights and gymnastic entertainments. Their female costume became astonishingly "modern" in style; their women wore corsets and flounced dresses. They had a system of writing which has not yet been deciphered.

It is the custom nowadays to make a sort of wonder of these achievements of the Cretans, as though they were a people of incredible artistic ability living in the dawn of civilization. But their great time was long past that dawn; as late as 2,000 B.C. It took them many centuries to reach their best in art and skill, and their art and luxury are by no means so great a wonder if we reflect that for 3,000 years they were immune from invasion, that for a thousand years they were at peace. Century after century their artizans could perfect their skill, and their men and women refine upon refinement. Wherever men of almost any race have been comparatively safe in this fashion for such a length of time, they have developed much artistic beauty. Given the opportunity, all races are artistic. Greek legend has it that it was in Crete that Dædalus attempted to make the first flying machine. Dædalus (=cunning artificer) was a sort of personified summary of mechanical skill. It is curious to speculate what germ of fact lies behind him and those waxen wings that, according to the legend, melted and plunged his son Icarus in the sea.

There came at last a change in the condition of the lives of these Cretans, for other peoples, the Greeks and the Phœnicians, were also coming out with powerful fleets upon the seas. We do not know what led to the disaster nor who inflicted it; but somewhen about 1,400 B.C. Cnossos was sacked and burnt, and though the Cretan life struggled on there rather lamely for another four centuries, there came at last a final blow about 1,000 B.C. (that is to say, in the days of the Assyrian ascendancy in the East). The palace at Cnossos was destroyed, and never rebuilt nor reinhabited. Possibly this was done by the ships of those new-comers

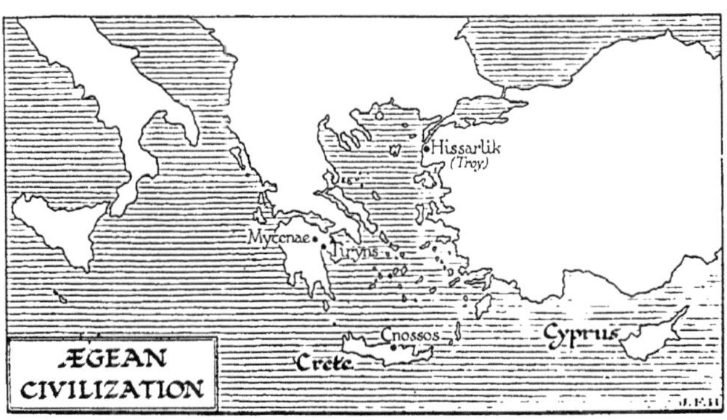

into the Mediterranean, the barbaric Greeks, a group of Aryan tribes, who may have wiped out Cnossos as they wiped out the city of Troy. The legend of Theseus tells of such a raid. He entered the Labyrinth (which may have been the Cnossos Palace) by the aid of Ariadne, the daughter of Minos, and slew the Minotaur.

J.F.H. *from photos. by British School at Athens*

Faience figure from Cnossos..... A votary of the Snake Goddess......

The *Iliad* makes it clear that destruction came upon Troy because the Trojans stole Greek women. Modern writers, with modern ideas in their heads, have tried to make out that the Greeks assailed Troy in order to secure a trade route or some such fine-spun commercial advantage. If so, the authors of the *Iliad* hid the motives of their characters very skilfully. It would be about as reasonable to say that the Homeric Greeks went to war with the Trojans in order to be well ahead with a station on the Berlin to Bagdad railway. The Homeric Greeks were a healthy barbaric Aryan people, with very poor ideas about trade and "trade routes"; they went to war with the Trojans because they were thoroughly annoyed about this stealing of women. It is fairly clear from the Minos legend and from the evidence of the Cnossos remains, that the Cretans kidnapped or stole youths and maidens to be slaves, bull-fighters, athletes, and perhaps sacrifices. They traded fairly with the Egyptians, but it may be they did not realize the gathering strength of the Greek barbarians; they "traded" violently with them, and so brought sword and flame upon themselves.[1]

Another great sea people were the Phœnicians. They were great seamen because they were great traders. Their colony of Carthage (founded before 800 B.C. by Tyre) became at last greater than any of the older Phœnician cities, but already before 1,500 B.C. both Sidon and Tyre had settlements upon the African coast. Carthage was comparatively inaccessible to the Assyrian and Babylonian hosts, and, profiting greatly by the long siege of Tyre by Nebuchadnezzar II, became the greatest maritime power the world had hitherto seen. She claimed the Western Mediterranean as her own, and seized every ship she could catch west of Sardinia. Roman writers accuse her of great cruelties. She fought the Greeks for Sicily, and later (in the second century B.C.) she fought the Romans. Alexander the Great formed plans for her conquest; but he died, as we shall tell later, before he could carry them out.

§ 3

At her zenith Carthage probably had the hitherto unheard-of population of a million. This population was largely industrial, and her woven goods were universally famous. As well as a coasting trade, she had a considerable land trade with Central Africa,[2] and she sold negro slaves, ivory, metals, precious stones and the like, to all the Mediterranean people; she worked Spanish copper mines, and her ships went out into the Atlantic and coasted along Portugal and France northward as far as the Cassiterides (the Scilly Isles, or Cornwall, in England) to get tin. About 520 B.C. a certain Hanno made a voyage that is still one of the most notable

[1] This is, I think, too dogmatic about Helen. True, raids on women were a real cause of war, but they were also a very favourite *ficelle* of fiction. A war with Troy might easily arise by the carrying off of a woman. But why was Troy destroyed six several times? It looks to me as if there was some strong motive for building just there, and an equally strong motive for great confederacies destroying the city when built.—G. M.

Walter Leaf in his *Homer and History* is in agreement with G. M. on this point.—G. Wh.

[2] There were no domesticated camels in Africa until after the Persian conquest of Egypt. This must have greatly restricted the desert routes. (See Bunbury, *History of Ancient Geography*, note to Chap. VIII.) But the Sahara desert of 3,000 or 2,000 years ago was less parched and sterile than it is to-day. From rock engravings we may deduce the theory that the desert was crossed from oasis to oasis by riding oxen and by ox-carts: perhaps, also, on horses and asses. The camel as a beast of transport was seemingly not introduced into North Africa till the Arab invasions of the seventh century A.D. The fossil remains of camels are found in Algeria, and wild camels may have lingered in the wastes of the Sahara and Somaliland till the domesticated camel was introduced. The Nubian wild ass also seems to have extended its range to the Sahara.—H. H. J.

in the world. This Hanno, if we may trust the *Periplus of Hanno*, the Greek translation of his account which still survives, followed the African coast southward from the Straits of Gibraltar as far as the confines of Liberia. He had sixty big ships, and his main task was to found or reinforce certain Carthaginian stations upon the Morocco coast. Then he pushed southward. He founded a settlement in the Rio de Oro (on Kerne or Herne Island), and sailed on past the Senegal River. The voyagers passed on for seven days beyond the Gambia, and landed at last upon some island. This they left in a panic, because, although the day was silent with the silence of the tropical forest, at night they heard the sound of flutes, drums, and gongs, and the sky was red with the blaze of the bush fires. The coast country for the rest of the voyage was one blaze of fire, from the burning of the bush. Streams of fire ran down the hills into the sea, and at length a blaze arose so loftily that it touched the skies. Three days further brought them to an island containing a lake (? Sherbro Island). In this lake was another island (? Macaulay Island), and on this were wild, hairy men and women, "whom the interpreters called gorilla." The Carthaginians, having caught some of the females of these "gorillas"—they were probably chimpanzees—turned back and eventually deposited the skins of their captives—who had proved impossibly violent guests to entertain on board ship—in the Temple of Juno.

A still more wonderful Phœnician sea voyage, long doubted, but now supported by some archæological evidence, is related by Herodotus, who declares that the Pharaoh Necho of the XXVIth Dynasty commissioned some Phœnicians to attempt the circumnavigation of Africa, and that starting from the Gulf of Suez southward, they did finally come back through the Mediterranean to the Nile delta. They took nearly three years to complete their voyage. Each year they landed, and sowed and harvested a crop of wheat before going on.

§ 4

The great trading cities of the Phœnicians are the most striking of the early manifestations of the peculiar and characteristic gift of the Semitic peoples to mankind, trade and exchange.[1] While the Semitic Phœnician peoples were spreading themselves upon the seas, another kindred Semitic people, the Arameans, whose occupation of Damascus we have already noted, were developing the caravan routes of the Arabian and Persian deserts, and becoming the chief trading people of Western Asia. The Semitic peoples, earlier civilized than the Aryan, have always shown, and still show to-day, a far greater sense of quality and quantity in marketable goods than the latter; it is to their need of account-keeping that the development of alphabetical writing is to be ascribed, and it is to them that most of the great advances in computation are due. Our modern numerals are Arabic; our arithmetic and algebra are essentially Semitic sciences.

The Semitic peoples, we may point out here, are to this day *counting peoples* strong in their sense of equivalents and reparation. The moral teaching of the Hebrews was saturated by such ideas. "With what measure ye mete, the same shall be meted unto you." Other races and peoples have imagined diverse and fitful and marvellous gods, but it was the trading Semites who first began to think of God as a Righteous Dealer, whose promises were kept, who failed not the humblest creditor, and called to account every spurious act.

The trade that was going on in the ancient world before the sixth or seventh century B.C. was almost entirely a barter trade. There was little or no credit or coined money. The ordinary standard of value with the early Aryans was cattle, as it still is with the Zulus and Kaffirs to-day. In the *Iliad*, the respective values of two shields are stated in head of cattle, and the Roman word for moneys, *pecunia*, is derived from *pecus*, cattle. Cattle as money had this advantage; it did not need to be carried from one owner to another, and if it needed attention and food, at any rate it bred. But it was inconvenient for ship or caravan transit. Many other substances have at various times been found convenient as a standard; tobacco was once legal tender in the colonial days in North America, and in West Africa fines are paid and bargains made in bottles of trade gin. The early Asiatic trade included metals; and weighed lumps of metal, since they were in general demand and were convenient for hoarding and storage, costing nothing for fodder and needing small house-room, soon asserted their superiority over cattle and sheep. Iron, which seems to have been first reduced from its ores by the Hittites, was, to begin with, a rare and much-

[1] There was Sumerian trade organized round the temples before the Semites got into Babylonia. See Hall and King, *Archæological Discoveries in Western Asia*.—E. B.

desired substance.[1] It is stated by Aristotle to have supplied the first currency. In the collection of letters found at Tel-el-Amarna, addressed to and from Amenophis III (already mentioned) and his successor Amenophis IV, one from a Hittite king promises iron as an extremely valuable gift. Gold, then as now, was the most precious, and therefore most portable, security. In early Egypt silver was almost as rare as gold until after the XVIIIth Dynasty. Later the general standard of value in the Eastern world became silver, measured by weight.

To begin with, metals were handed about in ingots and weighed at each transaction. Then they were stamped to indicate their fineness and guarantee their purity. The first recorded coins were minted about 600 B.C. in Lydia, a gold-producing country in the west of Asia Minor. The first-known gold coins were minted in Lydia by Crœsus, whose name has become a proverb for wealth; he was conquered, as we shall tell later, by that same Cyrus the Persian who took Babylon in 539 B.C. But very probably coined money had been used in Babylonia before that time. The "sealed shekel," a stamped piece of silver, came very near to being a coin. The promise to pay so much silver or gold on "leather" (=parchment) with the seal of some established firm is probably as old or older than coinage. The Carthaginians used such "leather money." We know very little of the way in which small traffic was conducted. Common people, who in those ancient times were in dependent positions, seem to have had no money at all; they did their business by barter. Early Egyptian paintings show this going on.[2]

§ 5

When one realizes the absence of small money or of any conveniently portable means of exchange in the pre-Alexandrian world, one perceives how impossible was private travel in those days.[3] The first "inns"—no doubt a sort of caravanserai—are commonly said to have come into existence in Lydia in the third or fourth century B.C. That, however, is too late a date. They are certainly older than that. There is good evidence of them at least as early as the sixth century. Æschylus twice mentions inns. His word is "all-receiver," or "all-receiving house."[4] Private travellers must have been fairly common in the Greek world, including its colonies, by this time. But such private travel was a comparatively new thing then. The early historians Hecatæus and Herodotus travelled widely. "I suspect," says Professor Gilbert Murray, "that this sort of travel 'for Historie' or 'for discovery' was rather a Greek invention. Solon is supposed to have practised it; and even Lycurgus." . . . The earlier travellers were traders travelling in a caravan or in a shipload, and carrying their goods and their minas and shekels of metal or gems or bales of fine stuff with them, or government officials travelling with letters of introduction and a proper retinue. Possibly there were a few mendicants, and, in some restricted regions, religious pilgrims.

That earlier world before 600 B.C. was one in which a lonely "stranger" was a rare and suspected and endangered being. He might suffer horrible cruelties, for there was little law to protect such as he. Few individuals strayed therefore. One lived and died attached and tied to some patriarchal tribe, if one was a nomad, or to some great household if one was civilized, or to one of the big temple establishments which we will presently discuss. Or one was a herded slave. One knew nothing, except for a few monstrous legends, of the rest of the world in which one lived. We know more to-day, indeed, of the world of 600 B.C. than any single living being knew at that time. We map it out, see it as a whole in relation to past and future. We begin to learn precisely what was going on at the same time in Egypt and Spain and Media and India and China. We can share in imagination, not only the wonder of Hanno's sailors, but of the men who lit the warning beacons on the shore. We know that those "mountains flaming to the sky" were only the customary burning of the dry grass at that season of the year. Year by year, more and more rapidly, our common knowledge increases. In the years to come men will understand still more of those lives in the past, until perhaps they will understand them altogether.

[1] Iron bars of fixed weight were used for coin in Britain. Cæsar, *De Bello Gallico*.—G. Wh.

[2] The earliest coinage of the west coast of Asia Minor was in electrum, a mixture of gold and silver, and there is an interesting controversy as to whether the first issues were stamped by cities, temples, or private bankers.—P. G.

[3] Small change was in existence before the time of Alexander. The Athenians had a range of exceedingly small silver coins running almost down to the size of a pinhead which were generally carried in the mouth; a character in Aristophanes was suddenly assaulted, and swallowed his change in consequence.—P. G.

[4] There is an inn-keeper in Aristophanes, but it may be inferred from the circumstance that she is represented as letting lodgings in hell, that the early inn left much to be desired.—P. G.

XVIII

WRITING

§ 1

IN the five preceding chapters (XIII to XVII) we have sketched in broad outline the development of the chief human communities from the primitive beginnings of the heliolithic culture to the great historical kingdoms and empires in the sixth century B.C. We must now study a little more closely the general process of social change, the growth of human ideas, and the elaboration of human relationships that was going on during these ages between 10,000 B.C. and 500 B.C. What we have done so far is to draw the map and name the chief kings and empires, to define the relations in time and space of Babylonia, Assyria, Egypt, Phœnicia, Cnossos, and the like; we come now to the real business of history, which is to get down below these outer forms to the thoughts and lives of individual men.

By far the most important thing that was going on during those fifty or sixty centuries of social development was the invention of writing and its gradual progress to importance in human affairs. It was a new instrument for the human mind, an enormous enlargement of its range of action, a new means of continuity. We have seen how in later Palæolithic and early Neolithic times the elaboration of articulate speech gave men a mental handhold for consecutive thought, and a vast enlargement of their powers of co-operation. For a time this new acquirement seems to have overshadowed their earlier achievement of drawing, and possibly it checked the use of gesture. But drawing presently reappeared again, for record, for signs, for the joy of drawing. Before real writing came picture-writing, such as is still practised by the Amerindians, the Bushmen, and savage and barbaric people in all parts of the world. It is essentially a drawing of things and acts, helped out by heraldic indications of proper names, and by strokes and dots to represent days and distances and such-like quantitative ideas.

Quite kindred to such picture-writing is the pictograph that one finds still in use to-day in international railway time-tables upon the continent of Europe, where a little black sign of a cup indicates a stand-up buffet for light refreshments; a crossed knife and fork, a restaurant; a little steamboat, a transfer to a steamboat; and a postilion's horn, a diligence. Similar signs are used in the well-known Michelin guides for automobilists in Europe, to show a post-office (envelope) or a telephone (telephone receiver). The quality of hotels is shown by an inn with one, two, three, or four gables, and so forth. Similarly, the roads of Europe are marked with wayside signs representing a gate, to indicate a level crossing ahead, a sinuous bend for a dangerous curve, and the like. From such pictographic signs to the first elements of Chinese writing is not a very long stretch.

In Chinese writing there are still traceable a number of pictographs. Most are now difficult to recognize. A mouth was originally written as a mouth-shaped hole, and is now, for convenience of brushwork, squared; a child, originally a recognizable little mannikin, is now a hasty wriggle and a cross; the sun, originally a large circle with a dot in the centre, has been converted, for the sake of convenience of combination, into a crossed oblong, which is easier to make with a brush. By combining these pictographs, a second order of ideas is expressed. For example, the pictograph for mouth combined with pictograph for vapour expressed "words." [1]

From such combinations one passes to what are called *ideograms:* the sign for "words" and the sign for "tongue" combine to make "speech"; the sign for "roof" and the sign for "pig" make "home"—for in the early domestic economy of China the pig was as important as it used to be in Ireland. But, as we have already noted earlier, the Chinese language consists of a comparatively few elementary monosyllabic sounds, which are all used in a great variety of meanings, and the Chinese

[1] See the *Encyclopædia Brit.*, Article *China*, p. 213.

soon discovered that a number of these *pictographs* and *ideographs* could be used also to express other ideas, not so conveniently pictured, but having the same sound. Characters so used are called *phonograms*. For example, the sound *fang* meant not only "boat," but "a place," "spinning," "fragrant," "inquire," and several other meanings according to the context. But while a boat is easy to draw, most of the other meanings are undrawable. How can one draw "fragrant" or "inquire"? The Chinese, therefore, took the same sign for all these meanings of "fang," but added to each of them another distinctive sign, the *determinative*, to show what sort of *fang* was intended. A "place" was indicated by the same sign as for "boat" (*fang*) and the determinative sign for "earth"; "spinning" by the sign for *fang* and the sign for "silk"; "inquire" by the sign for *fang*, and the sign for "words," and so on.

One may perhaps make this development of pictographs, ideograms, and phonograms a little clearer by taking an analogous case in English. Suppose we were making up a sort of picture-writing in English, then it would be very natural to use a square with a slanting line to suggest a lid, for the word and thing *box*. That would be a pictograph. But now suppose we had a round sign for money, and suppose we put this sign inside the box sign, that would do for "cash-box" or "treasury." That would be an ideogram. But the word "box" is used for other things than boxes. There is the box shrub which gives us boxwood. It would be hard to draw a recognizable box-tree distinct from other trees, but it is quite easy to put our sign "box," and add our sign for shrub as a determinative to determine that it is that sort of box and not a common box that we want to express. And then there is "box," the verb, meaning to fight with fists. Here, again, we need a determinative; we might add the two crossed swords, a sign which is used very often upon maps to denote a battle. A box at a theatre needs yet another determinative, and so we go on, through a long series of phonograms.

Now it is manifest that here in the Chinese writing is a very peculiar and complex system of sign-writing. A very great number of characters have to be learnt and the mind habituated to their use. The power it possesses to carry ideas and discussion is still ungauged by western standards, but we may doubt whether with this instrument it will ever be possible to establish such a wide, common mentality as the simpler and swifter alphabets of the western civilizations permit. In China it created a special reading-class, the mandarins, who were also the ruling and official class. Their necessary concentration upon words and classical

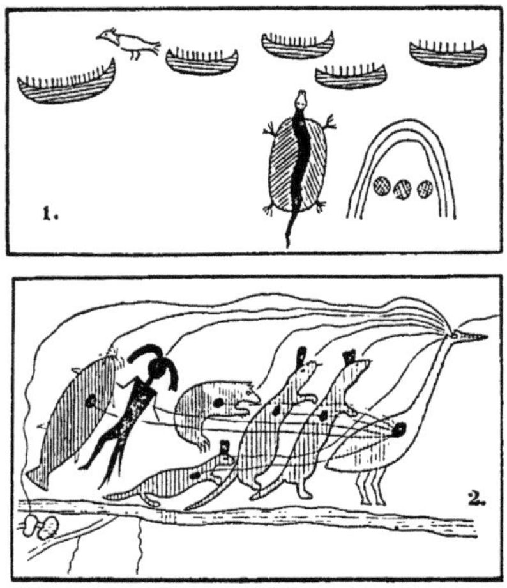

Specimens of American Indian picture-writing (after Schoolcraft.)

No. 1, painted on a rock on the shore of Lake Superior, records an expedition across the lake, in which five canoes took part. The upright strokes in each indicate the number of the crew, and the bird represents a chief, "The Kingfisher." The three circles (suns) under the arch (of heaven) indicate that the voyage lasted three days, and the tortoise, a symbol of land, denotes a safe arrival. No. 2 is a petition sent to the United States Congress by a group of Indian tribes, asking for fishing rights in certain small lakes. The tribes are represented by their totems, martens, bear, manfish, and catfish, led by the crane. Lines running from the heart and eye of each animal to the heart and eye of the crane denote that they are all of one mind; and a line runs from the eye of the crane to the lakes, shown in the crude little "map" in the lower left-hand corner.

forms, rather than upon ideas and realities, seems, in spite of her comparative peacefulness and the very high individual intellectual quality of her people, to have greatly hampered the social and economic development of China. Probably it is the complexity of her speech and writing, more than any other imaginable cause, that has made China to-day politically, socially, and individually a vast pool of backward people rather than the foremost power in the whole world.[1]

[1] The writer's friend, Mr. L. Y. Chen, thinks that this is only partially true. He thinks that the emperors insisted upon a minute and rigorous study of the set classics in order to check intellectual innovation. This was especially the case with the Ming emperors, the first of whom, when reorganizing the examination system on a narrower basis, said definitely, "This will bring all the intellectuals of the world into my trap." The Five Classics and the Four Books have imprisoned the mind of China.

§ 2

But while the Chinese mind thus made for itself an instrument which is probably too elaborate in structure, too laborious in use, and too inflexible in its form to meet the modern need for simple, swift, exact, and lucid communications, the growing civilizations of the west were working out the problem of a written record upon rather different and, on the whole, more advantageous lines. They did not seek to improve their script to make it swift and easy, but circumstances conspired to make it so. The Sumerian picture writing, which had to be done upon clay and with little styles, which made curved marks with difficulty and inaccurately, rapidly degenerated by a conventionalized dabbing down of wedged-shaped marks (cuneiform = wedge-shaped) into almost unrecognizable hints of the shapes intended. It helped the Sumerians greatly to learn to write, that they had to draw so badly. They got very soon to the Chinese pictographs, ideographs, and phonograms, and beyond them.

Most people know a sort of puzzle called a rebus. It is a way of representing words by pictures, not of the things the words represent, but by the pictures of other things having a similar sound. For example, two gates and a head is a rebus for Gateshead; a little streamlet (beck), a crowned monarch, and a ham, Beckingham. The Sumerian language was a language well adapted to this sort of representation. It was apparently a language of often quite vast polysyllables, made up of very distinct inalterable syllables; and many of the syllables taken separately were the names of concrete things. So that this cuneiform writing developed very readily into a syllabic way of writing, in which each sign conveys a syllable just as each act in a charade conveys a syllable. When presently the Semites conquered Sumeria, they adapted the syllabic system to their own speech, and so this writing became entirely a sign-for-a-sound writing. It was so used by the Assyrians and by the Chaldeans. But it was not a letter-writing, it was a syllable-writing. This cuneiform script prevailed for long ages over Assyria, Babylonia, and the Near East generally; there are vestiges of it in some of the letters of our alphabet to-day.

§ 3

But, meanwhile, in Egypt and upon the Mediterranean coast another system of writing grew up. Its beginnings are probably to be found in the priestly picture-writing (hieroglyphics) of the Egyptians, which also in the usual way became partly a sound-sign system. As we see it on the Egyptian monuments, the hieroglyphic writing consists of decorative but stiff and elaborate forms, but for such purpose as letter-writing and the keeping of recipes and the like, the Egyptian priests used a much simplified and flowing form of these characters, the *hieratic script*. Side by side with this hieratic script rose another, probably also derivative from the hieroglyphs, a script now lost to us, which was taken over by various non-Egyptian peoples in the Mediterranean, the Phœnicians, Libyans, Lydians, Cretans, and Celt-Iberians, and used for business purposes. Possibly a few letters were borrowed from the later cuneiform. In the hands of these foreigners this writing was, so to speak, cut off from its roots; it lost all but a few traces of its early pictorial character. It ceased to be pictographic or ideographic; it became simply a pure sound-sign system, an *alphabet*.

There were a number of such alphabets in the Mediterranean differing widely from each other.[1] It may be noted that the Phœnician alphabet (and perhaps others) omitted vowels. Possibly they pronounced their consonants very hard and had rather indeterminate vowels, as is said to be still the case with tribes of South Arabia. Quite probably, too, the Phœnicians used their alphabet at first not so much for writing as for single initial letters in their business accounts and tallies. One of these Mediterranean alphabets reached the Greeks, long after the time of the *Iliad*, who presently set to work to make it express the clear and beautiful sounds of their own highly developed Aryan speech. It consisted at first of consonants, and the Greeks added the vowels. They began to write for record, to help and fix their bardic tradition. . . .

§ 4

So it was by a series of very natural steps that writing grew out of the life of man. At first and for long ages it was the interest and the secret of only a few people in a special class, a mere accessory to the record of pictures. But there were certain very

[1] The Libyan alphabet survived in North Africa until a century ago, and was still used then for correspondence. It was supposed to be extinct, but in 1897 Sir Arthur Evans and Mr. J. L. Myres saw what looked like ancient Cretan lettering on some dyed skins from the Sahara in the bazaar at Tripoli. It was the ancient alphabet still in use for commercial signs.—E. B.

manifest advantages, quite apart from the increased expressiveness of mood and qualification, to be gained by making writing a little less plain than straightforward pictures, and in conventionalizing and codifying it. One of these was that so messages might be sent understandable by the sender and receiver, but not plain to the uninitiated. Another was that so one might put down various matters and help one's memory and the memory of one's friends, without giving away too much to the common herd. Among some of the earliest Egyptian writings, for example, are medical recipes and magic formulæ. Accounts, letters, recipes, name lists, itineraries; these were the earliest of written documents. Then, as the art of writing and reading spread, came that odd desire, that pathetic desire so common among human beings, to astonish some strange and remote person by writing down something striking, some secret one knew, some strange thought, or even one's name, so that long after one had gone one's way, it might strike upon the sight and mind of another reader. Even in Sumeria men scratched on walls, and all that remains to us of the ancient world, its rocks, its buildings, is plastered thickly with the names and the boasting of those foremost among human advertisers, its kings. Perhaps half the early inscriptions in that ancient world are of this nature, if, that is, we group with the name-writing and boasting the epitaphs, which were probably in many cases prearranged by the deceased.

For long the desire for crude self-assertion of the name-scrawling sort and the love of secret understandings kept writing within a narrow scope; but that other, more truly social desire in men, the desire to *tell*, was also at work. The profounder possibilities of writing, the possibilities of a vast extension and definition and settlement of knowledge and tradition, only grew apparent after long ages. But it will be interesting at this point and in this connection to recapitulate certain elemental facts about life, upon which we laid stress in our earlier chapters, because they illuminate not only the huge value of writing in the whole field of man's history, but also the rôle it is likely to play in his future.

1. Life had at first, it must be remembered, only a discontinuous repetition of consciousness, as the old died and the young were born.

Such a creature as a reptile has in its brain a capacity for experience, but when the individual dies, its experience dies with it. Most of its motives are purely instinctive, and all the mental life that it has is the result of heredity (birth inheritance).

2. But ordinary mammals have added to pure instinct *tradition*, a tradition of experience imparted by the imitated example of the mother, and in the case of such mentally developed animals as dogs, cats, or apes, by a sort of mute precept also. For example, the mother cat chastises her young for misbehaviour. So do mother apes and baboons.

3. Primitive man added to his powers of transmitting experience, representative art and speech. Pictorial and sculptured record and *verbal tradition* began.

Verbal tradition was developed to its highest possibility by the bards. They did much to make language what it is to the world to-day.

4. With the invention of writing, which developed out of pictorial record, human tradition was able to become fuller and much more exact. Verbal tradition, which had hitherto changed from age to age, began to be fixed. Men separated by hundreds of miles could now communicate their thoughts. An increasing number of human beings began to share a common written knowledge and a common sense of a past and a future. Human thinking became a larger operation in which hundreds of minds in different places and in different ages could react upon one another; it became a process constantly more continuous and sustained. . . .

5. For hundreds of generations the full power of writing was not revealed to the world, because for a long time the idea of multiplying writings by taking prints of a first copy did not become effective. The only way of multiplying writings was by copying one copy at a time, and this made books costly and rare. Moreover, the tendency to keep things secret, to make a cult and mystery of them, and so to gain an advantage over the generality of men, has always been very strong in men's minds. It is only nowadays that the great masses of mankind are learning to read, and reaching out towards the treasures of knowledge and thought already stored in books.

Nevertheless, from the first writings onward a new sort of tradition, an enduring and immortal tradition, began in the minds of men. Life, through mankind, grew thereafter more and more distinctly conscious of itself and its world. It is a thin streak of intellectual growth we trace in history, at first in a world of tumultuous ignorance and forgetfulness; it is like a mere line of light coming through the chink of an opening door into a darkened room; but slowly it widens, it grows. At last came a time in the history of Europe when the door, at the push of the printer, began to open more rapidly. Knowledge flared up, and as it flared it ceased to be the privilege of a favoured minority. For us now that door swings wider, and the light behind grows brighter. Misty it is still, glowing through clouds of dust and reek.

The door is not half open; the light is but a light new lit. Our world to-day is only in the beginning of knowledge.

XIX

GODS AND STARS, PRIESTS AND KINGS

§ 1

WE have already told what there is to tell of the social life of the Aryan tribes when they were settling down to the beginnings of civilized life; we have seen how they were associated in great households, grouped together under tribal leaders, who made a sort of informal aristocracy rather like that of the sixth form and prefects in an English boys' school; we have considered the rôle of the bards in the creation of an oral tradition, and we have glanced at their not very complex religious ideas. We may note one or two points of difference from the equivalent life of the nomadic Semites.

Like the early Aryan life, it was a life in a sort of family-tribe household. But it had differences due originally perhaps to the warmer, drier climate. Though both groups of races had cattle and sheep, the Aryans were rather herdsmen, the Semites shepherds. The Semites had no long winter evenings and no bardic singing. They never sat in hall. They have consequently no epics. They had stories, camp-fire stories, but not verbally beautified story recitations. The Semite also was more polygamous than the Aryan, his women less self-assertive,[1] and the tendency of his government more patriarchal. The head of the household or the tribe was less of a leader and more of a master, more like the Palæolithic Old Man. And the Semitic nomads were closer to the earlier civilizations, a thing that fitted in with their greater aptitude for trade and counting. But the religion of the nomadic Semite was as little organized as the religion of the Aryan. In either case the leading man performed most of the functions of the priest. The Aryan gods were little more than a kind of magical super-prince; they were supposed to sit in hall together, and to talk and make scenes with one another under Jupiter or Thor. The early Semitic gods, on the other hand, were thought of as tribal patriarchs. As peoples develop towards nomadism, they seem to lose even such primitive religion and magic as their Neolithic ancestors professed. Nomadism cuts men off from fixed temples and intense local associations; they take a broader and simpler view of the world. They tend towards religious simplification.

We write here of the nomadic peoples, the Aryan herdsmen and Semitic shepherds, and we write in the most general terms. They had their undercurrent of fables and superstitions, their phases of fear and abjection and sacrificial fury. These people were people like ourselves, with brains as busy and moody and inconsistent, and with even less training and discipline. It is absurd to suppose—as so many writers about early religion do seem to suppose—that their religious notions can be reduced to the consistent logical development of some one simple idea. We have already glanced, in Chapter XII, at the elements of religion that must have arisen necessarily in the

[1] The Sumerians allowed much more freedom and authority to women than the Semites. They had priestess-queens, and one of their great divinities was a goddess, Ishtar.

minds of those early peoples. But for most of the twenty-four hours these nomads were busy upon other things, and there is no sign that their houses, their daily routines, their ordinary acts, were dominated or their social order shaped, by any ideas that we should now call religious. As yet life and its ideas were too elementary for that.

But directly we turn our attention to these new accumulations of human beings that are beginning in Egypt and Mesopotamia, we find that one of the most conspicuous objects in every city is a temple or a group of temples. In some cases there arises beside it in these regions a royal palace, but as often the temple towers over the palace. This presence of the temple is equally true of the Phœnician cities and of the Greek and Roman as they arise. The palace of Cnossos, with its signs of comfort and pleasure-seeking, and the kindred cities of the Ægean peoples, include religious shrines, but in Crete there are also temples standing apart from the palatial city-households. All over the ancient civilized world we find them; wherever primitive civilization set its foot in Africa, Europe, or western Asia, a temple arose, and where the civilization is most ancient, in Egypt and in Sumer, there the temple is most in evidence. When Hanno reached what he thought was the most westerly point of Africa, he set up a temple to Hercules. We have, in fact, come now to a new stage in the history of mankind, the temple stage.

§ 2

In all these temples there was a shrine; dominating the shrine there was commonly a great figure usually of some monstrous half-animal form, before which stood an altar for sacrifices. This figure was either regarded as the god or as the image or symbol of the god, for whose worship the temple existed. And connected with the temple there were a number, and often a considerable number, of priests or priestesses, and temple servants, generally wearing a distinctive costume and forming an important part of the city population. They belonged to no household, as did the simple priest of the primitive Aryan; they made up a new kind of household of their own. They were a caste and a class apart, attracting intelligent recruits from the general population.

The primary duty of this priesthood was concerned with the worship of and the sacrifices to the god of the temple. And these things were done, not at any time, but at particular times and seasons. There had come into the life of man with his herding and agriculture a sense of a difference between the parts of the year and of a difference between day and day. Men were beginning to work—and to need days of rest. The temple, by its festivals, kept count. The temple in the ancient city was like the clock and calendar upon a writing-desk.

But it was a centre of other functions. It was in the early temples that the records and tallies of events were kept and that writing began. And there was knowledge there. The people went to the temple not only *en masse* for festivals, but individually for help. The early priests were also doctors and magicians. In the earliest temples we already find those little offerings for some private and particular end, which are still made in the chapels of catholic churches to-day, *ex votos*, little models of hearts relieved and limbs restored, acknowledgment of prayers answered and accepted vows.

It is clear that here we have that comparatively unimportant element in the life of the early nomad, the medicine-man, the shrine-keeper, and the memorist, developed, with the development of the community and as a part of the development of the community from barbarism to civilized settlement, into something of very much greater importance. And it is equally evident that those primitive fears of (and hopes of help from) strange beings, the desire to propitiate unknown forces, the primitive desire for cleansing and the primitive craving for power and knowledge have all contributed to crystallize out this new social fact of the temple.

The temple was accumulated by complex necessities, it grew from many roots and needs, and the god that dominated the temple was the creation of many imaginations and made up of all sorts of impulses, ideas, and half ideas. Here there was a god in which one sort of ideas predominated, and there another. It is necessary to lay some stress upon this confusion and variety of origin in gods, because there is a very abundant literature now in existence upon religious origins, in which a number of writers insist, some on this leading idea and some on that—we have noted several in our Chapter XII on "Early Thought"—as though it were the only idea. Professor Max Müller in his time, for example, harped perpetually on the idea of sun stories and sun worship. He would have had us think that

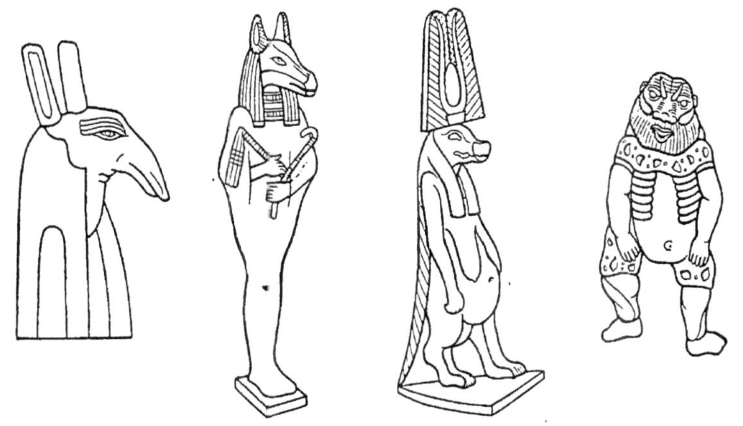

Set Egyptian god of darkness. **Anubis** a darkness god. **Typhon** wife of Anubis, also known as the Terrible One. The cheerful **Bes**.

early man never had lusts or fears, cravings for power, nightmares or fantasies, but that he meditated perpetually on the beneficent source of light and life in the sky. Now dawn and sunset are very moving facts in the daily life, but they are only two among many. Early men, three or four hundred generations ago, had brains very like our own. The fancies of our childhood and youth are perhaps the best clue we have to the ground-stuff of early religion, and anyone who can recall those early mental experiences will understand very easily the vagueness, the monstrosity, and the incoherent variety of the first gods. There were sun gods, no doubt, early in the history of temples, but there were also hippopotamus gods and hawk gods; there were cow deities, there were monstrous male and female gods, there were gods of terror and gods of an adorable quaintness, there were gods who were nothing but lumps of meteoric stone that had fallen amazingly out of the sky, and gods who were mere natural stones that had chanced to have a queer and impressive shape. Some gods, like Marduk of Babylon and the Baal (= the Lord) of the Phœnicians, Canaanites, and the like, were quite probably at bottom just legendary wonder beings, such as little boys will invent for themselves to-day. The early Semites, it is said, as soon as they thought of a god, invented a wife for him; most of the Egyptian and Babylonian gods were married. But the gods of the nomadic Semites had not this marrying disposition. Children were less eagerly sought by the inhabitants of the food-grudging steppes.

Even more natural than to provide a wife for a god is to give him a house to live in to which offerings can be brought. Of this house the knowing man, the magician would naturally become the custodian. A certain seclusion, a certain aloofness, would add greatly to the prestige of the god. The steps by which the early temple and the early priesthood developed so soon as an agricultural population settled and increased are all quite natural and understandable up to the stage of the long temple with the image, shrine and altar at one end and the long nave in which the worshippers stood. And this temple, because it had records and secrets, because it was a centre of power, advice, and instruction, because it sought and attracted imaginative and clever people for its service, naturally became a kind of brain in the growing community. The attitude of the common people who tilled the fields and herded the beasts towards the temple would remain simple and credulous. There, rarely seen and so imaginatively enhanced, lived the god whose approval gave prosperity, whose anger meant misfortune; he could be propitiated by little presents and the help of his servants could be obtained. He was wonderful, and of such power and knowledge that it did not do to

THE PYRAMIDS

Photo: Bonfils

"These unmeaning sepulchral piles of an almost incredible vastness, erected in an age when engineering science had scarcely begun, exhausted the resources of Egypt."

be disrespectful to him even in one's thoughts. Within the priesthood, however, a certain amount of thinking went on at a rather higher level than that.

§ 3[1]

And now we have to note a very interesting fact about the chief temples of Egypt and, so far as we know—because the ruins are not so distinct—of Babylonia, and that is that they were "oriented"—that is to say, that the same sort of temple was built so that the shrine and entrance always faced in the same direction.[2] In Babylonian temples this was most often due east, facing the sunrise on March 21st and September 21st, the equinoxes; and it is to be noted that it was at the spring equinox that the Euphrates and Tigris came down in flood. The Pyramids of Gizeh are also oriented east and west, and the Sphinx faces due east, but very many of the Egyptian temples to the south of the delta of the Nile do not point due east, but to the point where the sun rises at the longest day—and in Egypt the inundation comes close to that date. Others, however, pointed nearly northward, and others again pointed to the rising of the star Sirius or to the rising-point of other conspicuous stars. The fact of orientation links up with the fact that there early arose a close association between various gods and the sun and various fixed stars. Whatever the mass of people outside were thinking, the priests of the temples were beginning to link the movements of those heavenly bodies with the power in the shrine. They were thinking about the gods they served and thinking new meanings into them. They were brooding upon the mystery of the stars. It was very natural for them to suppose that these shining bodies, so irregularly distributed and circling so solemnly and silently, must be charged with portents to mankind.

Among other things, this orientation of the temples served to fix and help the great annual festival of the New Year. On one morning in the year, and one morning alone, in a temple oriented to the rising-place of the sun at Midsummer Day, the sun's first rays would smite down through the gloom of the temple and the long alley of the temple pillars, and light up the god above the altar and irradiate him with glory. The narrow, darkened structure of the ancient temples seems to be deliberately planned for such an effect. No doubt the people were gathered in the darkness before the dawn; in the darkness there was chanting and perhaps the offering of sacrifices; the god alone stood mute and invisible. Prayers and invocations would be made. Then upon the eyes of the worshippers, sensitized by the

[1] See Johnson's *Byeways of British Archæology*.

[2] Many Christian churches, almost all, indeed, built between the fifth century and the Renaissance, are oriented to the east. St. Peter's at Rome is oriented east and west.

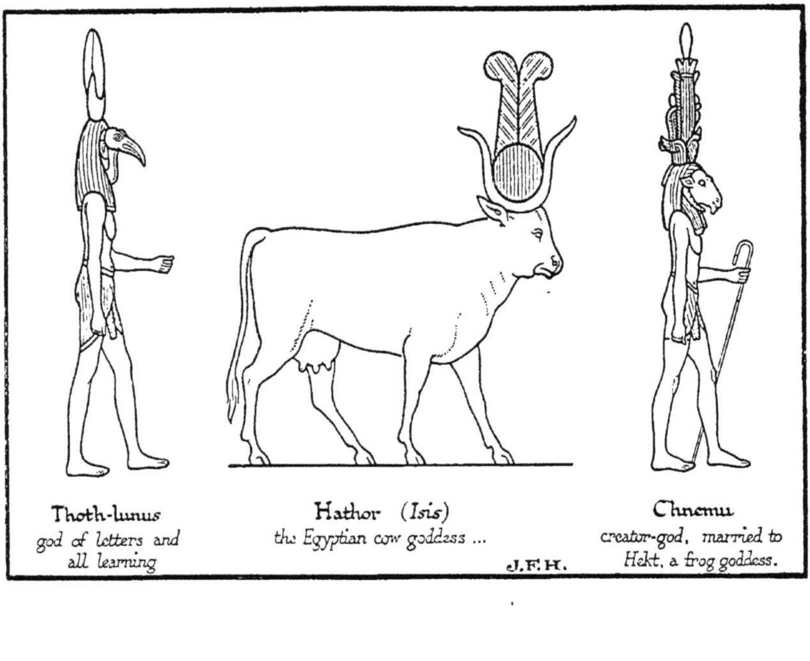

Thoth-lunus *god of letters and all learning* — **Hathor** (*Isis*) *the Egyptian cow goddess ...* — **Chnemu** *creator-god, married to Hekt, a frog goddess.* J.F.H.

darkness, as the sun rose behind them, the god would suddenly shine.

So, at least, one explanation of orientation is found by such students of orientation as Sir Norman Lockyer.[1] Not only is orientation apparent in most of the temples of Egypt, Assyria, Babylonia, and the east, it is found in the Greek temples; Stonehenge is oriented to the midsummer sunrise, and so are most of the megalithic circles of Europe; the Temple of Heaven in Peking is oriented to midwinter. In the days of the Chinese Empire, up to a few years ago one of the most important of all the duties of the Emperor of China was to sacrifice and pray in this temple upon midwinter's day for a propitious year.

The Egyptian priests had mapped out the stars into the constellations, and divided up the zodiac into twelve signs by 3,000 B.C. . . .

§ 4

This clear evidence of astronomical inquiry and of a development of astronomical ideas is the most obvious, but only the most obvious evidence of the very considerable intellectual activities that went on within the temple precincts in ancient times. There is a curious disposition among many modern writers to deprecate priesthoods and to speak of priests as though they had always been impostors and tricksters, preying upon the simplicity of mankind. But, indeed, they were for long the only writing class, the only reading public, the only learned and the only thinkers; they were all the professional classes of the time. You could have no intellectual life at all, you could not get access to literature or any knowledge except through the priesthood. The temples were not only observatories and libraries and clinics, they were museums and treasure-houses. The original *Periplus* of Hanno hung in one temple in Carthage, skins of his "gorillas" were hung and treasured in another. Whatever there was of abiding worth in the life of the community sheltered there. Herodotus, the early Greek historian (485–425 B.C.), collected most of his material from the priests of the countries in which he travelled, and it is evident they met him generously and put their very considerable resources completely at his disposal. Outside the temples the world was still a world of blankly illiterate and unspeculative human beings, living from day to day entirely for themselves. Moreover, there is little evidence that the commonalty felt cheated by the priests, or had anything but trust and affection for the early priesthoods. Even the great conquerors of later times were anxious to keep themselves upon the right side of the priests of the nations and cities whose obedience they desired, because of the immense popular influence of these priests.

No doubt there were great differences between temple and temple and cult and cult in the spirit and quality of the priesthood. Some probably were cruel, some vicious and greedy, many dull and doctrinaire, stupid with tradition, but it has to be kept in mind that there were distinct limits to the degeneracy or inefficiency of a priesthood. It had to keep its grip upon the general mind. It could not go beyond what people would stand—either towards the darkness or towards the light. Its authority rested, in the end, on the persuasion that its activities were propitious.

§ 5[2]

It is clear that the earliest civilized governments were essentially priestly governments. It was not kings and captains who first set men to the plough and a settled life. It was the ideas of the gods and plenty, working with the acquiescence of common men. The early rulers of Sumer we know were all priests, kings only because they were chief priests. And priestly government had its own weaknesses as well as its peculiar deep-rooted strength. The power of a priesthood is a power over their own people alone. It is a subjugation through mysterious fears and hopes. The priesthood can gather its people together for war, but its traditionalism and all its methods unfit it for military control. Against the enemy without, a priest-led people is feeble.

Moreover, a priest is a man vowed, trained, and consecrated, a man belonging to a special corps, and necessarily with an intense *esprit de corps*. He has given up his life to his temple and his god. This is a very excellent thing for the internal vigour of his own priesthood, his own temple. He lives or dies for the honour of his particular god. But in the next town or village is another temple with another god. It is his constant preoccupation to keep his people from that god. Religious cults and priesthoods are sectarian by nature; they will convert, they will overcome, but they will never coalesce. Our first perceptions of

[1] In his *Dawn of Astronomy*.

[2] Legrain's *Le Temps des Rois d'Ur* (Bibliothèque de l'École des Hautes Etudes) was useful here.

events in Sumer, in the dim uncertain light before history began, is of priests and gods in conflict; until the Sumerians were conquered by the Semites they were never united; and the same incurable conflict of priesthoods scars all the temple ruins of Egypt. It was impossible that it could have been otherwise, having regard to the elements out of which religion arose.

It was out of those two main weaknesses of all priesthoods, namely, the incapacity for efficient military leadership and their inevitable jealousy of all other religious cults, that the power of secular kingship arose. The foreign enemy either prevailed and set up a king over the people, or the priesthoods who would not give way to each other set up a common fighting captain, who retained more or less power in peace time. This secular king developed a group of officials about him and began, in relation to military organization, to take a share in the priestly administration of the people's affairs. So, growing out of priestcraft and beside the priest, the king, the protagonist of the priest, appears upon the stage of human history, and a very large amount of the subsequent experiences of mankind is only to be understood as an elaboration, complication, and distortion of the struggle, unconscious or deliberate, between these two systems of human control, the temple and the palace. And it was in the original centres of civilization that this antagonism was most completely developed. The Aryan peoples never passed through a phase of temple rule on their way to civilization; they came to civilization late; they found that drama already half-played. They took over the ideas of both temple and kingship, when those ideas were already elaborately developed, from the more civilized Hamitic or Semitic people they conquered.

The greater importance of the gods and the priests in the earlier history of the Mesopotamian civilization is very apparent, but gradually the palace won its way until it was at last in a position to struggle definitely for the supreme power. At first, in the story, the palace is ignorant and friendless in the face of the temple; the priests alone read, the priests alone know, the people are afraid of them. But in the dissensions of the various cults comes the opportunity of the palace. From other cities, from among captives, from defeated or suppressed religious cults, the palace gets men who also can read and who can do magic things.[1] The court also becomes a centre of writing and record; the king thinks for himself and becomes politic. Traders and foreigners drift to the court, and if the king has not the full records and the finished scholarship of the priests, he has a wider and fresher first-hand knowledge of many things. The priest comes into the temple when he is very young; he passes many years as a neophyte; the path of learning the clumsy letters of primitive times is slow and toilsome; he becomes erudite and prejudiced rather than a man of the world. Some of the more active-minded young priests may even cast envious eyes at the king's service.

An Assyrian King & his Chief Minister

[1] Cp. Moses and the Egyptian Magicians.

There are many complications and variations in this ages-long drama of the struggle going on beneath the outward conflicts of priest and king, between the made man and the born man, between learning and originality, between established knowledge and settled usage on the one hand, and creative will and imagination on the other. It is not always, as we shall find later, the priest who is the conservative and unimaginative antagonist. Sometimes a king struggles against narrow and obstructive priesthoods; sometimes priesthoods uphold the standards of civilization against savage, egotistical, or reactionary kings.

One or two outstanding facts and incidents of the early stages of this fundamental struggle in political affairs are all that we can note here between 4,000 B.C. and the days of Alexander.

§ 6

In the early days of Sumeria and Akkadia the city-kings were priests and medicine-men rather than kings, and it was only when foreign conquerors sought to establish their hold in relation to existing institutions that the distinction of priest and king became definite. But the god of the priests remained as the real overlord of the land and of priest and king alike. He was the universal landlord; the wealth and authority of his temples and establishments outshone those of the king. Especially was this the case within the city walls. Hammurabi, the founder of the first Babylonian empire, is one of the earlier monarchs whom we find taking a firm grip upon the affairs of the community. He does it with the utmost politeness to the gods. In an inscription recording his irrigation work in Sumeria and Akkadia, he begins: "When Anu and Bel entrusted me with the rule of Sumer and Akkad——." We possess a code of laws made by this same Hammurabi—it is the earliest known code of law—and at the head of this code we see the figure of Hammurabi receiving the law from its nominal promulgator, the god Shamash.

An act of great political importance in the conquest of any city was the carrying off of its god to become a subordinate in the temple of its conqueror. This was far more important than the subjugation of king by king. Merodach, the Babylonian Jupiter, was carried off by the Elamites, and Babylon did not feel independent until its return. But sometimes a conqueror was afraid of the god he had conquered. In the collection of letters addressed to Amenophis III and IV at Tel-Amarna in Egypt, to which allusion has already been made, is one from a certain king, Tushratta, King of Mitani, who has conquered Assyria and taken the statue of the goddess Ishtar. Apparently he has sent this statue into Egypt, partly to acknowledge the overlordship of Amenophis, but partly because he fears her anger. (Winckler.) In the Bible is related (Sam. i. v. 1) how the Ark of the Covenant of the God of the Hebrews was carried off by the Philistines, as a token of conquest, into the temple of the fish god, Dagon, at Ashdod, and how Dagon fell down and was broken, and how the people of Ashdod were smitten with disease. In the latter story particularly, the gods and priests fill the scene; there is no king in evidence at all.

Right through the history of the Babylonian and Assyrian empires no monarch seems to have felt his tenure of power secure in Babylon until he had "taken the hand of Bel"—that is to say, that he had been adopted by the priesthood of "Bel" as the god's son and representative. As our knowledge of Assyrian and Babylonian history grows clearer, it becomes plainer that the politics of that world, the revolutions, usurpations, changes of dynasty, intrigues with foreign powers, turned largely upon issues between the great wealthy priesthoods and the growing but still inadequate power of the monarchy. The king relied on his army, and this was usually a mercenary army of foreigners, speedily mutinous if there was no pay or plunder, and easily bribed. We have already noted the name of Sennacherib, the son of Sargon II, among the monarchs of the Assyrian empire. Sennacherib was involved in a violent quarrel with the priesthood of Babylon; he never "took the hand of Bel"; and finally struck at that power by destroying altogether the holy part of the city of Babylon (691 B.C.) and removing the statue of Bel-Marduk to Assyria. He was assassinated by one of his sons, and his successor, Esar-haddon (his son, but not the son who was his assassin), found it expedient to restore Bel-Marduk and rebuild his temple, and make his peace with the god.[1]

Assurbanipal (Greek, Sardanapalus), the

[1] According to Winckler, Sargon II, unlike his son, was pro-priest, and his usurpation of the throne was the result of an intrigue of the Babylonian priests against the feudal Assyrian military system of Tiglath Pileser III.

ASSURBANIPAL POURING A LIBATION OVER DEAD LIONS

British Museum

"In the early days the god of the priests remained as the real overlord of the land and of priest and king alike. Even the great conquerors were anxious to keep themselves on the right side of the priests."

son of this Esar-haddon, is a particularly interesting figure from this point of view of the relationship of priesthood and king. His father's reconciliation with the priests of Bel-Marduk went so far that Sardanapalus was given a Babylonian instead of a military Assyrian education. He became a great collector of the clay documents of the past, and his library, which has been unearthed, is now the most precious source of historical material in the world. But for all his learning he kept his grip on the Assyrian army; he made a temporary conquest of Egypt, suppressed a rebellion in Babylon, and carried out a number of successful expeditions. As we have already told in Chapter XVI, he was almost the last of the Assyrian monarchs. The Aryan tribes, who knew more of war than of priestcraft, and particularly the Scythians, the Medes and Persians, had long been pressing upon Assyria from the north and north-east. The Medes and Persians formed an alliance with the nomadic Semitic Chaldeans of the south for the joint undoing of Assyria. Nineveh, the Assyrian capital, fell to these Aryans in 606 B.C.

CHEPHREN

Sixty-seven years after the taking of Nineveh by the Aryans, which left Babylonia to the Semitic Chaldeans, the last monarch of the Chaldean Empire (the Second Babylonian Empire), Nabonidus, the father of Belshazzar, was overthrown by Cyrus, the Persian. This Nabonidus, again, was a highly educated monarch, who brought far too much intelligence and imagination and not enough of the short range wisdom of this world to affairs of state. He conducted antiquarian researches, and to his researches it is that we owe the date of 3,750 B.C., assigned to Sargon I and still accepted by many authorities. He was proud of this determination, and left inscriptions to record it. It is clear he was a religious innovator; he built and rearranged temples and attempted to centralize religion in Babylon by bringing a number of local gods to the temple of Bel-Marduk. No doubt he realized the weakness and disunion of his empire due to these conflicting cults, and had some conception of unification in his mind.

Events were marching too rapidly for any such development. His innovation had manifestly raised the suspicion and hostility of the priesthood of Bel. They sided with the Persians. "The soldiers of Cyrus entered Babylon without fighting." Nabonidus was taken prisoner, and Persian sentinels were set at the gates of the temple of Bel, "where the services continued without intermission."

Cyrus did, in fact, set up the Persian Empire in Babylon with the blessing of Bel-Marduk. He gratified the conservative instincts of the priests by packing off the local gods back to their ancestral temples. He also restored the Jews to Jerusalem.[1] These were merely matters of immediate policy to him. But in bringing in the irreligious Aryans, the ancient priesthood was paying too highly for the continuation of its temple services. It would have been wiser to have dealt with the innovations of Nabonidus, that earnest heretic, to have listened to his ideas, and to have met the needs of a changing world. Cyrus entered Babylon 539 B.C.; by 521 B.C. Babylon was in insurrection again, and in 520 B.C. another Persian monarch, Darius, was pulling down her walls. Within two hundred years the life had altogether gone out of those venerable rituals of Bel-Marduk, and the temple of Bel-Marduk was being used by builders as a quarry.

§ 7[2]

The story of priest and king in Egypt is similar to, but by no means parallel with, that of Babylonia. The kings of Sumeria and Assyria were priests who had become

[1] See the last two verses of the Second Book of Chronicles, and Ezra, ch. i.

[2] A book of the utmost interest and value here is Breasted's *Religion and Thought in Ancient Egypt*.

kings; they were secularized priests. The Pharaoh of Egypt does not appear to have followed precisely that line. Already in the very oldest records the Pharaoh has a power, and importance exceeding that of any priest. He is, in fact, a god, and more than either priest or king. We do not know how he got to that position. No monarch of Sumeria or Babylonia or Assyria could have induced his people to do for him what the great pyramid-building Pharaohs of the IVth Dynasty made their people do in those vast erections. The earlier Pharaohs were not improbably regarded as incarnations of the dominant god. The falcon god Horus sits behind the head of the great statue of Chephren. So late a monarch as Rameses III (XIXth Dynasty) is represented upon his sarcophagus (now at Cambridge) bearing the distinctive symbols of the three great gods of the Egyptian system.[1] He carries the two sceptres of Osiris, the god of Day and Resurrection; upon his head are the horns of the cow goddess Hathor, and also the sun ball and feathers of Ammon Ra. He is not merely wearing the symbols of these gods as a devout Babylonian might wear the symbols of Bel-Marduk; he *is* these three gods in one.

Relief on the cover of the sarcophagus (at Cambridge). After Sharpe.

Inscription (round the edges of cover) as far as decipherable:—

"Osiris, King of Upper and Lower Egypt, lord of the two countries . . . son of the Sun, beloved of the gods, lord of diadems, Rameses, prince of Heliopolis, triumphant! Thou art in the condition of a god, thou shalt arise as Usr: there is no enemy to thee, I give to thee triumph among them. . . ." BUDGE, *Catalogue, Egyptian Collection, Fitzwilliam Museum, Cambridge.*

The student will find much more in Sir J. G. Frazer's *Golden Bough* about the ancient use of human beings as well as statues to represent gods. Here we have merely to point to an apparent difference of idea between the Asiatic and African monarchies in this respect.

We find also a number of sculptures and paintings to enforce the idea that the Pharaohs were the actual sons of gods. The divine fathering and birth of Amenophis III, for instance (of the XVIIIth Dynasty), is displayed in extraordinary detail in a series of sculptures at Luxor. Moreover, it was held that the Pharaohs, being of so divine a strain, could not marry common clay, and consequently they were accustomed to marry blood relations within the degrees of consanguinity now prohibited, even marrying their sisters.

The struggle between palace and temple came into Egyptian history, therefore, at a different angle from that at which it came into Babylonia. Nevertheless, it came in. Professor Maspero (in his *New Light on Ancient Egypt*) gives a very interesting account of the struggle of Amenophis IV with the priesthoods, and particularly with priests of the great god, Ammon Ra, Lord of Karnak. The mother of Amenophis IV was not of the race of Pharaoh; it would seem that his father, Amenophis III, made a love match with a subject, a beautiful Syrian named Tii, and Professor Maspero finds in the possible opposition to and annoyance of this queen by the priests of Ammon Ra the beginnings of the quarrel. She may, he thinks, have inspired her son with a fanatical hatred of Ammon Ra. But Amenophis IV may have had a wider view. Like the Babylonian Nabonidus, who lived a thousand years later, he may have had in mind the problem of moral unity in his empire. We have already noted that Amenophis III ruled from Ethiopia to the Euphrates, and that the store of letters to himself and his son found at Tel Amarna show a very wide range of interest and influence. At any rate, Amenophis IV set himself to close all the Egyptian and Syrian temples, to put an end to all sectarian

[1] See S. Sharpe's *Egyptian Mythology and Egyptian Christianity*.

worship throughout his dominions, and to establish everywhere the worship of one god, Aton, the solar disk. He left his capital, Thebes, which was even more the city of Ammon Ra than later Babylon was the city of Bel-Marduk, and set up his capital at Tel Amarna; he altered his name from "Amenophis," which consecrated him to Ammon (Amen) to "Akhnaton," the Sun's Glory; and he held his own against all the priesthoods of his empire for eighteen years and died a Pharaoh.

Opinions upon Amenophis IV or Akhnaton, differ very widely. There are those who regard him as the creature of his mother's hatred of Ammon and the uxorious spouse of a beautiful wife. Certainly he loved his wife very passionately; he showed her great honour—Egypt honoured women, and was ruled at different times by several queens—and he was sculptured in one instance with his wife seated upon his knees, and in another in the act of kissing her in a chariot; but men who live under the sway of their womenkind do not sustain great empires in the face of the bitter hostility of the most influential organized bodies in their realm.[1] Others write of him as a "gloomy fanatic." Matrimonial bliss is rare in the cases of gloomy fanatics. It is much more reasonable to regard him as the Pharaoh who refused to be a god. It is not simply his religious policy and his frank display of natural affection that seem to mark a strong and very original personality. His æsthetic ideas were his own. He refused to have his portrait conventionalized into the customary smooth beauty of the Pharaoh god, and his face looks out at us across an interval of thirty-four centuries, a man amidst ranks of divine insipidities.

A reign of eighteen years was not long enough for the revolution he contemplated, and his son-in-law who succeeded him went back to Thebes and made his peace with Ammon Ra.

[1] Akhnaton lost some or all his father's Syrian conquests.
—G. W. B.

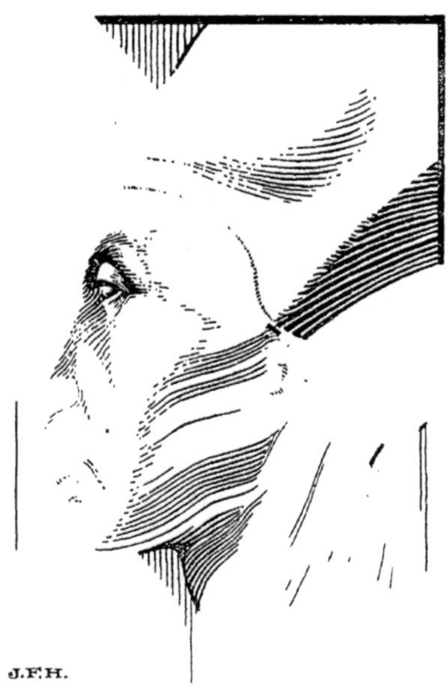

Akhnaton (Amenophis IV)
[based on the cast at Cairo, & the reliefs in the Berlin Museum.]

To the very end of the story the divinity of kings haunted the Egyptian mind, and infected the thoughts of intellectually healthier races. When Alexander the Great reached Babylon, the prestige of Bel-Marduk was already far gone in decay, but in Egypt, Ammon Ra was still god enough to make a snob of the conquering Grecian. The priests of Ammon Ra, about the time of the XVIIIth or XIXth Dynasty (*circa* 1,400 B.C.), had set up in an oasis of the desert a temple and oracle. Here was an image of the god which could speak, move its head, and accept or reject scrolls of inquiry. This oracle was still flourishing in 332 B.C. The young master of the world, it is related, made a special journey to visit it; he came into the sanctuary, and the image advanced out of the darkness at the back to meet him. There was an impressive exchange of salutations. Some such formula as this must have been used (says Professor Maspero): "Come, son of my loins, who loves me so that I give thee the royalty of Ra and the royalty of Horus! I give thee valiance, I give thee to hold all countries and all religions under thy feet; I give thee to strike all the peoples united together with thy arm!"

So it was that the priests of Egypt conquered their conqueror, and an Aryan monarch first became a god. . . .[2]

[2] Many authorities regard Alexander as a man with the ideas of a pushful nineteenth-century (A.D.) monarch, and consider this visit to Jupiter Ammon as a master-stroke of policy. He was, we are asked to believe, deliberately and cynically acquiring divinity as a "unifying idea." The writer is totally unable to accept anything of the sort. For a discussion of the question, see Ferguson's *Greek Imperialism.*

§ 8

The struggle of priest and king in China cannot be discussed here at any length. It was different again, as in Egypt it was different from Babylonia, but we find the same effort on the part of the ruler to break up tradition because it divides up the people. The Chinese Emperor, the "Son of Heaven," was himself a high-priest, and his chief duty was sacrificial; in the more disorderly phases of Chinese history he ceases to rule and continues only to sacrifice. The literary class was detached from the priestly class at an early date. It became a bureaucratic body serving the local kings and rulers. That is a fundamental difference between the history of China and any Western history. While Alexander was overrunning Western Asia, China, under the last priest-emperors of the Chow Dynasty, was sinking into a state of great disorder. Each province clung to its separate nationality and traditions, and the Huns spread from province to province. The King of T'sin (who lived about eighty years after Alexander the Great), impressed by the mischief tradition was doing in the land, resolved to destroy the entire Chinese literature, and his son, Shi Hwang-ti, the "first universal Emperor," made a strenuous attempt to seek out and destroy all the existing classics.[1] They vanished while he ruled, and he ruled without tradition, and welded China into a unity that endured for some centuries; but when he had passed, the hidden books crept out again. China remained united, though not under his descendants, but after a civil war under a fresh dynasty, the Han Dynasty (206 B.C.). The first Han monarch did not sustain this campaign of Shi Hwang-ti against the *literati*, and his successor made his peace with them and restored the texts of the classics.

XX

SERFS, SLAVES, SOCIAL CLASSES, AND FREE INDIVIDUALS

§ 1

WE have been sketching in the last four chapters the growth of civilized states out of the primitive Neolithic agriculture that began in Mesopotamia perhaps 15,000, perhaps 20,000, years ago. It was at first horticulture rather than agriculture; it was done with the hoe before the plough, and at first it was quite supplementary to the sheep, goat, and cattle tending that made the "living" of the family tribe. We have traced the broad outlines of the development in regions of exceptional fruitfulness of the first settled village communities into more populous towns and cities, and the growth of the village shrine and the village medicine-man into the city temple and the city priesthood. We have noted the beginnings of organized war, first as a bickering between villages, and then as a more disciplined struggle between the priest-king and god of one city and those of another. Our story has passed on rapidly from the first indications of conquest and empire in Sumer, perhaps 6,000 or 7,000 B.C., to the spectacle of great empires growing up, with roads and armies, with inscriptions and written documents

[1] "His reforming zeal made him unpopular with the upper classes. Schoolmen and pedants held up to the admiration of the people the heroes of the feudal times and the advantages of the system they administered. Seeing in this propaganda danger to the state, Shi Hwang-ti determined to break once and for all with the past. To this end he ordered the destruction of all books having reference to the past history of the empire, and many scholars were put to death for failing in obedience to it."—The late Sir R. K. Douglas in the *Encyclopædia Brit.*, article *China*.

Mr. L. Y. Chen does not agree with Sir R. K. Douglas here. He thinks that the motives of Shi Hwang-ti were obscurantist. His object was the intellectual slavery of the people. He collected a library for his own use.

with educated priesthoods and kings and rulers sustained by a tradition already ancient. We have traced in broad outline the appearance and conflicts and replacements of these empires of the great rivers. We have directed attention, in particular, to the evidence of a development of still wider political ideas as we find it betrayed by the actions and utterances of such men as Nabonidus and Amenophis IV. It has been an outline of the accumulations of human experience for ten or fifteen thousand years, a vast space of time in comparison with all subsequent history, but a brief period when we measure it against the succession of endless generations that intervenes between us and the first rude flint-using human creatures of the Pleistocene dawn. But for these last four chapters we have been writing almost entirely not about mankind generally, but only about the men who thought, the men who could draw and read and write, the men who were altering their world. Beneath their activities what was the life of the mute multitude ?

The life of the common man was, of course, affected and changed by these things, just as the lives of the domestic animals and the face of the cultivated country were changed; but for the most part it was a change suffered and not a change in which the common man upon the land had any voice or will. Reading and writing were not yet for the likes of him. He went on cultivating his patch, loving his wife and children, beating his dog and tending his beasts, grumbling at hard times, fearing the magic of the priests and the power of the gods, desiring little more except to be left alone by the powers above him. So he was in 10,000 B.C.; so he was, unchanged in nature and outlook, in the time of Alexander the Great; so over the greater part of the world he remains to-day. He got rather better tools, better seeds, better methods, a slightly sounder house, he sold his produce in a more organized market as civilization progressed. A certain freedom and a certain equality passed out of human life when men ceased to wander. Men paid in liberty for safety, shelter, and regular meals. By imperceptible degrees the common man found the patch he cultivated was not his own; it belonged to the god; and he had to pay a fraction of his produce to the god. Or the god had given it to the king, who exacted his rent and tax. Or the king had given it to an official, who was the lord of the common man. And sometimes the god or the king or the noble had work to be done, and then the common man had to leave his patch and work for his master.

How far the patch he cultivated was his own was never very clear to him. In ancient Assyria the land seems to have been held as a sort of freehold and the occupier paid taxes; in Babylonia the land was the god's, and he permitted the cultivator to work thereon. In Egypt the temples or Pharaoh-the-god or the nobles under Pharaoh were the owners and rent receivers. But the cultivator was not a slave; he was a peasant, and only bound to the land in so far that there was nothing else for him to do but cultivate, and nowhere else for him to go. He lived in a village or town, and went out to his work. The village, to begin with, was often merely a big household of related people under a patriarch headman, the early town a group of householders under its elders. There was no process of enslavement as civilization grew, but the headmen and leaderly men grew in power and authority, and the common men did not keep pace with them, and fell into a tradition of dependence and subordination.

On the whole, the common men were probably well content to live under lord or king or god and obey their bidding. It was safer. It was easier. All animals—and man is no exception—begin life as dependents. Most men never shake themselves loose from the desire for leading and protection.[1]

§ 2

The earlier wars did not involve remote or prolonged campaigns, and they were waged by levies of the common people. But war brought in a new source of possessions, plunder, and a new social factor, the captive. In the earlier, simpler days of war, the captive man was kept only to be tortured or sacrificed to the victorious god; the captive women and children were assimilated into the tribe. But later many captives were spared to be slaves because they had exceptional gifts or peculiar arts. It would be the kings and captains who would take these slaves at first, and it would speedily become apparent to them that these men were much more their own than were the peasant cultivators and common men

[1] There were literary expressions of social discontent in Egypt before 2,000 B.C. See "Social Forces and Religion" in Breasted's *Religion and Thought in Ancient Egypt* for some of the earliest complaints of the common man under the ancient civilizations.

of their own race.[1] The slave could be commanded to do all sorts of things for his master that the quasi-free common man would not do so willingly because of his attachment to his own patch of cultivation. From a very early period the artificer was often a household slave, and the manufacture of trade goods, pottery, textiles, metal ware, and so forth, such as went on vigorously in the household city of the Minos of Cnossos, was probably a slave industry from the beginning. Sayce, in his *Babylonians and Assyrians*,[2] quotes Babylonian agreements for the teaching of trades to slaves, and dealing with the exploitation of slave products. Slaves produced slave children, enslavement in discharge of debts added to the slave population; it is probable that as the cities grew larger, a larger part of the new population consisted of these slave artificers and slave servants in the large households. They were by no means abject slaves; in later Babylon their lives and property were protected by elaborate laws. Nor were they all outlanders. Parents might sell their children into slavery, and brothers their orphan sisters. Free men who had no means of livelihood would even sell themselves into slavery. And slavery was the fate of the insolvent debtor. Craft apprenticeship, again, was a sort of fixed-term slavery. Out of the slave population, by a converse process, arose the freed-man and freed-woman, who worked for wages and had still more definite individual rights. Since in Babylon slaves could themselves own property, many slaves saved up and bought themselves. Probably the town slave was often better off and practically as free as the cultivator of the soil, and as the rural population increased, its sons and daughters came to mix with and swell the growing ranks of artificers, some bound, some free.

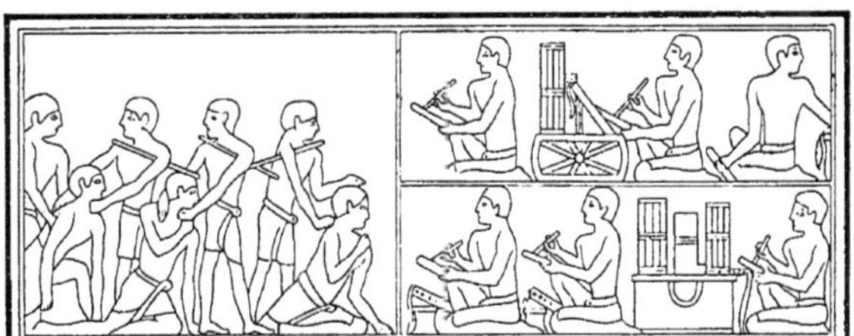

Egyptian peasants seized for non-payment of taxes... (Pyramid Age)

As the extent and complexity of government increased, the number of households multiplied. Under the king's household grew up the households of his great ministers and officials, under the temple grew up the personal households of temple functionaries; it is not difficult to realize how houses and patches of land would become more and more distinctly the property of the occupiers, and more and more definitely alienated from the original owner-god. The earlier empires in Egypt and China both passed into a feudal stage, in which families, originally official, became for a time independent noble families. In the later stages of Babylonian civilization we find an increasing propertied class of people appearing in the social structure, neither slaves nor peasants nor priests nor officials, but widows and descendants of such people, or successful traders and the like, and all *masterless* folk. Traders came in from the outside. Babylon was full of Aramean traders, who had great establishments, with slaves, freed-men, employees of all sorts. (Their book-keeping was a serious undertaking. It involved storing a great multitude of earthenware tablets in huge earthenware jars.) Upon this gathering mixture of more or less free and detached people would live other people, traders, merchants, small dealers, catering for their needs. Sayce (*op. cit.*) gives the particulars of an agreement for the setting up and stocking of a tavern and beerhouse, for example. The passer-by, the man who happened to be about, had come into existence.

But another and far less kindly sort of slavery also arose in the old civilization, and that was gang slavery. If it did not figure very largely in the cities, it was very much in evidence elsewhere. The king was to begin with, the chief *entrepreneur*. He made the canals and organized the irrigation (*e.g.* Hammurabi's enterprises noted in the previous chapter). He exploited mines. He seems (at Cnossos, *e.g.*) to have organized manufactures for export. The Pharaohs of the 1st Dynasty were already working the copper and turquoise mines in the peninsula

[1] The student should compare with this J. J. Atkinson's account (in his *Primal Law*) of the significance of marriage by capture and his theory of the origin of marriage.

[2] See also his shorter *Social Life of the Babylonians and Assyrians.*

of Sinai. For many such purposes gangs of captives were cheaper and far more controllable than levies of the king's own people. From an early period, too, captives may have tugged the oars of the galleys, though Torr (*Ancient Ships*) notes that up to the age of Pericles (450 B.C.) the free Athenians were not above this task. And the monarch also found slaves convenient for his military expeditions. They were uprooted men; they did not fret to go home, because they had no homes to go to. The Pharaohs hunted slaves in Nubia, in order to have black troops for their Syrian expeditions. Closely allied to such slave troops were the mercenary barbaric troops the monarchs caught into their service, not by positive compulsion, but by the bribes of food and plunder and under the pressure of need. As the old civilization developed, these mercenary armies replaced the national levies of the old order more and more, and servile gang labour became a more and more important and significant factor in the economic system. From mines and canal and wall building, the servile gang spread into cultivation. Nobles and temples adopted the gang-slave system for their works. Plantation gangs began to oust the patch cultivation of the labourer-serf in the case of some staple products. . . .

Brawl among boatmen... (From tomb of Ptah-hetep — —Pyramid Age).

§ 3

So, in a few paragraphs, we trace the development of the simple social structure of the early Sumerian cities to the complex city crowds, the multitude of individuals varying in race, tradition, education, and function, varying in wealth, freedom, authority, and usefulness, in the great cities of the last thousand years B.C. The most notable thing of all is the gradual increase amidst this heterogeneous multitude of what we may call *free individuals*, detached persons who are neither priests, nor kings, nor officials, nor serfs, nor slaves, who are under no great pressure to work, who have time to read and inquire. They appear side by side with the development of social security and private property. Coined money and monetary reckoning developed. The operations of the Arameans and such-like Semitic trading people led to the organization of credit and monetary security. In the earlier days almost the only property, except a few movables, consisted of rights in land and in houses; later, one could deposit and lend securities, could go away and return to find one's property faithfully held and secure. Towards the middle of the period of the Persian Empire there lived one free individual, Herodotus, who has a great interest for us because he was among the first writers of critical and intelligent history, as distinguished from a mere priestly or court chronicle. It is worth while to glance here very briefly at the circumstances of his life. Later on we shall quote from his history.

We have already noted the conquest of Babylonia by the Aryan Persians under Cyrus in 539 B.C. We have noted, further, that the Persian Empire spread into Egypt, where its hold was precarious; and it extended also over Asia Minor. Herodotus was born about 484 B.C. in a Greek city of Asia Minor, Halicarnassus, which was under the overlordship of the Persians, and directly under the rule of a political boss or tyrant. There is no sign that he was obliged either to work for a living or spend very much time in the administration of his property. We do not know the particulars of his affairs, but it is clear that in this minor Greek city, under foreign rule, he was able to obtain and read and study manuscripts of nearly everything that had been written in the Greek language before his time. He travelled, so far as one can gather, with freedom and comfort about the Greek archipelagoes; he stayed wherever he wanted to stay, and he seems to have found comfortable accommodation; he went to Babylon and to Susa, the new capital the Persians had set up in Babylonia to the east of the Tigris; he toured along the coast of the Black Sea, and accumulated a considerable amount of knowledge about the Scythians, the Aryan people who were then distributed over South Russia; he went to the south of Italy, explored the antiquities of Tyre, coasted Palestine, landed at Gaza, and made a long stay in Egypt. He went about Egypt looking at temples and monuments and gathering information. We know not only from him, but from other evidence, that in those days the older temples and the pyramids (which were already nearly three thousand years old) were visited by strings of tourists, a special sort of priests acting as guides. The inscriptions the sightseers scribbled upon the walls remain to this day, and many of them have been deciphered and published.

As his knowledge accumulated, he conceived the idea of writing a great history of the attempts of Persia to subdue Greece. But in order to introduce that history he composed an account of the past of Greece, Persia, Assyria, Babylonia, Egypt, Scythia, and of the geography and peoples of those countries. He then set himself it is said, to make his history known among his friends in Halicarnassus by reciting it to them, but they failed to appreciate it; and he then betook himself to Athens, the most flourishing of all Greek cities at that time. There his work was received with applause. We find him in the centre of a brilliant circle of intelligent and active-minded people, and the city authorities voted him a reward of ten talents (a sum of money equivalent to £2,400) in recognition of his literary achievement. . . .

But we will not complete the biography of this most interesting man, nor will we enter into any criticism of his garrulous, marvel-telling, and most entertaining history. It is a book to which all intelligent readers come sooner or later, abounding as it does in illuminating errors and Boswellian charm. We give these particulars here simply to show that in the fifth century B.C. a new factor was becoming evident in human affairs. Reading and writing had already long escaped from the temple precincts and the ranks of the court scribes. Record was no longer confined to court and temple. A new sort of people, these people of leisure and independent means, were asking questions, exchanging knowledge and views, and developing ideas. So beneath the march of armies and the policies of monarchs, and above the common lives of illiterate and incurious men, we note the beginnings of what is becoming at last nowadays a dominant power in human affairs, the *free intelligence of mankind.*

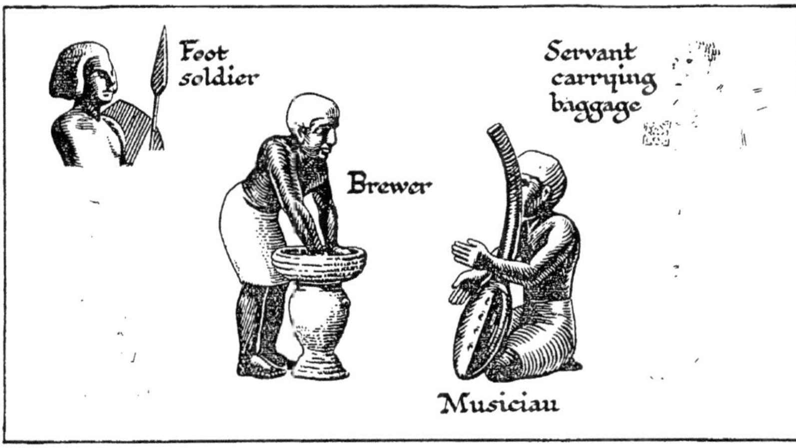

STATUETTES FROM MIDDLE-CLASS EGYPTIAN TOMBS SHOWING LOW-CLASS SOCIAL TYPES IN THE ANCIENT COMMUNITIES.

Of that free intelligence we shall have more to say when in a subsequent chapter we tell of the Greeks.

§ 4

We may summarize the discussion of the last two chapters here by making a list of the chief elements in this complicated accumulation of human beings which made up the later Babylonian and Egyptian civilizations of from two thousand five hundred to three thousand years ago. These elements grew up and became distinct one from another in the great river valleys of the

A ROYAL SCRIBE OF EGYPT

From the statue in the Louvre

"Under the Court system of 3,000 years ago, in Assyria, Babylon and Egypt were accumulated about the monarch his scribes . . . many had great establishments."

world in the course of five or six thousand years. They developed mental dispositions and traditions and attitudes of thought one to another. The civilization in which we live to-day is simply carrying on and still further developing and working out and rearranging these relationships. This is the world from which we inherit. It is only by the attentive study of their origins that we can detach ourselves from the prejudices and immediate ideas of the particular class to which we may belong, and begin to understand the social and political questions of our own time.

(1) First, then, came the priesthood, *the temple system*, which was the nucleus and the guiding intelligence about which the primitive civilizations grew. It was still in these later days a great power in the world, the chief repository of knowledge and tradition, an influence over the lives of every one, and a binding force to hold the community together. But it was no longer all-powerful, because its nature made it conservative and inadaptable. It no longer monopolized knowledge nor initiated fresh ideas. Learning had already leaked out to other less pledged and controlled people, who thought for themselves. About the temple system were grouped its priests and priestesses, its scribes, its physicians, its magicians, its lay brethren, treasurers, managers, directors, and the like. It owned great properties and often hoarded huge treasures.

(2) Over against the priesthood, and originally arising out of it, was the *court system*, headed by a king or a "king of kings," who was in later Assyria and Babylonia a sort of captain and lay controller of affairs, and in Egypt a god-man, who had released himself from the control of his priests. About the monarch were accumulated his scribes, counsellors, record keepers, agents, captains, and guards. Many of his officials, particularly his provincial officials, had great subordinate establishments, and were constantly tending to become independent. The nobility of the old river valley civilizations arose out of the court system. It was, therefore, a different thing in its origins from the nobility of the early Aryans, which was a republican nobility of elders and leading men.

(3) At the base of the social pyramid was the large and most necessary class in the community, *the tillers of the soil*. Their status varied from age to age and in different lands; they were free peasants paying taxes, or serfs of the god, or serfs or tenants of king or noble, or of a private owner, paying him a rent; in most cases tax or rent was paid in produce. In the states of the river valleys they were high cultivators, cultivating comparatively small holdings; they lived together for safety in villages, and had a common interest in maintaining their irrigation channels and a sense of community in their village life. The cultivation of the soil is an exacting occupation; the seasons and the harvest sunsets will not wait for men; children can be utilized at an early age, and so the cultivator class is generally a poorly educated, close-toiling class, superstitious by reason of ignorance and the uncertainty of the seasons, ill-informed and easily put upon. It is capable at times of great passive resistance, but it has no purpose in its round but crops and crops, to keep out of debt and hoard against bad times. So it has remained to our own days over the greater part of Europe and Asia.

(4) Differing widely in origin and quality from the tillers of the soil was *the artisan class*. At first, this was probably in part a town-slave class, in part it consisted of peasants who had specialized upon a craft. But in developing an art and mystery of its own, a technique that had to be learnt before it could be practised, each sort of craft probably developed a certain independence and a certain sense of community of its own. The artisans were able to get together and discuss their affairs more readily than the toilers on the land, and they were able to form guilds to restrict output, maintain rates of pay, and protect their common interest.

(5) As the power of the Babylonian rulers spread out beyond the original areas of good husbandry into grazing regions and less fertile districts, a class of *herdsmen* came into existence. In the case of Babylonia these were nomadic Semites, the Bedouin, like the Bedouin of to-day. They probably grazed their flocks over great areas much as the sheep ranchers of California do.[1] They were paid and esteemed much more highly than the husbandmen.

(6) The first *merchants* in the world were shipowners. like the people of Tyre and Cnossos, or nomads who carried and traded goods as they wandered between one area of primitive civilization and another. In the Babylonian and Assyrian world the traders were predominantly the Semitic Arameans, the ancestors of the modern

[1] See Mary Austin, *The Flock*.

Syrians. They became a distinct factor in the life of the community; they formed great households of their own. Usury developed largely in the last thousand years B.C. Traders needed accommodation; cultivators wished to anticipate their crops. Sayce (*op. cit.*) gives an account of the Babylonian banking-house of Egibi, which lasted through several generations and outlived the Chaldean Empire.

(7) A class of *small retailers*, one must suppose, came into existence with the complication of society during the later days of the first empires, but it was not probably of any great importance. It is difficult to understand how there could be much active retailing without small change, and there is little evidence of small change to be found either in Egypt or Mesopotamia.[1] Shekels and half-shekels of silver, weighing something between a quarter and half an ounce, are the lightest weights of stamped metal of which we find mention.

(8) A growing class of *independent property owners*.

(9) As the amenities of life increased, there grew up in the court, temples, and prosperous private houses a class of *domestic servants*, slaves or freed slaves, or young peasants taken into the household.

(10) *Gang workers.*—These were prisoners of war or debt slaves, or impressed or deported men.

(11) *Mercenary soldiers.*—These also were often captives or impressed men. Sometimes they were enlisted from friendly foreign populations in which the military spirit still prevailed.

(12) *Seamen.*

In modern political and economic discussions we are apt to talk rather glibly of "labour." Much has been made of the *solidarity of labour* and its sense of community. It is well to note that in these first civilizations, what we speak of as "labour" is represented by five distinct classes dissimilar in origin, traditions, and outlook—namely, classes 3, 4, 5, 9, 10, and the oar-tugging part of 12. The "solidarity of labour" is, we shall find when we come to study the mechanical revolution of the nineteenth century A.D., a new idea and a new possibility in human affairs.

[1] J. L. M. says this is the view of a Londoner. In a village or small town where everyone knows everyone, long credits are possible with barter. In Asia Minor there is much reckoning with quite imaginary money of account.

§ 5

Let us, before we leave this discussion of the social classes that were developing in these first civilizations, devote a little attention to their fixity. How far did they stand aloof from each other, and how far did they intermingle? So far as the classes we have counted as 9, 10, 11, and 12 go, the servants, the gang labourers and slaves, the gang soldiers, and, to a lesser extent the sailors, or at any rate the galley rowers among the sailors, they were largely recruited classes, they did not readily and easily form homes, they were not distinctively breeding classes; they were probably replenished generation after generation by captives, by the failures of other classes, and especially from the failures of the class of small retailers, and by persuasion and impressment from among the cultivators. But so far as the sailors go, we have to distinguish between the mere rower and the navigating and shipowning seamen of such ports as Tyre and Sidon. The shipowners pass, no doubt, by insensible gradations into the mercantile class, but the navigators must have made a peculiar community in the great seaports, having homes there and handing on the secrets of seacraft to their sons. The eighth class we have distinguished was certainly a precarious class, continually increased by the accession of the heirs and dependents, the widows and retired members of the wealthy and powerful, and continually diminished by the deaths or speculative losses of these people and the dispersal of their properties. The priests and priestesses too, so far as all this world west of India went, were not a very reproductive class; many priesthoods were celibate, and that class, too, may also be counted as a recruited class. Nor are servants, as a rule, reproductive. They live in the households of other people; they do not have households and rear large families of their own. This leaves us as the really vital classes of the ancient civilized community:

(*a*) The royal and aristocratic class, officials, military officers, and the like;
(*b*) The mercantile class;
(*c*) The town artisans;
(*d*) The cultivators of the soil; and
(*e*) The herdsmen.

Each of these classes reared its own children in its own fashion, and so naturally kept itself more or less continuously distinct from the others. General education was not organized in those ancient states, education was mainly a household matter (as it is still in many parts of India to-day), and so it was natural and necessary for the sons to follow in the footsteps of their father and to marry women accustomed to their own sort of household. Except during times of great political disturbance, therefore, there would be a natural and continuous separation of classes; which would not, however, prevent exceptional individuals from intermarrying or passing from one class to another. Poor aristocrats would marry rich members of the mercantile class; ambitious herdsmen, artisans, or sailors would become rich merchants. So far as one can gather, that was the general state of affairs in both Egypt and Babylonia. The idea was formerly entertained that in Egypt there was a fixity of classes, but this appears to be a misconception due to a misreading of Herodotus. The only exclusive class in Egypt which did not intermarry was, as in England to-day, the semi-divine royal family.

At various points in the social system there were probably developments of exclusiveness, an actual barring out of interlopers. Artisans of particular crafts possessing secrets, for example, have among all races and in all ages tended to develop guild organizations restricting the practice of their craft and the marriage of members outside their guild. Conquering people have also, and especially when there were marked physical differences of race, been disposed to keep themselves aloof from the conquered peoples, and have developed an aristocratic exclusiveness. Such organizations of restriction upon free intercourse have come and gone in great variety in the history of all long-standing civilizations. The natural boundaries of function were always there, but sometimes they have been drawn sharply and laid stress upon, and sometimes they have been made little of. There has been a general tendency among the Aryan peoples to distinguish noble (patrician) from common (plebeian) families; the traces of it are evident throughout the literature and life of Europe to-day, and it has received a picturesque enforcement in the "science" of heraldry. This tradition is still active even in democratic America. Germany, the most methodical of European countries, had in the Middle Ages a very clear conception of the fixity of such distinctions. Below the princes (who themselves constituted an exclusive class which did not marry beneath itself) there were the:

(*a*) Knights, the military and official caste, with heraldic coats-of-arms;

(*b* and *c*) The Bürgerstand, the merchants, shipping people, and artisans; and

(*d*) The Bauernstand, the cultivating serfs or peasants.

Mediæval Germany went as far as any of the Western heirs of the first great civilizations towards a fixation of classes. The idea is far less congenial both to the English-speaking people and to the French and Italians, who, by a sort of instinct, favour a free movement from class to class. Such exclusive ideas began at first among, and were promoted chiefly by, the upper classes, but it is a natural response and a natural Nemesis to such ideas that the mass of the excluded should presently range themselves in antagonism to their superiors. It was in Germany, as we shall see in the concluding chapters of this story, that the conception of a natural and necessary conflict, "the class war," between the miscellaneous multitudes of the disinherited ("the class-conscious proletariat" of the Marxist) and the rulers and merchants first arose. It was an idea more acceptable to the German mind than to the British or French. . . . But before we come to that conflict, we must traverse a long history of many centuries.

§ 6

If now we turn eastward from this main development of civilization in the world between Central Asia and the Atlantic, to the social development of India in the 2,000 years next before the Christian era, we find certain broad and very interesting differences. The first of these is that we find such a fixity of classes in process of establishment as no other part of the world can present. This fixity of classes is known to Europeans as the institution of *caste*;[1] its origins are still in complete obscurity, but it was certainly well rooted in the Ganges valley before the days of Alexander the Great. It is a complicated horizontal division of the social structure into classes or castes, the members of which may neither eat nor intermarry with persons of a lower caste under penalty of becoming outcasts, and who may also "lose caste" for various ceremonial negligences and defilements. By losing caste a man does not sink to a lower caste; he becomes outcast. The various subdivisions of caste are very complex; many are practically trade organizations. Each caste has its local organization which maintains discipline, distributes various charities, looks after its own poor, protects the common interests of its members, and

[1] From *casta*, a word of Portuguese origin; the Indian word is *varna*, colour.

examines the credentials of newcomers from other districts. (There is little to check the pretensions of a travelling Hindu to be of a higher caste than is legitimately his.) Originally, the four main castes seem to have been .

The Brahmins—the priests and teachers;
The Kshatriyas—the warriors;
The Vaisyas — herdsmen, merchants, moneylenders, and land-owners;
The Sudras;
And, outside the castes, the Pariahs.

But these primary divisions have long been superseded by the disappearance of the second and third primary castes, and the subdivision of the Brahmins and Sudras into a multitude of minor castes, all exclusive, each holding its members to one definite way of living and one group of associates.

Next to this extraordinary fission and complication of the social body we have to note that the Brahmins, the priests and teachers of the Indian world, unlike so many Western priesthoods, are a reproductive and exclusive class, taking no recruits from any other social stratum.

Whatever may have been the original incentive to this extensive fixation of class in India, there can be little doubt of the rôle played by the Brahmins as the custodians of tradition and the only teachers of the people in sustaining it. By some it is supposed that the first three of the four original castes, known also as the "twice born," were the descendants of the Vedic Aryan conquerors of India, who established these hard-and-fast separations to prevent racial mixing with the conquered Sudras and Pariahs. The Sudras are represented as a previous wave of northern conquerors, and the Pariahs are the original Dravidian inhabitants of India. But these speculations are not universally accepted, and it is, perhaps, rather the case that the uniform conditions of life in the Ganges valley throughout long centuries served to stereotype a difference of classes that have never had the same steadfastness of definition under the more various and variable conditions of the greater world to the west.

However caste arose, there can be no doubt of its extraordinary hold upon the Indian mind. In the sixth century B.C. arose Gautama, the great teacher of Buddhism, proclaiming, "As the four streams that flow into the Ganges lose their names as soon as they mingle their waters in the holy river, so all who believe in Buddha cease to be Brahmins, Kshatriyas, Vaisyas, and Sudras." His teaching prevailed in India for some centuries; it spread over China, Tibet, Japan, Burmah, Ceylon, Turkestan, Manchuria; it is to-day the religion of one-third of the human race, but it was finally defeated and driven out of Indian life by the vitality and persistence of the Brahmins and of their caste ideas. . . .

§ 7

In China we find a social system travelling along yet another, and only a very roughly parallel line to that followed by the Indian and Western civilizations. The Chinese civilization even more than the Hindu is organized for peace, and the warrior plays a small part in its social scheme. As in the Indian civilization, the leading class is an intellectual one; less priestly than the Brahmin and more official. But unlike the Brahmins, the mandarins, who are the literate men of China, are not a caste; one is not a mandarin by birth, but by education; they are drawn by education and examination from all classes of the community, and the son of a mandarin has no prescriptive right to succeed his father.[1] As a consequence of these differences, while the Brahmins of India are, as a class, ignorant even of their own sacred books, mentally slack, and full of a pretentious assurance, the Chinese mandarin has the energy that comes from hard mental work. But since his education so far has been almost entirely a scholarly study of the classical Chinese literature, his influence has been entirely conservative. Before the days of Alexander the Great, China had already formed itself and set its feet in the way in which it was still walking in the year 1900 A.D. Invaders and dynasties had come and gone, but the routine of life of the yellow civilization remained unchanged.

The traditional Chinese social system recognized four main classes below the priest-emperor.

(*a*) The literary class, which was equivalent partly to the officials of the Western world and partly to its teachers and clerics. In the time of Confucius its education included archery and horsemanship. Rites and music, history and mathematics completed the "Six Accomplishments."

(*b*) The cultivators of the land.

(*c*) The artisans.

(*d*) The mercantile class.

[1] In the time of Confucius classes were much more fixed than later. Under the Han dynasty the competitive examination system was not yet established. Scholars were recommended for appointments by local dignitaries, etc.—L. Y. C.

But since from the earliest times it has been the Chinese way to divide the landed possessions of a man among all his sons, there has never been in Chinese history any class of great land-owners, renting their land to tenants, such as most other countries have displayed. The Chinese land has always been cut up into small holdings, which are chiefly freeholds, and cultivated intensively. There are landlords in China who own one or a few farms and rent them to tenants, but there are no great, permanent estates. When a patch of land, by repeated division, is too small to sustain a man, it is sold to some prospering neighbour, and the former owner drifts to one of the great towns of China to join the mass of wage-earning workers there. In China, for many centuries, there have been these masses of town population with scarcely any property at all, men neither serfs nor slaves, but held to their daily work by their utter impecuniousness. From such masses it is that the soldiers needed by the Chinese Government are recruited, and also such gang labour as has been needed for the making of canals, the building of walls, and the like has been drawn.[1] The war captive and the slave class play a smaller part in Chinese history than in any more westerly record of these ages before the Christian era.

One fact, we may note, is common to all these three stories of developing social structure, and that is the immense power exercised by the educated class in the early stages before the crown or the commonalty began to read and, consequently, to think for itself. In India, by reason of their exclusiveness, the Brahmins, the educated class, retain their influence to this day; over the masses of China, along entirely different lines and because of the complexities of the written language, the mandarinate has prevailed. The diversity of race and tradition in the more various and eventful world of the West has delayed, and perhaps arrested for ever, any parallel organization of the specially intellectual elements of society into a class ascendancy. In the Western world, as we have already noted, education early "slopped over," and soaked away out of the control of any special class; it escaped from the limitation of castes and priesthoods and traditions into the general life of the community. Writing and reading had been simplified down to a point when it was no longer possible to make a cult and mystery of them. It may be due to the peculiar elaboration and difficulty of the Chinese characters, rather than to any racial difference, that the same thing did not happen to the same extent in China.

[1] The Grand Canal of China, the longer portion of which was made in the sixth century A.D., has a total length of nearly 900 miles. It was begun in the fifth century B.C. "Between Su-chow and Chin-kiang the canal is often 100 feet wide, and its sides are, in many places, faced with stone. It is spanned by fine stone bridges, and near its banks are many memorial arches and lofty pagodas." The Great Wall of China, which was begun in the third century B.C., was built originally to defend China against the Huns. It is about 1,500 miles long; its average height is between 20 and 30 feet, and every 200 yards there are towers 40 feet high.

§ 8

In these last six chapters we have traced in outline the whole process by which, in the course of 5,000 or 6,000 years—that is to say, in something between 150 and 200 generations—mankind passed from the stage of early Neolithic husbandry, in which the primitive skin-clad family tribe reaped and stored in their rude mud huts the wild-growing fodder and grain-bearing grasses with sickles of stone, to the days of the fourth century B.C., when all round the shores of the Mediterranean and up the Nile, and across Asia to India, and again over the great alluvial areas of China, spread the fields of human cultivation and busy cities, great temples, and the coming and going of human commerce. Galleys and lateen-sailed ships entered and left crowded harbours, and made their careful way from headland to headland and from headland to island, keeping always close to the land. Phœnician shipping under Egyptian owners was making its way into the East Indies and perhaps even further into the Pacific. Across the deserts of Africa and Arabia and through Turkestan toiled the caravans with their remote trade; silk was already coming from China, ivory from Central Africa, and tin from Britain to the centres of this new life in the world. Men had learnt to weave fine linen[2] and delicate fabrics of coloured wool; they could bleach and dye; they had iron as well as copper, bronze, silver, and gold; they had made the most beautiful pottery and porcelain; there was hardly a variety of precious stone in the world that they had not found and cut and polished; they could read and write; divert the course of rivers, pile pyramids, and make walls a thousand miles long. The fifty or sixty centuries in which all this had to be achieved may seem a long time in comparison with

[2] Damascus was already making Damask, and "Damascening" steel.

the threescore and ten years of a single human life, but it is utterly inconsiderable in comparison with the stretches of geological time. Measuring backward from these Alexandrian cities to the days of the first stone implements, the *rostro-carinate* implements of the Pliocene Age, gives us an extent of time fully a hundred times as long.

We have tried in this account, and with the help of maps and figures and time charts, to give a just idea of the order and shape of these fifty or sixty centuries. Our business is with that outline. We have named but a few names of individuals; though henceforth the personal names must increase in number. But the content of this outline that we have drawn here in a few diagrams and charts cannot but touch the imagination. If only we could look closelier, we should see through all these sixty centuries a procession of lives more and more akin in their fashion to our own. We have shown how the naked Palæolithic savage gave place to the Neolithic cultivator, a type of man still to be found in the backward places of the world. We have given an illustration of Sumerian soldiers copied from a carved stone that was set up long before the days when the Semitic Sargon I conquered the land. Day by day some busy brownish man carved those figures, and, no doubt, whistled as he carved. In those days the plain of the Egyptian delta was crowded with gangs of swarthy workmen unloading the stone that had come down the Nile to add a fresh course to the current pyramid. One might paint a thousand scenes from those ages: of some hawker merchant in Egypt spreading his stock of Babylonish garments before the eyes of some pretty, rich lady; of a miscellaneous crowd swarming between the pylons to some temple festival at Thebes; of an excited, dark-eyed audience of Cretans, like the Spaniards of to-day, watching a bull-fight, with the bull-fighters in trousers and tightly girded, exactly like any contemporary bull-fighter; of children learning their cuneiform signs—at Nippur the clay exercise tiles of a school have been found; of a woman with a sick husband at home slipping into some great temple in Carthage to make a vow for his recovery. Or perhaps it is a wild Greek, skin-clad and armed with a bronze axe, standing motionless on some Illyrian mountain crest, struck with amazement at his first vision of a many-oared Cretan galley crawling like a great insect across the amethystine mirror of the Adriatic Sea. He went home to tell his folk a strange story of a monster, Briareus with his hundred arms. Of millions of such stitches in each of these 200 generations is the fabric of this history woven. But unless they mark the presence of a primary seam or join, we cannot pause now to examine any of these stitches.

BOOK IV

JUDEA, GREECE, AND INDIA

XXI

THE HEBREW SCRIPTURES AND THE PROPHETS[1]

§ 1

WE are now in a position to place in their proper relationship to this general outline of human history the Israelites, and the most remarkable collection of ancient documents in the world, that collection which is known to all Christian peoples as the Old Testament. We find in these documents the most interesting and valuable lights upon the development of civilization, and the clearest indications of a new spirit that was coming into human affairs during the struggles of Egypt and Assyria for predominance in the world of men.

All the books that constitute the Old Testament were certainly in existence, and in very much their present form, at latest by the year 100 B.C. They were probably already recognized as sacred writings in the time of Alexander the Great (330 B.C.), and known and read with the utmost respect a hundred years before his time.[2] At that time some of them were of comparatively recent composition; others were already of very considerable antiquity. They were the sacred literature of a people, the Jews, who, except for a small remnant of common people, had recently been deported to Babylonia from their own country in 587 B.C. by Nebuchadnezzar II, the Chaldean. They had returned to their city, Jerusalem, and had rebuilt their temple there under the auspices of Cyrus, that Persian conqueror who, we have already noted, in 539 B.C. overthrew Nabonidus, the last of the Chaldean rulers in Babylon. The Babylonian Captivity had lasted about fifty years, and many authorities are of opinion that there was a considerable admixture during that period both of race and ideas with the Babylonians.

The position of the land of Judea and of Jerusalem, its capital, is a peculiar one. The country is a band-shaped strip between the Mediterranean to the west and the desert beyond the Jordan to the east; through it lies the natural high road between the Hittites, Syria, Assyria, and Babylonia to the north and Egypt to the south. It was a country predestined, therefore, to a stormy history. Across it Egypt, and whatever power was ascendant in the north, fought for empire; against its people they fought for a trade route. It had itself neither the area, the agricultural possibilities, nor the mineral wealth to be important. The story of its people that these scriptures have preserved runs like a commentary to the greater history of the two systems of civilization to the north and south and of the sea peoples to the west.

These scriptures consist of a number of different elements. The first five books, the *Pentateuch*, were early regarded with peculiar respect. They begin in the form of a universal history with a double account of the Creation of the world and mankind, of the early life of the race, and of a great Flood by which, except for certain favoured individuals, mankind was destroyed. Excavations have revealed Babylonian versions of both the Creation story and the Flood story of prior date to the restoration of the Jews, and it is therefore argued by Biblical critics that these opening chapters were acquired by the Jews during their captivity. They constitute the first ten chapters of Genesis. There follows a history of the fathers and founders of the Hebrew nation, Abraham, Isaac, and Jacob. They are presented as patriarchal Bedouin chiefs, living the life of nomadic shepherds in the country between Babylonia and Egypt. The existing Biblical account is said by the critics to be made up out of several pre-existing versions; but

[1] The *Encyclopædia Biblica* has been of great use here.

[2] This is probably much too early an estimate. The Book of Daniel was not written until 167-5 B.C. Ecclesiastes and several Psalms are later than Alexander.—G. W. B.

whatever its origins, the story, as we have it to-day, is full of colour and vitality. What is called Palestine to-day was at that time the land of Canaan, inhabited by a Semitic people called the Canaanites, closely related to the Phœnicians who founded Tyre and Sidon, and to the Amorites who took Babylon and, under Hammurabi, founded the first Babylonian Empire. The Canaanites were a settled folk in the days—which were perhaps contemporary with the days of Hammurabi—when Abraham's flocks and herds passed through the land. The God of Abraham, says the Bible narrative, promised this smiling land of prosperous cities to him and to his children. To the book of Genesis the reader must go to read how Abraham, being childless, doubted this promise, and of the births of Ishmael and Isaac. And in Genesis, too, he will find the lives of Isaac and Jacob, whose name was changed to Israel, and of the twelve sons of Israel; and how in the days of a great famine they went down into Egypt. With that, Genesis, the first book of the Pentateuch, ends. The next book, Exodus, is concerned with the story of Moses.

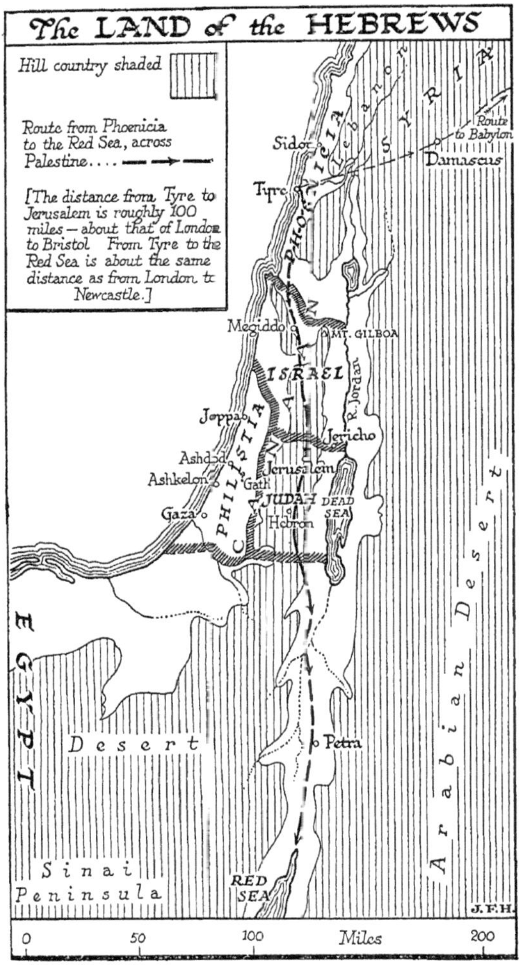

The story of the settlement and slavery of the children of Israel in Egypt is a difficult one. There is an Egyptian record of a settlement of certain Semitic peoples in the land of Goshen by the Pharaoh Rameses II, and it is stated that they were drawn into Egypt by want of food. But of the life and career of Moses there is no Egyptian record at all; there is no account of any plagues of Egypt or of any Pharaoh who was drowned in the Red Sea. There is much about the story of Moses that has a mythical flavour, and one of the most remarkable incidents in it, his concealment by his mother in an ark of bulrushes, has also been found in an ancient Sumerian inscription made at least a thousand years before his time by that Sargon I who founded the ancient Akkadian Sumerian Empire. It runs:

"Sargon, the powerful king, the king of Akkadia am I, my mother was poor, my father I knew not; the brother of my father lived in the mountains. . . . My mother, who was poor, secretly gave birth to me; she placed me in a *basket of reeds*, she shut up the mouth of it with bitumen, she abandoned me to the river, which did not overwhelm me. The river bore me away and brought me to Akki the irrigator. Akki the irrigator received me in the goodness of his heart. Akki the irrigator reared me to boyhood. Akki the irrigator made me a gardener. My service as a gardener was pleasing unto Istar and I became king."

This is perplexing. Still more perplexing

is the discovery of a clay tablet written by the Egyptian governors of a city in Canaan to the Pharaoh Amenophis IV, who came in the XVIIIth Dynasty before Rameses II, apparently mentioning the Hebrews by name and declaring that they are overrunning Canaan. Manifestly, if the Hebrews were conquering Canaan in the time of the XVIIIth Dynasty, they could not have been made captive and oppressed, before they conquered Canaan, by Rameses II of the XIXth Dynasty. But it is quite understandable that the Exodus story, written long after the events it narrates, may have concentrated and simplified, and perhaps personified and symbolized, what was really a long and complicated history of tribal invasions. One Hebrew tribe may have drifted down into Egypt and become enslaved, while the others were already attacking the outlying Canaanite cities. It is even possible that the land of the captivity was not Egypt (Hebrew, Misraim), but Misrim in the north of Arabia, on the other side of the Red Sea. These questions are discussed fully and acutely in the *Encyclopædia Biblica* (articles *Moses* and *Exodus*), to which the curious reader must be referred.[1]

Two other books of the Pentateuch, Deuteronomy and Leviticus, are concerned with the Law and the priestly rules. The book of Numbers takes up the wanderings of the Israelites in the desert and their invasion of Canaan.

Whatever the true particulars of the Hebrew invasion of Canaan may be, there can be no doubt that the country they invaded had changed very greatly since the days of the legendary promise, made centuries before, to Abraham. Then it seems to have been largely a Semitic land, with many prosperous trading cities. But great waves of strange peoples had washed along this coast. We have already told how the dark Iberian or Mediterranean peoples of Italy and Greece, the peoples of that Ægean civilization which culminated at Cnossos, were being assailed by the southward movement of Aryan-speaking races, such as the Italians and Greeks, and how Cnossos was sacked about 1,400 B.C., and destroyed altogether about 1,000 B.C. It is now evident that the people of these Ægean seaports were crossing the sea in search of securer land nests. They invaded the Egyptian delta and the African coast to the west, they formed alliances with the Hittites and other Aryan or Aryanized races. This happened after the time of Rameses II, in the time of Rameses III. Egyptian monuments record great sea fights, and also a march of these people along the coast of Palestine towards Egypt. Their transport was in the ox-carts characteristic of the Aryan tribes, and it is clear that these Cretans were acting in alliance with some early Aryan invaders. No connected narrative of these conflicts that went on between 1,300 B.C. and 1,000 B.C. has yet been made out, but it is evident from the Bible narrative, that when the Hebrews under Joshua pursued their slow subjugation of the promised land, they came against a new people, the Philistines, unknown to Abraham,[2] who were settling along the coast in a series of cities of which Gaza, Gath, Ashdod, Ascalon, and Joppa became the chief, who were really, like the Hebrews, newcomers, and probably chiefly these Cretans from the sea and from the north. The invasion, therefore, that began as an attack upon the Canaanites, speedily became a long and not very successful struggle for the coveted and promised land with these much more formidable newcomers, the Philistines.

It cannot be said that the promised land was ever completely in the grasp of the Hebrews. Following after the Pentateuch in the Bible come the books of Joshua, Judges, Ruth (a digression), Samuel I and II, and Kings I and II, with Chronicles repeating with variation much of the matter of Samuel II and Kings; there is a growing flavour of reality in most of this latter history, and in these books we find the Philistines steadfastly in possession of the fertile lowlands of the south, and the Canaanites and Phœnicians holding out against the Israelites in the north. The first triumphs of Joshua are not repeated. The book of Judges is a melancholy catalogue of failures. The people lose heart. They desert the worship of their own god Jehovah,[3] and worship Baal and Ashtaroth

[1] See also G. B. Gray, *A Critical Introduction to the Old Testament.*

[2] This may seem to contradict Genesis xx. 15, and xxi. and xxvi. various verses, but compare with this the *Encyclopædia Biblica* article *Philistines.*

[3] So this name should be spelt in English. It is now the fashion among the learned and among the sceptical to spell it Yahwe or Jahveh or Jahve, or in some such fashion. There is a justification for this in the fact that at first only the consonants were written in Hebrew, and then, for reasons into which we will not enter here, the wrong vowels were inserted in this name. But ever since the days of Tyndale's Bible, Jehovah has been established in English literature as the name of the God of Israel, and it is not to be lightly altered. There is at present a deplorable tendency to strange spelling among historians. Attention has already been called to the confusion that is being accumulated in people's minds by the variable spelling of Egyptologists, but the tendency is

(=Bel and Ishtar). They mixed their race with the Philistines, with the Hittites, and so forth, and became, as they have always subsequently been, a racially mixed people. Under a series of wise men and heroes they wage a generally unsuccessful and never very united warfare against their enemies. In succession they are conquered by the Moabites, the Canaanites, the Midianites, and the Philistines. The story of these conflicts, of Gideon and of Samson and the other heroes who now and then cast a gleam of hope upon the distresses of Israel, is told in the book of Judges. In the first book of Samuel is told the story of their great disaster at Ebenezer in the days when Eli was judge.

This was a real pitched battle in which the Israelites lost 30,000 (!) men. They had previously suffered a reverse and lost 4,000 men, and then they brought out their most sacred symbol, the Ark of the Covenant of God.

"And when the ark of the covenant of the Lord came into the camp, all Israel shouted with a great shout, so that the earth rang again. And when the Philistines heard the noise of the shout, they said, 'What meaneth the noise of this great shout in the camp of the Hebrews?' And they understood that the ark of the Lord was come into the camp. And the Philistines were afraid, for they said, 'God is come into the camp.' And they said, 'Woe unto us! for there hath not been such a thing heretofore. Woe unto us! who shall deliver us out of the hand of these mighty Gods? these are the Gods that smote the Egyptians with all the plagues in the wilderness. Be strong, and quit yourselves like men, O ye Philistines, that ye be not servants unto the Hebrews, as they have been to you: quit yourselves like men, and fight.'

"And the Philistines fought, and Israel was smitten, and they fled every man into his tent: and there was a very great slaughter, for there fell of Israel thirty thousand [1] footmen. And the ark of God was taken; and the two sons of Eli, Hophni and Phinehas, were slain.

"And there ran a man of Benjamin out of the army, and came to Shiloh the same day, with his clothes rent, and with earth upon his head. And when he came, lo, Eli sat upon a seat by the wayside watching: for his heart trembled for the ark of God. And when the man came into the city, and told it, all the city cried out. And when Eli heard the noise of the crying, he said, 'What meaneth the noise of this tumult?' And the man came in hastily, and told Eli. Now Eli was ninety and eight years old; and his eyes were dim that he could not see. And the man said unto Eli, 'I am he that came out of the army, and I fled to-day out of the army.' And he said, 'What is there done, my son?' And the messenger answered and said, 'Israel is fled before the Philistines, and there hath been also a great slaughter among the people, and thy two sons also, Hophni and Phinehas, are dead, and the ark of God is taken.' And it came to pass, when he made mention of the ark of God, that Eli fell from off the seat backward, by the side of the gate, and his neck brake, and he died: for he was an old man, and heavy. And he had judged Israel forty years.

"And his daughter in law, Phinehas' wife, was with child, near to be delivered: and when she heard the tidings that the ark of God was taken, and that her father in law and her husband were dead, she bowed herself and travailed: for her pains came upon

now almost universal among historical writers. In an otherwise admirable little book, *The Opening-up of Africa*, by Sir H. H. Johnston, for example, one finds him spelling Saul as Sha'ul, and Solomon as Shelomoh; Jerusalem becomes Yerusalim and the Hebrews, Habiru or Ibrim. Historians do not realize how the mind of the general reader is distressed and discouraged by these constantly fluctuating attempts to achieve phonetic exactitude. This treatment of old forms has much the same effect as the dazzle-painting of ships that went on during the submarine warfare. It is dazzle-spelling. The ordinary educated man is so confused that he fails altogether to recognize even his oldest friends under their modern disguises. He loses his way in the story hopelessly. The old events occur to novel names in unfamiliar places. He conceives a disgust for history in which no record seems to tally with any other record. Still more maddening and confusing is the variable spelling of Chinese names. A large part of the popular indifference to Chinese history may be due to the impossibility of holding on to the thread of a story in which one narrator talks of T'sin and another of Sin, and both forms mix themselves with Chin and T'chin. A boldly Europeanized name, such as Confucius, is far more readily grasped. Modern writers in their zeal for phonetics seem to have lost their sense of proportion. It is of far more importance not merely to civilization, but to the welfare, respect, and endowment of historians, that the general community should form clear and sound ideas of historical processes, than that it should pronounce the name Jehovah exactly as this or that learned gentleman believes it was pronounced by the Hebrews of the days of Ezra. A day may come in the future for one final, conclusive reform in the spelling of historical names. Meanwhile, it will probably save school teachers of history from endless confusion and muddle if they adhere firmly to the time-established spelling. Yet we have attempted no pedantic classicalism. The reader will find Peisistratus for Goldsmith's Pisistratus, the Arabic spelling of Muhammad, Kelt for Celt, and Habsburg taking the place of the older Hapsburg.

[1] Figures certainly exaggerated.—G. M.

her. And about the time of her death the women that stood by her said unto her, 'Fear not, for thou hast born a son.' But she answered not, neither did she regard it. And she named the child I-chabod,[1] saying, 'The glory is departed from Israel': because the ark of God was taken, and because of her father in law and her husband." (I. Sam., chap. iv.)

The successor of Eli and the last of the judges was Samuel, and at the end of his rule came an event in the history of Israel which paralleled and was suggested by the experience of the greater nations around. A king arose. We are told in vivid language the plain issue between the more ancient rule of priestcraft and the newer fashion in human affairs. It is impossible to avoid a second quotation.

"Then all the elders of Israel gathered themselves together, and came to Samuel unto Ramah, and said unto him: 'Behold, thou art old, and thy sons walk not in thy ways: now make us a king to judge us like all the nations.'

"But the thing displeased Samuel, when they said, 'Give us a king to judge us.' And Samuel prayed unto the Lord. And the Lord said unto Samuel, 'Hearken unto the voice of the people in all that they say unto thee: for they have not rejected thee, but they have rejected me, that I should not reign over them. According to all the works which they have done since the day that I brought them up out of Egypt even unto this day, wherewith they have forsaken me, and served other gods, so do they also unto thee. Now, therefore, hearken unto their voice: howbeit yet protest solemnly unto them, and shew them the manner of the king that shall reign over them.'

"And Samuel told all the words of the Lord unto the people that asked of him a king. And he said, 'This will be the manner of the king that shall reign over you: He will take your sons, and appoint them for himself, for his chariots, and to be his horsemen; and some shall run before his chariots. And he will appoint him captains over thousands, and captains over fifties; and will set them to ear his ground, and to reap his harvest, and to make his instruments of war, and instruments of his chariots. And he will take your daughters to be confectioners, and to be cooks, and to be bakers. And he will take your fields, and your vineyards, and your oliveyards, even the best of them, and give them to his servants. And he will take the tenth of your seed, and of your vineyards, and give to his officers, and to his servants. And he will take your menservants, and your maidservants, and your goodliest young men, and your asses, and put them to his work. He will take the tenth of your sheep: and ye shall be his servants. And ye shall cry out in that day because of your king which ye shall have chosen you; and the Lord will not hear you in that day.'

"Nevertheless, the people refused to obey the voice of Samuel; and they said, 'Nay; but we will have a king over us; that we also may be like all the nations; and that our king may judge us, and go out before us, and fight our battles.'" (I. Sam., chap. viii.)

§ 2

But the nature and position of their land was against the Hebrews, and their first king Saul was no more successful than their judges. The long intrigues of the adventurer David against Saul are told in the rest of the first book of Samuel, and the end of Saul was utter defeat upon Mount Gilboa. His army was overwhelmed by the Philistine archers.

"And it came to pass on the morrow, when the Philistines came to strip the slain, that they found Saul and his three sons fallen in mount Gilboa. And they cut off his head, and stripped off his armour, and sent into the land of the Philistines round about, to publish it in the house of their idols, and among the people. And they put his armour in the house of Ashtaroth; and they fastened his body to the wall of Beth-shan." (I. Sam., chap. xxxi.)

David (990 B.C. roughly) was more politic and successful than his predecessor, and he seems to have placed himself under the protection of Hiram, King of Tyre. This Phœnician alliance sustained him, and was the essential element in the greatness of his son Solomon. His story, with its constant assassinations and executions, reads rather like the history of some savage chief than of a civilized monarch. It is told with great vividness in the second book of Samuel.

The first book of Kings begins with the reign of King Solomon (960 B.C. roughly). The most interesting thing in that story, from the point of view of the general historian, is the relationship of Solomon to the national religion and the priesthood, and his dealings with the tabernacle, the priest Zadok, and the prophet Nathan.

The opening of Solomon's reign is as bloody

[1] That is, where is the glory?

as his father's. The last recorded speech of David arranges for the murder of Shimei; his last recorded word is "blood." "But his hoar head bring thou down to the grave with blood," he says, pointing out that though old Shimei is protected by a vow David had made to the Lord so long as David lives, there is nothing to bind Solomon in that matter. Solomon proceeds to murder his brother, who has sought the throne but quailed and made submission. He then deals freely with his brother's party. The weak hold of religion upon the racially and mentally confused Hebrews at that time is shown by the ease with which he replaces the hostile chief priest by his own adherent Zadok, and still more strikingly by the murder of Joab by Benaiah, Solomon's chief ruffian, in the tabernacle, while the victim is claiming sanctuary and holding to the very horns of Jehovah's altar. Then Solomon sets to work, in what was for that time a thoroughly modern spirit, to recast the religion of his people. He continues the alliance with Hiram, King of Sidon, who uses Solomon's kingdom as a high road by which to reach and build shipping upon the Red Sea, and a hitherto unheard-of wealth accumulates in Jerusalem as a result of this partnership. Gang labour appears in Israel; Solomon sends relays of men to cut cedarwood in Lebanon under Hiram, and organizes a service of porters through the land. (There is much in all this to remind the reader of the relations of some Central African chief to a European trading concern.) Solomon then builds a palace for himself, and a temple not nearly as big for Jehovah. Hitherto, the Ark of the Covenant, the divine symbol of these ancient Hebrews, had abode in a large tent, which had been shifted from one high place to another, and sacrifices had been offered to the God of Israel upon a number of different high places. Now the ark is brought into the golden splendours of the inner chamber of a temple of cedar-sheathed stone, and put between two great winged figures of gilded olivewood, and sacrifices are henceforth to be made only upon the altar before it.

This centralizing innovation will remind the reader of both Akhnaton and Nabonidus. Such things as this are done successfully only when the prestige and tradition and learning of the priestly order has sunken to a very low level.[1]

[1] But upon the question whether its "centralization" was the work of Solomon or a much later idea, cp. S. R. Driver, *Deuteronomy* (Int. Crit. Commentary.—G. W. B.

"And he appointed, according to the order of David his father, the courses of the priests to their service, and the Levites to their charges, to praise and minister before the priests, as the duty of every day required; the porters also by their courses at every gate; for so had David the man of God commanded. And they departed not from the commandment of the king unto the priests and Levites concerning any matter, or concerning the treasures."

Neither Solomon's establishment of the worship of Jehovah in Jerusalem upon this new footing, nor his vision of and conversation with his God at the opening of his reign, stood in the way of his developing a sort of theological flirtatiousness in his declining years. He married widely, if only for reasons of state and splendour, and he entertained his numerous wives by sacrificing to their national deities, to the Sidonian goddess Ashtaroth (Ishtar), to Chemosh (a Moabitish god), to Moloch, and so forth. The Bible account of Solomon does, in fact, show us a king and a confused people, both superstitious and mentally unstable, in no way more religious than any other people of the surrounding world.

A point of considerable interest in the story of Solomon, because it marks a phase in Egyptian affairs, is his marriage to a daughter of Pharaoh. This must have been one of the Pharaohs of the XXIst Dynasty. In the great days of Amenophis III, as the Tel Amarna letters witness, Pharaoh could condescend to receive a Babylonian princess into his harem, but he refused absolutely to grant so divine a creature as an Egyptian princess in marriage to the Babylonian monarch. It points to the steady decline of Egyptian prestige that now, three centuries later, such a petty monarch as Solomon could wed on equal terms with an Egyptian princess. There was, however, a revival with the next Egyptian dynasty (XXII); and the Pharaoh Shishak, the founder, taking advantage of the cleavage between Israel and Judah, which had been developing through the reigns of both David and Solomon, took Jerusalem and looted the all-too-brief splendours both of the new temple and of the king's house.

Shishak seems also to have subjugated Philistia. From this time onward it is to be noted that the Philistines fade in importance They had already lost their Cretan language and adopted that of the Semites they had conquered, and although their cities remain more or less independent, they merge gradually into the general Semitic life of Palestine.

There is evidence that the original rude but convincing narrative of Solomon's rule, of his various murders, of his association with Hiram, of his palace and temple building, and the extravagances that weakened and finally tore his kingdom in twain, has been subjected to extensive interpolations and expansions by a later writer, anxious to exaggerate his prosperity and glorify his wisdom. It is not the place here to deal with the criticism of Bible origins, but it is a matter of ordinary common sense rather than of scholarship to note the manifest reality and veracity of the main substance of the account of David and Solomon, an account explaining sometimes and justifying sometimes, but nevertheless relating facts, even the harshest facts, as only a contemporary or almost contemporary writer, convinced that they cannot be concealed, would relate them, and then to remark the sudden lapse into adulation when the inserted passages occur. It is a striking tribute to the power of the written assertion over realities in men's minds that this Bible narrative has imposed, not only upon the Christian, but upon the Moslem world, the belief that King Solomon was not only one of the most magnificent, but one of the wisest of men. Yet the first book of Kings tells in detail his utmost splendours, and beside the beauty and wonder of the buildings and organizations of such great monarchs as Thotmes III or Rameses II or half a dozen other Pharaohs, or of Sargon II or Sardanapalus or Nebuchadnezzar the Great, they are trivial. His temple measured internally was twenty cubits broad, about 35 feet [1]—that is, the breadth of a small villa residence—and sixty cubits say 100 feet, long. And as for his wisdom and statescraft, one need go no further than the Bible to see that Solomon was a mere helper in the wide-reaching schemes of the trader-king Hiram, and his kingdom a pawn between Phœnicia and Egypt. His importance was due largely to the temporary enfeeblement of Egypt, which encouraged the ambition of the Phœnician and made it necessary to propitiate the holder of the key to an alternate trade route to the East. To his own people Solomon was a wasteful and oppressive monarch, and already before his death his kingdom was splitting, visibly to all men.

With the reign of King Solomon the brief glory of the Hebrews ends; the northern and richer section of his kingdom, long oppressed by taxation to sustain his splendours, breaks off from Jerusalem to become the separate kingdom of Israel, and this split ruptures that linking connection between Sidon and the Red Sea by which Solomon's gleam of wealth was possible. There is no more wealth in Hebrew history. Jerusalem remains the capital of one tribe, the tribe of Judah, the capital of a land of barren hills, cut off by Philistia from the sea and surrounded by enemies.

The tale of wars, of religious conflicts, of usurpations, assassinations, and of fratricidal murders to secure the throne goes on for three centuries. It is a tale frankly barbaric. Israel wars with Judah and the neighbouring states; forms alliances first with one and then with the other. The power of Aramean Syria burns like a baleful star over the affairs of the Hebrews, and then there rises behind it the great and growing power of the last Assyrian empire. For three centuries the life of the Hebrews was like the life of a man who insists upon living in the middle of a busy thoroughfare, and is consequently being run over constantly by omnibuses and motor-lorries.

"Pul" (apparently the same person as Tiglath Pileser III) is, according to the Bible narrative, the first Assyrian monarch to appear upon the Hebrew horizon, and Menahem buys him off with a thousand talents of silver (738 B.C.). But the power of Assyria is heading straight for the now aged and decadent land of Egypt, and the line of attack lies through Judea; Tiglath Pileser III returns and Shalmaneser follows in his steps, the King of Israel intrigues for help with Egypt, that "broken reed," and in 721 B.C., as we have already noted, his kingdom is swept off into captivity and utterly lost to history. The same fate hung over Judah, but for a little while it was averted. The fate of Sennacherib's army in the reign of King Hezekiah (701 B.C.), and how he was murdered by his sons (II. Kings xix. 37), we have already mentioned. The subsequent subjugation of Egypt by Assyria finds no mention in Holy Writ, but it is clear that before the reign of Sennacherib, King Hezekiah had carried on a diplomatic correspondence with Babylon (700 B.C.), which was in revolt against Sargon II of Assyria. There followed the conquest of Egypt by Esarhaddon, and then for a time Assyria was occupied with her own troubles; the Scythians and Medes and Persians were pressing her on the north, and Babylon was in insurrection. As we have already noted,

[1] Estimates of the cubit vary. The greatest is 44 inches. This would extend the width to seventy-odd feet.

Egypt, relieved for a time from Assyrian pressure, entered upon a phase of revival, first under Psammetichus and then under Necho II.

Again the little country in between made mistakes in its alliances. But on neither side was there safety. Josiah opposed Necho, and was slain at the battle of Megiddo (608 B.C.). The king of Judah became an Egyptian tributary. Then when Necho, after pushing as far as the Euphrates, fell before Nebuchadnezzar II, Judah fell with him (604 B.C.). Nebuchadnezzar, after a trial of three puppet kings, carried off the greater part of the people into captivity in Babylon (586 B.C.), and the rest, after a rising and a massacre of Babylonian officials, took refuge from the vengeance of Chaldea in Egypt.

"And all the vessels of the house of God, great and small, and the treasures of the house of the Lord, and the treasures of the king, and of his princes; all these he brought to Babylon. And they burnt the house of God and brake down the wall of Jerusalem, and burnt all the palaces thereof with fire, and destroyed all the goodly vessels thereof. And them that had escaped from the sword carried he away to Babylon; where they were servants to him and his sons until the reign of the kingdom of Persia." (II. Chron. xxxvi. 18, 19, 20.)

So the four centuries of Hebrew kingship comes to an end. From first to last it was a mere incident in the larger and greater history of Egypt, Syria, Assyria, and Phœnicia. But out of it there were now to arise moral and intellectual consequences of primary importance to all mankind.

§ 3

The Jews who returned, after an interval of more than two generations, to Jerusalem from Babylonia in the time of Cyrus were a very different people from the warring Baal worshippers and Jehovah worshippers, the sacrificers in the high places and sacrificers at Jerusalem of the kingdoms of Israel and Judah. The plain fact of the Bible narrative is that the Jews went to Babylon barbarians and came back civilized. They went a confused and divided multitude, with no national self-consciousness; they came back with an intense and exclusive national spirit. They went with no common literature generally known to them, for it was only about forty years before the captivity that king Josiah is said to have discovered "a book of the law" in the temple (II. Kings xxii), and, besides that, there is not a hint in the record of any reading of books; and they returned with most of their material for the Old Testament. It is manifest that, relieved of their bickering and murderous kings, restrained from politics and in the intellectually stimulating atmosphere of that Babylonian world, the Jewish mind made a great step forward during the captivity.

It was an age of historical inquiry and learning in Babylonia. The Babylonian influences that had made Sardanapalus collect a great library of ancient writings in Nineveh were still at work. We have already told how Nabonidus was so preoccupied with antiquarian research as to neglect the defence of his kingdom against Cyrus. Everything, therefore, contributed to set the exiled Jews inquiring into their own history, and they found an inspiring leader in the prophet Ezekiel. From such hidden and forgotten records as they had with them, genealogies, contemporary histories of David, Solomon, and their other kings, legends and traditions, they made out and amplified their own story, and told it to Babylon and themselves. The story of the Creation and the Flood, much of the story of Moses, much of Samson, were probably incorporated from Babylonian sources.[1] When the Jews returned to Jerusalem, only the Pentateuch had been put together into one book, but the grouping of the rest of the historical books was bound to follow.

The rest of their literature remained for some centuries as separate books, to which a very variable amount of respect was paid. Some of the later books are frankly post-captivity compositions. Over all this literature were thrown certain leading ideas. There was an idea, which even these books themselves gainsay in detail, that all the people were pure-blooded children of Abraham; there was next an idea of a promise made by Jehovah to Abraham that he would exalt the Jewish race above all other races; and, thirdly, there was the belief first of all that Jehovah was the greatest and most powerful of tribal gods, and then that he was a god above all other gods, and at last that he was the only true god. The Jews became convinced at last, as a people, that they were the chosen people of the one God of all the earth.

And arising very naturally out of these three ideas, was a fourth, the idea of a

[1] But one version of the Creation story and the Eden story, though originally from Babylon, seem to have been known to the Hebrews before the exile.—G. W. B.

coming leader, a saviour, a Messiah who would realize the long-postponed promises of Jehovah.

This welding together of the Jews into one tradition-cemented people in the course of the "seventy years" is the first instance in history of the new power of the written word in human affairs. It was a mental consolidation that did much more than unite the people who returned to Jerusalem. This idea of belonging to a chosen race predestined to pre-eminence was a very attractive one. It possessed also those Jews who remained in Babylonia. Its literature reached the Jews now established in Egypt. It affected the mixed people who had been placed in Samaria, the old capital of the kings of Israel when the ten tribes were deported to Media. It inspired a great number of Babylonians and the like to claim Abraham as their father, and thrust their company upon the returning Jews. Ammonites and Moabites became adherents. The book of Nehemiah is full of the distress occasioned by this invasion of the privileges of the chosen. The Jews were already a people dispersed in many lands and cities, when their minds and hopes were unified and they became an exclusive people. But at first their exclusiveness is merely to preserve soundness of doctrine and worship, warned by such lamentable lapses as those of King Solomon. To genuine proselytes of whatever race, Judaism long held out welcoming arms.

To Phœnicians after the falls of Tyre and Carthage, conversion to Judaism must have been particularly easy and attractive. Their language was closely akin to Hebrew. It is possible that the great majority of African and Spanish Jews are really of Phœnician origin. There were also great Arabian accessions. In South Russia, as we shall note later, there were even Mongolian Jews.

§ 4

The historical books from Genesis to Nehemiah, upon which the idea of the promise to the chosen people had been imposed later, were no doubt the backbone of Jewish mental unity, but they by no means complete the Hebrew literature from which finally the Bible was made up. Of such books as Job, said to be an imitation of Greek tragedy, the Song of Solomon, the Psalms, Proverbs, and others, there is no time to write in this *Outline*, but it is necessary to deal with the books known as "the Prophets" with some fullness. For those books are almost the earliest and certainly the best evidence of the appearance of a new kind of leading in human affairs.[1]

These prophets are not a new class in the community; they are of the most various origins—Ezekiel was of the priestly caste and of priestly sympathies, and Amos was a shepherd; but they have this in common, that they bring into life a religious force outside the sacrifices and formalities of priesthood and temple. The earlier prophets seem most like the earlier priests, they are oracular, they give advice and foretell events; it is quite possible that at first, in the days when there were many high places in the land and religious ideas were comparatively unsettled, there was no great distinction between priest and prophet. The prophets danced, it would seem, somewhat after the Dervish fashion, and uttered oracles. Generally they wore a distinctive mantle of rough goatskin. They kept up the nomadic tradition as against the "new ways" of the settlement. But after the building of the temple and the organization of the priesthood, the prophetic type remains over and outside the formal religious scheme. They were probably always more or less of an annoyance to the priests. They became informal advisers upon public affairs, denouncers of sin and strange practices, "self-constituted," as we should say, having no sanction but an inner light. "Now the word of the Lord came unto"—so and so; that is the formula.

In the latter and most troubled days of the kingdom of Judah, as Egypt, North Arabia, Assyria, and then Babylonia closed like a vice upon the land, these prophets became very significant and powerful. Their appeal was to anxious and fearful minds, and at first their exhortation was chiefly towards repentance, the pulling down of this or that high place, the restoration of worship in Jerusalem, or the like. But through some of the prophecies there runs already a note like the note of what we call nowadays a "social reformer." The rich are "grinding the faces of the poor"; the luxurious are consuming the children's bread; influential and wealthy people make friends with and imitate the splendours and vices of foreigners, and sacrifice the common people to these new fashions; and this is hateful to Jehovah, who will certainly punish the land.

[1] For early Egyptian anticipations of the idea of a Messiah and of the prophetic style, see Breasted's *Development of Religion and Thought in Ancient Egypt*. A very good book on the Hebrew prophets is W. A. C. Allen's *Old Testament Prophets*.

But with the broadening of ideas that came with the Captivity, the tenor of prophecy broadens and changes. The jealous pettiness that disfigures the earlier tribal ideas of God gives place to a new idea of a god of universal righteousness. It is clear that the increasing influence of prophets was not confined to the Jewish people; it was something that was going on in those days all over the Semitic world. The breaking down of nations and kingdoms to form the great and changing empires of that age, the smashing up of cults and priesthoods, the mutual discrediting of temple by temple in their rivalries and disputes—all these influences were releasing men's minds to a freer and wider religious outlook. The temples had accumulated great stores of golden vessels and lost their hold upon the imaginations of men. It is difficult to estimate whether, amidst these constant wars, life had become more uncertain and unhappy than it had ever been before, but there can be no doubt that men had become more conscious of its miseries and insecurities. Except for the weak and the women, there remained little comfort or assurance in the sacrifices, ritual, and formal devotions of the temples. Such was the world to which the later prophets of Israel began to talk of the One God, and of a Promise that some day the world should come to peace and unity and happiness. This great God that men were now discovering lived in a temple "not made with hands, eternal in the heavens." There can be little doubt of a great body of such thought and utterance in Babylonia, Egypt, and throughout the Semitic east. The prophetic books of the Bible can be but specimens of the prophesyings of that time. . . .

We have already drawn attention to the gradual escape of writing and knowledge from their original limitation to the priesthood and the temple precincts, from the shell in which they were first developed and cherished. We have taken Herodotus as an interesting specimen of what we have called the free intelligence of mankind. Now here we are dealing with a similar overflow of moral ideas into the general community. The Hebrew prophets, and the steady expansion of their ideas towards one God in all the world, is a parallel development of the free conscience of mankind. From this time onward there runs through human thought, now weakly and obscurely, now gathering power, the idea of one rule in the world, and of a promise and possibility of an active and splendid peace and happiness in human affairs. From being a temple religion of the old type, the Jewish religion becomes, to a large extent, a prophetic and creative religion of a new type. Prophet succeeds prophet. Later on, as we shall tell, there was born a prophet of unprecedented power, Jesus, whose followers founded the great universal religion of Christianity. Still later Muhammad, another prophet, appears in Arabia and founds Islam. In spite of very distinctive features of their own, these two teachers do in a manner arise out of, and in succession to these Jewish prophets. It is not the place of the historian to discuss the truth and falsity of religion, but it is his business to record the appearance of great constructive ideas. Two thousand four hundred years ago, and six or seven or eight thousand years after the walls of the first Sumerian cities arose, the ideas of the moral unity of mankind and of a world peace had come into the world.[1]

[1] Fletcher H. Swift's *Education in Ancient Israel from Earliest Times to* A.D.70 is an interesting account of the way in which the Jewish religion, because it was a literature-sustained religion, led to the first efforts to provide elementary education for *all* the children in the community.

XXII

THE GREEKS AND THE PERSIANS[1]

§ 1

AND now our history must go back again to those Aryan-speaking peoples of whose early beginnings we have given an account in Chapters XIV and XV. We must, for the sake of precision, repeat here two warnings we have already given the reader: first, that we use the word Aryan in its widest sense, to express all the early peoples who spoke languages of the "Indo-Germanic" or "Indo-European" group; and, secondly, that when we use the word Aryan we do not imply any racial purity.

The original speakers of the fundamental Aryan language, 2,000 or 3,000 years B.C., were probably a specialized and distinctive Nordic race of fair white men, accustomed to forests and cattle, who wandered east of the Rhine and through the forests of the Danube valley, the Balkan peninsula, Asia Minor, and eastward to the north and west of the great Central Asian Sea; but very early they had encountered and mixed themselves extensively, and as they spread they continued to mix themselves with other races, with races of uncertain affinities in Asia Minor and with Iberian and Mediterranean peoples of the dark-haired white race. For instance, the Aryans, spreading and pressing westward in successive waves of Keltic-speaking peoples through Gaul and Britain and Ireland, mixed more and more with Iberian races, and were affected more and more by that Iberian blood and their speech by the characteristics of the language their Keltic tongue superseded. Other waves of Keltic peoples washed with diminishing force into Spain and Portugal, where to this day the pre-Keltic strain is altogether dominant although the languages spoken are Aryan. Northward, in Europe, the Aryan peoples were spreading into hitherto uninhabited country, and so remaining racially more purely Nordic blonds. They had already reached Scandinavia many centuries B.C.

From their original range of wandering, other Aryan tribes spread to the north as well as to the south of the Black Sea, and ultimately, as these seas shrank and made way for them, to the north and east of the Caspian, and so began to come into conflict with and mix also with Mongolian peoples of the Ural-Altaic linguistic group, the horse-keeping people of the grassy steppes of Central Asia. From these Mongolian races the Aryans seem to have acquired the use of the horse for riding and warfare. There were three or four prehistoric varieties or sub-species of horse in Europe and Asia, but it was the steppe or semi-desert lands that first gave horses of a build adapted to other than food uses.[2] All these peoples, it must be understood, shifted their ground rapidly, a succession of bad seasons might drive them many hundreds of miles, and it is only in a very rough and provisional manner that their "beats" can now be indicated. Every summer they went north, every winter they swung south again. This annual swing covered sometimes hundreds of miles. On our maps, for the sake of simplicity, we represent the shifting of nomadic peoples by a straight line; but really they moved in annual swings, as the broom of a servant who is sweeping out a passage swishes from side to side as she advances. Spreading round the north of the Black Sea, and probably to the north of the Caspian, from the range of the original Teutonic tribes of Central and North-central Europe to the Iranian peoples who became the Medes and Persians and (Aryan) Hindus, were the grazing lands of a confusion of tribes, about whom it is truer to be vague than precise, such as the Cimmerians, the Sarmatians, and

[1] Ridgeway's *Early History of Greece* has been used here, and Gilbert Murray's *Rise of the Greek Epic.*

[2] Roger Pocock's *Horses* is a good and readable book on these questions.

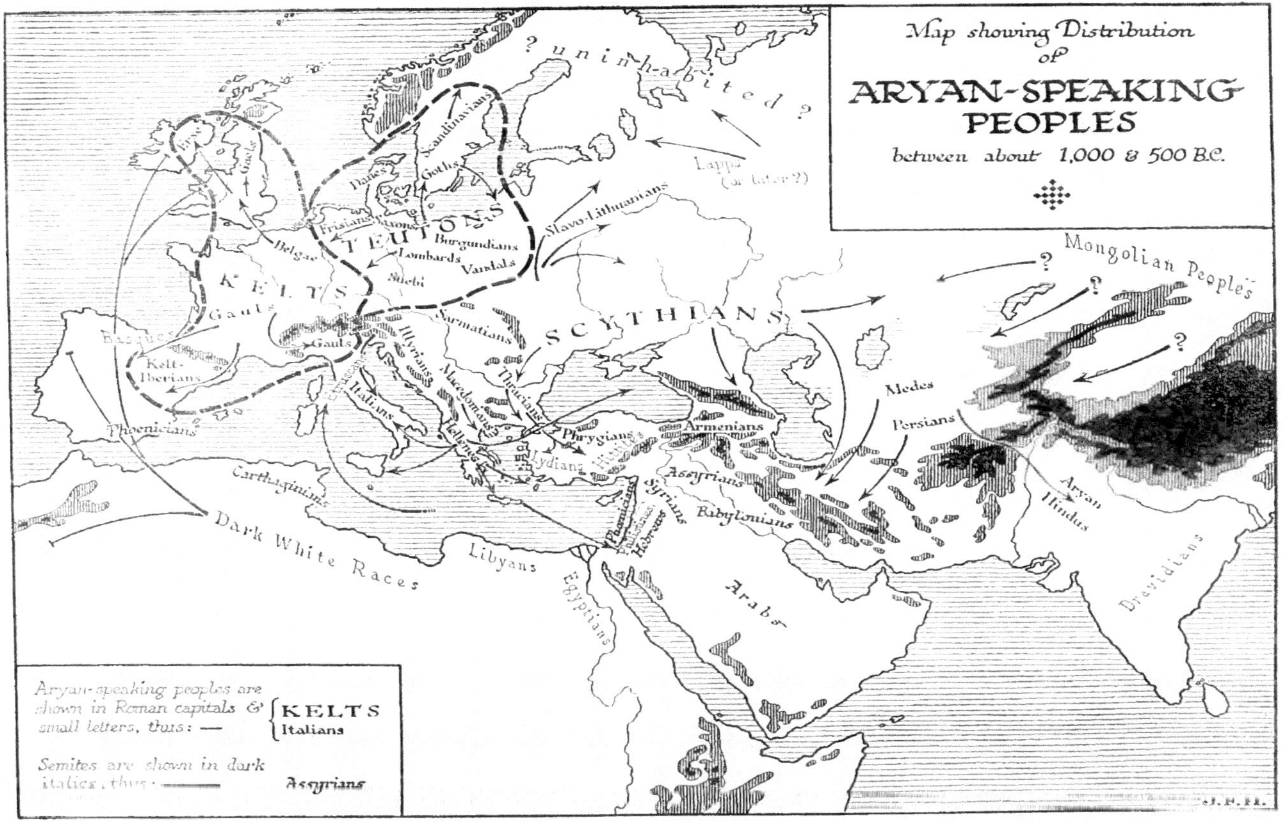
Map showing Distribution of
ARYAN-SPEAKING PEOPLES
between about 1,000 & 500 B.C.
? uninhabited ?
Lapps (or later?)
Mongolian Peoples
Scandinavians
Danes
Goths
Gaels
Erse
Frisians
Saxons
TEUTONS
Burgundians
Lombards
Vandals
Suebi
Belgae
KELTS
Gauls
Basques
Kelt-Iberians
Phoenicians
Slavo-Lithuanians
SCYTHIANS
Sarmatians
Illyrians
Etruscans
Italians
Macedonians
Thracians
Hellenes
Phrygians
Lydians
Hittites
Armenians
Assyrians
Syrians
Babylonians
Phoenicians
Philistines
Hebrews
Medes
Persians
Aryan Hindus
Dravidians
Arabs
Egyptians
Libyans
Carthaginians
Dark White Races
Aryan-speaking peoples are shown in Roman capitals & small letters, thus: — KELTS Italians
Semites are shown in dark italics, thus: — Assyrians
J.F.H.

those Scythians who, together with the Medes and Persians, came into effective contact with the Assyrian Empire by 1,000 B.C. or earlier.

East and south of the Black Sea, between the Danube and the Medes and Persians, and to the north of the Semitic and Mediterranean peoples of the sea coasts and peninsulas, ranged another series of equally ill-defined Aryan tribes, moving easily from place to place and intermixing freely—to the great confusion of historians. They seem, for instance, to have broken up and assimilated the Hittite civilization, which was probably pre-Aryan in its origin. They were, perhaps, not so far advanced along the nomadic line as the Scythians of the great plains.

The general characteristics of the original Aryan peoples we have already discussed in Chapter XV. They were a forest people, not a steppe people, and, consequently, wasteful of wood; they were a cattle people and not a horse people. The Greeks appear in the dim light before the dawn of history (say, 1,500 B.C.) as one of the wandering imperfectly nomadic Aryan peoples who were gradually extending the range of their pasturage southward into the Balkan peninsula and coming into conflict and mixing with that preceding Ægean civilization of which Cnossos was the crown.

In the Homeric poems these Greek tribes speak one common language, and a common tradition upheld by the epic poems keeps them together in a loose unity; they call their various tribes by a common name, *Hellenes*. They probably came in successive waves. Three main variations of the ancient Greek speech are distinguished: the Ionic, the Æolic, and the Doric. There was a great variety of dialects in Greece, almost every city having its own output of literature.[1] The Doric apparently constituted the last and most powerful wave of the migration. These Hellenic tribes conquered and largely destroyed the Ægean civilization that had preceded their arrival; upon its ashes they built up a civilization of their own. They took to the sea and crossed by way of the islands to Asia Minor; and, sailing through the Dardanelles and Bosphorus, spread their settlements along the south, and presently along the north borders of the Black Sea. They spread also over the south of Italy, which

[1] This is a little misleading. I may quote from C. D. Buch, *Introduction to the Study of Greek Dialects:* (*a*) "The great majority of the dialects play no rôle whatever in literature" (p. 14); (*b*) "In the course of literary development the dialects" (in a mixed and artificial form, *e.g.* the "epic" dialect) "came to be characteristic of certain classes of literature; and their rôle once established, the choice usually depended upon this factor, rather than upon the native dialect of the author" (p. 12). Speaking generally, each class of literature preserved the dialect of the region where it was first cultivated.

The following work is a most illuminating one on this subject: A. Meillet, *Aperçu d'une Histoire de la Langue Grecque* (Paris, 1913). —H. L. J.

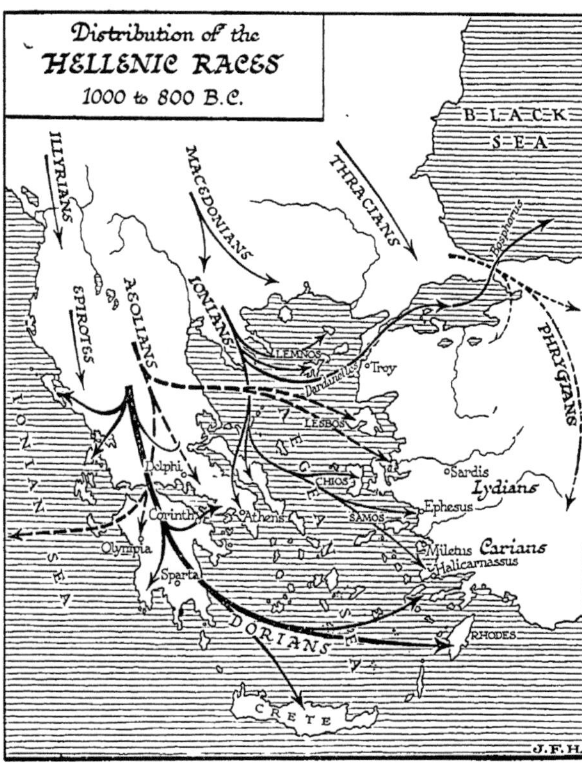

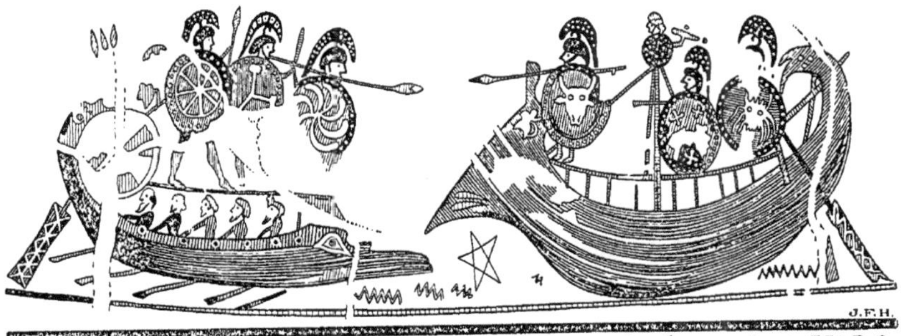

An early Greek sea-fight. From a painted vase, about 550 B.C.

was called at last Magna Græcia, and round the northern coast of the Mediterranean. They founded the town of Marseilles on the site of an earlier Phœnician colony. They began settlements in Sicily in rivalry with the Carthaginians as early as 735 B.C.

In the rear of the Greeks proper came the kindred Macedonians and Thracians; on their left wing, the Phrygians crossed by the Bosphorus into Asia Minor.

We find all this distribution of the Greeks effected before the beginnings of written history. By the seventh century B.C.—that is to say, by the time of the Babylonian captivity of the Jews—the landmarks of the ancient world of the pre-Hellenic civilization in Europe have been obliterated. Tiryns and Cnossos are unimportant sites; Mycenæ and Troy survive in legend; the great cities of this new Greek world are Athens, Sparta (the capital of Lacedemon), Corinth, Thebes, Samos, Miletus. The world our grandfathers called "Ancient Greece" had arisen on the forgotten ruins of a still more Ancient Greece, in many ways as civilized and artistic, of which to-day we are only beginning to learn through the labours of the excavator. But the newer Ancient Greece, of which we are now telling, still lives vividly in the imaginations and institutions of men because it spoke a beautiful and most expressive Aryan tongue akin to our own, and because it had taken over the Mediterranean alphabet and perfected it by the addition of vowels, so that reading and writing were now easy arts to learn and practise, and great numbers of people could master them and make a record for later ages.[1]

[1] Vowels were less necessary for the expression of a Semitic language. In the early Semitic alphabets only A, I, and U were provided with symbols, but for such a language as Greek, in which many of the inflectional endings are vowels, a variety of vowel signs was indispensable.

§ 2

Now this Greek civilization that we find growing up in South Italy and Greece and Asia Minor in the seventh century B.C., is a civilization differing in many important respects from the two great civilized systems whose growths we have already traced, that of the Nile and that of the Two Rivers of Mesopotamia. These civilizations grew through long ages where they are found; they grew slowly about a temple life out of a primitive agriculture; priest kings and god kings consolidated such early city states into empires. But the barbaric Greek herdsmen raiders came southward into a world whose civilization was already an old story. Shipping and agriculture, walled cities and writing were already there. The Greeks did not grow a civilization of their own; they wrecked one and put another together upon and out of the ruins.

To this we must ascribe the fact that there is no temple-state stage, no stage of priest kings, in the Greek record. The Greeks got at once to the city organization that in the east had grown round the temple. They took over the association of temple and city; the idea was ready-made for them. What impressed them most about the city was probably its wall. It is doubtful if they took to city life and citizenship straight away. At first they lived in open villages outside the ruins of the cities they had destroyed, but there stood the model for them, a continual suggestion. They thought first of a city as a safe place in a time of strife, and of the temple uncritically as a proper feature of the city. They came into this inheritance of a previous civilization with the ideas and traditions of the woodlands still strong in their minds. The heroic social system of the *Iliad* took possession of the land, and adapted itself to the new conditions. As history goes on the Greeks became more religious and superstitious as the faiths of the conquered welled up from below.[1]

We have already said that the social structure of the primitive Aryans was a two-class system of nobles and commoners, the classes not very sharply marked off from each other, and led in warfare by a king who was simply the head of one of the noble families, *primus inter pares*, a leader among his equals. With the conquest of the aboriginal population and with the building of towns there was added to this simple social arrangement of two classes a lower stratum of farm-workers and skilled and unskilled workers, who were for the most part slaves. But all the Greek communities were not of this "conquest" type. Some were "refugee" cities representing smashed communities, and in these the aboriginal substratum would be missing.

In many of the former cases the survivors of the earlier population formed a subject class, slaves of the state as a whole, as, for instance, the Helots in Sparta. The nobles and commoners became landlords and gentlemen farmers; it was they who directed the shipbuilding and engaged in trade. But some of the poorer free citizens followed mechanic arts, and, as we have already noted, would even pull an oar in a galley for pay. Such priests as there were in this Greek world were either the guardians of shrines and temples or sacrificial functionaries; Aristotle, in his *Politics*, makes them a mere subdivision of his official class. The citizen served as warrior in youth, ruler in his maturity, priest in his old age. The priestly *class*, in comparison with the equivalent class in Egypt and Babylonia, was small and insignificant. The gods of the Greeks proper, the gods of the heroic Greeks, were, as we have already noted, glorified human beings, and they were treated without very much fear or awe; but beneath these gods of the conquering freemen lurked other gods of the subjugated peoples, who found their furtive followers among slaves and women. The original Aryan gods were not expected to work miracles or control men's lives. But Greece, like most of the Eastern world in the thousand years B.C., was much addicted to consulting *oracles* or soothsayers. Delphi was particularly famous for its oracle. "When the Oldest Men in the tribe could not tell you the right thing to do," says Gilbert Murray, "you went to the blessed dead. All oracles were at the tombs of Heroes. They told you what was 'Themis,' what was the right thing to do, or, as religious people would put it now, what was the Will of the God."

The priests and priestesses of these temples were not united into one class, nor did they exercise any power as a class. It was the nobles and free commoners, two classes which, in some cases, merged into one common body of citizens, who constituted the Greek state. In many cases, especially in great city states, the population of slaves and unenfranchised strangers greatly outnumbered the citizens. But for them the state did not exist; it existed for the select body of citizens alone. It might or might not tolerate the outsider and the slave, but they had no legal voice in their treatment—any more than if it had been a despotism.[2]

This is a social structure differing widely from that of the Eastern monarchies. The exclusive importance of the Greek citizen

Rowers in an Athenian warship, about 400 B.C. (Fragment of relief found on the Acropolis)

[1] See Zimmern's *Greek Commonwealth*, Bury's *History of Greece*, and Barker's *Greek Political Theory*.

[2] "For them the state did not exist." This needs qualification. Cephalus, at whose house the conversation of Plato's *Republic* is placed, was a resident alien. He was a wealthy man in the best society, and taken as a type of the "happy man." His son, Lysias, was a leading orator. Even in the matter of the slaves: the Old Oligarch, in the "Constitution of Athens," complains that the Athenian slaves had no distinctive dress or manners, and so a gentleman could not even push one of them! In the *Republic* itself there is a description of the Democratic State, in which the slaves push you off the pavement. Moreover, even during the Peloponnesian War, there was no persecution of aliens and no expulsion of aliens from Athens. They were evidently a loyal and contented class. True, in time of food shortage, the claims of everybody to true citizenship were scrutinized more and more closely; but that was unavoidable.—G. M.

reminds one a little of the exclusive importance of the children of Israel in the later Jewish state, but there is no equivalent on the Greek side to the prophets and priests, nor to the idea of an overruling Jehovah.

Another contrast between the Greek states and any of the human communities to which we have hitherto given attention is their continuous and incurable division. The civilizations of Egypt, Sumeria, China, and no doubt North India, all began in a number of independent city states, each one a city with a few miles of dependent agricultural villages and cultivation around it, but out of this phase they passed by a process of coalescence into kingdoms and empires. But to the very end of their independent history the Greeks did not coalesce. Commonly, this is ascribed to the geographical conditions under which they lived. Greece is a country cut up into a multitude of valleys by mountain masses and arms of the sea that render intercommunication difficult; so difficult that few cities were able to hold many of the others in subjection for any length of time. Moreover, many Greek cities were on islands and scattered along remote coasts. To the end the largest city states of Greece remained smaller than many English counties; and some had an area of only a few square miles. Athens, the largest of the Greek cities, at the climax of its power had a population of perhaps a third of a million. Hardly any other Greek cities ever exceeded 50,000. Of this, half or more were slaves and strangers, and two-thirds of the free body women and children.

§ 3

The government of these city states varied very widely in its nature. As they settled down after their conquests the Greeks retained for a time the rule of their kings, but these kingdoms drifted back more and more to the rule of the aristocratic class. In Sparta (Lacedemon) kings were still distinguished in the sixth century B.C. The Lacedemonians had a curious system of a double kingship; two kings, drawn from different royal families, ruled together. But most of the Greek city states had become aristocratic republics long before the sixth century. There is, however, a tendency towards slackness and inefficiency in most families that rule by hereditary right; sooner or later they decline; and as the Greeks got out upon the seas and set up colonies and commerce extended, new rich families arose to jostle the old and bring new personalities into power. These *nouveaux riches* became members of an expanded ruling class, a mode of government known as oligarchy—in opposition to aristocracy—though, strictly, the term oligarchy (= government by the few) should of course include hereditary aristocracy as a special case.

In many cities persons of exceptional energy, taking advantage of some social conflict or class grievance, secured a more or less irregular power in the state. This combination of personality and opportunity has occurred in the United States of America, for example, where men exercising various kinds of informal power are called *bosses*. In Greece they were called *tyrants*. But the tyrant was rather more than a boss; he was recognized as a monarch, and claimed the authority of a monarch. The modern boss, on the other hand, shelters behind legal forms which he has "got hold of" and uses for his own ends. Tyrants were distinguished from kings, who claimed some sort of right, some family priority, for example, to rule. They were supported, perhaps, by the poorer class with a grievance; Peisistratus, for example, who was tyrant of Athens, with two intervals of exile, between 560 and 527 B.C., was supported by the poverty-struck Athenian hillmen. Sometimes, as in Greek Sicily, the tyrant stood for the rich against the poor. When, later on, the Persians began to subjugate the Greek cities of Asia Minor, they set up pro-Persian tyrants.

Aristotle, the great philosophical teacher, who was born under the hereditary Macedonian monarchy, and who was for some years tutor to the king's son, distinguishes in his *Politics* between kings who ruled by an admitted and inherent right, such as the King of Macedonia, whom he served, and tyrants who ruled without the consent of the governed. As a matter of fact, it is hard to conceive of a tyrant ruling without the consent of many, and the active participation of a substantial number of his subjects; and the devotion and unselfishness of your "true kings" has been known to rouse resentment and questioning. Aristotle was also able to say that while the king ruled for the good of the state, the tyrant ruled for his own good. Upon this point, as in his ability to regard slavery as a natural thing and to consider women unfit for freedom and political rights, Aristotle was in harmony with the trend of events about him.

A third form of government that prevailed increasingly in Greece in the sixth, fifth, and fourth centuries B.C., was known as *democracy*. As the modern world nowadays is constantly talking of democracy, and as the modern idea of democracy is something widely different from the democracy of the Greek city states, it will be well to be very explicit upon the meaning of democracy in Greece. Democracy then was government by the commonalty, the Demos; it was government by the whole body of the citizens, by the many as distinguished from the few. But let the modern reader mark that word "citizen." The slave was excluded, the freedman was excluded, the stranger; even the Greek born in the city, whose father had come eight or ten miles from the city beyond the headland, was excluded. The earlier democracies (but not all) demanded a property qualification from the citizen, and property in those days was land; this was subsequently relaxed, but the modern reader will grasp that here was something very different from modern democracy. At the end of the fifth century B.C. this property qualification had been abolished in Athens, for example; but Pericles, a great Athenian statesman of whom we shall have more to tell later, had established a law (451 B.C.) restricting citizenship to those who could establish Athenian descent on both sides. Thus, in the Greek democracies quite as much as in the oligarchies, the citizens formed *a close corporation*, ruling sometimes, as in the case of Athens in its great days, a big population of serfs, slaves, and "outlanders." A modern politician used to the idea, the entirely new and different idea, that democracy in its perfected form means that every adult man and woman shall have a voice in the government, would, if suddenly spirited back to the extremist Greek democracy, regard it as a kind of oligarchy. The only real difference between a Greek "oligarchy" and a Greek democracy was that in the former the poorer and less important citizens had no voice in the government, and in the latter every citizen had. Aristotle, in his *Politics*, betrays very clearly the practical outcome of this difference. Taxation sat lightly on the rich in the oligarchies; the democracies, on the other hand, taxed the rich, and generally paid the impecunious citizen a maintenance allowance and special fees. In Athens fees were paid to citizens even for attending the general assembly. But the generality of people outside the happy order of citizens worked and did what they were told, and if one desired the protection of the law, one sought a citizen to plead for one. For only the citizen had any standing in the law courts. Greek democracy was, in fact, a sort of government by a swarm of hereditary barristers. Our modern idea, that any one in the state is a citizen, would have shocked the privileged democrats of Athens profoundly.[1]

One obvious result of this monopolization of the state by the class of citizens was that the patriotism of these privileged people took an intense and narrow form. They would form alliances, but never coalesce with other city states. That would have obliterated every advantage by which they lived. There would have been no more fees, no more privileges. The narrow geographical limits of these Greek states added to the intensity of their feeling. A man's love for his country was reinforced by his love for his native town, his religion, and his home; for these were all one. Of course the slaves did not share in these feelings, and in the oligarchic states very often the excluded class got over its dislike of foreigners in its greater dislike of the class at home which oppressed it. But in the main, patriotism in the Greek was a personal passion of an inspiring and dangerous intensity. Like rejected love, it was apt to turn into something very like hatred. The Greek exile resembled the French or Russian *émigré* in being ready to treat his beloved country pretty roughly in order to save her from the devils in human form who had taken possession of her and turned *him* out.

In the fifth century B.C. Athens formed a system of relationships with a number of other Greek city states which is often spoken of by historians as the Athenian Empire. But all the other city states retained their own governments. One "new fact" added by the Athenian Empire was the complete and effective suppression of piracy; another was the institution of a sort of international law. The law indeed was Athenian law; but actions could now be brought and justice administered between citizens of the different states of the League, which of course had not been possible

[1] I do not agree with "hereditary barristers" or "fee-hunting." The Athenian dicasts were not barristers, but judges: they sat in panels (sometimes a panel of some hundreds) and judged. They had to be paid for attendance as judges (don't we pay jurymen?) because it took them away from their work as potters, dyers, and stone-masons. Pay was a genuine and good democratic institution; it was just what made possible the ordinary citizen's co-operation in the life of the state, and stopped its business from being the perquisite of the rich. I feel strongly that the text is unjust to Athens.—E. B.

See Zimmern's *Greek Commonwealth*, and Barker's *Greek Political Theory*, pp. 29-30.

before. The Athenian Empire had really developed out of a league of mutual defence against Persia; its seat had originally been in the island of Delos, and the allies had contributed to a common treasure at Delos; the treasure of Delos was carried off to Athens because it was exposed to a possible Persian raid. Then one city after another offered a monetary contribution instead of military service, with the result that in the end Athens was doing almost all the work and receiving almost all the money. She was supported by one or two of the larger islands. The "League" in this way became gradually an "Empire," but the citizens of the allied states remained, except where there were special treaties of intermarriage and the like, practically foreigners to one another. And it was chiefly the poorer citizens of Athens who sustained this empire by their most vigorous and incessant personal service. Every citizen was liable to military service at home or abroad between the ages of eighteen and sixty, sometimes on purely Athenian affairs and sometimes in defence of the cities of the Empire whose citizens had bought themselves off. There was probably no single man over twenty-five in the Athenian Assembly who had not served in several campaigns in different parts of the Mediterranean or Black Sea, and who did not expect to serve again. Modern imperialism is denounced by its opponents as the exploitation of the world by the rich; Athenian imperialism was the exploitation of the world by the poorer citizens of Athens.

Another difference from modern conditions, due to the small size of the Greek city states, was that in a democracy every citizen had the right to attend and speak and vote in the popular assembly. For most cities this meant a gathering of only a few hundred people; the greatest had no more than some thousands of citizens. Nothing of this sort is possible in a modern "democracy" with, perhaps, several million voters. The modern "citizen's" voice in public affairs is limited to the right to vote for one or other of the party candidates put before him. He, or she, is then supposed to have "assented" to the resultant government. Aristotle, who would have enjoyed the electoral methods of our modern democracies keenly, points out very subtly how the outlying farmer class of citizens in a democracy can be virtually disenfranchised by calling the popular assembly too frequently for their regular attendance. In the later Greek democracies (fifth century) the appointment of public officials, except in the case of officers requiring very special knowledge, was by casting lots. This was supposed to protect the general corporation of privileged citizens from the continued predominance of rich, influential, and conspicuously able men.

Some democracies (Athens and Miletus, *e.g.*) had an institution called the ostracism,[1] by which in times of crisis and conflict the decision was made whether some citizen should go into exile for ten years. This may strike a modern reader as an envious institution, but that was not its essential quality. It was, says Gilbert Murray, a way of arriving at a decision in a case when political feeling was so divided as to threaten a deadlock. There were in the Greek democracies parties and party leaders, but no regular government in office and no regular opposition. There was no way, therefore, of carrying out a policy, although it might be the popular policy, if a strong leader or a strong group stood out against it. But by the ostracism, the least popular or the least trusted of the chief leaders in the divided community was made to retire for a period without loss of honour or property. Professor Murray suggests that a Greek democracy, if it had found itself in such a position of deadlock as the British Empire did upon the question of Home Rule for Ireland in 1914, would have probably first ostracized Sir Edward Carson, and then proceeded to carry out the provisions of the Home Rule Bill.

This institution of the ostracism has immortalized one obscure and rather illiterate member of the democracy of Athens. A certain Aristides had gained a great reputation in the law court for his righteous dealing. He fell into a dispute with Themistocles upon a question of naval policy; Aristides was for the army, Themistocles was a "strong navy" man, and a deadlock was threatened. There was resort to an ostracism to decide between them. Plutarch relates that as Aristides walked through the streets while the voting was in progress, he was accosted by a strange citizen from the agricultural environs unaccustomed to the art of writing, and requested to write his own name on the proffered potsherd.

"But why?" he asked. "Has Aristides ever injured you?"

"No," said the citizen. "No. Never have I set eyes on him. But, oh! I am so *bored* by hearing him called Aristides the Just."

[1] From *ostrakon*, a tile; the voter wrote the name on a tile or shell.

ARISTIDES AND THE PEASANT

From the picture by E. E. Killemacker in the Dijon Museum

"A strange citizen accosted Aristides and requested him to write his own name on the proffered potsherd."

Whereupon, says Plutarch, without further parley Aristides wrote as the man desired. . . .

When one understands the true meaning of these Greek constitutions, and in particular the limitation of all power, whether in the democracies or the oligarchies, to a locally privileged class, one realizes how impossible was any effective union of the hundreds of Greek cities scattered about the Mediterranean region, or even of any effective co-operation between them for a common end. Each city was in the hands of a few or a few hundred men, to whom its separateness meant everything that was worth having in life. Only conquest from the outside could unite the Greeks, and until Greece was conquered they had no political unity. When at last they were conquered, they were conquered so completely that their unity ceased to be of any importance even to themselves; it was a unity of subjugation.

Yet there was always a certain tradition of unity between all the Greeks, based on a common language and script, on the common possession of the heroic epics, and on the continuous intercourse that the maritime position of the states made possible. And in addition, there were certain religious bonds of a unifying kind. Certain shrines, the shrines of the god Apollo in the island of Delos and at Delphi, for example, were sustained not by single states, but by leagues of states or Amphictyonies (=League of neighbours), which in such instances as the Delphic amphictyony became very wide-reaching unions. The league protected the shrine and the safety of pilgrims, kept up the roads leading thereunto, secured peace at the time of special festivals, upheld certain rules to mitigate the usages of war among its members, and—the Delian league especially—suppressed piracy. A still more important link of Hellenic union was the Olympian games that were held every four years at Olympia. Foot races, boxing, wrestling, javelin throwing, quoit throwing, jumping, and chariot and horse racing were the chief sports, and a record of victors and distinguished visitors was kept. From the year 776 B.C. onward [1] these games were held regularly for over a thousand years, and they did much to maintain that sense of a common Greek life (pan-Hellenic) transcending the narrow politics of the city states.

Such links of sentiment and association were of little avail against the intense "separatism" of the Greek political institutions. From the History of Herodotus the student will be able to gather a sense of the intensity and persistence of the feuds that kept the Greek world in a state of chronic warfare. In the old days (say, to the sixth century B.C.) fairly large families prevailed in Greece, and something of the old Aryan great household system (see Chap. XV), with its strong clan feeling and its capacity for maintaining an enduring feud, still remained. The history of Athens circles for many years about the feud of two great families, the Alcmæonidæ and the Peisistratidæ; the latter equally an aristocratic family, but founding its power on the support of the poorer class of the populace and the exploitation of their grievances. Later on, in the sixth and fifth centuries, a limitation of births and a shrinkage of families to two or three members—a process Aristotle notes without perceiving its cause—led to the disappearance of the old aristocratic clans, and the later wars were due rather to trade disputes and grievances caused and stirred up by individual adventurers than to family vendettas.

It is easy to understand, in view of this intense separatism of the Greeks, how readily the Ionians of Asia and of the islands fell first under the domination of the kingdom of Lydia, and then under that of the Persians when Cyrus overthrew Crœsus, the king of Lydia. They rebelled only to be reconquered. Then came the turn of European Greece. It is a matter of astonishment, the Greeks themselves were astonished, to find that Greece itself did not fall under the dominion of the Persians, these barbaric Aryan masters of the ancient civilizations of Western Asia. But before we tell of this struggle we must give some attention to these Asiatics against whom they were pitted; and particularly to these Medes and Persians who, by 538 B.C., were already in possession of the ancient civilizations of Assyria, Babylonia, and about to subjugate Egypt.

§ 4

We have had occasion to mention the kingdom of Lydia, and it may be well to give a short note here upon the Lydians before proceeding with our story. The original population of the larger part of Asia Minor may perhaps have been akin to the original population of Greece and Crete. If so, it was of "Mediterranean" race. Or it may have been another branch of those still

[1] 776 B.C. is the year of the First Olympiad, a valuable starting-point in Greek chronology.

more generalized and fundamental darkish peoples from whom arose the Mediterranean race to the west and the Dravidians to the east. Remains of the same sort of art that distinguishes Cnossos and Mycenæ are to be found scattered over Asia Minor. But just as the Nordic Greeks poured southward into Greece to conquer and mix with the aborigines, so did other and kindred Nordic tribes pour over the Bosphorus into Asia Minor. Over some areas these Aryan peoples prevailed altogether, and became the bulk of the inhabitants and retained their Aryan speech. Such were the Phrygians, a people whose language was almost as close to that of the Greeks as the Macedonian. But over other areas the Aryans did not so prevail. In Lydia the original race and their language held their own. The Lydians were a non-Aryan people speaking a non-Aryan speech, of which at the present time only a few words are known. Their capital city was Sardis.

Their religion was also non-Aryan. They worshipped a Great Mother goddess. The Phrygians also, though retaining their Greek-like language, became infected with mysterious religion, and much of the mystical religion and secret ceremonial that pervaded Athens at a later date was Phrygian (when not Thracian) in origin.

At first the Lydians held the western sea-coast of Asia Minor, but they were driven back from it by the establishment of Ionian Greeks coming by the sea and founding cities. Later on, however, these Ionian Greek cities were brought into subjection by the Lydian kings.

The history of this country is not clearly known, and were it known it would scarcely be of sufficient importance to be related in this historical outline, but in the eighth century B.C. one monarch, named Gyges, becomes noteworthy. The country under his rule was subjected to another Aryan invasion; certain nomadic tribes called the Cimmerians came pouring across Asia Minor, and they were driven back with difficulty by Gyges and his son and grandson. Sardis was twice taken and burnt by these barbarians. And it is on record that Gyges paid tribute to Sardanapalus, which serves to link him up with our general ideas of the history of Assyria, Israel, and Egypt. Later, Gyges rebelled against Assyria, and sent troops to help Psammetichus I to liberate Egypt from its brief servitude to the Assyrians.

It was Alyattes, the grandson of Gyges, who made Lydia into a considerable power. He reigned for seven years, and he reduced most of the Ionian cities of Asia Minor to subjection. The country became the centre of a great trade between Asia and Europe; it had always been productive and rich in gold, and now the Lydian monarch was reputed the richest in Asia. There was a great coming and going between the Black and Mediterranean Seas, and between the East and West. We have already noted that Lydia was reputed to be the first country in the world to produce coined money, and to provide the convenience of inns for travellers and traders. The Lydian dynasty seems to have been a trading dynasty of the type of Minos in Crete, with a banking and financial development. . . . So much we may note of Lydia by way of preface to the next section.

§ 5

Now while one series of Aryan-speaking invaders had developed along the lines we have described in Greece, Magna Græcia, and around the shores of the Black Sea, another series of Aryan-speaking peoples, whose originally Nordic blood was perhaps already mixed with a Mongolian element, were settling and spreading to the north and east of the Assyrian and Babylonian empires. We have already spoken of the arc-like dispersion of the Nordic Aryan peoples to the north of the Black and Caspian Seas; it was probably by this route that the Aryan-speaking races gradually came down into what is now the Persian country, and spread, on the one hand, eastward to India (? 2,000 to 1,000 B.C.), and on the other, increased and multiplied in the Persian uplands until they were strong enough to assail first Assyria (650 B.C.) and then Babylon (538 B.C.).

There is much that is not yet clear about the changes of climate that have been going on in Europe and Asia during the last 10,000 years. The ice of the last glacial age receded gradually, and gave way to a long period of steppe or prairie-like conditions over the great plain of Europe. About 12,000 or 10,000 years ago, as it is reckoned now, this state of affairs was giving place to forest conditions. We have already noted how, as a consequence of these changes, the Solutrian horse hunters gave place to Magdalenian fishers and forest deer hunters; and these, again, to the Neolithic herdsmen and agriculturists. For some thousands of years the European climate seems to have been warmer than it is to-day. A great sea spread from the coast of the Balkan peninsula far into Central Asia and extended northward into Central Russia, and the shrinkage of that sea and the consequent hardening of the climate of south Russia and Central Asia was going on contemporaneously with the development of the first civilizations in the river valleys. Many facts seem to point to a more genial climate in Europe and western Asia, and still more strongly to a greater luxuriance of plant and vegetable life, 4,000 to 3,000 years ago, than we find to-day. There were forests then in south Russia and in the country which is now Western Turkestan, where now steppes and deserts prevail. On the other hand, between 1,500 and 2,000 years ago, the Aral-Caspian region was probably drier and those seas smaller than they are at the present time.

We may note in this connection that Thotmes III (say, the fifteenth century B.C.), in his expedition beyond the Euphrates, hunted a herd of 120 elephants in that region. Again, an Ægean dagger from Mycenæ, dating about 2,000 B.C., shows a lion-hunt in progress. The hunters carry big shields and spears, and stand in rows one behind the other. The first man spears the lion, and when the wounded beast leaps at him, drops flat under the protection of his big shield, leaving the next man to repeat his stroke, and so on, until the lion is speared to death. This method of hunting is practised by the Masai to-day, and could only have been worked out by a people in a land where lions were abundant. But abundant lions imply abundant game, and that again means abundant vegetation. About 2,000 B.C. the hardening of the climate in the central parts of the Old World, to which we have already referred, which put an end to elephants and lions in Asia Minor and Greece,[1] was turning the faces of the nomadic Aryan peoples southward towards the fields and forests of the more settled and civilized nations.

These Aryan peoples come down from the East Caspian regions into history about the time that Mycenæ and Troy and Cnossos are falling to the Greeks. It is difficult to disentangle the different tribes and races that appear under a multitude of names in the records and inscriptions that record their first appearance, but, fortunately, these distinctions are not needed in an elementary outline such as this present history. A people called the Cimmerians appear in the districts of Lake Urumiya and Van, and shortly after Aryans have spread from Armenia to Elam. In the ninth century B.C., a people called the Medes, very closely related to the Persians to the east of them, appear in the Assyrian inscriptions. Tiglath Pileser III and Sargon II, names already familiar in this story, profess to have made them pay tribute. They are spoken of in the inscriptions as the "dangerous Medes." They are as yet a tribal people, not united under one king.

About the ninth century B.C. Elam and the Elamites, whose capital was Susa, a people which possessed a tradition and civilization at least as old as the Sumerian, suddenly vanish from history. We do not know what happened. They seem to have been overrun and the population absorbed by the conquerors. Susa is in the hands of the Persians.

A fourth people, related to these Aryan tribes, who appear at this time in the

[1] It is, at least, doubtful whether any change of climate expelled either lion or elephant from south-east Europe and Asia Minor; the cause of their gradual disappearance was—I think—nothing but Man, increasingly well armed for the chase. Lions lingered in the Balkan peninsula till about the fourth century B.C., if not later. Elephants had perhaps disappeared from western Asia by the eighth century B.C. The lion (much bigger than the existing form) stayed on in southern Germany till the Neolithic period. The panther inhabited Greece, southern Italy, and southern Spain likewise till the beginning of the historical period (say 1,000 B.C.).—H. H. J.

ONE OF THE FEW EXISTING REPRESENTATIONS OF THE ANCIENT SCYTHIANS: FROM A GREEK ELECTRUM VASE.

narrative of Herodotus, are the "Scythians." For a while the monarchs of Assyria play off these various kindred peoples, the Cimmerians, the Medes, the Persians, and the Scythians, against each other. Assyrian princesses (a daughter of Esarhaddon, *e.g.*) are married to Scythian chiefs. Nebuchadnezzar the Great, on the other hand, marries a daughter of Cyaxares, who has become king of all the Medes. The Aryan Scythians are for the Semitic Assyrians; the Aryan Medes for the Semitic Babylonians. It was this Cyaxares who took Nineveh, the Assyrian capital, in 606 B.C., and so released Babylon from the Assyrian yoke to establish, under Chaldean rule, the Second Babylonian Empire. The Scythian allies of Assyria drop out of the story after this. They go on living their own life away to the north without much interference with the peoples to the south. A glance at the map of this period shows how, for two-thirds of a century, the Second Babylonian Empire lay like a lamb within the embrace of the Median lion.

Into the internal struggles of the Medes and Persians, that ended at last in the accession of Cyrus "the Persian" to the throne of Cyaxares in 550 B.C., we will not enter. In that year Cyrus was ruling over an empire that reached from the boundaries of Lydia to Persia and perhaps to India. Nabonidus, the last of the Babylonian rulers, was, as we have already told, digging up old records and building temples in Babylonia.

Map showing the relation of the MEDIAN and Second BABYLONIAN (Chaldæan) EMPIRES in the reign of Nebuchadnezzar the Great

§ 6

But one monarch in the world was alive to the threat of the new power that lay in the hands of Cyrus. This was Crœsus, the Lydian king. His son had been killed in a very tragic manner, which Herodotus relates, but which we will not describe here. Says Herodotus:

"For two years then, Crœsus remained quiet in great mourning, because he was deprived of his son; but after this period of time, the overthrowing of the rule of the son of Cyaxares by Cyrus, and the growing greatness of the Persians, caused Crœsus to cease from his mourning, and led him to a care of cutting short the power of the Persians if by any means he might, while yet it was in growth and before they should have become great."

He then made trial of the various oracles. His method of trial we will not relate here, but it led him to the belief that the Delphi Oracle was alone trustworthy. What follows is rather a lengthy passage, but it is so characteristic of the garrulousness and wonder-loving mind of the Father of History, and with such a pleasant touch of spite against the Lacedemonians, that it is impossible to resist the quotation.

"After this, with great sacrifices, he endeavoured to win the favour of the god at Delphi: for of all the animals that are fit for sacrifice he offered three thousand of each kind, and he heaped up couches overlaid with gold and overlaid with silver, and cups of gold, and robes of purple, and tunics, making of them a great pyre, and this he burnt up, hoping by these means the more to win over the god to the side of the Lydians; and he proclaimed to all the Lydians that every one of them should make sacrifice with that which each man had. And when he had finished the sacrifice, he melted down a vast quantity of gold, and of it he wrought half-plinths, making them six palms in length and three in breadth, and in height one palm; and their number was one hundred and seventeen. Of these four were of pure gold weighing two talents and a half each, and the others of gold alloyed with silver weighing two talents. And he caused to be made also an image of a lion of pure gold weighing ten talents; which lion, when the temple at Delphi was being burnt down, fell from off the half-plinths, for upon these it was set, and is placed now in the treasury of the Corinthians, weighing six talents and a half, for three talents and a half were melted away from it. So Crœsus, having finished all these things, sent them to Delphi, and with them these besides: two mixing-bowls of great size, one of gold and the other of silver, of which the golden bowl was placed on the right hand as one enters the temple, and the silver on the left, but the places of these also were changed after the temple was burnt down. . . . Moreover, Crœsus sent four silver wine-jars, which stand in the treasury of the Corinthians, and two vessels for lustral water, one of gold and the other of silver, of which the gold one is inscribed 'from the Lacedemonians,' who say that it is their offering; therein, however, they do not speak rightly, for this also is from Crœsus, but one of the Delphians wrote the inscription upon it, desiring to gratify the Lacedemonians; and his name I know, but I will not make mention of it. . . . And many other votive offerings Crœsus sent with these, not specially distinguished, among which are certain castings of silver of a round shape, and also a golden figure of a woman three cubits high, which the Delphians say is a statue of the baker of Crœsus. Moreover, Crœsus dedicated the ornaments from his wife's neck and her girdles. . . .

"To the Lydians who were to carry these gifts to the temples Crœsus gave charge that they should ask the Oracles this question also: whether Crœsus should march against the Persians, and, if so, whether he should join with himself any army of men as his friends. And when the Lydians had arrived at the places to which they had been sent and had dedicated the votive offerings, they inquired of the Oracles, and said: 'Crœsus, king of the Lydians and of other nations, considering that these are the only true Oracles among men, presents to you gifts such as your revelations deserve, and asks you again now whether he shall march against the Persians, and, if so, whether he shall join with himself any army of men as allies.' They inquired thus, and the answers of both the Oracles agreed in one, declaring to Crœsus that if he should march against the Persians he should destroy a great empire. . . . So when the answers were brought back and Crœsus heard them, he was delighted with the Oracles, and expecting that he would certainly destroy the kingdom of Cyrus, he sent again to Pytho, and presented to the men of Delphi, having ascertained the number of them, two staters of gold for each man: and in return for this the Delphians gave to Crœsus and to the Lydians precedence in consulting the Oracle and freedom from all payments, and the right to front seats at the games, with this privilege also for all time, that any one of them who wished should be allowed to become a citizen of Delphi."

But here we may not run on as Herodotus loved to do. Suffice it to say that Crœsus made a defensive alliance both with the Lacedemonians and the Egyptians. We will not quote the story of how a great bronze mixing-bowl that the Lacedemonians sent to Crœsus went astray, but we will note a light on the life of the Medes and Persians of that time.

"Thus, then, it happened about the mixing-bowl; but meanwhile Crœsus, mistaking the meaning of the Oracle, was making a march into Cappadocia, expecting to overthrow Cyrus and the power of the Persians; and while Crœsus was preparing to march against the Persians, one of the Lydians, who even before this time was thought to be a wise man, but in consequence of this opinion got a very great name for wisdom among the Lydians, had advised Crœsus as follows: 'O king, thou art preparing to march against men who wear breeches of leather, and the rest of their clothing is of leather also; and they eat food not such as they desire, but such as they can obtain, dwelling in a land which is rugged; and, moreover, they make no use of wine but drink water; and no figs have they for dessert, nor any other good thing. On the one hand, if thou shalt overcome them, what wilt thou take away from them, seeing they have nothing? and, on the other hand, if thou shalt be overcome, consider how many good things thou wilt lose; for once having tasted our good things, they will cling to them fast, and it will not be possible to drive them away. I, for my own part, feel gratitude to the gods that they do not put it into the minds of the Persians to march against the Lydians.' Thus he spoke not persuading Crœsus; for it is true indeed that the Persians before they subdued the Lydians had no luxury nor any good thing."

Crœsus and Cyrus fought an indecisive battle at Pteria, from which Crœsus retreated. Cyrus followed him up, and he gave battle outside his capital town of Sardis. The chief strength of the Lydians lay in their cavalry; they were excellent, if undisciplined, horsemen, and fought with long spears.

"Cyrus, when he saw the Lydians being arrayed for battle, fearing their horsemen, did on the suggestion of Harpagos, a Mede, as follows: All the camels which were in the train of his army carrying provisions and baggage he gathered together, and he took off their burdens and set men upon them provided with the equipment of cavalry; and, having thus furnished them, forth he appointed them to go in front of the rest of the army towards the horsemen of Crœsus; and after the camel-troop he ordered the infantry to follow; and behind the infantry he placed his whole force of cavalry. Then, when all his men had been placed in their several positions, he charged them to spare none of the other Lydians, slaying all who might come in their way, but Crœsus himself they were not to slay, not even if he should make resistance when he was being captured. Such was his charge: and he set the camels opposite the horsemen for this reason—because the horse has a fear of the camel and cannot endure either to see his form or to scent his smell: for this reason then the trick had been devised, in order that the cavalry of Crœsus might be useless, that very force wherewith the Lydian king was expecting most to shine. And as they were coming together to the battle, so soon as the horses scented the camels and saw them, they turned away back, and the hopes of Crœsus were at once brought to nought. The Lydians, however, for their part did not upon that act as cowards, but when they perceived what was coming to pass, they leapt from their horses and fought with the Persians on foot. At length, however, when many had fallen on either side, the Lydians turned to flight; and having been driven within the wall of their fortress, they were besieged by the Persians."

In fourteen days Sardis was stormed and Crœsus taken prisoner. . . .

"So the Persians having taken him brought him into the presence of Cyrus; and he piled up a great pyre and caused Crœsus to go up upon it bound in fetters, and along with him twice seven sons of Lydians, whether it was that he meant to dedicate this offering as first-fruits of his victory to some god, or whether he desired to fulfil a vow, or else had heard that Crœsus was a god-fearing man, and so caused him to go up on the pyre because he wished to know if any one of the divine powers would save him, so that he should not be burnt alive. He, they say, did this; but to Crœsus as he stood upon the pyre there came, although he was in such evil case, a memory of the saying of Solon, how he had said with divine inspiration that no one of the living might be called happy. And when this thought came into his mind, they say that he sighed deeply and groaned aloud, having been for long silent, and three times he uttered the name of Solon. Hearing this, Cyrus bade the interpreters ask Crœsus who was this person on whom he called; and they came near and asked. And Crœsus for a time, it is said, kept silence when he was asked this, but afterwards, being pressed, he said: 'One whom more than much wealth I should have desired to have speech with all monarchs.' Then, since his words were of doubtful import, they asked again of that which he said; and as they were urgent with him and gave him no peace, he told how once Solon, an Athenian, had come and having inspected all his wealth had made light of it, with such and such words; and how all had turned out for him according as Solon had said, not speaking at all especially with a view to Crœsus himself, but with a view to the whole human race, and especially those who seem to themselves to be happy men. And while Crœsus related these things, already the pyre was lighted and the edges of it round about were burning. Then they say that Cyrus, hearing from the interpreters what Crœsus had said, changed his purpose and considered that he himself also was but a man, and that he was delivering another man, who had been not inferior to himself in felicity, alive to the fire; and, moreover, he feared the requital, and reflected that there was nothing of that which men possessed which was secure; therefore, they say, he ordered them to extinguish as quickly as possible the fire that was burning, and to bring down Crœsus and those who were with him from the pyre; and they, using endeavours, were not able now to get the mastery of the flames. Then it is related by the Lydians that Crœsus, having learned how Cyrus had changed his mind, and seeing that every one was trying to put out the fire, but that they were no longer able to check it, cried aloud, entreating Apollo that if any gift had ever been given by him which was acceptable to the god, he would come to his aid and rescue him from the evil which was now upon him. So he with tears entreated the god, and suddenly, they say, after clear sky and calm weather clouds gathered and a storm burst, and it rained with a very violent shower, and the pyre was extinguished. Then Cyrus, having perceived that Crœsus was a lover of the gods and a good man, caused him to be brought down from the pyre and asked him as follows: 'Crœsus, tell me who of all men was it who persuaded thee to march upon my land and so to become an enemy to me instead of a friend?' And he said: 'O king, I did this to thy felicity and to my own misfortune, and the causer of this was the god of the Hellenes, who incited me to march with my army. For no one is so senseless as to choose of his own will war rather than peace, since in peace the sons bury their fathers, but in war the fathers bury their sons. But it was pleasing, I suppose, to the divine powers that these things should come to pass thus.'"

But Herodotus is too alluring a companion for one who would write an Outline of History; and the rest of the life of Crœsus, and how he gave wise counsels to Cyrus, must be read in his ampler page.

When Lydia was subdued, Cyrus turned his attention to Nabonidus in Babylon. He defeated the Babylonian army, under Belshazzar, outside Babylon, and then laid siege to the town. He entered the town (538 B.C.), probably as we have already suggested, with the connivance of the priests of Bel.

§ 7

Cyrus was succeeded by his son Cambyses, who took an army into Egypt (525 B.C.). There was a battle in the delta, in which Greek mercenaries fought on both sides. Herodotus declares that he saw the bones of the slain still lying on the field fifty or sixty years later, and comments on the comparative thinness of the Persian skulls. After this battle Cambyses took Memphis and most of Egypt.

In Egypt, we are told, Cambyses went mad. He took great liberties with the Egyptian temples, and remained at Memphis "opening ancient tombs and examining the dead bodies." He had already murdered both Crœsus, ex-king of Lydia, and his own brother Smerdis before coming to Egypt, and he died in Syria on the way back to Susa of an accidental wound, leaving no heirs to succeed him. He was presently succeeded by Darius the Mede (521 B.C.), the son of Hystaspes, one of the chief councillors of Cyrus.

The empire of Darius I was larger than any one of the preceding empires whose growth we have traced. It included all Asia Minor and Syria, that is to say, the ancient Lydian and Hittite empires, all the old Assyrian and Babylonian empires, Egypt, the Caucasus and Caspian regions, Media, Persia, and it extended, perhaps, into India to the Indus. The nomadic Arabians alone of all the peoples of what is nowadays called the Near East, did not pay tribute to the satraps (provincial governors) of Darius. The organization of this great empire seems to have been on a much higher level of efficiency than any of its precursors. Great arterial roads joined province to province, and there was a system of royal posts;[1] at stated intervals post horses stood always ready to carry the government messenger, or the traveller if he had a government permit, on to the next stage of his journey. Apart from this imperial right-of-way and the payment of tribute, the local governments possessed a very considerable amount of local freedom. They were restrained from internecine conflict, which was all to their own good. And at first the Greek cities of the mainland of Asia paid the tribute and shared in this Persian Peace.

Darius was first incited to attack the Greeks in Europe by a homesick Greek physician at his court, who wanted at any cost to be back in Greece. Darius had already made plans for an expedition into Europe, aiming not at Greece, but to the northward of Greece, across the Bosphorus and Danube. He wanted to strike at South Russia, which he believed to be the home country of the Scythian nomads who threatened him on his northern and north-eastern frontiers. But he lent an attentive ear to the tempter, and sent agents into Greece.[2]

This great expedition of Darius opens out our view in this history. It lifts a curtain upon the Balkan country behind Greece about which we have said nothing hitherto; it carries us to and over the Danube. The

[1] But a thousand years earlier the Hittites seem to have had paved high roads running across their country.

[2] But cp. Bury's *History of Greece*, ch. vi., § 5.

nucleus of his army marched from Susa, gathering up contingents as they made their way to the Bosphorus. Here Greek allies (Ionian Greeks from Asia) had made a bridge of boats, and the army crossed over while the Greek allies sailed on in their ships to the Danube, and, two days' sail up from its mouth, landed to make another floating bridge. Meanwhile, Darius and his host advanced along the coast of what is now Bulgaria, but which was then called Thrace. They crossed the Danube, and prepared to give battle to the Scythian army and take the cities of the Scythians.

But the Scythians had no cities, and they evaded a battle, and the war degenerated into a tedious and hopeless pursuit of more mobile enemies. Wells were stopped up and pastures destroyed by the nomads. The Scythian horsemen hung upon the skirts of the great army, which consisted mostly of foot soldiers, picking off stragglers and preventing foraging; and they did their best to persuade the Ionian Greeks, who had made and were guarding the bridge across the Danube, to break up the bridge, and so ensure the destruction of Darius. So long as Darius continued to advance, however, the loyalty of his Greek allies remained unshaken.

But privation, fatigue, and sickness hindered and crippled the Persian army; Darius lost many stragglers and consumed his supplies, and at last the melancholy conviction dawned upon him that a retreat across the Danube was necessary to save him from complete exhaustion and defeat.

In order to get a start in his retreat he sacrificed his sick and wounded. He had these men informed that he was about to attack the Scythians at nightfall, and under this pretence stole out of the camp with the pick of his troops and made off southward, leaving the camp fires burning and the usual noises and movements of the camp behind him. Next day the men left in the camp realized the trick their monarch had played upon them, and surrendered themselves to the mercy of the Scythians; but Darius had got his start, and was able to reach the bridge of boats before his pursuers came upon him. They were more mobile than his troops, but they missed their quarry in the darkness. At the river the retreating Persians "were brought to an extremity of fear," for they found the bridge partially

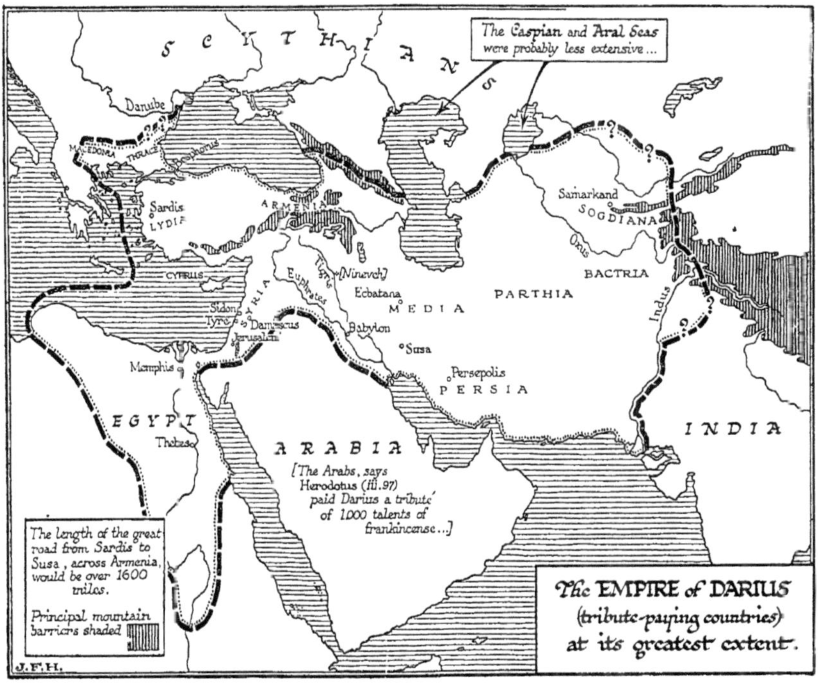

The EMPIRE of DARIUS (tribute-paying countries) at its greatest extent.

broken down and its northern end destroyed.

At this point a voice echoes down the centuries to us. We see a group of dismayed Persians standing about the Great King upon the bank of the streaming river; we see the masses of halted troops, hungry and war-worn; a trail of battered transport stretches away towards the horizon, upon which at any time the advance guards of the pursuers may appear. There is not much noise in spite of the multitude, but rather an inquiring silence. Standing out like a pier from the further side of the great stream are the remains of the bridge of boats, an enigma. . . . We cannot discern whether there are men over there or not. The shipping of the Ionian Greeks seems still to be drawn up on the further shore, but it is all very far away.

"Now there was with Darius an Egyptian who had a voice louder than that of any other man on earth, and this man Darius ordered to take his stand upon the bank of the Ister (Danube) and to call Histiæus of Miletus."

This worthy—a day is to come, as we shall presently tell, when his decapitated head will be sent to Darius at Susa—appears approaching slowly across the waters in a boat.

There is a parley, and we gather that it is "all right."

The explanation Histiæus has to make is a complicated one. Some Scythians have been and have gone again. Scouts, perhaps, these were. It would seem there had been a discussion between the Scythians and the Greeks. The Scythians wanted the bridge broken down; they would then, they said, undertake to finish up the Persian army and make an end of Darius and his empire, and the Ionian Greeks of Asia could then free their cities again. Miltiades, the Athenian, was for accepting this proposal. But Histiæus had been more subtle. He would prefer, he said, to see the Persians completely destroyed before definitely abandoning their cause. Would the Scythians go back and destroy the Persians to make sure of them while the Greeks on their part destroyed the bridge? Anyhow, whichever side the Greeks took finally, it was clear to him that it would be wise to destroy the northern end of the bridge, because otherwise the Scythians might rush it. Indeed, even as they parleyed the Greeks set to work to demolish the end that linked them to the Scythians as quickly as possible. In accordance with the suggestions of Histiæus the Scythians rode off in search of the Persians, and so left the Greeks safe in either event. If Darius escaped, they could be on his side; if he were destroyed, there was nothing of which the Scythians could complain.

Histiæus did not put it quite in that fashion to Darius. He had at least kept the shipping and most of the bridge. He represented himself as the loyal friend of Persia, and Darius was not disposed to be too critical. The Ionian ships came over. With a sense of immense relief the remnant of the wasted Persians were presently looking back at the steely flood of the Danube streaming wide between themselves and their pursuers. . . .

The pleasure and interest had gone out of the European expedition for Darius. He returned to Susa, leaving an army in Thrace, under a trusted general Megabazus. This Megabazus set himself to the subjugation of Thrace, and among other states which submitted reluctantly to Darius was a kingdom, which thus comes into our history for the first time, the kingdom of Macedonia, a country inhabited by a people so closely allied to the Greeks that one of its princes had already been allowed to compete and take a prize in the Olympian games.

Darius was disposed to reward Histiæus by allowing him to build a city for himself in Thrace, but Megabazus had a different opinion of the trustworthiness of Histiæus, and prevailed upon the king to take him to Susa, and, under the title of councillor, to keep him a prisoner there. Histiæus was at first flattered by this court position, and then realized its true meaning. The Persian court bored him, and he grew homesick for Miletus. He set himself to make mischief, and was able to stir up a revolt against the Persians among the Ionian Greeks on the mainland. The twistings and turnings of the story, which included the burning of Sardis by the Ionians and the defeat of a Greek fleet at the battle of Ladé (495 B.C.), are too complicated to follow here. It is a dark and intricate story of treacheries, cruelties, and hate, in which the death of the wily Histiæus shines almost cheerfully. The Persian governor of Sardis, through which town he was being taken on his way back to Susa as a prisoner, having much the same opinion of him as Megabazus had, and knowing his ability to humbug Darius, killed him there and then, and sent on the head only to his master.

Cyprus and the Greek islands were dragged into this contest that Histiæus had stirred up, and at last Athens. Darius realized the error he had made in turning to the right and not to the left when he had crossed the Bosphorus, and he now set himself to the conquest of all Greece. He began with the islands. Tyre and Sidon were subject to Persia, and ships of the Phœnician and of the Ionian Greeks provided the Persians with a fleet by means of which one Greek island after another was subjugated.

§ 8

The first attack upon Greece proper was made in 490 B.C. It was a sea attack upon Athens, with a force long and carefully prepared for the task, the fleet being provided with specially built transports for the conveyance of horses. This expedition made a landing near Marathon in Attica. The Persians were guided into Marathon by a renegade Greek, Hippias, the son of Peisistratus, who had been tyrant of Athens. If Athens fell, then Hippias was to be its tyrant, under the protection of the Persians. Meanwhile, so urgent was the sense of a crisis in the affairs of Hellas, that a man, a herald and runner, went from Athens to Sparta, forgetful of all feuds, to say: "Lacedemonians the Athenians make request of you to come to their help, and not to allow a city most anciently established among the Hellenes to fall into slavery by the means of Barbarians; for even now Eretria has been enslaved and Hellas has become the weaker by a city of renown." This man, Pheidippides, did the distance from Athens to Sparta, nearly a hundred miles as the crow flies, and much more if we allow for the contours and

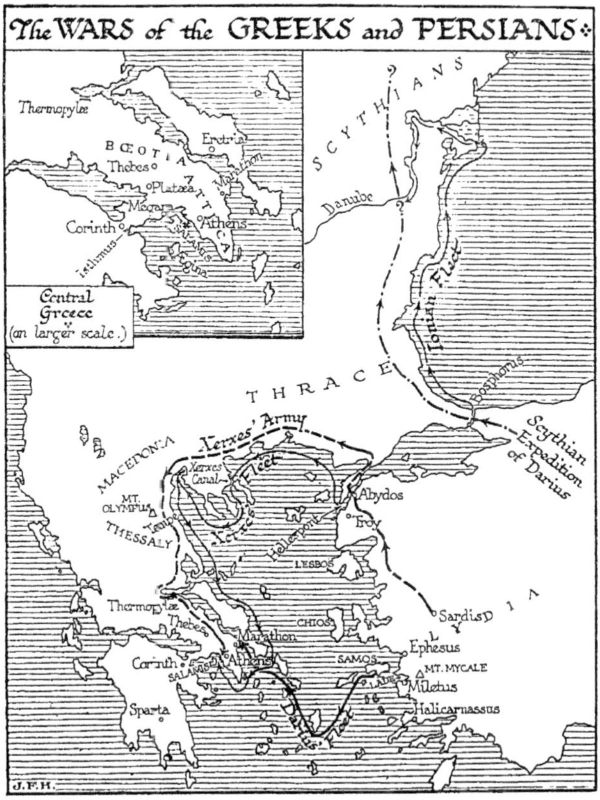

the windings of the way, in something under eight and forty hours.

But before the Spartans could arrive on the scene the battle was joined. The Athenians charged the enemy. They fought—"in a memorable fashion: for they were the first of all the Hellenes about whom we know who went to attack the enemy at a run, and they were the first also who endured to face the Median garments and the men who wore them, whereas up to this time the very name of the Medes was to the Hellenes a terror to hear."

The Persian wings gave before this impetuous attack, but the centre held. The Athenians, however, were cool as well as vigorous; they let the wings run and closed in on the flanks of the centre, whereupon the main body of the Persians fled to their ships. Seven vessels fell into the hands of the Athenians; the rest got away, and, after a futile attempt to sail round to Athens and seize the city before the army returned thither, the fleet made a retreat to Asia. Let Herodotus close the story with a paragraph that still further enlightens us upon the tremendous prestige of the Medes at this time:

"Of the Lacedemonians there came to Athens two thousand after the full moon, making great haste to be in time, so that they arrived in Attica on the third day after leaving Sparta: and though they had come too late for the battle, yet they desired to behold the Medes; and accordingly they went on to Marathon and looked at the bodies of the slain: then afterwards they departed home, commending the Athenians and the work which they had done."

§ 9

So Greece, unified for a while by fear, gained her first victory over Persia. The news came to Darius simultaneously with the news of a rebellion in Egypt, and he died while still undecided in which direction to turn. His son and successor, Xerxes, turned first to Egypt and set up a Persian satrap there; then for four years he prepared a second attack upon Greece. Says Herodotus, who was, one must remember, a patriotic Greek, approaching now to the climax of his History:

"For what nation did Xerxes not lead out of Asia against Hellas? and what water was not exhausted, being drunk by his host, except only the great rivers? For some supplied ships, and others were appointed to serve in the land army; to some it was appointed to furnish cavalry, and to others vessels to carry horses, while they served in the expedition themselves also; others were ordered to furnish ships of war for the bridges, and others again ships with provisions."

Xerxes passed into Europe, not as Darius did at the half-mile crossing of the Bosphorus, but at the Hellespont (= the Dardanelles). In his account of the assembling of the great army, and its march from Sardis to the Hellespont, the poet in Herodotus takes possession of the historian. The great host passes in splendour by Troy, and Xerxes, who although a Persian and a Barbarian, seems to have had the advantages of a classical education, turns aside, says our historian, to visit the citadel of Priam. The Hellespont was bridged at Abydos, and upon a hill was set a marble throne from which Xerxes surveyed the whole array of his forces.

"And seeing all the Hellespont covered over with the ships and all the shores and the

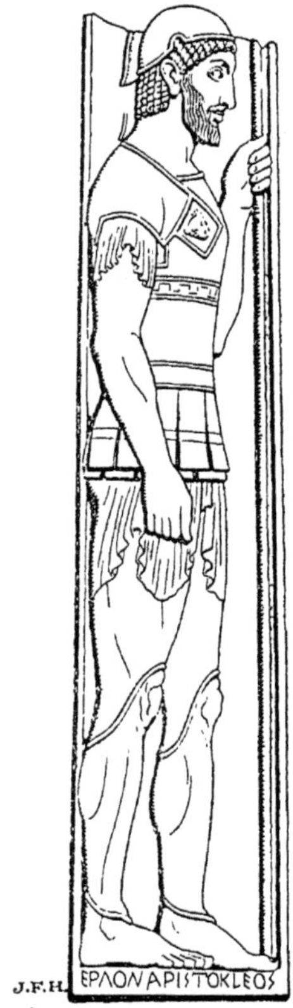

Monument of Athenian foot-soldier, found near Marathon.

plains of Abydos full of men, then Xerxes pronounced himself a happy man, and after that he fell to weeping. Artabanus, his uncle, therefore perceiving him—the same who at first boldly declared his opinion advising Xerxes not to march against Hellas—this man, I say, having observed that Xerxes wept, asked as follows: 'O king, how far different from one another are the things which thou hast done now and a short while before now! for having pronounced thyself a happy man, thou art now shedding tears.'

He said: 'Yea, for after I had reckoned up, it came into my mind to feel pity at the thought how brief was the whole life of man, seeing that of these multitudes not one will be alive when a hundred years have gone by.'"

This may not be exact history but it is great poetry. It is as splendid as anything in *The Dynasts*.

The Persian fleet, coasting from headland to headland, accompanied this land multitude during its march southward; but a violent storm did the fleet great damage and 400 ships were lost, including much corn transport. At first the united Hellenes marched out to meet the invaders at the Vale of Tempe near Mount Olympus, but afterwards retreated through Thessaly, and chose at last to await the advancing Persians at a place called Thermopylæ, where at that time—2,300 years have altered these things greatly—there was a great cliff on the landward side and the sea to the east, with a track scarcely wide enough for a chariot between. The great advantage to the Greeks of this position at Thermopylæ was that it prevented the use of either cavalry or chariots, and narrowed the battle front so as to minimize their numerical inequality. And there the Persians joined battle with them one summer day in the year 480 B.C.

For three days the Greeks held this great army, and did them much damage with small loss to themselves, and then on the third day a detachment of Persians appeared upon the rear of the Greeks, having learnt of a way over the mountains from a peasant. There were hasty discussions among the Greeks; some were for withdrawing, some for holding out. The leader of the whole force, Leonidas, was for staying; and with him he would keep, he said, 300 Spartans. The rest of the Greek army could, meanwhile, make good its retreat to the next defensible pass. The Thespian contingent of 700, however, refused to fall back. They preferred to stay and die with the Spartans. Also a contingent of 400 Thebans remained. As Thebes afterwards joined the Persians, there is a story that these Thebans were detained by force against their will, which seems on military as well as historical grounds improbable. These 1,400 stayed, and were, after a conflict of heroic quality, slain to a man. Two Spartans happened to be away, sick with ophthalmia. When they heard the news, one was too ill to move; the other made his helot guide him to the battle, and there struck blindly until he was killed. The other, Aristodemus, was taken away with the retreating troops, and returned to Sparta, where he was not actually punished for his conduct, but was known as Tresas, "the man who retreated." It was enough to distinguish him from all other Spartans, and he got himself killed at the Battle of Platæa a year later, performing prodigies of reckless courage. . . . For a whole day this little band had held the pass, assailed in front and rear by the whole force of the Persians. They had covered the retreat of the main Greek army, they had inflicted great losses on the invaders, and they had raised the prestige of the Greek warrior over that of the Mede higher even than the victory of Marathon had done.

The Persian cavalry and transport filtered slowly through the narrow passage of Thermopylæ, and marched on towards Athens, while a series of naval encounters went on at sea. The Hellenic fleet retreated before the advance of the Persian shipping, which suffered seriously through its comparative ignorance of the intricate coasts and of the tricks of the local weather. Weight of numbers carried the Persian army forward to Athens; now that Thermopylæ was lost, there was no line of defence nearer than the Isthmus of Corinth, and this meant the abandonment of all the intervening territory, including Athens. The population had either to fly or submit to the Persians. Thebes with all Bœotia submitted, and was pressed into the Persian army, except one town, Platæa, whose inhabitants fled to Athens. The turn of Athens came next, and great efforts were made to persuade her to make terms; but, instead, the whole population determined to abandon everything and take to the shipping. The women and non-combatants were carried to Salamis and various adjacent islands. Only a few people too old to move and a few dissentients remained in the town, which was occupied by the Persians and burnt. The sacred objects, statues, etc., which were burnt at this time, were afterwards buried in the Acropolis by the returning Athenians, and have been dug up in our own day with the marks of burning visible upon them. Xerxes sent off a mounted messenger to Susa with the news, and he invited the sons of Peisistratus, whom he had brought back with him, to enter upon their inheritance and sacrifice after the Athenian manner upon the Acropolis.

Meanwhile, the Hellenic confederate fleet had come round to Salamis, and in the council of war there were bitter differences of opinion. Corinth and the states behind the Isthmus wanted the fleet to fall back to that position, abandoning the cities of Megara and Ægina. Themistocles insisted with all his force on fighting in the narrows of Salamis. The majority was steadily in favour of retreat, when there suddenly arrived the news that retreat was cut off. The Persians had sailed round Salamis and held the sea on the other side. This news was brought by that Aristides the Just, of whose ostracism we have already told; his sanity and eloquence did much to help Themistocles to hearten the hesitating commanders. These two men had formerly been bitter antagonists; but, with a generosity rare in those days, they forgot their differences before the common danger. At dawn the Greek ships pulled out to battle.

The fleet before them was a fleet more composite and less united than their own. But it was about three times as great. On one wing were the Phœnicians, on the other Ionian Greeks from Asia and the Islands. Some of the latter fought stoutly; others remembered that they too were Greeks. The Greek ships, on the other hand, were mostly manned by freemen fighting for their homes. Throughout the early hours the battle raged confusedly. Then it became evident to Xerxes, watching the combat, that his fleet was attempting flight. The flight became disaster.

Xerxes had taken his seat to watch the battle. He saw his galleys rammed by the sharp prows of other galleys; his fighting-men shot down; his ships boarded. Much of the sea-fighting in those days was done by ramming; the big galleys bore down their opponents by superior weight of impact, or sheared off their oars and so destroyed their manœuvring power and left them helpless. Presently, Xerxes saw that some of his broken ships were surrendering. In the water he could see the heads of Greeks swimming to land; but "of the Barbarians the greater number perished in the sea, not knowing how to swim." The clumsy attempt of the hard-pressed first line of the Persian fleet to put about led to indescribable confusion. Some were rammed by the rear ships of their own side. This ancient shipping was poor, unseaworthy stuff by any modern standards. The west wind was blowing and many of the broken ships of Xerxes were now drifting away out of his sight to be wrecked on the coast beyond. Others were being towed towards Salamis by the Greeks. Others, less injured and still in fighting trim, were making for the beaches close beneath him that would bring them under the protection of his army. Scattered over the further sea, beyond the headlands, remote and vague, were ships in flight and Greek ships in pursuit. Slowly, incident by incident, the disaster had unfolded under his eyes. We can imagine something of the coming and going of messengers, the issuing of futile orders, the changes of plan, throughout the day. In the morning Xerxes had come out provided with tables to mark the most successful of his commanders for reward. In the gold of the sunset he beheld the sea power of Persia utterly scattered, sunken and destroyed, and the Greek fleet

Soldiers of the Persian body-guard (From frieze in the audience hall of Darius at Susa.)

over against Salamis unbroken and triumphant, ordering its ranks, as if still incredulous of victory.

The Persian army remained as if in indecision for some days close to the scene of this sea fight, and then began to retreat to Thessaly, where it was proposed to winter and resume the campaign. But Xerxes, like Darius I before him, had conceived a disgust for European campaigns. He was afraid of the destruction of the bridge of boats. With part of the army he went on to the Hellespont, leaving the main force in Thessaly under a general, Mardonius. Of his own retreat the historian relates:

"Whithersoever they came on the march

and to whatever nation they seized the crops of that people and used them for provisions; and if they found no crops, then they took the grass which was growing up from the earth, and stripped off the bark from the trees and plucked down the leaves and devoured them; alike of the cultivated trees and of those growing wild; and they left nothing behind them thus they did by reason of famine. Then plague too seized upon the army and dysentery, which destroyed them by the way, and some of them also who were sick the king left behind, laying charge upon the cities where at the time he chanced to be in his march, to take care of them and support them; of these he left some in Thessaly, and some at Siris in Paionia, and some in Macedonia. . . . . When, passing on from Thrace they came to the passage, they crossed over the Hellespont in haste to Abydos by means of the ships, for they did not find the floating bridges still stretched across, but broken up by a storm. While staying there for a time they had distributed to them an allowance of food more abundant than they had had by the way, and from satisfying their hunger without restraint and also from the changes of water there died many of those in the army who had remained safe till then. The rest arrived with Xerxes at Sardis."

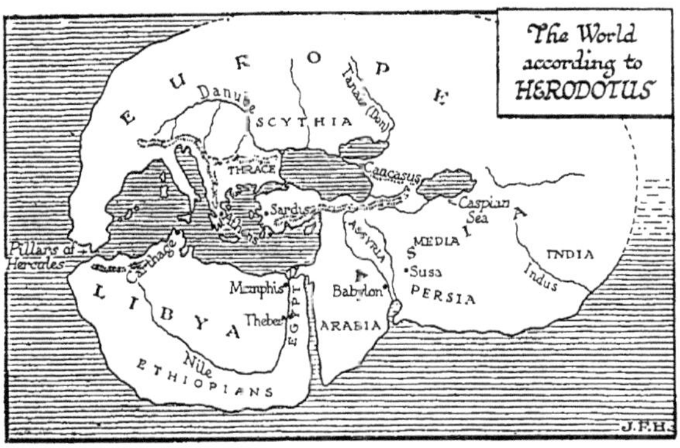

§ 10

The rest of the Persian army remained in Thessaly under the command of Mardonius, and for a year he maintained an aggressive campaign against the Greeks. Finally, he was defeated and killed in a pitched battle at Platæa (479 B.C.), and on the same day the Persian fleet and a land army met with joint disaster under the shadow of Mount Mycale on the Asiatic mainland, between Ephesus and Miletus. The Persian ships, being in fear of the Greeks, had been drawn up on shore and a wall built about them; but the Greeks disembarked and stormed this enclosure. They then sailed to the Hellespont to destroy what was left of the bridge of boats, so that later the Persian fugitives, retreating from Platæa, had to cross by shipping at the Bosphorus, and did so with difficulty.

Encouraged by these disasters of the imperial power, says Herodotus, the Ionian cities in Asia began for a second time to revolt against the Persians.

With this the ninth book of the *History of Herodotus* comes to an end. He was born about 484 B.C., so that at the time of the battle of Platæa he was a child of five years old. Much of the substance of his story was gathered by him from actors in, and eye-witnesses of, the great events he relates. The war still dragged on for a long time; the Greeks supported a rebellion against Persian rule in Egypt, and tried unsuccessfully to take Cyprus; it did not end until about 449 B.C. Then the Greek coasts of Asia Minor and the Greek cities in the Black Sea remained generally free, but Cyprus and Egypt continued under Persian rule. Herodotus, who had been born a Persian subject in the Ionian city of Halicarnassus, was five and thirty years old by that time, and he must have taken an early opportunity after this peace of visiting Babylon and Persia. He probably went to Athens, with his History ready to recite, about 438 B.C.

The idea of a great union of Greece for aggression against Persia was not altogether strange to Herodotus. Some of his readers suspect him of writing to enforce it. It was certainly in the air at that time. He describes Aristagoras, the son-in-law of Histiæus, as showing the Spartans "a tablet of bronze on which was engraved a map of the whole earth with all the seas and rivers." He makes Aristagoras say: "These Barbarians are not valiant in fight. You, on the other hand, have now attained to the utmost skill in war. They fight with bows and arrows and a short spear: they go into battle wearing trousers and having caps on their heads. You have perfected your weapons and discipline. They are easily to be conquered. Not all the other nations of the world have what they possess ; gold, silver, bronze, embroidered garments, beasts and slaves ; *all this you might have for yourselves, if you so desired.*"

It was a hundred years before these suggestions bore fruit.

Xerxes was murdered in his palace about 465 B.C., and thereafter Persia made no further attempts at conquest in Europe. We have no such knowledge of the things that were happening in the empire of the Great King as we have of the occurrences in the little states of Central Greece. Greece had suddenly begun to produce literature, and put itself upon record as no other nation had ever done hitherto. After 479 B.C. (Platæa) the spirit seems to have gone out of the government of the Medes and Persians. The empire of the Great King enters upon a period of decay. An Artaxerxes, a second Xerxes, a second Darius, pass across the stage ; there are rebellions in Egypt and Syria ; the Medes rebel ; a second Artaxerxes and a second Cyrus, his brother, fight for the throne. This history is even as the history of Babylonia, Assyria, and Egypt in the older times. It is autocracy reverting to its normal state of palace crime, blood-stained magnificence, and moral squalor. But the last-named struggle produced a Greek masterpiece, for this second Cyrus collected an army of Greek mercenaries and marched into Babylonia, and was there killed at the moment of victory over Artaxerxes II. Thereupon, the Ten Thousand Greeks, left with no one to employ them, made a retreat to the coast again (401 B.C.), and this retreat was immortalized in a book, one of the first of personal war books, the ***Anabasis***, by their leader Xenophon.

Murders, revolts, chastisements, disasters, cunning alliances, and base betrayals, and no Herodotus to record them. Such is the texture of Persian history. An Artaxerxes III, covered with blood, flourishes dimly for a time. "Artaxerxes III is said to have been murdered by Bagoas, who places Arses, the youngest of the king's sons, on the throne only to slay him in turn when he seemed to be contemplating independent action."[1] So it goes on. Beneath the crimes and disorders of the palaces, the life of the city and country ran a similar course.

Justice was fitful and law venal. Wars that were unmeaning catastrophes swept down upon any little gleam of prosperity or decency to which this or that community clambered. Athens, prospering for a time after the Persian repulse, was smitten by the plague, in which Pericles, its greatest ruler, died (428 B.C.). But, as a noteworthy fact amidst these confusions, the Ten Thousand of Xenophon were scattering now among the Greek cities, repeating from their own experience the declaration of Aristagoras that the Persian empire was a rich confusion which it would be very easy to conquer.

XXIII

GREEK THOUGHT AND LITERATURE[2]

§ 1. *The Athens of Pericles.*
§ 2. *Socrates.*
§ 3. *What was the Quality of the Common Athenians?*
§ 4. *Greek Tragedy and Comedy.*
§ 5. *Plato and the Academy.*
§ 6. *Aristotle and the Lyceum.*
§ 7. *Philosophy becomes Unworldly.*
§ 8. *The Quality and Limitations of Greek Thought.*

§ 1

GREEK history for the next forty years after Platæa and Mycale is a story of comparative peace and tranquillity. There were wars, but they were not intense wars. For a little while in Athens, for a section of the prosperous, there was leisure and opportunity. And by a combination of accidents and through the character of a small group of people, this leisure and opportunity produced the most remarkable and memorable results. A beautiful literature was produced ; the plastic arts flourished, and the foundations of modern science were laid. Then, after an interlude of fifty odd years, the long-smouldering

[1] Winckler, in Helmolt's *Universal History*.

[2] See in relation to this chapter, Zimmern's *Greek Commonwealth*. A very handy book for the student in this section is Abbott's *Skeleton Outline of Greek History*.

hostility between Athens and Sparta broke out into a fierce and exhausting war, which sapped at last the vitality of this creative movement.

This war is known in history as the Peloponnesian War; it went on for nearly thirty years, and wasted all the power of Greece. At first Athens was in the ascendant, then Sparta. Then arose Thebes, a city not fifty miles from Athens, to overshadow Sparta. Once more Athens flared into importance as the head of a confederation. The story must be told at considerable length or not told at all. It is a story of narrow rivalries and inexplicable hatreds that would have vanished long ago out of the memories of men, were it not that it is recorded and reflected in a great literature.

Through all this time Persia appears and reappears as the ally first of this league and then of that. About the middle of the fourth century B.C., Greece becomes aware of a new influence in its affairs, that of Philip, King of Macedonia. Macedonia does, indeed, arise in the background of this incurably divided Greece, as the Medes and Persians arose behind the Chaldean Empire. A time comes when the Greek mind turns round, so to speak, from its disputes, and stares in one united dismay at the Macedonian.

Planless and murderous squabbles are still planless and murderous squabbles even though Thucydides tells the story, even though the great beginnings of a new civilization are wrecked by their disorders; and in this general outline we can give no space at all to the particulars of these internecine feuds, to the fights and flights that sent first this Greek city and then that up to the sky in flames. Upon a one-foot globe Greece becomes a speck almost too small to recognize; and in a short history of mankind, all this century and more of dissension between the days of Salamis and Platæa and the rise of King Philip, shrinks to a little, almost inaudible clash of disputation, to a mere note upon the swift passing of opportunity for nations as for men.

But what does not shrink into insignificance, because it has entered into the intellectual process of all subsequent nations, because it is inseparably a part of our mental foundation, is the literature that Athens produced during such patches and gleams of tranquillity and security as these times afforded her.

Says Professor Gilbert Murray: [1]

"Their outer political history, indeed, like that of all other nations, is filled with war and diplomacy, with cruelty and deceit. It is the inner history, the history of thought and feeling and character, that is so grand. They had some difficulties to contend with which are now almost out of our path. They had practically no experience, but were doing everything for the first time; they were utterly weak in material resources, and their emotions, their '*desires and fears and rages,*' were probably wilder and fiercer than ours. Yet they produced the Athens of Pericles and of Plato."

This remarkable outbreak of creative power, which for three and twenty centuries has been to men of intelligence a guiding and inspiring beacon out of the past, flared up after the battles of Marathon and Salamis had made Athens free and fearless, and, without any great excesses of power, predominant in her world. It was the work of a quite small group of men. A number of her citizens lived for the better part of a generation under conditions which, in all ages, have disposed men to produce good and beautiful work; they were secure, they were free, and they had pride; and they were without that temptation of apparent and unchallenged power which disposes all of us to inflict wrongs upon our fellow men. When political life narrowed down again to the waste and crimes of a fratricidal war with Sparta, there was so broad and well-fed a flame of intellectual activity burning that it lasted through all the windy distresses of this war and beyond the brief lifetime of Alexander the Great, for a period altogether of more than a hundred years after the wars began.

Athens, it must be understood, was by far the largest of all the Greek city democracies. Flushed with victory and the sense of freedom fairly won, her people did for a time rise towards nobility. Under the guidance of a great demagogue, Pericles, the chief official of the Athenian general assembly, and a politician statesman rather of the calibre of Gladstone or Lincoln in modern history, they were set to the task of rebuilding their city and expanding their commerce. For a time they were capable of following a generous leader generously, and Fate gave them a generous leader. In Pericles there was mingled in the strangest fashion political ability with a real living passion for deep and high and beautiful things. He kept in power for over thirty years. He was a man of extraordinary vigour and liberality of mind. He stamped these qualities upon his time. As Winckler has remarked, the Athenian

[1] *Ancient Greek Literature*, by Gilbert Murray Heinemann, 1911).

democracy had for a time "the face of Pericles." He was sustained by what was probably a very great and noble friendship. There was a woman of unusual education, Aspasia, from Miletus, whom he could not marry because of the law that restricted the citizenship of Athens to the home-born, but who was in effect his wife. She played a large part in gathering about him men of unusual gifts. All the great writers of the time knew her, and several have praised her wisdom. Plutarch, it is true, accuses her of instigating a troublesome and dangerous but finally successful war against Samos, but, as he himself shows later, this was necessitated by the naval hostility of the Samians, which threatened the overseas trade of Athens, upon which all the prosperity of the republic depended.

Men's ambitions are apt to reflect the standards of their intimates. Pericles was content, at any rate, to serve as a leader in Athens rather than to dominate as a tyrant. Alliances were formed under his guidance, new colonies and trading stations were established from Italy to the Black Sea; and the treasures of the league at Delos were brought to Athens. Convinced of his security from Persia, Pericles spent the war hoard of the allies upon the beautification of his city. This was an unrighteous thing to do by our modern standards, but it was not a base or greedy thing to do. Athens had accomplished the work of the Delian League, and is not the labourer worthy of his hire? This sequestration made a time of exceptional opportunity for architects and artists. The Parthenon of Athens, whose ruins are still a thing of beauty, was but the crown set upon the clustering glories of the Athens Pericles rebuilt. Such sculptures as those of Phidias, Myron, and Polyclitus that still survive, witness to the artistic quality of the time.

The reader must bear in mind that illuminating remark of Winckler's, which says that this renascent Athens bore for a time the face of Pericles. It was the peculiar genius of this man and of his atmosphere that let loose the genius of men about him, and attracted men of great intellectual vigour to Athens. Athens wore his face for a time as one wears a mask, and then became restless and desired to put him aside. There was very little that was great and generous about the common Athenian. We have told of the spirit of one sample voter for the ostracism of Aristides, and Lloyd (in his *Age of Pericles*) declares that the Athenians would not suffer the name of Miltiades to be mentioned in connection with the battle of Marathon. The sturdy self-respect of the common voters revolted presently against the beautiful buildings rising about them; against the favours shown to such sculptors as Phidias over popular worthies in the same line of business; against the donations made to a mere foreigner like Herodotus of Halicarnassus; against the insulting preference of Pericles for the company and conversation of a Milesian woman. The public life of Pericles was conspicuously orderly, and that presently set the man in the street thinking that his private life must be very corrupt. One gathers that Pericles was "superior" in his demeanour; he betrayed at times a contempt for the citizens he served.

"Pericles acquired not only an elevation of sentiment, and a loftiness and purity of style far removed from the low expression of the vulgar, but likewise a gravity of countenance which relaxed not into laughter, a firm and even tone of voice, an easy deportment, and a decency of dress which no vehemence of speaking ever put into disorder. These things, and others of a like nature, excited admiration in all that saw him. Such was his conduct, when a vile and abandoned fellow loaded him a whole day with reproaches and abuse; he bore it with patience and silence, and continued in public for the despatch of some urgent affairs. In the evening he walked softly home, this impudent wretch following, and insulting him all the way with the most scurrilous language. And as it was dark when he came to his own door, he ordered one of his servants to take a torch and light the man home. The poet Ion, however, says he was proud and supercilious in conversation, and that there was a great deal of vanity and contempt of others mixed with his dignity of manner. . . . He appeared not in the streets except when he went to the forum or the senate house. He declined the invitations of his friends, and all social entertainments and recreations; insomuch that in the whole time of his administration, which was a considerable length, he never went to sup with any of his friends but once, which was at the marriage of his nephew Euryptolemus, and he stayed there only until the ceremony of libation was ended. He considered that the freedom of entertainments takes away all distinction of office, and that dignity is but little consistent with familiarity. . . ."[1]

There was as yet no gutter journalism to tell the world of the vileness of the conspicuous and successful; but the common man, a little out of conceit with himself,

[1] *Plutarch.*

found much consolation in the art of comedy, which flourished exceedingly. The writers of comedy satisfied that almost universal craving for the depreciation of those whose apparent excellence offends our self-love. They threw dirt steadily and industriously at Pericles and his friends. Pericles was portrayed in a helmet; a helmet became him, and it is to be feared he knew as much. This led to much joy and mirth over the pleasant suggestion of a frightfully distorted head, an onion head. The "goings on" of Aspasia were of course a fruitful vineyard for the inventions of the street. . . .

Athene of the Parthenon.

Dreaming souls, weary of the vulgarities of our time, have desired to be transferred to the sublime Age of Pericles. But, plumped down into that Athens, they would have found themselves in very much the atmosphere of the lower sort of contemporary music-hall, very much in the vein of our popular newspapers; the same hot blast of braying libel, foul imputation, greedy "patriotism," and general baseness would have blown upon them, the "modern note" would have pursued them. As the memories of Platæa and Salamis faded and the new buildings grew familiar, Pericles and the pride of Athens became more and more offensive to the homely humour of the crowd. He was never ostracized—his prestige with the quieter citizens saved him from that; but he was attacked with increasing boldness and steadfastness. He lived and died a poor man; he was perhaps the most honest of demagogues; but this did not save him from an abortive prosecution for peculation. Defeated in that, his enemies resorted to a more devious method; they began to lop away his friends.

Religious intolerance and moral accusations are the natural weapons of the envious against the leaders of men. His friend Damon was ostracized. Phidias was attacked for impiety. On the shield of the great statue of the goddess Athene, Phidias had dared to put, among the combatants in a fight between Greeks and Amazons, portraits of Pericles and himself. Phidias died in prison. Anaxagoras, a stranger welcomed to Athens by Pericles—when there were plenty of honest fellows already there quite willing to satisfy any reasonable curiosities—was saying the strangest things about the sun and stars, and hinting not obscurely that there were no gods, but only one animating spirit (*nous*) in the world.[1] The comedy writers suddenly found they had deep religious feelings that could be profoundly and even dangerously shocked, and Anaxagoras fled the threat of a prosecution. Then came the turn of Aspasia. Athens seemed bent upon deporting her, and Pericles was torn between the woman who was the soul of his life and the ungracious city he had saved, defended, and made more beautiful and unforgettable than any other city in history. He stood up to defend Aspasia, he was seized by a storm of very human emotion, and as he spoke he wept—a gleeful thing for the rabble. His tears saved Aspasia for a time.

The Athenians were content to humiliate Pericles, but he had served them so long that they were indisposed to do without him. He had been their leader now for a third of a century.

In 431 B.C. came the war with Sparta. Plutarch accuses Pericles of bringing it on, because he felt his popularity waned so fast that a war was needed to make him indispensable.

"And as he himself was become obnoxious to the people upon Phidias's account, and was afraid of being called in question for it, he urged on the war, which as yet was uncertain, and blew up that flame which till then was stifled and suppressed. By this means he hoped to obviate the accusations that threatened him, and to mitigate the rage of envy, because such was his dignity and

[1] For an account of his views, see Burnet's *Early Greek Philosophy*. Gomperz' *Greek Thinkers* is also a good book for this section.

power, that in all important affairs, and in every great danger, the republic could place its confidence in him alone."

But the war was a slow and dangerous war, and the Athenian people were impatient. A certain Cleon arose, ambitious to oust Pericles from his leadership. There was a great clamour for a swift ending of the war. Cleon set out to be "the man who won the war." The popular poets got to work in this fashion:

> "Thou king of satyrs . . . why boast thy prowess,
> Yet shudder at the sound of sharpened swords,
> Spite of the flaming Cleon?"

An expedition under the leadership of Pericles was unsuccessful, and Cleon seized the opportunity for a prosecution. Pericles was suspended from his command and fined. The story goes that his oldest son—this was not the son of Aspasia, but of a former wife—turned against him, and pursued him with vile and incredible accusations. This young man was carried off by the plague. Then the sister of Pericles died, and then his last legitimate son. When, after the fashion of the time, he put the funeral garlands on the boy he wept aloud. Presently he himself took the contagion and died (428 B.C.).

The salient facts of this brief summary will serve to show how discordant Pericles was with the normal life of his time and city. This intellectual and artistic outbreak in Athens was no doubt favoured by the conditions of the time, but it was also due in part to the appearance of some very unusual men. It was not a general movement; it was the movement of a small group of people exceptionally placed and gifted.

§ 2

Another leading figure in this Athenian movement, a figure still more out of harmony with the life around him, and quite as much an original source and stimulant of the enduring greatness of his age, was a man called Socrates, the son of a stone-mason. He was born about sixteen years later than Herodotus, and he was beginning to be heard of about the time when Pericles died. He himself wrote nothing, but it was his custom to talk in public places. There was in those days a great searching for wisdom going on; there was a various multitude of teachers called sophists who reasoned upon truth, beauty, and right living, and instructed the developing curiosities and imaginations of youth. This was so because there were no great priestly schools in Greece. And into these discussions this man came, a clumsy and slovenly figure, barefooted, gathering about him a band of admirers and disciples.

His method was profoundly sceptical; he believed that the only possible virtue was true knowledge; he would tolerate no belief, no hope that could not pass the ultimate acid test. For himself this meant virtue, but for many of his weaker followers it meant the loss of beliefs and moral habits that would have restrained their impulses. These weaklings became self-excusing, self-indulging scoundrels. Among his young associates were Plato, who afterwards immortalized his method in a series of philosophical dialogues, and founded the philosophical school of the Academy, which lasted nine hundred years, Xenophon, of the Ten Thousand, who described his death, and Isocrates, one of the wisest of Greek political thinkers; but there were also Critias, who, when Athens was utterly defeated by Sparta, was leader among the Thirty Tyrants appointed by the Spartans to keep the crushed city under;[1] Charmides, who was killed beside Critias when the Thirty were overthrown; and Alcibiades, a brilliant and complex traitor, who did much to lead Athens into the disastrous expedition against Syracuse which destroyed her strength, who betrayed her to the Spartans, and who was at last assassinated while on his way to the Persian court to contrive mischief against Greece. These latter pupils were not the only young men of promise whose vulgar faith and patriotism Socrates destroyed, to leave nothing in its place. His most inveterate enemy was a certain Anytus, whose son, a devoted disciple of Socrates, had become a hopeless drunkard. Through Anytus it was that Socrates was at

[1] "But it was not only against the lives, properties, and liberties of Athenian citizens that the Thirty made war. They were not less solicitous to extinguish the intellectual force and education of the city, a project so perfectly in harmony both with the sentiment and practice of Sparta, that they counted on the support of their foreign allies. Among the ordinances which they promulgated was one, expressly forbidding any one 'to teach the art of words.' The edict of the Thirty was, in fact, a general suppression of the higher class of teachers or professors, above the rank of the elementary (teacher of letters or) grammatist. If such an edict could have been maintained in force for a generation, combined with the other mandates of the Thirty—the city out of which Sophocles and Euripides had just died, and in which Plato and Isocrates were in vigorous age, would have been degraded to the intellectual level of the meanest community in Greece. It was not uncommon for a Grecian despot to suppress all those assemblies wherein youths came together for the purpose of common training, either intellectual or gymnastic, as well as the public banquets and clubs or associations, as being dangerous to his authority, tending to elevation of couragé, and to a consciousness of political rights among the citizens."—Grote's *History of Greece.*

last prosecuted for "corrupting" the youth of Athens, and condemned to death by drinking a poisonous draught made from hemlock (399 B.C.).

His death is described with great beauty in the dialogue of Plato called by the name of *Phædo*.

§ 3

The preceding section raised an interesting discussion between Professor Gilbert Murray and the writer upon the character and quality of the common Athenian citizen. Professor Murray thought several phrases used by the writer harsh and unjust. But what he had to say was so interesting and informing, and the writer was so entirely in agreement with his spirit, that it seemed better, instead of modifying what had been written in § 1, to leave that as it stood and to supplement it by quoting Professor Murray. He objected to the parallelism with a twentieth-century crowd. "What I want you to do," he wrote, "is to take them at the level of the people round them and before them and see how they differ. For example, the first thing that strikes one is that they use all their powers for a different purpose than most peoples: for intellectual and artistic things. No more enormous works here to glorify divine kings; no private splendour, no luxury, but a wonderful output of art, poetry, philosophy, and—within limits—science. Compare them with Rome.

"In the matter of slavery; all nations had slaves; some treated them very cruelly, some with moderate cruelty. The Greeks alone argued whether it was right to have them—and 'cranks' occasionally proposed emancipation. You get strong testimony, sometimes indignant testimony, that the Athenians were too soft altogether in their treatment of slaves. As soon as you get to Carthaginian or Roman history you get appalling cruelty (the 6,000 crucified by Crassus, the gladiatorial games, the habitual leg-breaking of slaves, etc.); such things seem never to have occurred in Greece. As soon as you get to Alexander you get, of course, the Oriental despotic touch—fantastic vanity and cruelty; and at length the recurrence of human sacrifice.

"The greatness of Greece comes out only in the art and literature and thought; not in the political and social history—except in dim flashes. By all means emphasize clearly to start with that the Greeks of, say, the ninth century, were practically savages, and those of even the sixth and in places right on to the fifth and fourth were in many things on the 'Lower Cultures' level. Clothes like Polynesians; tools very poor; religion . . . fragments of the Polynesian all about, when you got outside the educated Attic world. But the *characteristic* is that, on this very low level, you have extraordinary flashes of very high inspiration, as the poetry and art and philosophy witness. Also, an actual achievement in social life—what one calls 'Hellenism,' *i.e.*, republicanism, simplicity of life, sobriety of thought, almost complete abolition of torture, mutilation, etc., and an amazing emancipation of the individual and of the human intellect. It is impossible to speak, really, of the 'Greek view' of anything. Because all the different views are put forward and represented: polytheism, monotheism, atheism; pro-slavery, anti-slavery; duty to animals, no duty to animals; democracy, monarchy, aristocracy. The characteristic is that *human thought got free*. (Not absolutely, of course; only to an amazing extent.) This emancipation was paid for by all sorts of instability; awful political instability, because stability in such things is produced exactly by the opposite—by long firm tradition and cohesiveness.

"It is not fair to say I idealize the Athenian mob; see, for example, my *Euripides and his Age*. But I don't think it was like our music-hall mob. It was much more artistic, much more intellectual and yet more primitive, more indecent but less lascivious, more capable of atrocious misconduct; also probably more capable of idealism. But we don't really know much about the crowd. It is only a hostile average-sensual-man background against which the philosophers and poets stand out. There was no 'city mob,' as in Rome. They were nearly all small farmers or craftsmen. I can't help thinking that their badness was more like the faults of a superior South Sea Islander than like the viler side of the 'crowd' to-day."

§ 4

The most characteristic feature of the opening years of this brilliant century and a half (475 to 325 B.C.) of Greek intellectual life was the appearance of the great tragedies.

Before the age of Pericles the main literature of the Greek peoples had been their epic poetry, of which we have already said something in our account of the earlier nomadic Aryan life. It was made up of songs of free adventure, aristocratic and valiant in spirit. The main Greek epics were reduced to writing, and the text of the chief ones put in its present order in the time of the tyrant Peisistratus (*i.e.*, immediately before the first Persian wars). Chanted originally to the chiefs and leading men in hall, they were now recited at the public festivals. In addition, there were also poems of more homely character, love songs, war lyrics, and the like.

A third stream of poetry also ran into the Greek tradition, perhaps not of Aryan origin at all, but preserving the religious ideas of the dark whites whom the Greeks had conquered. There were religious chants and hymns associated with the secret religious practices of the worship of Demeter, the earth goddess, and of Orpheus and Dionysus. They are mixed up with ideas of self-abasement, self-mutilation, and the like, that were altogether foreign to the healthy directness of the hardy barbarians from the north. These ideas were creeping out from their hiding-places, and expressing themselves in Greek in Athens during this period in the Orphic religious poetry. It seems probable that in the Athenian population among all the Greek cities the pre-Aryan strain was unusually strong. This dark strain was subtle, artistic, creative—Cnossos witnesses to that; but it had no great courage of the mind; it was afraid of the stars and of life. Whenever that strain is found in any race, there is to be found also thoughts and legends of sacrificial murders.

And perhaps also indigenous to the Greek soil, rooted deeply there in the time of the world-wide ancient heliolithic culture, were religious dances. Such dances we can trace from the Atlantic to Peru. There is a drawing in a Spanish cave at Cogul, near the Ebro, which is supposed to represent a later palæolithic ritual dance. There is little evidence of the primitive Aryans engaging in religious dances. But running through the rural life of Greece was the tradition of a dressing-up and a dancing and chanting associated with the worship of another god, who is killed and lives again as a part of the ceremonies, the god Dionysus. After the coming of the Aryans into Greece, the vocal element became stronger in these proceedings, and thrust into the dance came a recitation. There was first one reciter, then two, and then three, and the rest of the company became the chorus to the declamations of these principal actors. Out of the public performance at festivals and anniversaries of these choir songs or dithyrambs with one actor grew the great art of tragedy with three and more. Side by side with tragedy, comedy developed from another and merrier series of dressings-up and singing. Here we can but name those who were supreme in these arts who flourished in the days of Pericles, Æschylus, Sophocles, and Euripides, the masters of tragedy, and Aristophanes, the writer of comedies. We can say nothing of the splendour and beauty of the former, nor of the fantastic invention and wit of the latter. Æschylus won his first prize for tragedy in the year that Herodotus was born (484 B.C.); Sophocles came some eighteen years later; Euripides was four years old when Æschylus was beginning his career. The mockery of Aristophanes broke out (427 B.C.) only when the days of great tragedy and sculpture and building were drawing to a close.[1]

§ 5

The influence of Socrates also began to bear fruit after the days of Pericles and Aspasia. This old questioner, at whose touch faith, speculation, and illusion shrivelled together, was the centre of a group of young men who lived through and after the years of the Peloponnesian War. Of all these young men, one stands out as the greatest of them all, Plato. He was born 427 B.C., the year of the first performance of the work of Aristophanes, and he lived for eighty years.

In mental temperament Plato was of an altogether different type from the older man. He was a most artistic and delicate writer, and Socrates could write nothing consecutive. He cared for beautiful things and Socrates despised them. He was supremely concerned with the ordering of public affairs and the scheming of happier human relationships, while Socrates, heedless of heat and cold and the opinion of his fellow creatures, concentrated his mind upon a serene disillusionment. Life, said Socrates, was deception; only the Soul lived. Plato had a very great affection for this rugged old teacher, he found his method of the utmost value in disentangling and cleaning up opinions, and he made him the central figure of his immortal dialogues; but his own thoughts and disposition turned him altogether away from the sceptical attitude. In many of the dialogues the voice is the voice of Socrates, but the thought is the thought of Plato. Plato was living in a time of doubt and questioning about all human relationships. In the great days of Pericles, before 450 B.C., there seems to have been a complete satisfaction in Athens

[1] A very good and useful account of this great literature for the reader who is not a classical student is Norwood's *Greek Tragedy*.

with social and political institutions. Then there seemed no reason for questioning. Men felt free; the community prospered; one suffered chiefly from jealousy. The History of Herodotus displays little or no dissatisfaction with Athenian political institutions.

But Plato, who was born about the time Herodotus died, and who grew up in the atmosphere of a disastrous war and great social distress and confusion, was from the first face to face with human discord and the misfit of human institutions. To that challenge his mind responded. One of his earlier works and his latest are bold and penetrating discussions of the possible betterment of social relations. Socrates had taught him to take nothing for granted, not even the common relations of husband and wife or parent and child. His *Republic*, the first of all Utopian books, is a young man's dream of a city in which human life is arranged according to a novel and a better plan; his last unfinished work, the *Laws*, is a discussion of the regulation of another such Utopia. There is much in Plato at which we cannot even glance here, but it is a landmark in this history, it is a new thing in the development of mankind, this appearance of the idea of wilfully and completely recasting human conditions. So far mankind has been living by tradition under the fear of the gods. Here is a man who says boldly to our race, and as if it were a quite reasonable and natural thing to say, "Take hold of your lives. Most of these things that distress you, you can avoid; most of these things that dominate you, you can overthrow. You can do as you will with them."

One other thing besides the conflicts of the time perhaps stimulated the mind of Plato in this direction. In the days of Pericles Athens had founded many settlements overseas, and the setting up of these settlements had familiarized men with the idea that a community need not grow, it could also be made.

Closely associated with Plato was a younger man, who later also maintained a school in Athens and lived to an even greater age. This was Isocrates. He was what we should call a publicist, a writer rather than an orator, and his peculiar work was to develop the idea of Herodotus, the idea of a unification of Greece against the Persian Empire, as a remedy for the baseness and confusion of her politics and the waste and destruction of her internecine wars. His political horizon was in some respects broader than Plato's, and in his later years he looked towards monarchy, and particularly towards the Macedonian monarchy of Philip, as a more unifying and broadening method of government than city democracy. The same drift to monarchist ideas had occurred in the case of that Xenophon whose *Anabasis* we have already mentioned. In his old age this retired mercenary wrote the *Cyropædia*, a "vindication both theoretically and practically of absolute monarchy as shown in the organization of the Persian Empire." [1]

§ 6

Plato taught in the Academy. To him in his old age came a certain good-looking youngster from Stagira in Macedonia, Aristotle, who was the son of the Macedonian king's physician, and a man with a very different type of mind from that of the great Athenian. He was naturally sceptical of the imaginative will, and with a great respect for and comprehension of established fact. Later on, after Plato was dead, he set up a school at the Lyceum in Athens and taught, criticizing Plato and Socrates with a certain hardness. When he taught, the shadow of Alexander the Great lay across the freedom of Greece, and he favoured slavery and constitutional kings. He had previously been the tutor of Alexander for several years at the court of Philip of Macedon.[2] Intelligent men were losing heart in those days, their faith in the power of men to make their own conditions of life was fading. There were no more Utopias. The rush of events was manifestly too powerful for such organized effort as was then practicable between men of fine intelligence. It was possible to think of recasting human society when human society was a little city of a few thousand citizens, but what was happening about them was something cataclysmal; it was the political recasting of the whole known world, of the affairs of what even then must have amounted to something between fifty and a hundred million people. It was recasting upon a scale no human mind was yet equipped to grasp. It drove thought back upon the idea of a vast and implacable Fate. It made men snatch at whatever looked stable and unifying. Monarchy, for instance, for all its manifest vices, was a conceivable government for millions; it had, to a certain extent, *worked;* it imposed a ruling will

[1] Mahaffy.

[2] There is not a single sentence in praise of Alexander, no dedication, no compliments, in all Aristotle. On the other hand, he never mentions Demosthenes nor quotes him in the Rhetoric.—G. M.

THE ACADEMY AT ATHENS

By James Clark, R.I.

"Plato taught in the Academy. To him, in his old age, came Aristotle, a good-looking youngster from Stagira."

where it would seem that a collective will was impossible. This change of the general intellectual mood harmonized with Aristotle's natural respect for existing fact. If, on the one hand, it made him approve of monarchy and slavery and the subjection of women as reasonable institutions, on the other hand it made him eager to understand fact and to get some orderly knowledge of these realities of nature and human nature that were now so manifestly triumphant over the creative dreams of the preceding generation. He is terribly sane and luminous, and terribly wanting in self-sacrificial enthusiasm. He questions Plato when Plato would exile poets from his Utopia, for poetry is a power; he directs his energy along a line diametrically opposed to Socrates' depreciation of Anaxagoras. He anticipates Bacon and the modern scientific movement in his realization of the importance of ordered knowledge. He set himself to the task of gathering together and setting down knowledge. He was the first natural historian. Other men before him had speculated about the nature of things, but he, with every young man he could win over to the task, set himself to classify and compare things. Plato says in effect: "Let us take hold of life and remodel it"; this soberer successor: "Let us first know more of life and meanwhile serve the king." It was not so much a contradiction as an immense qualification of the master.

The peculiar relation of Aristotle to Alexander the Great enabled him to procure means for his work such as were not available again for scientific inquiry for long ages. He could command hundreds of talents (a talent=about £240) for his expenses. At one time he had at his disposal a thousand men scattered throughout Asia and Greece, collecting matter for his natural history.[1] [2] They were, of course, very untrained observers, collectors of stories rather than observers; but nothing of the kind had ever been attempted, had even been thought of, so far as we know, before his time. Political as well as natural science began. The students of the Lyceum under his direction made an analysis of 158 political constitutions. . . .

This was the first gleam of organized science in the world. The early death of Alexander and the breaking up of his empire almost before it had begun, put an end to endowments on this scale for 2,000 years. Only in Egypt at the Alexandria Museum did any scientific research continue, and that only for a few generations. Fifty years after Aristotle's death the Lyceum had already dwindled to insignificance.

[1] Wheeler.

[2] Bauer, in *Vom Griechentum zum Christentum*, says that Alexander sent a mission of exploration to Abyssinia to enable Aristotle to settle the question of the cause of the Nile inundations (melting of mountain snows), and that he also had tropical flora and other material collected for him.—E. B.

M

§ 7

The general drift of thought in the concluding years of the fourth century B.C. was not with Aristotle, nor towards the laborious and necessary accumulation of ordered knowledge. It is possible that without his endowments from the king he would have made but a small figure in intellectual history. Through them he was able to give his splendid intelligence substance and effect. The ordinary man prefers easy ways so long as they may be followed, and is almost wilfully heedless whether they end at last in a cul-de-sac. Finding the stream of events too powerful to control at once, the generality of philosophical teachers drifted in those days from the scheming of model cities and the planning of new ways of living into the elaboration of beautiful and consoling systems of evasion.

Perhaps that is putting things coarsely and unjustly. But let Professor Gilbert Murray speak upon this matter.[3]

"The Cynics cared only for virtue and the relation of the soul to God; the world and its learning and its honours were as dross to them. The Stoics and Epicureans, so far apart at first sight, were very similar in their ultimate aim. What they really cared about was ethics—the practical question how a man should order his life. Both, indeed, gave themselves to some science—the Epicureans to physics, the Stoics to logic and rhetoric—but only as a means to an end. The Stoic tried to win men's hearts and convictions by sheer subtlety of abstract argument and dazzling sublimity of thought and expression. The Epicurean was determined to make Humanity go its way without cringing to capricious gods and without sacrificing Free-Will. He condensed his gospel into four maxims: "God is not to be feared; Death cannot be felt; the Good can be won; all that we dread can be borne and conquered."

And meanwhile the stream of events flowed on, with a reciprocal indifference to philosophy.

[3] *Ancient Greek Literature.*

§ 8

If the Greek classics are to be read with any benefit by modern men, they must be read as the work of men like ourselves. Regard must be had to their traditions, their opportunities, and their limitations. There is a disposition to exaggeration in all human admiration; men will treat the rough notes of Thucydides or Plato for work they never put in order as miracles of style, and the errors of their transcribers as hints of unfathomable mysteries; most of our classical texts are very much mangled, and all were originally the work of human beings in difficulties, living in a time of such darkness and narrowness of outlook as makes our own age by comparison a period of dazzling illumination. What we shall lose in reverence by this familiar treatment, we shall gain in sympathy for that group of troubled, uncertain, and very modern minds. The Athenian writers were, indeed, the first of modern men. They were discussing questions that we still discuss; they began to struggle with the great problems that confront us to-day. Their writings are our dawn.[1]

They began an inquiry, and they arrived at no solutions. We cannot pretend to-day that we have arrived at solutions to most of the questions they asked. The mind of the Hebrews, as we have already shown, awoke suddenly to the endless miseries and disorders of life, saw that these miseries and disorders were largely due to the lawless acts of men, and concluded that salvation could come only through subduing ourselves to the service of the one God who rules heaven and earth. The Greek, rising to the same perception, was not prepared with the same idea of a patriarchal deity; he lived in a world in which there was not God but the gods; if perhaps he felt that the gods themselves were limited, then he thought of Fate behind them, cold and impersonal. So he put his problem in the form of an enquiry as to what was right living, without any definite correlation of the right-living man with the will of God. . . . To us, looking at the matter from a standpoint purely historical, the common problem can now be presented in a form that, for the purposes of history, covers both the Hebrew and Greek way of putting it. We have seen our kind rising out of the unconsciousness of animals to a continuing racial self-consciousness, realizing the unhappiness of its wild diversity of aims, realizing the inevitable tragedy of individual self-seeking, and feeling its way blindly towards some linking and subordinating idea to save it from the pains and accidents of mere individuality. The gods, the god-king, the idea of the tribe, the idea of the city; here are ideas that have claimed and held for a time the devotion of men, ideas in which they have a little lost their individual selfishness and escaped to the realization of a more enduring life. Yet, as our wars and disasters prove, none of these greater ideas have yet been great enough. The gods have failed to protect, the tribe has proved itself vile and cruel, the city ostracized one's best and truest friends, the god-king made a beast of himself. . . .

As we read over the speculative literature of this great period of the Greeks, we realize three barriers set about the Greek mind, from which it rarely escaped, but from which we now perhaps are beginning to escape.

The first of these limitations was the obsession of the Greek mind by the idea of the city as the ultimate state. In a world in which empire had followed empire, each greater than its predecessor, in a world through which men and ideas drove ever more loosely and freely, in a world visibly unifying even then, the Greeks, because of their peculiar physical and political circumstances, were still dreaming impossibly of a compact little city state, impervious to outer influences, valiantly secure against the whole world. Plato's estimate of the number of citizens in a perfect state varied between 1,000 (the *Republic*) and 5,040 (the *Laws*) citizens.[2]

[1] Jung in his *Psychology of the Unconscious* is very good in his chapter I, on the differences between ancient (pre-Athenian) thought and modern thought. The former he calls Undirected Thinking, the latter Directed Thinking. The former was a thinking in images, akin to dreaming; the latter a thinking in words. Science is an organization of directed thinking. The Antique spirit (before the Greek thinkers i.e.) created not science but mythology. The ancient human world was a world of subjective fantasies like the world of children and uneducated young people to-day, and like the world of savages and dreams. Infantile thought and dreams are a re-echo of the prehistoric and savage. Myths are the mass dreams of peoples, and dreams the myths of individuals. The work of hard and disciplined thinking by means of carefully analysed words and statements which was begun by the Greek thinkers and resumed by the scholastic philosophers of whom we shall tell in the middle ages, was a necessary preliminary to the development of modern science.

[2] "For the proper administration of justice and for the distribution of authority it is necessary that the citizens be acquainted with each other's characters, so that, where this cannot be, much mischief ensues, both in the use of authority and in the administration of justice; for it is not just to decide arbitrarily, as must be the case with excessive population." Aristotle's *Politics*, quoted by Wheeler, who adds,

THE DEATH OF DEMOSTHENES

From the picture by Bramtott

"A voice in Athens began to clamour like a watch-dog . . it was the orator Demosthenes, hurling warnings and threats and denunciations at King Philip of Macedon."

This state was to go to war and hold its own against other cities of the same size. And this was not a couple of generations after the hosts of Xerxes had crossed the Hellespont!

Perhaps these Greeks thought the day of world empires had passed for ever, whereas it was only beginning. At the utmost their minds reached out to alliances and leagues. There must have been men at the court of Artaxerxes thinking far away beyond these little ideas of the rocky creek, the island, and the mountain-encircled valley. But the need for unification against the greater powers that moved outside the Greek-speaking world, the Greek mind disregarded wilfully. These outsiders were barbarians, not to be needlessly thought about; they were barred out now from Greece for ever. One took Persian money; everybody took Persian money; what did it matter? Or one enlisted for a time in their armies (as Xenophon did) and hoped for his luck with a rich prisoner. Athens took sides in Egyptian affairs, and carried on minor wars with Persia, but there was no conception of a common policy or a common future for Greece. . . . Until at last a voice in Athens began to shout "Macedonia!" to clamour like a watch-dog, "Macedonia!" This was the voice of the orator and demagogue, Demosthenes, hurling warnings and threats and denunciations at King Philip of Macedon, who had learnt his politics not only from Plato and Aristotle, but also from Isocrates and Xenophon, and from Babylon and Susa, and who was preparing quietly, ably, and steadfastly to dominate all Greece, and through Greece to conquer the known world. . . .

There was a second thing that cramped the Greek mind, the institution of domestic slavery. Slavery was implicit in Greek life; men could conceive of neither comfort nor dignity without it. But slavery shuts off one's sympathy not only from a class of one's fellow subjects; it puts the slave-owner into a class and organization against all stranger men. One is of an elect tribe. Plato, carried by his clear reason and the noble sanity of his spirit beyond the things of the present, would have abolished slavery; much popular feeling and the New Comedy were against it; the Stoics and Epicureans, many of whom were slaves, condemned it as unnatural, but finding it too strong to upset, decided that it did not affect the soul and might be ignored. With the wise there was no bound or free. To the matter-of-fact Aristotle, and probably to most practical men, its abolition was inconceivable. So they declared that there were in the world men "naturally slaves." . . .

Finally, the thought of the Greeks was hampered by a want of knowledge that is almost inconceivable to us to-day. They had no knowledge of the past of mankind at all; at best they had a few shrewd guesses. They had no knowledge of geography beyond the range of the Mediterranean basin and the frontiers of Persia. We know far more to-day of what was going on in Susa, Persepolis, Babylon, and Memphis in the time of Pericles than he did. Their astronomical ideas were still in the state of rudimentary speculations. Anaxagoras, greatly daring, thought the sun and moon were vast globes, so vast that the sun was probably "as big as all the Peloponnesus." The forty-seventh proposition of the first book of Euclid was regarded as one of the supreme triumphs of the human mind. Their ideas in physics and chemistry were the results of profound cogitation; it is wonderful that they did guess at atomic structure. One has to remember their extraordinary poverty in the matter of experimental apparatus. They had coloured glass for ornament, but no white glass; no accurate means of measuring the minor intervals of time, no really efficient numerical notation, no very accurate scales, no rudiments of telescope or microscope. A modern scientific man dumped down in the Athens of Pericles would have found the utmost difficulty in demonstrating the elements of his knowledge, however crudely, to the men he would have found there. He would have had to rig up the simplest apparatus under every disadvantage, while Socrates pointed out the absurdity of seeking Truth with pieces of wood and string and metal such as small boys use for fishing. And our professor of science would also have been in constant danger of a prosecution for impiety.

Our world to-day draws upon relatively immense accumulations of knowledge of fact. In the age of Pericles scarcely the first stone of our comparatively tremendous cairn of things recorded and proved had been put in place. When we reflect upon this difference, then it ceases to be remarkable that the Greeks, with all their aptitude for political speculation, were blind to the insecurities of their civilization from without and from within, to the necessity for effective

"Aristotle comes to the conclusion that the natural 'limit to the size of the state must be found in the capability of being easily taken in at a glance.'" But Murray notes that the word Eusunopton means also "capable of being comprehended as a unity"—a very different and wider idea.

unification, to the swift rush of events that was to end for long ages these first brief freedoms of the human mind.

It is not in the results it achieved, but in the attempts it made that the true value for us of this group of Greek talkers and writers lies. It is not that they answered questions, but that they dared to ask them. Never before had man challenged his world and the way of life to which he found his birth had brought him. Never had he said before that he could alter his conditions. Tradition and a seeming necessity had held him to life as he had found it grown up about his tribe since time immemorial. Hitherto he had taken the world as children still take the homes and habits in which they have been reared.

So in the fifth and fourth centuries B.C. we perceive, most plainly in Judea and in Athens, but by no means confined to those centres, the beginnings of a moral and an intellectual process in mankind, an appeal to righteousness and an appeal to the truth from the passions and confusions and immediate appearances of existence. It is like the dawn of the sense of responsibility in a youth, who suddenly discovers that life is neither easy nor aimless. Mankind is growing up. The rest of history for three and twenty centuries is threaded with the spreading out and development and interaction and the clearer and more effective statement of these main leading ideas. Slowly more and more men apprehend the reality of human brotherhood, the needlessness of wars and cruelties and oppression, the possibilities of a common purpose for the whole of our kind. In every generation thereafter there is the evidence of men seeking for that better order to which they feel our world must come. But everywhere and wherever in any man the great constructive ideas have taken hold, the hot greeds, the jealousies, the suspicions and impatience that are in the nature of every one of us, war against the struggle towards greater and broader purposes. The last twenty-three centuries of history are like the efforts of some impulsive, hasty immortal to think clearly and live rightly. Blunder follows blunder; promising beginnings end in grotesque disappointments; streams of living water are poisoned by the cup that conveys them to the thirsty lips of mankind. But the hope of men rises again at last after every disaster. . . .

We pass on now to the story of one futile commencement, one glorious shattered beginning of human unity. There was in Alexander the Great knowledge and imagination, power and opportunity, folly, egotism, detestable vulgarity, and an immense promise broken by the accident of his early death while men were still dazzled by its immensity.

XXIV

THE CAREER OF ALEXANDER THE GREAT[1]

§ 1

THE true hero of the story of Alexander is not so much Alexander as his father Philip. The author of a piece does not shine in the limelight as the actor does, and it was Philip who planned much of the greatness that his son achieved, who laid the foundations and forged the tools, who had indeed already begun the Persian expedition at the time of his death. Philip, beyond doubting, was one of the greatest monarchs the world has ever seen; he was a man of the utmost intelligence and ability, and his range of ideas was vastly beyond the scope of his time. He made Aristotle his friend; he must have discussed with him those schemes for the organization of real knowledge which the philosopher was to realize later through Alexander's endowments. Philip, so far as we can judge, seems to have been Aristotle's "Prince";

[1] Benjamin Ide Wheeler's *Alexander the Great* and G. D. Hogarth's *Philip and Alexander* have been very useful here.

to him Aristotle turned as men turn only to those whom they admire and trust. To Philip also Isocrates appealed as the great leader who should unify and ennoble the chaotic public life of Greece.

In many books it is stated that Philip was a man of incredible cynicism and of uncontrolled lusts. It is true that at feasts, like all the Macedonians of his time, he was a hard drinker and sometimes drunken—it was probably considered unamiable not to drink excessively at feasts; but of the other accusations there is no real proof, and for evidence we have only the railings of such antagonists as Demosthenes, the Athenian demagogue and orator, a man of reckless rhetoric. The quotation of a phrase or so will serve to show to what the patriotic anger of Demosthenes could bring him. In one of the *Philippics*, as his denunciations of Philip are called, he gives vent in this style:

"Philip—a man who not only is no Greek, and no way akin to the Greeks, but is not even a barbarian from a respectable country—no, a pestilent fellow of Macedon, a country from which we never get even a decent slave." And so on and so on. We know, as a matter of fact, that the Macedonians were an Aryan people very closely akin to the Greeks, and that Philip was probably the best educated man of his time. This was the spirit in which the adverse accounts of Philip were written.

When Philip became king of Macedonia in 359 B.C., his country was a little country without a seaport or industries or any considerable city. It had a peasant population, Greek almost in language and ready to be Greek in sympathies, but more purely Nordic in blood than any people to the south of it. Philip made this little barbaric state into a great one; he created the most efficient military organization the world had so far seen, and he had brought most of Greece into one confederacy under his leadership at the time of his death. And his extraordinary quality, his power of thinking out beyond the current ideas of his time, is shown not so much in those matters as in the care with which he had his son trained to carry on the policy he had created. He is one of the few monarchs in history who cared for his successor. Alexander was, as few other monarchs have ever been, a specially educated king; he was educated for empire. Aristotle was but one of the several able tutors his father chose for him. Philip confided his policy to him, and entrusted him with commands and authority by the time he was sixteen. He commanded the cavalry at Chæronea under his father's eye. He was nursed into power—generously and unsuspiciously.

To any one who reads his life with care it is evident that Alexander started with an equipment of training and ideas of unprecedented value. As he got beyond the wisdom of his upbringing he began to blunder and misbehave—sometimes with a dreadful folly. The defects of his character had triumphed over his upbringing long before he died.

Philip of Macedon

Philip was a king after the old pattern, a leader-king, first among his peers, of the ancient Nordic Aryan type. The army he found in Macedonia consisted of a general foot levy and a noble equestrian order called the "companions." The people were farmers and hunters and somewhat drunken in their habits, but ready for discipline and good fighting stuff. And if the people were homely, the government was intelligent and alert. For some generations the court language had been Attic (=Athenian) Greek, and the court had been sufficiently civilized to shelter and entertain such great figures as Euripides, who died there in 406 B.C., and Zeuxis the artist. Moreover, Philip, before his accession, had spent some years as a hostage in Greece. He had had as good an education as Greece could give at that time. He was, therefore, quite familiar with what we may call the idea of Isocrates—the idea of a great union of the Greek states in Europe to dominate the Eastern world; and he knew, too, how incapable was the Athenian democracy, because of its constitution and tradition, of taking the opportunity that lay before it. For it was an opportunity that would have to be shared. To the Athenians or the Spartans it would mean letting in a "lot of foreigners" to the advantages of citizenship. It would mean lowering themselves to the level of equality and fellowship with Macedonians—a people from whom "*we*" do not get "even a decent slave."[1]

There was no way to secure unanimity

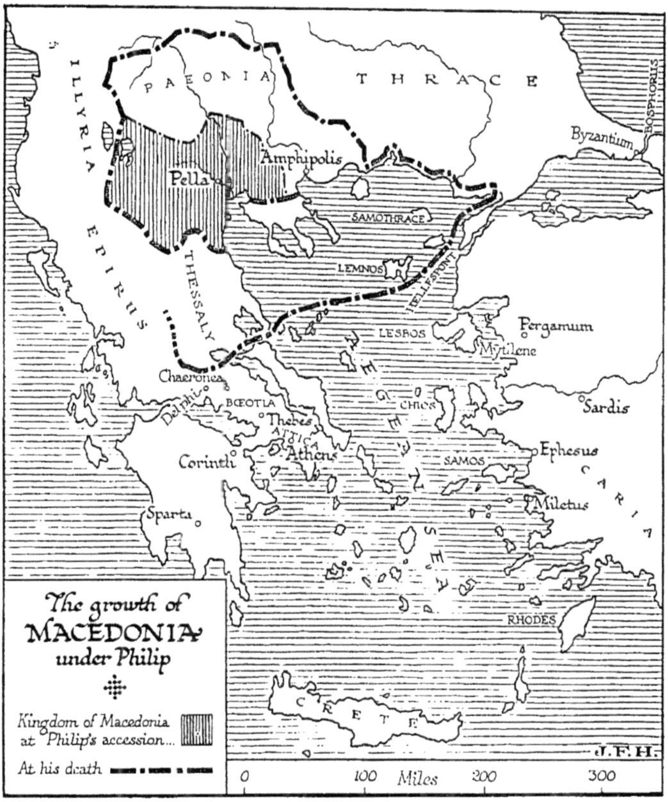

The growth of MACEDONIA under Philip

Kingdom of Macedonia at Philip's accession...

At his death

among the Greeks for the contemplated enterprise except by some revolutionary political action. It was no love of peace that kept the Greeks from such an adventure; it was their political divisions. The resources of the several states were exhausted in a series of internecine wars—wars arising out of the merest excuses and fanned by oratorical wind. The ploughing of certain sacred lands near Delphi by the Phocians was, for example, the pretext for a sanguinary Sacred War.

Philip's first years of kingship were devoted to the discipline of his army. Hitherto most of the main battle fighting in the world had been done by footmen in formation. In the very ancient Sumerian battle-pieces we see spearmen in close order forming the main battle, just as they did in the Zulu armies of the nineteenth century; the Greek troops of Philip's time were still fighting in that same style; the Theban phalanx was a mass of infantry holding spears, the hinder ranks thrusting their longer spears between the front-line men. Such a formation went through anything less disciplined that opposed it. Mounted archers could, of course, inflict considerable losses on such a mass of men, and accordingly, as the horse came into warfare, horsemen appeared on

[1] To the common Athenians, that is. But to many thoughtful Greeks the rôle of Macedonia in their future was a matter of earnest speculation. Herodotus (viii. 137) tells a long story of a prophecy by which the inheritance of Perdiccas, the ancestor of the Macedonian kings, was to embrace at last the whole round world. This was written a hundred years before Philip and Alexander.

either side as an accessory to this main battle. The reader must remember that the horse did not come into very effective use in western war until the rise of the Assyrians, and then at first only as a chariot horse. The chariots drove full tilt at the infantry mass and tried to break it. Unless its discipline was very solid they succeeded. The Homeric fighting is chariot fighting. It is not until the last thousand years B.C. that we begin to find mounted soldiers, as distinct from charioteers, playing a part in warfare. At first they appear to have fought in a scattered fashion, each man doing his personal feats. So the Lydians fought against Cyrus. It was Philip who seems to have created charging cavalry. He caused his "companions" to drill for a massed charge. And also he strengthened his phalanx by giving the rear men longer spears than had been used hitherto, and so deepening its mass. The Macedonian phalanx was merely a more solid version of the Theban phalanx. None of these massed infantry formations was flexible enough to stand a flank or rear attack. They had very slight manœuvring power. Both Philip's and his son's victories followed, therefore, with variations, one general scheme of co-operation between these two arms. The phalanx advanced in the centre and held the enemy's main body; on one wing or the other the cavalry charges swept away the enemy cavalry, and then swooped round upon the flank and rear of the enemy phalanx, the front of which the Macedonian phalanx was already smiting. The enemy main battle then broke and was massacred. As Alexander's military experience grew, he also added a use of catapults in the field, big stone-throwing affairs, to break up the enemy infantry. Before his time catapults had been used in sieges, but never in battles. He invented "artillery preparation."

With the weapon of his new army in his hand, Philip first turned his attention to the north of Macedonia. He carried expeditions into Illyria and as far as the Danube; he also spread his power along the coast as far as the Hellespont. He secured possession of a port, Amphipolis, and certain gold mines adjacent. After several Thracian expeditions he turned southward in good earnest. He took up the cause of the Delphic amphictyony against those sacrilegious Phocians, and so appeared as the champion of Hellenic religion.

There was a strong party of Greeks, it must be understood, a Pan-Hellenic party, in favour of the Greek headship of Philip. The chief writer of this Pan-Hellenic movement was Isocrates. Athens, on the other hand was the head and front of the opposition to Philip, and Athens was in open sympathy with Persia, even sending emissaries to the Great King to warn him of the danger to him of a united Greece. The comings and goings of twelve years cannot be related here. In 338 B.C. the long struggle between division and pan-Hellenism came to a decisive issue, and at the battle of Chæronea Philip inflicted a crushing defeat upon Athens and her allies. He gave Athens peace upon astonishingly generous terms; he displayed himself steadfastly resolved to propitiate and favour that implacable city; and in 338 B.C. a congress of Greek states recognized him as captain-general for the war against Persia.

He was now a man of forty-seven. It seemed as though the world lay at his feet. He had made his little country into the leading state in a great Græco-Macedonian confederacy. That unification was to be the prelude to a still greater one, the unification of the Western world with the Persian empire into one world state of all known peoples. Who can doubt he had that dream? The writings of Isocrates convince us that he had it. Who can deny that he might have realized it? He had a reasonable hope of living for perhaps another quarter century of activity. In 336 B.C. his advanced guard crossed into Asia. . . .

But he never followed with his main force. He was assassinated.

§ 2

It is necessary now to tell something of the domestic life of King Philip. The lives of both Philip and his son were pervaded by the personality of a restless and evil woman, Olympias, the mother of Alexander.

She was the daughter of the king of Epirus, a country to the west of Macedonia, and, like Macedonia, a semi-Greek land. She met Philip, or was thrown in his way, at some religious gathering in Samothrace. Plutarch declares the marriage was a love-match, and there seems to be at least this much in the charges against Philip that, like many energetic and imaginative men, he was prone to impatient love impulses. He married her when he was already a king, and Alexander was born to him three years later.

It was not long before Olympias and Philip were bitterly estranged. She was jealous of him, but there was another and graver source of trouble in her passion for religious mysteries. We have already noted that beneath the fine and restrained Nordic religion of the Greeks the land abounded with religious cults of a darker and more ancient kind, aboriginal cults with secret initiations, orgiastic celebrations, and often with cruel and obscene rites. These religions of the shadows, these practices of the women and peasants and slaves, gave Greece her Orphic, Dionysic, and Demeter cults; they have lurked in the tradition of Europe down almost to our own times. The witchcraft of the Middle Ages, with its resort to the blood of babes, scraps of executed criminals, incantations and magic circles, seems to have been little else than the lingering vestiges of these solemnities of the dark whites. In these matters Olympias was an expert and an enthusiast, and Plutarch

mentions that she achieved considerable celebrity by a use of tame serpents in these pious exercises. The snakes invaded her domestic apartments, and history is not clear whether Philip found in them matter for exasperation or religious awe. These occupations of his wife must have been a serious inconvenience to Philip, for the Macedonian people were still in that sturdy stage of social development in which neither enthusiastic religiosity nor uncontrollable wives are admired.

The evidence of a bitter hostility between mother and father peeps out in many little things in the histories. She was evidently jealous of Philip's conquests; she hated his fame. There are many signs that Olympias did her best to set her son against his father and attach him wholly to herself. A story survives (in Plutarch's *Life*) that "whenever news was brought of Philip's victories, the capture of a city or the winning of some great battle, he never seemed greatly rejoiced to hear it; on the contrary he used to say to his play-fellows: 'Father will get everything in advance, boys; he won't leave any great task for me to share with you.'" . . .

It is not a natural thing for a boy to envy his father in this fashion without some inspiration. That sentence sounds like an echo.

We have already pointed out how manifest it is that Philip planned the succession of Alexander, and how eager he was to thrust fame and power into the boy's hands. He was thinking of the political structure he was building—but the mother was thinking of the glory and pride of that wonderful lady Olympias. She masked her hatred of her husband under the cloak of a mother's solicitude for her son's future. When in 337 B.C. Philip, after the fashion of kings in those days, married a second wife who was a native Macedonian, Cleopatra, "of whom he was passionately enamoured," Olympias made much trouble.

Plutarch tells of a pitiful scene that occurred at Philip's marriage to Cleopatra There was much drinking of wine at the banquet, and Attalus, the father of the bride, being "intoxicated with liquor," betrayed the general hostility to Olympias and Epirus by saying he hoped there would be a child by the marriage to give them a truly Macedonian heir. Whereupon Alexander, taut for such an insult, cried out, "What then am I?" and hurled his cup at Attalus. Philip, enraged, stood up and, says Plutarch, drew his sword, only to stumble and fall. Alexander, blind with rage and jealousy, taunted and insulted his father.

"Macedonians," he said. "See there the general who would go from Europe to Asia! Why! he cannot get from one table to another!"

How that scene lives still, the sprawl, the flushed faces, the angry voice of the boy! Next day Alexander departed with his mother—and Philip did nothing to restrain them. Olympias went home to Epirus; Alexander departed to Illyria. Thence Philip persuaded him to return.

Fresh trouble arose. Alexander had a brother of weak intellect, Aridæus, whom the Persian governor of Caria sought as a son-in-law. "Alexander's friends and his mother now infused notions into him again, though perfectly groundless, that by so noble a match, and the support consequent upon it, Philip designed the crown for Aridæus.

Alexander, in the uneasiness these suspicions gave him, sent one Thessalus, a player, into Caria, to desire the grandee to pass by Aridæus, who was of spurious birth, and deficient in point of understanding, and to take the lawful heir to the crown into his alliance. Pixodarus was infinitely more pleased with this proposal. But Philip no sooner had intelligence of it, than he went to Alexander's apartment, taking along with him Philotas, the son of Parmenio, one of his most intimate friends and companions, and, in his presence, reproached him with his degeneracy and meanness of spirit, in thinking of being son-in-law to a man of Caria, one of the slaves of a barbarian king. At the same time he wrote to the Corinthians, insisting that they should send Thessalus to him in chains. Harpalus and Niarchus, Phrygius and Ptolemy, some of the other companions of the prince, he banished. But Alexander afterwards recalled them, and treated them with great distinction."

There is something very touching in this story of the father pleading with the son he manifestly loved, and baffled by the web of mean suggestion which had been spun about the boy's imagination.

It was at the marriage of his daughter to her uncle, the king of Epirus and the brother of Olympias, that Philip was stabbed. He was walking in a procession into the theatre unarmed, in a white robe, and he was cut down by one of his bodyguard. The murderer had a horse waiting, and would have got away, but the foot of his horse caught in a wild vine and he was thrown from the saddle by the stumble and slain by his pursuers. . . .

So at the age of twenty Alexander was at the end of his anxiety about the succession, and established king in Macedonia.

Olympias then reappeared in Macedonia, a woman proudly vindicated. It is said that she insisted upon paying the same funeral honours to the memory of the murderer as to Philip, and that she consecrated the fatal weapon to Apollo, inscribed with the name Myrtalis, by which Philip had been wont to address her when their loves first began.[1] In Greece there were great rejoicings over this auspicious event, and Demosthenes, when he had the news, although it was but seven days after the death of his own daughter, went into the public assembly at Athens in gay attire wearing a chaplet.

[1] Goldsmith's *History of Greece*. The picturesque disposition of the novelist, rather than the austere method of the historian, is apparent here.

Whatever Olympias may have done about her husband's assassin, history does not doubt about her treatment of her supplanter, Cleopatra. So soon as Alexander was out of the way—and a revolt of the hillmen in the north called at once for his attention—Cleopatra's newly born child was killed in its mother's arms, and Cleopatra—no doubt after a little taunting—was then strangled. These excesses of womanly feeling are said to have shocked Alexander, but they did not prevent him from leaving his mother in a position of considerable authority in Macedonia. She wrote letters to him upon religious and political questions, and he showed a dutiful disposition in sending her always a large share of the plunder he made.

§ 3

These stories have to be told because history cannot be understood without them. Here was the great world of men between India and the Adriatic ready for union, ready as it had never been before for a unifying control. Here was the wide order of the Persian empire with its roads, its posts, its general peace and prosperity, ripe for the fertilizing influence of the Greek mind. And these stories display the quality of the human beings to whom those great opportunities came. Here was this Philip who was a very great and noble man, and yet he was drunken, he could keep no order in his household. Here was Alexander in many ways gifted above any man of his time, and he was vain, suspicious, and passionate, with a mind set awry by his mother.

We are beginning to understand something of what the world might be, something of what our race might become, were it not for our still raw humanity. It is barely a matter of seventy generations between ourselves and Alexander; and between ourselves and the savage hunters our ancestors, who charred their food in the embers or ate it raw, intervene some four or five hundred generations. There is not much scope for the modification of a species in four or five hundred generations. Make men and women only sufficiently jealous or fearful or drunken or angry, and the hot red eyes of the cave-men will glare out at us to-day. We have writing and teaching, science and power; we have tamed the beasts and schooled the lightning; but we are still only shambling towards the light. We have tamed and bred the beasts, but we have still to tame and breed ourselves.

From the very beginning of his reign the

deeds of Alexander showed how well he had assimilated his father's plans, and how great were his own abilities. A map of the known world is needed to show the course of his life. At first, after receiving assurances from Greece that he was to be captain-general of the Grecian forces, he marched through Thrace to the Danube; he crossed the river and burnt a village, the second great monarch to raid the Scythian country beyond the Danube; then recrossed it and marched westward and so came down by Illyria. By that time the city of Thebes was in rebellion, and his next blow was at Greece. Thebes—unsupported of course by Athens—was taken and looted; it was treated with extravagant violence; all its buildings, except the temple and the house of the poet Pindar, were razed, and thirty thousand people sold into slavery. Greece was stunned, and Alexander was free to go on with the Persian campaign.

This destruction of Thebes betrayed a streak of crazy violence in the new master of human destinies. It was too heavy a blow to have dealt. It was a barbaric thing to do. No Greeks would have gone so far with conquered Greeks. If the spirit of rebellion was killed, so also was the spirit of help. The Greek states remained inert thereafter, neither troublesome nor helpful. They would not support Alexander with their shipping, a thing which was to prove a very grave embarrassment to him.[1]

There is a story told by Plutarch about this Theban massacre, as if it redounded to the credit of Alexander, but indeed it shows only how his saner and his crazy sides were in conflict. It tells of a Macedonian officer and a Theban lady. This officer was among the looters, and he entered this woman's house, inflicted unspeakable insults and injuries upon her, and at last demanded whether she had gold or silver hidden. She told him all her treasures had been put into the well, conducted him thither, and, as he stooped to peer down, pushed him suddenly in and killed him by throwing great stones upon him. Some allied soldiers came upon this scene and took her forthwith to Alexander for judgment.

She defied him. Already the extravagant impulse that had ordered the massacre was upon the wane, and he not only spared her, but had her family and property and freedom restored to her. This Plutarch makes out to be a generosity, but the issue is more complicated than that. It was Alexander who was outraging and plundering and enslaving all Thebes. That poor crumpled Macedonian brute in the well had been doing only what he had been told he had full liberty to do. Is a commander first to give cruel orders, and then to forgive and reward those who slay his instruments? This gleam of remorse at the instance of one woman who was not perhaps wanting in tragic dignity and beauty, is a poor set-off to the murder of a great city.

Mixed with the craziness of Olympias in Alexander was the sanity of Philip and the teachings of Aristotle. This Theban business certainly troubled the mind of Alexander. Whenever afterwards he encountered Thebans, he tried to show them special favour. Thebes, to his credit, haunted him.

Yet the memory of Thebes did not save three other great cities from similar brain storms; Tyre he destroyed, and Gaza, and a city in India, in the storming of which he was knocked down in fair fight and wounded; and of the latter place not a soul, not a child, was spared. He must have been badly frightened to have taken so evil a revenge.

At the outset of the war the Persians had this supreme advantage, they were practically masters of the sea. The ships of the Athenians and their allies sulked unhelpfully. Alexander, to get at Asia, had to go round by the Hellespont; and if he pushed far into the Persian empire, he ran the risk of being cut off completely from his base. His first task, therefore, was to cripple the enemy at sea, and this he could only do by marching along the coast of Asia Minor and capturing port after port until the Persian sea bases were destroyed. If the Persians had avoided battle and hung upon his lengthening line of communications they could probably have destroyed him, but this they did not do. A Persian army not very much greater than his own gave battle on the banks of the Granicus (334 B.C.) and was destroyed. This left him free to take Sardis, Ephesus, Miletus, and, after a fierce struggle, Halicarnassus. Meanwhile the Persian fleet was on his right flank and between him and Greece, threatening much but accomplishing nothing.

In 333 B.C., pursuing this attack upon the sea bases, he marched along the coast as far as the head of the gulf now called the Gulf of Alexandretta. A huge Persian army, under the great king Darius III, was inland of his

[1] But Phocis was treated in the same way by Philip and his friends in 346, and Mantinea by Sparta in 385. It was a regular Greek punishment of a city to break it up into villages; and as for selling into slavery, Callicratidas the Spartan, in the Peloponnesian War, was held to be very noble when he said he would not sell Greeks into slavery. Anyhow, the destruction of Thebes was due to the *Greek* enemies of Thebes, who pressed it on Alexander.—E. B.

THE BATTLE OF ISSUS
Alexander the Great defeats Darius

By Dudley Tennant

"Darius encamped on the plain of Issus; there Alexander struck him. The cavalry charge and the phalanx smashed this great brittle host. It was routed."

line of march, separated from the coast by mountains, and Alexander went right beyond this enemy force before he or the Persians realized their proximity. Scouting was evidently very badly done by Greek and Persian alike. The Persian army was a vast, ill-organized assembly of soldiers, transport, camp followers, and so forth. Darius, for instance, was accompanied by his harem, and there was a great multitude of harem slaves, musicians, dancers, and cooks. Many of the leading officers had brought their families to witness the hunting down of the Macedonian invaders. The troops had been levied from every province in the empire; they had no tradition or principle of combined action. Seized by the idea of cutting off Alexander from Greece, Darius moved this multitude over the mountains to the sea; he had the luck to get through the passes without opposition, and he encamped on the plain of Issus between the mountains and the shore. And there Alexander, who had turned back to fight, struck him. The cavalry charge and the phalanx smashed this great brittle host as a stone smashes a bottle. It was routed. Darius escaped from his war chariot—that out-of-date instrument—and fled on horseback, leaving even his harem in the hands of Alexander.

All the accounts of Alexander after this battle show him at his best. He was restrained and magnanimous. He treated the Persian princesses with the utmost civility. And he kept his head; he held steadfastly to his plan. He let Darius escape, unpursued, into Syria, and he continued his march upon the naval bases of the Persians

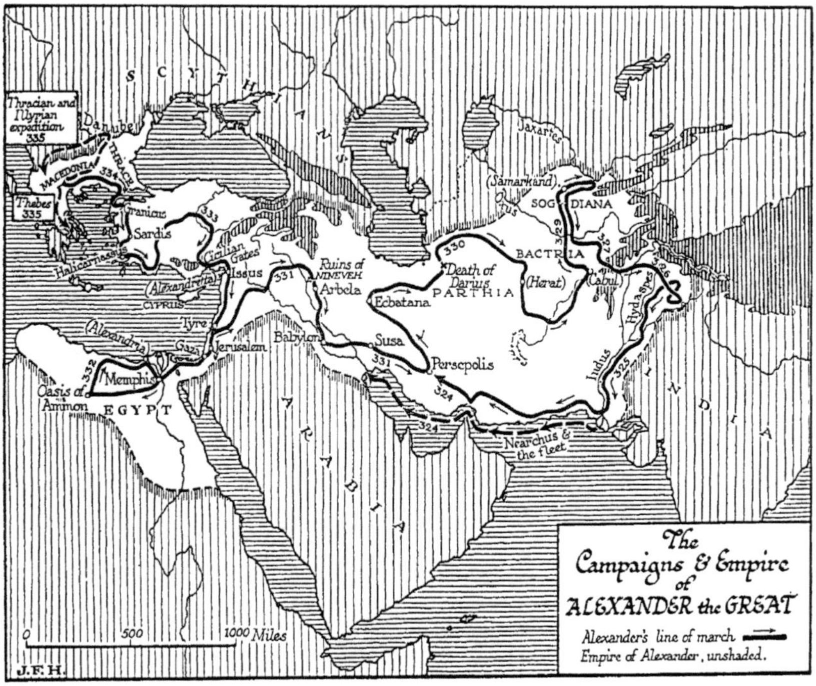

—that is to say, upon the Phœnician ports of Tyre and Sidon.

Sidon surrendered to him; Tyre resisted.

Here, if anywhere, we have the evidence of great military ability on the part of Alexander. His army was his father's creation, but Philip had never shone in the siege of cities. When Alexander was a boy of sixteen, he had seen his father repulsed by the fortified city of Byzantium upon the Bosphorus. Now he was face to face with an inviolate city which had stood siege after siege, which had resisted Nebuchadnezzar the Great for fourteen years. For the standing of sieges Semitic peoples hold the palm. Tyre was then an island half a mile from the shore, and her fleet was unbeaten. On the other hand,

Alexander had already learnt much by the siege of the citadel of Halicarnassus; he had gathered to himself a corps of engineers from Cyprus and Phœnicia, the Sidonian fleet was with him, and presently the king of Cyprus came over to him with a hundred and twenty ships, which gave him the command of the sea. Moreover, great Carthage, either relying on the strength of the mother city or being disloyal to her, and being furthermore entangled in a war in Sicily, sent no help.

The first measure of Alexander was to build a pier from the mainland to the island, a dam which remains to this day; and on this, as it came close to the walls of Tyre, he set up his towers and battering-rams. Against the walls he also moored ships in which towers and rams were erected. The Tyrians used fire-ships against this flotilla, and made sorties from their two harbours. In a big surprise raid that they made on the Cyprian ships they were caught and badly mauled; many of their ships were rammed, and one big galley of five banks of oars and one of four were captured outright. Finally a breach in the walls was made, and the Macedonians, clambering up the debris from their ships, stormed the city.

The siege had lasted seven months. Gaza held out for two. In each case there was a massacre, the plundering of the city, and the selling of the survivors into slavery. Then towards the end of 332 B.C. Alexander entered Egypt, and the command of the sea was assured. Greece, which all this while had been wavering in its policy, decided now at last that it was on the side of Alexander, and the council of the Greek states at Corinth voted its "captain-general" a golden crown of victory. From this time onward the Greeks were with the Macedonians.

The Egyptians also were with the Macedonians. But they had been for Alexander from the beginning. They had lived under Persian rule for nearly two hundred years, and the coming of Alexander meant for them only a change of masters; on the whole, a change for the better. The country surrendered without a blow. Alexander treated its religious feelings with extreme respect. He unwrapped no mummies as Cambyses had done; he took no liberties with Apis, the sacred bull of Memphis. Here, in great temples and upon a vast scale, Alexander found the evidences of a religiosity, mysterious and irrational to remind him of the secrets and mysteries that had entertained his mother and impressed his childhood. During his four months in Egypt he flirted with religious emotions.

He was still a very young man, we must remember, divided against himself. The strong sanity he inherited from his father had made him a great soldier; the teaching of Aristotle had given him something of the scientific outlook upon the world. He had destroyed Tyre; in Egypt, at one of the mouths of the Nile, he now founded a new city, Alexandria, to replace that ancient centre of trade. To the north of Tyre, near Issus, he founded a second port, Alexandretta. Both of these cities flourish to this day, and for a time Alexandria was perhaps the greatest city in the world. The sites, therefore, must have been wisely chosen. But also Alexander had the unstable emotional imaginativeness of his mother, and side by side with such creative work he indulged in religious adventures. The gods of Egypt took possession of his mind. He travelled four hundred miles to the remote oasis of the oracle of Ammon. He wanted to settle certain doubts about his true parentage. His mother had inflamed his mind by hints and vague speeches of some deep mystery about his parentage. Was so ordinary a human being as Philip of Macedon really his father?

For nearly four hundred years Egypt had been a country politically contemptible, overrun now by Ethiopians, now by Assyrians, now by Babylonians, now by Persians. As the indignities of the present became more and more disagreeable to contemplate, the past and the other world became more splendid to Egyptian eyes. It is from the festering humiliations of peoples that arrogant religious propagandas spring. To the triumphant the downtrodden can say, "It is naught in the sight of the true gods." So the son of Philip of Macedon, the master-general of Greece, was made to feel a small person amidst the gigantic temples. And he had an abnormal share of youth's normal ambition to impress everybody. How gratifying then for him to discover presently that he was no mere successful mortal, not one of these modern vulgar Greekish folk, but ancient and divine, the son of a god, the Pharaoh god, son of Ammon Ra!

Already in a previous chapter we have given a description of that encounter in the desert temple.

Not altogether was the young man convinced. He had his moments of conviction; he had his saner phases when the thing was almost a jest. In the presence of Macedonians and Greeks he doubted if he was divine. When it thundered loudly, the ribald Aristarchus could ask him: "Won't *you* do something of the sort, oh Son of Zeus?" But the crazy notion was, nevertheless, present henceforth in his brain, ready to be inflamed by wine or flattery.

Next spring (331 B.C.) he returned to Tyre, and marched thence round towards Assyria, leaving the Syrian desert on his right. Near the ruins of forgotten Nineveh he found a great Persian army, that had been gathering since the battle of Issus, awaiting him. It was another huge medley of contingents, and it relied for its chief force upon that now antiquated weapon, the war chariot. Of these Darius had a force of two hundred, and each chariot had scythes attached to its wheels and to the pole and body of the chariot. There seem to have been four horses to each chariot, and it will be obvious that if one of those horses was wounded by javelin or arrow, that chariot was incapacitated. Against broken footmen or a crowd of individualist fighters such vehicles might be formidable; but Darius began the battle by flinging these instruments against the cavalry and light infantry. Few reached their objective, and those that did were readily disposed of. There was some manœuvring for position. The well-drilled Macedonians moved obliquely across the Persian front, keeping good order; the Persians, following this movement to the flank, opened gaps in their array. Then suddenly the disciplined Macedonian cavalry charged at one of these torn places and smote the centre of the Persian host. The infantry followed close upon their charge. The centre and left of the Persians crumpled up. For a while the light cavalry on the Persian right gained ground against Alexander's left, only to be cut to pieces by the cavalry from Thessaly, which by this time had become almost as good as its Macedonian model. The Persian forces ceased to resemble an army. They dissolved into a vast multitude of fugitives streaming under great dust clouds and without a single rally across the hot plain towards Arbela. Through the dust and the flying crowd rode the victors, slaying and slaying until darkness stayed the slaughter. Darius led the retreat.

Such was the battle of Arbela. It was fought on October the 1st, 331 B.C. We know its date so exactly, because it is recorded that, eleven days before it began, the soothsayers on both sides had been greatly exercised by an eclipse of the moon.

Darius fled to the north into the country of the Medes. Alexander marched on to Babylon. The ancient city of Hammurabi (who had reigned seventeen hundred years before) and of Nebuchadnezzar the Great and of Nabonidus, unlike Nineveh, was still a prosperous and important centre. Like the Egyptians, the Babylonians were not greatly concerned at a change of rule to Macedonian from Persian. The temple of Bel-Marduk was in ruins, a quarry for building material, but the tradition of the Chaldean priests still lingered, and Alexander promised to restore the building. Thence he marched on to Susa, once the chief city of the vanished and forgotten Elamites, and now the Persian capital. He went on to Persepolis, where, as the climax of a drunken carouse, he burnt down the great palace of the king of kings. This he afterwards declared was the revenge of Greece for the burning of Athens by Xerxes.

§ 4

And now begins a new phase in the story of Alexander. For the next seven years he wandered with an army chiefly of Macedonians in the north and east of what was then the known world. At first it was a pursuit of Darius. Afterwards it became——? Was it a systematic survey of a world he meant to consolidate into one great order, or was it a wild-goose chase? His own soldiers, his own intimates, thought the latter, and at last stayed his career beyond the Indus. On the map it looks very like a wild-goose chase; it seems to aim at nothing in particular and to get nowhere.

The pursuit of Darius III soon came to a pitiful end. After the battle of Arbela his own generals seem to have revolted against his weakness and incompetence; they made him a prisoner, and took him with them in spite of his desire to throw himself upon the generosity of his conqueror. Bessus, the satrap of Bactria, they made their leader. There was at last a hot and exciting chase of the flying caravan which conveyed the captive king of kings. At dawn, after an all-night pursuit, it was sighted far ahead. The flight became a headlong bolt. Baggage, women, everything was abandoned by Bessus and his captains; and one other impediment also they left behind. By the side of a pool of water far away from the road a Macedonian trooper presently found a deserted mule-cart with its mules still in the traces. In this cart lay Darius, stabbed in a score of places and bleeding to death. He had refused to go on with Bessus, refused to mount the horse that was brought to him. So his captains had run him through with their spears and left him. . . . He asked his captors for water. What else he may have said we do not know. The historians have seen fit to fabricate a quite impossible last dying speech for him. Probably he said very little. . . .

When, a little after sunrise, Alexander came up, Darius was already dead. . . .

To the historian of the world the wanderings of Alexander have an interest of their own quite apart from the light they throw upon his character. Just as the campaign of Darius I lifted the curtain behind Greece and Macedonia, and showed us something of the silent background to the north of the audible and recorded history of the early civilizations, so now Alexander's campaigns take us into regions about which there had hitherto been no trustworthy record made.

We discover they were not desert regions, but full of a gathering life of their own.

He marched to the shores of the Caspian, thence he travelled eastward across what is now called Western Turkestan. He founded a city that is now known as Herat; whence he went northward by Cabul and by what is now Samarkand, right up into the mountains of Central Turkestan. He returned southward, and came down into India by the Khyber Pass. He fought a great battle on the Upper Indus against a very tall and chivalrous king, Porus, in which the Macedonian infantry encountered an array of elephants and defeated them. Possibly he would have pushed eastward across the deserts to the Ganges valley, but his troops refused to go further. Possibly, had they not done so, then or later he would have gone on until he vanished eastward out of history. But he was forced to turn about. He built a fleet and descended to the mouth of the Indus. There he divided his forces. The main army he took along the desolate coast back to the Persian Gulf, and on the way it suffered dreadfully and lost many men through thirst. The fleet followed him by sea, and rejoined him at the entrance to the Persian Gulf. In the course of this six-year tour he fought battles, received the submission of many strange peoples, and founded cities. He saw the dead body of Darius in June, 330 B.C.; he returned to Susa in 324 B.C. He found the empire in disorder: the provincial satraps raising armies of their own, Bactria and Media in insurrection, and Olympias making government impossible in Macedonia. Harpalus, the royal treasurer, had bolted with all that was portable of the royal treasure, and was making his way, bribing as he went, towards Greece. Some of the Harpalus money is said to have reached Demosthenes.

But before we deal with the closing chapter of the story of Alexander, let us say a word or so about these northern regions into which he wandered. It is evident that from the Danube region right across South Russia, right across the country to the north of the Caspian, right across the country to the east of the Caspian, as far as the mountain masses of the Pamir Plateau and eastward into the Tarim basin of Eastern Turkestan, there spread then a series of similar barbaric tribes and peoples all at about the same stage of culture, and for the most part Aryan in their language and possibly Nordic in their race. They had few cities, mostly they were nomadic; at times they settled temporarily to cultivate the land. They were certainly already mingling in Central Asia with Mongolian tribes, but the Mongolian tribes were not then prevalent there.

An immense process of drying up and elevation has been going on in these parts of the world during the last ten thousand years. Ten thousand years ago there was probably a continuous water barrier between the basin of the Obi and the Aral-Caspian sea. As this had dried up and the marshy land had become steppe-like country, Nordic nomads from the west and Mongolian nomads from the east had met and mixed, and the riding horse had come back into the western world. It is evident this great stretch of country was becoming a region of accumulation for these barbaric peoples. They were very loosely attached to the lands they occupied. They lived in tents and wagons rather than houses. A brief cycle of plentiful and healthy years or a cessation of tribal warfare under some strong ruler, would lead to considerable increases of population; then two or three hard years would suffice to send the tribes wandering again in search of food.

From before the dawn of recorded history this region of human accumulation between the Danube and China had been, as it were, intermittently *raining* out tribes southward and westward. It was like a cloud bank behind the settled landscape that accumulated and then precipitated invaders. We have noted how the Keltic peoples drizzled westward, how the Italians, the Greeks, and their Epirote, Macedonian, and Phrygian kindred came south. We have noted too the Cimmerian drive from the east, like a sudden driving shower of barbarians across Asia Minor, the southward coming of the Scythians and Medes and Persians, and the Aryan descent into India. About a century before

Alexander there had been a fresh Aryan invasion of Italy by a Keltic people, the Gauls, who had settled in the valley of the Po. Those various races came down out of their northern obscurity into the light of history; and meanwhile beyond that light the reservoir accumulated for fresh discharges. Alexander's march in Central Asia brings now into our history names that are fresh to us; the Parthians, a race of mounted bowmen who were destined to play an important rôle in history a century or so later, and the Bactrians who lived in the sandy native land of the camel. Everywhere he seems to have met Aryan-speaking peoples. The Mongolian barbarians to the northeastward were still unsuspected, no one imagined there was yet another great cloud bank of population beyond the Scythians and their kind, in the north of China, that was presently also to begin a drift westward and southward, mixing as it came with the Nordic Scythians and every other people of kindred habits that it encountered. As yet only China knew of the Huns; there were no Turks in Western Turkestan or anywhere else then, no Tartars in the world.

This glimpse of the state of affairs in Turkestan in the fourth century B.C. is one of the most interesting aspects of the wanderings of Alexander; another is his raid through the Punjab. From the point of view of the teller of the human story it is provocative that he did not go on into the Ganges country, and that consequently we have no independent accounts by Greek writers of the life in ancient Bengal. But there is a considerable literature in various Indian languages dealing with Indian history and social life that still needs to be made accessible to European readers.

§ 5

Alexander had been in undisputed possession of the Persian empire for six years. He was now thirty-one. In those six years he had created very little. He had retained most of the organization of the Persian provinces, appointing fresh satraps or retaining the former ones; the roads, the ports, the organization of the empire was still as Cyrus, his greater predecessor, had left them; in Egypt he had merely replaced old provincial governors by new ones; in India he had defeated Porus, and then left him in power much as he found him, except that Porus was now called a satrap by the Greeks. Alexander had, it is true, planned out a number of towns, and some of them were to grow into great towns; seventeen Alexandrias he founded altogether;[1] but he had destroyed Tyre, and with Tyre the security of the sea routes which had hitherto been the chief westward outlet for Mesopotamia. Historians say that he Hellenized the east. But Babylonia and Egypt swarmed with Greeks before his time; he was not the cause, he was a part of the Hellenization. For a time the whole world, from the Adriatic to the Indus, was under one ruler; so far he had realized the dreams of Isocrates and Philip his father. But how far was he making this a permanent and enduring union? How far as yet was it anything more than a dazzling but transitory flourish of his own magnificent self?

He was making no great roads, setting up no sure sea communications. It is idle to accuse him of leaving education alone, because the idea that empires must be cemented by education was still foreign to human thought. But he was forming no group of statesmen about him; he was thinking of no successor; he was creating no tradition—nothing more than a personal legend. The idea that the world would have to go on after Alexander, engaged in any other employment than the discussion of his magnificence, seems to have been outside his mental range. He was still young, it is true, but well before Philip was one and thirty he had been thinking of the education of Alexander.

Was Alexander a statesman at all?

Some students of his career assure us that he was; that now at Susa he planned a mighty world empire, seeing it not simply as a Macedonian conquest of the world, but as a melting together of racial traditions. He did one thing, at any rate, that gives colour to this idea; he held a great marriage feast, in which he and ninety of his generals and friends were married to Persian brides. He himself married a daughter of Darius, though already he possessed an Asiatic wife in Roxana, the daughter of the king of Samarkand. This wholesale wedding was made a very splendid festival, and at the same time all of his Macedonian soldiers, to the number of several thousands, who had married Asiatic brides, were given wedding gifts. This has been called the Marriage of Europe and Asia; the two continents were to be joined, wrote Plutarch, "in lawful wedlock and by community of offspring." And next he began to train recruits from Persia and the north,

[1] Mahaffy. Their names have undergone various changes—*e.g.* Candahar (Iskender) and Secunderabad.

Parthians, Bactrians, and the like, in the distinctive disciplines of the phalanx and the cavalry. Was that also to assimilate Europe and Asia, or was it to make himself independent of his Macedonians? They thought the latter, at any rate, and mutinied, and it was with some difficulty that he brought them to a penitent mood and induced them to take part in a common feast with the Persians. The historians have made a long and eloquent speech for him on this occasion, but the gist of it was that he bade his Macedonians begone, and gave no sign of how he proposed they should get home out of Persia. After three days of dismay they submitted to him and begged his forgiveness.

Alexander the Great
(silver coin of Lysimachus, 321-281 B.C.)

Here is the matter for a very pretty discussion. Was Alexander really planning a racial fusion or had he just fallen in love with the pomp and divinity of an Oriental monarch, and wished to get rid of these Europeans to whom he was only a king-leader? The writers of his own time, and those who lived near to his time, lean very much to the latter alternative. They insist upon his immense vanity. They relate how he began to wear the robes and tiara of a Persian monarch. "At first only before the barbarians and privately, but afterwards he came to wear it in public when he sat for the dispatch of business." And presently he demanded Oriental prostrations from his friends.

One thing seems to support the suggestion of great personal vanity in Alexander. His portrait was painted and sculptured frequently, and always he is represented as a beautiful youth, with wonderful locks flowing backward from a broad forehead. Previously most men had worn beards. But Alexander, enamoured of his own youthful loveliness, would not part with it; he remained a sham boy at thirty-two; he shaved his face, and so set a fashion in Greece and Italy that lasted many centuries.

The stories of violence and vanity in his closing years cluster thick upon his memory. He listened to tittle-tattle about Philotas, the son of Parmenio, one of his most trusted and faithful generals. Philotas, it was said, had boasted to some woman he was making love to that Alexander was a mere boy; that, but for such men as his father and himself, there would have been no conquest of Persia, and the like. Such assertions had a certain element of truth in them. The woman was brought to Alexander, who listened to her treacheries. Presently Philotas was accused of conspiracy, and, upon very insufficient evidence, tortured and executed. Then Alexander thought of Parmenio, whose other two sons had died for him in battle. He sent swift messengers to assassinate the old man before he could hear of his son's death! Now Parmenio had been one of the most trusted of Philip's generals; it was Parmenio who had led the Macedonian armies into Asia before the murder of Philip. There can be little doubt of the substantial truth of this story, nor about the execution of Callisthenes, the nephew of Aristotle, who refused Alexander divine honours, and "went about with as much pride as if he had demolished a tyranny, while the young men followed him as the only freeman among thousands." Mixed with such incidents we have the very illuminating story of the drunken quarrel in which he killed Clitus. The monarch and his company had been drinking hard, and the drink had made the talk loud and free. There was much flattery of the "young god," much detraction of Philip, at which Alexander had smiled with satisfaction.[1] Was he not the son of a god? This drunken self-complacency was more than the honest Macedonians could stand; it roused Clitus, his foster-brother, to a frenzy. Clitus reproached Alexander with his Median costume and praised Philip, there was a loud quarrel, and, to end it, Clitus was hustled out of the room by his friends. He was, however, in the obstinate phase of drunkenness, and he returned by another entrance. He was

[1] D. G. Hogarth.

heard outside quoting Euripides "in a bold and disrespectful tone":

> "Are these your customs? Is it thus that Greece
> Rewards her combatants? Shall one man claim
> The trophies won by thousands?"

Whereupon Alexander snatched a spear from one of his guards and ran Clitus through the body as he lifted the curtain to come in. . . .

One is forced to believe that this was the real atmosphere of the young conqueror's life. Then the story of his frantic and cruel display of grief for Hephæstion can scarcely be all invention. If it is true, or in any part true, it displays a mind ill-balanced and altogether wrapped up in personal things, to whom empire was no more than opportunity for egoistic display, and all the resources of the world, stuff for freaks of that sort of "generosity" which robs a thousand people to extort the admiration of one astounded recipient.

Hephæstion, being ill, was put upon a strict diet, but in the absence of his physician at the theatre he ate a roasted fowl and drank a flagon of iced wine, in consequence of which he died. Thereupon Alexander decided upon a display of grief. It was the grief of a lunatic. He had the physician crucified! He ordered every horse and mule in Persia to be shorn, and pulled down the battlements of the neighbouring cities. He prohibited all music in his camp for a long time, and, having taken certain villages of the Cusæans, he caused all the adults to be massacred, as a sacrifice to the manes of Hephæstion. Finally he set aside ten thousand talents (a talent = £240) for a tomb. For those days this was an enormous sum. None of which things did any real honour to Hephæstion, but they served to demonstrate to an awe-stricken world what a tremendous thing the sorrow of Alexander could be.

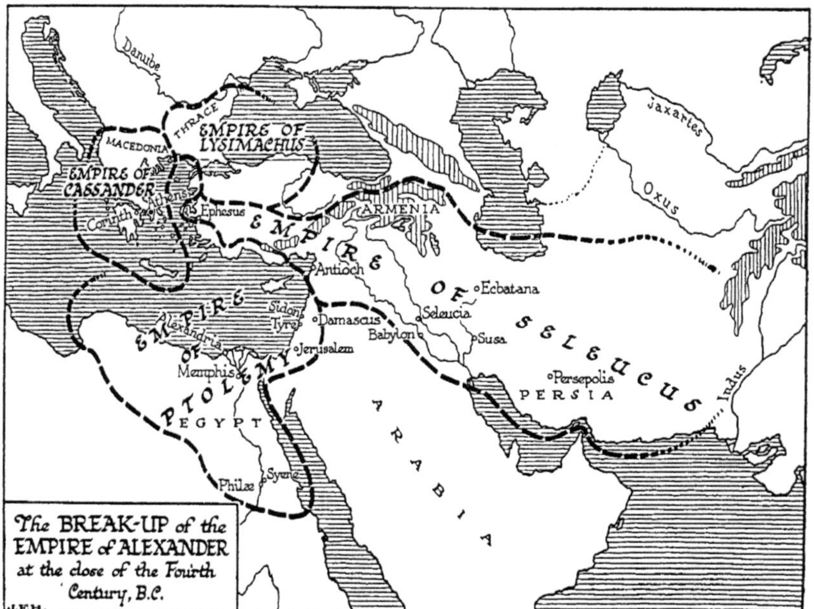

The BREAK-UP of the EMPIRE of ALEXANDER at the close of the Fourth Century, B.C.

This last story and many such stories may be lies or distortions or exaggerations. But they have a vein in common. After a bout of hard drinking in Babylon a sudden fever came upon Alexander (323 B.C.), and he sickened and died. He was still only thirty-three years of age. Forthwith the world empire he had snatched at and held in his hands, as a child might snatch at and hold a precious vase, fell to the ground and was shattered to pieces.

Whatever appearance of a worldwide order may have gleamed upon men's imaginations, vanished at his death. The story becomes the story of a barbaric autocracy in confusion. Everywhere the provincial rulers set up for themselves. In the course of a few years the entire family of Alexander had been destroyed. Roxana, his barbarian wife, was prompt to murder, as a rival, the daughter of Darius. She herself presently bore Alexander a posthumous son, who was also called Alexander. He was murdered, with her, a few years later (311 B.C.). Hercules, the only other son of Alexander, was murdered also. So too was Aridæus, the weak-minded half-brother (see § 2). Plutarch gives a last glimpse of Olympias during a brief interval of power in Macedonia, accusing

Tetradrachm with head of Seleucus I.

first this person and then that of poisoning her wonderful son. Many she killed in her fury. The bodies of some of his circle who had died after his death she caused to be dug up, but we do not know if any fresh light was shed upon his death by these disinterments. Finally Olympias was killed in Macedonia by the friends of those she had slain.

§ 6

From this welter of crime there presently emerged three leading figures. Much of the old Persian empire, as far as the Indus eastward and almost to Lydia in the west, was held by one general Seleucus, who founded a dynasty, the Seleucid Dynasty; Macedonia fell to another Macedonian general, Antigonus; a third Macedonian, Ptolemy, secured Egypt, and making Alexandria his chief city, established a sufficient naval ascendancy to keep also Cyprus and most of the coast of Phœnicia and Asia Minor. The Ptolemaic and Seleucid empires lasted for a considerable time; the forms of government in Asia Minor and the Balkans were more unstable. Two maps will help the reader to a sense of the kaleidoscopic nature of the political boundaries of the third century B.C. Antigonus was defeated and killed at the battle of Ipsus (301), leaving Lysimachus, the governor of Thrace, and Cassander, of Macedonia and Greece, as equally transitory successors. Minor governors carved out smaller states. Meanwhile the barbarians swung down into the broken-up and enfeebled world of civilization from the west and from the east. From the west came the Gauls, a people closely related to the Kelts. They raided down through Macedonia and Greece to Delphi, and (227 B.C.) two sections of them crossed the Bosphorus into Asia Minor, being first employed as mercenaries and then setting up for themselves as independent plunderers; and after raiding almost to the Taurus, they settled in the old Phrygian land, holding the people about them to tribute. (These Gauls of Phrygia became the Galatians of St. Paul's Epistle.) Armenia and the southern shores of the Black Sea became a confusion of changing rulers. Kings with Hellenistic ideas appeared in Cappadocia, in Pontus (the south shore of the Black Sea), in Bithynia, and in Pergamum. From the east the Scythians and the Parthians and Bactrians also drove southward. . . . For a time there were Greek-ruled Bactrian states becoming more and more Orientalized; in the second century B.C. Greek adventurers from Bactria raided down into North India and founded short-lived kingdoms there, the last eastward fling of the Greek; then gradually barbarism fell again like a curtain between the Western civilizations and India.[1]

§ 7

Amidst all these shattered fragments of the burst bubble of Hellenic empire one small state stands out and demands at least a brief section to itself, the kingdom of Pergamum. We hear first of this town as an independent centre during the struggle that ended in the battle of Ipsus. While the tide of the Gaulish invasion swirled and foamed to and fro about Asia Minor between the years 277 and 241, Pergamum for a time paid them tribute, but she retained her general independence, and at last, under Attalus I, refused her tribute and defeated them in two decisive battles. For more than a century thereafter (until 133 B.C.) Pergamum re-

[1] The stages by which Bactria degenerated into Afghanistan may be studied neatly in the progressive deterioration of its coinage from a decent standard of Hellenic accomplishment into the vague flourishes of Orientalism; it began by displaying a Heracles of pure Greek blood and a pair of horsemen who would hardly have seemed out of place on the frieze of the Parthenon, and it fell steadily to a level of incompetence only equalled by the crude imitations of Roman currency that were being made in pre-Roman Britain about the same time.—P. G.

mained free, and was perhaps during that period the most highly civilized state in the world. On the hill of the Acropolis was reared a rich group of buildings, palaces, temples, a museum, and a library, rivals of those of Alexandria of which we shall presently tell, and almost the first in the world. Under the princes of Pergamum, Greek art blossomed afresh, and the reliefs of the altar of the temple of Zeus and the statues of the fighting and dying Gauls which were made there, are among the great artistic treasures of mankind.

In a little while, as we shall tell later, the influence of a new power began to be felt in the Eastern Mediterranean, the power of the Roman republic, friendly to Greece and to Greek civilization; and in this power the Hellenic communities of Pergamum and Rhodes found a natural and useful ally and supporter against the Galatians and against the Orientalized Seleucid empire. We shall relate how at last the Roman power came into Asia, how it defeated the Seleucid empire at the battle of Magnesia (190 B.C.), and drove it out of Asia Minor and beyond the Taurus mountains, and how finally in 133 B.C. Attalus III, the last king of Pergamum, bowing to his sense of an inevitable destiny, made the Roman republic the heir to his kingdom, which became then the Roman province of "Asia."

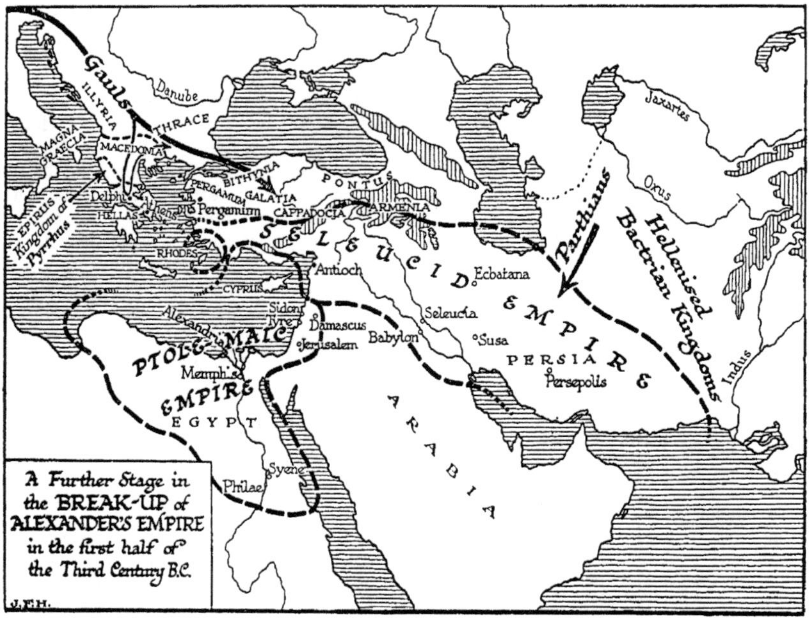

A Further Stage in the BREAK-UP of ALEXANDER'S EMPIRE in the first half of the Third Century B.C.

§ 8

Nearly all historians are disposed to regard the career of Alexander the Great as marking an epoch in human affairs. It drew together all the known world, excepting only the western Mediterranean, into one drama. But the opinions men have formed of Alexander himself vary enormously. They fall, most of them, into two main schools. One type of scholar is fascinated by the youth and splendour of this young man. These Alexander-worshippers seem disposed to take him at his own valuation, to condone every crime and folly either as the mere ebullience of a rich nature or as the bitter necessity to some gigantic scheme, and to regard his life as framed upon a design, a scheme of statesmanship, such as all the wider knowledge and wider ideas of these later times barely suffice to bring into the scope of our understanding. On the other hand, there are those who see him only as a wrecker of the slowly maturing possibilities of a free and tranquil Hellenized world.

Before we ascribe to Alexander or to his father Philip schemes of world policy such as a twentieth-century historian-philosopher might approve, we shall do well to consider very carefully the utmost range of knowledge and thought that was possible in those days. The world of Plato, Isocrates, and Aristotle had practically no historical perspective at all; there had not been such a thing as history in the world, history, that is, as distinguished from mere priestly chronicles, until the last couple of centuries. Even highly educated men had the most circumscribed ideas of geography and foreign countries. For most men the world was still flat and limitless. The only systematic political philosophy was based on the experiences of minute city states, and took no thought of empires. Nobody knew anything of the origins of civilization. No one had speculated upon economics.[1] No one had worked out the reaction of one social class upon another. We are too apt to consider the career of Alexander as the crown of some process that had long been afoot; as the climax of a crescendo. In a sense, no doubt, it was that; but much more true is it that it was not so much an end as a beginning; it was the first revelation to the human imagination of the oneness of human affairs. The utmost reach of the thought of Greece before his time was of a Persian empire Hellenized, a predominance in the world of Macedonians and Greeks. But before Alexander was dead, and much more after he was dead and there had been time to think him over, the conception of a world law and organization was a practicable and assimilable idea for the minds of men.

For some generations Alexander the Great was for mankind the symbol and embodiment of world order and world dominion. He became a fabulous being. His head, adorned with the divine symbols of the demi-god Hercules or the god Ammon Ra, appears on the coins of such among his successors as could claim to be his heirs. Then the idea of world dominion was taken up by another great people, a people who for some centuries exhibited considerable political genius, the Romans; and the figure of another conspicuous adventurer, Cæsar, eclipsed for the western half of the old world the figure of Alexander.

So by the beginning of the third century B.C. we find already arisen in the Western civilization of the old world three of the great structural ideas that rule the mind of contemporary mankind. We have already traced the escape of writing and knowledge from the secrets and mysteries and initiations of the old-world priesthoods, and the development of the idea of a universal knowledge, of a universally understandable and communicable history and philosophy. We have taken the figures of Herodotus and Aristotle as typical exponents of this first great idea, the idea of *science*—using the word science in its widest and properest sense, to include history and signify a clear vision of man in relation to the things about him. We have traced also the generalization of religion among the Babylonians, Jews, and other Semitic peoples, from the dark worship in temples and consecrated places of some local or tribal god to the open service of *one universal God of Righteousness*, whose temple is the whole world. And now we have traced also the first germination of the idea of *a world polity*. The rest of the history of mankind is very largely the history of those three ideas of science, of a universal righteousness, and of a human commonweal, spreading out from the minds of the rare and exceptional persons and peoples in which they first originated, into the general consciousness of the race, and giving first a new colour, then a new spirit, and then a new direction to human affairs.

[1] Before that time. But such speculation was going on then. There is some interesting economic theory in Plato's *Republic*, and, Aristotle was writing the *œconomica*. Xenophon wrote on Athenian revenues and other economic matters. Thucycides wrote an excellent passage on the Greek past, and Aristotle dealt with barbaric customs.—E. B.

XXV

SCIENCE AND RELIGION AT ALEXANDRIA[1]

§ 1. *The Science of Alexandria.* § 2. *Philosophy of Alexandria.* § 3. *Alexandria as a Factory of Religions.*

§ 1

ONE of the most prosperous fragments of the brief world empire of Alexander the Great was Egypt, which fell to the share of the Ptolemy whose name we have already noted as one of the associates of Alexander whom King Philip had banished. The country was at a secure distance from plundering Gaul or Parthian, and the destruction of Tyre and the Phœnician navy, and the creation of Alexandria gave Egypt a temporary naval ascendancy in the Eastern Mediterranean. Alexandria grew to proportions that rivalled Carthage; eastward she had an overseas trade through the Red Sea with Arabia and India; and westward her traffic competed with the Carthaginian. In the Macedonian and Greek governors of the Ptolemies, the Egyptians found a government more sympathetic and tolerable than any they had ever known since they ceased to be a self-governing empire. Indeed it is rather that Egypt conquered and annexed the Ptolemies politically, than that the Macedonians ruled Egypt.

There was a return to Egyptian political ideas, rather than any attempt to Hellenize the government of the country. Ptolemy became Pharaoh, the god king, and his administration continued the ancient tradition of Pepi, Thotmes, Rameses, and Necho. Alexandria, however, for her town affairs, and subject to the divine overlordship of Pharaoh, had a constitution of the Greek city type. And the language of the court and administration was Attic Greek. Greek became so much the general language of educated people in Egypt that the Jewish community there found it necessary to translate their Bible into the Greek language, many men of their own people being no longer able to understand Hebrew. Attic Greek for some centuries before and after Christ was the language of all educated men from the Adriatic to the Persian Gulf.

Of all Alexander's group of young men, Ptolemy seems to have done most to carry out those ideas of a systematic organization of knowledge with which Aristotle had no doubt familiarized the court of Philip of Macedon. Ptolemy was a man of very extraordinary intellectual gifts, at once creative and modest, with a certain understandable cynicism towards the strain of Olympias in the mind of Alexander. His contemporary history of Alexander's campaigns has perished; but it was a source to which all the surviving accounts are deeply indebted.

The Museum he set up in Alexandria was in effect the first university in the world. As its name implies, it was dedicated to the service of the Muses, which was also the case with the Peripatetic school at Athens. It was, however, a religious body only in form, in order to meet the legal difficulties of endowment in a world that had never foreseen such a thing as a secular intellectual process. It was essentially a college of learned men engaged chiefly in research and record, but also to a certain extent in teaching. At the outset, and for two or three generations, the Museum at Alexandria presented such a scientific constellation as even Athens at its best could not rival. Particularly sound and good was the mathematical and geographical work. The names of Euclid, familiar to every schoolboy, Eratosthenes, who measured the size of the earth and came within fifty miles of the true diameter, Apollonius, who wrote on conic sections, stand out. Hipparchus made the first attempt to catalogue and map the stars with a view to checking any changes that might be occurring in the heavens. Hero devised the first steam engine. Archimedes came to Alexandria to study, and remained a frequent correspondent of the Museum. The medical school of Alexandria was equally famous. For the first time in the world's history a standard of professional knowledge was set up. Herophilus, the greatest of the Alexandrian anatomists, is said to have conducted vivisections upon condemned criminals.[2] Other teachers, in opposition to Herophilus,

[1] *Vide* Mahaffy's *Greek Life and Thought* and his *Progress of Hellenism in Alexander's Empire*, Marvin's *Living Past*, Legge's *Forerunners and Rivals of Christianity*, and Reinach's *Orpheus*.

[2] The question whether the vivisection of human beings, or, indeed, whether any vivisection at all occurred at Alexandria, is one of considerable importance because of the light it throws upon the moral

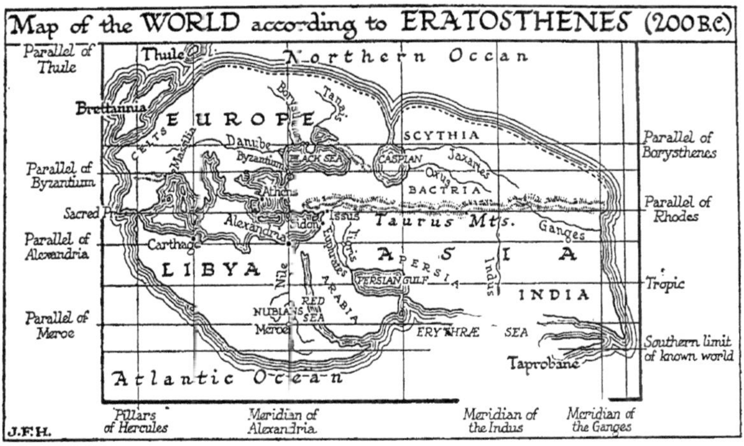

condemned the study of anatomy and developed the science of drugs. But this scientific blaze at Alexandria did not endure altogether for more than a century. The organization of the Museum was not planned to ensure its mental continuity. It was a "royal" college; its professors and fellows (as we may call them) were appointed and paid by Pharaoh. "The republican character of the private corporations called the schools or academies at Athens was far more stable and independent."[1] Royal patronage

and intellectual quality of the time. One of the editors of this book was inclined to throw doubt upon it, as a thing antipathetic to the Greek spirit. The writer has taken some pains to find out the facts of the case, and he has been so fortunate as to have the help of Dr. Singer, one of the greatest living authorities upon the history of medicine. There are statements made by Tertullian (*De Anima*, chap. xxv.), but he was a biased and untrustworthy witness. The conclusive passage is taken from Celsus, who wrote during the reign of Tiberius, three centuries after the great days of Alexandria. "If you are to have one witness," writes Dr. Singer, "you could hardly have a better. In my own mind I am satisfied with the evidence of Celsus, and I have asked Dr. E. T. Withington, our best authority on Greek medicine, and he also is satisfied."

The following is a translation of the passage in Celsus, *De Re Medica*. One school says that "it is necessary to dissect the bodies of the dead, and to examine their viscera and intestines. Herophilus and Erasistratus adopted by far the best method, for they obtained criminals from prison by royal permission, and dissected them alive, and they examined, while they still breathed, the parts which Nature had concealed, noting their position, warmth (or possibly 'colour'—*colorem* instead of *calorem*), shape, size, relation, hardness, softness, smoothness, and feel; also the projections and depressions of each and how they fit into one another. For if there happen any inward pain, he who has not learned where the viscera and intestines are placed, cannot know where the pain is; nor can the diseased part be cured by one who does not know what part it is. Again, if the viscera of any one are exposed by a wound, he who is ignorant of the natural colour of that part in the healthy state cannot know whether it be sound or corrupted, and therefore cannot cure the corrupted part. Moreover remedies can be applied more appropriately externally when the position, shape, and size of the internal parts is known, and the same argument holds for all the other matters that we have mentioned. Nor is it a cruel act, as many would have it, to seek remedies for innocent mankind throughout the ages by torture of a few criminals."

Against this view, says Celsus, the other school argues that "to cut open the abdomen and thorax of living men, and thus to turn that art which concerns itself with the health of mankind not only into an instrument of death (*pestem*—lit. 'a plague'), but (death) in its most horrible form, and this although some of the things that we seek thus barbarously can by no means be known, while others may be learned without cruelty. For the colour, smoothness, softness, hardness, and all their like are not the same when the body is cut open as when it is whole; and, moreover, even in bodies that have not been thus ravaged, these properties are often changed by fear, grief, want of food, or of digestion, fatigue, and a thousand other lesser causes. It is thus more likely that the inner organs, which are more tender, and to which the light is a new experience, are changed by serious wounds and by mangling.

"Further, nothing can be more foolish than to think that any things are the same in a live man as in a moribund one, or, rather, in one practically dead. It is indeed true that the abdomen, with which our argument is less concerned, can be opened while a man yet lives, but as soon as the knife reaches the thorax (præcordium), and cuts the transverse septum, which is a membrane dividing the superior parts from the inferior and called diaphragma by the Greeks, the man at once gives up the ghost, and thus it is the breast and its viscera of a dead and not a living man which the murderous physician examines. He has thus but performed a cruel murder, and has not learned what the viscera of a living man are like."

Celsus' own judgment is given a little later: "To dissect a living body is both cruel and unnecessary; to dissect dead bodies is necessary."

It is to be noted, says Professor Murray, that Herophilus and Erasistratus were not living in a Greek city state, but under an *oriental despot.*

[1] Mahaffy.

was all very well so long as Pharaoh was Ptolemy I, or Ptolemy II, but the strain degenerated, and the long tradition of Egyptian priestcraft presently swallowed up the Ptolemies—and destroyed the Aristotelian mentality of the Museum altogether. The Museum had not existed for a hundred years before its scientific energy was extinct.

Side by side with the Museum, Ptolemy I created a more enduring monument to himself in the great library. This was a combination of state library and state publishing upon a scale hitherto unheard of. It was to be altogether encyclopædic. If any stranger brought an unknown book to Egypt, he had to have it copied for the collection, and a considerable staff of copyists was engaged continually in making duplicates of all the more popular and necessary works. The library, like a university press, had an outward trade. It was a book-selling affair. Under Callimachus, the head of the library during the time of Ptolemy II and III, the arrangement and cataloguing of the accumulations was systematically undertaken. In those days, it must be remembered, books were not in pages, but rolled like the music-rolls of the modern piano-player, and in order to refer to any particular passage, a reader had to roll back or roll forward very tediously, a process which wore out books and readers together. One thinks at once of a simple and obvious little machine by which such a roll could have been quickly wound to and fro for reference, but nothing of the sort seems to have been used. Every time a roll was read it was handled by two perspiring hands. It was to minimize the waste of time and trouble that Callimachus broke up long works, such as the History of Herodotus

into "books" or volumes, as we should call them, each upon a separate roll. The library of Alexandria drew a far vaster crowd of students than the teachers of the Museum. The lodging and catering for these visitors from all parts of the world became a considerable business interest for the Alexandrian population.

It is curious to note how slowly the mechanism of the intellectual life improves. Contrast the ordinary library facilities of a middle-class English home, such as the present writer is now working in, with the inconveniences and deficiencies of the equipment of an Alexandrian writer, and one realizes the enormous waste of time, physical exertion, and attention that went on through all the centuries during which that library flourished. Before the present writer lie half a dozen books, and there are good indices to three of them. He can pick up any one of these six books, refer quickly to a statement, verify a quotation, and go on writing. Contrast with that the tedious unfolding of a rolled manuscript. Close at hand are two encyclopædias, a dictionary, an atlas of the world, a biographical dictionary, and other books of reference. They have no marginal indices, it is true; but that perhaps is asking for too much at present. There were no such resources in the world in 300 B.C. Alexandria had still to produce the first grammar and the first dictionary. This present book is being written in manuscript; it is then taken by a typist and typewritten very accurately. It can then, with the utmost convenience, be read over, corrected amply, rearranged freely, retyped, and recorrected. The Alexandrian author had to dictate or recopy every word he wrote. Before he could turn back to what he had written previously, he had to dry his last words by waving them in the air or pouring sand over them; he had not even blotting-paper. Whatever an author wrote had to be recopied again and again before it could reach any considerable circle of readers, and every copyist introduced some new error.[1] Whenever a need for maps or diagrams arose, there were fresh difficulties. Such a science as anatomy, for example, depending as it does upon accurate drawing, must have been enormously hampered by the natural limitations of the copyist. The transmission of geographical fact again must have been almost incredibly tedious. No doubt a day will come when a private library and writing-desk of the year A.D. 1919 will seem quaintly clumsy and difficult; but, measured by the standards of Alexandria, they are astonishingly quick, efficient, and economical of nervous and mental energy.

No attempt seems to have been made at Alexandria to print anything at all. That strikes one at first as a very remarkable fact. The world was crying out for books, and not simply for books. There was an urgent public need for notices, proclamations, and the like. Yet there is nothing in the history of the Western civilizations that one can call printing until the fifteenth century A.D. It is not as though printing was a recondite art or dependent upon any precedent and preliminary discoveries. Printing is the most obvious of dodges. In principle it has always been known. As we have already stated, there is ground for supposing that the Palæolithic men of the Magdalenian period may have printed designs on their leather garments. The "seals" of ancient Sumeria again were printing devices. Coins are print. Illiterate persons in all ages have used wooden or metal stamps for their signatures; William I, the Norman Conqueror of England, for example, used such a stamp with ink to sign documents. In China the classics were being printed by the second century A.D. Yet either because of a complex of small difficulties about ink or papyrus or the form of books, or because of some protective resistance on the part of the owners of the slave copyists, or because the script was too swift and easy to set men thinking how to write it still more easily, as the Chinese character or the Gothic letters did, or because of a gap in the social system between men of thought and knowledge and men of technical skill, printing was not used—not even used for the exact reproduction of illustrations.

The chief reason for this failure to develop printing systematically lies, no doubt, in the fact that there was no abundant supply of printable material of a uniform texture and convenient form. The supply of papyrus was strictly limited, strip had to be fastened to strip, and there was no standard size of sheet. Paper had yet to come from China to release the mind of Europe. Had there been presses, they would have had to stand idle while the papyrus rolls were slowly made. But this explanation does not account for the failure to use block printing in the case of illustrations and diagrams.

[1] It has been suggested that new books were perhaps dictated to a roomful of copyists, and so issued in a first edition of some hundreds at least. In Rome, Horace and Virgil seem to have been issued in quite considerable editions.

These limitations enable us to understand why it was that Alexandria could at once achieve the most extraordinary intellectual triumphs—for such a feat as that of Eratosthenes, for instance, having regard to his poverty of apparatus, is sufficient to put him on a level with Newton or Pasteur—and yet have little or no effect upon the course of politics or the lives and thoughts of people round about her. Her Museum and library were a centre of light, but it was light in a dark lantern hidden from the general world. There were no means of carrying its results even to sympathetic men abroad except by tedious letter-writing. There was no possibility of communicating what was known there to the general body of men. Students had to come at great cost to themselves to this crowded centre because there was no other way of gathering even scraps of knowledge. At Athens and Alexandria there were bookstalls where manuscript note-books of variable quality could be bought at reasonable prices, but any extension of education to larger classes and other centres would have produced at once a restrictive shortage of papyrus. Education did not reach into the masses at all; to become more than superficially educated one had to abandon the ordinary life of the times and come for long years to live a hovering existence in the neighbourhood of ill-equipped and overworked sages. Learning was not indeed so complete a withdrawal from ordinary life as initiation into a priesthood, but it was still something in that nature.

And very speedily that feeling of freedom, that openness and directness of statement which is the vital air of the true intellectual life, faded out of Alexandria. From the first the patronage even of Ptolemy I set a limit to political discussion. Presently the dissensions of the schools let in the superstitions and prejudices of the city mob to scholastic affairs.

Wisdom passed away from Alexandria and left pedantry behind. For the use of books was substituted the worship of books. Very speedily the learned became a specialized queer class with unpleasant characteristics of its own. The Museum had not existed for half a dozen generations before Alexandria was familiar with a new type of human being; shy, eccentric, unpractical, incapable of essentials, strangely fierce upon trivialities of literary detail, as bitterly jealous of the colleague within as of the unlearned without, the bent Scholarly Man. He was as intolerant as a priest, though he had no altar; as obscurantist as a magician, though he had no cave. For him no method of copying was sufficiently tedious and no rare book sufficiently inaccessible. He was a sort of by-product of the intellectual process of mankind. For many precious generations the new-lit fires of the human intelligence were to be seriously banked down by this by-product.

Right thinking is necessarily an open process, and the only science and history of full value to men consist of what is generally and clearly known; this is surely a platitude, but we have still to discover how to preserve our centres of philosophy and research from the caking and darkening accumulations of narrow and dingy-spirited specialists. We have still to ensure that a man of learning shall be none the less a man of affairs, and that all that can be thought and known is kept plainly, honestly, and easily available to the ordinary men and women who are the substance of mankind.

§ 2

At first the mental activities of Alexandria centred upon the Museum, and were mainly scientific. Philosophy, which in a more vigorous age had been a doctrine of power over self and the material world, without abandoning these pretensions, became in reality a doctrine of secret consolation. The stimulant changed into an opiate. The philosopher let the world, as the vulgar say, *rip*, the world of which he was a part, and consoled himself by saying in very beautiful and elaborate forms that the world was illusion and that there was in him something quintessential and sublime, outside and above the world. Athens,[1] politically insignificant, but still a great and crowded mart throughout the fourth century, decaying almost imperceptibly so far as outer seeming went, and treated with a strange respect that was half contempt by all the warring powers and adventurers of the world, was the fitting centre of such philosophical teaching. It was quite a couple of centuries before the schools of Alexandria became as important in philosophical discussion.

But of Philo the Jew in the first century A.D., and of Plotinus in the third, interesting as the thought and influence of these men were, the scale of this outline will not permit us to treat.

§ 3

If Alexandria was late to develop a distinctive philosophy, she was early prominent

[1] See Ferguson's *Hellenistic Athens.*

as a great factory and exchange of religious ideas.

The Museum and Library represented only one of the three sides of the triple city of Alexandria. They represented the Aristotelian, the Hellenic, and Macedonian element. But Ptolemy I had brought together two other factors to this strange centre. First there was a great number of Jews, brought partly from Palestine, but largely also from those settlements in Egypt which had never returned to Jerusalem; these latter were the Jews of the Diaspora or Dispersion, a race of Jews who, as we have already noted in Chapter XXI, had not shared the Babylonian Captivity, but who were nevertheless in possession of the Bible and in close correspondence with their co-religionists throughout the world. These Jews populated so great a quarter of Alexandria that the town became the largest Jewish city in the world, with far more Jews in it than there were in Jerusalem. We have already noted that they had found it necessary to translate their scriptures into Greek. And, finally, there was a great population of native Egyptians, also for the most part speaking Greek, but with the superstitious temperament of the dark whites and with the vast tradition of forty centuries of temple religion and temple sacrifices at the back of their minds. In Alexandria three types of mind and spirit met, the three main types of the white race, the clear-headed criticism of the Aryan Greek, the moral fervour and monotheism of the Semitic Jew, and the deep Mediterranean tradition of mysteries and sacrifices that we have already seen at work in the secret cults and occult practices of Greece, ideas which in Hamitic Egypt ruled proudly in great temples in the open light of day.

These three were the permanent elements of the Alexandrian blend. But in the seaport and markets mingled men of every known race, comparing their religious ideas and customs. It is even related that in the third century B.C. Buddhist missionaries came from the court of King Asoka in India. Aristotle remarks in his *Politics* that the religious beliefs of men are apt to borrow their form from political institutions, "men assimilate the lives no less than the bodily forms of the gods to their own," and this age of Greek-speaking great empires under autocratic monarchs was bearing hardly upon those merely local celebrities, the old tribal and city deities. Men were requiring deities with an outlook at least as wide as the empires, and except where the interests of powerful priesthoods stood in the way, a curious process of assimilation of gods was going on. Men found that though there were many gods, they were all very much alike. Where there had been many gods, men came to think there must be really only one god under a diversity of names. He had been everywhere—under an alias. The Roman Jupiter, the Greek Zeus, the Egyptian Ammon, the putative father of Alexander and the old antagonist of Amenophis IV the Babylonian Bel-Marduk, were all sufficiently similar to be identified.

> "Father of all in every age, in every clime adored
> By saint, by savage and by sage, Jehovah, Jove or Lord."

Where there were distinct differences, the difficulty was met by saying that these were different *aspects* of the same god. Bel-Marduk, however, was now a very decadent god indeed, who hardly survived as a pseudonym; Assur, Dagon, and the like, poor old gods of fallen nations, had long since passed out of memory, and did not come into the amalgamation. Osiris, a god popular with the Egyptian commonalty, was already identified with Apis, the sacred bull in the temple of Memphis, and somewhat confused with Ammon. Under the name of Serapis he became the great god of Hellenic Alexandria.[1] He was Jupiter-Serapis. The Egyptian cow goddess, Hathor or Isis, was also represented now in human guise as the wife of Osiris, to whom she bore the infant Horus, who grew up to be Osiris again. These bald statements sound strange, no doubt, to a modern mind, but these identifications and mixing up of one god with another are very illustrative of the struggle the quickening human intelligence was making to cling still to religion and its emotional bonds and fellowship, while making its gods more reasonable and universal.

This fusing of one god with another is called *theocrasia*, and nowhere was it more vigorously going on than in Alexandria. Only two peoples resisted it in this period: the Jews, who already had their faith in the One God of Heaven and Earth, Jehovah, and the Persians, who had a monotheistic sun worship.

It was Ptolemy I who set up not only the Museum in Alexandria, but the Serapeum, devoted to the worship of a trinity of gods which represented the result of a process of theocrasia applied more particularly to the gods of Greece and Egypt.

[1] Serapis sounds like a compound of Apis and Osiris, but there is reason for supposing that the name is really of Chaldean origin. See Cumont, *Oriental Religions in Roman Paganism.*

HORUS PRESENTING ANI TO OSIRIS

Papyrus in British Museum

"Osiris (sitting), a popular Egyptian god, to whom Horus, his son, is presenting Ani (a teacher and scribe), whose heart has been weighed and found righteous and true. Ani

This trinity consisted of the god Serapis (=Osiris+Apis), the goddess Isis (=Hathor, the cow-moon goddess), and the child-god Horus. In one way or another almost every other god was identified with one or other of these three aspects of the one God, even the sun god Mithras of the Persians. And they were each other; they were three, but

Isis and Horus

they were also one. They were worshipped with great fervour, and the jangling of a peculiar instrument, the *sistrum*, a frame set with bells and used rather after the fashion of the tambourine in the proceedings of the modern Salvation Army, was a distinctive accessory to the ceremonies. And now for the first time we find the idea of immortality becoming the central idea of a religion that extended beyond Egypt. Neither the early Aryans nor the early Semites seem to have troubled very much about immortality, it has affected the Mongolian mind very little, but the continuation of the individual life after death had been from the earliest times an intense preoccupation of the Egyptians. It played now a large part in the worship of Serapis. In the devotional literature of his cult he is spoken of as "the saviour and leader of souls, leading souls to the light and receiving them again." It is stated that "he raises the dead, he shows forth the longed-for light of the sun to those who see, whose holy tombs contain multitudes of sacred books"; and again, "we never can escape him, he will save us, after death we shall still be the care of his providence." [1]

[1] Legge, *Forerunners and Rivals of Christianity.*

The ceremonial burning of candles and the offering of ex-votos, that is to say of small models of parts of the human body in need of succour, was a part of the worship of the Serapeum. Isis attracted many devotees, who vowed their lives to her. Her images stood in the temple, crowned as the Queen of Heaven and bearing the infant Horus in her arms. The candles flared and guttered before her, and the wax ex-votos hung about the shrine. The novice was put through a long and careful preparation, he took vows of celibacy, and when he was initiated his head was shaved and he was clad in a linen garment. . . .

In this worship of Serapis, which spread very widely throughout the civilized world in the third and second centuries B.C., we see the most remarkable anticipations of usages and forms of expression that were destined to dominate the European world throughout the Christian era. The essential idea, the living spirit, of Christianity was, as we shall presently show, a new thing in the

Serapis

history of the mind and will of man; but the garments of ritual and symbol and formula that Christianity has worn, and still in many countries wears to this day, were certainly woven in the cult and temples of Jupiter, Serapis, and Isis that spread now from Alexandria throughout the civilized world in the age of theocrasia in the second and first centuries before Christ.[2]

[2] See for much light on the syncretic religions before Christianity, Franz Cumont, *Oriental Religions in Roman Paganism.* This is a very able and thoroughly interesting book.

XXVI

THE RISE AND SPREAD OF BUDDHISM[1]

§ 1

IT is interesting to turn from the mental and moral activities of Athens and Alexandria, and the growth of human ideas in the Mediterranean world, to the almost entirely separate intellectual life of India. Here was a civilization which from the first seems to have grown up upon its own roots and with a character of its own. It was cut off from the civilizations to the west and to the east by vast mountain barriers and desert regions. The Aryan tribes who had come down into the peninsula soon lost touch with their kindred to the west and north, and developed upon lines of their own. This was more particularly the case with those who had passed on into the Ganges country and beyond. They found a civilization already scattered over India, the Dravidian civilization. This had arisen independently, just as the Sumerian, Cretan, and Egyptian civilizations seem to have arisen, out of that widespread development of the neolithic culture, the heliolithic culture, whose characteristics we have already described. They revived and changed this Dravidian civilization much as the Greeks did the Ægean or the Semites the Sumerian.

These Indian Aryans were living under different conditions from those that prevailed to the north-west. They were living in a warmer climate, in which a diet of beef and fermented liquor was destructive; they were forced, therefore, to a generally vegetarian dietary, and the prolific soil, almost unasked, gave them all the food they needed. There was no further reason for them to wander; the crops and seasons were trustworthy. They wanted little clothing or housing. They wanted so little that trade was undeveloped. There was still land for every one who desired to cultivate a patch—and a little patch sufficed. Their political life was simple and comparatively secure; no great conquering powers had arisen as yet in India, and her natural barriers sufficed to stop the early imperialisms to the west of her and to the east. Thousands of comparatively pacific little village republics and chieftainships were spread over the land. There was no sea life, there were no pirate raiders, no strange traders. One might write a history of India coming down to four hundred years ago and hardly mention the sea.

The history of India for many centuries had been happier, less fierce, and more dreamlike than any other history. The noblemen, the rajahs, hunted; life was largely made up of love stories. Here and there a maharajah arose amidst the rajahs and built a city, caught and tamed many elephants, slew many tigers, and left a tradition of his splendour and his wonderful processions.

It was somewhen between 500 and 600 B.C., when Crœsus was flourishing in Lydia and Cyrus was preparing to snatch Babylon from Nabonidus, that the founder of Buddhism was born in India. He was born in a small republican tribal community in the north of Bengal under the Himalayas, in what is now overgrown jungle country on the borders of Nepal. The little state was ruled by a family, the Sakya clan, of which this man Siddhattha Gautama, was a member. Siddhattha was his personal name, like Caius or John; Gautama, or Gôtama, his family name, like Cæsar or Smith; Sakya his clan name, like Julius. The institution of caste was not yet fully established in India, and the Brahmins, though they were privileged and influential, had not yet struggled to the head of the system; but there were already strongly marked class distinctions and a practically impermeable partition between the noble Aryans and the darker common people. Gautama belonged to the former race. His teaching, we may note, was called the Aryan Path, the Aryan Truth.

It is only within the last half-century that the increasing study of the Pali language, in which most of the original sources were written, has given the world a real knowledge of the life and actual thought of

[1] Rhys Davids' *Buddhism* and other writings by him have been our chief guide here.

[2] Pronounced Ashoka.

Gautama. Previously his story was overlaid by monstrous accumulations of legend, and his teaching violently misconceived. But now we have a very human and understandable account of him.

He was a good-looking, capable young man of fortune, and until he was twenty-nine he lived the ordinary aristocratic life of his time. It was not a very satisfying life intellectually. There was no literature except the oral tradition of the Vedas, and that was chiefly monopolized by the Brahmins; there was even less knowledge. The world was bound by the snowy Himalayas to the north and spread indefinitely to the south. The city of Benares, which had a king, was about a hundred miles away. The chief amusements were hunting and love-making. All the good that life seemed to offer, Gautama enjoyed. He was married at nineteen to a beautiful cousin. For some years they remained childless. He hunted and played and went about in his sunny world of gardens and groves and irrigated rice-fields. And it was amidst this life that a great discontent fell upon him. It was the unhappiness of a fine brain that seeks employment. He lived amidst plenty and beauty, he passed from gratification to gratification, and his soul was not satisfied. It was as if he heard the destinies of the race calling to him. He felt that the existence he was leading was not the reality of life, but a holiday—a holiday that had gone on too long.

While he was in this mood he saw four things that served to point his thoughts. He was driving on some excursion of pleasure, when he came upon a man dreadfully broken down by age. The poor bent, enfeebled creature struck his imagination. "Such is the way of life," said Channa, his charioteer, and "to that we must all come." While this was yet in his mind he chanced upon a man suffering horribly from some loathsome disease. "Such is the way of life," said Channa. The third vision was of an unburied body, swollen, eyeless, mauled by passing birds and beasts and altogether terrible. "That is the way of life," said Channa.

The sense of disease and mortality, the insecurity and the unsatisfactoriness of all happiness, descended upon the mind of Gautama. And then he and Channa saw one of those wandering ascetics who already existed in great numbers in India. These men lived under severe rules, spending much time in meditation and in religious discussion. For many men before Gautama in that land of uneventful sunshine had found life distressing and mysterious. These ascetics were all supposed to be seeking some deeper reality in life, and a passionate desire to do likewise took possession of Gautama.

He was meditating upon this project, says the story, when the news was brought to him that his wife had been delivered of his first-born son. "This is another tie to break," said Gautama.

He returned to the village amidst the rejoicings of his fellow clansmen. There was a great feast and a Nautch dance to celebrate the birth of this new tie, and in the night Gautama awoke in a great agony of spirit, "like a man who is told that his house is on fire." In the ante-room the dancing girls were lying in strips of darkness and moonlight. He called Channa, and told him to prepare his horse. Then he went softly to the threshold of his wife's chamber, and saw her by the light of a little oil lamp, sleeping sweetly, surrounded by flowers, with his infant son in her arm. He felt a great craving to take up the child in one first and last embrace before he departed, but the fear of waking his wife prevented him, and at last he turned away and went out into the bright Indian moonshine to Channa waiting with the horses, and mounted and stole away.

As he rode through the night with Channa, it seemed to him that Mara, the Tempter of Mankind, filled the sky and disputed with him. "Return," said Mara, "and be a king, and I will make you the greatest of kings. Go on, and you will fail. Never will I cease to dog your footsteps. Lust or malice or anger will betray you at last in some unwary moment; sooner or later you will be mine."

Very far they rode that night, and in the morning he stopped outside the lands of his clan, and dismounted beside a sandy river. There he cut off his flowing locks with his sword, removed all his ornaments, and sent them and his horse and sword back to his house by Channa. Then going on he presently met a ragged man and exchanged clothes with him, and so having divested himself of all worldly entanglements, he was free to pursue his search after wisdom. He made his way southward to a resort of hermits and teachers in a hilly spur running into Bengal northward from the Vindhya Mountains, close to the town of Rajgir. There a number of wise men lived in a warren of caves, going into the town for their simple supplies and imparting their knowledge by word of mouth to such as cared to come to them.

This instruction must have been very much in the style of the Socratic discussions that were going on in Athens a couple of centuries later. Gautama became versed in all the metaphysics of his age. But his acute intelligence was dissatisfied with the solutions offered him.

The Indian mind has always been disposed to believe that power and knowledge may be obtained by extreme asceticism, by fasting, sleeplessness, and self-torment, and these ideas Gautama now put to the test. He betook himself with five disciple companions to the jungle in a gorge in the Vindhya Mountains, and there he gave himself up to fasting and terrible penances. His fame spread, "like the sound of a great bell hung in the canopy of the skies." [1] But it brought him no sense of truth achieved. One day he was walking up and down, trying to think in spite of his enfeebled state. Suddenly he staggered and fell unconscious. When he recovered, the preposterousness of these semi-magic ways of attempting wisdom was plain to him.

He amazed and horrified his five companions by demanding ordinary food and refusing to continue his self-mortifications. He had realized that whatever truth a man may reach is reached best by a nourished brain in a healthy body. Such a conception was absolutely foreign to the ideas of the land and age. His disciples deserted him, and went off in a melancholy state to Benares. The boom of the great bell ceased. Gautama the wonderful had fallen.

For a time Gautama wandered alone, the loneliest figure in history, battling for light.

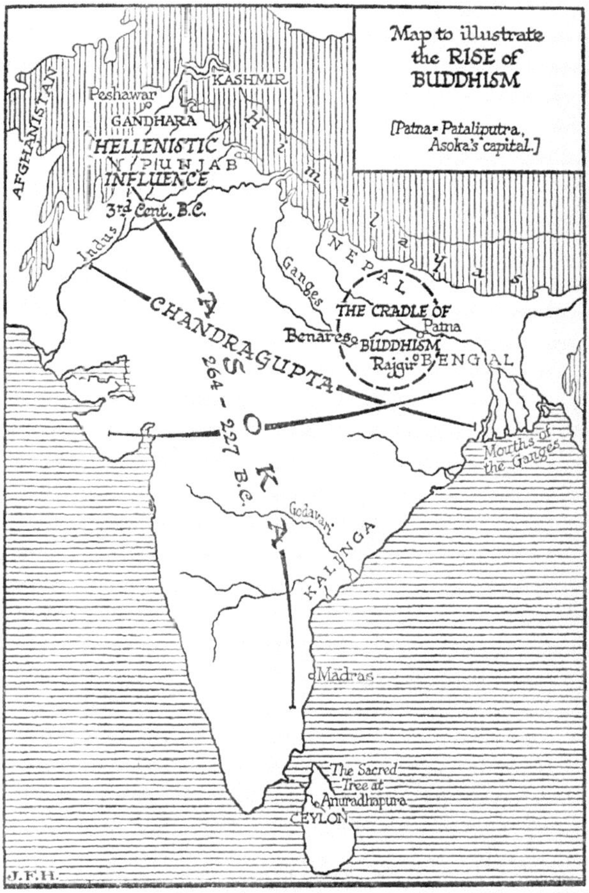

Map to illustrate the RISE of BUDDHISM

[Patna = Pataliputra, Asoka's capital.]

[1] The *Burmese Chronicle*, quoted by Rhys Davids.

BUDDHA PREACHING
Sculpture discovered at Sarnath
Photo: India Office

"Gautama Buddha's fame spread 'like the sound of a great bell hung in the canopy of the skies.'"

When the mind grapples with a great and intricate problem, it makes its advances, it secures its positions step by step, with but little realization of the gains it has made, until suddenly, with an effect of abrupt illumination, it realizes its victory. So it would seem it happened to Gautama. He had seated himself under a great tree by the side of a river to eat, when this sense of clear vision came to him. It seemed to him that he saw life plain. He is said to have sat all day and all night in profound thought, and then he rose up to impart his vision to the world.

§ 2

Such is the plain story of Gautama as we gather it from a comparison of early writings. But common men must have their cheap marvels and wonders.

It is nothing to them that this little planet should at last produce upon its surface a man thinking of the past and the future and the essential nature of existence. And so we must have this sort of thing by some worthy Pali scribe, making the most of it:

"When the conflict began between the Saviour of the World and the Prince of Evil a thousand appalling meteors fell. . . . Rivers flowed back towards their sources; peaks and lofty mountains where countless trees had grown for ages rolled crumbling to the earth. . . . the sun enveloped itself in awful darkness, and a host of headless spirits filled the air." [1]

Of which phenomena history has preserved no authentication. Instead we have only the figure of a lonely man walking towards Benares.

Extraordinary attention has been given to the tree under which Gautama had this sense of mental clarity. It was a tree of the fig genus, and from the first it was treated with peculiar veneration. It was called the Bo Tree. It has long since perished, but close at hand lives another great tree which may be its descendant, and in Ceylon there grows to this day a tree, the oldest historical tree in the world, which we know certainly to have been planted as a cutting from the Bo Tree in the year 245 B.C. From that time to this it has been carefully tended and watered; its great branches are supported by pillars, and the earth has been terraced up about it so that it has been able to put out fresh roots continually. It helps us to realize the shortness of all human history to see so many generations spanned by the endurance of one single tree. Gautama's disciples unhappily have cared more for the preservation of his tree than of his thought, which from the first they misconceived and distorted.

[1] The *Madhuratha Vilasini*, quoted by Rhys Davids.

At Benares Gautama sought out his five pupils, who were still leading the ascetic life. There is an account of their hesitation to receive him when they saw him approaching. He was a backslider. But there was some power of personality in him that prevailed over their coldness, and he made them listen to his new convictions. For five days the discussion was carried on. When he had at last convinced them that he was now enlightened, they hailed him as the Buddha. There was already in those days a belief in India that at long intervals Wisdom returned to the earth and was revealed to mankind through a chosen person known as the Buddha. According to Indian belief there have been many such Buddhas; Gautama Buddha is only the latest one of a series. But it is doubtful if he himself accepted that title or recognized that theory. In his discourses he never called himself the Buddha.

He and his recovered disciples then formed a sort of Academy in the Deer Park at Benares. They made themselves huts, and accumulated other followers to the number of threescore or more. In the rainy season they remained in discourse at this settlement, and during the dry weather they dispersed about the country, each giving his version of the new teachings. All their teaching was done, it would seem, by word of mouth. There was probably no writing yet in India at all. We must remember that in the time of Buddha it is doubtful if even the Iliad had been committed to writing. Probably the Mediterranean alphabet, which is the basis of most Indian scripts, had not yet reached India. The master, therefore, worked out and composed pithy and brief verses, aphorisms, and lists of "points," and these were expanded in the discourse of his disciples. It greatly helped them to have these points and aphorisms numbered. The modern mind is apt to be impatient of the tendency of Indian thought to a numerical statement of things, the Eightfold Path, the Four Truths, and so on, but this enumeration was a mnemonic necessity in an undocumented world.

§ 3

The fundamental teaching of Gautama, as it is now being made plain to us by the study of original sources, is clear and simple and in the closest harmony with modern ideas. It is beyond all dispute the achievement of one of the most penetrating intelligences the world has ever known.

We have what are almost certainly the authentic heads of his discourse to the five disciples which embodies his essential doctrine. All the miseries and discontents of life he traces to insatiable selfishness. Suffering, he teaches, is due to the craving individuality, to the torment of greedy desire. Until a man has overcome every sort of personal craving his life is trouble and his end sorrow. There are three principal forms the craving of life takes, and all are evil. The first is the desire to gratify the senses, sensuousness. The second is the desire for personal immortality. The third is the desire for prosperity, worldliness. All these must be overcome—that is to say, a man must no longer be living for himself—before life can become serene. But when they are indeed overcome and no longer rule a man's life, when the first personal pronoun has vanished from his private thoughts, then he has reached the higher wisdom, Nirvana, serenity of soul. For Nirvana does not mean, as many people wrongly believe, extinction, but the extinction of the futile personal aims that necessarily make life base or pitiful or dreadful.

Now here, surely we have the completest analysis of the problem of the soul's peace. Every religion that is worth the name, every philosophy, warns us to lose ourselves in something greater than ourselves. "Whosoever would save his life, shall lose it;" there is exactly the same lesson.

The teaching of history, as we are unfolding it in this book, is strictly in accordance with this teaching of Buddha. There is, as we are seeing, no social order, no security, no peace or happiness, no righteous leadership or kingship, unless men lose themselves in something greater than themselves. The study of biological progress again reveals exactly the same process—the merger of the narrow globe of the individual experience in a wider being (compare what has been said in Chaps. XII and XVIII). To forget oneself in greater interests is to escape from a prison.

The self-abnegation must be complete. From the point of view of Gautama, that dread of death, that greed for an endless continuation of his mean little individual life which drove the Egyptian and those who learnt from him with propitiations and charms into the temples, was as mortal and ugly and evil a thing as lust or avarice or hate. The religion of Gautama is flatly opposite to the "immortality" religions. And his teaching is set like flint against asceticism, as a mere attempt to win personal power by personal pains.

But when we come to the rule of life, the Aryan Path, by which we are to escape from the threefold base cravings that dishonour human life, then the teaching is not so clear. It is not so clear for one very manifest reason, Gautama had no knowledge nor vision of history; he had no clear sense of the vast and many-sided adventure of life opening out in space and time. His mind was confined within the ideas of his age and people, and their minds were shaped into notions of perpetual recurrence, of world following world and of Buddha following Buddha, a stagnant circling of the universe. The idea of mankind as a great Brotherhood pursuing an endless destiny under the God of Righteousness, the idea that was already dawning upon the Semitic consciousness in Babylon at this time, did not exist in his world. Yet his account of the Eightfold Path is, nevertheless, within these limitations, profoundly wise.

Let us briefly recapitulate the eight elements of the Aryan Path. First, Right Views; Gautama placed the stern examination of views and ideas, the insistence upon *truth* as the first research of his followers. There was to be no clinging to tawdry superstitions. He condemned, for instance, the prevalent belief in the transmigration of souls. In a well-known early Buddhist dialogue there is a destructive analysis of the idea of an enduring individual soul. Next to Right Views came Right Aspirations; because nature abhors a vacuum, and since base cravings are to be expelled, other desires must be encouraged—love for the service of others, desire to do and secure justice and the like. Primitive and uncorrupted Buddhism aimed not at the destruction of desire, but at the change of desire. Devotion to science and art, or to the betterment of things manifestly falls into harmony with the Buddhistic Right Aspirations, provided such aims are free from jealousy or the craving for fame. Right Speech, Right Conduct, and Right Livelihood, need no expansion here. Sixthly in this list came Right Effort, for Gautama had no toleration for good intentions and slovenly application; the disciple had to keep a keenly critical eye upon his activities. The seventh element of the path, Right Mindfulness, is the constant guard against a lapse into personal feeling or glory for whatever is done or not done. And, finally, comes

Right Rapture, which seems to be aimed against the pointless ecstacics of the devout, such witless baseline glorying, for instance, as those that went to the jingle of the Alexandrian sistrum.

We will not discuss here the Buddhistic doctrine of *Karma*, because it belongs to a world of thought that is passing away. The good or evil of every life was supposed to determine the happiness or misery of some subsequent life, that was in some inexplicable way identified with its predecessor. Nowadays we realize that a life goes on in its consequences for ever, but we find no necessity to suppose that any particular life resumes again. The Indian mind was full of the idea of cyclic recurrence; everything was supposed to come round again. This is a very natural supposition for men to make; so things seem to be until we analyse them. Modern science has made clear to us that there is no such exact recurrence as we are apt to suppose; every day is by an infinitesimal quantity a little longer than the day before; no generation repeats the previous generation precisely; history never repeats itself; change, we realize now, is inexhaustible; all things are eternally new. But these differences between our general ideas and those Buddha must have possessed need not in any way prevent us from appreciating the unprecedented wisdom, the goodness, and the greatness of this plan of an emancipated life as Gautama laid it down somewhen in the sixth century before Christ.

And if he failed in theory to gather together all the wills of the converted into the one multifarious activity of our race battling against death and deadness in time and space, he did in practice direct his own life and that of all his immediate disciples into one progressive adventure, which was to preach and spread the doctrine and methods of Nirvana or soul-serenity throughout our fevered world. For them at least his teaching was complete and full. But all men cannot preach or teach; doctrine is but one of many of the functions of life that are fundamentally righteous. To the modern mind it seems at least equally acceptable that a man may, though perhaps against greater difficulties, cultivate the soil, rule a city, make roads, build houses, construct engines, or seek and spread knowledge, in perfect self-forgetfulness and serenity. As much was inherent in Gautama's teaching, but the stress was certainly laid upon the teaching itself, and upon withdrawal from rather than upon the ennoblement of the ordinary affairs of men.

In certain other respects this primitive Buddhism differed from any of the religions we have hitherto considered. It was primarily a religion of conduct, not a religion of observances and sacrifices. It had no temples, and since it had no sacrifices, it had no sacred order of priests. Nor had it any theology. It neither asserted nor denied the reality of the innumerable and often grotesque gods who were worshipped in India at that time. It passed them by.

§ 4

From the very first this new teaching was misconceived. One corruption was perhaps inherent in its teaching. Because the world of men had as yet no sense of the continuous progressive effort of life, it was very easy to slip from the idea of renouncing self to the idea of renouncing active life. As Gautama's own experiences had shown, it is easier to flee from this world than from self. His early disciples were strenuous thinkers and teachers, but the lapse into mere monastic seclusion was a very easy one, particularly easy in the climate of India, where an extreme simplicity of living is convenient and attractive, and exertion more laborious than anywhere else in the world.

And it was early the fate of Gautama, as it has been the fate of most religious founders since his days, to be made into a wonder by his less intelligent disciples in their efforts to impress the outer world. We have already noted how one devout follower could not but believe that the moment of the master's mental irradiation must necessarily have been marked by an epileptic fit of the elements. This is one small sample of the vast accumulation of vulgar marvels that presently sprang up about the memory of Gautama.

There can be no doubt that for the great multitude of human beings then as now the mere idea of an emancipation from self is a very difficult one to grasp. It is probable that even among the teachers Buddha was sending out from Benares there were many who did not grasp it and still less were able to convey it to their hearers. Their teaching quite naturally took on the aspect of salvation not from oneself—that idea was beyond them—but from misfortunes and sufferings here and hereafter. In the existing superstitions of the people, and especially in the idea of the transmigration of the soul after death, though this idea was contrary to the Master's own teaching, they found stuff of fear they could work upon. They urged virtue upon the people lest they should live again in degraded or miserable forms, or fall into some one of the innumerable hells of torment with which the Brahminical teachers had already familiarized their minds. They represented Buddha as the saviour from almost unlimited torment.

There seems to be no limit to the lies that honest but stupid disciples will tell for the glory of their master and for what they regard as the success of their propaganda. Men

Hariti (painting from Chinese Turkestan, 6th Cent.y A.D.)

[after Foucher]

who would scorn to tell a lie in everyday life will become unscrupulous cheats and liars when they have given themselves up to propagandist work; it is one of the perplexing absurdities of our human nature. Such honest souls, for most of them were indubitably honest, were presently telling their hearers of the miracles that attended the Buddha's birth—they no longer called him Gautama, because that was too familiar a name—of his youthful feats of strength, of the marvels of his everyday life, winding up with a sort of illumination of his body at the moment of death. Of course it was impossible to believe that Buddha was the son of a mortal father. He was miraculously conceived through his mother dreaming of a beautiful white elephant! Previously he had himself been a marvellous elephant with six tusks; he had generously given them all to a needy hunter—and even helped him to saw them off. And so on.

Moreover, a theology grew up about Buddha. He was discovered to be a god. He was one of a series of divine beings, the Buddhas. There was an undying "Spirit of all the Buddhas"; there was a great series of Buddhas past and Buddhas (or Buddisatvas) yet to come. But we cannot go further into these complications of Asiatic theology. "Under the overpowering influence of these sickly imaginations the moral teachings of Gautama have been almost hid from view. The theories grew and flourished; each new step, each new hypothesis, demanded another; until the whole sky was filled with forgeries of the brain, and the nobler and simpler lessons of the founder of the religion were smothered beneath the glittering mass of metaphysical subtleties." [1]

In the third century B.C. Buddhism was gaining wealth and power, and the little groups of simple huts in which the teachers of the Order gathered in the rainy season were giving place to substantial monastic buildings. To this period belong the beginnings of Buddhistic art. Now if we remember how recent was the adventure of Alexander, that all the Punjab was still under Seleucid rule, that all India abounded with Greek adventurers, and that there was still quite open communication by sea and land with Alexandria, it is no great wonder to find that this early Buddhist art was strongly Greek in character, and that the new Alexandrian cult of Serapis and Isis was extraordinarily influential in its development.

The kingdom of Gandhara on the northwest frontier near Peshawar, which flourished in the third century B.C., was a typical meeting-place of the Hellenic and Indian worlds. Here are to be found the earliest Buddhist sculptures, and interwoven with them are figures which are recognizably the figures of Serapis and Isis and Horus already worked into the legendary net that gathered about Buddha. No doubt the Greek artists who came to Gandhara were loth to relinquish a familiar theme. But Isis, we are told, is no longer Isis but Hariti, a pestilence goddess whom Buddha converted and made benevolent. Foucher traces Isis from this centre into China, but here other influences were also at work, and the story becomes too complex for us to disentangle in this *Outline*.[2] China had a Taoist deity,

[1] Rhys Davids, *Buddhism*.

[2] See R. F. Johnston, *Buddhist China*.—L. C. B.

A BUDDHIST APOSTLE
Tang Dynasty, A.D. 618-906.

Statue in British Museum.

"Buddhism spread because many of the early Buddhists were sweet and gentle, helpful and noble and admirable people, who compelled belief in this sustaining faith."

the Holy Mother, the Queen of Heaven, who took on the name (originally a male name) of Kuan-yin and who came to resemble the Isis figure very closely. The Isis figures, we feel, must have influenced the treatment of Kuan-yin. Like Isis she was also Queen of the Seas. Stella Maris. In Japan she was called Kwannon. There seems to have been a constant exchange of the outer forms of religion between east and west. We read in Huc's Travels how perplexing he and his fellow missionary found this possession of a common tradition of worship. "The cross," he says, "the mitre, the dalmatica, the cope, which the Grand Lamas wear on their journeys, or when they are performing some ceremony out of the temple; the service with double choirs, the psalmody, the exorcisms, the censer, suspended from five chains, which you can open or close at pleasure; the benedictions given by the Lamas by extending the right hand over the heads of the faithful; the chaplet, ecclesiastical celibacy, spiritual retirement, the worship of the saints, the fasts, the processions, the litanies, the holy water, all these are analogies between the Buddhists and ourselves." [1]

The cult and doctrine of Gautama, gathering corruptions and variations from Brahminism and Hellenism alike, was spread throughout India by an increasing multitude of teachers in the fourth and third centuries B.C. For some generations at least it retained much of the moral beauty and something of the simplicity of the opening phase. Many people who have no intellectual grasp upon the meaning of self-abnegation and disinterestedness have nevertheless the ability to appreciate a splendour in the reality of these qualities. Early Buddhism was certainly producing noble lives, and it is not only through reason that the latent response to nobility is aroused in our minds. It spread rather in spite of than because of the concessions that it made to vulgar imaginations. It spread because many of the early Buddhists were sweet and gentle, helpful and noble and admirable people, who compelled belief in their sustaining faith.

Quite early in its career Buddhism came into conflict with the growing pretensions of the Brahmins. As we have already noted, this priestly caste was still only struggling to dominate Indian life in the days of Gautama. They had already great advantages. They had the monopoly of tradition and religious sacrifices. But their power was being challenged by the development of kingship, for the men who became clan-leaders and kings were usually not of the Brahminical caste.

Kingship received an impetus from the Persian and Greek invasions of the Punjab. We have already noted the name of King Porus whom, in spite of his elephants, Alexander defeated and turned into a satrap. There came also to the Greek camp upon the Indus a certain low-caste [2] adventurer named Chandragupta Maurya, whom the Greeks called Sandracottus, with a scheme for conquering the Ganges country. The scheme was not welcome to the Macedonians, who were in revolt against marching any further into India, and he had to fly the camp. He wandered among the tribes upon the north-west frontier, secured their support, and after Alexander had departed, overran the Punjab, ousting the Macedonian representatives. He then conquered the Ganges country (321 B.C.), waged a successful war (303 B.C.) against Seleucus (Seleucus I) when the latter attempted to recover the Punjab, and consolidated a great empire reaching across all the plain of northern India from the western to the eastern sea. And this King Chandragupta came into much the same conflict with the growing power of the Brahmins, into the conflict between crown and priesthood, that we have already noted as happening in Babylonia and Egypt and China. He saw in the spreading doctrine of Buddhism an ally against the growth of priestcraft and caste. He supported and endowed the Buddhistic Order, and encouraged its teachings.

CHINESE IMAGE OF KUAN-YIN.

He was succeeded by his son, who conquered Madras and was in turn succeeded by Asoka (264 to 227 B.C.), one of the great monarchs of history, whose dominions extended from Afghanistan to Madras. He is the only military monarch on record who abandoned warfare after victory. He had invaded Kalinga (255 B.C.), a country along

[1] Huc's *Travels in Tartary, Thibet, and China.*

[2] Rhys Davids. He was the son of a king by a low-caste mother.

the east coast of Madras, perhaps with some intention of completing the conquest of the tip of the Indian peninsula. The expedition was successful, but he was disgusted by what he saw of the cruelties and horrors of war. He declared, in certain inscriptions that still exist, that he would no longer seek conquest view of the ends and way of life. He made vast benefactions to the Buddhist teaching orders, and tried to stimulate them to a better study of their own literature. All over the land he set up long inscriptions rehearsing the teaching of Gautama, and it is the simple and human teaching and not

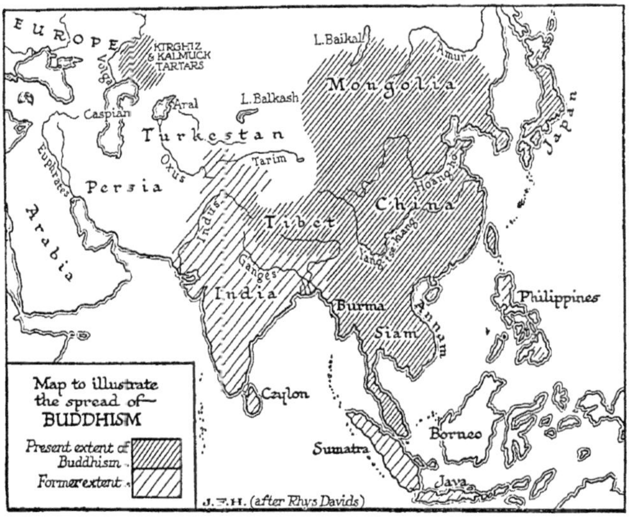

by war, but by religion, and the rest of his life was devoted to the spreading of Buddhism throughout the world.

He seems to have ruled his vast empire in peace and with great ability. He was no mere religious fanatic. But in the year of his one and only war he joined the Buddhist community as a layman, and some years later he became a full member of the Order, and devoted himself to the attainment of Nirvana by the Eightfold Path. How entirely compatible that way of living then was with the most useful and beneficent activities his life shows. Right Aspiration, Right Effort, and Right Livelihood distinguished his career. He organized a great digging of wells in India, and the planting of trees for shade. He appointed officers for the supervision of charitable works. He founded hospitals and public gardens. He had gardens made for the growing of medicinal herbs. Had he had an Aristotle to inspire him, he would no doubt have endowed scientific research upon a great scale. He created a ministry for the care of the aborigines and subject races. He made provision for the education of women. He made, he was the first monarch to make, an attempt to educate his people into a common the preposterous accretions. Thirty-five of his inscriptions survive to this day. Moreover, he sent missionaries to spread the noble and reasonable teaching of his master throughout the world, to Kashmir, to Ceylon, to the Seleucids, and the Ptolemies. It was one of these missions which carried that cutting of the Bo Tree, of which we have already told, to Ceylon.

For eight and twenty years Asoka worked sanely for the real needs of men. Amidst the tens of thousands of names of monarchs that crowd the columns of history, their majesties and graciousnesses and serenities and royal highnesses and the like, the name of Asoka shines, and shines almost alone, a star. From the Volga to Japan his name is still honoured. China, Tibet, and even India, though it has left his doctrine, preserve the tradition of his greatness. More living men cherish his memory to-day than have ever heard the names of Constantine or Charlemagne.

§ 5

It is thought that the vast benefactions of Asoka finally corrupted Buddhism by attracting to its Order great numbers of mercenary and insincere adherents, but there can be no doubt that its rapid extension throughout Asia was very largely due to his stimulus.

It made its way into Central Asia through Afghanistan and Turkestan, and so reached China. Buddhist teaching had spread widely in China before 200 B.C.[1] Buddhism found there a popular and prevalent religion, Taoism, a development of very ancient and primitive magic and occult practices. It was reorganized as a distinctive cult by Chang Daoling in the days of the Han dynasty. Tao means the Way, which corresponds closely with the idea of the Aryan Path. The two religions spread side by side and underwent similar changes, so that nowadays their outward practice is very similar. Buddhism also encountered Confucianism, which was even less theological and even more a code of personal conduct. And finally it encountered the teachings of Lao Tse, "anarchist, evolutionist, pacifist and moral philosopher,"[2] which were not so much a religion as a philosophical rule of life. The teachings of this Lao Tse were later to become incorporated with the Taoist religion by Chen Tuan, the founder of modern Taoism.

Confucius, the founder of Confucianism, like the great southern teacher Lao Tse and Gautama, lived also in the sixth century B.C. His life has some interesting parallelisms with that of some of the more political of the Greek philosophers of the fifth and fourth. The sixth century B.C. falls into the period assigned by Chinese historians to the Chow Dynasty, but in those days the rule of that dynasty had become little more than nominal; the emperor conducted the traditional sacrifices of the Son of Heaven, and received a certain formal respect. Even his nominal empire was not a sixth part of the China of to-day. In Chapter XVI we have already glanced at the state of affairs in China at this time; practically China was a multitude of warring states open to the northern barbarians. Confucius was a subject in one of those states, Lu; he was of aristocratic birth, but poor; and, after occupying various official positions, he set up a sort of Academy in Lu for the discovery and imparting of Wisdom. And we also find Confucius travelling from state to state in China, seeking a prince who would make him his counsellor and become the centre of a reformed world. Plato, two centuries later, in exactly the same spirit, went as adviser to the tyrant Dionysius of Syracuse, and we have already noted the attitudes of Aristotle and Isocrates towards Philip of Macedonia.

The teaching of Confucius centred upon the idea of a noble life which he embodied in a standard or ideal, the Aristocratic Man. This phrase is often translated into English as the Superior Person, but as "superior" and "person," like "respectable" and "genteel," have long become semi-humorous terms of abuse, this rendering is not fair to Confucianism. He did present to his time the ideal of a devoted public man. The public side was very important to him. He was far more of a constructive political thinker than Gautama or Lao Tse. His mind was full of the condition of China, and he sought to call the Aristocratic Man into existence very largely in order to produce the noble state. One of his sayings may be quoted here: "It is impossible to withdraw from the world, and associate with birds and beasts that have no affinity with us. With whom should I associate but with suffering men? The disorder that prevails is what requires my efforts. If right principles ruled through the kingdom, there would be no necessity for me to change its state."

The political basis of his teaching seems to be characteristic of Chinese moral ideas; there is a much directer reference to the State than is the case with most Indian and European moral and religious doctrine. For a time he was appointed magistrate in Chung-tu, a city of the dukedom of Lu, and here he sought to regulate life to an extraordinary extent, to subdue every relationship and action indeed to the rule of an elaborate etiquette. "Ceremonial in every detail, such as we are wont to see only in the courts of rulers and the households of high dignitaries, became obligatory on the people at large, and all matters of daily life were subject to rigid rule. Even the food which the different classes of people might eat was regulated; males and females were kept apart in the streets; even the thickness of coffins and the shape and situation of graves were made the subject of regulations.[3]

This is all, as people say, very Chinese. No other people have ever approached moral order and social stability through the channel of manners. Yet in China, at any rate, the methods of Confucius have had an enormous effect, and no nation in the world to-day has such a universal tradition of decorum and self-restraint.

[1] See Giles, *Confucianism and its Rivals.*

[2] S. N. Fu.

[3] Hirth's *The Ancient History of China.*

Vishnu Brahma Siva

Later on the influence of Confucius over his duke was undermined, and he withdrew again into private life. His last days were saddened by the deaths of some of his most promising disciples. "No intelligent ruler," he said, "arises to take me as his master, and my time has come to die." . . .

But he died to live. Says Hirth, "There can be no doubt that Confucius has had a greater influence on the development of the Chinese national character than many emperors taken together. He is, therefore, one of the essential figures to be considered in connection with any history of China. That he could influence his nation to such a degree was, it appears to me, due more to the peculiarity of the nation than to that of his own personality. Had he lived in any other part of the world, his name would perhaps be forgotten. As we have seen, he had formed his character and his personal views on man's life from a careful study of documents closely connected with the moral philosophy cultivated by former generations. What he preached to his contemporaries was, therefore, not all new to them; but, having himself, in the study of old records, heard the dim voice of the sages of the past, he became, as it were, the megaphone phonograph through which were expressed to the nation those views which he had derived from the early development of the nation itself. . . . The great influence of Confucius's personality on national life in China was due not only to his writings and his teachings as recorded by others, but also to his doings. His personal character, as described by his disciples and in the accounts of later writers, some of which may be entirely legendary, has become the pattern for millions of those who are bent on imitating the outward manners of a great man. . . . Whatever he did in public was regulated to the minutest detail by ceremony. This was no invention of his own, since ceremonial life had been cultivated many centuries before Confucius; but his authority and example did much to perpetuate what he considered desirable social practices."

The Chinese speak of Buddhism and the doctrines of Lao Tse and Confucius as the Three Teachings. Together they constitute the basis and point of departure of all later Chinese thought. Their thorough study is a necessary preliminary to the establishment of any real intellectual and moral community between the great people of the East and the Western world.[1]

There are certain things to be remarked in common of all these three teachers, of whom Gautama was indisputably the greatest and profoundest, whose doctrines to this day dominate the thought of the great majority of human beings; there are certain features in which their teaching contrasts with the thoughts and feelings that were soon to take possession of the western world. Primarily they are personal and tolerant doctrines; they are doctrines of a Way, of a

[1] The reader will find a footnote to Chap. XXXI, § 8, signed L. C. B., which gives the main differences between the teachings of Confucius and Lao Tse.

Path, of a Nobility, and not doctrines of a church or a general rule. And they offer nothing either for or against the existence and worship of the current gods. The Athenian philosophers, it is to be noted, had just the same theological detachment; Socrates was quite willing to bow politely or sacrifice formally to almost any divinity,—reserving his private thoughts. This attitude is flatly antagonistic to the state of mind that was growing up in the Jewish communities of Judea, Egypt, and Babylonia, in which the thought of the one God was first and foremost. Neither Gautama nor Lao Tse nor Confucius had any inkling of this idea of a *jealous* God, a God who would have "none other gods," a God of terrible Truth, who would not tolerate any lurking belief in magic, witchcraft, or old customs, or any sacrificing to the god-king or any trifling with the stern unity of things.

§ 6

The intolerance of the Jewish mind did keep its essential faith clear and clean. The theological disregard of the great Eastern teachers, neither assenting nor denying, did on the other hand permit elaborations of explanation and accumulations of ritual from the very beginning. Except for Gautama's insistence upon Right Views, which was easily disregarded, there was no *self-cleansing* element in either Buddhism, Taoism, or Confucianism. There was no effective prohibition of superstitious practices, spirit raising, incantations, prostrations, and supplementary worships. At an early stage a process of encrustation began, and continued. The new faiths caught almost every disease of the corrupt religions they sought to replace; they took over the idols and the temples, the altars and the censers.

Tibet to-day is a Buddhistic country, yet Gautama, could he return to earth, might go from end to end of Tibet seeking his own teaching in vain. He would find that most ancient type of human ruler, a god king, enthroned, the Dalai Lama, the "living Buddha." At Lhassa he would find a huge temple filled with priests, abbots, and lamas —he whose only buildings were huts and who made no priests—and above a high altar he would behold a huge golden idol, which he would learn was called "Gautama Buddha"! He would hear services intoned before this divinity, and certain precepts, which would be dimly familiar to him, murmured as responses. Bells, incense, prostrations, would play their part in these amazing proceedings. At one point in the service a bell would be rung and a mirror lifted up, while the whole congregation, in an access of reverence, bowed lower. . . .

About this Buddhist countryside he would discover a number of curious little mechanisms, little wind-wheels and water-wheels spinning, on which brief prayers were inscribed. Every time these things spin, he would learn, it counts as a prayer. "To whom?" he would ask. Moreover, there would be a number of flagstaffs in the land

Krishna   Kali, *as an impersonation of Vengeance*   Ganesa

carrying beautiful silk flags, silk flags which bore the perplexing inscription, "*Om Mani padme hum*," "the jewel is in the lotus." Whenever the flag flaps, he would learn, it was a prayer also, very beneficial to the gentleman who paid for the flag and to the land generally. Gangs of workmen, employed by pious persons, would be going about the country cutting this precious formula on cliff and stone. And this, he would realize at last, was what the world had made of his religion! Beneath this gaudy glitter was buried the Aryan Way to serenity of soul.[1]

We have already noted the want of any progressive idea in primitive Buddhism. In that again it contrasted with Judaism. The idea of a Promise gave to Judaism a quality no previous or contemporary religion displayed; it made Judaism historical and dramatic. It justified its fierce intolerance because it pointed to an aim. In spite of the truth and profundity of the psychological side of Gautama's teaching, Buddhism stagnated and corrupted for the lack of that directive idea. Judaism, it must be confessed, in its earlier phases, entered but little into the souls of men; it let them remain lustful, avaricious, worldly or superstitious; but because of its persuasion of a promise and of a divine leadership to serve divine ends, it remained in comparison with Buddhism bright and expectant, like a cared-for sword.

[1] See Huc's *Travels in Tartary, Thibet, and China.*

§ 7

For some time Buddhism flourished in India. But Brahminism, with its many gods and its endless variety of cults, always flourished by its side, and the organization of the Brahmins grew more powerful, until at last they were able to turn upon this caste-denying cult and oust it from India altogether. The story of that struggle is not to be told here; there were persecutions and reactions, but by the eleventh century, except for Orissa, Buddhist teaching was extinct in India. Much of its gentleness and charity had, however, become incorporated with Brahminism.

Over great areas of the world, as our map has shown, it still survives; and it is quite possible that in contact with western science, and inspired by the spirit of history, the original teaching of Gautama, revived and purified, may yet play a large part in the direction of human destiny.

But with the loss of India the Aryan Way ceased to rule the lives of any Aryan peoples. It is curious to note that while the one great Aryan religion is now almost exclusively confined to Mongolian peoples, the Aryans themselves are under the sway of two religions, Christianity and Islam, which are, as we shall see, essentially Semitic. And both Buddhism and Christianity wear garments of ritual and formula that seem to be derived through Hellenistic channels from that land of temples and priestcraft, Egypt, and from the mentality of the brown Hamitic peoples.

BOOK V

THE RISE AND COLLAPSE OF THE ROMAN EMPIRE

XXVII

THE TWO WESTERN REPUBLICS[1]

§ 1

IT is now necessary to take up the history of the two great republics of the Western Mediterranean, Rome and Carthage, and to tell how Rome succeeded in maintaining for some centuries an empire even greater than that achieved by the conquests of Alexander. But this new empire was, as we shall try to make clear, a political structure differing very profoundly in its nature from any of the great Oriental empires that had preceded it. Great changes in the texture of human society and in the conditions of social interrelations had been going on for some centuries. The flexibility and transferability of money was becoming a power and, like all powers in inexpert hands, a danger in human affairs. It was altering the relations of rich men to the state and to their poorer fellow citizens. This new empire, the Roman empire, unlike all the preceding empires, was not the creation of a great conqueror. No Sargon, no Thothmes, no Nebuchadnezzar, no Cyrus nor Alexander nor Chandragupta, was its fountain head. It was made by a republic. It grew by a kind of necessity through new concentrating and unifying forces that were steadily gathering power in human affairs.

But first it is necessary to give some idea of the state of affairs in Italy in the centuries immediately preceding the appearance of Rome in the world's story.

Before 1200 B.C., that is to say before the rise of the Assyrian empire, the siege of Troy, and the final destruction of Cnossos, but after the time of Amenophis IV, Italy, like Spain, was probably still inhabited mainly by dark white people of the more fundamental Iberian or Mediterranean race.[2] This aboriginal population was probably a thin and backward one. But already in Italy, as in Greece, the Aryans were coming southward. By 1000 B.C. immigrants from the north had settled over most of the north and centre of Italy, and, as in Greece, they had intermarried with their darker predecessors and established a group of Aryan languages, the Italian group, more akin to the Keltic (Gaelic)[3] than to any other, of which the most interesting from the historical point of view was that spoken by the Latin tribes in the plains south and east of the river Tiber. Meanwhile the Greeks had been settling down in Greece, and now they were taking

[1] A very convenient handbook for this and the next two chapters is Matheson's *Skeleton Outline of Roman History.*

[2] For Italian pre-history see Modestov's *Introduction à l'histoire Romaine,* and Peet's *Stone and Bronze Age in Italy and Sicily.*

[3] See Lloyd's *Making of the Roman People.*

to the sea and crossing over to South Italy and Sicily and establishing themselves there. Subsequently they established colonies along the French Riviera and founded Marseilles upon the site of an older Phœnician colony. Another interesting people also had come into Italy by sea. These were a brownish sturdy people, to judge from the pictures they have left of themselves; very probably they were a tribe of those Ægean "dark whites" who were being driven out of Greece and Asia Minor and the islands in between by the Greeks. We have already told the tale of Cnossos (Chapter XVII) and of the settlement of the kindred Philistines in Palestine (Chapter XXI, § 1) These Etruscans, as they were called in Italy, were known even in ancient times to be of Asiatic origin, and it is tempting, but probably unjustifiable, to connect this tradition with the Æneid, the sham epic of the Latin poet Virgil, in which the Latin civilization is ascribed to Trojan immigrants from Asia Minor. (But the Trojans themselves were probably an Aryan people allied to the Phrygians.) These Etruscan people conquered most of Italy north of the Tiber from the Aryan tribes who were scattered over that country. Probably the Etruscans ruled over a subjugated Italian population, so reversing the state of affairs in Greece, in which the Aryans were uppermost.

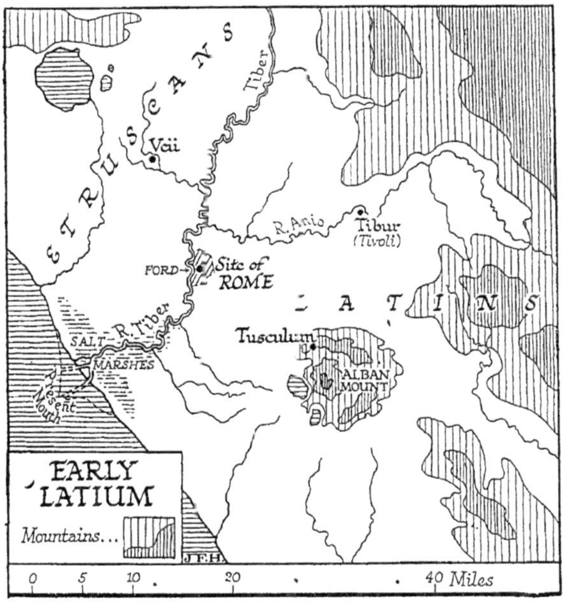

Our map, which may be taken to represent roughly the state of affairs about 750 B.C., also shows the establishments of the Phœnician traders, of which Carthage was the chief, along the shores of Africa and Spain.

Of all the peoples actually in Italy, the Etruscans were by far the most civilized. They built sturdy fortresses of the Mycænean type of architecture; they had a metal industry; they used imported Greek pottery of a very fine type. The Latin tribes on the other side of the Tiber were by comparison barbaric.

The Latins were still a rude farming people. The centre of their worship was a temple to the tribal god Jupiter, upon the Alban Mount. There they gathered for their chief festivals very much after the fashion of the early tribal gathering we have already imagined at Avebury (Chapter XII). This gathering-place was not a town. It was a high place of assembly. There was no population permanently there. There were, however, twelve townships in the Latin league. At one point upon the Tiber there was a ford, and here there was a trade between Latins and Etruscans. At this ford Rome had its beginnings. Traders assembled there, and refugees from the twelve towns found an asylum and occupation at this trading centre. Upon the seven hills near the ford a number of settlements sprang up, which finally amalgamated into one city.

Most people have heard the story of the two brothers Romulus and Remus, who founded Rome, and the legend of how they were exposed as infants and sheltered and suckled by a wolf. Little value is now attached to this tale by modern historians.

The peninsula of Italy was not then the smiling land of vineyards and olive orchards it has since become. It was still a rough country of marsh and forest, in which the farmers grazed their cattle and made their clearings. Rome, on the boundary between Latin and Etruscan, was not in a very strong position for defence. At first there were perhaps Latin kings in Rome, then it

AN ETRUSCAN SARCOPHAGUS, FROM CERVETRI SIXTH CENTURY, B.C.

British Museum

"These Etruscan people were by far the most civilized in Italy—Rome fell into their hands, but tyrannous conduct led to their expulsion in the sixth century, B.C."

would seem the city fell into the hands of Etruscan rulers whose tyrannous conduct led at last to their expulsion, and Rome became a Latin-speaking republic. The Etruscan kings were expelled from Rome in the sixth century B.C., while the successors of Nebuchadnezzar were ruling by the sufferance of the Medes in Babylon, while Confucius was seeking a king to reform the disorders of China, and while Gautama was teaching the Aryan Way to his disciples at Benares.

Etruscan painting of a Ceremonial Burning of the Dead

Of the struggle between the Romans and the Etruscans we cannot tell in any detail here. The Etruscans were the better armed, the more civilized, and the more numerous, and it would probably have gone hard with the Romans if they had had to fight them alone. But two disasters happened to the Etruscans which so weakened them that the Romans were able at last to master them altogether. The first of these was a war with the Greeks of Syracuse in Sicily which destroyed the Etruscan fleet (474 B.C.), and the second was a great raid of the Gauls from the north into Italy. These latter people swarmed into North Italy and occupied the valley of the Po towards the end of the fifth century B.C., as a couple of centuries later their kindred were to swarm down into Greece and Asia Minor and settle in Galatia. The Etruscans were thus caught between hammer and anvil, and after a long and intermittent war the Romans were able to capture Veii, an Etruscan fortress, a few miles from Rome, which had hitherto been a great threat and annoyance to them.

It is to this period of struggle against the Etruscan monarchs, the Tarquins, that Macaulay's *Lays of Ancient Rome*, familiar to every schoolboy, refer.

But the invasion of the Gauls was one of those convulsions of the nations that leave nothing as it has been before. They carried their raiding right down the Italian peninsula, devastating all Etruria. They took and sacked Rome (390 B.C.). According to Roman legends—on which doubt is thrown—the citadel on the Capitol held out, and this also the Gauls would have taken by surprise at night, if certain geese had not been awakened by their stealthy movements and set up such a cackling as to arouse the garrison. After that the Gauls, who were ill-equipped for siege operations, and perhaps suffering from disease in their camp, were bought off, and departed to the northward again, and, though they made subsequent raids, they never again reached Rome.

The leader of the Gauls who sacked Rome was named Brennus. It is related of him that as the gold of the ransom was being weighed, there was some dispute about the justice of the counterpoise, whereupon he flung his sword into the scale, saying, "*Væ victis!*" ("Woe to the vanquished!")—a phrase that has haunted the discussions of all subsequent ransoms and indemnities down to the present time.

For half a century after this experience Rome was engaged in a series of wars to establish herself at the head of the Latin tribes. For the burning of the chief city seems to have stimulated rather than crippled her energies. However much she had suffered, most of her neighbours seem to have suffered more. By 290 B.C. Rome was the mistress city of all Central Italy from the Arno to south of Naples. She had conquered the Etruscans altogether, and her boundaries marched with those of the Gauls to the north and with the regions of Italy under Greek dominion (Magna Græcia) to the south. Along the Gaulish boundary she had planted garrisons and colonial cities, and no doubt it was because of that line

Greek statuette of a Gaul..

(From Myrina)

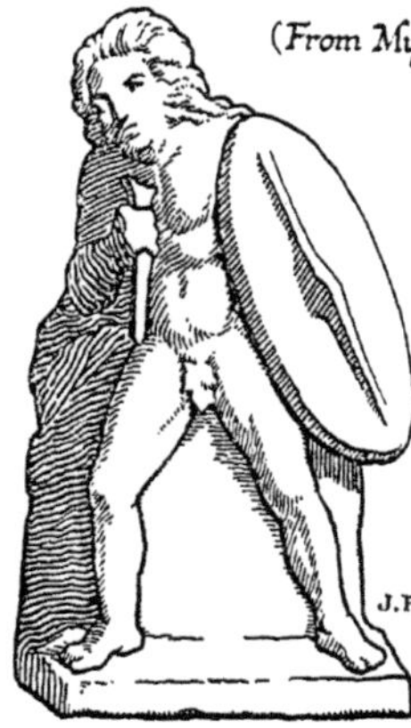

of defence that the raiding enterprises of the Gauls were deflected eastward into the Balkans.

After what we have already told of the history of Greece and the constitutions of her cities, it will not surprise the reader to learn that the Greeks of Sicily and Italy were divided up into a number of separate city governments, of which Syracuse and Tarentum (the modern Taranto) were the chief, and that they had no common rule of direction or policy. But now, alarmed at the spread of the Roman power, they looked across the Adriatic for help, and found it in the ambitions of Pyrrhus, the king of Epirus. Between the Romans and Pyrrhus these Greeks of Magna Græcia were very much in the same position that Greece proper had

The ROMAN POWER after the SAMNITE WARS

Samnite warriors . . . . (from painted vases.)

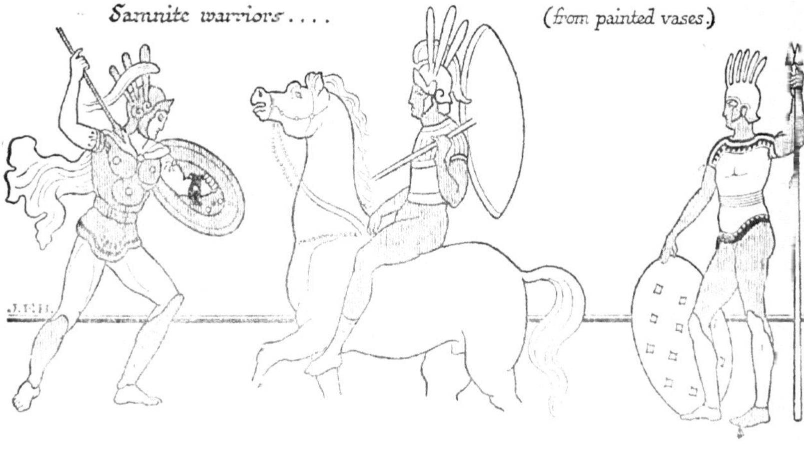

been in, between the Macedonians and the Persians half a century before.

The reader will remember that Epirus, the part of Greece that is closest to the heel of Italy, was the native land of Olympias, the mother of Alexander. In the kaleidoscopic changes of the map that followed the death of Alexander, Epirus was sometimes swamped by Macedonia, sometimes independent. This Pyrrhus was a kinsman of Alexander the Great, and a monarch of ability and enterprise, and he seems to have planned a career of conquest in Italy and Sicily. He commanded an admirable army, against which the comparatively inexpert Roman levies could at first do little. His army included all the established military devices of the time, an infantry phalanx, Thessalian cavalry and twenty fighting elephants from the east. He routed the Romans at Heraclea (280 B.C.), and, pressing after them, defeated them again at Ausculum (279 B.C.) in their own territory. Then, instead of pursuing the Romans further, he made a truce with them, turned his attention to the subjugation of Sicily, and so brought the sea power of Carthage into alliance against him. For Carthage could not afford to have a strong power established so close to her as Sicily. Rome in those days seemed to the Carthaginians a far less serious threat than the possibility of another Alexander the Great ruling Sicily. A Carthaginian fleet appeared off the mouth of the Tiber, therefore, to encourage or induce the

Romans to renew the struggle, and Rome and Carthage were definitely allied against the invader.

This interposition of Carthage was fatal to Pyrrhus. Without any decisive battle his power wilted, and, after a disastrous repulse in an attack upon the Roman camp of Beneventum, he had to retire to Epirus (275 B.C.).

It is recorded that when Pyrrhus left Sicily, he said he left it to be the battleground of Rome and Carthage. He was killed three years later in a battle in the streets of Argos. The war against Pyrrhus was won by the Carthaginian fleet, and Rome reaped a full half of the harvest of victory. Sicily fell completely to Carthage, and Rome came down to the toe and heel of Italy, and looked across the Straits of Messina at her new rival. In eleven years' time (264 B.C.) the prophecy of Pyrrhus was fulfilled, and the first war with Carthage, the first of the three Punic [1] Wars, had begun.

[1] Latin *Pœni* = Carthaginians. *Punicus* (*adj.*) = Carthaginian, i.e. Phœnician.

§ 2[1]

But we write "Rome" and the "Romans," and we have still to explain what manner of people these were who were playing a rôle of conquest that had hitherto been played only by able and aggressive monarchs.

Their state was, in the fifth century B.C., a republic of the Aryan type very similar to a Greek aristocratic republic. The earliest accounts of the social life of Rome give us a picture of a very primitive Aryan com-

ROMAN COIN STRUCK TO COMMEMORATE THE VICTORY OVER PYRRHUS AND HIS ELEPHANTS.

munity. "In the second half of the fifth century before Christ, Rome was still an aristocratic community of free peasants, occupying an area of nearly 400 square miles, with a population certainly not exceeding 150,000, almost entirely dispersed over the country-side and divided into seventeen districts or rural tribes. Most of the families had a small holding and a cottage of their own, where father and sons lived and worked together, growing corn for the most part, with here and there a strip of vine or olive. Their few head of cattle were kept at pasture on the neighbouring common land; their clothes and simple implements of husbandry they made for themselves at home. Only at rare intervals and on special occasions would they make their way into the fortified town, which was the centre at once of their religion and their government. Here were the temples of the gods, the houses of the wealthy, and the shops of the artizans and traders, where corn, oil, or wine could be bartered in small quantities for salt or rough tools and weapons of iron."[2]

This community followed the usual tradition of a division into aristocratic and common citizens, who were called in Rome patricians and plebeians. These were the citizens; the slave or outlander had no more part in the state than he had in Greece. But the constitution differed from any Greek constitution in the fact that a great part of the ruling power was gathered into the hands of a body called the Senate, which was neither purely a body of hereditary members nor directly an elected and representative one. It was a nominated one, and in the earlier period it was nominated solely from among the patricians. It existed before the expulsion of the kings, and in the time of the kings it was the king who nominated the senators. But after the expulsion of the kings (510 B.C.), the supreme government was vested in the hands of two elected rulers, the *consuls*; and it was the consuls who took over the business of appointing senators. In the early days of the Republic only patricians were eligible as consuls or senators, and the share of the plebeians in the government consisted merely in a right to vote for the consuls and other public officials. Even for that purpose their votes did not have the same value as those of their patrician fellow citizens. But their votes had at any rate sufficient weight to induce many of the patrician candidates to profess a more or less sincere concern for plebeian grievances. In the early phases of the Roman state, moreover, the plebeians were not only excluded from public office, but from intermarriage with the patrician class. The administration was evidently primarily a patrician affair.

The early phase of Roman affairs was therefore an aristocracy of a very pronounced type, and the internal history of Rome for the two centuries and a half between the expulsion of the last Etruscan king, Tarquin the Proud, and the beginning of the first Punic War (264 B.C.), was very largely a struggle for mastery between those two orders, the patricians and the plebeians. It was, in fact, closely parallel with the struggle of aristocracy and democracy in the city states of Greece, and, as in the case of Greece, there were whole classes in the community, slaves, freed slaves, unpropertied free men, outlanders, and the like, who were entirely outside and beneath the struggle. We have already noted the essential difference of Greek democracy and what is called democracy in the world to-day. Another misused word is the Roman term *proletariat*, which in modern jargon means all the unpropertied people in a modern state. In Rome the *proletarii* were a voting division of fully qualified citizens whose property was less than 10,000 copper asses (= £275). They were an enrolled class; their value to the state consisted in their raising families

[1] See Pelham, *Outlines of Roman History*; Mommsen, *History of Rome*; and the histories of the Roman Empire by Bury, H. Stuart Jones, and W. E. Heitland.

[2] Ferrero, *The Greatness and Decline of Rome*.

ROME SAVED BY THE SACRED GEESE OF JUNO

By Henri Paul Motte

"The Gauls would have taken the Capitol itself if the cackling of the geese—disturbed by the stealthy movements—had not aroused the garrison"

of citizens (proles = offspring), and from their ranks were drawn the colonists who went to form new Latin cities or to garrison important points. But the proletarii were quite distinct in origin from slaves or freedmen or the miscellaneous driftage of a town slum, and it is a great pity that modern political discussion should be confused by an inaccurate use of a term which has no exact modern equivalent and which expresses nothing real in modern social classification.

The mass of the details of this struggle between patricians and plebeians we can afford to ignore in this outline. It was a struggle which showed the Romans to be a people of a curiously shrewd character, never forcing things to a destructive crisis, but being within the limits of their discretion grasping hard dealers. The patricians made a mean use of their political advantages to grow rich through the national conquests at the expense not only of the defeated enemy, but of the poorer plebeian, whose farm had been neglected and who had fallen into debt during his military service. The plebeians were ousted from any share in the conquered lands, which the patricians divided up among themselves. The introduction of money [1] probably increased the facilities of the usurer and the difficulties of the borrowing debtor.

Three sorts of pressure won the plebeians a greater share in the government of the country and the good things that were coming to Rome as she grew powerful. The first of these (1) was the general strike of plebeians; the plebeians seem to have invented the strike, which now makes its first appearance in history. Twice they actually marched right out of Rome, threatening to make a new city higher up the Tiber, and twice this threat proved conclusive. The second method of pressure (2) was the threat of a tyranny. Just as in Attica (the little state of which Athens was the capital), Peisistratus raised himself to power on the support of the poorer districts, so there was to be found in most periods of plebeian discontent some ambitious man ready to figure as a leader and wrest power from the senate. For a long time the Roman patricians were clever enough to beat every such potential tyrant by giving in to a certain extent to the plebeians. And finally (3) there were patricians big-minded and far-seeing enough to insist upon the need of reconciliation with the plebeians.

Thus in 509 B.C., Valerius Poplicola (3), the consul, enacted that whenever the life or rights of any citizen were at stake, there should be an appeal from the magistrates to the general assembly. This Lex Valeria was "the Habeas Corpus of Rome," and it freed the Roman plebeians from the worst dangers of class vindictiveness in the law courts.

In 494 B.C. occurred the first strike (1). "After the Latin war the pressure of debt had become excessive, and the plebeians saw with indignation their friends, who had often served the state bravely in the legions, thrown into chains and reduced to slavery at the demand of patrician creditors. War was raging against the Volscians; but the legionaries, on their victorious return, refused any longer to obey the consuls, and marched, though without any disorder, to the Sacred Mount beyond the Anio (up the Tiber). There they prepared to found a new city, since the rights of citizens were denied to them in the old one. The patricians were compelled to give way, and the plebeians, returning to Rome from the "First Secession," received the privilege of having officers of their own, tribunes and ædiles." [2]

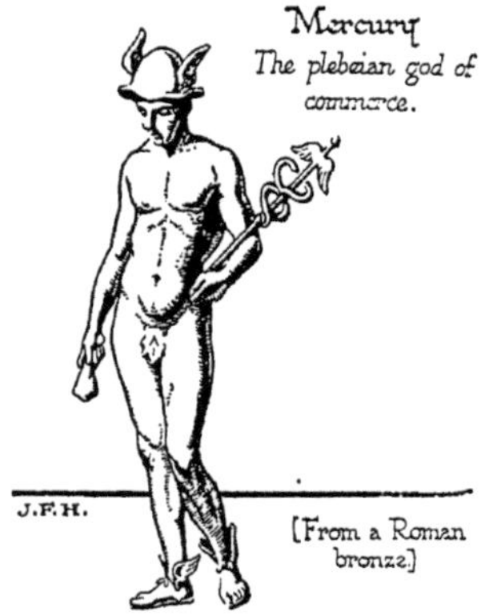

Mercury
The plebeian god of commerce.

[From a Roman bronze]

In 486 B.C. arose Spurius Cassius (2), a consul who carried an Agrarian Law securing public land for the plebeians. But the next year he was accused of aiming at royal power, and condemned to death. His law never came into operation.

There followed a long struggle on the part of the plebeians to have the laws of Rome written down, so that they would no longer

[1] J. Wells, *Short History of Rome to the Death of Augustus.*

[2] J. Wells.

have to trust to patrician memories. In 451–450 B.C. the law of the Twelve Tables was published, the basis of all Roman law.

But in order that the Twelve Tables should be formulated, a committee of ten (the *decemvirate*) was appointed in the place of the ordinary magistrates. A second decemvirate, appointed in succession to the first, attempted a sort of aristocratic counter-revolution under Appius Claudius. The plebeians withdrew again a second time to the Sacred Mount, and Appius Claudius committed suicide in prison.

In 440 came a famine, and a second attempt to found a popular tyranny upon the popular wrongs, by Spurius Mælius, a wealthy plebeian, which ended in his assassination.

After the sack of Rome by the Gauls (390 B.C.), Marcus Manlius, who had been in command of the Capitol when the geese had saved it, came forward as a popular leader. The plebeians were suffering severely from the after-war usury and profiteering of the patricians, and were incurring heavy debts in rebuilding and restocking their farms. Manlius spent his fortune in releasing debtors. He was accused by the patricians of tyrannous intentions, condemned, and suffered the fate of condemned traitors in Rome, being flung from the Tarpeian Rock, the precipitous edge of that same Capitoline Hill he had defended.

In 376 B.C., Licinius, who was one of the ten tribunes for the people, began a long struggle with the patricians by making certain proposals called the Licinian Rogations, that there should be a limit to the amount of public land taken by any single citizen, so leaving some for everybody, that outstanding debts should be forgiven without interest upon the repayment of the principal, and that henceforth one at least of the two consuls should be a plebeian. This precipitated a ten-year struggle. The plebeian power to stop business by the veto of their representatives, the tribunes, was fully exercised. In cases of national extremity it was the custom to set all other magistrates aside and appoint one leader, the Dictator. Rome had done such a thing during times of military necessity before, but now the patricians set up a Dictator in a time of profound peace, with the idea of crushing Licinius altogether. They appointed Camillus, who had besieged and taken Veii from the Etruscans. But Camillus was a wiser man than his supporters; he brought about a compromise between the two orders in which most of the demands of the plebeians were conceded (366 B.C.), dedicated a temple to Concord, and resigned his power.

Thereafter the struggle between the orders abated. It abated because, among other influences, the social differences between patricians and plebeians were diminishing. Trade was coming to Rome with increasing political power, and many plebeians were growing rich and many patricians becoming relatively poor. Intermarriage had been rendered possible by a change in the law, and social intermixture was going on. While the rich plebeians were becoming, if not aristocratic, at least oligarchic in habits and sympathy, new classes were springing up in Rome with fresh interests and no political standing. Particularly abundant were the freedmen, slaves set free, for the most part artisans, but some of them traders, who were growing wealthy. And the Senate, no longer a purely patrician body—since various official positions were now open to plebeians, and such plebeian officials became senators—was becoming now an assembly of all the wealthy, able, energetic, and influential men in the state. The Roman power was expanding, and as it expanded these old class oppositions of the early Latin community were becoming unmeaning. They were being replaced by new associations and new antagonisms. Rich men of all origins were being drawn together into a common interest against the communistic ideas of the poor.

In 390 B.C. Rome was a miserable little city on the borders of Etruria, being sacked by the Gauls; in 275 B.C. she was ruling and unifying all Italy, from the Arno to the Straits of Messina. The compromise of Camillus (367 B.C.) had put an end to internal dissensions, and left her energies free for expansion. And the same queer combination of sagacity and aggressive selfishness that had distinguished the war of her orders at home and enabled her population to worry out a balance of power without any catastrophe, marks her policy abroad. She understood the value of allies; she could assimilate; abroad as at home she could in those days at least "give and take" with a certain fairness and sanity. There lay the peculiar power of Rome. By that it was she succeeded where Athens, for example, had conspicuously failed.

The Athenian democracy suffered much from that narrowness of "patriotism," which is the ruin of all nations. "Athens for the Athenians" was the guiding principle of her rule, and "tax the foreigner" her substitute for political wisdom.[1] Even Pericles used the funds of the allies to beautify the capital city. So Athens was disliked and envied by her own empire; her disasters were not felt and shared as disasters by her subject-cities. The shrewder, nobler Roman senators of the great years of Rome, before the first Punic War overstrained her moral strength and began her degeneration, were not only willing in the last resort to share their privileges with the mass of their own people, but eager to incorporate their sturdiest antagonists upon terms of equality with themselves. They extended their citizenship cautiously but steadily. Some cities became Roman, with even a voting share in the government. Others had self-government and the right to trade or marry in Rome, without full Roman citizenship. Garrisons of full citizens were set up at strategic points, and colonies with variable privileges established amidst the purely conquered peoples. The need to keep communications open in this great and growing mass of citizenship was evident from the first. Printing and paper were not yet available for intercourse, but a system of high roads followed the Latin speech and the Roman rule. The first of these, the Appian Way, ran from Rome ultimately into the heel of Italy. It was begun by the censor Appius Claudius (who must not be confused with the decemvir Appius Claudius of a century earlier) in 312 B.C.

According to a census made in 265 B.C., there were already in the Roman dominions, that is to say in Italy south of the Arno, 300,000 citizens. They all had a common interest in the welfare of the state; they were all touched a little with the diffused kingship of the republic. This was, we have to note, an absolutely new thing in the history of mankind. All considerable states and kingdoms and empires hitherto had been communities by mere obedience to some head, some monarch, upon whose moods and character the public welfare was helplessly dependent. No republic had hitherto succeeded in being anything more than a city state. The so-called Athenian "empire" was simply a city state directing its allies and its subjugated cities. In a few decades the Roman republic was destined to extend its citizenship into the valley of the Po, to assimilate the kindred Gauls, replacing their language by Latin, and to set up a Latin city, Aquileia, at the very head of the Adriatic Sea. In 89 B.C. all free inhabitants of Italy became Roman citizens; in 212 A.D. the citizenship was extended to all free men in the empire.[2]

This extraordinary political growth was manifestly the precursor of all modern states of the western type. It is as interesting to the political student, therefore, as a carboniferous amphibian or an *archæopteryx* to the student of zoological development. It is the primitive type of the now dominant order. Its experiences throw light upon all subsequent political history.

One natural result of this growth of a democracy of hundreds of thousands of citizens scattered over the greater part of Italy was the growth in power of the Senate. There had been in the development of the Roman constitution a variety of forms of the popular assembly, the plebeian assembly, the assembly by tribes, the assembly by centuries, and the like, into which variety we cannot enter here with any fullness; but the idea was established that with the popular assembly lay the power of initiating laws. It is to be noted that there was a sort of parallel government in this system. The assembly by tribes or by centuries was an assembly of the *whole citizen body*, patrician and plebeian together; the assembly of the plebeians was of course an assembly only of the plebeian class. Each assembly had its own officials; the former, the consuls, etc.; the latter, the tribunes. While Rome was a little state, twenty miles square, it was possible to assemble something like a representative gathering of the people, but it will be manifest that with the means of communication existing in Italy at that time,

[1] But note that Athens had (1) no taxes on foreigners, and inflicted no disabilities on them except absence of citizenship. No "expulsions of aliens" such as were regular at Sparta, and common in most places. This is a frequent Athenian boast. Cp. Thucydides ii. 39, "Our city is thrown open to the world. We never expel a foreigner or prevent him from seeing and learning anything of which the secret, if revealed, might be useful to an enemy." (2) Practically Free Trade; only a general 5 per cent. import duty. (3) Great interest in foreign places, constitutions, customs, etc. Athens was very oppressive—by modern standards—to its subject-allies; chiefly because there was no representation, and because she was so much at war. But even here, after her defeat in 404, they voluntarily gathered to her again. The second Athenian Empire was not in any way forced upon them.—G. M.

[2] Haverfield says—and I think he is right—that Rome had a great advantage in her imperial development—viz.. that she was a city and not a nation. A nation implies some unity of race, and race prejudice. A city is based on the mere fact of citizenship. We should have said to St. Paul: "Citizen or no citizen, you are only a Levantine Jew." But a Roman, apparently, did not think of saying so. Hence the great freedom with which emperors and senators are taken from other races.—G. M.

it was now impossible for the great bulk of the citizens even to keep themselves informed of what was going on at Rome, much less to take any effective part in political life there. Aristotle in his *Politics* had already pointed out the virtual disenfranchisement of voters who lived out of the city and were preoccupied with agricultural pursuits, and this sort of disenfranchisement by mechanical difficulties applied to the vast majority of Roman citizens. With the growth of Rome an unanticipated weakness crept into political life through these causes, and the popular assembly became more and more a gathering of political hacks and the city riffraff, and less and less a representation of the ordinary worthy citizens. The popular assembly came nearest to power and dignity in the fourth century B.C. From that period it steadily declined in influence, and the new Senate, which was no longer a patrician body, with a homogeneous and on the whole a noble tradition, but a body of rich men, ex-magistrates, powerful officials, bold adventurers and the like, pervaded by a strong disposition to return to the idea of hereditary qualification, became for three centuries the ruling power in the Roman world.

There are two devices since known to the world which might have enabled the popular government of Rome to go on developing beyond its climax in the days of Appius Claudius the Censor, at the close of the fourth century B.C., but neither of them occurred to the Roman mind. The first of these devices was a proper use of print. In our account of early Alexandria we have already remarked upon the strange fact that printed books did not come into the world in the fourth or third century B.C. This account of Roman affairs forces us to repeat that remark. To the modern mind it is clear that a widespread popular government demands, as a necessary condition for health, a steady supply of correct information upon public affairs to all the citizens and a maintenance of interest. The popular governments in the modern states that have sprung up on either side of the Atlantic during the last two centuries have been possible only through the more or less honest and thorough ventilation of public affairs through the press. But in Italy the only way in which the government at Rome could communicate with any body of its citizens elsewhere was by the antiquated device of sending a herald, and with the individual citizen it could hold no communication by any means at all.

The second device, for which the English are chiefly responsible in the history of mankind, which the Romans never used, was the almost equally obvious one of representative government. For the old Popular Assembly (in its threefold form) it would have been possible to have substituted a gathering of delegates. Later on in history, the English did, as the state grew, realize this necessity. Certain men, the Knights of the Shire, were called up to Westminster to speak and vote for local feeling, and were more or less formally elected for that end. The Roman situation seems to a modern mind to have called aloud for such a modification. It was never made.[1]

The method of assembling the *comitia tributa*[2] (one of the three main forms of the Popular Assembly) was by the proclamation of a herald, who was necessarily inaudible to most of Italy, seventeen days before the date of the gathering. The augurs, the priests of divination whom Rome had inherited from the Etruscans, examined the entrails of sacrificial beasts on the night before the actual assembly, and if they thought fit to say that these gory portents were unfavourable, the *comitia tributa* dispersed. But if the augurs reported that the livers were propitious, there was a great blowing of horns from the Capitol and from the walls of the city, and the assembly went on. It was held in the open air, either in the little Forum beneath the Capitol or in a still smaller recess opening out of the Forum, or in the military exercising ground, the Campus Martius, now the most crowded part of modern Rome, but then an open space. Business began at dawn with prayer. There were no seats, and this probably helped to reconcile the citizen to the rule that everything ended at sunset.

After the opening prayer came a discussion

[1] The point raised here that Rome never developed representation is a very interesting one. There was a golden chance in the Social War (90 B.C.). The allies of Rome (socii) revolted, and set up a counter Rome in Corfinium. Now, to our minds, the obvious thing for them to do was (1) to make Corfinium just a capital; (2) to set up a parliament there, consisting of representatives drawn from the allies, who lived, of course, all over Italy. Not a bit of it. They made Corfinium a city state (not a capital), and feigned themselves all to be citizens of it, meeting in a primary assembly there. They also set up, it is true, a senate of 500; but this was just a copy of the Roman senate, and not a representative body (see Mommsen, vol. iii. pp. 237–8, Eng. trans.). Under the Roman Empire there were germs of representation in provincial assemblies: see Bury, *Student's Roman Empire*, on the *concilium Lugdunense* in Gaul and τὰ κοινά in Asia Minor.—E. B.

[2] Seyffert's *Dictionary of Classical Antiquities*. (Nettleship Sandys.)

of the measures to be considered by the assembly, and the proposals before the meeting were read out. Is it not astonishing that there were no printed copies distributed? If any copies were handed about, they must have been in manuscript, and each copy must have been liable to errors and deliberate falsification. No questions seem to have been allowed, but private individuals might address the gathering with the permission of the presiding magistrate.

The multitude then proceeded to go into enclosures like cattle-pens according to their tribes, and each tribe voted upon the measure under consideration. The decision was then taken not by the majority of the citizens, but by the majority of tribes, and it was announced by the heralds.

The Popular Assembly by centuries, *comitia centuriata*, was very similar in its character, except that instead of thirty-five tribes there were, in the third century B.C., 373 centuries, and there was a sacrifice as well as prayer to begin with. The centuries, originally military (like the "hundreds" of primitive English local government), had long since lost any connection with the number one hundred. Some contained only a few people; some very many. There were eighteen centuries of knights (equites), who were originally men in a position to maintain a horse and serve in the cavalry, though later the Roman knighthood, like knighthood in England, became a vulgar distinction of no military, mental, or moral significance. (These equites became a very important class as Rome traded and grew rich; for a time they were the real moving class in the community. There was as little chivalry left among them at last as there is in the "honours list" knights of England of to-day. The senators from about 200 B.C. were excluded from trade. The equites became, therefore, the great business men, *negotiatores*, and as *publicani* they farmed the taxes.) There were, in addition, eighty (!) centuries of wealthy men (worth over 100,000 asses), twenty-two of men worth over 75,000 asses, and so on. There were two centuries each of mechanics and musicians, and the *proletarii* made up one century. The decision in the *comitia centuriata* was by the majority of centuries.

Is it any wonder that with the growth of the Roman state and the complication of its business, power shifted back from such a Popular Assembly to the Senate, which was a comparatively compact body varying between three hundred as a minimum, and, at the utmost, nine hundred members (to which it was raised by Cæsar), men who had to do with affairs and big business, who knew each other more or less, and had a tradition of government and policy? The power of nominating and calling up the senators vested in the Republic first with the consuls, and when, some time after, "censors" were created, and many of the powers of the consuls had been transferred to them, they were also given this power. Appius Claudius, one of the first of the censors to exercise it, enrolled freedmen in the tribes and called sons of freedmen to the Senate. But this was a shocking arrangement to the conservative instincts of the time; the consuls would not recognize his Senate, and the next censors (304 B.C.) set aside his invitations. His attempt, however, serves to show how far the Senate had progressed from its original condition as a purely patrician body. Like the contemporary British House of Lords, it had become a gathering of big business men, energetic politicians, successful adventurers, great landowners, and the like; its patrician dignity was a picturesque sham; but, unlike the British House of Lords, it was unchecked legally by anything but the inefficient Popular Assembly we have already described, and by the tribunes elected by the plebeian assembly. Its legal control over the consuls and proconsuls was not great; it had little executive power; but in its prestige and experience lay its strength and influence. The interests of its members were naturally antagonistic to the interests of the general body of citizens, but for some generations that great mass of ordinary men was impotent to express its dissent from the proceedings of this oligarchy. Direct popular government of a state larger than a city state had already failed therefore in Italy, because as yet there was no public education, no press, and no representative system; it had failed through these mere mechanical difficulties, before the first Punic War. But its appearance is of enormous interest, as the first appearance of a set of problems with which the whole political intelligence of the world wrestles at the present time.

The Senate met usually in a Senate House in the Forum, but on special occasions it would be called to meet in this or that temple; and when it had to deal with foreign ambassadors or its own generals (who were not allowed to enter the city while in command of troops), it assembled in the Campus Martius outside the walls.

§ 3

It has been necessary to deal rather fully with the political structure of the Roman republic because of its immense importance to this day. The constitution of Carthage [1] need not detain us long.

Italy under Rome was a republican country; Carthage was that much older thing, a republican city. She had an "empire," as Athens had an "empire," of tributary states which did not love her, and she had a great and naturally disloyal industrial slave population.

In the city there were two elected "kings," as Aristotle calls them, the *suffetes*, who were really equivalent to the Roman censors; their Semitic name was the same as that used for the Jewish *judges*. There was an impotent public assembly and a senate of leading personages; but two committees of this senate, nominally elected, but elected by easily controlled methods, the Hundred and Four and the Thirty, really constituted a close oligarchy of the richest and most influential men. They told as little as they could to their allies and fellow citizens, and consulted them as little as possible. They pursued schemes in which the welfare of Carthage was no doubt subordinated to the advantage of their own group. They were hostile to new men or novel measures, and confident that a sea ascendancy that had lasted two centuries must be in the very nature of things.

Carthaginian coins.

§ 4

It would be interesting, and not altogether idle, to speculate what might have happened to mankind if Rome and Carthage could have settled their differences and made a permanent alliance in the Western world. If Alexander the Great had lived, he might have come westward and driven these two powers into such a fusion of interests. But that would not have suited the private schemes and splendours of the Carthaginian oligarchy, and the new Senate of greater Rome was now growing fond of the taste of plunder and casting covetous eyes across the Straits of Messina upon the Carthaginian possessions in Sicily. They were covetous, but they were afraid of the Carthaginian sea-power. Roman popular "patriotism," however, was also jealous and fearful of these Carthaginians, and less inclined to count the cost of a conflict. The alliance Pyrrhus had forced upon Rome and Carthage held good for eleven years, but Rome was ripe for what is called in modern political jargon an "offensive defensive" war. The occasion arose in 264 B.C.

At that time Sicily was not completely in Carthaginian hands. The eastward end was still under the power of the Greek king of Syracuse, Hiero, a successor of that Dionysius to whom Plato had gone as resident court philosopher. A band of mercenaries who had been in the service of Syracuse seized upon Messina (289 B.C.), and raided the trade of Syracuse so that at last Hiero was forced to take measures to suppress them (270 B.C.). Thereupon Carthage, which was also vitally concerned in the suppression of piracy, came to his aid, and put in a Carthaginian garrison at Messina. This was an altogether justifiable proceeding. Now that Tyre had been destroyed, the only capable guardian of sea law in the Mediterranean was Carthage, and the suppression of piracy was her task by habit and tradition.

The pirates of Messina appealed to Rome, and the accumulating jealousy and fear of Carthage decided the Roman people to help them. An expedition was dispatched to Messina under the consul Appius Claudius (the third Appius Claudius we have had to mention in this history).

So began the first of the most wasteful and disastrous series of wars that has ever darkened the history of mankind. But this is how one historian, soaked with the fantastic political ideas of our times, is pleased to write of this evil expedition. "The Romans knew they were entering on war

[1] Aristotle, *Politics*, Bk. ii. ch. xi.; and J. Wells, *Rome to the Death of Augustus*.

with Carthage; but the political instincts of the people were right, for a Carthaginian garrison on the Sicilian Straits would have been a dangerous menace to the peace of Italy." So they protected the peace of Italy from this "menace" by a war that lasted nearly a quarter of a century. They wrecked their own slowly acquired political *moral* in the process.

The Romans captured Messina, and Hiero deserted from the Carthaginians to the Romans. Then for some time the struggle centred upon the town Agrigentum. This the Romans besieged, and a period of trench warfare ensued. Both sides suffered greatly from plague and irregular supplies; the Romans lost 30,000 men; but in the end (261 B.C.) the Carthaginians evacuated the place and retired to their fortified towns on the western coast of the island of which Lilybæum was the chief. These they could supply easily from the African mainland, and, as long as their sea ascendancy held, they could exhaust any Roman effort against them.

And now a new and very extraordinary phase of the war began. The Romans came out upon the sea, and to the astonishment of the Carthaginians and themselves defeated the Carthaginian fleet. Since the days of Salamis there had been a considerable development of naval architecture. Then the ruling type of battleship was a trireme, a galley with three banks (rows) of oars; now the leading Carthaginian battleship was a quinquereme, a much bigger galley with five banks of oars, which could ram or shear the oars of any feebler vessel. The Romans had come into the war with no such shipping. Now they set to work to build quinqueremes, being helped, it is said, in their designing by one of these Carthaginian vessels coming ashore. In two months they built a hundred quinqueremes and thirty triremes. But they had no skilled navigators, no experienced oarsmen, and these deficiencies they remedied partly with the assistance of their Greek allies and partly by the invention of new tactics. Instead of relying upon ramming or breaking the oars of the adversary, which demanded more seamanship than they possessed, they decided to board the enemy, and they constructed a sort of long drawbridge on their ships, held up to a mast by a pulley and with grappling-hooks and spikes at the end. They also loaded their galleys with soldiers. Then as the Carthaginian rammed or swept alongside, this *corvus*, as it was called, could be let down and the boarders could swarm aboard him.

Simple as this device was, it proved a complete success. It changed the course of the war and the fate of the world. The small amount of invention needed to counteract the *corvus* was not apparently within the compass of the Carthaginian rulers. At the battle of Mylæ (260 B.C.) the Romans gained their first naval victory and captured or destroyed fifty vessels. At the great battle of Ecnomus (256 B.C.), "probably the greatest naval engagement of antiquity,"[1] in which seven or eight hundred big ships were engaged, the Carthaginians showed that they had learnt nothing from their former disaster. According to rule they outmanœuvred and defeated the Romans, but the *corvus* again defeated them. The Romans sank thirty vessels and captured sixty-four.

Thereafter the war continued with violent fluctuations of fortune, but with a continuous demonstration of the greater energy, solidarity, and initiative of the Romans. After Ecnomus the Romans invaded Africa by sea, and sent an insufficiently supported army, which after many successes and the capture of Tunis (within ten miles of Carthage) was completely defeated. They lost their sea ascendancy through a storm, and regained it by building a second fleet of two hundred and twenty ships within three months. They captured Palermo, and defeated a great Carthaginian army there (251 B.C.), capturing one hundred and four elephants, and making such a triumphal procession into Rome as that city had never seen before. They made an unsuccessful siege of Lilybæum, the chief surviving Carthaginian stronghold in Sicily. They lost their second fleet in a great naval battle at Drepanum (249 B.C.), losing one hundred and eighty out of two hundred and ten vessels; and a third fleet of one hundred and twenty battleships and eight hundred transports was lost in the same year partly in battle and partly in a storm.

For seven years a sort of war went on between the nearly exhausted combatants, a war of raids and feeble sieges, during which the Carthaginians had the best of it at sea. Then by a last supreme effort Rome launched a fourth fleet of two hundred keels, and defeated the last strength of the Carthaginians at the battle of the Ægatian Isles (241 B.C.), after which Carthage (240 B.C.) sued for peace.

By the terms of this peace, all Sicily, except for the dominions of Hiero of Syracuse, became an "estate" of the Roman people.

[1] J. Wells, *op. cit.*

There was no such process of assimilation as had been practised in Italy; Sicily became a conquered province, paying tribute and yielding profit like the provinces of the older empires. And, in addition, Carthage paid a war indemnity of 3,200 talents (=£788,000).

§ 5

For twenty-two years there was peace between Rome and Carthage. It was peace without prosperity. Both combatants were suffering from the want and disorganization that follow naturally and necessarily upon all great wars. The territories of Carthage seethed with violent disorder; the returning soldiers could not get their pay, and mutinied and looted; the land went uncultivated. We read of horrible cruelties in the suppression of these troubles by Hamilcar, the Carthaginian general; of men being crucified by the thousand. Sardinia and Corsica revolted. The "peace of Italy" was scarcely happier. The Gauls rose and marched south; they were defeated, and 40,000 of them killed at Telamon. It is manifest that Italy was incomplete until it reached the Alps. Roman colonies were planted in the valley of the Po, and the great northward artery, the Via Flaminia was begun. But it shows the moral and intellectual degradation of this post-war period that when the Gauls were threatening Rome, human sacrifices were proposed and carried out. The old Carthaginian sea law was broken up—it may have been selfish and monopolistic, but it was at least orderly—the Adriatic swarmed with Illyrian pirates, and as the result of a quarrel arising out of this state of affairs, Illyria, after two wars, had to be annexed as a second "province." By sending expeditions to annex Sardinia and Corsica, which were Carthaginian provinces in revolt, the Romans prepared the way for the Second Punic War.

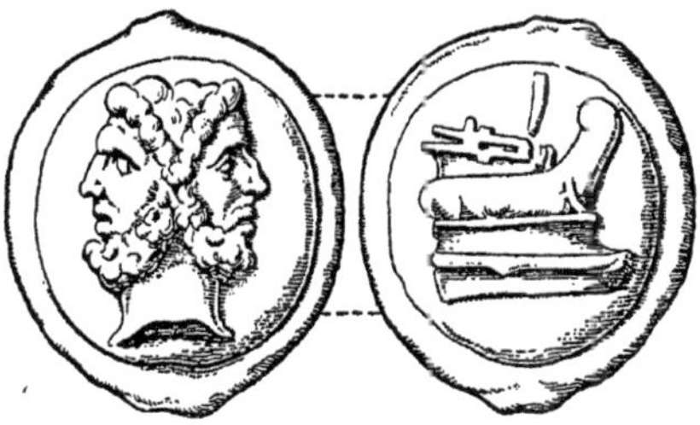

Roman As (bronze, 4th Cent. B.C. Half size.)

The First Punic War had tested and demonstrated the relative strength of Rome and Carthage. With a little more wisdom on either side, with a little more magnanimity on the part of Rome, there need never have been a renewal of the struggle. But Rome was an ungracious conqueror. She seized Corsica and Sardinia on no just grounds, she increased the indemnity by 1,200 talents, she set a limit, the Ebro, to Carthaginian developments in Spain. There was a strong party in Carthage, led by Hanno, for the propitiation of Rome; but it was natural that many Carthaginians should come to regard their national adversary with a despairing hatred.

So began that age-long hostility between the lands north and south of the Mediterranean which lasts down to our own day, the conflict of the Semiticized Berber and the Aryanized south European, in spite of the fact that these two divisions of Mediterranean man have so much physically in common. Henceforth they took different sides in religion, in language, in costume and culture.

Hatred is one of the passions that can master a life, and there is a type of temperament very prone to it, ready to see life in terms of vindictive melodrama, ready to find stimulus and satisfaction in frightful demonstrations of "justice" and revenge. The fears and jealousies of the squatting-place and the cave still bear their dark blossoms in our lives; we are not four hundred generations yet from the old Stone Age. Great wars, as all Europe knows, give this "hating" temperament the utmost scope, and the greed and pride and cruelty that the First Punic War had released were now producing a rich crop of anti-foreign monomania. The outstanding figure upon the side of Carthage was a great general and administrator, Hamilcar Barca, who now set himself to circumvent and shatter Rome. He was the father-in-law of Hasdrubal and the father of a boy Hannibal, destined to be the most dreaded enemy that ever scared the Roman Senate. The most obvious course before Carthage was the reconstruction of its fleet and naval administration, and the recovery of sea power, but this, it would seem, Hamilcar could not effect. As an alternative he resolved to organize Spain as the base of a land attack upon Italy. He went to Spain as governor in 236 B.C., and Hannibal related afterwards that his father then—he was a boy of eleven—made him vow deathless hostility to the Roman power.

This quasi-insane concentration of the gifts and lives of the Barca family upon revenge is but one instance of the narrowing and embitterment of life that the stresses and universal sense of insecurity of this great struggle produced in the minds of men. A quarter of a century of war had left the whole western world miserable and harsh. While the eleven-year-old Hannibal was taking his vow of undying hatred, there was running about a farmhouse of Tusculum a small but probably very disagreeable child of two named Marcus Porcius Cato. This boy lived to be eighty-five years old, and his ruling passion seems to have been hatred for any human happiness but his own. He was a good soldier, and had a successful political career. He held a command in Spain, and distinguished himself by his cruelties. He posed as a champion of religion and public morality, and under this convenient cloak carried on a lifelong war against everything that was young, gracious, or pleasant. Whoever roused his jealousy incurred his moral disapproval. He was energetic in the support and administration of all laws against dress, against the personal adornment of women, against entertainments and free discussion. He was so fortunate as to be made censor, which gave him great power over the private lives of public people. He was thus able to ruin public opponents through private scandals. He expelled Manlius from the Senate for giving his wife a kiss in the daytime in the sight of their daughter. He persecuted Greek literature, about which, until late in life, he was totally ignorant. Then he read and admired Demosthenes. He wrote in Latin upon agriculture and the ancient and lost virtues of Rome. From these writings much light is thrown upon his qualities. One of his maxims was that when a slave was not sleeping he should be working. Another was that old oxen and slaves should be sold off. He left the war horse that had carried him through his Spanish campaigns behind him when he returned to Italy in order to save freight. He hated other people's gardens, and cut off the supply of water for garden use in Rome. After entertaining company, when dinner was over he would go out to correct any negligence in the service with a leather thong. He admired his own virtues very greatly, and insisted upon them in his writings. There was a battle at Thermopylæ against Antiochus the Great, of which he wrote, "those who saw him charging the enemy, routing and pursuing them, declared that Cato owed less to the people of Rome, than the people of Rome owed to Cato."[1] In his old age Cato became lascivious and misconducted himself with a woman slave. Finally, when his son protested against this disorder of their joint household, he married a young wife, the daughter of his secretary, who was not in a position to refuse his offer. (What became of the woman slave is not told. Probably he sold her.) This compendium of all the old Roman virtues died at an advanced age, respected and feared. Almost his last public act was to urge on the Third Punic War and the final destruction of Carthage. He had gone to Carthage as a commissioner to settle certain differences between Carthage and Numidia, and he had been shocked and horrified to find some evidences of prosperity and even of happiness in that country.

[1] Plutarch, *Life of Cato.*

From the time of that visit onward Cato concluded every speech he made in the Senate by croaking out "*Delenda est Carthago*" ("Carthage must be destroyed").

Such was the type of man that rose to prominence in Rome during the Punic struggle, such was the protagonist of Hannibal and the Carthaginian *revanche*, and by him and by Hannibal we may judge the tone and quality of the age.

The two great western powers, and Rome perhaps more than Carthage, were strained mentally and morally by the stresses of the First War. The evil side of life was uppermost. The history of the Second and Third Punic Wars (219 to 201 and 149 to 146 B.C.), it is plain, is not the history of perfectly sane peoples. It is nonsense for historians to write of the "political instincts" of the Romans or Carthaginians. Quite other instincts were loose. The red eyes of the ancestral ape had come back into the world. It was a time when reasonable men were howled down or murdered; the true spirit of the age is shown in the eager examination for signs and portents of the still quivering livers of those human victims who were sacrificed in Rome during the panic before the battle of Telamon. The western world was indeed black with homicidal monomania. Two great peoples, both very necessary to the world's development, fell foul of one another, and at last Rome succeeded in murdering Carthage.

§ 6

We can only tell very briefly here of the particulars of the Second and Third Punic Wars. We have told how Hamilcar began to organize Spain, and how the Romans forbade him to cross the Ebro. He died in 228 B.C., and was followed by his son-in-law Hasdrubal, who was assassinated in 221 B.C., and succeeded by Hannibal, who was now twenty-six. The actual war was precipitated by the Romans making a breach of their own regulations, and interfering with affairs south of the Ebro. Whereupon Hannibal marched straight through the south of Gaul, and crossed the Alps (218 B.C.) into Italy.

The history of the next fifteen years is the story of the most brilliant and futile raid in history. For fifteen years Hannibal held out in Italy, victorious and unconquered. The Roman generals were no match for the Carthaginian, and whenever they met him they were beaten. But one Roman general, P. Cornelius Scipio, had the strategic sense to take a course that robbed all Hannibal's victories of fruit. At the outbreak of the war he had been sent by sea to Marseilles to intercept Hannibal; he arrived three days late, and, instead of pursuing him, he sent on his army into Spain to cut up Hannibal's supplies and reinforcements. Throughout all the subsequent war there remained this Roman army of Spain between Hannibal and his base. He was left "in the air," incapable of conducting sieges or establishing conquests.

Whenever he met the Romans in open fight he beat them. He gained two great victories in North Italy, and won over the Gauls to his side. He pressed south into Etruria, and ambushed, surrounded, and completely destroyed a Roman army at Lake Trasimene. In 216 B C. he was assailed by a vastly superior Roman force under Varro at Cannæ, and destroyed it utterly. Fifty thousand men are said to have been killed and ten thousand prisoners taken. He was, however, unable to push on and capture Rome because he had no siege equipment.

But Cannæ produced other fruits. A large part of Southern Italy came over to Hannibal, including Capua, the city next in size to Rome, and the Macedonians allied themselves with him. Moreover, Hiero of Syracuse, the faithful ally of Rome, was now dead, and his successor Hieronymus turned over to the Carthaginians. The Romans carried on the war, however, with great toughness and resolution; they refused to treat with Hannibal after Cannæ, they pressed a slow but finally successful blockade and siege of Capua, and a Roman army set itself to reduce Syracuse. The siege of Syracuse is chiefly memorable for the brilliant inventions of the philosopher Archimedes, which long held the Romans at bay. We have already named this Archimedes as one of the pupils and correspondents of the school of the Alexandrian Museum. He was killed in the final storm of the town. Tarentum (209 B.C.), Hannibal's chief port and means of supply from Carthage, at last followed Syracuse (212 B.C.) and Capua (211 B.C.), and his communications became irregular.

Spain also was wrested bit by bit from the Carthaginian grip. When at last reinforcements for Hannibal under his brother Hasdrubal (not to be confused with his brother-in-law of the same name who was assassinated) struggled through into Italy, they were destroyed at the battle of the Metaurus (207 B.C.), and the first news that came to Hannibal of the disaster was the hacked-off head of his brother thrown into his camp.

Thereafter Hannibal was blockaded into Calabria, the heel of Italy. He had no forces for further operations of any magnitude, and he returned at last to Carthage in time to command the Carthaginians in the last battle of the war.

This last battle, the battle of Zama (202 B.C.), was fought close to Carthage.

It was the first defeat Hannibal experienced and so it is well to give a little attention to the personality of his conqueror, Scipio Africanus the Elder, who stands out in history as a very fine gentleman indeed, a great soldier and a generous man. We have already mentioned a certain P. Cornelius Scipio who struck at Hannibal's base in Spain; this was his son; until after Zama this son bore the same name of P. Cornelius Scipio, and then the surname of Africanus was given him. (The younger Scipio Africanus, Scipio Africanus Minor, who was later to end the Third Punic War, was the adopted son of the son of this first Scipio Africanus the Elder.) Scipio Africanus was everything that aroused the distrust, hatred, and opposition of old-fashioned Romans of the school of Cato. He was young, he was happy and able, he spent money freely, he was well versed in Greek literature, and inclined rather to Phrygian novelties in religion than to the sterner divinities of Rome. And he did not believe in the extreme discretion that then ruled Roman strategy.

After the early defeats of the Second Punic War, Roman military operations were dominated by the personality of a general, Fabius, who raised the necessity of avoiding battle with Hannibal into a kind of sacred principle. For ten years "Fabian tactics" prevailed in Italy. The Romans blockaded, cut up convoys, attacked stragglers, and ran away whenever Hannibal appeared. No doubt it was wise for a time after their first defeats to do this sort of thing, but the business of the stronger power, and Rome was the stronger power throughout the Second Punic War, is not to tolerate an interminable war, but to repair losses, discover abler generals, train better armies, and destroy the enemy power. Decision is one of the duties of strength.

To such men as young Scipio, the sly, ineffective artfulness of Fabianism, which was causing both Italy and Carthage to bleed slowly to death, was detestable. He clamoured for an attack upon Carthage itself.

"But Fabius, on this occasion, filled the city with alarms, as if the commonwealth was going to be brought into the most extreme danger by a rash and indiscreet young man; in short, he scrupled not to do or say anything he thought likely to dissuade his countrymen from embracing the proposal. With the Senate he carried his point. But the people believed that his opposition to Scipio proceeded either from envy of his success, or from a secret fear that if this young hero should perform some signal exploit, put an end to the war, or even remove it out of Italy, his own slow proceedings through the course of so many years might be imputed to indolence or timidity. . . . He applied to Crassus, the colleague of Scipio, and endeavoured to persuade him not to yield that province to Scipio, but, if he thought it proper to conduct the war in that manner, to go himself against Carthage. Nay, he even hindered the raising of money for that expedition, so that Scipio was obliged to find the supplies as he could. . . . He endeavoured to prevent the young men who offered to go as volunteers from giving in their names, and loudly declared, both in the Senate and Forum, 'That Scipio did not only himself avoid Hannibal, but intended to carry away with him the remaining strength of Italy, persuading the young men to abandon their parents, their wives, and native city, while an unsubdued and potent enemy was still at their doors.' With these assertions he so terrified the people, that they allowed Scipio to take with him only the legions that were in Sicily, and three hundred of those men who had served him with so much fidelity in Spain. . . . After Scipio was gone over into Africa, an account was soon brought to Rome of his glorious and wonderful achievements. This account was followed by rich spoils, which confirmed it. A Numidian king was taken prisoner; two camps were burned and destroyed; and in them a vast number of men, arms, and horses; and the Carthaginians sent orders to Hannibal to quit his fruitless hopes in Italy, and return home to defend his own country. Whilst every tongue was applauding these exploits of Scipio, Fabius proposed that his successor should be appointed, without any shadow of reason for it, except what this well-known maxim implies: viz., 'That it is dangerous to trust affairs of such importance to the fortune of one man, because it is not likely that he will be always successful.' . . . Nay, even when Hannibal embarked his army and quitted Italy, Fabius ceased not to disturb the general joy and to damp the spirits of Rome, for he took the liberty to affirm, 'That the commonwealth was now come to her last and worst trial; that she had the most reason to dread the efforts of Hannibal when he should arrive in Africa, and attack her sons under the walls of Carthage; that Scipio would have to do with an army yet warm with the blood of so many Roman generals, dictators, and consuls.' The city was alarmed with these declamations, and though the war was removed into Africa, the danger seemed to approach nearer Rome than ever."

Before the battle of Zama there were a brief truce and negotiations, which broke down through the fault of the Carthaginians. As with the battle of Arbela, so the exact day of the battle of Zama can be fixed by an eclipse, which in this case occurred during the fighting. The Romans had been joined by the Numidians, the hinterland people of Carthage, under their king Massinissa, and this gave them—for the first time in any battle against Hannibal—a great superiority of cavalry. Hannibal's cavalry wings were driven off, while at the same time the sounder discipline of Scipio's infantry enabled them to open lanes for the charge of the Carthaginian war elephants without being thrown into confusion. Hannibal attempted to extend his infantry line to envelop the Roman infantry mass, but while at Cannæ all the advantage of training and therefore of manœuvring power had been on his side, and he had been able to surround and massacre a crowd of infantry, he now found against him an infantry line better than his own. His own line broke as it extended the Roman legion charged home, and the day was lost. The Roman cavalry came back from the pursuit of Hannibal's horse to turn what was already a defeat into a disastrous rout.

Carthage submitted without any further struggle. The terms were severe, but they left it possible for her to hope for an honourable future. She had to abandon Spain to Rome, to give up all her war fleet except ten vessels, to pay 10,000 talents (£2,400,000), and, what was the most difficult condition of all, to agree not to wage war without the permission of Rome. Finally a condition was added that Hannibal, as the great enemy of Rome, should be surrendered. But he saved his countrymen from this humiliation by flying to Asia.

These were exorbitant conditions, with which Rome should have been content. But there are nations so cowardly that they dare not merely conquer their enemies; they must *mak siccar* and destroy them. The generation of Romans that saw greatness and virtue in a man like Cato the Censor, necessarily made their country a mean ally and a cowardly victor.

§ 7

The history of Rome for the fifty-six years that elapsed between the battle of Zama and the last act of the tragedy, the Third Punic War, tells of a hard ungracious expansion of power abroad and of a slow destruction, by the usury and greed of the rich, of the free agricultural population at home.

The spirit of the nation had become harsh and base; there was no further extension of citizenship, no more generous attempts at the assimilation of congenial foreign populations. Spain was administered badly, and settled slowly and with great difficulty. Complicated interventions led to the reduction of Illyria and Macedonia to the position of tribute-paying provinces; Rome, it was evident, was going to "tax the foreigner" now and release her home population from taxation. After 168 B.C. the old land tax was no longer levied in Italy, and the only revenue derived from Italy was from the state domains and through a tax on imports from overseas. The revenues from the province of "Asia" defrayed the expenses of the Roman state.[1] At home men of the Cato type were acquiring farms by loans and foreclosure, often the farms of men impoverished by war service; they were driving the free citizens off their land, and running their farms with the pitilessly driven slave labour that was made cheap and abundant. Such men regarded alien populations abroad merely as unimported slaves. Sicily was handed over to the greedy enterprise of tax-farmers. Corn could be grown there by rich men using slaves, and imported very profitably into Rome, and so the home land could be turned over to cattle and sheep feeding. Consequently a drift of the uprooted Italian population to the towns, and particularly to Rome, began.

Of the first conflicts of the spreading power of Rome with the Seleucids, and how she formed an alliance with Egypt, we can tell little here, nor of the tortuous fluctuations of the Greek cities under the shadow of her advance until they fell into actual subjugation. A map must suffice to show the extension of her empire at this time.

The general grim baseness of the age was not without its protesting voices. We have already told how the wasting disease of the Second Punic War, a disease of the state which was producing avaricious rich men exactly as diseases of the body will sometimes produce great pustules, was ended by the vigour of Scipio Africanus. When it had seemed doubtful whether the Senate would let him go as the Roman general, he had threatened an appeal to the people. Thereafter he was a marked man for the senatorial gang, who were steadily changing Italy from a land of free cultivators to a land of slave-worked cattle ranches; they attempted to ruin him before ever he reached Africa; they gave him forces insufficient, as they hoped, for victory; and after the war they barred him strictly from office. Interest and his natural malice alike prompted Cato to attack him.

Scipio Africanus the Elder seems to have been of a generous and impatient temperament, and indisposed to exploit the popular discontent with current tendencies and his own very great popularity to his own advantage. He went as subordinate to his brother Lucius Scipio, when the latter commanded the first Roman army to pass into Asia. At Magnesia in Lydia a great composite army under Antiochus III, the Seleucid monarch, suffered the fate (190 B.C.) of the very similar Persian armies of a hundred and forty years before. This victory drew down upon Lucius Scipio the hostility of the Senate, and he was accused of misappropriating moneys received from Antiochus. This filled Africanus with honest rage. As Lucius stood up in the Senate with his accounts in his hands ready for the badgering of his accusers, Africanus snatched the documents from him, tore them up, and flung the fragments down. His brother, he said, had paid into the treasury 200,000 sestertia (=£2,000,000). Was he now to be pestered and tripped up upon this or that item? When, later on, Lucius was prosecuted and condemned, Africanus rescued him by force. Being impeached, he reminded the people that the day

[1] Mommsen says the other provinces cost as much as they paid.

The EXTENT of the ROMAN POWER & its ALLIANCES about 150 B.C.
[i.e., on the eve of the Third Punic War.]
GAUL
SPAIN
ALPS
Rhine
Rhone
CISALPINE GAUL
CORSICA
SARDINIA
Rome
SICILY
Cannae
Carthage
NUMIDIA
DALMATIA
Danube
ILLYRIA
MACEDONIA
GREECE
THRACE
BITHYNIA
PONTUS
PERGAMUM
GALATIA
Magnesia
RHODES
CRETE
CYPRUS
TAURUS MTS.
ARMENIA
CAUCASUS
CASPIAN
PARTHIANS
Antioch
SYRIA
SELEUCID EMPIRE
Seleucia
Jerusalem
Alexandria
Memphis
PTOLEMAIC EMPIRE
Philae
ARABIA
AFRICA
Roman power . . . .
Ptolemaic Empire . .
Other Allies of Rome
J.F.H.

was the anniversary of the battle of Zama, and defied the authorities amidst the plaudits of the crowd.

The Roman people seem to have liked and supported Scipio Africanus, and, after an interval of two thousand years, men must like him still. He was able to throw torn paper in the face of the Senate, and when Lucius was attacked again, one of the tribunes of the people interposed his veto and quashed the proceedings. But Scipio Africanus lacked that harder alloy which makes men great democratic leaders. He was no Cæsar. He had none of the qualities that subdue a man to the base necessities of political life. After these events he retired in disgust from Rome to his estates, and there he died in the year 183 B.C.

In the same year died Hannibal. He poisoned himself in despair. The steadfast fear of the Roman Senate had hunted him from court to court. In spite of the indignant protests of Scipio, Rome in the peace negotiations had demanded his surrender from Carthage, and she continued to make this demand of every power that sheltered him. When peace was made with Antiochus III, this was one of the conditions. He was run to earth at last in Bithynia; the king of Bithynia detained him in order to send him to Rome, but he had long carried the poison he needed in a ring, and by this he died.

It adds to the honour of the name of Scipio that it was another Scipio, Scipio Nasica, who parodied Cato's *Delenda est Carthago* by ending all his speeches in the Senate with "Carthage must stand." He had the wisdom to see that the existence and stimulus of Carthage contributed to the general prosperity of Rome.[1]

Yet it was the second Scipio Africanus, the adopted grandson of Scipio Africanus the Elder, who took and destroyed Carthage.[2] The sole offence of the Carthaginians, which brought about the third and last Punic War, was that they continued to trade and prosper. Their trade was not a trade that competed with that of Rome; when Carthage was destroyed, much of her trade died with her, and North Africa entered upon a phase of economic retrogression; but her prosperity aroused that passion of envy which was evidently more powerful even than avarice in the "old Roman" type. The rich Equestrian order resented any wealth in the world but its own. Rome provoked the war by encouraging the Numidians to encroach upon Carthage until the Carthaginians were goaded to fight in despair. Rome then pounced upon Carthage, and declared she had broken the treaty! She had made war without permission.

The Carthaginians sent the hostages Rome demanded, they surrendered their arms, they prepared to surrender territory. But submission only increased the arrogance of Rome and the pitiless greed of the rich Equestrian order which swayed her counsels. She now demanded that Carthage should be abandoned, and the population removed to a spot at least ten miles from the sea. This demand they made to a population that subsisted almost entirely by overseas trade!

This preposterous order roused the Carthaginians to despair. They recalled their exiles and prepared for resistance. The military efficiency of the Romans had been steadily declining through a half-century of narrow-minded and base-spirited government, and the first attacks upon the town in 149 B.C. almost ended in disaster. Young Scipio, during these operations, distinguished himself in a minor capacity. The next year was also a year of failure for the incom-

[1] But it was this Scipio Nasica who was responsible for the killing of Tiberius Gracchus. On the whole, he seems to have been a statesman of very distinguished abilities. He was the means of bringing the Asiatic Great Mother Goddess to Rome. "People at Rome generally were beginning to see that they would have to take over Asia. Had they any right? Nasica was sent on a mission to invite the Magna Mater at Pessinus to come to Rome. Her image nodded 'yes.' She was brought and installed in Rome. Now this is a policy of peaceful assimilation. Just as in Babylon you get gods of other cities brought to Babylon, just as Nabonidus (see Chap. xix. § 6) was trying to get an amicable pantheon as a way of peaceful assimilation, and failing to do so because he did not bring the priesthoods as well as the gods, so Rome was at this time thinking on the same lines. Camillus had shown the way when he suggested the invitation of Juno of Veii to Rome. Now Nasica, it may be suggested, wanted to treat Carthage in the same fashion. He opposed the destruction of Carthage in 146 (Mommsen iii. p. 23, p. 39). If he had had his way, one may guess, he would have invited the Carthaginian gods to Rome, and the corollary would have been the enfranchisement of the Carthaginian population—the treatment of the Carthaginians as equals, whose gods had been received in Rome, and stood in Rome. Mummius did the same in carrying off the statues of Greek gods to Rome, only, being stupid he did not understand why (146 B.C.)."

Nasica's visit to Pessinus was as important as the testament of Attalus. His policy is not the policy of Rome the conqueror, but Rome the assimilator. He is trying to get a nexus by a common pantheon. If this had been done, the Republic might have survived. As it was, the deification of the ruler had to provide the nexus, as in Alexander's empire. The "Synœcism of gods" or the "deification of rulers," those are the only ways of amalgamating peoples. It is a pity Alexander and Rome did not attempt the former.—J. L. M. and E. B.

[2] The intervening Scipio was a man of learning and high character who died young.—G. M.

petents of the Senate. That august body then passed from a bullying mood to one of extreme panic. The Roman populace was even more seriously scared. Young Scipio, chiefly on account of his name, although he was under the proper age, and in other respects not qualified for the office, was made consul, and bundled off to Africa to save his precious country.

There followed the most obstinate and dreadful of sieges. Scipio built a mole across the harbour, and cut off all supplies by land or sea. The Carthaginians suffered horribly from famine; but they held out until the town was stormed. The street fighting lasted for six days, and when at last the citadel capitulated, there were fifty thousand Carthaginians left alive out of an estimated population of half a million. These survivors went into slavery, the whole city was burnt, the ruins were ploughed to express final destruction, and a curse was invoked with great solemnities upon anyone who might attempt to rebuild it.

In the same year (146 B.C.) the Roman Senate and Equestrians also *murdered* another great city that seemed to limit their trade monopolies, Corinth. They had a justification, for Corinth had been in arms against them, but it was an inadequate justification.

§ 8

We must note here, in a brief section, a change in the military system of Rome, after the Second Punic War, that was of enormous importance in her later development. Up to that period the Roman armies had been levies of free citizens. Fighting power and voting power were closely connected; the public assembly by centuries followed the paraphernalia of a military mobilization, and marched, headed by the Equestrian centuries, to the Campus Martius. The system was very like that of the Boers before the last war in South Africa. The ordinary Roman citizen, like the ordinary Boer, was a farmer; at the summons of his country he went "on commando." The Boers were, indeed, in many respects, the last survivors of Aryanism, They fought extraordinarily well, but at the back of their minds was an anxious desire to go back to their farms. For prolonged operations, such as the siege of Veii, the Romans reinforced and relieved their troops in relays; the Boers did much the same at the siege of Ladysmith.

The necessity for subjugating Spain after the Second Punic War involved a need for armies of a different type. Spain was too far off for periodic reliefs, and the war demanded a more thorough training than was possible with these on and off soldiers. Accordingly men were enlisted for longer terms and *paid*. So the paid soldier first appeared in Roman affairs. And to pay was added booty. Cato distributed silver treasure among his command in Spain; and it is also on record that he attacked Scipio Africanus for distributing booty among his troops in Sicily. The introduction of military pay led on to a professional army, and this, a century later, to the disarmament of the ordinary Roman citizen, who was now drifting in an impoverished state into Rome and the larger towns. The great wars had been won, the foundations of the empire had been well and truly laid by the embattled farmers of Rome before 200 B.C. In the process the embattled farmers of Rome had already largely disappeared. The change that began after the Second Punic War was completed towards the close of the century in the reorganization of the army by Marius, as we will tell in its place. After his time we shall begin to write of "the army," and then of "the legions," and we shall find we are dealing with a new kind of army altogether, no longer held together in the solidarity of a common citizenship. As that tie fails, the legions discover another in *esprit de corps*, in their common difference from and their common interest against the general community. They begin to develop a warmer interest in their personal leaders, who secure them pay and plunder. Before the Punic Wars it was the tendency of ambitious men in Rome to court the plebeians; after that time they began to court the legions.

§ 9

The history of the Roman Republic thus far, is in many respects much more modern in flavour, especially to the American or Western European reader, than anything that has preceded it. For the first time we have something like a self-governing "nation," something larger than a mere city state, seeking to control its own destinies. For the first time we have a wide countryside under one conception of law. We get in the Senate and the popular assembly a conflict of groups and personalities, an argumentative process of control, far more stable and enduring than any autocracy can be, and far more flexible and adaptable than any priesthood. For the first time also we encounter social conflicts comparable to our own. Money has superseded barter, and financial capital has become fluid and free; not perhaps so fluid and free as it is to-day, but much more so than it had ever been before. The Punic Wars were wars of peoples, such as were no other wars we have yet recorded. Indubitably the broad lines of our present world, the main ideas, the chief oppositions, were appearing in those days.

But, as we have already pointed out, certain of the elementary facilities and some of the current political ideas of our time were still wanting in the Rome of the Punic Wars. There were no newspapers,[1] and there was practically no use of elected representatives in the popular assemblies. And another deficiency, very understandable to us nowadays, but quite beyond the scope of anyone then, was the absence of any general elementary political education at all. The plebeians of Rome had shown some glimmering of the idea that without knowledge votes cannot make men free, when they had insisted upon the publication of the law of the Twelve Tables; but they had never been able, it was beyond the possibilities of the time, to imagine any further extension of knowledge to the bulk of the people. It is only nowadays that men are beginning to understand fully the political significance of the maxim that "knowledge is power." Two British Trade Unions, for example, have recently set up a Labour College to meet the special needs of able working-men in history, political and social science, and the like. But education in republican Rome was the freak of the individual parent, and the privilege of wealth and leisure. It was mainly in the hands of Greeks, who were in many cases slaves. There was a thin small stream of very fine learning and very fine thinking up to the first century of the monarchy, let Lucretius and Cicero witness, but it did not spread into the mass of the people. The ordinary Roman was not only blankly ignorant of the history of mankind, but also of the conditions of foreign peoples; he had no knowledge of economic laws nor of social possibilities. Even his own interests he did not clearly understand.

Of course, in the little city states of Greece and in that early Roman state of four hundred square miles, men acquired by talk and observation a sufficient knowledge for the ordinary duties of citizenship, but by the beginning of the Punic Wars the business was already too big and complicated for illiterate men. Yet nobody seems to have observed the gap that was opening between the citizen and his state, and so there is no record at all of any attempt to enlarge the citizen by instruction to meet his enlarged duties. From the second century B.C. and onward everyone is remarking upon the ignorance of the common citizen and his lack of political wisdom, everything is suffering from the lack of political solidarity due to this ignorance, but no one goes on to what we should now consider the inevitable corollary, no one proposes to destroy the ignorance complained of. There existed no means whatever for the instruction of the masses of the people in a common political and social ideal. It was only with the development of the great propagandist religions in the Roman world, of which Christianity was the chief and the survivor, that the possibility of such a systematic instruction of great masses of people became apparent in the world. That very great political genius, the Emperor Constantine the Great, six centuries later, was the first to apprehend and to attempt to use this possibility for the preservation and the mental and moral knitting-together of the world community over which he ruled.

But it is not only in these deficiencies of news and of education and of the expedient of representative government that this political system of Rome differed from our own. True, it was far more like a modern civilized state than any other state we have considered hitherto, but in some matters it was strangely primordial and "sub-civilized." Every now and then the reader of Roman history, reading it in terms of debates and measures, policies and campaigns, capital and labour, comes upon something that gives him much the same shock he would feel if he went down to an unknown caller in his house and extended his hand to meet the misshapen hairy paw of *Homo Neanderthalensis* and looked up to see a chinless, bestial face. We have noted the occurrence of human sacrifice in the third century B.C., and much that we learn of the religion of republican Rome carries us far back beyond

[1] Julius Cæsar (60 B.C.) caused the proceedings of the Senate to be published by having them written up upon bulletin boards, *in albo* (upon the white). It had been the custom to publish the annual edict of the prætor in this fashion. There were professional letter-writers who sent news by special courier to rich country correspondents, and these would copy down the stuff upon the Album (white board). Cicero, while he was governor in Cilicia, got the current news from such a professional correspondent. He complains in one letter that it was not what he wanted; the expert was too full of the chariot races and other sporting intelligence, and failed to give any view of the political situation. Obviously this news-letter system was available only for public men in prosperous circumstances.

CICERO AT HIS VILLA

After the picture by R. Wilson, R.A.

"Cicero got the current news from a professional correspondent. This news-letter system was available only for public men in prosperous circumstances."

he days of decent gods, to the age of shamanism and magic. We talk of a legislative gathering, and the mind flies to Westminster; but how should we feel if we went to see the beginning of a session of the House of Lords, and discovered the Lord Chancellor, with bloody fingers, portentously fiddling about among the entrails of a newly killed sheep? The mind would recoil from Westminster to the customs of Benin. And the slavery of Rome was a savage slavery, altogether viler than the slavery of Babylon. We have had a glimpse of the virtuous Cato among his slaves in the second century B.C. Moreover, in the third century B.C., when King Asoka was ruling India in light and gentleness, the Romans were reviving an Etruscan sport, the setting on of slaves to fight for their lives. One is reminded of West Africa again in the origin of this amusement; it grew out of the prehistoric custom of a massacre of captives at the burial of a chief. There was a religious touch about this sport, the slaves with hooks, who dragged the dead bodies out of the arena, wore masks to represent the infernal ferryman-god, Charon. In 264 B.C., the very year in which Asoka began to reign and the First Punic War began, the first recorded gladiatorial combat took place in the forum at Rome, to celebrate the funeral of a member of the old Roman family of Brutus. This was a modest display of three couples, but soon gladiators were fighting by the hundred. The taste for these combats grew rapidly, and the wars supplied an abundance of captives. The old Roman moralists, who were so severe upon kissing and women's ornaments and Greek philosophy, had nothing but good to say for this new development. So long as pain was inflicted, Roman morality, it would seem, was satisfied.

If republican Rome was the first of modern self-governing national communities, she was certainly the "Neanderthal" form of them.

In the course of the next two or three centuries the gladiatorial shows of Rome grew to immense proportions. To begin with, while wars were frequent, the gladiators were prisoners of war. They came with their characteristic national weapons, tattooed Britons, Moors, Scythians, negroes, and the like, and there was perhaps some military value in these exhibitions. Then criminals of the lower classes[1] condemned to death were also used. The ancient world did not understand that a criminal condemned to death still has rights, and at any rate the use of a criminal as a gladiator was not so bad as his use as "material" for the vivisectors of the Museum at Alexandria. But as the profits of this sort of show business grew and the demand for victims increased, ordinary slaves were sold to the trainers of gladiators, and any slave who had aroused his owner's spite might find himself in an establishment for letting out gladiators. And dissipated young men who had squandered their property, and lads of spirit would go voluntarily into the trade for a stated time, trusting to their prowess to survive. As the business developed, a new use was found for gladiators as armed retainers; rich men would buy a band, and employ it as a bodyguard or hire it out for profit at the shows. The festivities of a show began with a ceremonial procession (*pompa*) and a sham fight (*prœlusio*). The real fighting was heralded by trumpets. Gladiators who objected to fight for any reason were driven on by whips and hot irons. A wounded man would sometimes call for pity by holding up his forefinger. The spectators would then either wave their handkerchiefs in token of mercy, or condemn him to death by holding out their

Gladiators (from a wall-painting at Pompeii)

[1] Seyffert, *op. cit.*

clenched fists with the thumbs down.[1] The slain and nearly dead were dragged out to a particular place, the *spoliarium*, where they were stripped of their arms and possessions, and those who had not already expired were killed.

This organization of murder as a sport and show serves to measure the great gap in moral standards between the Roman community and our own. No doubt cruelties and outrages upon human dignity as monstrous as this still go on in the world, but they do not go on in the name of the law and without a single dissentient voice. For it is true that until the time of Seneca (first century A.D.) there is no record of any plain protest against this business. The conscience of mankind was weaker and less intelligent then than now. Presently a new power was to come into the human conscience through the spread of Christianity. The spirit of Jesus in Christianity became the great antagonist in the later Roman state of these cruel shows and of slavery, and, as Christianity spread, these two evil things dwindled and disappeared.[2]

XXVIII

FROM TIBERIUS GRACCHUS TO THE GOD EMPEROR IN ROME

§ 1

WE have already twice likened the self-governing community of Rome to a "Neanderthal" variety of the modern "democratic" civilized state, and we shall recur again to this comparison. In form the two things, the first great primitive essay and its later relations, are extraordinarily similar; in spirit they differ very profoundly. Roman political and social life, and particularly Roman political and social life in the century between the fall of Carthage and the rise of Cæsar and Cæsarism, has a very marked general resemblance to the political and social life in such countries as the United States of America or the British Empire to-day. The resemblance is intensified by the common use, with a certain inaccuracy in every case, of such terms as "senate," "democracy," "proletariat," and the like. But everything in the Roman

[1] Authorities differ here. Mayor says thumbs up (to the breast) meant death and thumbs down meant "Lower that sword." The popular persuasion is that thumbs down meant death. Seyffert's *Dict. Class. Antiq.* gives this view. See the *Encyclopædia Britannica*, article "Gladiators."

[2] "A little more needs to be said on this matter. The Greeks cited gladiatorial shows as a reason for regarding the Romans as *Barbaroi*, and there were riots when some Roman proconsul tried to introduce them in Corinth. Among Romans, the better people evidently disliked them, but a sort of shyness prevented them from frankly denouncing them as cruel. For instance, Cicero, when he had to attend the Circus, took his tablets and his secretary with him, and didn't look. He expresses particular disgust at the killing of an elephant; and somebody in Tacitus (Drusus, Ann. 1. 76) was unpopular because he was too fond of gladiatorial bloodshed—"*quamquam vili sanguine nimis gaudens*" ("rejoicing too much in blood, worthless blood though it was"). The games were unhesitatingly condemned by Greek philosophy, and at different times two Cynics and one Christian gave their lives in the arena, protesting against them, before they were abolished.

"I do not think Christianity had any such relation to slavery as is here stated. St. Paul's action in sending back a slave to his master, and his injunction, 'Slaves, obey your masters,' were regularly quoted on the pro-slavery side, down to the nineteenth century; on the other hand, both the popular philosophies and the Mystery religions were against slavery in their whole tendency, and Christianity of course in time became the chief representative of these movements. Probably the best test is the number of slaves who occupied posts of honour in the religious and philosophic systems, like Epictetus, for instance, or the many slaves who hold offices in the Mithraic Inscriptions. I do not happen to know if any slaves were made Christian bishops, but by analogy I should think it likely that some were. In all the Mystery religions, as soon as you entered the community, and had communion with God, earthly distinctions shrivelled away."—G. M.

The Spirit of Jesus is something different from formal Christianity, which I regard as the vehicle, the largely unsympathetic vehicle, by which that spirit was carried about the world.—H. G. W.

CICERO AND CATILINE IN THE SENATE

From the picture by Professor C. Maccari

"Roman political life had a very marked resemblance to that of the United States of America or the British Empire to-day."

state was earlier, cruder, and clumsier; the injustices were more glaring, the conflicts harsher. There was comparatively little knowledge and few general ideas. Aristotle's scientific works were only beginning to be read in Rome in the first century B.C.; Ferrero,[1] it is true, makes Cæsar familiar with the Politics of Aristotle, and ascribes to him the dream of making a "Periclean Rome," but in doing so, Ferrero seems to be indulging in one of those lapses into picturesque romancing which are at once the joy and the snare of all historical writers.

Attention has already been drawn to the profound difference between Roman and modern conditions due to the absence of a press, of any popular education or of the representative idea in the popular assembly. Our world to-day is still far from solving the problem of representation and from producing a public assembly which will really summarize, crystallize, and express the thought and will of the community; our elections are still largely an ingenious mockery of the common voter who finds himself helpless in the face of party organizations which reduce his free choice of a representative to the less unpalatable of two political hacks, but, even so, his vote, in comparison with the vote of an ordinary honest Roman citizen, is an effective instrument. Too many of our histories dealing with this period of Roman history write of "the popular party," and of the votes of the people and so forth, as though such things were as much working realities as they are to-day. But the senators and politicians of Rome saw to it that such things never did exist as clean and wholesome realities. These modern phrases are very misleading unless they are carefully qualified.

We have already described the gatherings of the popular comitia; but that clumsy assembly in sheep pens does not convey the full extent to which the gerrymandering of popular representation could be carried in Rome. Whenever there was a new enfranchisement of citizens in Italy, there would be the most elaborate trickery and counter-trickery to enrol the new voters into as few or as many of the thirty old "tribes" as possible, or to put them into as few as possible new tribes. Since the vote was taken by tribes, it is obvious that however great the number of new additions made, if they were all got together into one tribe, their opinion would only count for one tribal vote, and similarly if they were crowded into just a few tribes, old or new. On the other hand, if they were put into too many tribes, their effect in any particular tribe might be inconsiderable. Here was the sort of work to fascinate every smart knave in politics. The *comitia tributa* could be *worked* at times so as to vote right counter to the general feeling of the people. And as we have already noted, the great mass of voters in Italy were also disenfranchised by distance. About the middle period of the Carthaginian wars there were upwards of 300,000 Roman citizens; about 100 B.C. there were more than 900,000, but in effect the voting of the popular assembly was confined to a few score thousand resident in and near Rome, and mostly men of a base type. And the Roman voters were "organized" to an extent that makes the Tammany machine of New York seem artless and honest. They belonged to clubs, *collegia sodalicia*, having usually some elegant religious pretensions; and the rising politician working his way to office went first to the usurers and then with the borrowed money to these clubs. If the outside voters were moved enough by any question to swarm into the city, it was always possible to put off the voting by declaring the omens unfavourable. If they came in unarmed, they could be intimidated; if they brought in arms, then the cry was raised that there was a plot to overthrow the republic, and a massacre would be organized.

There can be no doubt that all Italy, all the empire was festering with discomfort, anxiety, and discontent in the century after the destruction of Carthage; a few men were growing very rich, and the majority of people found themselves entangled in an inexplicable net of uncertain prices, jumpy markets, and debts; but yet there was no way at all of stating and clearing up the general dissatisfaction. There is no record of a single attempt to make the popular assembly a straightforward and workable public organ. Beneath the superficial appearances of public affairs struggled a mute giant of public opinion and public will, who sometimes made some great political effort a rush to vote or such like, and sometimes broke into actual violence. So long as there was no actual violence, the Senate and the financiers kept on in their own disastrous way. Only when they were badly frightened would governing cliques or parties desist from some nefarious policy and heed the common good. The real method of popular expression in Italy in those days was not the *comitia tributa*, but the strike and insurrection, the righteous and necessary methods of all cheated or suppressed peoples. We have seen

[1] *Greatness and Decline of Rome*, bk. i. ch. xi.

in our own days in Great Britain a decline in the prestige of parliamentary government and a drift towards unconstitutional methods on the part of the masses through exactly the same cause, through the incurable disposition of politicians to gerrymander the electoral machine until the community is driven to explosion.

For insurrectionary purposes a discontented population needs a leader, and the political history of the concluding century of Roman republicanism is a history of insurrectionary leaders and counter-revolutionary leaders. Most of the former are manifestly unscrupulous adventurers who try to utilize the public necessity and unhappiness for their own advancement. Many of the historians of this period betray a disposition to take sides, and are either aristocratic in tone or fiercely democratic; but, indeed, neither side in these complex and intricate disputes has a record of high aims or clean hands. The Senate and the rich equestrians were vulgar and greedy spirits, hostile and contemptuous towards the poor mob; and the populace was ignorant, unstable, and at least equally greedy. The Scipios in all this record shine by comparison, a group of gentlemen. To the motives of one or the other figures of the time, to Tiberius Gracchus, for example, we may perhaps extend the benefit of the doubt. But for the rest, they do but demonstrate how clever and cunning men may be, how subtle in contention, how brilliant in pretence, and how utterly wanting in wisdom or grace of spirit. "A shambling, hairy, brutish, but probably very cunning creature with a big brain *behind*;" so someone, I think it was Sir Harry Johnston, has described *Homo Neanderthalensis*.

To this day we must still use similar terms to describe the soul of the politician. The statesman has still to oust the politician from his lairs and weapon heaps. History has still to become a record of human dignity.

§ 2

Another respect in which the Roman system was a crude anticipation of our own, and different from any preceding political system we have considered, was that it was a cash and credit-using system. Money had been in the world as yet for only a few centuries. But its use had been growing; it was providing a fluid medium for trade and enterprise, and changing economic conditions profoundly. In republican Rome, the financier and the "money" interest began to play a part recognizably similar to their rôles to-day.

We have already noted—in our account of Herodotus—that a first effect of money was to give freedom of movement and leisure to a number of people who could not otherwise have enjoyed these privileges. And that is the peculiar value of money to mankind. Instead of a worker or helper being paid in kind and in such a way that he is tied as much in his enjoyment as in his labour, money leaves him free to do as he pleases amidst a wide choice of purchasable aids, eases, and indulgences. He may eat his money or drink it or give it to a temple or spend it in learning something or save it against some foreseen occasion. That is the good of money, the freedom of its universal convertibility. But the freedom money gives the poor man is nothing to the freedom money has given the rich man. With money rich men ceased to be tied to lands, houses, stores, flocks and herds. They could change the nature and locality of their possessions with an unheard-of freedom. In the third and second century B.C., this release, this untethering of wealth, began to tell upon the general economic life of the Roman and Hellenized world. People began to buy land and the like not for use, but to sell again at a profit; people borrowed to buy, speculation developed. No doubt there were bankers in the Babylon of 1,000 B.C., but they lent in a far more limited and solid way, bars of metal and stocks of goods. That earlier world was a world of barter and payment in kind, and it went slowly—and much more staidly and stably—for that reason. In that state the vast realm of China has remained almost down to the present time.

The big cities before Rome were trading and manufacturing cities. Such were Corinth and Carthage and Syracuse. But Rome never produced a very considerable industrial population, and her warehouses never rivalled those of Alexandria. The little port of Ostia was always big enough for her needs. Rome was a political and financial capital, and in the latter respect, at least, she was a new sort of city. She imported profits and tribute, and very little went out from her in return. The wharves of Ostia were chiefly busy unloading corn from Sicily and Africa and loot from all the world.

After the fall of Carthage the Roman imagination went wild with the hitherto unknown possibilities of finance. Money, like most other inventions, had "happened" to mankind, and men had still to develop—

to-day they have still to perfect—the science and morality of money. One sees the thing "catching on" in the recorded life and the writings of Cato the Censor. In his early days he was bitterly virtuous against usury; in his later he was devising ingenious schemes for safe usury.

In this curiously interesting century of Roman history we find man after man asking, "What has happened to Rome?" Various answers are made—a decline in religion, a decline from the virtues of the Roman forefathers, Greek "intellectual poison," and the like. We who can look at the problem with a large perspective, can see that what had happened to Rome was "money"—the new freedoms and chances and opportunities that money opened out. Money floated the Romans off the firm ground, everyone was getting hold of money, the majority by the simple expedient of running into debt; the eastward expansion of the empire was very largely a hunt for treasure in strong rooms and temples to keep pace with the hunger of the new need. The Equestrian order, in particular, became the money power. Everyone was developing property. Farmers were giving up corn and cattle, borrowing money, buying slaves, and starting the more intensive cultivation of oil and wine. Money was young in human experience and wild, nobody had it under control. It fluctuated greatly. It was now abundant and now scarce. Men made sly and crude schemes to corner it, to hoard it, to send up prices by releasing hoarded metals. A small body of very shrewd men was growing immensely rich. Many patricians were growing poor and irritated and unscrupulous. Among the middle sort of peoples there was much hope, much adventure, and much more disappointment. The growing mass of the expropriated was permeated by that vague, baffled, and hopeless sense of being inexplicably bested, which is the preparatory condition for all great revolutionary movements.

§ 3

The first conspicuous leader to appeal to the gathering revolutionary feeling in Italy was Tiberius Gracchus. He looks more like an honest man than any other figure in this period of history, unless it be Scipio Africanus the Elder. At first Tiberius Gracchus was a moderate reformer of a rather reactionary type. He wished to restore the yeoman class to property, very largely because he believed that class to be the backbone of the army, and his military experience in Spain before and after the destruction of Carthage had impressed upon him the declining efficiency of the legions. He was what we should call nowadays a "Back-to-the-land" man. He did not understand and few people understand to-day, how much easier it is to shift population from the land into the towns, than to return it to the laborious and simple routines of agricultural life. He wanted to revive the Licinian laws, which had been established when Camillus built his temple of Concord nearly two centuries and a half before (see Chap. xxvii, § 2), so far as they broke up great estates and restrained slave labour.

These Licinian laws had repeatedly been revived and repeatedly lapsed to a dead letter again. It was only when the big proprietors in the Senate opposed this proposal that Tiberius Gracchus turned to the people and began a furious agitation for popular government. He created a commission to inquire into the title of all landowners. In the midst of his activities occurred one of the most extraordinary incidents in history. Attalus, the king of the rich country of Pergamum in Asia Minor, died (133 B.C.), and left his kingdom to the Roman people.

It is difficult for us to understand the motives of this bequest. Pergamum was a country allied to Rome, and so moderately secure from aggression; and the natural consequence of such a will was to provoke a violent scramble among the senatorial gangs and a dispute between them and the people for the spoils of the new acquisition. Practically Attalus handed over his country to be looted. The act is so amazing that one is driven towards the hypothesis of forgery.[1] There were of course many Italian business people established in the country and a strong party of native rich men in close relations with Rome. To them, no doubt, a coalescence with the Roman system would have been acceptable. Josephus bears witness to such a desire for annexation among the rich men of Syria, a desire running counter to the wishes of both king and people. This Pergamum bequest, astonishing in itself, had the still more astonishing result of producing

[1] There is no evidence of forgery and no contemporary suggestion of the sort. The bequest of Attalus, even if it was a forgery (Mommsen accepts it, iii. p. 55), is of importance, as showing that a great many people did think that Rome was the best administrator. Otherwise, the story (if it is only a story) could not have caught on. *A priori* there seems good reason for the testament. The Attalid dynasty was "petering out"; there were troublesome Gauls about (Mommsen, iii. p. 53).—J. L. M. and E. B.

imitations in other quarters. In 96 B.C. Ptolemy Apion bequeathed Cyrenaica, in North Africa, to the Roman people; in 81 B.C. Alexander II, King of Egypt, followed suit with Egypt, a legacy too big for the courage if not for the appetite of the Senators, and they declined it; in 74 B.C. Nicomedes, King of Bithynia, demised Bithynia. Of these latter testamentary freaks we will say no more here. But it will be manifest how great an opportunity was given Tiberius Gracchus by the bequest of Attalus, of accusing the rich of greed and of proposing to decree the treasures of Attalus to the commonalty. He proposed to use this new wealth to provide seed, stock, and agricultural implements for the resettlement of the land.

His movement was speedily entangled in the complexities of the Roman electoral system—without a simple and straightforward electoral method, all popular movements in all ages necessarily become entangled and maddened in constitutional intricacies, and almost as necessarily lead to bloodshed. It was needed, if his work was to go on, that Tiberius Gracchus should continue to be tribune, and it was illegal for him to be tribune twice in succession. He overstepped the bounds of legality, and stood for the tribuneship a second time; the peasants who came in from the countryside to vote for him came in armed; the cry that he was aiming at a tyranny, the cry that had long ago destroyed Mælius and Manlius, was raised in the Senate, the friends of "law and order" went to the Capitol in state, accompanied by a rabble of dependents armed with staves and bludgeons; there was a conflict, or rather a massacre of the revolutionaries, in which nearly three hundred people were killed, and Tiberius Gracchus was beaten to death with the fragments of a broken bench by two Senators.

Thereupon the Senators attempted a sort of counter-revolution, and proscribed many of the followers of Tiberius Gracchus; but the state of public opinion was so sullen and threatening that this movement was dropped and Scipio Nasica, who was implicated in the death of Tiberius, though he occupied the position of pontifex maximus and should have remained in Rome for the public sacrifices which were the duties of that official, went abroad to avoid trouble.

The uneasiness of Italy next roused Scipio Africanus the Younger to propose the enfranchisement of all Italy. But he died suddenly before he could carry the proposal into effect.

Then followed the ambiguous career of Caius Gracchus, the brother of Tiberius, who followed some tortuous "policy" that still exercises the mind of historians. He increased the burthens of taxation laid upon the provinces, it is supposed with the idea of setting the modern financiers (the Equites) against the senatorial landowners. He gave the former the newly bequeathed taxes of Asia to farm, and, what is worse, he gave them control of the special courts set up to prevent extortion. He started enormous public works and particularly the construction of new roads, and he is accused of making a political use of the contracts. He revived the proposal to enfranchise Italy. He increased the distribution of subsidized cheap corn to the Roman citizens. . . . Here we cannot attempt to disentangle his schemes, much less to judge him. But that his policy was offensive to the groups that controlled the Senate there can be no doubt whatever. He was massacred by the champions of "law and order," with about three thousand of his followers, in the streets of Rome in 121 B.C. His decapitated head was carried to the Senate on the point of a pike.

(A reward of its weight in gold, says Plutarch, had been offered for this trophy; and its captor, acting in the true spirit of a champion of "big business," filled the braincase with lead on its way to the scales.)

In spite of these prompt firm measures the Senate was not to enjoy the benefits of peace and the advantages of a control of the imperial resources for long. Within ten years the people were in revolt again.

In 118 B.C. the throne of Numidia, the semi-barbaric kingdom that had arisen in North Africa upon the ruins of the civilized Carthaginian power, was seized by a certain able Jugurtha, who had served with the Roman armies in Spain, and had a knowledge of the Roman character. He provoked the military intervention of Rome. But the Romans found that their military power, under a Senate of financiers and landlords, was very different from what it had been even in the days of the younger Scipio Africanus. "Jugurtha bought over the Commissioners sent out to watch him, the Senators charged with their prosecution, and the generals in command against him."[1] There is a mistaken Roman proverb: "*pecunia non olet*" (money does not stink), for the money of Jugurtha stank even in Rome. There was an angry agitation; and a capable soldier of lowly origin, Marius, was carried to the consulship (107 B.C.) on the wave of popular indignation. Marius made

[1] Ferrero.

no attempt on the model of the Gracchi to restore the backbone of the army by rehabilitating the yeoman class. He was a professional soldier with a high standard of efficiency and a disposition to take short cuts. He simply raised troops from among the poor, whether countrymen or townsmen, paid them well, disciplined them thoroughly, and (106 B.C.) ended the seven years' war with Jugurtha by bringing that chieftain in chains to Rome. It did not occur to anybody that incidentally Marius had also created a professional army with no interest to hold it together but its pay. He then held on to the consulship more or less illegally for several years, and in 102 and 101 B.C. repelled a threatening move of the Germans (who thus appear in our history for the first time), who were raiding through Gaul towards Italy. He gained two victories; one on Italian soil. He was hailed as the saviour of his country, a second Camillus (100 B.C.).

The social tensions of the time mocked that comparison with Camillus. The Senate benefited by the greater energy in foreign affairs and the increased military efficiency that Marius had introduced, but the sullen, shapeless discontent of the mass of the people was still seeking some effective outlet. The rich grew richer and the poor poorer. It was impossible to stifle the consequences of that process for ever by political trickery. The Italian people were still unenfranchised. Two extreme democratic leaders, Saturninus and Glaucia, were assassinated, but that familiar senatorial remedy failed to assuage the populace on this occasion. In 92 B.C. an aristocratic official, Rutilius Rufus, who had tried to restrain the exactions of the financiers in Asia Minor, was condemned on a charge of corruption so manifestly trumped up that it deceived no one; and in 91 B.C., Livius Drusus, a newly elected tribune of the people, who was making capital out of the trial of Rutilius Rufus, was assassinated. He had proposed a general enfranchisement of the Italians, and he had foreshadowed not only another land law, but a general abolition of debts. Yet for all this vigour on the part of the senatorial usurers, landgrabbers, and forestallers, the hungry and the anxious were still insurgent. The murder of Drusus was the last drop in the popular cup; Italy blazed into a desperate insurrection.

There followed two years of bitter civil war, the Social War. It was a war between the idea of a united Italy and the idea of the rule of the Roman Senate. It was not a "social" war in the modern sense, but a war between Rome and her Italian allies (allies = Socii). "Roman generals, trained in the traditions of colonial warfare, marched ruthlessly up and down Italy, burning farms, sacking towns, and carrying off men, women, and children, to sell them in the open market or work them in gangs upon their estates."[1] Marius and an aristocratic general, Sulla, who had been with him in Africa and who was his bitter rival, both commanded on the side of Rome. But though the insurgents experienced defeats and looting, neither of these generals brought the war to an end. It was ended in a manner (89 B.C.) by the practical surrender of the Roman Senate to the idea of reform. The spirit was taken out of the insurrection by the concession of their demands "in principle"; and then as soon as the rebels had dispersed, the usual cheating of the new voters, by such methods as we have explained in § 1 of this chapter, was resumed.

By the next year (88 B.C.) the old round had begun again. It was mixed up with the personal intrigues of Marius and Sulla against each other; but the struggle had taken on another complexion through the army reforms of Marius, which had created a new type of legionary, a landless professional soldier with no interest in life but pay and plunder, and with no feeling of loyalty except to a successful general. A popular tribune, Sulpicius, was bringing forward some new laws affecting debt, and the consuls were dodging the storm by declaring a suspension of public business. Then came the usual resort to violence, and the followers of Sulpicius drove the consuls from the forum. But here it is that the new forces which the new army had made possible came into play. King Mithridates of Pontus, the Hellenized king of the southern shores of the Black Sea east of Bithynia, was pressing Rome into war. One of the proposed laws of Sulpicius was that Marius should command the armies sent against this Mithridates. Whereupon Sulla marched the army he had commanded throughout the Social War to Rome, Marius and Sulpicius fled, and a new age, an age of military pronunciamentos, began.

Of how Sulla had himself made commander against Mithridates and departed, and of how legions friendly to Marius then seized power, how Marius returned to Italy and enjoyed a thorough massacre of his political opponents and died, sated, of fever, we cannot tell in any detail. But one measure during the Marian reign of terror did much to relieve the social tension, and that was the abolition

[1] Ferrero

of three-quarters of all outstanding debts. Nor can we tell here how Sulla made a discreditable peace with Mithridates (who had massacred a hundred thousand Italians in Asia Minor) in order to bring his legions back to Rome, defeat the Marians at the battle of the Colline Gate of Rome, and reverse the arrangements of Marius. Sulla restored law and order by the proscription and execution of over five thousand people. He desolated large parts of Italy, restored the Senate to power, repealed many of the recent laws, though he was unable to restore the cancelled burden of debt, and then, feeling bored by politics and having amassed great riches, he retired with an air of dignity into private life, gave himself up to abominable vices, and so presently died, eaten up with some disgusting disease produced by debauchery.[1]

§ 4

Political life in Italy was not so much tranquillized as stunned by the massacres and confiscations of Marius and Sulla. The scale upon which this history is planned will not permit us to tell here of the great adventurers who, relying more and more on the support of the legions, presently began to scheme and intrigue again for dictatorial power in Rome. In 73 B.C. all Italy was terrified by a rising of the slaves, and particularly of the gladiators, led by a gladiator from Thessaly, Spartacus. He and seventy others had fled out from a gladiatorial "farm" at Capua. Similar risings had already occurred in Sicily. The forces under Spartacus necessarily became a miscellaneous band drawn from east and west, without any common idea except the idea of dispersing and getting home; nevertheless, he held out in southern Italy for two years, using the then apparently extinct crater of Vesuvius for a time as a natural fortress. The Italians, for all their love of gladiatorial display, failed to appreciate this conversion of the whole country into an arena, this bringing of the gladiatorial sword to the door, and when at last Spartacus was overthrown, their terror changed to frantic cruelty, six thousand of his captured followers were crucified—long miles of nailed and drooping victims—along the Appian Way.

Here we cannot deal at any length with Lucullus, who invaded Pontus and fought Mithridates, and brought the cultivated cherry-tree to Europe; nor can we tell how ingeniously Pompey the Great stole the triumph and most of the prestige Lucullus had won in Armenia beyond Pontus. Lucullus, like Sulla, retired into an opulent private life, but with more elegance and with a more gracious end. We cannot relate in any detail how Julius Cæsar accumulated reputation in the west, by conquering Gaul, defeating the German tribes upon the Rhine, and pushing a punitive raid across the Straits of Dover into Britain. More and more important grow the legions; less and less significant are the Senate and the assemblies of Rome. But there is a certain grim humour about the story of Crassus that we cannot altogether neglect.

This Crassus was a great money-lender and forestaller. He was a typical man of the new Equestrian type, the social equivalent of a modern munition profiteer. He first grew rich by buying up the property of those proscribed by Sulla. His earliest exploits in the field were against Spartacus, whom finally he crushed by great payments and exertions after a prolonged and expensive campaign. He then, as the outcome of complicated bargains, secured the command in the east and prepared to emulate the glories of Lucullus, who had pushed east from Pergamum and Bithynia into Pontus, and of Pompey, who had completed the looting of Armenia.

His experiences serve to demonstrate the gross ignorance with which the Romans were conducting their affairs at that time. He crossed the Euphrates, expecting to find in Persia another Hellenized kingdom like Pontus. But, as we have already intimated, the great reservoirs of nomadic peoples that stretched round from the Danube across Russia into Central Asia, had been raining back into the lands between the Caspian Sea and the Indus that Alexander had conquered for Hellenism. Crassus found himself against the "Scythian" again; against mobile tribes of horsemen led by a monarch in Median costume.[2] The particular variety of "Scythian" he encountered was called the Parthian. It is possible that in the Parthians a Mongolian (Turanian) element was now mingled with the Aryan strain; but the campaign of Crassus beyond the Euphrates is curiously like the campaign of Darius beyond the Danube; there is the same heavy thrusting of an infantry force against elusive light horsemen. But Crassus was less quick than Darius to realize the need

[1] Plutarch. To which, however, G. M. adds the following note. "It is generally believed that Sulla died through bursting a blood-vessel in a fit of temper. The story of abominable vices seems to be only the regular slander of the Roman mob against anyone who did not live in public."

[2] Plutarch.

of withdrawal, and the Parthians were better bowmen than the Scythians Darius met. They seem to have had some sort of noisy projectile of unusual strength and force, something different from an ordinary arrow.[1] The campaign culminated in that two days' massacre of the hot, thirsty, hungry, and weary Roman legions, which is known as the battle of Carrhæ (53 B.C.). They toiled through the sand, charging an enemy who always evaded their charge and rode round them and shot them to pieces. Twenty thousand of them were killed, and ten thousand marched on eastward as prisoners into slavery in Iran.

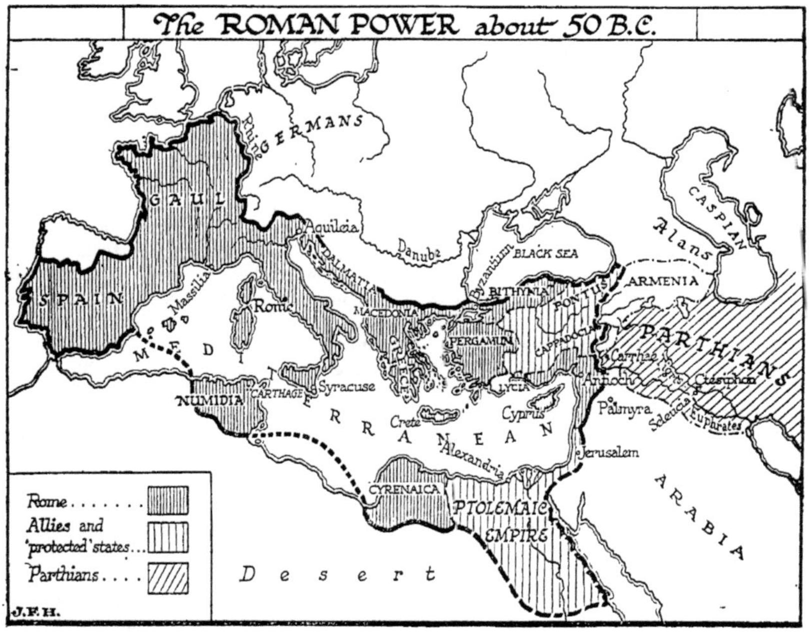

What became of Crassus is not clearly known. There is a story, probably invented for our moral benefit and suggested by his usuries, that he fell alive into the hands of the Parthians and was killed by having molten gold poured down his throat.

But this disaster has a very great significance indeed to our general history of mankind. It serves to remind us that from the Rhine to the Euphrates, all along to the north of the Alps and Danube and Black Sea, stretched one continuous cloud of nomadic and semi-nomadic peoples, whom the statescraft of imperial Rome was never able to pacify and civilize, nor her military science subdue. We have already called attention to a map showing how the Second Babylonian Empire, the Chaldean Empire, lay like a lamb in the embrace of the Median power. In exactly the same way the Roman Empire lay like a lamb in the embrace of this great crescent of outer barbarians. Not only was Rome never able to thrust back or assimilate that superincumbent crescent, but she was never able to organize the Mediterranean Sea into a secure and orderly system of communication between one part of her empire and another. Quite unknown as yet to Rome, the Mongolian tribes from North-eastern Asia, the Huns and their kin, walled back and driven out from China by the Tsi and Han dynasties, were drifting and pressing westward, mixing with the Parthians, the Scythians, the Teutons and the like, or driving them before them.

[1] The bow was probably the composite bow, so-called because it is made of several plates (five or so) of horn, like the springs of a carriage: it discharges a high-speed arrow with a twang. This was the bow the Mongols used. This short composite bow (it was not a long bow) was quite old in human experience. It was the bow of Odysseus; the Assyrians had it in a modified form. It went out in Greece, but it survived as the Mongol bow. It was quite short, very stiff to pull, with a flat trajectory, a remarkable range, and a great noise (cp. Homer's reference to the twang of the bow). It went out in the Mediterranean because the climate was not good for it, and because there were insufficient animals to supply the horn.—J. L. M.

Never at any time did the Romans succeed in pushing their empire beyond Mesopotamia, and upon Mesopotamia their hold was never very secure. Before the close of the republic that power of assimilation which had been the secret of their success was giving way to "patriotic" exclusiveness and "patriotic" greed. Rome plundered and destroyed Asia Minor and Babylonia, which were the necessary basis for an eastward extension to India, just as she had destroyed and looted Carthage and so had no foothold for extension into Africa, and just as she had destroyed Corinth and so cut herself off from an easy way into the heart of Greece. Western European writers, impressed by the fact that later on Rome Romanized and civilized Gaul and South Britain and restored the scene of her earlier devastations in Spain to prosperity, are apt to ignore that over far greater areas to the south and east her influence was to weaken and so restore to barbarism the far wider conquests of Hellenic civilization.

§ 5

But among the politicians of Italy in the first century B.C. there were no maps of Germany and Russia, Africa and Central Asia, and no sufficient intelligence to study them had they existed. Rome never developed the fine curiosities that sent Hanno and the sailors of Pharaoh Necho down the coasts of Africa. When, in the first century B.C., the emissaries of the Han dynasty reached the eastern shores of the Caspian Sea, they found only stories of a civilization that had receded. The memory of Alexander still lived in these lands, but of Rome men only knew that Pompey had come to the western shores of the Caspian and gone away again, and that Crassus had been destroyed. Rome was pre-occupied at home. What mental energy remained over in the Roman citizen from the attempt to grow personally rich and keep personally safe was intent upon the stratagems and strokes and counter-strokes of the various adventurers who were now manifestly grappling for the supreme power.

It is the custom of historians to treat these struggles with extreme respect. In particular the figure of Julius Cæsar is set up as if it were a star of supreme brightness and importance in the history of mankind.[1] Yet a dispassionate consideration of the known facts fails altogether to justify this demi-god theory of Cæsar. Not even that precipitate wrecker of splendid possibilities, Alexander the Great, has been so magnified and dressed up for the admiration of careless and uncritical readers. There is a type of scholar who, to be plain, sits and *invents* marvellous world policies for the more conspicuous figures in history with the merest scraps of justification or with no justification at all. We are told that Alexander planned the conquest of Carthage and Rome and the complete subjugation of India, and that only his death shattered these schemes. What we know for certain is that he conquered the Persian Empire, and never went far beyond its boundaries; and that when he was supposed to be making these vast and noble plans, he was in fact indulging in such monstrous antics as his mourning for his favourite Hephæstion, and as his main occupation he was drinking himself to death. So too Julius Cæsar is credited with the intention of doing just that one not impossible thing which would have secured the Roman Empire from its ultimate collapse—namely, the systematic conquest and civilization of Europe as far as the Baltic and the Dnieper. He was to have marched upon Germany, says Plutarch, through Parthia and Scythia, round the north of the Caspian and Black Seas. Yet the fact we have to reconcile with this wise and magnificent project is that at the crest of his power, Cæsar, already a bald, middle-aged man, past the graces and hot impulses of youthful love, spent the better part of a year in Egypt, feasting and entertaining himself in amorous pleasantries with the Egyptian queen Cleopatra. And afterwards he brought her with him to Rome, where her influence over him was bitterly resented. Such complications with a woman mark the elderly sensualist or sentimentalist—he was fifty-four at the commencement of the *affaire*—rather than the master-ruler of men.

On the side of the superman idea of Cæsar, we have to count a bust in the Naples Museum. It represents a fine and intellectual face, very noble in its expression, and we can couple with that the story that his head, even at birth, was unusually large and finely formed. But there is really no satisfying evidence that this well-known bust does represent Cæsar, and it is hard to reconcile its austere serenity with the reputation for violent impulse and disorderliness that clung to him. Other busts

[1] For a good compact account of Cæsar, much more appreciative of him than our text, see Warde Fowler's *Julius Cæsar*.

THE MURDER OF CÆSAR

From the picture by Carl T. Von Piloty

"He was beset in the Senate and stabbed in three-and-twenty places."

of a quite different man are also, with more probability, ascribed to him.

There can be little doubt that he was a dissolute and extravagant young man—the scandals cluster thick about his sojourn in Bithynia, whither he fled from Sulla; he was the associate of the reprobate Clodius and the conspirator Catiline, and there is nothing in his political career to suggest any aim higher or remoter than his own advancement to power, and all the personal glory and indulgence that power makes possible. We will not attempt to tell here of the turns and devices of his career. Although he was of an old patrician family, he came into politics as the brilliant darling of the people. He spent great sums and incurred heavy debts to provide public festivals on the most lavish scale. He opposed the tradition of Sulla, and cherished the memory of Marius, who was his uncle by marriage. For a time he worked in conjunction with Crassus and Pompey, but after the death of Crassus he and Pompey came into conflict. By 49 B.C. he and Pompey, with their legions, he from the west and Pompey from the east, were fighting openly for predominance in the Roman state. He had broken the law by bringing his legions across the Rubicon, which was the boundary between his command and Italy proper. At the battle of Pharsalos in Thessaly (48 B.C.), Pompey was routed, and, fleeing to Egypt, was murdered, leaving Cæsar more master of the Roman world than ever Sulla had been.

He was then created dictator for ten years in 46 B.C., and early in 45 B.C. he was made dictator for life. This was monarchy; if not hereditary monarchy, it was at least electoral life monarchy. It was unlimited opportunity to do his best for the world. And by the spirit and quality of his use of this dictatorial power during these four years we are bound to judge him. A certain reorganization of local administration he effected, and he seems to have taken up what was a fairly obvious necessity of the times, a project for the restoration of the two murdered seaports of Corinth and Carthage, whose destruction had wrecked the sea-life of the Mediterranean. But much more evident was the influence of Cleopatra and Egypt upon his mind. Like Alexander before him, his head seems to have been turned by the king-god tradition, assisted no doubt in his case by the adulation of that charming hereditary goddess, Cleopatra. We find evidence of exactly that same conflict upon the score of divine pretensions, between him and his personal friends, that we have already recorded in the case of Alexander. So far as the Hellenized east was concerned, the paying of divine honours to rulers was a familiar idea; but it was still repulsive to the lingering Aryanism of Rome.

Antony, who had been his second in command at Pharsalos, was one of the chief of his flatterers. Plutarch describes a scene at the public games in which Antony tried to force a crown upon Cæsar, which Cæsar, after a little coyness and in face of the manifested displeasure of the crowd, refused. But he had adopted the ivory sceptre

JVLIVS CÆSAR
(from the Naples bust)

and throne, which were the traditional insignia of the ancient kings of Rome. His image was carried amidst that of the gods in the opening *pompa* of the arena, and his statue was set up in a temple with an inscription, "To the Unconquerable God!" Priests even were appointed for his godhead. These things are not the symptoms of greatmindedness, but of a common man's megalomania. Cæsar's record of vulgar scheming for the tawdriest mockeries of personal worship is a silly and shameful record; it is incompatible with the idea that he was a wise and wonderful superman setting the world to rights.

Finally (44 B.C.) he was assassinated by a group of his own friends and supporters, to whom these divine aspirations had become intolerable. He was beset in the Senate, and stabbed in three and twenty places, dying at the foot of the statue of his fallen rival Pompey the Great. The scene marks the complete demoralization of the old Roman governing body. Brutus, the ringleader of the murderers, would have addressed the senators, but, confronted by this crisis, they were scuttling off in every direction. For the best part of a day Rome did not know what to make of this event; the murderers marched about with their bloody weapons through an undecided city, with no one gainsaying them and only a few joining them; then public opinion turned against them, some of their houses were attacked, and they had to hide and fly for their lives.

§ 6

But the trend of things was overwhelmingly towards monarchy. For thirteen years more the struggle of personalities went on. One single man is to be noted as inspired by broad ideas and an ambition not entirely egoistic, Cicero. He was a man of modest origin, whose eloquence and literary power had won him a prominent place in the Senate. He was a little tainted by the abusive tradition of Demosthenes, nevertheless he stands out, a noble and pathetically ineffective figure, pleading with the now utterly degenerate, base, and cowardly Senate for the high ideals of the Republic. He was a writer of great care and distinction, and the orations and private letters he has left us make him one of the most real and living figures of this period to the modern reader.[1] He was proscribed and killed in 43 B.C., the year after the murder of Julius Cæsar, and his head and hands were nailed up in the Roman forum. Octavian, who became at last the monarch of Rome, seems to have made an effort to save Cicero; that murder was certainly not his crime.

Here we cannot trace out the tangle of alliances and betrayals that ended in the ascendancy of this Octavian, the adopted heir of Julius Cæsar. The fate of the chief figures is interwoven with that of Cleopatra.

After the death of Cæsar, she set herself to capture the emotions and vanity of Antony, a much younger man than Cæsar, with whom she was probably already acquainted. For a time Octavian and Antony and a third figure, Lepidus, divided the Roman world just as Cæsar and Pompey had divided it before their final conflict. Octavian took the hardier west, and consolidated his power; Antony had the more gorgeous east—and Cleopatra. To Lepidus fell that picked bone, Carthaginian Africa. He seems to have been a good man of good traditions, set upon the restoration of Carthage rather than upon wealth or personal vanities. The mind of Antony succumbed to those same ancient ideas of divine kingship that had already proved too much for the mental equilibrium of Julius Cæsar. In the company of Cleopatra he gave himself up to love, amusements, and a dream of sensuous glory, until Octavian felt that the time was ripe to end these two Egyptian divinities.

In 32 B.C. Octavian induced the Senate to depose Antony from the command of the east, and proceeded to attack him. A great naval battle at Actium (31 B.C.) was decided by the unexpected desertion of Cleopatra with sixty ships in the midst of the fight. It is quite impossible for us to decide now whether this was due to premeditated treachery or to the sudden whim of a charming woman. The departure of these ships threw the fleet of Antony into hopeless confusion, which was increased by the headlong flight of this model lover in pursuit. He went off in a swift galley after her without informing his commanders. He left his followers to fight and die as they thought fit, and for a time they were incredulous that he had gone. The subsequent encounter of the two lovers and their reconciliation is a matter for ironical speculation on the part of Plutarch.

Octavian's net closed slowly round his rival. It is not improbable that there was some sort of understanding between Octavian and Cleopatra, as perhaps in the time of Julius Cæsar there may have been between the queen and Antony. Antony gave way to much mournful posturing, varied by love scenes, during this last stage of his little drama. For a time he posed as an imitator of the cynic Timon, as one who had lost all faith in mankind, though one may think that his deserted sailors at Actium had better reason for such an attitude. Finally he found himself and Cleopatra besieged by Octavian in Alexandria. There were some sallies and minor successes, and Antony was loud with challenges to Octavian to decide the matter by personal combat. Being led to believe that Cleopatra had committed suicide, this star of romance stabbed himself, but so ineffectually as to die lingeringly, and he was carried off to expire in her presence (30 B.C.).

Plutarch's account of Antony, which was derived very largely from witnesses who had seen and known him, describes him as of

[1] See Strachan Davidson's *Cicero*, or, better, his own letters to Atticus.

THE DEATH OF CLEOPATRA

By the Hon. J. Collier
Permission, Oldham Art Gallery

"When Cleopatra found that Octavian's care for her was chiefly that he might exhibit her in a triumphal procession in Rome, she committed suicide."

heroic mould. He is compared to the demi-god Hercules, from whom indeed he claimed descent, and also to the Indian Bacchus. There is a disgusting but illuminating description of a scene in the Senate when he attempted to speak while drunk, and was overtaken by one of the least dignified concomitants of intoxication.

For a little while Cleopatra still clung to life, and perhaps to the hope that she might reduce Octavian to the same divine rôle that had already been played by Julius Cæsar and Antony. She had an interview with Octavian, in which she presented herself as beauty in distress and very lightly clad. But when it became manifest that Octavian lacked the godlike spark, and that his care for her comfort and welfare was dictated chiefly by his desire to exhibit her in a triumphal procession through the streets of Rome, she also committed suicide. An asp was smuggled to her past the Roman sentries, concealed in a basket of figs, and by its fangs she died.

Octavian seems to have been almost entirely free from the divine aspirations of Julius Cæsar and Antony. He was neither God nor romantic hero; he was a man. He was a man of far greater breadth and capacity than any other player in this last act of the Republican drama in Rome. All things considered, he was perhaps the best thing that could have happened to Rome at that time. He "voluntarily resigned the extraordinary powers which he had held since 43, and, to quote his own words, 'handed over the republic to the control of the senate and the people of Rome.' The old constitutional machinery was once more set in motion; the senate, assembly, and magistrates resumed their functions, and Octavian himself was hailed as the 'restorer of the commonwealth and the champion of freedom.' It was not so easy to determine what relation he himself, the actual master of the Roman world, should occupy towards this revived republic. His abdication, in any real sense of the word, would have simply thrown everything back into confusion. The interests of peace and order required that he should retain at least the substantial part of his authority; and this object was in fact accomplished, and the rule of the emperors founded, in a manner which has no parallel in history. Any revival of the kingly title was out of the question, and Octavian himself expressly refused the dictatorship. Nor was any new office created or any new official title invented for his benefit. But by senate and people he was invested according to the old constitutional forms with certain powers, as many citizens had been before him, and so took his place by the side of the lawfully appointed magistrates of the republic; only, to mark his pre-eminent dignity, as the first of them all, the senate decreed that he should take as an additional cognomen that of 'Augustus,' while in common parlance he was henceforth styled Princeps, a simple title of courtesy, familiar to republican usage and conveying no other idea than that of a recognized primacy and precedence over his fellow-citizens. The ideal sketched by Cicero in his *De Republica*, of a constitutional president of a free republic, was apparently realized; but it was only in appearance. For in fact the special prerogatives conferred upon Octavian gave him back in substance the autocratic authority he had resigned, and as between the restored republic and its new *princeps* the balance of power was overwhelmingly on the side of the latter."[1]

§ 7

In this manner it was that Roman republicanism ended in a *princeps* or ruling prince, and the first great experiment in a self-governing community on a scale larger than that of tribe or city, collapsed and failed.

The essence of its failure was that it could not sustain unity. In its early stages its citizens, both patrician and plebeian, had a certain tradition of justice and good faith, and of the loyalty of all citizens to the law, and of the goodness of the law for all citizens; it clung to this idea of the importance of the law and of law-abidingness nearly into the first century B.C. But the unforeseen invention and development of money, the temptations and disruptions of imperial expansion, the entanglement of electoral methods, weakened and swamped this tradition by presenting old issues in new disguises under which the judgment did not recognize them, and by enabling men to be loyal to the professions of citizenship and disloyal to its spirit. The bond of the Roman people had always been a moral rather than a religious bond; their religion was sacrificial and superstitious; it embodied no such great ideas of a divine leader and of a sacred mission as Judaism was developing. As the idea of citizenship failed and faded before the new occasions, there remained no inner, that is to say no real, unity in the system at

[1] H. S. Jones in *The Encyclopædia Britannica*, article "Rome." His contribution is admirably verified and exact, and we are greatly indebted to it.

all. Every man tended more and more to do what was right in his own eyes.

Under such conditions there was no choice between chaos and a return to monarchy, to the acceptance of some chosen individual as the one unifying will in the state. Of course in that return there is always hidden the expectation that the monarch will become as it were magic, will cease to be merely a petty human being, and will think and feel as something greater and more noble, as indeed a state personage: and of course monarchy invariably fails to satisfy that expectation. We shall glance at the extent of this failure in the brief review we shall presently make of the emperors of Rome. We shall find at last one of the more constructive of these emperors, Constantine the Great, conscious of his own inadequacy as a unifying power, turning to the faith, the organization, and teaching network of one of the new religious movements in the empire, to supply just that permeating and correlating factor in men's minds that was so manifestly wanting.

With Cæsar, the civilization of Europe and Western Asia went back to monarchy, and, through monarchy, assisted presently by organized Christianity, it sought to achieve peace, righteousness, happiness and world order for close upon eighteen centuries. Then almost suddenly it began reverting to republicanism, first in one country and then in another, and, assisted by the new powers of printing and the press and of organized general education, and by the universalist religious ideas in which the world had been soaked for generations, it has now resumed again the effort to create a republican world-state and a world-wide scheme of economic righteousness which the Romans had made so prematurely and in which they had so utterly and disastrously failed.

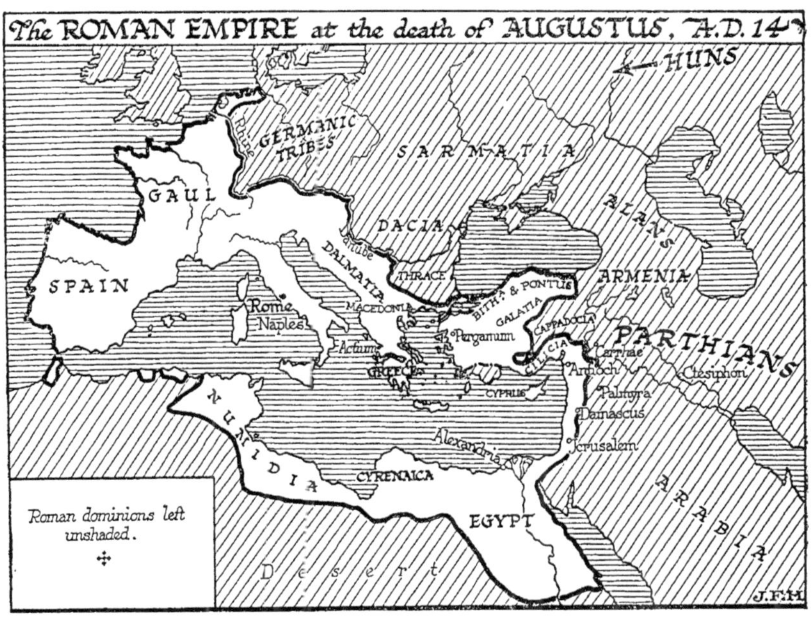

The ROMAN EMPIRE at the death of AUGUSTUS, A.D. 14

Certain conditions, we are now beginning to perceive, are absolutely necessary to such a creation; conditions which it is inconceivable that any pre-Christian Roman could have regarded as possible. We may still think the attainment of these conditions a vastly laborious and difficult and uncertain undertaking, but we understand that the attempt must be made because no other prospect before us gives even a promise of happiness or self-respect or preservation of our kind. The first of these conditions is that there should be a common political idea in the minds of all men, an idea of the state thought of as the personal possession of each individual and as the backbone fact of his scheme of duties. In the early days of Rome, when it was a little visible state, twenty miles square, such notions could be and were developed in children in their homes, and by what they saw and heard of the political lives of their fathers ; but in a larger country such as Rome had already become before the war with Pyrrhus, there was a need of an organized teaching of the history, of the main laws, and of the general intentions of the state towards everyone if this moral unity was to be maintained. But the need was never realized, and no attempt at any such teaching was ever made. At the time it could not have been made. It is inconceivable that it could have been made. The knowledge was not there, and there existed no class from which the needed teachers could be drawn and no conception of an organization for any such systematic moral and intellectual training as the teaching organization of Christianity, with its creeds and catechisms and sermons and confirmations, presently supplied.

Moreover, we know nowadays that even a universal education of this sort supplies only the basis for a healthy republican state. Next to education there must come abundant, prompt, and truthful information of what is going on in the state, and frank and free discussion of the issues of the time. Even nowadays these functions are performed only very imperfectly and badly by the press we have and by our publicists and politicians ; but badly though it is done, the thing is done, and the fact that it is done at all argues that it may ultimately be done well. In the Roman state it was not even attempted. The Roman citizen got his political facts from rumour and the occasional orator. He stood wedged in the forum, imperfectly hearing a distant speaker. He probably misconceived every issue upon which he voted.

And of the monstrous ineffectiveness of the Roman voting system we have already written.

Unable to surmount or remove these obstacles to a sane and effective popular government, the political instincts of the Roman mind turned towards monarchy. But it was not monarchy of the later European type, not hereditary monarchy, which was now installed in Rome. The *princeps* was really like an American war-time president elected not for four years, but for life, able to appoint senators instead of being restrained by an elected senate, and with a rabble popular meeting in the place of the house of representatives. He was also *pontifex maximus*, chief of the sacrificial priests, a function unknown at Washington ; and in practice it became usual for him to designate and train his successor and to select for that honour a son or an adopted son or a near relation whom he could trust. The power of the *princeps* was in itself enormous to entrust to the hands of a single man without any adequate checks, but it was further enhanced by the tradition of monarch-worship which had now spread out from Egypt over the entire Hellenized east. and which was coming to Rome in the head of every Oriental slave and immigrant. By natural and imperceptible degrees the idea of the god-emperor came to dominate the whole Romanized world.

Only one thing presently remained to remind the god-emperor that he was mortal, and that was the army. The god-emperor was never safe upon the Olympus of the Palatine Hill at Rome. He was only secure while he was the beloved captain of his legions. And as a consequence only the hardworking emperors who kept their legions active and in close touch with themselves had long reigns. The sword overhung the emperor and spurred him to incessant activity. If he left things to his generals, one of those generals presently replaced him. This spur was perhaps the redeeming feature of the Roman Imperial system. In the greater, compacter, and securer empire of China there was not the same need of legions, and so there was not the same swift end for lazy or dissipated or juvenile monarchs that overtook such types in Rome.

XXIX

THE CÆSARS BETWEEN THE SEA AND THE GREAT PLAINS OF THE OLD WORLD[1]

§ 1

WESTERN writers are apt, through their patriotic predispositions, to overestimate the organization, civilizing work, and security of the absolute monarchy that established itself in Rome after the accession of Augustus Cæsar. From it we derive the political traditions of Britain, France, Spain, Germany, and Italy, and these countries loom big in the perspectives of European writers. By the scale of a world history the Roman Empire ceases to seem so overwhelmingly important. It lasted about four centuries in all before it was completely shattered. The Byzantine Empire was no genuine continuation of it; it was a resumption of the Hellenic Empire of Alexander; it spoke Greek; its monarch had a Roman title no doubt, but so for that matter had the late Tsar of Bulgaria. During its four centuries of life the empire of Rome had phases of division and complete chaos; its prosperous years, if they are gathered together and added up, do not amount in all to a couple of centuries. Compared with the quiet steady expansion, the security, and the civilizing task of the contemporary Chinese Empire, or with Egypt between 4,000 and 1,000 B.C., or with Sumeria before the Semitic conquest, this amounts to a mere incident in history. The Persian Empire of Cyrus again, which reached from the Hellespont to the Indus, had as high a standard of civilization; and its homelands remained unconquered and fairly prosperous for over two hundred years. Its predecessor, the Median Empire, had endured for half a century. After a brief submergence by Alexander the Great, it rose again as the Seleucid Empire, which endured for some centuries. The Seleucid dominion shrank at last to the west of the Euphrates, and became a part of the Roman Empire; but Persia, revived by the Parthians as a new Persian Empire, first under the Arsacids and then under the Sassanids, outlived the empire of Rome. The Sassanids repeatedly carried war into the Byzantine Empire, and held the line of the Euphrates steadfastly. In 616 A.D. under Chosroes II, they were holding Damascus, Jerusalem, and Egypt, and threatening the Hellespont. But there has been no tradition to keep alive the glories of the Sassanids. The reputation of Rome has flourished through the prosperity of her heirs. The tradition of Rome is greater than its reality.

History distinguishes two chief groups of Roman emperors who were great administrators. The first of these groups began with:—

Augustus Cæsar (27 B.C. to 14 A.D.), the Octavian of the previous section, who worked hard at the reorganization of the provincial governments and at financial reform. He established a certain tradition of lawfulness and honesty in the bureaucracy, and he restrained the more monstrous corruptions and tyrannies by giving the provincial citizen the right to appeal to Cæsar. But he fixed the European boundaries of the empire along the Rhine and Danube, so leaving Germany, which is the necessary backbone of a safe and prosperous Europe, to barbarism; and he made a similar limitation in the east at the Euphrates, leaving Armenia independent, to be a constant bone of contention with the Arsacids and Sassanids. It is doubtful whether he considered that he was fixing the final boundaries of the empire along these lines, or whether he thought it desirable to consolidate for some years before any further attempts at expansion.

Tiberius (14 to 37 A.D.) is also described as a capable ruler, but he became intensely unpopular in Rome, and it would seem that he was addicted to gross and abominable vices. But his indulgence in these and his personal tyrannies and cruelties did not interfere with the general prosperity of the empire. It is difficult to judge him; nearly all our sources of information are manifestly hostile to him.

Caligula (37 to 41 A.D.) was insane, but the empire carried on during four years of

[1] The best book in a compact compass for expanding this chapter is H. Stuart Jones's *The Roman Empire.*

A ROMAN CHARIOT RACE

From the picture by U. Checa
By permission of Messrs. L. H. Lefèvre & Son, owners of the copyright

"Cæsar, the brilliant darling of the people, provided public festivals on a most lavish scale."

eccentricity at its head. Finally he was murdered in his palace by his servants, and there seems to have been an attempt to restore the senatorial government, an attempt which was promptly suppressed by the household legions.

Claudius (41 to 54 A.D.), the uncle of Caligula, upon whom the choice of the soldiers fell, was personally uncouth, but he seems to have been a hardworking and fairly capable administrator. He advanced the westward boundary of the empire by annexing the southern half of Britain. He was poisoned by Agrippina, the mother of his adopted son, Nero, and a woman of great charm and force of character.

Nero (54 to 68 A.D.), like Tiberius, is credited with monstrous vices and cruelties, but the empire had acquired sufficient momentum to carry on through his fourteen years of power. He certainly murdered his devoted but troublesome mother and his wife, the latter as a mark of devotion to a lady, Poppæa, who then married him; but the domestic infelicities of the Cæsars are no part of our present story. The reader greedy for criminal particulars must go to the classical source, Suetonius. These various Cæsars and their successors and their womenkind were probably no worse essentially than most weak and passionate human beings, but they had no real religion, being themselves gods; they had no wide knowledge on which to build high ambitions, their women were fierce and often illiterate, and they were under no restraints of law or custom. They were surrounded by creatures ready to stimulate their slightest wishes and to translate their vaguest impulses into action. What are mere passing black thoughts and angry impulses with most of us became therefore deeds with them. Before a man condemns Nero as a different species of being from himself, he should examine his own secret thoughts very carefully. Nero became intensely unpopular in Rome, and it is interesting to note that he became unpopular not because he murdered and poisoned his intimate relations, but because there was an insurrection in Britain under a certain Queen Boadicea, and the Roman forces suffered a great disaster (61 A.D.), and because there was a destructive earthquake in Southern Italy. The Roman population, true to its Etruscan streak, never religious and always superstitious, did

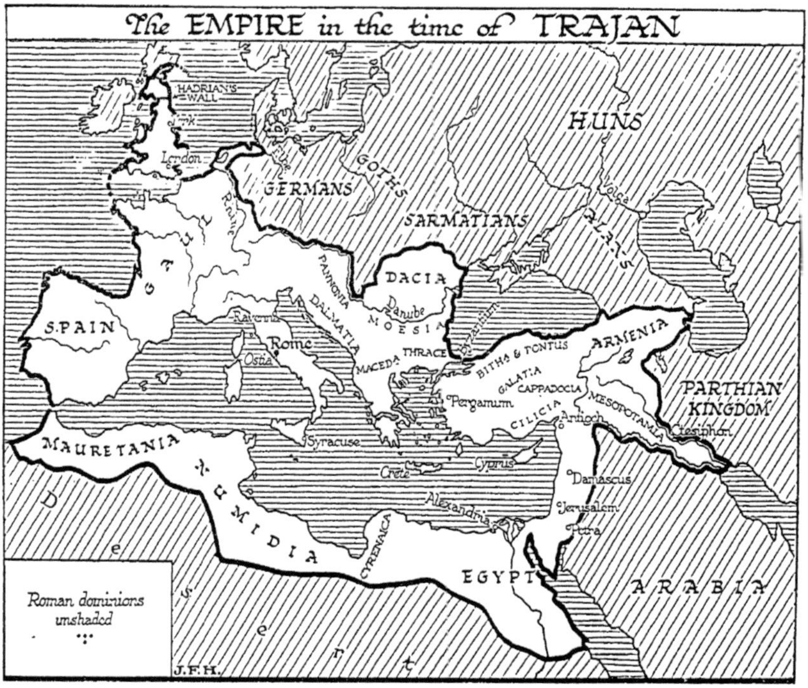

The EMPIRE in the time of TRAJAN

not mind a wicked Cæsar, but it did object strongly to an unpropitious one. The Spanish legions rose in insurrection under an elderly general of seventy-three, Galba, whom they acclaimed emperor. He advanced upon Rome carried in a litter. Nero, hopeless of support, committed suicide (68 A.D.).

Galba, however, was only one of a group of would-be emperors. The generals in command of the Rhine legions, the Palatine troops, and the eastern armies, each attempted to seize power. Rome saw four emperors in a year, Galba, Otho, Vitellus, and Vespasian; the fourth, Vespasian (69–79 A.D.), from the eastern command, had the firmest grip, and held and kept the prize. But with Nero the line of Cæsars born or adopted ended. Cæsar ceased to be the family name of the Roman emperors, and became a title, Divus Cæsar, the Cæsar god. The monarchy took a step forward towards orientalism by an increased insistence upon the worship of the ruler.

Vespasian (69 to 79 A.D.) and his sons Titus (79 A.D.) and Domitian (81 A.D.) constitute, as it were, a second dynasty, the Flavian; then after the assassination of Domitian came a group of emperors related to one another not by blood, but by adoption, the adoptive emperors. Nerva (96 A.D.) was the first of this line, and Trajan (98 A.D.) the second. They were followed by the indefatigable Hadrian (117 A.D.), Antoninus Pius (138 A.D.), and Marcus Aurelius (161 to 180 A.D.). Under both the Flavians and the Antonines the boundaries of the empire crept forward again. North Britain was annexed in 84 A.D., the angle of the Rhine and Danube was filled in, and what is now Transylvania was made into a new province, Dacia. Trajan also invaded Parthia and annexed Armenia, Assyria, and Mesopotamia. Under his rule the empire reached its maximum extent. Hadrian, his successor, was of a cautious and retractile disposition. He abandoned these new eastern conquests of Trajan's, and he also abandoned North Britain. He adopted the Chinese idea of the limiting wall against barbarism, an excellent idea so long as the pressure of population on the imperial side of the wall is greater than the pressure from without, but worthless otherwise. He built Hadrian's wall across Britain, and a palisade between the Rhine and the Danube. The full tide of Roman expansion was past, and in the reign of his successor the North European frontier was already actively on the defensive against the aggression of Teutonic and Slavic tribes.

Marcus Aurelius Antoninus is one of those figures in history about which men differ widely and intensely. To some critics he seems to have been a priggish person; he dabbled in religions, and took a pleasure in conducting priestly ceremonies in priestly garments—a disposition offensive to common men—and they resent his alleged failure to restrain the wickedness of his wife Faustina. The stories of his domestic infelicity, however, rest on no very good foundations, though certainly his son Commodus was a startling person for a good home to produce. On the other hand, he was unquestionably a devoted and industrious emperor, holding social order together through a series of disastrous years of vile weather, great floods, failing harvests and famine, barbaric raids and revolts, and at last a terrible universal pestilence. Says F. W. Farrar, quoted in the *Encyclopædia Britannica*, "He regarded himself as being, in fact, the servant of all. The registry of the citizens, the suppression of litigation, the elevation of public morals, the care of minors, the retrenchment of public expenses, the limitation of gladiatorial games and shows, the care of roads, the restoration of senatorial privileges, the appointment of none but worthy magistrates, even the regulation of street traffic, these and numberless other duties so completely absorbed his attention that, in spite of indifferent health, they often kept him at severe labour from early morning till long after midnight. His position, indeed, often necessitated his presence at games and shows; but on these occasions he occupied himself either in reading, or being read to, or in writing notes. He was one of those who held that nothing should be done hastily, and that few crimes were worse than waste of time."

But it is not by these industries that he is now remembered. He was one of the greatest exponents of the Stoical philosophy, and in his *Meditations*, jotted down in camp and court, he has put so much of a human soul on record as to raise up for himself in each generation a fresh series of friends and admirers.

With the death of Marcus Aurelius this phase of unity and comparatively good government came to an end, and his son Commodus inaugurated an age of disorder. Practically the empire had been at peace within itself for two hundred years. Now for a hundred years the student of Roman history must master the various criminology of a number of inadequate emperors, while the frontier crumbled and receded under barbarian pressure. One or two names only seem to be the names of able men: such were Septimius Severus, Aurelian, and

Probus. Septimius Severus was a Carthaginian, and his sister was never able to master Latin. She conducted her Roman household in the Punic language, which must have made Cato the elder turn in his grave. The rest of the emperors of this period were chiefly adventurers too unimportant to the general scheme of things for us to note. At times there were separate emperors ruling in different parts of the distracted empire. From our present point of view the Emperor Decius, who was defeated and killed during a great raid of the Goths into Thrace in 251 A.D., and the Emperor Valerian, who, together with the great city of Antioch, was captured by the Sassanid Shah of Persia in 260 A.D., are worthy of notice because they mark the insecurity of the whole Roman system, and the character of the outer pressure upon it. So too is Claudius, "the Conqueror of the Goths," because he gained a great victory over these people at Nish in Serbia (270 A.D.), and because he died, like Pericles, of the plague.

Through all these centuries intermittent pestilences were playing a part in weakening races and altering social conditions, a part that has still to be properly worked out by historians. There was, for instance, a great plague throughout the empire between the years 164 and 180 A.D. in the reign of the Emperor Marcus Aurelius. It probably did much to disorganize social life and prepare the way for the troubles that followed the accession of Commodus. This same pestilence devastated China, as we shall note in § 4 of this chapter. Considerable fluctuations of climate had also been going on in the first and second centuries, producing stresses and shiftings of population, whose force historians have still to appraise. But before we go on to tell of the irruptions of the barbarians and the attempts of such later emperors as Diocletian (284 A.D.) and Constantine the Great (312 A.D.) to hold together the heaving and splitting vessel of the state, we must describe something of the conditions of human life in the Roman Empire during its two centuries of prosperity.

§ 2

The impatient reader of history may be disposed to count the two centuries of order between 27 B.C. and 180 A.D. as among the wasted opportunities of mankind. It was an age of spending rather than of creation, an age of architecture and trade in which the rich grew richer and the poor poorer and the soul and spirit of man decayed. Looked at superficially, as a man might have looked at it from an aeroplane a couple of thousand feet in the air, there was a considerable flourish of prosperity. Everywhere, from York to Cyrene and from Lisbon to Antioch, he would have noted large and well-built cities, with temples, theatres, amphitheatres, markets, and the like; thousands of such cities, supplied by great aqueducts and served by splendid high roads, whose stately remains astonish us to this day. He would have noted an abundant cultivation, and have soared too high to discover that this cultivation was the grudging work of slaves. Upon the Mediterranean and the Red Sea a considerable traffic would be visible; and the sight of two ships alongside each other would not at that altitude reveal the fact that one was a pirate and plundering the other.

And even if the observer came down to a closer scrutiny, there would still be much accumulated improvement to note. There had been a softening of manners and a general refinement since the days of Julius Cæsar. With this there had been a real increase of humane feeling. During the period of the Antonines, laws for the protection of slaves from extreme cruelty came into existence, and it was no longer permissible to sell them to the gladiatorial schools. Not only were the cities outwardly more splendidly built, but within the homes of the wealthy there had been great advances in the art of decoration. The gross feasting, animal indulgence, and vulgar display of the earlier days of Roman prosperity were now tempered by a certain refinement. Dress had become richer, finer, and more beautiful. There was a great trade in silk with remote China, for the mulberry tree and the silkworm had not yet begun to move west. By the time silk had ended its long and varied journey to Rome it was worth its weight in gold. Yet it was used abundantly, and there was a steady flow of the precious metals eastward in exchange. There had been very considerable advances in gastronomy and the arts of entertainment. Petronius describes a feast given by a wealthy man under the early Cæsars, a remarkable succession of courses, some delicious, some amazing, exceeding anything that even the splendours and imagination of modern New York could produce; and the festival was varied by music and by displays of tight-rope dancing, juggling, Homeric recitations, and the like. There was a considerable amount of what we may describe as "rich men's culture" throughout the empire. Books were far more plentiful than they had been before the time of the Cæsars. Men prided themselves upon their libraries, even when the cares and responsibilities of property made them too busy to give their literary treasures much more than a passing examination. The knowledge of Greek spread eastward and of Latin westward, and if the prominent men of this or that British or Gallic city lacked any profound Greek culture themselves, they could always turn to some slave or other, whose learning had been guaranteed of the highest quality by the slave-dealer, to supply the deficiency.

The generation of Cato had despised Greeks and the Greek language, but now all that was changed. The prestige of Greek learning of an approved and settled type was as high in the Rome of Antoninus Pius as it was in the Oxford and Cambridge of Victorian England. The Greek scholar received the same mixture of unintelligent deference and practical contempt. There was a very considerable amount of Greek scholarship, and of written criticism and commentary. Indeed there was so great an admiration for Greek letters as almost completely to destroy the Greek spirit; and the recorded observations of Aristotle were valued so highly as to preclude any attempt to imitate his organization of further inquiry. It is noteworthy that while Aristotle in the original Greek fell like seed upon stony soil in the Roman world, he was, in Syrian and Arabic translations, immensely stimulating to the Arabic civilization of a thousand years later. Nor were the æsthetic claims of Latin neglected in this heyday of Greek erudition. As Greece had her epics and so forth, the Romans felt that they too must have their epics. The age of Augustus was an age of imitative literature. Virgil in the Æneid set himself modestly but resolutely, and with an elegant sort of successfulness, to parallel Homer, just as Lord Tennyson, the poet laureate of Queen Victoria, using the mediæval literature about King Arthur as his material, did a similar service for Great Britain in his *Idylls of the King*.

All this wide-spread culture of the wealthy householder is to the credit of the early Roman Empire, and Gibbon makes the most of it in the sunny review of the age of the Antonines with which he opens his *Decline and Fall of the Roman Empire*. His design for that great work demanded a prelude of splendour and tranquillity. But he was far too shrewd and subtle not to qualify his apparent approval of the conditions he describes. "Under the Roman Empire," he writes, "the labour of an industrious and ingenious people was variously but incessantly employed in the service of the rich. In their dress, their table, their houses, and their furniture, the favourites of fortune united every refinement of convenience, of elegance, and of splendour, whatever could soothe their pride, or gratify their sensuality. Such refinements, under the odious name of luxury, have been severely arraigned by the moralists of every age; and it might perhaps be more conducive to the virtue, as well as happiness, of mankind, if all possessed the necessaries, and none the superfluities of life. But in the present imperfect condition of society, luxury, though it may proceed from vice or folly, seems to be the only means that can correct the unequal distribution of property. The diligent mechanic and the skilful artist, who have obtained no share in the division of the earth, receive a voluntary tax from the possessors of land; and the latter are prompted, by a sense of interest, to improve those estates, with whose produce they may purchase additional pleasure. This operation, the particular effects of which are felt in every society, acted with much more diffuse energy in the Roman world. The provinces would soon have been exhausted of their wealth, if the manufactures and commerce of luxury had not insensibly restored to the industrious subjects the sums which were exacted from them by the arms and authority of Rome." And so on, with a sting of satire in every fold of the florid description.

If we look a little more widely than a hovering aeroplane can do at the movement of races upon the earth, or a little more closely than an inspection of streets, amphitheatres, and banquets goes, into the souls and thoughts of men, we shall find that this impressive display of material prosperity is merely the shining garment of a polity blind to things without and things within, and blind to the future. If, for instance, we compare the two centuries of Roman ascendancy and opportunity, the first and second centuries A.D., with the two centuries of Greek and Hellenic life beginning about 466 B.C. with the supremacy of Pericles in Athens, we are amazed by—we cannot call it an inferiority, it is a complete absence of science. The incuriousness of the Roman rich and the Roman rulers was more massive and monumental even than their architecture.

In one field of knowledge particularly we might have expected the Romans to have been alert and enterprising, and that was geography. Their political interests demanded a steadfast inquiry into the state of affairs beyond their frontiers, and yet that inquiry was never made. There is practically no literature of Roman travel beyond the imperial limits, no such keen and curious accounts as Herodotus gives of the Scythians, the Africans, and the like. There is nothing in Latin to compare with the early descriptions of India and Siberia that are to be found in Chinese. The Roman legions went at one time into Scotland, yet there remains no really intelligent account of Picts or Scots, much less any glance at the seas beyond. Such explorations as those of Hanno or Pharaoh Necho seem to have been altogether beyond the scope of the Roman imagination. It is probable that after the destruction of Carthage the amount of shipping that went out into the Atlantic through the Straits of Gibraltar fell to inconsiderable proportions. Still more impossible in this world of vulgar wealth, enslaved intelligence, and bureaucratic rule was any further development of the astronomy and physiography of Alexandria. The Romans do not seem even to have inquired what manner of men wove the silk and prepared the spices or collected the amber and the pearls that came into their markets. Yet the channels of inquiry were open and easy; pathways led in every direction to the most convenient "jumping-off places" for explorers it is possible to imagine.

"The most remote countries of the ancient world were ransacked to supply the pomp and delicacy of Rome. The forests of Scythia afforded some valuable furs. Amber was brought overland from the shores of the Baltic to the Danube, and the barbarians were astonished at the price which they received in exchange for so useless a commodity. There was a considerable demand for Babylonian carpets and other manufactures of the East; but the most important branch of foreign trade was carried on with Arabia and India. Every year, about the time of the summer solstice, a fleet of a hundred and twenty vessels sailed from Myos-hormos, a port of Egypt on the Red Sea. By the periodical assistance of the monsoons, they traversed the ocean in about forty days. The coast of Malabar, or the island of Ceylon, was the usual term of their navigation, and it was in those markets that the merchants from the more remote countries of Asia expected their arrival. The return of the fleet to Egypt was fixed to the months of December or January, and as soon as their rich cargo had been transported, on the backs of camels, from the Red Sea to the Nile, and had descended that river as far as Alexandria, it was poured, without delay, into the capital of the empire."[1]

Yet Rome was content to feast, exact, grow rich, and watch its gladiatorial shows without the slightest attempt to learn anything of India, China, Persia or Scythia, Buddha or Zoroaster, or about the Huns, the Negroes, the people of Scandinavia, or the secrets of the western sea.

When we realize the uninspiring quality of the social atmosphere which made this indifference possible, we are able to account for the failure of Rome during its age of opportunity to develop any physical or chemical science, and as a consequence to gain any increased control over matter. Most of the physicians in Rome were Greeks and many of them slaves—for the Roman wealthy did not even understand that a bought mind is a spoilt mind. Yet this was not due to any want of natural genius among the Roman people; it was due entirely to their social and economic conditions. From the Middle Ages to the present day Italy has produced a great number of brilliant scientific men. And one of the most shrewd and inspired of scientific writers was an Italian, Lucretius, who lived between the time of Marius and Julius Cæsar (about 100 B.C. to about 55 B.C.). This amazing man was of the quality of Leonardo da Vinci (also an Italian) or Newton. He wrote a long Latin poem about the processes of Nature, *De Rerum Natura*, in which he guessed with astonishing insight about the constitution of matter and about the early history of mankind. Osborn in his *Old Stone Age* quotes with admiration long passages from Lucretius about primitive man, so good and true are they to-day. But this was an individual display, a seed that bore no fruit. Roman science was stillborn, into a suffocating atmosphere of vile wealth and military oppression. The true figure to represent the classical Roman attitude to science is not Lucretius, but that Roman soldier who hacked Archimedes to death at the storming of Syracuse.

And if physical and biological science wilted and died on the stony soil of Roman prosperity, political and social science never had a chance to germinate. Political discussion would have been treason to the emperor, social or economic inquiry would have threatened the rich. So Rome, until disaster fell upon her, never examined into her own social health, never questioned the ultimate value of her hard officialism.

[1] Gibbon.

Consequently, there was no one who realized the gravity of her failure to develop any intellectual imagination to hold her empire together, any general education in common ideas that would make men fight and work for the empire as men will fight and work for a dear possession. But the rulers of the Roman Empire did not want their citizens to fight for anything in any spirit at all. The rich had eaten the heart out of their general population, and they were content with the meal they had made. The legions were filled with Germans, Britons, Numidians, and the like; and until the very end the wealthy Romans thought they could go on buying barbarians to defend them against the enemy without and the rebel poor within. How little was done in education by the Romans is shown by an account of what was done. Says Mr. H. Stuart Jones,[1] "Julius Cæsar bestowed Roman citizenship on 'teachers of the liberal arts'; Vespasian endowed professorships of Greek and Latin oratory at Rome; and later emperors, especially Antoninus Pius, extended the same benefits to the provinces. Local enterprise and munificence were also devoted to the cause of education; we learn from the correspondence of the younger Pliny that public schools were founded in the towns of Northern Italy. But though there was a wide diffusion of knowledge under the empire, there was no true intellectual progress. Augustus, it is true, gathered about him the most brilliant writers of his time, and the debut of the new monarchy coincided with the Golden Age of Roman literature; but this was of brief duration, and the beginnings of the Christian era saw the triumph of classicism and the first steps in the decline which awaits all literary movements which look to the past rather than the future."

There is a diagnosis of the intellectual decadence of the age in a treatise upon the sublime by a Greek writer who wrote somewhen in the second, third, or fourth century A.D., and who may possibly have been Longinus Philologus,[2] which states very distinctly one manifest factor in the mental sickness of the Roman world. He is cited by Gibbon: "The sublime Longinus, who, in somewhat a later period and in the court of a Syrian queen, preserved the spirit of ancient Athens, observes and laments the degeneracy of his contemporaries, which debased their sentiments, enervated their courage, and depressed their talents. 'In the same manner,' says he, 'as some children always remain pigmies, whose infant limbs have been too closely confined, thus our tender minds, fettered by the prejudices and habits of a just servitude, are unable to expand themselves or to attain that well-proportioned greatness which we admire in the ancients; who, living under a popular government, wrote with all the same freedom as they acted.'"

But this critic grasped only one aspect of the restraints upon mental activity. The leading-strings that kept the Roman mind in a permanent state of infantilism constituted a double servitude; they were economic as well as political. The account Gibbon gives of the life and activities of a certain Herodes Atticus, who lived in the time of Hadrian, shows just how little was the share of the ordinary citizen in the outward magnificence of the time. This Atticus had an immense fortune, and he amused himself by huge architectural benefactions to various cities. Athens was given a racecourse, and a theatre of cedar, curiously carved, was set up there to the memory of his wife; a theatre was built at Corinth, a racecourse was given to Delphi, baths to Thermopylæ, an aqueduct to Canusium, and so on and so on. One is struck by the spectacle of a world of slaves and common people who were not consulted and over whose heads, without any participation on their part, this rich man indulged in his displays of "taste."[3] Numerous inscriptions in Greece and Asia still preserve the name of Herodes Atticus, "patron and benefactor," who ranged about the empire as though it was his private garden, commemorating himself by these embellishments. He did not confine himself to splendid buildings. He was also a philosopher, though none of his wisdom has survived. He had a large villa near Athens, and there philosophers were welcome guests so long as they convinced their patron of the soundness of their pretensions, received his discourses with respect, and did not offend him by insolent controversy.

The world, it is evident, was not progressing during these two centuries of Roman prosperity. But was it happy in its stagna-

[1] *Encyclopædia Britannica*, article "Rome."

[2] See *Encyclopædia Britannica*, article "Longinus." The Syrian queen referred to by Gibbon is Zenobia. Longinus was put to death by Aurelian. See ch. xxxii., § 2.

[3] The natural result of a plutocratic rule above was a vigorous trade-unionism intent only on short hours and high wages below, and as indifferent as the rich to the common weal. See Hubbard's *Fate of Empires*, a very stimulating book, differing widely in its spirit and conclusions from those of the writer.

A ROMAN TRIUMPH

By Frank W. W. Topham, A.R.I., R.O.I.

Permission, Museum and Art Gallery Committee, Leicester Corporation

"Rome was content to feast, exact, grow rich, watch its shews . . . . yet the great mass of human beings in the Empire was probably very acutely miserable beneath its outward magnificence."

tion? There are signs of a very unmistakable sort that the great mass of human beings in the empire, a mass numbering something between a hundred and a hundred and fifty millions, was not happy, was probably very acutely miserable, beneath its outward magnificence. True there were no great wars and conquests within the empire, little of famine or fire or sword to afflict mankind; but, on the other hand, there was a terrible restraint by government, and still more by the property of the rich, upon the free activities of nearly everyone. Life for the great majority who were neither rich nor official, nor the womankind and the parasites of the rich and official, must have been laborious, tedious, and lacking in interest and freedom to a degree that a modern mind can scarcely imagine.

Three things in particular may be cited to sustain the opinion that this period was a period of widespread unhappiness. The first of these is the extraordinary apathy of the population to political events. They saw one upstart pretender to empire succeed another with complete indifference. Such things did not seem to matter to them; hope had gone. When presently the barbarians poured into the empire, there was nothing but the legions to face them. There was no popular uprising against them at all. Everywhere the barbarians must have been outnumbered if only the people had resisted. But the people did not resist. It is manifest that to the bulk of its inhabitants the Roman Empire did not seem to be a thing worth fighting for. To the slaves and common people the barbarian probably seemed to promise more freedom and less indignity than the pompous rule of the imperial official and grinding employment by the rich. The looting and burning of palaces and an occasional massacre did not shock the folk of the Roman underworld as it shocked the wealthy and cultured people to whom we owe such accounts as we have of the breaking down of the imperial system. Great numbers of slaves and common people probably joined the barbarians, who knew little of racial or patriotic prejudices, and were openhanded to any promising recruit. No doubt in many cases the population found that the barbarian was a worse infliction even than the tax-gatherer and the slave-driver. But that discovery came too late for resistance or the restoration of the old order.

And as a second symptom that points to the same conclusion that life was hardly worth living for the poor and the slaves and the majority of people during the age of the Antonines, we must reckon the steady depopulation of the empire. People refused to have children. They did so, we suggest, because their homes were not safe from oppression, because in the case of slaves there was no security that the husband and wife would not be separated, because there was no pride nor reasonable hope in children any more. In modern states the great breeding-ground has always been the agricultural countryside where there is a more or less secure peasantry; but under the Roman Empire the peasant and the small cultivator was either a worried debtor, or he was held in a network of restraints that made him a spiritless serf, or he had been ousted altogether by the gang production of slaves.

A third indication that this outwardly flourishing period was one of deep unhappiness and mental distress for vast multitudes, is to be found in the spread of new religious movements throughout the population. We have seen how in the case of the little country of Judea a whole nation may be infected by the persuasion that life is unsatisfactory and *wrong*, and that something is needed to set it right. The mind of the Jews, as we know, had crystallized about the idea of the Promise of the One True God and the coming of a Saviour or Messiah. Rather different ideas from these were spreading through the Roman Empire. They were but varying answers to one universal question: "What must we do for salvation?" A frequent and natural consequence of disgust with life as it is, is to throw the imagination forward to an after-life, which is to redeem all the miseries and injustices of this one. The belief in such compensation is a great opiate for present miseries. Egyptian religion had long been saturated with anticipations of immortality, and we have seen how central was that idea to the cult of Serapis and Isis at Alexandria. The ancient mysteries of Demeter and Orpheus, the mysteries of the Mediterranean race, revived and made a sort of *theocrasia* with these new cults.

A second great religious movement was Mithraism, a development of Zoroastrianism, a religion of very ancient Aryan origin, traceable back to the Indo-Iranian people before they split into Persians and Hindus. We cannot here examine its mysteries in any detail.[1] Mithras was a god of light, a Sun of Righteousness, and in the shrines of the cult he was always represented as slaying a sacred bull whose blood was the seed of life.

[1] See Legge, *Forerunners and Rivals of Christianity.*

Suffice it that, complicated with many added ingredients, this worship of Mithras came into the Roman Empire about the time of Pompey the Great, and began to spread very widely under the Cæsars and Antonines. Like the Isis religion, it promised immortality. Its followers were mainly slaves, soldiers, and distressed people. In its methods of worship, in the burning of candles before the altar and so forth, it had a certain superficial resemblance to the later developments of the ritual of the third great religious movement in the Roman world, Christianity.

Christianity also was a doctrine of immortality and salvation, and it too spread at first chiefly among the lowly and unhappy. Christianity has been denounced by modern writers as a "slave religion." It was. It took the slaves and the downtrodden, and it gave them hope and restored their self-respect, so that they stood up for righteousness like men and faced persecution and torment. But of the origins and quality of Christianity we will tell more fully in a later chapter.

§ 3

We have already shown reason for our statement that the Roman imperial system was a very unsound political growth indeed. It is absurd to write of its statecraft; it had none. At its best it had a bureaucratic administration which kept the peace of the world for a time and failed altogether to secure it.

Let us note here the main factors in its failure.

The clue to all its failure lies in the absence of any free mental activity and any organization for the increase, development, and application of knowledge. It respected wealth and it despised science. It gave government to the rich, and imagined that wise men could be bought and bargained for in the slave markets when they were needed. It was, therefore, a colossally ignorant and unimaginative empire. It foresaw nothing.

It had no strategic foresight, because it was blankly ignorant of geography and ethnology. It knew nothing of the conditions of Russia, Central Asia, and the East. It was content to keep the Rhine and Danube as its boundaries, and to make no effort to Romanize Germany. But we need only look at the map of Europe and Asia showing the Roman Empire to see that a willing and incorporated Germany was absolutely essential to the life and security of Western Europe. Excluded, Germany became a wedge that needed only the impact of the Hunnish hammer to split up the whole system.

Moreover, this neglect to push the boundaries northward to the Baltic left that sea and the North Sea as a region of experiment and training and instruction in seamanship for the Northmen of Scandinavia, Denmark, and the Frisian coast. But Rome went on its way quite stupidly, oblivious to the growth of a newer and more powerful piracy in the north.

The same unimaginative quality made the Romans leave the seaways of the Mediterranean undeveloped. When presently the barbarians pressed down to the warm water, we read of no swift transport of armies from Spain or Africa or Asia to the rescue of Italy and the Adriatic coasts. Instead, we see the Vandals becoming masters of the western Mediterranean without so much as a naval battle.

The Romans had been held at the Euphrates by an array of mounted archers. It was clear that as the legion was organized it was useless in wide open country, and it should have been equally clear that sooner or later the mounted nomads of east Germany, south Russia or Parthia were bound to try conclusions with the empire. But the Romans, two hundred years after Cæsar's time, were still marching about, the same drilled and clanking cohorts they had always been, easily ridden round and shot to pieces. The empire had learnt nothing even from Carrhæ.

The incapacity of the Roman imperialism for novelty in methods of transport again is amazing. It was patent that their power and unity depended upon the swift movement of troops and supplies from one part of the empire to another. The republic made magnificent roads; the empire never improved upon them. Four hundred years before the Antonines, Hero of Alexandria had made the first steam-engine. Beautiful records of such beginnings of science were among the neglected treasures of the rich men's libraries throughout the imperial domains. They were seed lying on stony ground. The armies and couriers of Marcus Aurelius drudged along the roads exactly as the armies of Scipio Africanus had done three centuries before them.

The Roman writers were always lamenting the effeminacy of the age. It was their favourite cant. They recognized that the free men of the forest and steppes and desert were harder and more desperate fighters than their citizens, but the natural corollary of developing the industrial power of their accumulations of population to make a countervailing equipment never entered their heads. Instead they took the barbarians into their legions, taught them the arts of war, marched them about the empire, and returned them, with their lesson well learnt, to their own people.

In view of these obvious negligences, it is no wonder that the Romans disregarded that more subtle thing, the soul of the empire, altogether, and made no effort to teach or train or win its common people into any conscious participation with its life. Such teaching or training would indeed have run counter to all the ideas of the rich men and the imperial officials. They had made a tool of religion; science, literature, and education they had entrusted to the care of slaves, who were bred and trained and sold like dogs or horses; ignorant, pompous, and base, the Roman adventurers of finance and property who created the empire, lorded it with a sense of the utmost security while their destruction gathered without the empire and within.

By the second and third centuries A.D. the overtaxed and overstrained imperial machine was already staggering towards its downfall.

§ 4[1]

And now it is necessary, if we are to understand clearly the true situation of the Roman Empire, to turn our eyes to the world beyond its northern and eastern borders, the world of the plains, that stretches, with scarcely a break, from Holland across Germany and Russia to the mountains of Central Asia and Mongolia, and to give a little attention to the parallel empire in China that was now consolidating and developing a far tougher and more enduring moral and intellectual unity than the Romans ever achieved.

"It is the practice," says Mr. E. H. Parker, "even amongst our most highly educated men in Europe, to deliver sonorous sentences about being 'masters of the world,' 'bringing all nations of the earth under her sway,' and so on, when in reality only some corner of the Mediterranean is involved or some ephemeral sally into Persia and Gaul. Cyrus and Alexander, Darius and Xerxes, Cæsar and Pompey, all made very interesting excursions, but they were certainly not on a larger scale or charged with greater human interest than the campaigns which were going on at the other end of Asia. Western civilization possessed much in art and science for which China never cared, but, on the other hand, the Chinese developed a historical and critical literature, a courtesy of demeanour, a luxury of clothing, and an administrative system of which Europe might have been proud. In one word, the history of the Far East is quite as interesting as that of the Far West. It only requires to be able to read it. When we brush away contemptuously from our notice the tremendous events which took place on the plains of Tartary, we must not blame the Chinese too much for declining to interest themselves in the doings of what to them appear insignificant states dotted round the Mediterranean and Caspian, which, at this time, was practically all the world of which we knew in Europe." [2]

We have already mentioned (in chap. xvi. and elsewhere) the name of Shi-Hwang-Ti, who consolidated an empire much smaller, indeed, than the present limits of China, but still very great and populous, spreading from the valleys of the Hwang-ho and the Yang Tse. He became king of Ch'in in 246 B.C. and emperor in 220 B.C., and he reigned until 210 B.C., and during this third of a century he effected much the same work of consolidation that Augustus Cæsar carried out in Rome two centuries later. At his death there was dynastic trouble for four years, and then (206 B.C.) a fresh dynasty, the Han, established itself and ruled for two hundred and twenty-nine years. The opening quarter century of the Christian era was troubled by a usurper; then what is called the Later Han Dynasty recovered power and ruled for another century and a half, until China, in the time of the Antonines, was so devastated by an eleven-year pestilence as to fall into disorder. This same pestilence, we may note, also helped to produce a century of confusion in the Western world (see § 1). But altogether until this happened, for more than four hundred years Central China was generally

[1] No really good, full, and popular descriptive history, with maps and illustrations, of early and medieval China, nor of the Mongol (Hun) and Turkish peoples, seems to exist in the English language. The writer has consulted Skrine and Ross's *Heart of Asia*, Hirth's *Ancient History of China*, S. Wells Williams' *History of China*, *A Thousand Years of the Tartars*, by E. H. Parker, H. H. Howorth's *History of the Mongols*, and has found much useful material scattered through Ratzel and Helmolt. He has later on made a useful section from Watters' translation and commentary upon the *Travels of Yuan Chwang*, supplemented by the *Life of Yuan Chwang*, edited by L. Cranmer Byng. Yule's edition of Marco Polo has also been a very inspiring source of material.

[2] E. H. Parker, *A Thousand Years of the Tartars*.

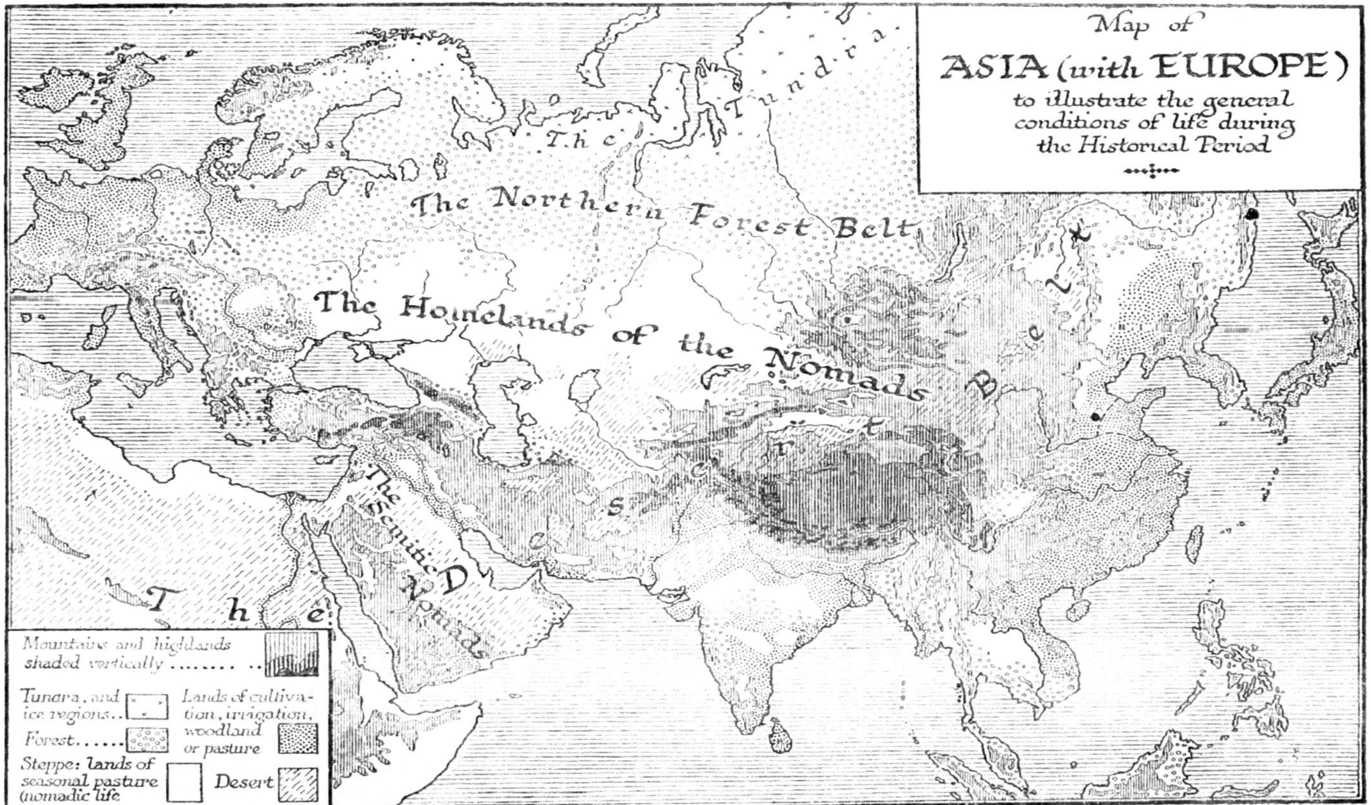
Map of
ASIA (with EUROPE)
to illustrate the general
conditions of life during
the Historical Period
The Tundra
The Northern Forest Belt
The Homelands of the Nomads
Belt
The Semitic Nomads
The Desert
Mountains and highlands shaded vertically
Tundra, and ice regions
Lands of cultivation, irrigation, woodland or pasture
Forest
Steppe: lands of seasonal pasture (nomadic life
Desert

at peace, and on the whole well governed, a cycle of strength and prosperity unparalleled by anything in the experience of the Western world.

Only the first of the Han monarchs continued the policy of Shi-Hwang-Ti against the *literati*. His successor restored the classics, for the old separatist tradition was broken, and in the uniformity of learning throughout the empire lay, he saw, the cement of Chinese unity. While the Roman world was still blind to the need of any universal mental organization, the Han emperors were setting up a uniform system of education and of literary degrees throughout China that has maintained the intellectual solidarity of that great and always expanding country into modern times. The bureaucrats of Rome were of the most miscellaneous origins and traditions; the bureaucrats of China were, and are still, made in the same mould, all members of one tradition. Since the Han days China has experienced great vicissitudes of political fortune, but they have never changed her fundamental character; she has been divided, but she has always recovered her unity; she has been conquered, and she has always absorbed and assimilated her conquerors.

But from our present point of view, the most important consequences of this consolidation of China under Shi-Hwang-Ti and the Hans was in its reaction upon the unsettled tribes of the northern and western border of China. Throughout the disordered centuries before the time of Shi-Hwang-Ti, the Hiung-nu or Huns had occupied Mongolia and large portions of Northern China, and had raided freely into China and interfered freely in Chinese politics. The new power and organization of the Chinese civilization began to change this state of affairs for good and all.

We have already, in our first account of Chinese beginnings, noted the existence of these Huns. It is necessary now to explain briefly who and what they were. Even in using this word Hun as a general equivalent for the Hiung-nu, we step on to controversial ground. In our accounts of the development of the Western world we have had occasion to name the Scythians, and to explain the difficulty of distinguishing clearly between Cimmerians, Sarmatians, Medes, Persians, Parthians, Goths, and other more or less nomadic, more or less Aryan peoples who drifted to and fro in a great arc between the Danube and Central Asia. While sections of the Aryans were moving south and acquiring and developing civilization, these other Aryan peoples were developing mobility and nomadism; they were learning the life of the tent, the wagon, and the herd. They were learning also to use milk as a food basis, and were probably becoming less agricultural, less disposed to take even snatch crops, than they had been. Their development was being aided by a slow change in climate that was replacing the swamps and forests and parklands of South Russia and Central Asia by steppes, by wide grazing lands that is, which favoured a healthy, unsettled life, and necessitated an annual movement between summer and winter pasture. These peoples had only the lowest political forms; they split up, they mingled together; the various races had identical social habits; and so it is that the difficulty, the impossibility of sharp distinctions between them arises. Now the case of the Mongolian races to the north and north-west of the Chinese civilization is very parallel. There can be little doubt that the Hiung-nu, the Huns, and the later people called the Mongols, were all very much the same people, and that the Turks and Tartars presently branched off from this same drifting Mongolian population. Kalmucks and Buriats are later developments of the same strain. Here we shall favour the use of the word "Hun" as a sort of general term for these tribes, just as we have been free and wide in our use of "Scythian" in the West.

The consolidation of China was a very serious matter for these Hunnish peoples. Hitherto their overflow of population had gone adventuring southward into the disorders of divided China as water goes into a sponge. Now they found a wall built against them, a firm government, and disciplined armies cutting them off from the grass plains. And though the wall held them back, it did not hold back the Chinese. They were increasing and multiplying through these centuries of peace, and as they increased and multiplied, they spread steadily with house and plough wherever the soil permitted. They spread westward into Tibet and northward and north-westwardly, perhaps to the edge of the Gobi desert. They spread into the homes and pasturing and hunting-grounds of the Hunnish nomads, exactly as the white people of the United States spread westward into the hunting-grounds of the Red Indians. And in spite of raid and massacre, they were just as invincible because they had the pressure of numbers and a strong avenging government behind them. Even without the latter support the cultivating civilization of China has enormous powers of permeation and extension. It has spread slowly and continuously for three thousand years. It is spreading in Manchuria and Siberia to-day. It roots deeply where it spreads.

Partly the Huns were civilized and assimilated by the Chinese. The more northerly Huns were checked and their superabundant energies were turned westward. The southern Huns were merged into the imperial population.

If the reader will examine the map of Central Asia, he will see that very great mountain barriers separate the Southern, Western, and Eastern peoples of Asia. (But he should be wary of forming his ideas from a map upon Mercator's projection, which enormously exaggerates the areas and distances of Northern Asia and Siberia.) He will find that from the central mountain masses three great mountain systems radiate eastward; the Himalayas going south-eastward, south of Tibet, the Kuen Lun eastward, north of Tibet, and the Thien Shan north-eastward to join the Altai mountains. Further to the north is the great plain, still steadily thawing and drying. Between the Thien Shan and the Kuen Lun is an area, the Tarim Basin (=roughly Eastern Turkestan), of rivers that never reach the sea but end in swamps and intermittent lakes. This basin was much more fertile in the past than it is now. The mountain barrier to the west of this Tarim Basin is high, but not forbidding; there are many practicable routes downward into Western Turkestan, and it is possible to travel either along the northern foothills of the Kuen Lun or by the Tarim valley westward from China to Kashgar (where the roads converge), and so over the mountains to Kokand, Samarkand, and Bokhara. Here then is the natural meeting-place in history of Aryan and Mongolian. Here or round by the sea.

We have already noted how Alexander the Great came to one side of the barrier in 329 B.C. High among the mountains of Turkestan a lake preserves his name. Indeed, so living is the tradition of his great raid, that almost any stone ruin in Central Asia is still ascribed to "Iskander." After this brief glimpse, the light of history upon this region fades again, and when it becomes bright once more it is on the eastern and not upon the western side. Far away to the east Shi-Hwang-ti had routed the Huns and walled them out of China proper. A portion of these people remained in the north of China, a remnant which was destined to amalgamate with Chinese life under the Hans, but a considerable section had turned westward and (second and first centuries B.C.) driven before them a kindred people called the Yueh-Chi, driving them from the eastern to the western extremity of the Kuen Lun, and at last right over the barrier into the once Aryan region of Western Turkestan.[1] These Yueh-Chi conquered the slightly Hellenized kingdom of Bactria, and mixed with Aryan people there. Later on these Yueh-Chi became, or were merged with Aryan elements into, a people called the Indo-Scythians, who went on down the Khyber Pass and conquered northern portions of India as far as Benares (100–150 A.D.), wiping out the last vestiges of Hellenic rule in India. This big splash over of the Mongolian races westward was probably not the first of such splashes, but it is the first recorded splash. In the rear of the Yueh-Chi were the Huns, and in the rear of the Huns and turning them now northward was the vigorous Han Dynasty of China. In the reign of the greatest of the Han monarchs, Wu-Ti (140–86 B.C.), the Huns had been driven northward out of the whole of Eastern Turkestan or subjugated, the Tarim Basin swarmed with Chinese settlers, and caravans were going over westward with silk and lacquer and jade to trade for the gold and silver of Armenia and Rome.

The splash over of the Yueh-Chi is recorded, but it is fairly evident that much westward movement of sections of the Hunnish peoples is not recorded. From 200 B.C. to 200 A.D. the Chinese Empire maintained a hard, resolute, advancing front towards nomadism, and the surplus of the nomads drifted steadily west. There was no such settling down behind a final frontier on the part of the Chinese as we see in the case of the Romans at the Rhine and Danube. The drift of the nomads before this Chinese thrust, century by century, turned southward at first towards Bactria. The Parthians of the first century B.C. probably mingled Scythian and Mongolian elements. The "singing arrows" that destroyed the army of Crassus came, it would seem, originally from the Altai and the Thien Shan. After the first century B.C. the line of greater attraction and least resistance lay for a time towards the north of the Caspian. In a century or so all the country known as Western Turkestan was "Mongolized," and so it remains to this day. A second great

[1] Even in Eastern Turkestan there are still strong evidences of Nordic blood in the physiognomy of the people. See Ella and Percy Sykes, *Through Deserts and Oases of Central Asia.*

thrust by China began about 75 A.D., and accelerated the westward drift of the nomads. In 102, Pan Chau, a great Chinese general, was sending explorers from his advanced camp upon the Caspian (or, as some authorities say, the Persian Gulf) to learn particulars of the Roman power. But their reports decided him not to proceed.

By the first century A.D. nomadic Mongolian peoples are in evidence upon the eastern boundaries of Europe, already greatly mixed with Aryan nomads and with uprooted Aryan elements from the Caspian-Pamir region. There are Hunnish peoples established between the Caspian Sea and the Urals. West of them were the Alans, probably also a Mongolian people with Aryan elements; they had fought against Pompey the Great when he was in Armenia in 65 B.C. These are as yet the furthest westward peoples of the new Mongolian advance, and they made no further westward push until the fourth century A.D. To the north-west the Finns, a Mongolian people, had long been established as far west as the Baltic.

West of the Huns, beyond the Don, there were Aryan tribes, the Goths. These Goths had spread south-eastward from their region of origin in Scandinavia. They were a Teutonic people, and we have already marked them crossing the Baltic in the map on page 148. They continued to move south-eastward across Russia, using the rivers and never forgetting their Baltic watercraft. No doubt they assimilated much Scythian population as they spread down to the Black Sea. In the first century A.D. they were in two main divisions, the Ostrogoths, the east Goths, who were between the Don and the Dnieper, and the Visigoths, or West Goths, west of the Dnieper. During the first century there was an air of quiescence over the great plains, but population was accumulating and the tribes were fermenting. The second and third centuries seem to have been a phase of comparatively moist seasons and abundant grass. Presently in the fourth and fifth centuries the weather grew drier and the grass became scanty, and the nomads stirred afresh.

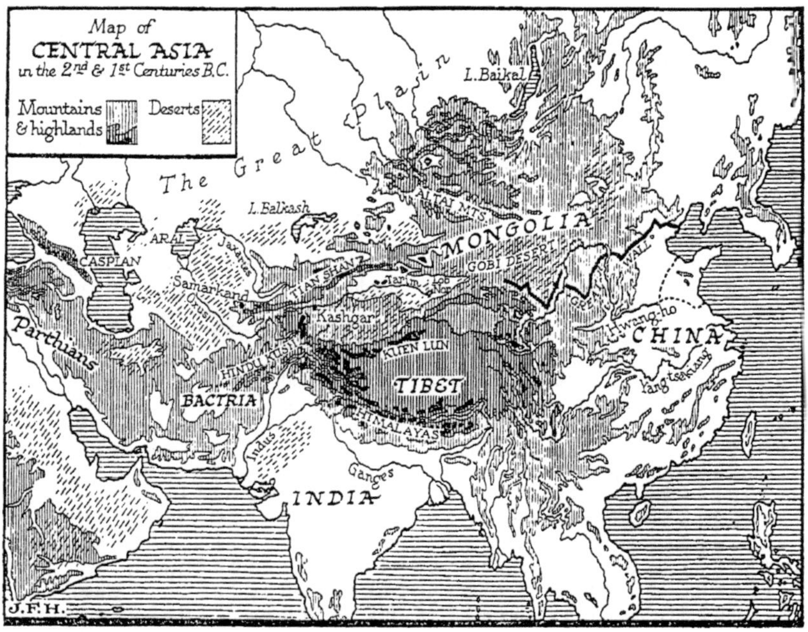

But it is interesting to note that in the opening century of the Christian era, the Chinese Empire was strong enough to expel and push off from itself the surplus of this Mongolian nomadism to the north of it which presently conquered North India and gathered force and mingled with Aryan nomadism, and fell at last like an avalanche upon the weak-backed Roman Empire.

Before we go on to tell of the blows that now began to fall upon the Roman Empire and of the efforts of one or two great men to arrest the collapse, we may say a few words about the habits and quality of these westward-drifting barbaric Mongolian peoples who were now spreading from the limits of China towards the Black and Baltic Seas. It is still the European custom to follow the lead of the Roman writers and write of these Huns and their associates as of something incredibly destructive and cruel. But such accounts as we have from the Romans were written in periods of panic, and the Roman could lie about his enemies with a freedom and vigour that must arouse the envy even of the modern propagandist. He could talk of "Punic faith" as a byword for perfidy while committing the most abominable treacheries against Carthage, and his railing accusations of systematic cruelty against this people or that were usually the prelude and excuse for some frightful massacre or enslavement or robbery on his own part. He had quite a modern passion for self-justification. We must remember that these accounts of the savagery and frightfulness of the Huns came from a people whose chief amusement was gladiatorial shows, and whose chief method of dealing with insurrection and sedition was nailing the offender to a cross to die. From first to last the Roman Empire must have killed hundreds of thousands of men in that way. A large portion of the population of this empire that could complain of the barbarism of its assailants consisted of slaves subject practically to almost any lust or caprice at the hands of their owners. It is well to bear these facts in mind before we mourn the swamping of the Roman Empire by the barbarians as though it was an extinction of all that is fine in life by all that is black and ugly.

The facts seem to be that the Hunnish peoples were the eastern equivalent of the primitive Aryans of whom we have given an account in Chapter XV, and that, in spite of their profound racial and linguistic differences, they mixed with the nomadic and semi-nomadic residuum of the Aryan races north of the Danube and Persia very easily and successfully. Instead of killing, they enlisted and intermarried with the peoples they invaded. They had that necessary gift for all peoples destined to political predominance, tolerant assimilation. They came rather later in time, and their nomadic life was more highly developed than that of the primitive Aryans. The primitive Aryans were a forest and ox-wagon people who took to the horse later. The Hunnish peoples had grown up with the horse. Somewhen about 1,200 or 1,000 years B.C. they began to ride the horse. The bit, the saddle, the stirrup, these are not primitive things, but they are necessary if man and horse are to keep going for long stretches. It is well to bear in mind how modern a thing is riding. Altogether man has not been in the saddle for much more than three thousand years.[1] We have already noted the gradual appearance of the war-chariot, the mounted man, and finally of disciplined cavalry in this history. It was from the Mongolian regions of Asia that these things came. To this day men in Central Asia go rather in the saddle than on their proper feet. Says Ratzel,[2] "Strong, long-necked horses are found in enormous numbers on the steppes. For Mongols and Turcomans riding is not a luxury; even the Mongol shepherds tend their flocks on horseback. Children are taught to ride in early youth; and the boy of three years old often takes his first riding-lesson on a safe child's saddle and makes quick progress."

It is impossible to suppose that the Huns and the Alans could have differed very widely in character from the present nomads of the steppe regions, and nearly all observers are agreed in describing these latter as open and pleasant people. They are thoroughly honest and free-spirited. "The character of the herdsmen of Central Asia," says Ratzel,[3] "when unadulterated, is ponderous eloquence, frankness, rough good-nature, pride, but also indolence, irritability, and a tendency to vindictiveness. Their faces show a considerable share of frankness combined with amusing naïveté. . . . Their courage is rather a sudden blaze of pugnacity than cold boldness. Religious fanaticism they have none. Hospitality is universal." This is not an entirely disagreeable picture. Their personal bearing, he says further, is quieter and more dignified than that of the townsmen of Turkestan and Persia. Add to this that the nomadic life prevents any great class inequalities or any extensive development of slavery.

Of course these peoples out of Asia were totally illiterate and artistically undeveloped. But we must not suppose, on that account, that they were primitive barbarians, and that their state of life was at the level from which the agricultural civilization had long ago arisen. It was not. They too had developed, but they had developed along a different line, a line with less intellectual complication, more personal dignity perhaps, and certainly with a more intimate contact with wind and sky.

[1] See Roger Pocock, *Horses*, a very interesting and picturesque little book.

[2] *The History of Mankind*, book v., C.

[3] *Ibid.*

§ 5

The first serious irruptions of the German tribes into the Roman Empire began in the third century with the decay of the central power.[1] We will not entangle the reader here with the vexed and intricate question of the names, identity, and inter-relationships of the various Germanic tribes. Historians find great difficulties in keeping them distinct, and these difficulties are enhanced by the fact that they themselves took little care to keep themselves distinct. We find in 236 A.D. a people called the Franks breaking bounds upon the Lower Rhine, and another, the Alamanni, pouring into Alsace. A much more serious push southward was that of the Goths. We have already noted the presence of these people in South Russia, and their division by the Dnieper into Western and Eastern Goths. They had become a maritime people again upon the Black Sea—probably their traditional migration from Sweden was along the waterways, for it is still possible to row a boat, with only a few quite practicable portages, from the Baltic right across Russia to either the Black or Caspian Sea—and they had wrested the command of the eastern seas from the control of Rome. They were presently raiding the shores of Greece. They also crossed the Danube in a great land raid in 247, and defeated and killed the Emperor Decius in what is now Serbia. The province of Dacia vanished from Roman history. In 270 they were defeated at Nish in Serbia by Claudius, and in 276 they were raiding Pontus. It is characteristic of the invertebrate nature of the empire that the legions of Gaul found that the most effective method of dealing with the Franks and the Alamanni at this time was by setting up a separate emperor in Gaul and doing the job by themselves.

Then for a while the barbarians were held, and the Emperor Probus in 276 forced the Franks and the Alamanni back over the Rhine. But it is significant of the general atmosphere of insecurity created by these raids that Aurelian (270–275) fortified Rome, which had been an open and secure city for all the earlier years of the empire.

In 321 A.D. the Goths were again over the Danube, plundering what is now Serbia and Bulgaria. They were driven back by Constantine the Great, of whom we shall have more to tell in the next chapter. About the end of his reign (337 A.D.) the Vandals, a people closely kindred to the Goths, being pressed by them, obtained permission to cross the Danube into Pannonia, which is now that part of Hungary west of the river.

But by the middle of the fourth century the Hunnish people to the east were becoming aggressive again. They had long subjugated the Alani, and now they made the Ostrogoths, the east Goths, tributary. The Visigoths (or west Goths) followed the example of the Vandals, and made arrangements to cross the Danube into Roman territory. There was some dispute upon the terms of this settlement, and the Visigoths, growing fierce, assumed the offensive, and at Adrianople defeated the Emperor Valens, who was killed in this battle. They were then allowed to settle in what is now Bulgaria, and their army became nominally a Roman army, though they retained their own chiefs, the foremost of whom was Alaric. It exhibits the complete "barbarization" of the Roman empire that had already occurred, that the chief opponent of Alaric the Goth, Stilicho, was a Pannonian Vandal. The legions in Gaul were under the command of a Frank, and the Emperor Theodosius I (emp. 379–395) was a Spaniard chiefly supported by Gothic auxiliaries.

The empire was now splitting finally into an eastern (Greek-speaking) and a western (Latin-speaking) half. Theodosius the Great was succeeded by his sons Arcadius at Constantinople and Honorius at Ravenna. Alaric made a puppet of the eastern monarch and Stilicho of the western. Huns now first appear within the empire as auxiliary troops enlisted under Stilicho. In this struggle of East and West, the frontier—if we can still speak of a frontier between the unauthorized barbarian without and the barbarian in possession within—gave way. Fresh Vandals, more Goths, Alans, Suevi, marched freely westward, living upon the country. Amidst this confusion occurred a crowning event. Alaric the Goth marched down Italy, and after a short siege captured Rome (410).

By 425 or so, the Vandals (whom originally we noted in East Germany) and a portion of the Alani (whom we first mentioned in South-east Russia) had traversed Gaul and the Pyrenees, and had amalgamated and settled in the south of Spain. There were Huns in possession of Pannonia and Goths in Dalmatia. Into Bohemia and Moravia came and settled a Slavic people, the Czechs (451). In Portugal and north of the Vandals in Spain were Visigoths and Suevi. Gaul was divided among Visigoths, Franks, and Burgundians. Britain was being invaded by

[1] See *Migrations*, by Flinders Petrie, the 1906 Huxley Lecture of the Royal Anthrop. Institute.

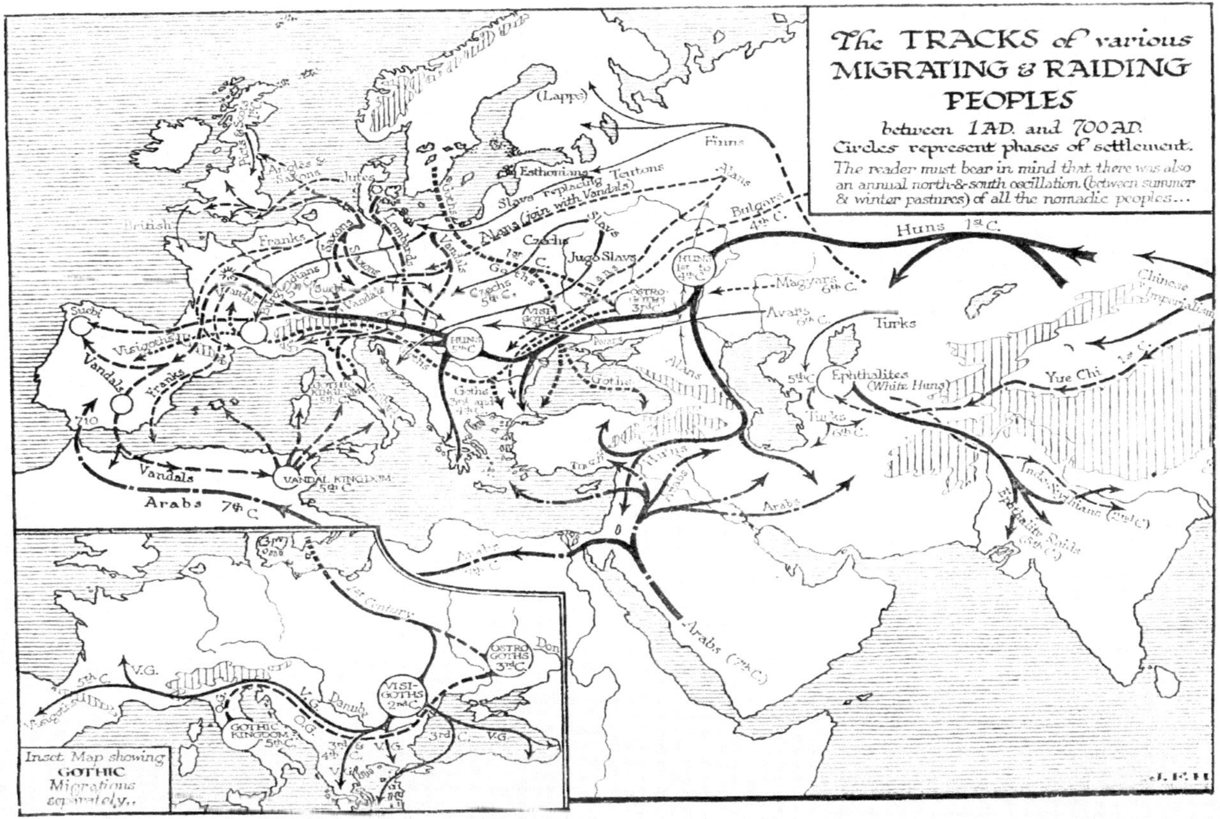
The TRACKS of various MIGRATING & RAIDING PEOPLES
between 1 A.D. and 700 A.D.
Circles represent phases of settlement.
The reader must bear in mind that there was also an annual north-&-south oscillation (between summer & winter pastures) of all the nomadic peoples...
Huns 1st C.
Chinese Imperialism
Yue Chi 1st C.
Turks
Ephthalites (White Huns)
Indo-Scythians (2nd C.)
Ephthalite Raids (6th C.)
Magyars 6th C.
Avars 6th C.
Bulgars 4th C.
Finns
Alans
Teutons
Esthonians
Slavs replacing Teutons
Alans (join with Vandals)
Czechs
Jugo Slavs
Slavs
(Lapps)
Angles & Saxons
Jutes
Picts & Scots
British
Franks
Saxons
Lombards
Vandals
Goths
Czechs 5th C.
Visigoths
Suebi
Vandal Kingdom 5th C.
Arabs 7th C.
Arabs (7th C.)
Arabs
Huns
Huns 5th C.
Huns 1st to 4th C.
Ostrogoths 3rd C.
710
Inset Map showing GOTHIC Migrations separately..
1st Century
Ostrogoths 3rd C.
Visigoths 2nd C.
Gothic Kingdom 5th C.
V.G.
O.G.
Danube
Don
J.F.H.

Low German tribes, the Jutes, Angles and Saxons, before whom the Keltic British of the south-west were flying across the sea to what is now Brittany in France. The usual date given for this invasion is 449, but it was probably earlier.[1] And as the result of intrigues between two imperial politicians, the Vandals of the south of Spain, under their king Genseric, embarked *en masse* for North Africa (429), became masters of Carthage (439), secured the mastery of the sea, raided, captured, and pillaged Rome (455), crossed into Sicily, and set up a kingdom in West Sicily, which endured there for a hundred years (up to 534). At the time of its greatest extent (477) this Vandal kingdom included also Corsica, Sardinia, and the Balearic Isles, as well as much of North Africa.

About this Vandal kingdom facts and figures are given that show very clearly the true nature of these barbarian irruptions. They were not really the conquest and replacement of one people or race by another; what happened was something very different, it was a social revolution started and masked by a superficial foreign conquest. The whole Vandal nation, men, women, and children, that came from Spain to Africa, for example, did not number more than eighty thousand souls. We know this because we have particulars of the transport problem. In their struggle for North Africa, Dr. Schurtz tells us,[2] "there is no trace of any serious resistance offered by the inhabitants; Boniface (the Roman governor of North Africa) had defended Hippo with Gothic mercenaries, while the native population lent no appreciable assistance, and the nomad tribes of the country either adopted a dubious attitude or availed themselves of the difficulties of the Roman governor to make attacks and engage in predatory expeditions. This demoralization resulted from social conditions, which had perhaps developed more unfavourably in Africa than in other parts of the Roman Empire. The free peasants had long ago become the serfs of the great landed proprietors, and were little superior in position to the masses of slaves who were everywhere to be found. And the great landowners had become in their turn easy victims of the policy of extortion followed by unscrupulous governors to an increasingly unprecedented extent in proportion as the dignity of the imperial power sank lower. No man who had anything to lose would now take a place in the senate of the large towns, which had once been the goal of the ambitious, for the senators were required to make up all deficiencies in the revenue, and such deficiencies were now frequent and considerable. . . . Bloody insurrections repeatedly broke out, always traceable ultimately to the pressure of taxation. . . ."

Manifestly the Vandals came in as a positive relief to such a system.[3] They exterminated the great landowners, wiped out all debts to Roman money-lenders, and abolished the last vestiges of military service. The cultivators found themselves better off; the minor officials kept their places; it was not so much a conquest as a liberation from an intolerable deadlock.

It was while the Vandals were still in Africa that a great leader, Attila, arose among the Huns. The seat of his government was in the plains east of the Danube. For a time he swayed a considerable empire of Hunnish and Germanic tribes, and his rule stretched from the Rhine into Central Asia. He negotiated on equal terms with the Chinese emperor. He bullied Ravenna and Constantinople for ten years. Honoria, the grand-daughter of Theodosius II, Emperor of the Eastern empire, one of those passionate young ladies who cause so much trouble in the world, having been put under restraint because of a love affair with a court chamberlain, sent her ring to Attila and called upon him to be her husband and deliverer. He was also urged to attack the Eastern empire by Genseric the Vandal, who was faced by an alliance of the Western and Eastern emperors. He raided southward to the very walls of Constantinople, completely destroying, says Gibbon, seventy cities in his progress, and forcing upon the emperor an onerous peace, which apparently did not involve the liberation of Honoria to her hero.

At this distance of time we are unable to guess at the motives for this omission. Attila continued to speak of her as his affianced bride, and to use the relationship as a pretext for aggressions. In the subsequent negotiations a certain Priscus accompanied an embassy to the camp of the Hunnish monarch, and the fragments that still survive of the narrative he wrote give us a glimpse of the camp and way of living of the great conqueror.

The embassy was itself a curiously constituted body. Its head was Maximin, an honest diplomatist who went in good faith. Quite unknown to him and, at the time, to

[1] E. B.

[2] In Helmolt's *History of the World*.

[3] E. B. disagrees with this view. He regards it as the pro-Teutonic view of the German historians.

Priscus, Vigilius, the interpreter of the expedition, had also a secret mission from the court of Theodosius which was to secure by bribery the assassination of Attila. The little expedition went by way of Nish; it crossed the Danube in canoes, dug out of a single tree, and it was fed by contributions from the villages on the route. Differences in dietary soon attracted the attention of the envoys. Priscus mentions mead in the place of wine, millet for corn, and a drink either distilled[1] or brewed from barley. The journey through Hungary will remind the reader in many of its incidents of the journeys of travellers in Central Africa during the Victorian period. The travellers were politely offered temporary wives.

Attila's capital was rather a vast camp and village than a town. There was only one building of stone, a bath constructed on the Roman model. The mass of the people were in huts and tents; Attila and his leading men lived in timber palaces in great stockaded enclosures with their numerous wives and ministers about them. There was a vast display of loot, but Attila himself affected a nomadic simplicity; he was served in wooden cups and platters, and never touched bread. He worked hard, kept open court before the gate of his palace, and was commonly in the saddle. The primitive custom of both Aryans and Mongols of holding great feasts in hall still held good, and there was much hard drinking. Priscus describes how bards chanted before Attila. They "recited the verses which they had composed, to celebrate his valour and his victories. A profound silence prevailed in the hall, and the attention of the guests was captivated by the vocal harmony, which revived and perpetuated the memory of their own exploits; a martial ardour flashed from the eyes of the warriors, who were impatient for battle; and the tears of the old men expressed their generous despair, that they could no longer partake the danger and glory of the field. This entertainment, which might be considered as a school of military virtue, was succeeded by a farce that debased the dignity of human nature. A Moorish and Scythian buffoon successively excited the mirth of the rude spectators by their deformed figures, ridiculous dress, antic gestures, absurd speeches, and the strange, unintelligible confusion of the Latin, the Gothic, and the Hunnish languages, and the hall resounded with loud and licentious peals of laughter. In the midst of this intemperate riot, Attila alone, without change of countenance, maintained his steadfast and inflexible gravity."[2]

Although Attila was aware, through the confession of the proposed assassin, of the secret work of Vigilius, he allowed this embassy to return in safety, with presents of numerous horses and the like, to Constantinople. Then he despatched an ambassador to Theodosius II to give that monarch, as people say, a piece of his mind. "Theodosius," said the envoy, "is the son of an illustrious and respectable parent; Attila, likewise, is descended from a noble race; and *he* has supported, by his actions, the dignity which he inherited from his father Munzuk. But Theodosius has forfeited his parental honours, and, by consenting to pay tribute, has degraded himself to the condition of a slave. It is therefore just that he should reverence the man whom fortune and merit have placed above him; instead of attempting, like a wicked slave, clandestinely to conspire against his master."

This straightforward bullying was met by abject submission. The emperor sued for pardon, and paid a great ransom.

In 451 Attila declared war on the western empire. He invaded Gaul. So far as the imperial forces were concerned, he had things all his own way, and he sacked most of the towns of France as far south as Orleans. Then the Franks and Visigoths and the imperial forces united against him, and a great and obstinate battle at Troyes (451), in which over 150,000 men were killed on both sides, ended in his repulse and saved Europe from a Mongolian overlord. This disaster by no means exhausted Attila's resources. He turned his attention southward, and overran North Italy. He burnt Aquileia and Padua, and looted Milan, but he made peace at the entreaty of Pope Leo I. He died in 453. . . .

Hereafter the Huns, so far as that name goes in Europe, the Huns of Attila, disappeared out of history. They dissolve into the surrounding populations. They were probably already much mixed, and rather Aryan than Mongolian. They did not become, as one might suppose, the inhabitants of Hungary, though they have probably left many descendants there. About a hundred years after came another Hunnish or mixed people, the Avars, out of the east into Hungary, but these were driven out eastward again by Charlemagne in 791–5. The Magyars, the modern Hungarians, came westward later. They were a Turko-Finnish people. The Magyar is a language belonging to the

[1] Gibbon.

[2] Gibbon.

Finno-Ugrian division of the Ural-Altaic tongues. The Magyars were on the Volga about 550. They settled in Hungary about 900. . . . But we are getting too far on in our story, and we must return to Rome.

In 493 Theodoric, a Goth, became King of Rome, but already for seventeen years there had been no Roman emperor. So it was in utter social decay and collapse that the great slave-holding "world-ascendancy" of the God-Cæsars and the rich men of Rome came to an end.

§ 6

But though throughout the whole of Western Europe and North Africa the Roman imperial system had collapsed, though credit had vanished, luxury production had ceased and money was hidden, though creditors were going unpaid and slaves masterless, the tradition of the Cæsars was still being carried on in Constantinople. We have already had occasion to mention as two outstanding figures among the late Cæsars, Diocletian (284) and Constantine the Great (312), and it was to the latter of these that the world owes the setting up of a fresh imperial centre at Constantinople. Very early during the imperial period the unsuitability of the position of Rome as a world capital, due to the Roman failure to use the sea, was felt. The destruction of Carthage and Corinth had killed the shipping of the main Mediterranean sea-routes. For a people who did not use the sea properly, having the administrative centre at Rome meant that every legion, every draft of officials, every order, had to travel northward for half the length of Italy before it could turn east or west. Consequently nearly all the more capable emperors set up their headquarters at some subordinate centre in a more convenient position. Sirmium (on the River Save), Milan, Lyons, and Nicomedia (in Bithynia) were among such supplementary capitals. For a time under Diocletian, Durazzo was the imperial capital. Ravenna, near the head of the Adriatic, was the capital of the last Roman emperors in the time of Alaric and Stilicho.

It was Constantine the Great who determined upon the permanent transfer of the centre of imperial power to the Bosphorus. We have already noted the existence of the city of Byzantium, which Constantine chose to develop into his new capital. It played a part in the story of the intricate Histiæus (chap. xxii, § 4); it repulsed Philip of Macedon (chap. xxiv, § 3). If the reader will examine its position, he will see that in the hands of a line of capable emperors, and

as the centre of a people with some solidarity and spirit and seacraft (neither of which things were vouchsafed to it), it was extraordinarily well placed. Its galleys could have penetrated up the rivers to the heart of Russia and outflanked every barbarian advance. It commanded practicable trade routes to the east, and it was within a reasonable striking distance of Mesopotamia, Egypt, Greece, and all the more prosperous and civilized regions of the world at that period. And even under the rule of a series of inept monarchs and under demoralized social conditions, the remains of the Roman Empire centring at Constantinople held out for nearly a thousand years.

It was the manifest intention of Constantine the Great that Constantinople should be the centre of an undivided empire. But having regard to the methods of travel and transport available at the time, the geographical conditions of Europe and Western Asia do not point to any one necessary centre of government. If Rome faced westward instead of eastward, and so failed to reach out beyond the Euphrates, Constantinople on the other hand was hopelessly remote from Gaul. The enfeebled Mediterranean civilization, after a certain struggle for Italy, did in fact let go of the west altogether and concentrated upon what were practically the central vestiges, the stump, of the empire of Alexander. The Greek language resumed its sway which had never been very seriously undermined by the official use of Latin. This "Eastern" or longer in Greece, but Alexandria. Its mentality was no longer the mentality of free-minded plain-speaking citizens, of the Stagirite Aristotle and the Greek Plato; its mentality was the mentality of the pedants and of men politically impotent; its philosophy was a pompous evasion of real things, and its scientific impulse was dead. Nevertheless, it was Hellenic. The Roman had come, and he had gone again. Indeed he had gone very extensively from the west

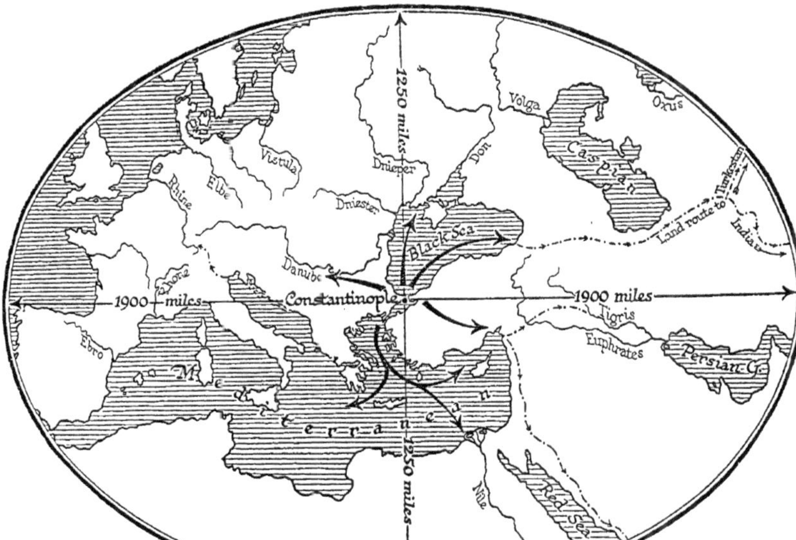

Map to illustrate the geographical advantages of CONSTANTINOPLE

Byzantine empire is generally spoken of as if it were a continuation of the Roman tradition. It is really far more like a resumption of Alexander's.

The Latin language had not the intellectual vigour behind it, it had not the literature and the science, to make it a necessity to intelligent men and so to maintain an ascendancy over the Greek. For no language, whatever officialdom may do, can impose itself in competition with another that can offer the advantages of a great literature or encyclopædic information. Aggressive languages must bring gifts, and the gifts of Greek were incomparably greater than the gifts of Latin. The Eastern empire was from the beginnings of its separation Greek-speaking, and a continuation, though a degenerate continuation, of the Hellenic tradition. Its intellectual centre was no also. By the sixth century A.D. the populations of Europe and North Africa had been stirred up like sediment. When presently in the seventh and eighth centuries the sediment begins to settle down again and populations begin to take on a definite localized character, the Roman is only to be found by name in the region about Rome. Over large parts of his Western empire we find changed and changing modifications of his Latin speech; in Gaul, where the Frank is learning a Gallic form of Latin and evolving French in the process; in Italy, where, under the influence of Teutonic invaders, the Lombards and Goths, Latin is being modified into various Italian dialects; in Spain and Portugal, where it is becoming Spanish and Portuguese. The fundamental Latinity of the languages in these regions serves to remind us of the numerical unimportance of the various Frankish, Vandal, Avar, Gothic, and the like German-speaking invaders, and serves to justify our statement that what happened to the Western empire was not so much conquest and the replacement of one population by another as a political and social revolution. The district of Valais in South Switzerland also retained a fundamentally Latin speech and so did the Canton Grisons; and, what is more curious and interesting, is that in Dacia and Mœsia Inferior, large parts of which to the north of the Danube became the modern Roumania (=Romania), although these regions were added late to the empire and lost soon, the Latin speech also remained.

In Britain Latin was practically wiped out by the conquering Anglo-Saxons, from among whose various dialects the root stock of English presently grew.

But while the smashing of the Roman social and political structure was thus complete, while in the east it was thrown off by the older and stronger Hellenic tradition, and while in the west it was broken up into fragments that began to take on a new and separate life of their own, there was one thing that did not perish, but grew, and that was the tradition of the world empire of Rome and of the supremacy of the Cæsars. When the reality was destroyed, the legend had freedom to expand. Removed from the possibility of verification, the idea of a serene and splendid Roman world-supremacy grew up in the imagination of mankind, and still holds it to this day.

Ever since the time of Alexander, human thought has been haunted by the possible political unity of the race. All the sturdy chiefs and leaders and kings of the barbarians, who raided through the prostrate but vast disorder of the decayed empire, were capable of conceiving of some mighty king of kings greater than themselves and giving a real law for all men, and they were ready to believe that elsewhere in space and time, and capable of returning presently to resume his supremacy, Cæsar had been such a king of kings. Far above their own titles, therefore, they esteemed and envied the title of Cæsar. The international history of Europe from this time henceforth is largely the story of kings and adventurers setting up to be Cæsar and Imperator (Emperor). We shall tell of some of them in their places. So universal did this "Cæsaring" become, that the Great War of 1914–18 mowed down no fewer than four Cæsars, the German Kaiser (=Cæsar), the Austrian Kaiser, the Tsar (=Cæsar) of Russia, and that fantastic figure, the Tsar of Bulgaria. The French "Imperator" (Napoleon III) had already fallen in 1871. There is now (1920) no one left in the world to carry on the Imperial title or the tradition of Divus Cæsar except the Turkish Sultan and the British monarch. The former commemorates his lordship over Constantinople as Kaisar-i-Roum [1]; the latter is called the Cæsar of India (a country no real Cæsar ever looked upon), Kaisar-i-Hind.

[1] The spread and the vitality of the place-name "Rome" were even greater than the vogue of the title "Cæsar." All the countries which had formed part of the Eastern and Western divisions of the Roman empire (excepting the ephemeral extension of Roman rule over Mesopotamia) were known to the Saracens, the Arabs, the Berbers as "Rum," and their peoples as "Rumis," "Rumas." And this name was applied without, in all cases, carrying with it the signification of "Christian" or "Christendom." Thus the Spanish Moors were, and their descendants are, styled by the Moroccan Moors and the Algerians and Tunisians: "Rumas." When expelled from Spain most of them took service under the Sharifian Emperors of Morocco, and brought with them a European knowledge of fire-arms. Thus you are told in Algeria that "Romans" (i.e. Spanish Moors) conquered the Upper Niger basin for Morocco in the seventeenth century; their descendants remain there till to-day between Jenné and Timbuktu, still known to the French as "Roumas." Some Spanish Moors even penetrated to the coast of eastern equatorial Africa and carried the name of "Rome" into the fierce expulsion of the Portuguese from those parts which was begun by the Omani Arabs.—H. H. J.

Printed by
Cassell & Company, Limited,
La Belle Sauvage, London, E.C.4

Lightning Source UK Ltd.
Milton Keynes UK
UKHW021127161219
355473UK00018B/4331/P

9 781290 835633